Exam 70-271: Supporting Users and Troubleshooting a Microsoft Windows XP Operating System

Objective	Chapter	Lesson
1. Installing a Windows Desktop Operating System		
1.1. Perform and troubleshoot an attended installation of a Windows XP operating system.		
1.1.1. Answer end-user questions related to performing an attended installation of a Windows XP operating system.	2	1
1.1.2. Troubleshoot and complete installations in which an installation does not start. Tasks include configuring the device boot order and ascertaining probable cause of the failure to start.	2	2
1.1.3. Troubleshoot and complete installations in which an installation fails to complete. Tasks include reviewing setup log files and providing needed files.	2	2
1.1.4. Perform postinstallation configuration. Tasks include customizing installations for individual users and applying service packs.	2	3
1.2. Perform and troubleshoot an unattended installation of a Windows desktop operating system		
1.2.1. Answer end-user questions related to performing an unattended installation of a Windows XP operating system. Tasks include starting an installation, answering questions asked by an end user during an installation, and performing postinstallation tasks.	2	1
1.2.2. Configure a PC to boot to a network device and start installation of a Windows XP operating system. Tasks include configuring PXE compliant network cards.	2	1
1.2.3. Perform an installation by using unattended installation files.	2	1
1.3. Upgrade from a previous version of Windows.		
1.3.1. Answer end-user questions related to upgrading from a previous version of Windows. Considerations include available upgrade paths and methods for transferring user state data.	2	1
1.3.2. Verify hardware compatibility for upgrade. Considerations include minimum hardware and system resource requirements.	2	1
1.3.3. Verify application compatibility for upgrade. Tasks include ascertaining which applications can and cannot run, and using the application compatibility tools.	2	1
1.3.4. Migrate user state data from an existing PC to a new PC	2	1
1.3.5. Install a second instance of an operating system on a computer	2	1
2. Managing and Troubleshooting Access to Resources		
2.1. Monitor, manage, and troubleshoot access to files and folders.		
2.1.1. Answer end-user questions related to managing and troubleshooting access to files and folders.	5	1–5
2.1.2. Monitor, manage, and troubleshoot NTFS file permissions.	5	2
2.1.3. Manage and troubleshoot simple file sharing.	5	4
2.1.4. Manage and troubleshoot file encryption.	5	1
2.2. Manage and troubleshoot access to shared folders.		
2.2.1. Answer end-user questions related to managing and troubleshooting access to shared folders.	5	3
2.2.2. Create shared folders.	5	3
2.2.3. Configure access permission for shared folders on NTFS partitions.	5	3
2.2.4. Troubleshoot and interpret Access Denied messages.	5	3
2.3. Connect to local and network print devices.		
2.3.1. Answer end-user questions related to printing locally.	9	1
2.3.2. Configure and manage local printing.	9	1
2.3.3. Answer end-user questions related to network-based printing.	9	1
2.3.4. Connect to and manage printing to a network-based printer.	9	1
2.4. Manage and troubleshoot access to and synchronization of offline files.		
2.4.1. Answer end-user questions related to configuring and synchronizing offline files.	5	5
2.4.2. Configure and troubleshoot offline files.	5	5
2.4.3. Configure and troubleshoot offline file synchronization.	5	5
3. Configuring and Troubleshooting Hardware Devices and Drivers		
3.1. Configure and troubleshoot storage devices.		
3.1.1. Answer end-user questions related to configuring hard disks and partitions or volumes.	8	1
3.1.2. Manage and troubleshoot disk partitioning.	8	1
3.1.3. Answer end-user questions related to optical drives such as CD-ROM, CD-RW, DVD, and DVD-R.	8	2
3.1.4. Configure and troubleshoot removable storage devices such as pen drives, flash drives, and memory cards.	7	2
3.2. Configure and troubleshoot display devices.		
3.2.1. Answer end-user questions related to configuring desktop display settings.	7	1
3.2.2. Configure display devices and display settings.	7	1
3.2.3. Troubleshoot display device settings.	7	1
3.3. Configure and troubleshoot Advanced Configuration and Power Interface (ACPI).		
3.3.1. Answer end-user questions related to configuring ACPI settings.	7	3
3.3.2. Configure and troubleshoot operating system power settings.	7	3
3.3.3. Configure and troubleshoot system standby and hibernate settings.	7	3

Microsoft®

Note: Exam objectives are subject to change at anytime without prior notice and at Microsoft's sole discretion. Please visit Microsoft's Training & Certification Web site (www.microsoft.com/traincert) for the most current listing of exam objectives.

Microsoft

MCDST Self-Paced Training Kit (Exam 70-271):

Supporting Users and Troubleshooting a Microsoft® Windows® XP Operating System, Second Edition

Walter Glenn

Tony Northrup

PUBLISHED BY
Microsoft Press
A Division of Microsoft Corporation
One Microsoft Way
Redmond, Washington 98052-6399

Library of Congress Control Number 2005932149

Printed and bound in the United States of America.

1 2 3 4 5 6 7 8 9   QWT   8 7 6 5

Distributed in Canada by H.B. Fenn and Company Ltd. A CIP catalogue record for this book is available from the British Library.

Microsoft Press books are available through booksellers and distributors worldwide. For further information about international editions, contact your local Microsoft Corporation office or contact Microsoft Press International directly at fax (425) 936-7329. Visit our Web site at www.microsoft.com/mspress. Send comments to tkinput@microsoft.com.

Acquisitions Editor: Ken Jones
Project Editor: Karen Szall

Body Part No. X11-45182

For my kids, Liam and Maya

-Walter

For Sam

-Tony

Contents at a Glance

Practices

Tables

Troubleshooting Labs

Case Scenario Exercises

Contents

What do you think of this book? We want to hear from you!	Microsoft is interested in hearing your feedback about this publication so we can continually improve our books and learning resources for you. To participate in a brief online survey, please visit: *www.microsoft.com/learning/booksurvey/*

9   Managing Local and Network Printers   9-1

10   Supporting Network Connectivity   **10-1**

16   Configuring and Troubleshooting the Desktop and User Environments (4.0)   16-1

17   Troubleshooting Network Protocols and Services (5.0)   17-1

System Requirements

Acknowledgments

Getting a book like this written, edited, and published doesn't happen without the help of a lot of people. This book has been an enormous project, and we'd like to extend our thanks to everyone who worked on it. Maureen Zimmerman, our development editor, and Karen Szall, our project editor, both did an amazing job making sure that the book was of the highest quality and that everyone involved turned in their best effort. Bob Hogan, our technical editor, provided a detailed technical review. Thanks also to Martin DelRe for his advice and support along the way.

We'd also like to tip our hats to Daniel Akins, who wrote the defrag.vbs script for running Disk Defragmenter automatically so that it can be scheduled. This tool is included on the book's CD.

And, as always, thanks to Neil Salkind and everyone else at StudioB for helping put this project together.

—Walter Glenn and Tony Northrup

About This Book

Welcome to *MCDST Self-Paced Training Kit (Exam 70-271): Supporting Users and Troubleshooting a Microsoft Windows XP Operating System*, Second Edition. This book teaches you how to resolve end-user requests for configuring and troubleshooting Microsoft Windows XP Home Edition or Windows XP Professional Edition.

You will learn how to talk to end users about problems, isolate and troubleshoot problems, and then propose and document solutions. This book focuses on the following:

- Installing Windows XP Professional and Home Edition
- Managing and troubleshooting access to resources
- Configuring and troubleshooting hardware devices and drivers
- Configuring and troubleshooting the desktop and user environments
- Troubleshooting network protocols and services

Note For more information about becoming a Microsoft Certified Professional (MCP) or Microsoft Certified Desktop Support Technician (MCDST), see the section titled "The Microsoft Certified Professional Program" later in this introduction.

Intended Audience

This book was developed for information technology (IT) professionals who plan to take the related Microsoft Certified Professional exam 70-271, Supporting Users and Troubleshooting a Microsoft Windows XP Operating System. It was also developed for IT professionals who run Windows XP Professional in a corporate or small business environment or run Windows XP Home Edition in a home environment.

Note Exam skills are subject to change without prior notice and at the sole discretion of Microsoft.

Prerequisites

This training kit requires that students meet the following prerequisites:

- Have a working knowledge of the Windows XP operating system
- Have a basic understanding of using Microsoft Internet Explorer 6

- Have a basic knowledge of computer hardware

- Have a basic understanding of networking technologies

About the CD-ROM

This book includes two companion CD-ROMs. The first contains a variety of informational aids to complement the book content:

- The Microsoft Press Readiness Review Suite Powered by MeasureUp. This suite of practice tests and objective reviews contains questions of varying degrees of complexity and offers multiple testing modes. You can assess your understanding of the concepts presented in this book and use the results to develop a learning plan that meets your needs.

- An electronic version of this book (eBook). For information about using the eBook, see the "The eBook" section later in this introduction.

- Any tools recommended in the book.

- An eBook of the *Microsoft Encyclopedia of Networking*, Second Edition, and *Microsoft Encyclopedia of Security*, which provide complete and up-to-date reference materials for networking and security.

The second CD-ROM contains a 120-day evaluation edition of Microsoft Windows XP Professional Edition with Service Pack 2.

Caution   The 120-day evaluation edition that is provided with this training kit is not the full retail product; it is provided only for the purpose of training and evaluation. Microsoft Technical Support does not support this evaluation edition.

For additional support information regarding this book and the CD-ROMs (including answers to commonly asked questions about installation and use), visit the Microsoft Press Technical Support website at *http://www.microsoft.com/learning/support/books/*. You can also e-mail tkinput@microsoft.com or send a letter to Microsoft Press, Attention: *MCDST Self-Paced Training Kit (Exam 70-271): Supporting Users and Troubleshooting a Microsoft Windows XP Operating System*, Second Edition, One Microsoft Way, Redmond, WA 98052-6399.

Features of This Book

This book has two parts. Use Part 1 to learn at your own pace and to practice what you learn with practical exercises. Part 2 contains questions and answers you can use to test yourself on what you learned.

Part 1: Learn at Your Own Pace

Each chapter identifies the exam objectives covered within the chapter, provides an overview of why the topics matter by identifying how the information is applied in the real world, and lists any prerequisites that must be met to complete the lessons presented in the chapter.

The chapters are divided into lessons. Lessons contain practices that include one or more hands-on exercises. These exercises give you an opportunity to use the skills being presented or to explore the part of the application being described.

After the lessons, you are given an opportunity to apply what you learned in a case scenario exercise. In this exercise, you work through a multistep solution for a realistic case scenario. You are also given an opportunity to work through a troubleshooting lab that explores difficulties you might encounter on the job when applying what you learned.

Each chapter ends with a short summary of key concepts and a short section summarizing key topics and listing key terms you need to know before taking the exam.

Real World   Helpful Information

You will find sidebars like this one that contain related information you might find helpful. "Real World" sidebars contain specific information gained through the experience of IT professionals just like you.

Part 2: Prepare for the Exam

Part 2 helps to familiarize you with the types of questions you will encounter on the MCP exam. By reviewing the objectives and sample questions, you can focus on the specific skills you need to improve on before taking the exam.

See Also   For a complete list of MCP exams and their related objectives, go to *http://www.microsoft.com/learning/mcp/*.

Part 2 is organized by the exam's objectives. Each chapter covers one of the primary groups of objectives, referred to as *Objective Domains*. Each chapter lists the tested skills you need to master to answer the exam questions, and it includes a list of further readings to help you improve your ability to perform the tasks or skills specified by the objectives.

Within each Objective Domain, you will find the related objectives that are covered on the exam. Each objective provides you with several practice exam questions. The answers are accompanied by explanations of each correct and incorrect answer.

> **Note**   These questions are also available on the companion CD as a practice test.

Informational Notes

Several types of reader aids appear throughout the training kit.

- **Tip** contains methods of performing a task more quickly or in a not-so-obvious way.

- **Important** contains information that is essential to completing a task.

- **Note** contains supplemental information.

- **Caution** contains valuable information about possible loss of data; be sure to read this information carefully.

- **Warning** contains critical information about possible physical injury; be sure to read this information carefully.

- **See Also** contains references to other sources of information.

- **Planning** contains hints and useful information that should help you to plan the implementation.

- **On the CD** points you to supplementary information or files that you need that are on the companion CD.

- **Security Alert** highlights information you need to know to maximize security in your work environment.

- **Exam Tip** flags information you should know before taking the certification exam.

- **Off the Record** contains practical advice about the real-world implications of information presented in the lesson.

Notational Conventions

The following conventions are used throughout this book:

- Characters or commands that you type appear in **bold** type.

- *Italic* in syntax statements indicates placeholders for variable information. *Italic* is also used for book titles.

- Names of files and folders appear in Title caps, except when you are to type them directly. Unless otherwise indicated, you can use all lowercase letters when you type a file name in a dialog box or at a command prompt.

- File name extensions appear in all UPPERCASE.

- Acronyms appear in all UPPERCASE.

- Monospace type represents code samples, examples of screen text, or entries that you might type at a command prompt or in initialization files.

- Square brackets [ ] are used in syntax statements to enclose optional items. For example, [*filename*] in command syntax indicates that you can choose to type a file name with the command. Type only the information within the brackets, not the brackets themselves.

- Braces { } are used in syntax statements to enclose required items. Type only the information within the braces, not the braces themselves.

Keyboard Conventions

- A plus sign (+) between two key names means that you must press those keys at the same time. For example, "Press ALT+TAB" means that you hold down ALT while you press TAB.

- A comma (,) between two or more key names means that you must press each of the keys consecutively, not together. For example, "Press ALT, F, X" means that you press and release each key in sequence. "Press ALT+W, L" means that you first press ALT and W at the same time, and then release them and press L.

Getting Started

This training kit contains hands-on exercises to help you learn about supporting applications in Windows XP. Use this section to prepare your self-paced training environment.

Hardware Requirements

To follow the practices in this book, it is recommended that you use a computer that is not your primary workstation because you will be called on to make changes to the operating system and application configuration. The computer you use must have the following minimum configuration (all hardware should be listed in the Microsoft Windows Catalog):

- Personal computer with a 233 MHz or higher processor (Pentium III recommended) in the Intel Pentium/Celeron family, the AMD K6/Athlon/Duron family, or compatible (300 MHz processor recommended)

- 64 MB of RAM or higher (128 MB is recommended)

- 1.8 GB of available hard disk space

- CD-ROM drive or DVD-ROM drive

- Super VGA (800 x 600) or higher resolution monitor

- Keyboard and Microsoft Mouse, Microsoft IntelliMouse, or compatible pointing device

- Internet connection

Software Requirements

The following software is required to complete the procedures in this training kit. (A 120-day evaluation edition of Microsoft Windows XP Professional Edition with SP2 is included on one of the CD-ROMs.)

- Microsoft Windows XP Professional Edition with SP2

Caution The 120-day evaluation edition that is provided with this training kit is not the full retail product and is provided only for the purposes of training and evaluation. Microsoft Technical Support does not support these evaluation editions. For additional support information regarding this book and the CD-ROMs (including answers to commonly asked questions about installation and use), visit the Microsoft Press Technical Support website at *http://www.microsoft.com/learning/support/books/*. You can also e-mail tkinput@microsoft.com or send a letter to Microsoft Press, Attn: *MCDST Self-Paced Training Kit (Exam 70-271): Supporting Users and Troubleshooting a Microsoft Windows XP Operating System*, Second Edition, One Microsoft Way, Redmond, WA 98052-6399.

Setup Instructions

Set up your computer according to the manufacturer's instructions.

Caution If your computer is part of a larger network, you *must* verify with your network administrator that the computer name, domain name, and other information used in configuring Windows XP in several chapters of this book do not conflict with network operations. If they do conflict, ask your network administrator to provide alternative values and use those values throughout all the exercises in this book.

The Readiness Review Suite

The companion CD-ROM includes a practice test made up of 300 sample exam questions and an objective-by-objective review with an additional 125 questions. Use these tools to reinforce your learning and to identify any areas in which you need to gain more experience before taking the exam.

▶ **To Install the Practice Test and Objective Review**

    1. Insert the companion CD-ROM into your CD-ROM drive.

> **Note**   If AutoRun is disabled on your machine, refer to the Readme.txt file on the CD-ROM.

    2. Click Readiness Review Suite on the user interface menu.

Practice Files

The \Tools folder on the CD-ROM contains the Defrag tool that is referenced in Chapter 12.

The eBook

The CD-ROM includes an electronic version of the Training Kit. The eBook is in Portable Document Format (PDF) and can be viewed by using Adobe Acrobat Reader.

▶ **To Use the eBook**

    1. Insert the companion CD-ROM into your CD-ROM drive.

> **Note**   If AutoRun is disabled on your machine, refer to the Readme.txt file on the CD-ROM.

    2. Click eBook on the user interface menu. You can also review any of the other eBooks that are provided for your use.

The Microsoft Certified Professional Program

The Microsoft Certified Professional (MCP) program provides the best method to prove your command of current Microsoft products and technologies. The exams and corresponding certifications are developed to validate your mastery of critical competencies as you design and develop, or implement and support, solutions with Microsoft products and technologies. Computer professionals who become Microsoft-certified are recognized as experts and are sought after industry-wide. Certification brings a variety of benefits to the individual and to employers and organizations.

See Also   For a full list of MCP benefits, go to *http://www.microsoft.com/learning/itpro/ default.asp.*

Certifications

The MCP program offers multiple certifications, based on specific areas of technical expertise:

- *Microsoft Certified Professional (MCP)*. Demonstrated in-depth knowledge of at least one Microsoft Windows operating system or architecturally significant platform. An MCP is qualified to implement a Microsoft product or technology as part of a business solution for an organization.

- *Microsoft Certified Desktop Support Technician (MCDST)*. Individuals who support end users and troubleshoot desktop environments running on the Windows operating system.

- *Microsoft Certified Solution Developer (MCSD)*. Professional developers qualified to analyze, design, and develop enterprise business solutions with Microsoft development tools and technologies including the Microsoft .NET Framework.

- *Microsoft Certified Application Developer (MCAD)*. Professional developers qualified to develop, test, deploy, and maintain powerful applications using Microsoft tools and technologies including Microsoft Visual Studio .NET and XML Web services.

- *Microsoft Certified Systems Engineer (MCSE)*. Qualified to effectively analyze the business requirements and design and implement the infrastructure for business solutions based on the Microsoft Windows and Microsoft Server 2003 operating system.

- *Microsoft Certified Systems Administrator (MCSA)*. Individuals with the skills to manage and troubleshoot existing network and system environments based on the Microsoft Windows and Microsoft Server 2003 operating systems.

- *Microsoft Certified Database Administrator (MCDBA)*. Individuals who design, implement, and administer Microsoft SQL Server databases.

- *Microsoft Certified Trainer (MCT)*. Instructionally and technically qualified to deliver Microsoft Official Curriculum through a Microsoft Certified Technical Education Center (CTEC).

Requirements for Becoming a Microsoft Certified Professional

The certification requirements differ for each certification and are specific to the products and job functions addressed by the certification.

To become a Microsoft Certified Professional, you must pass rigorous certification exams that provide a valid and reliable measure of technical proficiency and expertise. These exams are designed to test your expertise and ability to perform a role or task with a product, and are developed with the input of professionals in the industry. Questions in the exams reflect how Microsoft products are used in actual organizations, giving them "real-world" relevance.

- Microsoft Certified Professional (MCP) candidates are required to pass one current Microsoft certification exam. Candidates can pass additional Microsoft certification exams to further qualify their skills with other Microsoft products, development tools, or desktop applications.

- Microsoft Certified Solution Developers (MCSDs) are required to pass three core exams and one elective exam. (MCSD for Microsoft .NET candidates are required to pass four core exams and one elective.)

- Microsoft Certified Application Developers (MCADs) are required to pass two core exams and one elective exam in an area of specialization.

- Microsoft Certified Systems Engineers (MCSEs) are required to pass five core exams and two elective exams.

- Microsoft Certified Systems Administrators (MCSAs) are required to pass three core exams and one elective exam that provide a valid and reliable measure of technical proficiency and expertise.

- Microsoft Certified Database Administrators (MCDBAs) are required to pass three core exams and one elective exam that provide a valid and reliable measure of technical proficiency and expertise.

- Microsoft Certified Trainers (MCTs) are required to meet instructional and technical requirements specific to each Microsoft Official Curriculum course they are certified to deliver. The MCT program requires ongoing training to meet the requirements for the annual renewal of certification. For more information about becoming a Microsoft Certified Trainer, visit *http://www.microsoft.com/learning/ mcp/mct/* or contact a regional service center near you.

Technical Support

Every effort has been made to ensure the accuracy of this book and the contents of the companion disc. If you have comments, questions, or ideas regarding this book or the companion disc, please send them to Microsoft Press by using either of the following methods:

E-mail: tkinput@microsoft.com

Postal Mail: Microsoft Press
                 Attn: *MCDST Self-Paced Training Kit (Exam 70-271): Supporting Users and Troubleshooting a Microsoft Windows XP Operating System,* Second Edition, Editor
                 One Microsoft Way
                 Redmond, WA 98052-6399

For additional support information regarding this book and the CD-ROMs (including answers to commonly asked questions about installation and use), visit the Microsoft Press Technical Support website at *http://www.microsoft.com/learning/support/books/*. To connect directly to the Microsoft Knowledge Base and enter a query, visit *http://support.microsoft.com/search/*. For support information regarding Microsoft software, please connect to *http://support.microsoft.com*.

Evaluation Edition Software Support

The 120-day evaluation edition provided with this training is not the full retail product and is provided only for the purposes of training and evaluation. Microsoft and Microsoft Technical Support do not support this evaluation edition.

Caution   The evaluation edition of Microsoft Windows XP Professional Edition included with this book should not be used on a primary work computer. The evaluation edition is unsupported. For online support information relating to the full version of Microsoft Windows XP Professional Edition that *might* also apply to the evaluation edition, you can connect to *http://support.microsoft.com/*.

Information about any issues relating to the use of the evaluation edition with this training kit is posted to the Support section of the Microsoft Press website (*http://www.microsoft.com/learning/support/books/*). For information about ordering the full version of any Microsoft software, please call Microsoft Sales at (800) 426-9400 or visit *http://www.microsoft.com*.

Part 1
Learn at Your Own Pace

1 Introduction to Desktop Support

Exam Objectives in this Chapter:

- This first chapter serves as an overview to the desktop support role and environment; it does not specifically cover any exam objective.

Why This Chapter Matters

As a desktop support technician (DST), your job is to isolate and solve problems. To do this, you must understand your role in the support environment. You must also know how to talk to and how to listen to users with different levels of experience—how to ask questions, how to interpret what users say, and how to suggest changes. You must know where to search for answers to problems and how to apply and document the solutions to those problems.

The goal of this chapter is to introduce you to desktop support and common network configurations and to teach you how best to support the end user in these varied settings. The chapter begins with an introduction to supporting users and then discusses corporate environments, the help and support tier structure, and common job titles and duties. A discussion of workgroups, domains, and reasons for multiple domains is also included. Noncorporate environments are introduced, including Internet service providers (ISPs), call centers, and large and small repair shops. The chapter also introduces you to basic troubleshooting techniques, including how to gather information about a problem, research and implement solutions, and document your activities.

Lessons in this Chapter:

Before You Begin

The purpose of this training kit is to teach you to support end users who run Microsoft Windows XP Professional in a corporate environment or Windows XP Home Edition in a home or small business environment and to prepare you for the 70-271 MCDST exam. This training kit assumes that you have approximately six months of hands-on experience and the following prerequisite knowledge:

- Basic experience using a Windows operating system such as Windows XP

- Basic understanding of Windows accessories, including Microsoft Internet Explorer

- Basic understanding of core operating system technologies, including installation and configuration

- Basic understanding of hardware components and their functions

- Basic understanding of the major desktop components and interfaces and their functions

- Basic understanding of Transmission Control Protocol/Internet Protocol (TCP/IP) settings

- Basic understanding of using command-line utilities to manage the operating system

- Basic understanding of technologies that are available for establishing Internet connectivity

Lesson 1: Introduction to Supporting Users

Being a DST involves much more than answering the telephone and resolving a problem. It also involves understanding, communicating with, and pleasing the end user. You must be able to listen to a customer, gather information from that customer, diagnose and resolve the problem (or refer the problem to a senior technician or system administrator), and properly document the resolution of the problem in the manner that is dictated by company policy. The end user must also be satisfied with the solution and believe that he or she was treated fairly and with respect.

After this lesson, you will be able to

- Identify the types of end users that you will encounter.
- Explain how previous interactions with desktop support could have gone better.
- Discuss traits of a qualified DST.
- Identify what end users expect from you.

Estimated lesson time: 15 minutes

The End User's Level of Expertise

There are many types of end users. Each user has a different level of expertise, and each one has expertise to varying degrees. Some end users have no computer experience at all and barely understand basic computer terms; some have targeted experience while others have many years of experience. Table 1-1 shows the different types of users you might encounter.

Table 1-1   End Users Have Varying Skill Levels

Skill Level	Description
Highly experienced	These users are extremely experienced and most likely know more than you do concerning the problem at hand. Their problems generally need to be escalated quickly.
Generally experienced	These users can use e-mail and the Internet, download and install programs, follow wizards, install and configure programs, set up simple networks, and do minor troubleshooting. Tier-1 or tier-2 support personnel can generally assist these users.
Targeted experience	These users have experience in one or two applications that they use daily to do their jobs. Other than this experience, they have almost no computing skills. Depending on the application in question, tier-1 or tier-2 support personnel can generally assist these users.

Table 1-1   End Users Have Varying Skill Levels

Skill Level	Description
No experience	These users are completely new to computing and have little or no experience with using e-mail, accessing the Internet, or installing or using applications. Tier-1 personnel should be able to handle most of these calls.

After you gain some experience as a DST, you will be able to determine how experienced the user is after speaking with him or her for only a few minutes. In the interim, you will learn how to work with and assist the different types of end users by communicating with them through written scripts and by following specific (and proven) troubleshooting guidelines.

Tip   Keep in mind at all times that you will assist all levels of users; never assume that the user knows less than you do.

Real World   Leveraging the Expert User

As you work in the desktop support world, you will run into many users who have expertise that you can use. Whether the users have more general computing experience than you do, are hardware hobbyists, or are simply gurus in particular applications, it is in your best interest to recognize their expertise and learn from it.

Especially in the corporate world (which you will learn more about in Lesson 2), expert users are worth their weight in gold. You will not have time to become an expert in every application that is running within a company, so knowing whom to go to with your questions can help keep things running smoothly. You are also likely to find a user or two in each department who can help field questions when you are not available or whom you can ask to sit down at a user's desk if that user is having trouble explaining the problem to you.

In the noncorporate world, expert users offer a good source for your own continuing education. Listen to what they have to say and learn from the techniques they use when troubleshooting their own problems.

Previous Experiences with Technical Support

Chances are that the end user with whom you are speaking on the phone or visiting at his or her desk has dealt with a DST before. If that experience was not satisfactory, you might have to deal with an angry, dissatisfied, or frustrated client. You might also be the second or third DST who tried to solve the problem, or the problem might be a recurring one. If this is the case, concentrate on verifying the problem, be polite and respectful, and use whatever resources it takes to solve the problem quickly and effectively.

Traits of a Qualified DST

Companies and clients want to hire and keep the best DSTs that they can find, and they look for several specific traits and qualities. It does not matter whether you work in a corporate environment or offer in-home computer repair services; the traits and skills are the same. To be the best DST you can be, work to demonstrate as many of the following qualities as possible.

- **Excellent customer service skills**   Successful DSTs have the ability and emotional intelligence to teach highly technical content to users with any level of experience. They can speak to any user about any problem and define that problem in terms that the user can understand (without making the user feel inadequate or stupid). Successful DSTs have skills that any successful customer service employee has: They are polite, are concerned for the customer, and have a sincere desire to service the customer's needs. Beyond emotional intelligence, they also have social intelligence, which is the ability to handle their (or others') anxieties, anger, and sadness; to be self-motivated; and to have empathy for others.

- **Talent for communicating**   Qualified DSTs can communicate with end users of any level of experience, any personality, and any level on the corporate ladder. They can communicate technical information to nontechnical users and can acquire technical information from those who cannot explain the problem clearly. Qualified DSTs also take the time to explain in simple terms why the problem occurred, how it can be avoided in the future, and how and where to get help when no DST is available. Qualified DSTs document the problems, their communications with users, and the solutions they try so that they can communicate even better with users the next time around.

- **Ability to multitask and stay calm under pressure**   DSTs must deal with ongoing problems, multiple open troubleshooting tickets, deadlines for meeting **service-level agreements (SLAs)**, accountability to upper management and end users, and ambiguous problems. While dealing with these demands, DSTs must be able to work effectively and calmly under pressure. DSTs must also respond calmly when an end user becomes frustrated or angry and must maintain a professional demeanor at all times.

- **Technical aptitude**   DSTs have a natural aptitude for computers, hardware, and software and for configuring each. They enjoy working with the technologies; have workstations at home at which they troubleshoot problems in their spare time; welcome new technologies; and show a talent for seeing the big picture in terms of networks, components, shared files and folders, and problems. Having the ability to see the big picture is the first step to becoming an expert in your field.

- **Capacity to solve problems**   Talented DSTs have the capacity to solve problems quickly. They are good at solving logic problems, uncovering hidden clues, chasing leads, and discovering and attempting solutions without complicating the problem further. Communication and linear and logical troubleshooting abilities are the top DST skills that employers seek. The technical aspect can be taught much more easily than these skills, which have far more to do with overall intelligence, personality, and social abilities than do technical skills. You must strive to develop critical thinking and problem-solving skills and learn to "read the signs" when dealing with a problem. The better you are at seeing the signs and the big picture, the better you will be as a DST. The capacity to solve problems can be improved through training, experience, trial and error, observation, and working with higher-level DSTs.

Lesson Review

The following questions are intended to reinforce key information presented in this lesson. If you are unable to answer a question, review the lesson materials and try the question again. You can find answers to the questions in the "Questions and Answers" section at the end of this chapter.

1. Give yourself five minutes to list as many traits as you can that relate to the three categories listed here:

    ❑ Communication skills

    ❑ Aptitude skills

    ❑ Personal skills

    _____

    _____

2. You are working as a tier-1 support technician. You are speaking to a user whom you quickly assess as being highly experienced. The user starts the conversation by telling you what she has already tried and what she suspects is the cause of her problem. What is the likely outcome of this support call?

    _____

    _____

3. You are speaking with a user who has been on hold for almost 20 minutes. The first thing the customer tells you is that he has already spoken with two other DSTs that day, and the "fixes" they recommended have made things worse. How should you handle this?

_____

_____

Lesson Summary

■ As a DST, you will encounter users of all skill levels. Never assume that you know more than the user to whom you are talking.

■ DSTs must have technical knowledge in many areas, including the configuration and troubleshooting of the desktop interface, hardware, network connectivity, and more.

■ DSTs should be adept at getting information from people who might not be able to explain the problem clearly and should be good at explaining technical information to nontechnical users.

Lesson 2: Overview of Corporate Environments

There are several types of environments in which you might be employed. Understanding these environments and your place in them is crucial to your success. This section provides a brief overview of the corporate environment, including common network setups, tier structure, job titles, and job requirements.

After this lesson, you will be able to

■ Explain the types of networks that you might encounter.

■ Define the tier structure and explain the responsibilities of each tier.

■ Identify common support job titles and the responsibilities of those jobs.

Estimated lesson time: 25 minutes

Types of Networks

From a user's perspective, there are three basic types of logical networks: **workgroups**, **domains**, and **multiple domains**. In each of these environments, users can share common resources such as files, folders, and printers. There are security measures available that keep users' personal data, network resources, and company data secure and protected from outside forces.

Exam Tip   Different types of networks involve different capabilities, security measures, and policies. Identifying the scope of a problem (and, therefore, correctly providing an answer) hinges on correctly identifying the type of network involved. Deciding on the scope should be your first step on the exam and in the real world.

Workgroups

Workgroups, which are logical groupings of networked computers that share resources, are often referred to as peer-to-peer networks. Of the three network types, the workgroup is the easiest to set up and maintain, but it is the least secure. Each computer maintains its own local security database, which contains the valid user accounts for logging onto and using that computer. The user accounts secure data on the computer and protect the computer from unwanted access. Because no single computer provides centralized security of user accounts for all the computers on the network, the network is considered decentralized. Figure 1-1 shows an example of a workgroup.

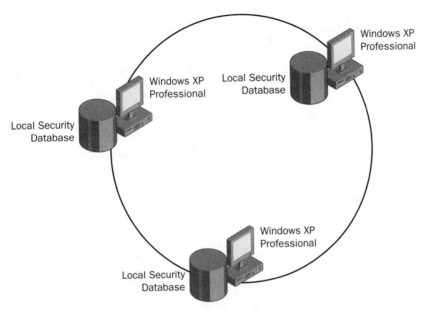

Figure 1-1 A workgroup is often referred to as a peer-to-peer network.

Note Workgroups are typically configured for home networks, small home offices, and small businesses in which the computers are in close proximity to one another and can be connected using a hub, switch, or router. Because they are not the most secure option for a network, they are not often used in larger corporations.

Domains

Domains are logical groupings of networked computers that share a common database of users and centrally managed security on a single server (or group of servers) called a domain controller. A single domain must have one or more domain controllers, and these computers provide Microsoft **Active Directory** directory services such as providing access to resources, security, and a single point of administration. Domains are logical groupings, so they are independent of the actual physical structure of the network. Domains can span a building, city, state, country, or even the globe or they can be configured for a small office. The computers can be connected by dial-up, Ethernet, Integrated Services Digital Network (ISDN) lines, satellite, or even wireless connections. Figure 1-2 shows an example of a domain with two domain controllers.

> **Note**   Domains are typically configured for networks in larger companies and corporations because they are the most secure option for a network, offer centralized security and management, and are extensible. Smaller companies generally opt against domains because they have more overhead, are more expensive, and require more attention than workgroups do.

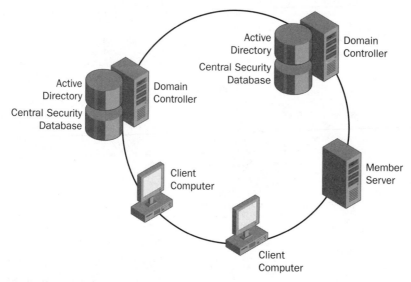

Figure 1-2   Domains share a common database and are centrally managed.

> **Note**   Workgroups, domains, and multiple domains describe the logical grouping of computers. Do not confuse this logical grouping with the physical layout of the network. A small network of three computers connected by a single hub can be logically grouped into a domain, just as a larger network consisting of thousands of computers across multiple subnets can also be grouped into a domain. The reason for the distinction between logical and physical structures is one of abstraction. The physical layout has to do with where computers are located and how they are connected to the network. The logical layout has to do with the function of the computer, how it is used, and how it is managed. By separating the two, the administration of computers does not have to be affected by the network infrastructure.

Multiple Domains

Networks can also be arranged into multiple domains, which are still managed as a single, cohesive, yet decentralized unit. Multiple administrators manage the network, and the domains represent specific parts of a larger organization. Multiple domains are generally created when the network (and corporation) spans multiple countries or when two established companies merge. In a multiple domain configuration, there must be at least one domain controller in each domain.

See Also   To learn more about domains and Active Directory, visit *http://technet.microsoft.com/default.aspx* and search using the keywords "Active Directory."

Tier Structure

Corporations define technical support roles in tiers; generally, there are four tiers, as detailed in Table 1-2. Each of these four tiers can also have its own tier structure. The tier position that we are concerned with is tier 1, which is italicized in the table. The employees in the corporate tier-1 group are also categorized in three additional internal tiers. The internal tier-1 employees usually provide front-line support and internal tiers 2, 3, and 4 accept escalations. These roles are defined with more detail in the section "Telephone Call Centers" later in this chapter. Your position in the corporation will be in the tier 1, help desk position.

Table 1-2   An Overview of the Corporate Tier Structure

Tier	Description
Tier 4, architect	Strategic: Analyzes and designs enterprises. Makes budget and purchasing decisions.
Tier 3, engineer	Tactical: Analyzes and designs within a single technology and implements the technology. Handles complex troubleshooting, including escalations from administrators.
Tier 2, administrator	Operational: Provides day-to-day server and software troubleshooting. Performs operating system management and support.
Tier 1, help desk	*Support: Supports day-to-day client operating systems, applications, and hardware troubleshooting. Follows prescriptive guidelines and provides end-user phone support.*

Corporate tier structures allow for growth by clearly defining technical support roles and requirements for moving up the tier ladder. The Microsoft Certified Desktop Support Technician (MCDST) certification prepares candidates for jobs in the tier-1 environment and provides a good foundation for moving up in the corporation.

Job Titles and Requirements

As a tier-1 entry-level technical support employee, your job is to provide direct end-user support. At a high level, you should be prepared to perform the following tasks:

- Perform general troubleshooting of the operating system and installed applications

- Provide customer service, including listening to the customer, defining and solving the problem, and educating the user about how to avoid the problem in the future

- Install, configure, and upgrade software, including applications and operating systems

- Monitor and maintain systems

- Document calls and close them or escalate them as required by company policy and time limits set by SLAs

Note   An SLA defines the parameters of service provided by a company to a user. SLAs typically cover the services to be delivered, fees and expenses, customer responsibilities, documentation requirements, and support policies.

More specifically, you will be consulted to troubleshoot and provide information about a variety of aspects of the operating system. You will be called on to resolve installation and connectivity issues; configure and troubleshoot users' desktop environments; troubleshoot multiple boot or multiuser computers; and install, configure, and troubleshoot hardware. You will be expected to resolve or escalate 80 percent of the incident requests you receive from end users, employ proper procedures to document the incident, and operate within the environment's SLAs. SLAs might require that a call be resolved in a particular amount of time or within a specified budget.

There are various job titles and job roles for DSTs; common tier-1 entry-level job titles are listed here. When creating a resumé, looking for employment, or interviewing, make sure that you are familiar with these titles. Each of these job titles is a tier-1 entry-level job, and all are quite similar.

- Call center support representative
- Customer service representative
- Help desk specialist (or technician)
- Product support specialist
- PC support specialist

Tip   To supplement your DST training, join a relevant newsgroup. With a newsgroup, you can exchange ideas, ask for help, and get answers to common questions quickly. For more information, visit *http://www.microsoft.com/windowsxp/expertzone/newsgroups.mspx*.

Practice: Identify Tasks in a Corporate Environment

In this practice, you will explore some of the tasks that are associated with the various tiers. If you are unable to answer a question, review the lesson materials and try the question again. You can find answers to the questions in the "Questions and Answers" section at the end of this chapter.

Scenario

You are a technical support administrator at Proseware, Inc., which supports end users of video games. Proseware also runs online servers for its multiplayer games. You have been asked to separate support into three categories: help desk, administrator, and engineer. You have been told that the help desk will handle client-side questions concerning configuration issues within the game. Administrators will handle configuration problems that the help desk fails to solve, and they will handle all operating system and hardware issues. The engineer group will handle any technical problems that occur on the server.

Group the following list of tasks according to which support tier you think would handle them. (Tiers are tier 1—Help Desk, tier 2—Administrator, and tier 3—Engineer.)

- Adjust display settings.
- Troubleshoot video driver problems.
- Troubleshoot registration problems that occur on the server.
- Adjust audio settings.
- Troubleshoot joystick problems.
- Configure the game to play on a home network.
- Troubleshoot networking issues preventing a customer's computer from connecting to the server.
- Register the product online.
- Deal with server crashes resulting from too many requests for service.

Lesson Review

The following questions are intended to reinforce key information presented in this lesson. If you are unable to answer a question, review the lesson materials and try the question again. You can find answers to the questions in the "Questions and Answers" section at the end of this chapter.

1. Briefly, what types of businesses, corporations, or companies would choose to configure a workgroup? A domain? A multiple domain? Why?

   _____

   _____

   _____

2. Which of the following is not a job function of a tier-1 corporate desktop support technician? (Choose all that apply.)

   A. Perform general troubleshooting of the operating system.

   B. Perform general troubleshooting of operating system components, such as Internet Explorer.

   C. Troubleshoot network problems that do not directly affect the end user.

   D. Install, configure, and upgrade software, including applications and operating systems.

   E. Set group or local security policies for end users, including which security settings a user should have, and determine what he or she can or cannot access on the network.

3. For each of the following descriptions, decide whether it refers to a workgroup, a domain, or multiple domain network configurations. If the description applies to more than one network configuration, list all that apply.

   A. This network configuration is a logical grouping of computers created for the purpose of sharing resources such as files and printers.

   B. This network configuration does not use Active Directory services.

   C. This network configuration can include multiple domain controllers.

   D. This network configuration provides a single point of administration for security.

   E. This network configuration is easy to design and implement, and is best configured for users in close proximity to one another.

Lesson Summary

- DSTs must be prepared to work in various environments, including workgroups, domains, and multiple domains.

- A DST's place in the corporate, ISP, or company hierarchy is generally the tier-1 position, which is considered an entry-level position.

- The MCDST certification opens a doorway into tier-1 jobs, identifies the employee as qualified to hold the desired job, and identifies the business owner as qualified to determine and resolve home end-user problems.

Lesson 3: Overview of Noncorporate Environments

Not all DSTs acquire or hold jobs in a large corporate environment; many obtain employment through telephone call centers, repair shops, private businesses, and ISPs.

After this lesson, you will be able to

■ Identify common types of noncorporate support jobs.

■ Describe the job activities found in noncorporate support jobs.

Estimated lesson time: 10 minutes

Telephone Call Centers

Telephone call centers accept calls from end users and resolve problems over the telephone. These calls can be hardware- or software-related, depending on the company and its clients. A DST's place in these environments is defined by using a tier system similar to that in a corporate environment. Table 1-3 shows a general tier structure for a telephone call center. An entry-level DST falls in either of the first two tiers (italicized in the table), depending on experience.

Table 1-3   Overview of the Telephone Call Center Tier Structure

Experience	Scope of Responsibilities
Tier 4: 4+ years of experience	Receives calls that are escalated from tier-3 personnel and tries to resolve them. This involves complex troubleshooting; employees in this tier are hardware and software engineers and architects.
Tier 3: 1 to 2 years of experience	Receives calls that are escalated from tier-2 personnel and tries to resolve them. This involves a combination of experience, directed training in specific hardware and software, and application of previous knowledge. These employees might have other certifications.
Tier 2: 6 months to 1 year of experience	*Receives calls that are escalated from tier 1 personnel and tries to resolve them. Like tier-1 employees, tier-2 employees work by using a set of prescribed questions and solutions. Supports operating system, application, and hardware troubleshooting.*
Tier 1: Less than 6 months of experience	*Answers the phone and works using a script. The tier-1 employee instructs the user to reboot the computer, disconnect and reconnect, stop and restart an application, and perform other common troubleshooting tasks. Determines the appropriate time to escalate calls to tier-2 personnel.*

Repair Shops and Private Businesses

DSTs also find their niche as members of small repair shops, large repair shop chains, computer sales chains, computer manufacturers, or hardware testing labs. They can also start their own computer-repair businesses.

If you intend to work as a DST in any of these settings, you should also be either A+ or Network+ certified. Unlike a DST, an employee at a repair shop or one who owns his or her own business has much more hands-on computer work than those who answer phones. These DSTs replace hardware, add memory, repair printers, and perform similar tasks in addition to the tasks required of a DST.

Internet Service Providers

ISPs are companies that provide Internet access to subscribers for a monthly fee. Subscribers can be individuals or entire corporations. Some ISPs do more than offer Internet access, however: They design Web pages, consult with businesses, provide feedback concerning Web page traffic, and send out virus warnings. Some also set up, secure, and maintain e-commerce websites for clients.

If you choose to work for an ISP, you will most likely answer the phones and perform general help-desk duties, as previously defined. The most common tasks required of an ISP DST include the following:

- Set up new accounts using Microsoft Office Outlook or Outlook Express, Netscape Mail, Apple OSX Mail, Eudora, and other e-mail clients
- Configure settings to filter spam by creating rules and blocking senders
- Troubleshoot Internet and e-mail access
- Troubleshoot servers and physical connections
- Resolve problems with various connection types, including dial-up modems, digital subscriber line (DSL), cable, and wireless connections
- Resolve and escalate calls when necessary

ISP DSTs must be familiar with Internet technologies, Domain Name System (DNS) name resolution, connection types, available modems, and other common ISP tools. ISPs, like other DST employers, generally work using a tier system, and moving up the tier is dependent on experience, education, and training.

Lesson Review

The following questions are intended to reinforce key information presented in this lesson. If you are unable to answer a question, review the lesson materials and try the question again. You can find answers to the questions in the "Questions and Answers" section at the end of this chapter.

1. You have just gotten a job at an ISP and have been assigned a tier-1 position. Which of the following can you expect in your first week at work? (Choose all that apply.)

   A. To walk users through re-creating their e-mail accounts or reconfiguring their Internet security settings

   B. To configure local security policies

   C. To answer phones and instruct users to reboot their computers, close and restart applications, and disconnect from and reconnect to the ISP

   D. To read from a script of questions and make decisions based on users' answers

   E. To help users reinstall their e-mail clients

2. Taking into account what you have learned about workgroups and domains, network topologies, corporate and noncorporate tier structures, call center environments, hands-on repair shops, and ISPs, describe the environment in which you would most like to work. Cite five reasons for your decision.

   _____

   _____

Lesson Summary

- Noncorporate environments in which a DST might work include telephone call centers, repair shops, private businesses, and ISPs.

- Each of the noncorporate environments requires different skills, but in each instance you must be friendly, helpful, capable, and competent.

- If you work for a telephone call center or an ISP, you will likely work in a tier structure similar to the structures found in corporate environments.

Lesson 4: Overview of Basic Troubleshooting

This lesson discusses the techniques involved with resolving service calls. The most important part of troubleshooting is asking pertinent questions and listening to and making notes on the answers. After you have asked the proper questions and made notes on the answers, you will need to formulate a plan of action for researching and isolating the problem and then for resolving the call.

After this lesson, you will be able to

- Describe the questions that you should ask to help determine the problem.
- Explain what the answers to those questions can tell you.
- Explain general troubleshooting procedures.
- Describe places you can turn to for help locating answers.
- Explain how to attempt solutions without making the problem worse.

Estimated lesson time: 50 minutes

Asking Who, When, What, Why, and How

A reporter or police officer asks these questions to obtain the required information to perform his or her job, and you will ask the same questions in your role as a DST. The information that you acquire helps you determine why the problem occurred. Then, with that knowledge, you can often resolve the problem on your own. The following sections list some common questions and possible answers.

Who?

The following questions will help you identify the person affected by a problem.

- Who was using the computer when the problem first occurred?
- Who else has been using the computer, and has he or she experienced similar problems?
- Who has worked on this problem previously (if it has happened before)?
- Who has the same problem on another computer (that you know of)?

The answers to these questions tell you who has firsthand knowledge of the problem and whether other users who access the same computer (under a different account) also encounter the problem. If multiple users have access, but only one user encounters the problem, you have already narrowed the issue. You will also learn from these questions who has worked on the problem before (you might find out that the user has) and whether other users on the network are having the same problem on their computers. If the latter is true, the problem could be a networkwide problem, such as a security policy issue, a virus, or some other glitch in the entire system.

When?

The following questions will help you determine when a problem occurred and establish a timeline of activities that might relate to the problem.

- When did this problem occur the first time, and has it occurred since?
- When was the last time you downloaded or installed an application?
- When was the last time you installed new hardware?
- When did you last clean your hard drive with Disk Cleanup or Disk Defragmenter, delete temporary files or cookies, or perform similar deletions of data?
- When was the last time you uninstalled an application?

The answers to these questions tell you how long the user has had this problem, whether the problem occurred after the user installed a new piece of hardware or a new application, and whether the user routinely maintains the computer. If the problem occurred after installing or uninstalling hardware or software, you have a good lead. Asking pointed questions about maintenance can also be helpful for finding out whether the user has recently cleaned out program or system folders, or has deleted any necessary files.

What?

The following questions will help you find information about what the user thinks may be the cause of the problem and any solutions the user has already attempted.

- What are your thoughts on what caused the problem?
- What have you tried doing to troubleshoot the problem yourself?
- What do you think can be done to solve the problem?

The answers to these questions tell you what the user believes happened and give you an opportunity to involve him or her in the solution. Asking the user what he or she thinks can be done to solve the problem could also reveal a very simple solution. If the user recently reconfigured settings for a program or uninstalled a necessary file or program, you know where to begin. If the user has already tried to troubleshoot the problem, you need to know what changes he or she has made. Finally, if the user thinks that reconfiguring the e-mail account will solve the problem, he or she might have been doing something to that account earlier, but does not want to admit it.

Why and How?

The following questions often can produce a solution quickly.

- Why do you think the problem occurred?

- How do you think the problem occurred?

If the user says, "The problem occurred because I spilled coffee on the keyboard," or "The problem occurred because I opened an attachment in an e-mail," you know exactly where to start. Keep in mind, however, that these answers will not always be useful; they might sometimes even be misleading. (A user might have opened an attachment, but might tell you he or she did not, for instance.) Remember, you are the expert.

As you work through these questions with an end user, document the answers carefully, listen to everything he or she has to say, be polite and professional, and make notes of possible solutions as you think of them. If you need to, leave the situation for a few minutes to digest the information and then check company documentation, online support, or other resources for answers.

> **Real World   Your Changing Role**
>
> When you begin working at a telephone call center, a company, a home business, or an ISP as a tier-1 DST, you should expect to ask your end users specific questions that are already written for you in the form of a script. However, as you move up the ladder and work through the natural progression of gaining expertise and experience, you will move from following a script to building your own repertoire of queries. As you internalize your knowledge, you will start to learn and understand how to resolve problems on your own. Keeping in mind that you will probably start your first tier-1 position reading questions already written for you, in this section you will learn what types of questions to ask when you are required to work through the resolution process on your own.

Reproducing the Problem

If you or the end user can reproduce the problem, you will have quite a bit of additional information to work with. Problems that cannot be reproduced, such as applications that shut down for no apparent reason, are much more difficult to diagnose than problems that can be reproduced, such as being unable to send or receive e-mail. If the end user can reproduce the problem, make a note of which applications were open and which components were being used, and then troubleshoot those applications and their configurations.

> **Caution**   Do not try to reproduce any problem that has previously caused loss of data or is a known network problem, such as a virus or worm. Doing so can cause additional problems and further damage.

Understanding General Troubleshooting Procedures

If you work for an ISP or a telephone call center, your plan of action might involve only reading a set of directions from a script and escalating the call up a tier, but it is still a course of action. If you have already determined a solution and solved the problem, you need to only document your solution.

If you own your own business or are otherwise on your own when fielding a service call, solving the problem might involve more groundwork. When physically assisting users in their homes or at their desks, it is not quite so easy to turn the call over to someone else. If you own your own business, conferring with someone else can cost you time and money, as well as clients. If you walk across the corporate campus to field a call, calling in someone else means waiting for them to arrive and then explaining the problem again. In either instance, when you are given more responsibility for servicing calls, you must have a plan of action for uncovering, documenting, and resolving the call without another DST. In this section, you will learn the steps involved in resolving a service call on your own, instead of calling in another DST or escalating the call. In general, a specific procedure should be followed, and a common technique is listed here.

To locate answers and to determine a solution after speaking with the end user, follow these general steps. (Each step is detailed in the following sections.)

1. Locate a solution by searching the computer's Help And Support Center. If you find a solution, attempt to solve the problem and document the solution. If the solution does not work, document that as well, and undo any changes made to the computer.

2. Locate a solution by searching the company's support files. If you find a solution, attempt to solve the problem and document the solution. If the solution does not work, document that as well, and undo any changes made to the computer.

3. Search manufacturers' websites. If you find a solution, attempt to solve the problem and document the solution. If the solution does not work, document that as well, and undo any changes made to the computer.

4. Search technical sites. If you find a solution, attempt to solve the problem and document the solution. If the solution does not work, document that as well, and undo any changes made to the computer.

5. Search newsgroups. If you find a solution, attempt to solve the problem and document the solution. If the solution does not work, document that as well, and undo any changes made to the computer.

6. If you do not find a solution, document the information and attempted solutions, and undo any changes made to the computer during the troubleshooting process.

7. Escalate the call.

8. When the problem is solved, document the solution.

The troubleshooting process covered in the preceding steps is shown in further detail in the flowchart in Figure 1-3.

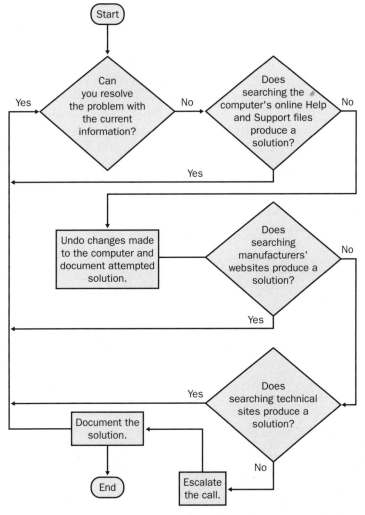

Figure 1-3   Troubleshooting a problem is best done systematically.

Locating the Answers

There are several places to look for help in troubleshooting a computer problem, and if you have good research skills, you will most likely be able to locate a solution without escalating the call. Because escalations require more work, more downtime, and more expense for both you and the end user, you should do all you can to resolve calls without having to call in someone else to help. As for finding a solution, chances are good that this is not the first time an end user has encountered this problem, and the answer will probably be easy to find either in company documents or on the Internet.

Tip   The ability to research and find answers is not an innate skill; a good researcher learns where to look for answers.

Help And Support Center

The Help And Support Center should be the first place you look for information about common operating system problems. Windows Help And Support Center offers information ranging from performing basic tasks, such as logging on and off, to complex ones, such as working remotely. It also offers tools to help you access advanced system information, check network diagnostics, and run software and hardware troubleshooting wizards. Figure 1-4 shows the default Help And Support Center for Microsoft Windows XP Professional. It is easy to use; simply browse the categories or type in a few keywords.

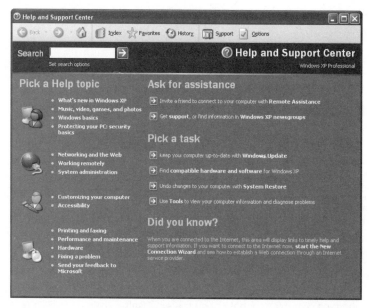

Figure 1-4   The Windows XP Professional default Help And Support Center page offers an abundance of information.

Company Documentation

As time passes, more and more businesses customize the help files in the Help And Support Center so that the files offer resources to end users that are specific to their department, job role, company, or domain. This localized help information is useful—not only to the end user, but also to DSTs who do not work for the company and are instead hired as vendors or contract employees. Computer manufacturers already personalize help files for home users and include help files directly related to the user's specific computer configuration.

> **Exam Tip**   Always determine the manufacturer and model of a computer first. Some manufacturers change default Windows settings, include modified help files, and install custom diagnostics software. Often, you can take advantage of these inclusions. At a minimum, you should be aware of their presence when proposing solutions.

Targeted help such as this enables users to locate answers to their own problems easily, and it allows you to access information quickly as well. Figure 1-5 shows an example of a customized Help And Support Center interface created by Sony Corporation for the home user. Notice that there are additional help topics, including "VAIO User Guide," "VAIO Multimedia," and "VAIO Support Agent Help." These topics are specific to the machine, and they can be quite helpful for troubleshooting computer problems.

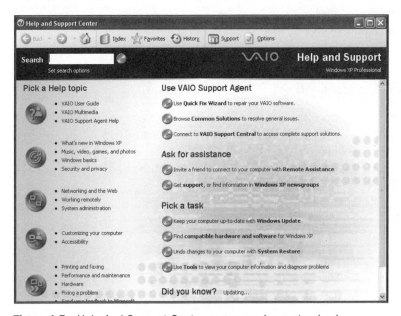

Figure 1-5   Help And Support Center pages can be customized.

Depending on your work environment, this type of customized documentation might be available. At the very least, almost every company offers some access to a database that contains answers to commonly asked questions. If you cannot find the answer to your troubleshooting query using the Windows Help And Support Center, try the manufacturer's website.

Manufacturers' Websites

Many times, a problem occurs because a piece of hardware has failed. A **device driver** is corrupt, for example, or new software is incompatible with Windows XP or other installed software, or a computer's **basic input/output system (BIOS)** needs updating. You can research these problems and others through a manufacturer's website. Websites are an especially appropriate tool when troubleshooting a home user's computer or a computer that has recently been upgraded from one operating system to another. If you have yet to find the problem and a troubleshooting wizard has listed hardware, software, or BIOS problems as the culprit, visit the manufacturer's website for help and updates.

Tip   Home users are more likely to install new drivers, applications, and third-party utilities than office users—mainly because companies place more limitations on office users. Office users are often not allowed to install devices and applications because of network policies. When troubleshooting a home user's computer, make sure that you know what has been installed recently; a new hardware device might be causing the problem. When troubleshooting for an office user, make sure that the user is (or you are) allowed to implement the proposed solutions.

The Microsoft Knowledge Base

The Microsoft Knowledge Base (available at *http://support.microsoft.com/default.aspx*) offers answers to known issues and can be of significant help when you are trying to solve seemingly unresolvable issues. Figure 1-6 shows the Microsoft Help And Support website, in which Knowledge Base and other resources can be accessed. Notice that you can also access announcements, link to visitors' top links, acquire downloads and updates, get product support, and locate other support centers (for Microsoft Outlook, Windows 2000, and so on).

Figure 1-6   The Microsoft Knowledge Base offers solutions to known issues.

The Knowledge Base contains support articles that are identified by an ID number, and you can search for information using that number or using keywords. These articles address known issues with the operating system, third-party software, and hardware; they also provide workarounds and solutions. The Knowledge Base also offers how-to articles, such as KB 291252, "How To Publish Pictures to the Internet in Windows XP," and KB 813938, "How to Set Up a Small Network with Windows Home Edition" (the first part of a series of articles on the subject).

Search the Knowledge Base after you have tried the previous options and when you need to know the following:

- Why a specific piece of hardware such as a camera, scanner, printer, or other device does not work as expected and the problem can be reproduced easily

- Why a specific third-party application does not install, does not start, does not work as expected, or produces error messages

- How to resolve operating system errors, including boot errors, problems during installation, access violation errors, and standby problems; and how to resolve other known issues

- How to create boot disks, view system requirements, configure file associations, or perform other common tasks

- How to resolve errors that occur when accessing operating system components, such as when configuring system properties or using System Restore

- What a stop error message means and how to resolve it

- How to resolve errors that occur after installing updates

Note   Search the Knowledge Base for the specific error message if a text message exists. This is an especially helpful resource when the error is caused by third-party software or hardware. Information about third-party tools is not available in the Windows XP help files.

TechNet

Microsoft TechNet (*http://technet.microsoft.com/default.aspx*) offers comprehensive help on applications; operating systems; and components such as Active Directory, Microsoft Internet Explorer, and Windows XP Professional—including planning, deployment, maintenance, and support. You can also access information about security, get downloads, read how-to articles, read columns, and access troubleshooting and support pages. Because your job will revolve around troubleshooting and resolving end-user requests, you will likely spend most of your time accessing the troubleshooting pages. A sample TechNet page is shown in Figure 1-7.

Figure 1-7   A TechNet page provides a wealth of information that is written for IT professionals.

Much of the information available from TechNet, including the Knowledge Base, is also available through the Microsoft Help And Support website, but TechNet is more geared toward information technology (IT) professionals. You will find that the articles from TechNet are often more technical and sometimes more slanted toward large organizations and networks. Both the TechNet and the Microsoft Help And Support websites are useful sites, and you will develop a feel for which is the most useful in different situations.

Search the TechNet support pages after you have tried the Microsoft Help And Support Website and when you need to do any of the following:

■ Locate product documentation

■ View the latest security bulletins

■ Get information about service packs, Windows updates, and drivers

- Get help with dynamic-link library (DLL) errors

- Subscribe to TechNet

- Locate highly technical information about technologies

> **Note**   TechNet offers two types of annual subscriptions for a single user or a single server: TechNet Standard and TechNet Plus. Subscription prices range from about $350 to $1,000 (U.S.). A one-year subscription delivers up-to-date technical information every month, including the complete Knowledge Base and the latest resource kits, service packs, drivers and patches, deployment guides, white papers, evaluation guides, and much more. This information is on a set of CDs or DVDs that can be accessed anywhere and at any time—even when you cannot get online. Installing service packs from a disc is much faster than downloading them, which is another reason to consider the subscription. Finally, TechNet Plus offers beta and evaluation software, allowing you to gain experience with software before it is released to the public.

Newsgroups

Newsgroups are a valuable resource for locating answers that you are unable to resolve using any other method. Members of newsgroups are your peers in IT, computer enthusiasts, beginners, and advanced business or home users, and they have various abilities. Some are looking for answers, and some frequent the newsgroup to provide answers to issues they have resolved and to share their expertise. You can join a newsgroup that addresses the application or operating system you need help with, immediately post your question, and almost as quickly receive an answer. Sometimes, answers even come from Microsoft experts, such as Microsoft Most Valuable Professionals (MVPs). Microsoft MVPs are chosen based on their practical expertise in Microsoft technologies, and these MVPs are deemed experts in their fields.

You can access newsgroups in a number of ways, including the following:

- To access newsgroups through a newsreader (the best method because you can access all the newsgroups, and it is easiest to stay current this way), configure your newsreader to access the *msnews.microsoft.com* news server.

- To access a full list of available newsgroups through the Web (a good choice if you do not have newsreader software), visit *http://www.microsoft.com/communities/ newsgroups/en-us/default.aspx.*

- To access newsgroups through the Microsoft Help And Support website, the Windows XP Expert Zone, or the TechNet website, visit those sites and click the Newsgroups link. Some people favor this method because the newsgroups are more clearly identified and are a bit more accessible. However, the newsgroups presented on these sites are just a subset of what is available.

You will find newsgroups for a variety of applications, operating systems, components, and levels of end user. Table 1-4 lists some of the available newsgroup categories, although each category can have multiple newsgroups (such as different newsgroups on Windows XP for subjects such as hardware, customizing, and networking).

Table 1-4   Selecting the Right Newsgroup

For Help With...	Join These Knowledge Base Newsgroups
Operating systems	*microsoft.public.windowsxp*
	microsoft.public.windowsme
	microsoft.public.windows.server
Internet Explorer	*microsoft.public.windows.inetexplorer*
Connectivity and networking	*microsoft.public.windowsxp.network_web*
	microsoft.public.windows.networking
	microsoft.public.certification.networking
Security	*microsoft.public.security*
	microsoft.public.security.virus
	microsoft.public.windowsxp.security_admin

Working through Possible Solutions

Working through a solution after you have found it requires a little more know-how than simply clicking the mouse a few times and then walking away or hanging up the phone. You will have to perform some prerepair and post-repair tasks such as ordering the solutions (if there are more than one), backing up the user's data, and attempting the solutions and documenting the results. If a solution does not work, you will have to undo it, try another, and possibly escalate the problem as required by your company.

Attempting Solutions

Most of the time, after researching your problem, you will find a single solution, and working through that solution will resolve the problem. Solutions you will uncover in a tier-1 position generally involve running a command-line utility, reconfiguring an e-mail account, installing an update, re-creating a network connection, reseating a card on the motherboard, or even simply rebooting the computer or removing a floppy disk from the A drive. However, no matter how simple the solution seems, you should always prepare for the worst. Before attempting any solution (besides removing a floppy disk or rebooting), perform as many of the following tasks as you can within your time frame, job scope, and corporate limitations:

- Locate and make a note of previous settings so that you can revert to those if your solution fails or causes additional problems.

- Order the solutions by listing solutions obtained from reputable sources first. (List Help And Support Center, Knowledge Base, TechNet, the manufacturer's website, and so on first; then list solutions found through newsgroups or third-party sites.)

- Back up the end-user's data to a network resource, CD-R, or external hard disk.

- Create a System Restore point.

- Perform any additional tasks required by your company.

- Completely document all attempted solutions and their results.

The higher you move up the tier ladder, the more of these tasks you will need to perform or be able to perform. If you provide phone support and work from a script, you might not be able to perform any of these tasks, but if you own your own business and visit the user onsite (or if you go to a user's desk to solve the problem), you will likely have more leeway (and responsibility) and can do more.

Caution Protect the end-user's data at all costs. If that means postponing an attempt at a risky or an undocumented solution until another DST can back up the data or until you can bring in a CD-R drive to back up a home user's data, you must wait.

While working to repair the problem, if you attempt a solution that does not work, you must undo any changed settings, configurations, uninstalled programs, or other specific alterations to a computer before you attempt another solution. This is especially critical if you need to escalate the call; the next DST needs to see the computer in its previous state. In addition, fully test the solution that you think resolves the problem. For instance, verify that e-mail can be sent and received after you have changed Post Office Protocol version 3 (POP3) e-mail settings, or make sure that the user can access a website after you have changed Internet Explorer's privacy settings. Attempt solutions that are within your realm of responsibility; do not perform a repair installation if that task is not on your list of repair options.

Documenting the Problem and Attempted Solutions

Documenting the problem, attempted solutions, and solutions that work are a major part of a DST's job. Although companies, call centers, ISPs, repair shops, and small business owners each has its own way of documenting, documentation tasks usually involve creating (or accessing) a file for a specific client, subscriber, end user, or company computer and then updating that file each time there is a service call regarding it. The documentation might be handwritten on a documentation worksheet and then transferred to a computer file later (for home or desktop technical support), or it might be immediately entered into a computer (for call center or ISP technical support).

Depending on the job you hold and your position in the tier structure, you might be required to fill in only a few fields of a documentation worksheet. However, if you own your own company and keep your own records, you will want to keep much more detailed information. Here are a few items that you should almost always document, regardless of the type of job or position that you hold:

- The date and time the service call was initiated
- The name, address, phone number, logon information, and any other pertinent data that identifies the end user
- The computer ID, operating system version, connection type, and installed applications, as appropriate
- The problem in definite terms, with as much detail as time allows
- The attempted solutions and the results
- The solution or escalation information
- Whether the issue has been resolved and how long the resolution took

Keeping customer and service call documentation (with even minimal information) is crucial to being a good DST, running a successful business, acquiring experience, or advancing in your field. Keeping a separate log of problems and solutions that you have dealt with can also become quite a reference tool; you can refer to your own personal documentation when the problem arises again with another client. In the next section, you will learn how to create a personal knowledge base.

Creating a Personal Knowledge Base

There are several options for collecting and maintaining the data you will compile while performing your job as a DST. Microsoft Office Excel and Microsoft Office Access make good database and organizational tools, and third-party software might also be appropriate, depending on how much data you want to keep. Keeping your own personal knowledge base of problems you have encountered and their solutions can make it easier for you to access the answers to those problems the next time they arise.

When creating a personal knowledge base of problems and their solutions, document the following:

■ The problem in detail, using keywords so that a search for the problem or one similar to it will produce results

■ The cause of the problem, using keywords so that a search for the problem or one similar to it will produce results

■ The resource that offered a solution to the problem, including a Uniform Resource Locator (URL)

■ The solution

■ Problems that resulted from the solution (if any)

■ How many times the problem has been encountered and solved

Lesson Review

The following questions are intended to reinforce key information presented in this lesson. If you are unable to answer a question, review the lesson materials and try the question again. You can find answers to the questions in the "Questions and Answers" section at the end of this chapter.

1. Questions asked of clients often trigger quick solutions to basic problems. Match the question on the left to the solution it triggered on the right.

1. Who is affected by this problem?

A. The user states that she recently deleted all temporary files and cookies from her computer, explaining why she is no longer able to sign in automatically to websites she visits.

2. When was the first time you noticed the problem? Was it after a new installation of software or hardware?

B. John cannot send or receive messages using Outlook. It is determined that the problem is related only to his configuration of Outlook because other users who log on to the same computer under a different account can use Outlook to send and receive e-mail messages without any problems.

3. Has the user recently deleted any files or performed any maintenance?

C. The keyboard keys are sticky because coffee was spilled on the keyboard.

4. How did this problem occur?

D. The user states that the first time the computer acted strangely was after he installed a new screen saver.

2. Decide where to look first for solutions to the problems that are listed here. Match each question on the left to the appropriate choice on the right.

1. After a recent upgrade to Windows XP Professional, a user's scanner no longer functions as it should. The user remembers that the scanner was listed as incompatible during the upgrade, and you believe that it might be a driver issue. Where will you likely find the new driver?

A. Newsgroup

2. A user cannot access a network application. The application was designed specifically for the company and is not a Microsoft product or any other common third-party application. Where will you likely find information about this application?

B. TechNet

3. You have searched the Knowledge Base and TechNet for the solution to a problem, but have not had any luck. Where should you look now?

C. Knowledge Base

4. You need to search through the latest security bulletins to find out whether the problem you are having is related to a known security problem. Which online resource offers access to these bulletins?

D. Manufacturer's website

5. You need to find out why a home user's camera does not work with the Windows Picture And Fax Viewer. Specifically, the Rotate tool causes the computer to freeze up each time it is used. Where should you look first?

E. Company documentation

6. You want to access the Hardware Troubleshooter to resolve a problem with a user's sound card. Where can this troubleshooter be found?

F Help And Support Center

3. Create three simple questions you could ask an end user who is having a problem accessing data on the network server that would in turn provide answers to common connectivity problems. Explain what each solution might uncover. For instance, a "yes" answer to the question, "Has the computer been moved or bumped recently?" could indicate that a network card inside the computer is loose.

_____

_____

Lesson Summary

- To resolve a service call, you must gather information, determine a solution, find and attempt solutions or escalate the call, test any solutions that you implement, and inform the end user of your findings.

- To solve a problem, first get answers to the questions who, when, what, why, and how. The answers often point to a solution quickly.

- To find a solution, search these resources in the following order: Help And Support Center, Help And Support website, company documentation, manufacturers' websites, technical sites, and newsgroups. Apply possible solutions in the same order.

- Before attempting any solution, back up the user's data, create a System Restore point, and document previous settings and configurations if doing so is within your job role.

- Always document the service call fully, including the user's name, the computer ID, the problem, the attempted solution, the result, and how long it took to resolve the call.

Case Scenario Exercises

In the following scenarios, you must use what you have learned throughout the lessons in this chapter to answer questions based on a real-world scenario. Read each scenario and answer the questions. If you have trouble, review the chapter and try again. You can find answers in the "Questions and Answers" section at the end of this chapter.

Scenario 1.1

John earned his MCDST and is in the process of obtaining an entry-level IT job. He enjoys working with people, but he also enjoys the hands-on aspect of the technology. He has several computers at home, and he has connected them and configured a small domain just for the fun of it. He likes working inside the computer, too, adding memory, replacing cards, and so on. He is certain that someday he wants to own his own computer-repair or network-consulting business. He wants to make sure that he gets the best work experience possible.

1. What type of entry-level job do you think is best for John as he works to meet his goals? Why?

_____

_____

_____

Scenario 1.2

You recently earned your A+ certification and are currently working in a small family-owned repair shop. You work in the repair section of the shop and do a lot of hands-on computer work, but you do not have much interaction with the public. Although you have exceptionally good problem-solving skills and are extremely talented at repairing hardware, adding memory, repairing printers, and performing similar tasks, you know that you lack some of the delicate personal skills required of a successful DST. Your boss has even mentioned that you could be a little more personable.

   1. Which of the following offer the best solutions to this problem? (Select two.)

      A. Consider moonlighting two or three nights a week as a telephone call support technician. There, you will learn some of the basic personal skills required of a good DST.

      B. Quit the repair shop and go to work immediately for an ISP. You can learn to create websites, you will learn about e-commerce, and if you are lucky, you will have to deal with people face-to-face only occasionally.

      C. Take a course on interpersonal skills at your local community college. There you will learn basic communication skills, such as how to listen and how to converse effectively with all types of people.

      D. Consider a different line of work. Communication skills, ability, talent, and personal skills come naturally to good DSTs and cannot be taught.

Scenario 1.3

An end user calls to report a problem with a locally attached printer. The user is in an office on the other side of the corporate complex, you are busy, and no other DST is available. You find out, after asking a few questions, that the printer actually works fine; it just prints slowly. You will not be able to visit the user's desk in person until tomorrow, and you have learned from the user that she has quite a bit of experience with computers.

   1. Which of the following solutions (they are all valid) is best under these circumstances?

      A. Tell the user to join a printer newsgroup and ask other users for advice.

      B. Tell the user to open Help And Support Center, locate the printer trouble-shooter, and work through the options. There is an option to allow Windows to investigate the problem, and this might produce a solution.

      C. Tell the user to visit *http://www.windrivers.com* and download a new driver for the printer.

      D. Tell the user to uninstall and reinstall the printer.

Chapter Summary

- As a DST, you will encounter users of all skill levels. Never assume that you know more than the user to whom you are talking.

- DSTs must have technical knowledge in many areas, including the operating system; components, such as Microsoft Office Outlook Express and Internet Explorer; and applications, including Outlook, Excel, and Access.

- DSTs must be good at gathering information from people who might not be able to explain the problem clearly and must be good at explaining technical information to nontechnical users.

- DSTs must be prepared to work in various environments, including workgroups, domains, and multiple domains.

- A DST's place in the corporate, ISP, or company hierarchy is generally the tier-1 position, which is considered an entry-level position.

- The MCDST certification opens a doorway into tier-1 jobs, identifies the employee as qualified to hold the desired job, and identifies the business owner as qualified to determine and resolve home end-user problems.

- Noncorporate environments in which a DST might work include telephone call centers, repair shops, private businesses, and ISPs.

- Each of the noncorporate environments requires different skills, but you must be friendly, helpful, capable, and competent in each instance.

- If you work for a telephone call center or an ISP, you will likely work in a tier structure much like the structures found in corporate environments.

- To solve a problem, first get answers to the questions who, when, what, why, and how. The answers often point quickly to a solution.

- To find a solution, search these resources in the following order: Help And Support Center, Help And Support website, company documentation, manufacturers' websites, technical sites, and newsgroups. Apply possible solutions in the same order.

- Before attempting any solution, back up the user's data, create a System Restore point, and document previous settings and configurations if doing so is within your job role.

- Always document the service call fully, including the user's name, the computer ID, the problem, the attempted solution, the result, and how long it took to resolve the call.

Exam Highlights

Before taking the exam, review the key topics and terms that are presented in this chapter. You need to know this information.

Key Points

- Learn to recognize quickly the skill level of the user you are helping. This helps you get the right information from the user and create solutions that the user is comfortable implementing.

- Always identify the scope of a problem. Is it isolated to a single application? A single computer? Is it a network problem? What type of network is involved—peer-to-peer or domain?

- Always try one possible solution at a time. If the solution does not work, undo the solution before moving on to the next one. This takes extra time, but helps ensure the stability of the user's system and gives you a better idea of what worked and what did not.

Key Terms

Active Directory   A single point of administration database that contains information about a network's users, workstations, servers, printers, and other resources. Active Directory (found on a domain controller) determines who can access what and to what degree. Active Directory is essential to maintaining, organizing, and securing the resources on a larger network. It allows network administrators to centrally manage resources, and it is extensible—meaning that it can be configured to grow and be personalized for any company.

basic input/output system (BIOS)   A computer's BIOS program determines in what order the computer searches for system files on startup, it manages communication between the operating system and the attached devices on boot up, and it is an integral part of the computer.

device driver   A software component that permits a computer system to communicate with a device. In most cases, the driver also manipulates the hardware to transmit the data to the device. Device drivers that are incompatible, corrupt, outdated, or the wrong version for the hardware can cause errors that are difficult to diagnose.

service-level agreement (SLA)   An agreement between parties (such as a call center and the company that hires it) that defines how long a call should take, how much should be spent on each incident, and which reports and documents must be maintained. The SLA also defines penalties for not meeting those requirements.

Questions and Answers

Lesson 1 Review

Page 1-8   **1.** Give yourself five minutes to list as many traits as you can that relate to the three categories listed here:

- ❑ Communication skills

- ❑ Aptitude skills

- ❑ Personal skills

Communication skills are vital because DSTs are often the only people in an organization with whom users work directly. DSTs should be able to communicate with users who have varying experience and job titles; explain technical problems to nontechnical users; obtain technical information from nontechnical users; explain in simple terms how the problem occurred, how to avoid it, and how the user can repair it on his or her own; and leave the user happy and satisfied, with the problem solved.

Having an aptitude for the technology you support is also vital. Qualified DSTs enjoy working with computers and new technologies, and like to tinker with computers in their spare time; they see the big picture when diagnosing a problem. They have considerable capacity to solve problems quickly, are good at logic problems and puzzles, and excel at finding solutions to difficult queries.

DSTs also require a number of personal skills. You should be able to react calmly under pressure, meet deadlines, document problems and solutions, multitask, and work with end users who might become frustrated or who have had prior unresolved problems.

2. You are working as a tier-1 support technician. You are speaking to a user whom you quickly assess as being highly experienced. The user starts the conversation by telling you what she has already tried and what she suspects is the cause of her problem. What is the likely outcome of this support call?

If you think the user is right in her assessment of the problem, it is likely that you will escalate her call quickly unless it is a simple service that you can provide.

3. You are speaking with a user who has been on hold for nearly 20 minutes. The first thing the customer tells you is that he has already spoken with two other DSTs that day, and the "fixes" they recommended have made things even worse. How should you handle this?

Of course, your first goal is to be polite and respectful. It is likely that the user will be confrontational about your suggestions and maybe even about your qualifications. Stay calm. You can often put a person at ease with a statement as simple as, "I am sorry you are still having problems. Let us see what we can do about them." Give the user a chance to tell the story of what has happened and what the other DSTs have recommended. You will likely pick up valuable clues along the way, and it will give the user a chance to be heard and to calm down.

Lesson 2 Practice: Identify Tasks in a Corporate Environment

Page 1-15 Group the following list of tasks according to which support tier you think would handle them. (Tiers are tier 1—Help Desk, tier 2—Administrator, and tier 3—Engineer.)

- Adjust display settings.

- Troubleshoot video driver problems.

- Troubleshoot registration problems that occur on the server.

- Adjust audio settings.

- Troubleshoot joystick problems.

- Configure the game to play on a home network.

- Troubleshoot networking issues preventing a customer's computer from connecting to the server.

- Register the product online.

- Deal with server crashes resulting from too many requests for service.

Answers will vary widely, but following are some of the types of activities that each level will handle:

- Tier 1—Help Desk
    - ❏ Adjust display settings.
    - ❏ Adjust audio settings.
    - ❏ Configure the game to play on a home network.
    - ❏ Register the product online.
- Tier 2—Administrator
    - ❏ Troubleshoot video driver problems.
    - ❏ Troubleshoot joystick problems.
    - ❏ Troubleshoot networking issues preventing a customer's computer from connecting to the server.
- Tier 3—Engineer
    - ❏ Troubleshoot registration problems that occur on the server.
    - ❏ Deal with server crashes resulting from too many requests for service.

Lesson 2 Review

Page 1-16 **1.** Briefly, what types of businesses, corporations, or companies would choose to configure a workgroup? A domain? A multiple domain? Why?

Small businesses and home users generally choose workgroups because they are easy to set up and maintain while still offering the security they need. Medium-sized companies and larger corporations choose domains because of their single point of administration for security and their Active Directory features. Domains are much more secure than workgroups, and security is extremely important in these settings. Large multinational corporations or corporations that have merged use multiple domains so that each country or merged business can control its own networks.

2. Which of the following is not a job function of a tier-1 corporate desktop support technician? (Choose all that apply.)

  A. Perform general troubleshooting of the operating system.

  B. Perform general troubleshooting of operating system components, such as Internet Explorer.

  C. Troubleshoot network problems that do not directly affect the end user.

  D. Install, configure, and upgrade software, including applications and operating systems.

  E. Set group or local security policies for end users, including which security settings a user should have, and determine what he or she can or cannot access on the network.

Answers A, B, and D correctly identify the duties of a tier-1 DST. Answer C is incorrect because DSTs troubleshoot only problems that directly affect end users; they are not responsible for the company's network. Answer E is incorrect because DSTs do not set security policies; that work is done by network administrators in tier 2 or tier 3.

3. For each of the following descriptions, decide whether it refers to a workgroup, a domain, or multiple domain network configurations. If the description applies to more than one network configuration, list all that apply.

  A. This network configuration is a logical grouping of computers created for the purpose of sharing resources such as files and printers.

  Workgroups, domains, and multiple domains. All networks are created for the purpose of sharing resources; it does not matter what logical grouping they use.

  B. This network configuration does not use Active Directory services.

  Workgroup. Workgroups do not use a single point of administration database (domain controller), so they therefore do not use Active Directory.

  C. This network configuration can include multiple domain controllers.

  Domains and multiple domains. Domain controllers are used in all types of domain configurations.

D. This network configuration provides a single point of administration for security.

Domains and multiple domains. There is not a single point of administration for security in workgroups, but there is in domains.

E. This network configuration is easy to design and implement, and is best configured for users in close proximity to one another.

Workgroup. Workgroups are best used for small groups of computers that are in close proximity to one another. It is the easiest type of logical network to configure.

Lesson 3 Review

Page 1-20 **1.** You have just gotten a job at an ISP and have been assigned a tier-1 position. Which of the following can you expect in your first week at work? (Choose all that apply.)

A. To walk users through re-creating their e-mail accounts or reconfiguring their Internet security settings

B. To configure local security policies

C. To answer phones and instruct users to reboot their computers, close and restart applications, and disconnect from and reconnect to the ISP

D. To read from a script of questions and make decisions based on users' answers

E. To help users reinstall their e-mail clients

Answers C and D are correct. A DST's first week will require that he or she be placed in the lowest level of the larger tier-1 group. The job duties and responsibilities at this level are minimal, and answers c and d define these clearly. Answers A, B, and E involve more complex tasks that are performed by tier-2 or tier-3 DSTs.

2. Taking into account what you have learned about workgroups and domains, network topologies, corporate and noncorporate tier structures, call center environments, hands-on repair shops, and ISPs, describe which environment you would most like to work in. Cite five reasons for your decision.

Sample answer: I want to work in a corporate environment because I want to learn more about domains, domain controllers, and Active Directory; I want to learn about security, scalability, and databases; I see more room for advancement in a corporate environment than in any other option; I want to have health insurance and a pension plan; I am sure I do not want to work in a call center.

Lesson 4 Review

Page 1-36 **1.** Questions asked of clients often trigger quick solutions to basic problems. Match the question on the left to the solution it triggered on the right.

1. Who is affected by this problem?

A. The user states that she recently deleted all temporary files and cookies from her computer, explaining why she is no longer able to sign in automatically to websites she visits.

2. When was the first time you noticed the problem? Was it after a new installation of software or hardware?

B. John cannot send or receive messages using Outlook. It is determined that the problem is related only to his configuration of Outlook because other users who log on to the same computer under a different account can use Outlook to send and receive e-mail messages without any problems.

3. Has the user recently deleted any files or performed any maintenance?

C. The keyboard keys are sticky because coffee was spilled on the keyboard.

4. How did this problem occur?

D. The user states that the first time the computer acted strangely was after he installed a new screen saver.

Answer 1-B is correct. Because only one person is affected by this problem, the "Who?" question produces a solution to the problem. John's configuration of Outlook must need attention. 2-D is correct because asking "When?" produces the information needed to solve the problem. The problem occurred after the user installed a screen saver. 3-A is correct because asking what has been deleted recently produces the cause of the problem. The user recently deleted cookies and temporary files. 4-C is correct because the question "How?" produces the simple answer to why the keys are sticky.

2. Decide where to look first for solutions to the problems that are listed here. Match each question on the left to the appropriate choice on the right.

1. After a recent upgrade to Windows XP Professional, a user's scanner no longer functions as it should. The user remembers that the scanner was listed as incompatible during the upgrade, and you believe that it might be a driver issue. Where will you likely find the new driver?

A. Newsgroup

2. A user cannot access a network application. The application was designed specifically for the company and is not a Microsoft product or any other common third-party application. Where will you likely find information about this application?

B. TechNet

3. You have searched the Knowledge Base and TechNet for the solution to a problem, but have not had any luck. Where should you look now?

C. Knowledge Base

4. You need to search through the latest security bulletins to find out whether the problem you are having is related to a known security problem. Which online resource offers access to these bulletins?

D. Manufacturer's website

5. You need to find out why a home user's camera does not work with the Windows Picture And Fax Viewer. Specifically, the Rotate tool causes the computer to freeze up each time it is used. Where should you look first?

E. Company documentation

6. You want to access the Hardware Troubleshooter to resolve a problem with a user's sound card. Where can this trouble-shooter be found?

F. Help And Support Center

Answer 1-D is correct. Manufacturers often offer new drivers when new operating systems become available. 2-E is correct. Because the application is a company product, the company documentation offers the best place to search for answers. 3-A is correct. After searching the Knowledge Base and TechNet, newsgroups are a good place to look. 4-B is correct. TechNet offers these resources. 5-C is correct. The Knowledge Base offers information about known issues between the operating system and third-party hardware and software. 6-F is correct. The Hardware Troubleshooter is available from the Help And Support Center.

3. Create three simple questions you could ask an end user who is having a problem accessing data on the network server that would in turn provide answers to common connectivity problems. Explain what each solution might uncover. For instance, a yes answer to the question, "Has the computer been moved or bumped recently?" could indicate that a network card is loose inside the computer.

The specific questions that you might ask will vary, but the following are typical questions that you could ask:

a. Have you or anyone else who uses the computer changed any settings recently? Changes to computer settings, such as the computer name, can render a computer unable to connect.

b. Is the network cable plugged in to both the computer and the outlet or hub?

c. Did you log on properly when the computer booted up? Failing to log on to the domain will cause access to network resources to be denied.

Case Scenario Exercises: Scenario 1.1

Page 1-38 **1.** What type of entry-level job do you think is best for John while he works to meet his goals? Why?

> Although answers will vary, a corporate job might be the best thing for John. There, he can gain some hands-on experience with clients at their desks, but he will also gain experience doing telephone work. He will work with networks that are domains, and he will have the opportunity to enhance his hands-on skills by checking physical connections and cards and repairing general computer problems. John will also learn how to communicate with many types of people with many levels of experience, thus gaining the personal traits required of a good DST.

Case Scenario Exercises: Scenario 1.2

Page 1-39 **1.** Which of the following offer the best solutions to this problem? (Select two.)

   A. Consider moonlighting two or three nights a week as a telephone call support technician. There, you will learn some of the basic personal skills required of a good DST.

   B. Quit the repair shop and go to work immediately for an ISP. You can learn to create websites, you will learn about e-commerce, and if you are lucky, you will have to deal with people face-to-face only occasionally.

   C. Take a course on interpersonal skills at your local community college. There you will learn basic communication skills, such as how to listen and how to converse effectively with all types of people.

   D. Consider a different line of work. Communication skills, ability, talent, and personal skills come naturally to good DSTs and cannot be taught.

> Answers A and C are the best responses to this question. Answer A is correct because you will learn how to deal with people over the phone, you will learn some basic communication skills, and you will learn how to be polite and empathetic with a customer. At two or three nights a week, the experience will not be too stressful. Answer C is correct because interpersonal skills can be learned, and taking a class can help you improve in this area. Answers B and D are incorrect. Quitting and considering a different line of work are drastic ways to deal with this situation. Communication and personal skills do not always come naturally, but, like technical skills, you can learn them with practice, experience, mental fortitude, and instruction.

Case Scenario Exercises: Scenario 1.3

Page 1-39 **1.** Which of the following solutions (they are all valid) is best under these circumstances?

   A. Tell the user to join a printer newsgroup and ask other users for advice.

   B. Tell the user to open Help And Support Center, locate the printer trouble-shooter, and work through the options. There is an option to allow Windows to investigate the problem, and this might produce a solution.

   C. Tell the user to visit *http://www.windrivers.com* and download a new driver for the printer.

   D. Tell the user to uninstall and reinstall the printer.

   Answer B is correct. The Help And Support Center offers many valuable troubleshooters that both DSTs and end users can employ. Answers A, C, and D are not the best choices under these circumstances because they will not quickly produce a dependable, acceptable, and valid solution.

2 Installing Windows XP

Exam Objectives in this Chapter:

- Perform and troubleshoot an attended installation of a Microsoft Windows XP operating system
    - ❑ Answer end-user questions related to performing an attended installation of a Windows XP operating system
    - ❑ Troubleshoot and complete installations in which an installation does not start
    - ❑ Troubleshoot and complete installations in which an installation fails to complete
    - ❑ Perform postinstallation configuration
- Perform and troubleshoot an unattended installation of a Windows XP operating system
    - ❑ Answer end-user questions related to performing an unattended installation of a Windows XP operating system
    - ❑ Configure a computer to boot to a network device and start installation of a Windows XP operating system
    - ❑ Perform an installation by using unattended installation files
- Upgrade from a previous version of Windows
    - ❑ Answer end-user questions related to upgrading from a previous version of Windows
    - ❑ Verify hardware compatibility for upgrade
    - ❑ Verify application compatibility for upgrade
    - ❑ Migrate user state data from an existing PC to a new PC
    - ❑ Install a second instance of an operating system on a computer

Why This Chapter Matters

This chapter teaches you how to install Microsoft Windows XP. It addresses actions that you must take prior to installing Windows XP, such as verifying that a computer meets minimum hardware requirements, and prepares you for decisions that you must make during the installation process. This chapter examines three primary types of installations: clean installations (those in which an operating system is not already installed on the computer), upgrades from previous versions of Windows, and multiple-boot installations. To help users install Windows XP and troubleshoot failed installations, you must understand the various phases of the installation process and be able to identify where trouble can occur in the installation process. You must also be able to resolve these problems and complete a successful installation. This chapter also covers postinstallation tasks, such as activating and updating Windows XP.

Lessons in this Chapter:

Before You Begin

Before you begin this chapter, you should have a basic familiarity with working in a Windows-based operating system. To complete the practices in this chapter, you must have a computer on which you can install Windows XP Professional.

Lesson 1: Installing Windows XP

As a desktop support technician (DST), you will be called upon to troubleshoot problems with computers on which Windows XP is already installed. Occasionally, however, users will ask you to help them install Windows XP or troubleshoot an installation. If you are working in a corporate environment, chances are high that a network administrator will have an automated (or semiautomated) installation method in place, so you must be familiar with the types of automated installations that you may encounter. If you are supporting a home user or a small network, it is more likely that you will help users install Windows XP from CD-ROM, so you must be familiar with the decisions that must be made during installation.

After this lesson, you will be able to

- Identify the hardware requirements for installing Windows XP.
- Verify that hardware is supported in Windows XP by checking the Windows Catalog.
- Prepare a computer for installation of Windows XP.
- Identify the methods that are available for installing Windows XP.
- Perform an attended installation of Windows XP.
- Upgrade to Windows XP from a previous version of Windows.

Estimated lesson time: 70 minutes

Note   Although this lesson takes a little more than an hour, one of the practices at the end of the lesson requires that you install Windows XP. This process can take from 30 to 90 additional minutes.

Meeting the System Requirements

Before installing Windows XP, you must determine whether the computer meets the minimum hardware requirements for the installation. The hardware requirements for Windows XP Professional and Windows XP Home Edition are as follows:

- **CPU**   Windows XP requires a 233-megahertz (MHz) Intel Pentium II/Celeron or AMD-compatible processor, although a 300-MHz processor (or faster) is strongly recommended. Windows XP Professional supports up to two processors.

- **Memory**   Windows XP requires a minimum of 64 MB of random access memory (RAM), although 128 MB or more is recommended. Generally, the more memory a computer running Windows XP has, the better the performance. Windows XP supports a maximum of 4 gigabytes (GB) of RAM.

- **Hard disk space** Windows XP requires 1.5 GB of free space for installation. However, you may need additional disk space, depending on the applications and features you choose to install.

- **Display** Windows XP requires a Super Video Graphics Array (SVGA)–compatible or better display adapter, with a monitor resolution of 800 x 600 dots per inch (dpi).

- **Input devices** The computer must have a keyboard and a Microsoft Mouse, Microsoft IntelliMouse, or other pointing device.

- **CD-ROM** The computer must have a CD-ROM or DVD-ROM drive if you will be performing Setup from CD-ROM.

- **Floppy disk drive** The computer must have a high-density 3.5-inch drive if you perform Setup across the network using a network client or boot disk or if your computer does not support booting with the Windows XP installation CD.

- **Network adapter card** The computer must have a network adapter card appropriate for your network if you perform Setup from a network installation point.

Exam Tip You should memorize the basic hardware requirements—especially the amount of CPU, RAM, and hard disk space—and be able to determine if a computer with certain specifications can run Windows XP.

Checking the Windows Catalog

Microsoft maintains the Windows Catalog, which lists devices that Microsoft has tested and supports for use with Windows XP. If a device in the computer is not listed in the catalog, Microsoft does not support it. However, you can contact the device's manufacturer to determine whether the manufacturer provides drivers and support for the device under Windows XP. You should be aware that even if the manufacturer supports the device, there is no guarantee that it will function correctly with Windows XP. You can find the Windows Catalog at *http://www.microsoft.com/windows/catalog*.

Preparing the BIOS

A computer's basic input/output system (BIOS) is a set of basic software routines that resides in a special area of permanent memory on a computer. When you turn on a computer, BIOS tests and initializes the computer's hardware, and then starts the operating system. If a computer has an outdated BIOS, it can often cause problems with disk partitioning, power management, peripheral configuration, and Windows installation.

Before you install Windows XP, you should check with the manufacturer of the computer (or of the computer's motherboard) to determine whether the BIOS supports Windows XP. You may need to download and apply a BIOS update prior to installation.

Understanding Installation Types

You can install Windows XP using three types of installation. The type of installation you choose greatly affects the decisions you will make during installation. The three types of installations that are available in Windows XP are the following:

- **Clean installation**   A clean installation is one in which there is no existing operating system on the computer or one in which you do not want to preserve the existing installation. You will always perform a clean installation on a computer on which an operating system is not already installed. The biggest advantage of performing a clean installation is that you can be certain that nothing is carried over from a previous installation, which usually results in somewhat better performance and stability. The only real disadvantage of performing a clean installation over an upgrade is that you will have to reinstall all your applications and reconfigure your Windows settings. However, even that disadvantage presents you with the opportunity to "clean house," as it were.

> **Note**   It is possible to perform a clean installation on a computer that is already running a previous version of Windows. In this case, Windows Setup leaves the existing data on the hard drive intact (including application folders, document folders, and so on) and installs Windows XP into its own folder. However, you still cannot use the existing applications until you reinstall them. The only advantage of performing this kind of clean installation is if you do not have a way to back up the data on your hard disk prior to installation.

- **Upgrade**   An upgrade installation is one in which Windows XP is installed over an existing installation of a previous version of Windows. The advantage of an upgrade over a clean installation is that you can retain application installations and user settings. Following a successful upgrade, you should be able to log on to Windows XP and start working again right away. The disadvantage of an upgrade is really the same as the advantage: Windows XP retains all settings and applications, and these are often settings and applications that users could do without. Although performing a clean install takes more time, it ensures that the user has a more stable and less cluttered system.

- **Multiple-boot installation**   A multiple-boot installation is one in which multiple operating systems are installed on a computer, and the user can select which operating system to use during system startup. If you install Windows XP as an additional operating system on a computer, you still have to reinstall any applications you want to use when running Windows XP. The advantage of using a multiple-boot installation over an upgrade or clean installation is that you can retain the previous operating system and installed applications. This is useful if you want to test or experiment with Windows XP, or if you have important applications that you know will not run on Windows XP.

> **Note**   The terminology regarding computers that have more than one operating system installed can be confusing. You will hear such computers referred to as "multiboot," "multiple boot," and "dual-boot." The objectives for this exam use the term "multiboot," but this chapter uses the term "multiple boot" for one important reason: the majority of articles you will find on TechNet and in the Microsoft Knowledge Base also use the term "multiple boot" (although they occasionally use "dual-boot," as well). When you are reading this chapter (and when taking the exam), understand that the terms "multiboot," "multiple boot," and "dual-boot" all refer to the same basic setup: a computer running more than one operating system. When you search online for help on this subject, be sure to check for articles that mention both "multiple boot" and "dual-boot."

Understanding Installation Methods

After you have identified the type of installation you want to perform, you should next decide on a method for the installation. The different methods of installing Windows XP are as follows:

- **Standard (attended) installation**   The standard installation is the one with which you are probably already familiar and it is the method most likely used by home and small business users. During a standard installation, the user remains at the computer to supply information that is needed by Windows.

- **Network installation**   A network installation is one in which the Windows XP installation files are located on a network share. This is the method that is used in some small businesses and corporations. Network installations remove the need for the user to have an installation CD.

- **Automated installation**   An automated installation is one that does not require a user to provide information during setup. There are several ways to automate an installation, but they all share a common purpose: reducing or eliminating the amount of user intervention that is required during the setup process. Automated installations are most often used on larger corporate networks.

Starting a Standard (Attended) Installation

A standard installation of Windows XP requires that the person performing the setup provide information during the installation process. This information includes the location for the Windows files (and whether to create and format a partition to use as that location), the name of the computer, and basic network settings. As a DST, you will be called on to help users with standard installations and possibly to perform the installation yourself.

There are several ways to start a standard installation:

- If the computer is already running a previous version of Windows, you can simply insert the Windows XP installation CD and use a setup wizard to begin the installation. Setup gives you the choice of upgrading the existing operating system or performing a clean installation.

- Whether the computer is already running a previous version of Windows or has no operating system installed, you can start the computer from the installation CD. If you start a computer by using the installation CD, you can only perform a clean installation; upgrading is not an option. The computer's BIOS must support booting using the CD-ROM drive to use this option. Check the BIOS to ensure that the CD-ROM drive is a supported boot device. You should also ensure that the order of boot devices listed in BIOS places the CD-ROM drive ahead of the hard drive in the boot sequence.

- If a computer does not support booting from CD, you can create a set of floppy disks that will start the computer and then initiate setup from the CD. After the installation has started, this method proceeds just as if booting from CD.

See Also   Microsoft makes the tools for creating boot floppy disks for Windows XP Professional Edition and Windows XP Home Edition available for download. Visit *http:// www.microsoft.com/downloads* and search by using the keywords "Windows XP boot floppy" to locate these utilities.

- You can also start Windows XP installation from the command line. You can use the command **winnt.exe** to start the installation from the command prompt in MS-DOS or Windows 3.x. This command is especially useful for starting the Windows XP installation when booting using a DOS boot disk. You can use the command **winnt32.exe** to start installation from the command prompt in Microsoft Windows 95, Windows 98, Windows Millennium Edition (Me), or Windows 2000.

> **See Also**   Starting Windows XP installation from a command line is used mostly when starting Setup after starting the computer with an MS-DOS boot disk or when performing unattended installations. The commands also allow a number of advanced parameters. You can learn more about using these commands by searching for "winnt" or "winnt32" in the Help And Support Center.

Network Installation

Installing an operating system by booting from the CD is practical only when there are a limited number of installations to perform. On larger networks, it is inconvenient to carry CDs around to many computers. Also, because Windows XP is often licensed for numerous installations, there may not actually be such a CD.

A network installation differs from a standard installation only in the location of the installation files. For network installations, the Windows XP installation files are stored in a shared network folder. You can start either an upgrade or a clean installation from a network installation point.

When you perform a network installation, the computer on which you are installing Windows XP must have a way to connect to the network share that contains the installation files. If you are starting Setup on a computer on which an operating system is already installed, you likely already have network connectivity. To start the installation, you can simply locate the shared folder and run the Setup program (**setup.exe**).

Starting a network installation on a computer that does not already have an operating system installed is a little more complex. The most common way to start such an installation is to use an MS-DOS boot disk that contains DOS-based network drivers and client software. After starting the computer with this disk, you can connect to the network share and start the installation by using the **winnt.exe** command. It is also possible that network administrators will have created a boot disk with a batch file (a text file that automatically executes commands) that starts the computer, initializes the network, locates the installation files, and then starts the installation automatically.

Automated Installation

An automated installation is simply one in which little or no user intervention is required during the setup process. As a DST, you will not normally be responsible for designing or creating automated installations. However, you should understand which methods are available for automated installations and be able to help a user start and troubleshoot such an installation, if necessary.

There are several methods for performing automated installations, including the following:

- An unattended installation is one in which an administrator uses a program named Setup Manager to specify answers to many of the options that are required during setup, such as the computer name, administrator password, installation folder, network settings, and so on. Setup Manager creates a text file called an answer file from which Windows XP Setup can pull this information.

- Administrators can also use disk duplication to automate installations. First, the administrator installs Windows XP on a standardized computer. Next, the administrator creates an image of the hard disk on that computer, which is essentially a single file that contains all the information on the hard disk. Finally, the administrator uses a tool named System Preparation to strip machine-specific settings from the disk image. The image is then copied to other computers using third-party disk duplication utilities.

- Remote Installation Services (RIS) is a service that is available for servers running Windows 2000 and Windows 2003. The RIS server is a disk image server that contains as many disk images as are necessary to support the different configurations of Windows XP on a network. A RIS client is a computer that connects to the RIS server and downloads an image. The RIS server might be configured in advance to download a particular image to a client computer, or the user might be able to select an image manually from the RIS Administration menu.

Supporting Unattended Installations by Using Answer Files   At several points during a standard installation, Setup requires that the user provide information, such as the time zone, network settings, and so on. One way to automate an installation is to create an answer file that supplies the required information. As a DST, you will not be responsible for using Setup Manager to create answer files, but you should understand how answer files are used during installation to troubleshoot setup problems.

Answer files are really just text files that contain responses to some, or all, of the questions that Setup asks during the installation process. After an answer file is created, it can be applied to as many computers as necessary. However, there also are certain settings that must be unique to each computer, such as the computer name. To answer this need, Setup Manager also allows the creation of a file called a uniqueness database file (UDF), which is used in conjunction with the standard answer file. The UDF contains the settings that are unique to each computer.

Exam Tip   Remember that a standard answer file is used to provide the common configuration settings for all computers that are affected during an unattended installation. A UDF provides the unique settings that each computer needs to distinguish it from other computers.

If you are helping a user start Setup from the command line (the most common way to start an unattended installation), you must use a specific parameter and indicate the location of the answer file.

To use the **winnt.exe** command from an MS-DOS or Windows 3.x command prompt to perform a clean installation of Windows XP, you must use the following syntax:

winnt [/**s**:SourcePath] [/**u:**answer file] [/**udf:**ID [,UDB_file]]

To use the **winnt32.exe** command from a Windows 95, Windows 98, Windows Me, or Windows 2000 command prompt to perform a clean installation of Windows XP, you must use the following syntax:

winnt32 [/**unattend**[num]:[answer_file] [/**udf:**ID [,UDB_file]]

Note   You can also use the **winnt32.exe** command to upgrade from a previous installation of Windows. In this case, you do not need to specify an answer file because Setup takes settings from the previous installation. To use the **winnt32.exe** command to perform an upgrade, just type **winnt32 /unattend** at the command prompt.

See Also   For more information about answer file structure, syntax, and configurable options, see the Deployment User Tools Guide on the Windows XP Professional CD. You can find it in \Support\Tools\Deploy.cab\Deploy.chm.

Disk Duplication   Windows XP Professional includes a program named System Preparation (sysprep.exe) that allows administrators to prepare images of a Windows XP installation for distribution by removing machine-specific information from the image. The first step in creating a disk image is for the administrator to install Windows XP onto a reference computer. The reference computer can contain just the Windows XP Professional operating system or it can contain the operating system and any number of installed applications. After the reference computer is configured properly, the administrator uses a disk-duplication utility to create a base disk image. The disk image is simply a compressed file that contains the contents of the entire hard disk on which the operating system is installed.

Many settings on a Windows XP Professional computer must be unique, such as the Computer Name and the security identifier (SID), which is a number used to track an object through the Windows security subsystem. The System Preparation tool removes the SID and all other user- and computer-specific information from a disk image.

When a client computer starts Windows XP Professional for the first time after loading a disk image that has been prepared with Sysprep, Windows automatically generates a unique SID, initiates Plug and Play detection, and starts the Mini Setup Wizard. The Mini Setup Wizard prompts the user for user- and computer-specific information, such as the following:

- End-User License Agreement (EULA)
- Regional options
- User name and company
- Product key
- Computer name and administrator password
- Time zone selection

> **Note**   When an administrator creates a disk image, all the hardware settings of the refer-
> ence computer become part of the image. Thus, the reference computer should have the
> same (or similar) hardware configuration as the destination computers. If the destination
> computers contain Plug and Play devices that are not present in the reference computer, they
> are automatically detected and configured at the first startup following installation. The user
> must install any non–Plug and Play devices manually. (You will learn more about installing
> devices in Chapter 6, "Installing and Managing Hardware.")

Remote Installation Services (RIS)   As a DST, you will not be responsible for configuring or managing RIS servers. However, you might be called on to help a user start a
RIS installation on a client computer.

To start an installation from a RIS client, use one of the following:

- On computers that are equipped with a Preboot Execution Environment (PXE)–
  compliant network adapter, you can start the computer from a server on a
  network instead of using a floppy disk, CD, or hard disk. A computer with a PXE-
  compliant network adapter broadcasts its presence on the network. A server then
  provides the computer with the information that is necessary to access the RIS
  server. After the computer starts, installation can happen automatically, or the RIS
  server can allow the user to select an operating system to install.

- On computers that do not have a PXE-compliant network adapter, the user must start the computer with a RIS disk that is supplied by a network administrator. The computer starts, loads the appropriate network drivers from the RIS disk, and then emulates a PXE boot environment. After the client computer connects to a RIS server, installation works the same way as when the computer has a PXE-compliant network adapter.

See Also   For more information about RIS, see "Remote Installation Services" at *http://www.microsoft.com/technet/prodtechnol/windowsserver2003/library/ServerHelp/c62e5951-5eb9-42f1-95ae-490e5d7a5551.mspx.*

Preparing the Hard Disk

Before you install Windows XP, you must understand some basic concepts regarding hard disks, including hard disk partitions and file systems.

Understanding Disk Partitions

A disk partition is a logical section of a hard disk on which the computer may write data. Partitions offer a way to divide the space on a single physical hard disk into multiple areas, each of which is treated as a different disk within Windows.

Partition information is stored in the master boot record of a hard drive and is independent of any operating systems installed on the computer. You must partition every hard disk before you can use it. Most often, you will configure a hard disk as one big partition that takes all the space on the disk, but you can also divide a disk into several partitions. When you partition a disk, you must decide how much disk space to allocate to each partition.

Some people create separate partitions to help organize their files. For example, you might store the Windows system files and application files on one partition, user-created documents on another partition, and backup files on another partition.

Another reason to use multiple partitions is to isolate operating systems from one another when you install more than one operating system on a computer. Although it is technically possible to install some operating systems on the same partition, Microsoft does not recommend or support this practice. You should always create a separate partition for each operating system.

You can create the following types of disk partitions on a hard drive:

- **Primary**   You can configure as many as four primary partitions on a computer running a Windows operating system (three, if you also have an extended partition on the disk). You can configure any primary partition as the active (or bootable) drive, but only one primary partition is active at a time. When you configure a multiple boot computer, you should create a primary partition for each operating system, and then install each operating system onto a different primary partition.

■ **Extended**   An extended partition provides a way to bypass the four primary partition limit. You cannot format an extended partition with any file system. Rather, extended partitions serve as a shell in which you can create any number of logical partitions.

■ **Logical**   You can create any number of logical partitions inside an extended partition. You cannot set a logical partition as an active partition, however, so you cannot use logical partitions to hold most operating systems. Instead, logical partitions are normally used for organizing files. All logical partitions are visible, no matter which operating system is started, so logical partitions provide a good method for making files available to any of the operating systems installed on a multiple boot computer.

Figure 2-1 shows an example of a hard drive with several disk partitions. There are two primary partitions: one with Windows XP installed and the other with Windows 2000 installed. There is a single extended partition that holds two logical partitions: One logical partition is used to store documents and the other is used to store backup files.

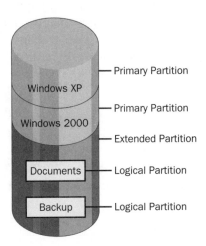

Figure 2-1   Partitions offer a way to divide hard drive space for different purposes.

You can create disk partitions by using a number of methods. Windows XP Setup provides basic partitioning utilities that you can use after you have started the installation. You can also create a partition by using a partitioning utility prior to starting the installation of Windows XP. Some partitioning utilities, such as the FDISK utility that is included with MS-DOS or Microsoft Windows 95 and Windows 98, are limited in the size and number of partitions that they can create. Third-party disk-partitioning utilities are often much more flexible.

Managing System and Boot Partitions

Regardless of how you configure disk partitions on a computer, you must also decide which partitions will hold the two major sets of files that are required to start the operating system: hardware-specific boot files and operating system files. The disk partition that holds the initial hardware-specific boot files is referred to as the **system partition**. The disk partition that holds the Windows operating system files is referred to as the **boot partition**.

> **Tip**   Unfortunately, the names of the system and boot partitions are a little confusing. The system partition holds hardware boot files, and the boot partition holds operating system files. It helps if you think of the system partition as holding files necessary for starting the physical components of the system and think of the boot partition as holding the files necessary to start the operating system.

On computers with only one operating system installed, the system partition and the boot partition are typically found on the same primary disk partition. You will not have to decide which partition contains the different system and boot files.

On computers with multiple operating systems installed, things are a little more complicated. Assuming that you follow the recommended procedure and install each operating system onto its own disk partition, each operating system will have its own boot partition. The system partition on a multiple boot computer may share a disk partition with one of the operating system's boot partitions, or the system partition may be given a disk partition of its own.

Selecting a File System

After you decide how to partition a hard disk, you must then decide what file system to use to format the partition onto which you will install Windows XP. Windows XP supports two file systems: **NT file system (NTFS)** and the **file allocation table (FAT)**.

Using NTFS   NTFS is the preferred file system for Windows XP. Microsoft recommends that you always use NTFS unless there is a specific reason to use another file system (such as when you are installing more than one operating system on a computer and one of those operating systems does not recognize NTFS partitions). NTFS provides many features that the other file systems do not have, such as the following:

■ **File and folder security**   In Windows XP Professional, NTFS allows you to control which users can access applications and data. Windows XP Home Edition offers only simple file sharing, so you cannot configure NTFS file permissions. You can learn more about configuring NTFS partitions in Chapter 5, "Supporting Windows XP File and Folder Access."

- **Increased performance**   NTFS uses a more efficient mechanism for locating and retrieving information from the hard disk than FAT or FAT32.

- **Disk quotas**   In Windows XP Professional, NTFS provides the ability to control how much disk space each user can have. Windows XP Home Edition does not support disk quotas.

- **Disk compression**   NTFS can compress files to create more available disk space.

- **File encryption**   In Windows XP Professional, NTFS allows you to encrypt data that is stored on the hard disk. Windows XP Home Edition does not support file encryption.

File Allocation Table (FAT)   Windows XP uses the term FAT to refer to two related file systems: the original FAT file system and its 32-bit successor, FAT32. When you format a partition by using FAT during Windows XP Setup, Windows uses FAT for partitions that are smaller than 2 GB and FAT32 for partitions that are larger than 2 GB.

> **Note**   Windows XP Setup cannot create a FAT32 partition that is smaller than 2 GB. It also cannot create a FAT32 partition larger than 32 GB; it forces you to use NTFS. This is not a limitation of the FAT32 file system. You can use third-party formatting utilities to configure FAT32 partitions smaller than 2 GB and greater than 32 GB.

All Microsoft operating systems support FAT. FAT32 is supported by Windows 95 Service Pack 2 (SP2) and later, Windows 98, Windows Me, Windows 2000, and Windows XP. Note that Windows NT 3.5 and 4.0 do not support FAT32.

File System Considerations on Multiple Boot Computers   Table 2-1 shows the file systems that are supported in various Microsoft operating systems. Keep in mind that the support that is listed here refers to the local file system only. Any operating system that can access network shares can do so regardless of the file system that is used on the computer that is sharing the data.

Table 2-1   Supported File Systems

Operating System	Supports FAT	Supports FAT32	Supports NTFS
MS-DOS	Yes	No	No
Windows 3.1	Yes	No	No
Windows NT Server and Workstation	Yes	No	Yes
Windows 95	Yes	No	No
Windows 95 OSR2	Yes	Yes	No
Windows 98	Yes	Yes	No

Table 2-1   Supported File Systems

Operating System	Supports FAT	Supports FAT32	Supports NTFS
Windows Me	Yes	Yes	No
Windows 2000 Professional and Server	Yes	Yes	Yes
Windows XP	Yes	Yes	Yes
Windows Server 2003	Yes	Yes	Yes

Exam Tip   The *only* reason to use FAT32 on a system running Windows XP is if the system is also configured to run an operating system that does not support NTFS. If a computer runs only Windows XP, you should always use NTFS.

File system access problems can occur when a user is logged on to one operating system and tries to access a file or folder on another partition that is using a file system that the operating system does not support. For example, assume that a computer has one partition that is formatted with NTFS, on which Windows XP is installed, and another partition that is formatted with FAT32, on which Windows 98 is installed. When the computer is running Windows XP, the operating system can access both partitions. When the computer is running Windows 98, the operating system can access only the FAT32 partition because Windows 98 cannot recognize NTFS partitions. An operating system that can access only a FAT partition does not recognize any files on a FAT32 or NTFS partition; an operating system that can access only FAT or FAT32 partitions does not recognize an NTFS partition.

Understanding the Installation Process

Regardless of how you install Windows—whether it is an unattended or attended installation, a clean installation, or an upgrade—the installation process is almost the same. The differences in the various installation methods affect how a user starts the installation and whether the user is required to supply information during setup.

Installation takes place in the following phases:

1. Setup copies a number of installation files from the installation source to the local hard disk. These files are used to start the installation after you restart the computer. If you start an installation by using the installation CD, Setup does not perform this step and loads files directly from the CD instead of first copying them to the hard disk.

2. Text mode setup begins. During a clean installation, this phase of Setup initializes the storage devices on your computer, allows you to select or create a disk partition (as shown in Figure 2-2), and then allows you to format the partition prior to installation. At the end of the text mode installation, Setup copies the Windows files to the selected Windows folder, and then restarts the computer.

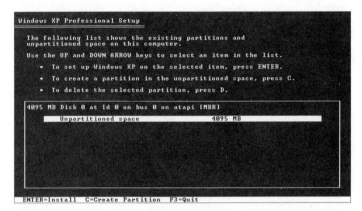

Figure 2-2   Create or select a partition during the text mode phase of Setup.

3. Graphical user interface (GUI) mode setup begins after the computer restarts. This is the graphical portion of Windows Setup, shown in Figure 2-3, and is also referred to as the Setup Wizard. In a clean attended installation, this phase is when you select regional settings, such as language and time zone, and enter details such as the product key, computer name, and administrator password.

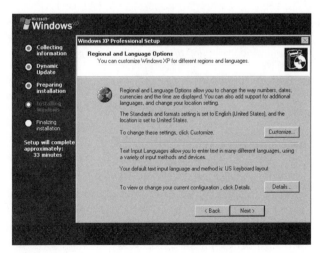

Figure 2-3   Specify regional, time zone, and other settings during the GUI mode phase of Setup.

4. The network setup phase begins during the graphical portion of Setup if Setup detects networking hardware on the computer, as shown in Figure 2-4. You must choose one of the following networking options:

❑ Choose Typical Settings if you want Setup to configure networking components automatically. Typical components include Client for Microsoft Networks, File And Print Sharing for Microsoft Networks, and Transmission Control Protocol/Internet Protocol (TCP/IP). TCP/IP is configured to automatically obtain an Internet Protocol (IP) address from a Dynamic Host Configuration Protocol (DHCP) server by default.

❑ Choose Custom Settings if you need to configure IP settings manually, install additional protocols or services, or both.

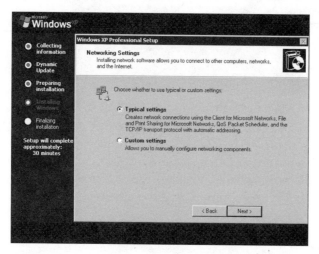

Figure 2-4   Specify network settings during the network setup phase.

5. After the network setup is finished, the graphical portion of the installation ends and the computer restarts. Windows starts for the first time and gives you the option to create user accounts and activate Windows.

Upgrading from a Previous Version of Windows

If a computer is already running Windows 98, Windows Me, Windows NT Workstation 4.0 Service Pack 5 (SP5), or Windows 2000 Professional, you can upgrade it directly to Windows XP. This includes computers with partitions that are formatted by using FAT or NTFS because Windows XP can recognize both file systems. You cannot directly upgrade computers running earlier versions of Windows such as Windows 95 or Windows NT Workstation 3.51. These operating systems require interim upgrades to a version of Windows that supports a direct upgrade to Windows XP. Table 2-2 shows the available Windows XP upgrade paths.

> **Note**   Although you can upgrade previous versions of Windows operating systems by using interim upgrades, keep in mind that the computer on which the older operating systems are running most likely will not meet the minimum hardware requirements for Windows XP Professional.

Table 2-2   Windows XP Upgrade Paths

Current Operating System	Upgrade Path
Windows 95	Must first be upgraded to Windows 98 and then to Windows XP
Windows 98	Direct upgrade to Windows XP
Windows Me	Direct upgrade to Windows XP
Windows NT 3.51 Workstation	Must first be upgraded to Windows NT 4.0 SP5 and then to Windows XP
Windows NT 4.0 Workstation without SP5 or later	Must first have SP5 applied and then be upgraded to Windows XP
Windows NT 4.0 Workstation with SP5 or later	Direct upgrade to Windows XP
Windows 2000 Professional	Direct upgrade to Windows XP
Windows XP Home	Direct upgrade to Windows XP Professional

> **Note**   You cannot upgrade computers running Windows NT 4.0 Server and Windows 2000 Server directly to Windows XP. In addition, you cannot upgrade computers running Small Business Server or trial editions of older Windows versions to Windows XP.

Before starting an upgrade, there are a few considerations that you should take into account. These considerations include the following:

- Ensure that the computer meets the hardware and software compatibility requirements for Windows XP. Consult the Windows Catalog on the Web for supported hardware.

- You should also generate a system compatibility report prior to starting the upgrade process. This report analyzes potential problems that you might encounter after an upgrade and provides possible solutions. You can generate this report by selecting the Check System Compatibility option on the splash screen that appears when you insert the installation CD. You can also generate the report when starting Setup from the command line by typing **winnt32 /Checkupgradeonly**. If the compatibility check reports any hardware or software incompatibilities, you should obtain and apply the proper updates before proceeding with the upgrade.

- Uninstall any incompatible software until you can load new compatible replacements.

- Check the system's basic input/output system (BIOS) version to verify that the version is the latest revision available. You should also verify that BIOS-based virus protection is disabled before initiating the Windows XP upgrade. BIOS antivirus features interpret attempts by Setup to modify the boot sector as virus-like activity and prevents the modifications, causing Setup to fail.

- Back up important files and data before performing an upgrade to avoid potential loss. There is always the possibility of system failure during any major operation.

- Scan for viruses and remove them from the computer before performing an upgrade.

- Uncompress any drive that is compressed with anything other than NTFS compression before performing an upgrade. The only type of compression that is supported by Windows XP is NTFS compression. Windows XP does not support DriveSpace, DoubleSpace, or any third-party compression formats.

Real World When Not to Upgrade

Upgrading to Windows XP from a previous version of Windows has advantages, the most important of which are that applications that are already installed remain accessible, and that most user settings are retained. However, installing Windows XP to a blank hard drive presents a great opportunity to clean out some of the mess that accumulates when a user has been running Windows for a long time (and has possibly already upgraded the computer once or twice).

Unless time is a limiting factor, talk to the user about the advantages of backing up their computer, reformatting the hard drive, installing Windows XP, and then installing only the applications that the user needs. Although this method takes more time and requires more care (especially in making sure everything is backed up), the user is also ensured a more stable and less-cluttered computer.

Migrating Existing User Environments

You can use two tools to transfer the files and user settings from an old computer to a new computer running Windows XP: the **Files and Settings Transfer Wizard** and the **User State Migration Tool (USMT)**. Both tools transfer many of the same items, but each tool is useful in a different setting:

- **Files And Settings Transfer Wizard**   The Files and Settings Transfer Wizard is designed for home and small business users. It uses a simple wizard interface that allows you to copy files and user settings from an old computer to removable media or across a network and then import those files and settings into a user pro-file on a computer running Windows XP.

- **User State Migration Tool (USMT)**   The USMT allows administrators to transfer user configuration settings and files from computers running Windows 95 or later to a new Windows XP installation (does not work with upgrades). Unlike the Files And Settings Transfer Wizard, you can configure the USMT for different environments by using INF files to control the items that are transferred. Also, administrators can incorporate USMT into scripts because USMT relies on two command-line tools: scanstate.exe for copying files and loadstate.exe for importing them.

By default, both utilities transfer many settings, including the following:

- The majority of user interface settings, such as display properties, fonts, mapped network drives, network printers, browser settings, folder options, taskbar options, and many files and settings that are associated with the configuration of Microsoft Office

- The My Documents, My Pictures, Desktop, and Favorites folders

- Files with extensions such as .ch3, .csv, .dif, .doc, .dot, .dqy, .iqy, .mcw, .oqy, .pot, .ppa, .pps, .ppt, .pre, .rqy, .scd, .sh3, .txt, .wpd, .wps, .wql, .wri, and .xls

Note   The information and procedures in this chapter are based on a default installation of Windows XP Professional. Some of the information and procedures might change if you have installed Windows XP Service Pack 2.

▶ Using the Files And Settings Transfer Wizard

Using the Files And Settings Transfer Wizard requires that you perform two distinct steps. First, copy the files and settings from the old computer. Then transfer these files and settings to your Windows XP computer.

To copy files and settings from the old computer by using the Files And Settings Transfer Wizard, use the following steps:

1. On the old computer, insert the Windows XP installation CD. When the splash screen loads, close the screen and use Windows Explorer to locate the \Support\Tools folder on the CD.

2. Double-click the file named Fastwiz.exe to start the Files And Settings Transfer Wizard.

3. To continue, click Next in the Welcome to the Files And Settings Transfer Wizard window. Note that you are reminded to close any other programs before continuing.

4. On the Which Computer Is This? page, select the Old Computer option and click Next.

5. After the wizard gathers information, it displays the Select A Transfer Method page, which allows you to choose where you want to save the files and settings. Choose an appropriate location, and then click Next.

6. On the What Do You Want To Transfer? page, select Both Files And Settings, and then click Next.

7. The wizard may display a window informing you that certain programs need to be installed before you transfer information to the new computer. Make note of these programs and click Next.

8. After the wizard collects the files and settings, you are prompted to provide the storage media for the transfer. After you have indicated a location, click OK and then Finish to complete the process.

To transfer the copied files and settings to the new computer running Windows XP, use the following steps:

1. Log on to the new computer running Windows XP as the user for which you want to restore files and settings.

2. On the Start menu, point to All Programs, Accessories, System Tools; and then select Files And Settings Transfer Wizard.

3. Click Next to advance past the Welcome page.

4. On the Which Computer Is This? page, select New Computer and then click Next.

5. Select the I Don't Need The Wizard Disk. I Have Already Collected My Files And Settings From My Old Computer option, and then click Next.

6. On the Where Are The Files And Settings? page, select the same transfer method that you selected when copying the files and settings from the old computer. Click Next.

7. If you selected Floppy Drive Or Other Removable Media, you are prompted to insert the first disk. Do so, and then click OK.

8. Click Finish.

9. When the wizard is finished, it displays a message letting you know that you must log off for the changes to take effect. Click Yes to log off.

10. Log on to the computer to apply your transferred settings.

Practice: Install Windows XP

In this practice, you will determine whether your computer meets the minimum requirements specified by Microsoft to run Windows XP Professional and whether the hardware in your computer is in the Windows Catalog. You will then perform a clean installation of Windows XP Professional using an installation CD.

Exercise 1: Gather Information About Your Computer

1. On the Start menu, select Run.

2. In the Run dialog box, type **msinfo32** and then click OK.

3. The System Information utility opens to show a summary of your system. Use this information to fill out the following table and determine whether your computer meets the minimum hardware requirements.

Component	Minimum Required	Your Computer
CPU	233 MHz Pentium- or AMD-compatible	
Memory	64 MB RAM	
Hard Disk Space	2 GB hard disk with 1.5 GB free disk space	
Display	SVGA-compatible (800 x 600)	
Input Devices	Keyboard and Microsoft Mouse (or other pointing device)	
Other	CD-ROM or DVD-ROM	

Exercise 2: Verify That Your Hardware Is in the Windows Catalog

1. Locate the documentation that came with your computer, including any information about the motherboard, expansion cards, network adapters, video display adapters, and sound cards. Use this documentation and information provided by the System Information tool to complete as much as you can of the following table (N/A means "not applicable"):

Hardware	Manufacturer	BIOS Date	BIOS Version	Model	Version	Chipset Version
System Board				N/A	N/A	N/A
Video Display		N/A			N/A	N/A
Hard Disk Interface		N/A	N/A			N/A

Hardware	Manufacturer	BIOS Date	BIOS Version	Model	Chipset Version	Version
Network Interface Card		N/A			N/A	N/A
Sound		N/A	N/A		N/A	
SCSI		N/A			N/A	N/A

2. Compare your findings with those in the Windows Catalog.

3. If any of your current hardware is not on the list, contact the manufacturer to determine if Windows XP supports the product.

Exercise 3: Perform a Clean Installation of Windows XP from CD-ROM

> **Note**   This practice assumes that you have a computer on which you can boot using the installation CD, and that you are willing to format your hard disk and install a fresh copy of Windows XP.

To perform an attended installation of Windows XP Professional, use the following steps:

1. Make sure that your computer is set up to start from the CD-ROM drive. If you are not sure how to do this, consult your computer documentation for information about accessing the BIOS settings.

2. Insert the Windows XP Professional with Service Pack 2 installation CD into your CD-ROM drive and restart the computer. When the computer restarts, the text mode portion of the installation begins. During this time, you will be asked if you need to install any third-party drivers. You only have a few seconds to press the F6 key and install the drivers before the installation continues.

3. Windows loads a number of files needed for setup and after a few minutes, the Welcome To Setup screen appears. You can use this screen to set up Windows XP or to repair an existing installation. Press ENTER to continue with the installation.

4. The Windows XP Licensing Agreement appears. After reading the terms of the license, press F8 to accept the terms and continue the installation. If you do not accept the agreement, Setup will not continue.

5. After you accept the Licensing Agreement, Setup proceeds to the Disk Partitioning portion. If you have multiple partitions, Setup will list them and allow you to you choose which one to install XP Professional to. If you have no partitions configured, you can create one at this point.

6. After you have determined which partition to install to, press Enter to continue.

7. The Format screen appears, which is where you decide how the drive should be formatted (FAT or NTFS). Select Format The Partition Using The NTFS File System and press Enter.

8. Setup displays a screen warning that formatting the disk will delete all files from it. Press F to format the drive and continue.

9. After the format process is complete, Setup copies the files needed to complete the next phase of the install process and then restarts the computer.

10. After the computer restarts, Setup enters the graphical user interface (GUI) mode portion of the installation.

11. Setup continues the installation for several minutes, and then displays the Regional And Language Options page. Make sure that the settings are correct for your area, and then click Next.

12. The Personalize Your Software page appears. Fill in the appropriate information and click Next.

13. The Product Key entry page appears. Enter the 25-digit product ID and click Next.

14. The Computer Name And Administrator Password page appears. Enter a name for your computer and choose a password for the Administrator account.

15. The Date And Time Settings page appears. Make sure that the information is correct for your area and click Next.

16. If Setup detects an installed network adapter, Setup will install network components next.

17. The Network Settings page appears. You should select the Typical Settings option if you want Setup to automatically configure networking components. Typical components include Client for Microsoft Networks, File and Print Sharing for Microsoft Networks, and Transmission Control Protocol/Internet Protocol (TCP/IP). Click Next.

18. After you choose the network settings, Setup displays the Workgroup Or Computer Domain name page. Enter the appropriate information and click Next.

19. After you click Next in the Workgroup Or Computer Domain page, Setup continues with the final portion of the installation. It may take from 15 to 60 minutes for the process to finish. When the installation is complete, the computer restarts and you are prompted to log on for the first time.

Lesson Review

The following questions are intended to reinforce key information presented in this lesson. If you are unable to answer a question, review the lesson materials and try the question again. You can find answers to the questions in the "Questions and Answers" section at the end of this chapter.

1. What are the minimum requirements for installing Windows XP?

   _____

   _____

2. A Windows XP Professional volume that is formatted with FAT32 cannot support which of the following? (Choose all that apply.)

   A. Disk quotas

   B. Disk compression

   C. File encryption

   D. Drives larger than 2 GB

3. What are the two files that are created by Setup Manager that you can use to automate the Windows XP installation process? (Choose two.)

   A. Standard answer files

   B. Remote installation files

   C. Uniqueness database files

   D. System information files

4. From which of the following versions of Windows can you upgrade directly to Windows XP Professional?

   A. Windows 95 OSR2

   B. Windows 98

   C. Windows NT 4.0 Workstation (with Service Pack 3)

   D. Windows NT 4.0 Workstation (with Service Pack 5)

   E. Windows 2000 Professional

5. List the tools that are available for copying files and settings from an old computer running a previous version of Windows to a new computer running Windows XP. What are the differences between the tools?

   _____

   _____

Lesson Summary

- Before installing Windows XP, you must ensure that the computer meets or exceeds the hardware requirements for the operating system. You should also make sure that all hardware devices are listed in Microsoft's Windows Catalog.

- Windows XP supports three types of installations: clean installations, upgrades, and multiple boot installations.

- Windows XP also supports three methods of installations: standard (attended), network, and automated.

- A standard (attended) installation is controlled manually, requiring that someone be present to make installation decisions and perform the initial configuration. This method is suitable for home and smaller business installations.

- Unattended installations rely on scripted programs that simulate the presence of a human administrator and answer questions presented during the installation process.

- The Files And Settings Transfer Wizard and the USMT can both be used to transfer files and settings. The Files and Settings Transfer Wizard is intended for home and small business users and provides a simple wizard interface. USMT is intended for IT professionals on larger networks.

Lesson 2: Troubleshooting Windows XP Installations

As you learned in Lesson 1, the best way to avoid trouble when installing Windows XP is to properly prepare the computer for the installation and understand the decisions that you will be required to make during the installation process. Unforeseen problems do sometimes occur, and as a DST, you are likely to be the first person called to troubleshoot a failed installation. To deal with issues that may occur during the installation of Windows XP, you must be familiar with the Windows installation process, typical symptoms that are produced by different types of failures, and corrective actions you can use to remedy the issue.

After this lesson, you will be able to

- Troubleshoot common Windows XP installation errors.
- Troubleshoot CD-ROM-based Windows XP installations.
- Troubleshoot upgrades.
- Troubleshoot unattended installations.

Estimated lesson time: 15 minutes

Troubleshooting Common Installation Problems

Fortunately, installation problems do not happen often and are usually minor issues. Although good preparation can help avoid almost all installation problems, you may not always have that luxury as a DST. More than likely, a user will call you after a failed installation attempt rather than get your help preparing an installation. Table 2-3 summarizes common installation errors that can occur during a Windows XP installation and suggests actions for solving the problem.

Table 2-3   Common Windows XP Installation Errors

Error Condition	Suggested Action
Insufficient hard disk space	If the user is upgrading to Windows XP, you may need to delete files or remove programs to free up some disk space. If that is not possible, the user could install an additional hard disk or create an additional partition to hold Windows XP. Help the user determine the best course to take.
Setup failure during early text mode portion of Setup	Verify that Windows XP supports the mass storage devices that are on the computer. If there are unsupported devices, press F6 when prompted and supply the necessary drivers for these devices from a floppy disk with drivers from the manufacturer.

Table 2-3   Common Windows XP Installation Errors

Error Condition	Suggested Action
During Setup, the computer's BIOS-based virus scanner gives an error message indicating that a virus is attempting to infect the boot sector. Setup fails.	When Setup attempts to write to the boot sector of the hard disk so that it can start Windows XP, BIOS-based virus scanners might interpret the action as an attempt by a virus to infect the computer. Disable the virus protection in the BIOS and enable it again after Windows XP is fully installed.
Setup fails during hardware detection or component installation.	Verify that all hardware is in the Windows Catalog. Remove non-supported devices to try to get past the error. If you are unsure which devices are not supported, consider removing all devices except those that are necessary to run the computer (such as the motherboard, display adapter, memory, and so on) during the installation and then reconnecting them after Windows is installed.
Errors accessing the CD	Clean the CD. If that does not resolve the issue and you have another CD available, try the other CD. If it works, then you know the first CD is bad. If you do not have another installation CD, you can also try to use a different CD-ROM drive.
Inability to join the domain during Setup	This will most likely occur because the computer cannot locate a domain controller. This lack of connectivity can occur because the network card is not functioning correctly, the network configuration is incorrect, or the client cannot contact the appropriate servers. This connectivity problem can also occur if the computer does not have an account in the domain and the user does not have permission to create an account in the domain. To try and resolve the issue, join a workgroup to complete Setup, troubleshoot the issue, and join the domain after the issue has been resolved. After installation, you can add the computer to the domain from the Computer Name tab in the Properties of My Computer.

Using the Windows XP Setup Logs

The Setup utility creates two log files in the installation folder that you can use to help you in the troubleshooting process:

- **Setupact.log** Contains information about the files that are copied during Setup and other Setup activity

- **Setupapi.log** Contains information about device driver files that are copied during Setup

These logs are text documents that you can view in Notepad, WordPad, or Microsoft Word. Some of the documents are very large. Consider searching the document for the word "fail," which can help you locate instances in the log files that contain information on failed operations.

Troubleshooting Stop Errors

Stop errors, also referred to as blue screen errors, occur when the computer detects a condition from which it cannot recover. The computer stops responding and displays a screen of information, as shown in Figure 2-5. The most likely time when you may experience stop errors is after the text mode phase of Setup has finished, your computer restarts, and the GUI mode phase begins. During this transition, Windows XP loads the newly installed operating system kernel for the first time and initializes new hardware drivers.

Figure 2-5   Stop errors are most likely to occur when the GUI mode phase of Setup begins.

Stop errors are identified by a 10-digit hexadecimal number. The two most common stop errors you will encounter during Windows XP installation are Stop: 0x0000000A and Stop: 0x0000007B.

Resolving Stop: 0x0000000A Errors   The Stop error 0x0000000A error usually indicates that Windows attempted to access a particular memory address at too high of a process internal request level (IRQL). This error usually occurs when a hardware driver uses an incorrect memory address. This error can also indicate an incompatible device driver or a general hardware problem.

To troubleshoot this error, take the following actions:

- Confirm that your hardware is listed in the Windows Catalog.

- Disable all caching in the computer's BIOS, including L2, BIOS, and write-back caching on disk controllers. Consult the documentation for the computer or motherboard for details on disabling these options.

- Remove all unnecessary hardware, including network cards, modems, sound cards, and additional drives.

- If the installation drive is Small Computer System Interface (SCSI)–based, you must obtain the correct device driver from the manufacturer, confirm that termination is set properly and that you have no ID conflicts, and then turn off sync negotiation at the SCSI host adapter.

- If the installation drive is an Integrated Device Electronics (IDE) drive, verify that the installation drive is attached to the primary channel and that it is set to be the master drive.

- Verify that your memory modules are compatible with each other and that you have not mixed types, speeds, or manufacturers. A defective memory module can also produce this type of error message.

- Verify that the motherboard BIOS is current and compatible with Windows XP. The manufacturer's website will contain information about each motherboard it produces. You may need to update the BIOS with a newer version.

- Turn off any BIOS-based virus protection or disk write protection that may be enabled.

Resolving Stop: 0x0000007B Errors   The Stop: 0X0000007B error normally indicates that you have an inaccessible boot device, meaning that Windows cannot access your hard disk. The common causes for this type of error are as follows:

- **Boot sector virus**   You must eliminate all boot sector viruses before proceeding with the installation of Windows XP. The exact removal process depends on which virus has infected the drive. You must scan the drive with an up-to-date virus-scanning utility and then check the antivirus manufacturer's website for the proper procedure to repair the disk.

- **Defective or incompatible hardware**   Verify that all the hardware on the computer is in the Windows Catalog and that no components are defective.

- **Defective or missing third-party device driver**   If any third-party device drivers are required to install Windows XP, you will be prompted to press F6 during the first phase of the installation process. You may need to obtain the latest drivers for your controller card before proceeding with the installation of Windows XP. With the correct drivers on a floppy disk, restart the installation of Windows XP, press F6 when prompted, and insert the driver disk.

> **Tip**   Although these are the two most common stop errors you will see during Windows XP installation, you may encounter other stop errors. If a user gets a stop error, have the user write down the stop error number and the parameters that follow the error. Search the Knowledge Base by using the number as your keyword, and you will find information on resolving the error.

Troubleshooting CD-ROM-Based Installations

Installing Windows XP from the installation CD is perhaps the most common installation method. Although troubleshooting issues that occur during this type of installation also include using the general Windows XP troubleshooting steps that are listed in the previous section, there are a few issues that are specific to CD-based installations.

Problems specific to CD-based installations include the following:

- If you try to start the computer by using the installation CD, but Windows Setup does not start, check the BIOS settings on the computer to make sure that the CD-ROM drive is a valid start device and that the current order of boot devices has the CD-ROM drive ahead of the hard disk.

- If a computer does not support starting from a CD, create a set of boot floppy disks for Windows XP.

- If the computer supports starting from a CD, and the order of boot devices is correct, you may have a damaged installation CD or CD-ROM drive. Verify that the CD-ROM drive is operational by using another disk in the CD drive. It is also possible that the CD-ROM drive lens needs cleaning; there are several commercial products available to clean CD-ROM drive lenses.

- If the CD-ROM drive appears functional, try cleaning the installation CD and starting Setup again. If this fails, it is possible that the installation CD is damaged and needs to be replaced.

Troubleshooting Upgrades

You can prevent most upgrade-specific problems by taking a few measures before starting the upgrade. Before upgrading any computer, you should perform all the following actions:

- Ensure that the computer meets minimum hardware requirements
- Check the compatibility of programs and hardware
- Run the Windows XP Upgrade Advisor
- Back up all data on the computer and verify that the data can be restored
- Update the computer BIOS
- Turn off any power management and antivirus features in the computer's BIOS
- Remove all antivirus software
- Uncompress all hard disks
- Run ScanDisk and ScanReg
- Download available driver updates
- Stop all running programs

Troubleshooting Problems with Answer Files

When troubleshooting problems with answer files, by far the most common problem is an answer file that was not configured correctly. If an answer file was configured incorrectly or incompletely, you can either edit the file directly by using any text editor—Microsoft Notepad, for example—or you can re-create the answer file. However, if you are working as a DST, you must be careful to ensure that you are authorized to reconfigure the answer file. More than likely, your responsibility is simply to notify an administrator of the failure. You should also be prepared to provide the administrator with setup logs and an explanation of problems that occurred during setup.

Lesson Review

The following questions are intended to reinforce key information presented in this lesson. If you are unable to answer a question, review the lesson materials and try the question again. You can find answers to the questions in the "Questions and Answers" section at the end of this chapter.

1. A user calls and tells you that she is trying to install Windows XP Professional by using the installation CD-ROM. However, she cannot get the computer to start using the CD-ROM. What steps should you take?

_____

_____

_____

_____

2. You are helping a user perform a remote installation from a RIS server on his notebook computer. He has a boot disk that his administrator told him will force the computer to boot from the network and start the installation. However, when he tries to start the computer by using the boot disk, he receives an error stating that a supported network card could not be found. You verify that the user's network adapter is functional by installing it on another computer and connecting to the network. What is the likely problem?

_____

_____

_____

_____

Lesson Summary

- Common reasons for a Windows XP installation failure include insufficient disk space, a BIOS-based virus scanner that is preventing Setup from running properly, incompatible or malfunctioning hardware, and problems with the installation CD (or accessing the installation files on the network).

- You can use the Windows Setup log files (Setupact.log and Setupapi.log) to view information about the setup process and help identify the cause of installation failures.

- Stop errors occur when the computer detects a condition from which it cannot recover. You can look up specific stop errors in the Knowledge Base.

- Troubleshooting upgrade problems follows the same procedure as troubleshooting installation problems. However, there are a number of actions you should take before performing an upgrade to ensure that the process goes as smoothly as possible. The most important of these actions is making sure that the computer meets the minimum hardware requirements, that software and hardware are compatible, that the computer is backed up, and that all programs (especially antivirus software) are stopped.

Lesson 3: Activating and Updating Windows XP

After installing Windows XP for a home or small business user, you must activate Windows. If not activated, Windows can be used for only 30 days. Corporate installations typically do not need to be activated because most corporations use a volume licensing system. You will also need to install any available updates and preferably configure Windows to download and install critical updates automatically.

After this lesson, you will be able to

- Activate Windows XP following installation.
- Use the Microsoft Update site to scan a computer, display available updates, and apply the updates.
- Configure Automatic Updates to download and install updates automatically.
- Apply service packs.

Estimated lesson time: 30 minutes

Activating Windows Following Installation

Windows XP Professional requires that the operating system be activated with Microsoft within 30 days of installation. If the operating system is not activated within this time, Windows ceases to function until it is activated. You are not allowed to log on to the computer until you contact one of Microsoft's product activation centers.

Windows Product Activation (WPA) requires each installation to have a unique product key. When you enter the 25-character product key during Windows installation, the Setup program generates a 20-character product ID (PID). During activation, Windows combines the PID and a hardware ID to form an installation ID. Windows sends this installation ID to a Microsoft license clearinghouse, in which the PID is verified to ensure that it is valid and that it has not already been used to activate another installation. If this check passes, the license clearinghouse sends a confirmation ID to your computer, and Windows XP Professional is activated. If the check fails, activation fails.

Windows XP prompts you to perform activation the first time Windows starts after installation. If you do not perform the activation, Windows continues to prompt you at regular intervals until you activate the product.

Note   Microsoft does not collect any personal information during the activation process. Instead, an identification key is generated based on the types of hardware that are on your computer.

Using the Microsoft Update Site

Microsoft Update is an online service that provides updates to the Windows family of operating systems and select Microsoft products, such as Microsoft Office. Product updates such as critical and security updates, general updates, and device driver updates are all easily accessible. When you connect to the Microsoft Update website, shown in Figure 2-6, the site scans your computer (a process that happens locally without sending any information to Microsoft) to determine what is already installed and then presents you with available updates for your computer.

Figure 2-6   Using the Microsoft Update site

You can access Microsoft Update in the following ways:

■   Through Internet Explorer, by selecting Windows Update from the Tools menu

■   Through any Web browser by using the URL *http://update.microsoft.com/ windowsupdate*

■   Through the Help And Support Center by selecting Windows Update

- Through the Start menu by selecting All Programs and then Windows Update

- Through Device Manager by selecting Update Driver in the Properties dialog box of any device

▶ **Using the Microsoft Update Site**

To obtain updates manually from the Microsoft Update site, follow these steps:

1. Click the Start menu, point to All Programs, and then click Windows Update.

   The Microsoft Update site determines whether you have the latest version of the software that scans your computer and recommends necessary updates. Microsoft Update might need to install the software before you can continue. After the latest version of the software is installed, Microsoft Update provides two choices: Express and Custom.

2. Click Express to quickly scan the computer for critical and security updates only, and then automatically download and install such available updates. Usually, you will not need to restart the computer after an Express install. If you choose Express, this is the last step you need to perform. Clicking Custom allows you to select the updates you want to install. The remainder of this procedure details the steps of a custom installation.

3. After clicking Custom, Microsoft Update scans your computer. After the scan is complete (a process that is performed locally—no information is sent to Microsoft's servers), select a category under Select By Type, and then click Add for each update you want to install. After the updates have been selected, click Review And Install Updates. The following categories are available:

   ❏ **High Priority updates** High Priority updates include critical and security updates. These updates are crucial to the operation of the computer, so you should *always* install them. These updates provide solutions to known issues, include patches for security vulnerabilities, and might contain updates to the operating system or other applications. Service packs are also included as critical updates.

   ❏ **Software Optional updates** Software Optional updates are less critical than the previously detailed updates and range from application updates for Microsoft software to updates for previously applied operating system service packs. Not everyone needs all updates, however, so you should read the descriptions prior to adding them to the installation list and add only necessary updates.

❑ **Hardware Optional updates** Hardware Optional updates include new and updated drivers for a user's particular computer and setup. When Microsoft Update scans the computer, it acquires information about the modem, network card, printer, and similar hardware, and then offers any available driver updates. Users often find that driver updates enhance the performance of the computer.

4. The Microsoft Update site selects all high-priority updates and service packs for you automatically. You must add optional updates to the installation manually. Pay attention to the updates that you select; some updates must be installed independently of other updates.

5. After selecting the updates you want to install, click Review And Install Updates.

6. Review the updates you have selected, and then click Install Updates.

7. If Windows displays a license agreement, read it and then click I Accept. Wait while the updates are installed and then restart the computer if prompted.

Configuring Automatic Updates

Windows XP also supports Automatic Updates, a feature that automatically downloads and installs new critical updates on the computer when the updates become available. The first time a computer starts after Windows XP is installed (or after Windows XP Service Pack 2 is installed, if it is installed separately), Windows displays a dialog box that allows you to turn on Automatic Updates. You should encourage users to configure the Automatic Updates feature in Windows XP so that it downloads and installs critical updates automatically.

If a user reports problems acquiring updates, you should verify that Automatic Updates is enabled and configured appropriately. Use the following steps to turn on Automatic Updates:

1. Click Start, and then click Control Panel.

2. In the Control Panel (in Category View), click Performance And Maintenance.

3. In the Performance And Maintenance window, click System.

On the Automatic Updates tab, select Automatic (Recommended), as shown in Figure 2-7. This setting configures Windows XP to download and install updates automatically at the configured time (3:00 A.M., by default). You can also specify whether the user should be notified before downloading and installation, have downloads happen automatically and be notified before installation, or download and install automatically according to a schedule. For the highest level of security (and the least intervention required by users), use the fully automatic option and configure a time when the computer will not be used.

Figure 2-7   You can configure Automatic Updates in many ways.

4. Click OK.

Exam Tip   Enabling Automatic Updates and configuring it to download and install updates automatically according to a preset schedule is the recommended way to handle critical updates for Windows XP. To obtain critical updates for Office, you must visit the Microsoft Office Online site at *http://office.microsoft.com/home/default.aspx/*.

Applying Service Packs

Microsoft periodically releases service packs for Windows XP. A service pack is a collection of all updates released to that point and often includes new features. You must be familiar with the deployment of service packs to ensure that all operating systems on the network are up-to-date and to avoid issues later.

Windows XP ships with a utility called Winver.exe, which you can use to determine the version of Windows you are running and what level of service pack (if any) is installed. Figure 2-8 displays the output of Winver.exe prior to any service pack being installed. If a service pack has been installed, the version is noted after the build number.

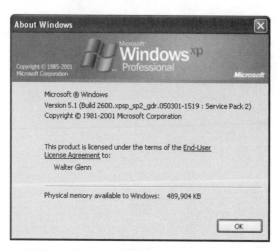

Figure 2-8 Use Winver.exe to determine the current Windows version and service pack.

Obtaining a Service Pack

Service packs are free, and you can get them in the following ways:

- Use Microsoft Update to update a single computer with a service pack.

- Download the service pack from Microsoft Update to deploy to many computers. The download is a single, large, self-extracting executable, which will have a different name depending on the service pack version that you are installing. The file is quite large (85 MB or more), so be sure that you have sufficient bandwidth available to support the download.

- Order the service pack CD. You can order the service pack CD from Microsoft for a nominal fee that covers the cost of manufacture and shipping. In addition to containing the service pack, the CD contains operating system enhancements and other advanced utilities.

- Use Microsoft subscription services. Microsoft has several subscription services, such as Microsoft TechNet, which will automatically provide you with service packs with the next issue after the release of the service pack.

Installing a Service Pack

Service pack setup programs can have various names. Some Windows Service Packs use a program named Update.exe, while some use a name based on the service pack version. Regardless of the file name, most Microsoft Windows updates support the same command-line parameters, which control how the service pack deploys. Table 2-4 lists these parameters.

Table 2-4   Command-Line Parameters for Windows Updates

Switch	Function
/f	Forces all applications to close prior to restarting the computer.
/n	Does not back up Uninstall files. You cannot uninstall the service pack if this switch is used.
/o	Overwrites original equipment manufacturer (OEM)-provided files without prompting the user.
/q	Installation runs in quiet mode with no user interaction required (requires –o to update OEM-supplied files).
/s:[path to distribution folder]	Creates an integration installation point.
/u	Unattended installation (requires –o to update OEM-supplied files).
/x	Extracts files without starting Setup. This is useful if you want to move installation files to another location.
/z	Disables automatic restart when installation is finished.

Service pack installations require a significant amount of disk space (hundreds of MBs). The uninstall folder consumes the majority of this disk space. You can install a service pack without saving uninstall files by using the –n switch when you install the service pack.

When applying service packs, you must choose an installation method from the following options:

- **Update installation**   The service pack executable is started locally, across the network, or through Microsoft Update.

- **Integrated installation**   Also called slipstreaming, this installation is one in which the service pack is applied to the installation files on a distribution server by using the –s switch, integrating the installation files and the service pack into a single set of updated installation files. You can then perform new installations that include the service pack by using the integrated distribution point. This eliminates the need to apply the service pack after the installation. However, you cannot uninstall the service pack if it is applied using this method.

On the CD One of the CDs accompanying this book contains a trial version of Windows XP Professional with Service Pack 2. Service Pack 2 has been slipstreamed into the Windows XP Professional installation files.

■ **Combination installation** This installation involves using a combination of an integrated installation, an answer file to control the installation process, and a Cmdlines.txt file to launch additional application setup programs after the operating system setup has completed.

When you install new operating system components after installing a service pack, Setup will require the location of both the operating system and service pack installation files. This allows Setup to install the updated version of the component.

Uninstalling a Service Pack

By default, the service pack setup program automatically creates a backup of the files and settings that are changed during the service pack installation and places them in an uninstall folder named \$NTServicepackUninstall$. You can uninstall the service pack by using Add/Remove Programs in Control Panel or from a command line by running Spuninst.exe in the \$NTServicepackUninstall\Spunints folder.

Note If you installed a service pack without creating a backup, you cannot uninstall the service pack.

Practice: Update Windows XP

In this practice, you will configure Automatic Updates to download and install critical updates automatically. You will also use the Microsoft Update site to manually update Windows XP.

Exercise 1: Configure Automatic Updates

1. From the Start menu, click Control Panel.

2. In the Control Panel window (in Category View), click Performance And Maintenance.

3. In the Performance and Maintenance window, click System.

4. On the Automatic Updates tab, select Automatic (Recommended).

5. Click OK.

Exercise 2: Update Windows XP using the Microsoft Update Site

1. Log onto Windows XP using an account with administrator permissions.

2. From the Start menu, point to All Programs, and then click Windows Update.

3. If you see a Security Warning dialog box, click Yes.

4. The Microsoft Update site spends some time checking for updates to the scanning software that the site uses to scan your computer. When this scan finishes, on the Welcome To Microsoft Update page, click Express .

5. If you see a dialog box asking whether you accept the End-User License Agreement, click I Agree or Accept (whichever is displayed).

6. A Microsoft Update dialog box appears and displays progress. After installation is complete, you might receive a Microsoft Internet Explorer message box asking if you want to restart the computer. If so, click OK.

Lesson Review

The following questions are intended to reinforce key information presented in this lesson. If you are unable to answer a question, review the lesson materials and try the question again. You can find answers to the questions in the "Questions and Answers" section at the end of this chapter.

1. List the types of updates that are available from the Microsoft Update site and explain the differences between them.

   _____

   _____

   _____

   _____

2. What is the recommended way to configure the Automatic Updates feature in Windows XP?

   _____

   _____

   _____

   _____

3. How many days will Windows XP function if you do not activate Windows or are not part of a volume licensing agreement?

A. 10 days

B. 14 days

C. 30 days

D. 60 days

E. 120 days

Lesson Summary

- You can use the Microsoft Update site to scan a computer and display available critical, Windows, and driver updates.

- Automatic Updates is a Windows XP feature that downloads and installs critical and security updates automatically. Although you can specify that Automatic Updates prompts users before downloading or installing, Microsoft recommends that you configure it to download and install automatically according to a preset schedule.

- Service packs are collections of updates (and sometimes new features) that Microsoft has tested to ensure that they work together correctly. Microsoft occasionally issues new service packs for its products.

Lesson 4: Troubleshooting Windows XP Startup Problems

After you install Windows XP, the first opportunity for problems to occur happens when Windows XP starts. Understanding how Windows XP starts up is an important part of understanding Windows XP. After you understand the startup procedure, you will have a better idea of what you can modify about the way that Windows starts and how to troubleshoot startup problems. This lesson examines the startup process and covers important startup troubleshooting tools and techniques.

After this lesson, you will be able to

- Explain how a computer starts.
- Explain how Windows starts.
- Check Event Viewer for startup problems.
- Configure advanced boot options.
- Use the Recovery Console to troubleshoot startup problems.

Estimated lesson time: 30 minutes

Understanding How a Computer Starts

When you press the power button on a computer, power is provided to all the components and the boot process begins. This process happens as follows:

1. When you supply power to the motherboard on a computer, the BIOS begins a process called power-on self test (POST). During POST, the BIOS tests important hardware that is on the computer, including the display adapter, memory, storage devices, and the keyboard.

2. BIOS first gives control of the testing process to the display adapter, which has its own testing routine built in. This is why the first screen you see when starting a computer is usually a blank screen with information at the top about your display adapter.

3. The display adapter then gives control back to the POST routine, and the main POST screen appears, as shown in Figure 2-9.

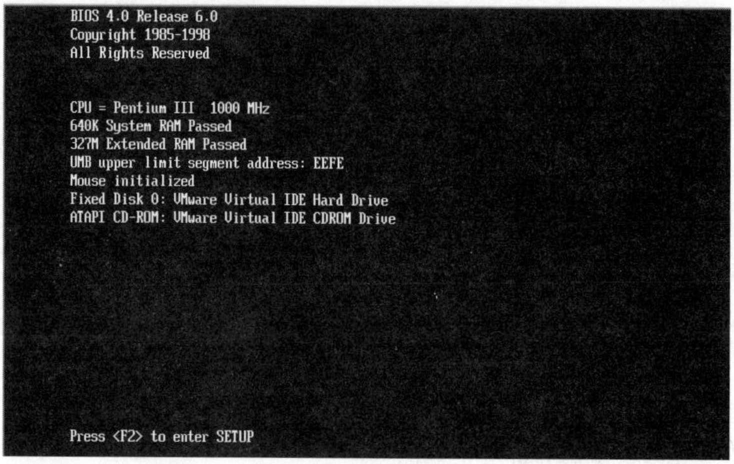

```
BIOS 4.0 Release 6.0
Copyright 1985-1998
All Rights Reserved


CPU = Pentium III  1000 MHz
640K System RAM Passed
327M Extended RAM Passed
UMB upper limit segment address: EEFE
Mouse initialized
Fixed Disk 0: VMware Virtual IDE Hard Drive
ATAPI CD-ROM: VMware Virtual IDE CDROM Drive











Press <F2> to enter SETUP
```

Figure 2-9 The main POST screen displays information about the hardware on a computer.

4. POST tests your processor and displays the processor version on the screen.

5. After the processor test is complete, POST gives control of your computer back to the BIOS. At this point, you can press the DELETE key (or whatever key allows you to enter the BIOS setup on your computer) to configure BIOS settings.

6. Assuming that you do not enter BIOS setup, BIOS tests your memory next. This step (the memory countdown) is probably the one that you will be the most familiar with. The memory is displayed on the next line after the processor.

7. BIOS then checks the connections to your various hard drives, CD drives, and floppy drives. If no connections are present, or if connections are different from what is listed in the BIOS settings, BIOS displays an error message, and the boot process halts. You must enter BIOS setup to correct these problems.

8. Assuming that all goes well, BIOS next displays a screen that summarizes the state of your computer.

9. BIOS then calls a special software code named the BIOS operating system bootstrap interrupt (Int 19h). This code locates a bootable disk by attempting to load each disk that is configured as a bootable in the BIOS settings.

10. After BIOS finds a bootable disk, it loads the program that is found at the Master Boot Record (MBR) of the disk into your computer's memory and gives control of the computer to that program. Assuming that BIOS gives control to the MBR on the boot partition that contains Windows XP, the startup phase now moves from the starting of your computer to the starting of Windows.

Understanding How Windows XP Starts

After the computer starts and hands off the process to the operating system, Windows XP continues to load in the following manner:

1. The MBR is a small program typically found on the first sector of a hard drive. Because the MBR is so small, it cannot do much. In fact, the MBR that is used in Windows XP has only one function: it loads a program named NTLDR into memory.

> **Tip**   NTLDR is probably a name that you recognize. When a computer tries to start from a disk that is not bootable, but has been formatted with a file system that is compatible with Windows XP, you will often see the message "NTLDR is missing. Press CTRL+ALT+DEL to restart" (or something like it). If you see this message, Windows is telling you that either the disk that you are trying to start from is not a valid boot disk (maybe a floppy disk is still in the drive) or that the NTLDR file is invalid.

2. NTLDR switches your computer to a flat memory model (thus bypassing the 640 KB memory restrictions placed on PCs) and then reads the contents of a file named BOOT.INI. The BOOT.INI file contains information on the different boot sectors that exist on your computer.

3. If a computer has multiple bootable partitions, NTLDR uses the information in the BOOT.INI file to display a menu. That menu contains options on the various operating systems that you can load. If a computer has only one bootable partition, NTLDR bypasses the menu and loads Windows XP.

4. Before Windows XP loads, NTLDR opens yet another program into memory named NTDETECT.COM. NTDETECT.COM performs a complete hardware test on your computer. After determining the hardware that is present, NTDETECT.COM gives that information back to NTLDR.

5. NTLDR then attempts to load the version of Windows XP that you selected in Step 3 (if you selected one). It does this by finding the NTOSKRNL file in the System32 folder of your Windows XP directory. NTOSKRNL is the root program of the Windows operating system: the kernel. After the kernel is loaded into memory, NTLDR passes control of the boot process to the kernel and to another file named HAL.DLL. HAL.DLL controls Windows' famous hardware abstraction layer (HAL), which is the protective layer between Windows and a computer's hardware that enables such stability in the Windows XP environment.

6. NTOSKRNL handles the rest of the boot process. First, it loads several low-level system drivers. Next, NTOSKRNL loads all the additional files that make up the core Windows XP operating system.

7. Next, Windows verifies whether there is more than one hardware profile configured for the computer (see Chapter 6 for more information about hardware profiles). If there is more than one profile, Windows displays a menu from which to choose. If there is only one hardware profile, Windows bypasses the menu and loads the default profile.

8. After Windows knows which hardware profile to use, Windows next loads all the device drivers for the hardware on your computer. By this time, you are looking at the Welcome To Windows XP boot screen.

9. Finally, Windows starts any services that are scheduled to start automatically. While services are starting, Windows displays the logon screen.

Using Advanced Boot Options

In addition to displaying the regular boot menu, there is another menu behind the scenes of the Windows startup process. Pressing the F8 function key during the Windows XP boot process displays the Advanced Options menu. Table 2-5 summarizes the functionality of each of the options on the Advanced Options menu. Options that require further description are explained in detail in the sections immediately following the table.

Table 2-5   Summary of Advanced Boot Options

Option	Summary Description
Safe Mode	Loads only the basic devices and drivers that are required to start the computer. Devices that are initialized include mass storage devices, standard Video Graphics Adapter (VGA), mouse, keyboard, and other essential drivers and computer services.
Safe Mode With Networking	Same as Safe Mode, but with the addition of networking drivers and services. Use when troubleshooting problems that require network connectivity.
Safe Mode With Command Prompt	Same as Safe Mode, but starts a command prompt (Cmd.exe) instead of the Windows Explorer GUI. Generally used when Safe Mode does not function.
Enable Boot Logging	Starts the computer normally, but records driver loading and initialization information to a text file for subsequent analysis.
Enable VGA Mode	Currently installed video driver loaded in 640x480 mode. Useful when the display adapter is configured to a resolution that the monitor cannot support.
Last Known Good Configuration	The computer is started with the configuration that was in use the last time a user was able to log on successfully.

Table 2-5   Summary of Advanced Boot Options

Option	Summary Description
Debug Mode	Enables debugging mode on the computer, allowing debug information to be sent over the computer's COM2 serial port.
Boot Normally	Performs a standard Windows XP boot.

Exam Tip   The Safe Mode and Last Known Good Configuration options are two of the most useful tools to try first when troubleshooting Windows startup. Enabling Boot Logging is also useful when you are having trouble locating the source of the problem.

Using Safe Mode

Safe mode is one of the most important tools for solving startup problems. In safe mode, Windows loads only essential drivers and services. Windows does not load programs referenced in the Startup folders and through the Run options in the Registry. Windows also does not process local or group policies when starting in safe mode.

Loading only essential driver and service items makes safe mode a useful tool for troubleshooting and resolving issues with faulty services, device drivers, and application programs that are automatically loaded at startup. From safe mode, you can make configuration changes that are necessary to solve a problem, and then restart the computer normally. Figure 2-10 displays the Windows XP desktop when started in safe mode.

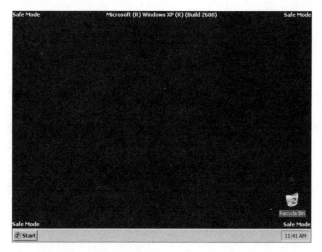

Figure 2-10   Safe mode often allows you to change settings you cannot change in normal mode.

You can use safe mode for troubleshooting the following types of situations:

- The computer no longer starts after loading a new device driver or application program. If this is the case, start in safe mode and use Event Viewer to check the event logs. Most likely an error will be associated with the driver or application. If the error indicates that a reconfiguration is necessary, attempt to correct the problem and start normally. If you cannot correct the problem, start in safe mode, remove the newly installed component, and contact the manufacturer for further information.

- The video is not displaying correctly (selecting the Enable VGA Mode option from the Advanced Options menu is also useful in this situation). This situation most commonly occurs when the computer is configured to a resolution that the monitor does not support. Starting in safe mode loads a standard VGA driver, and you can then reconfigure the resolution or load a different display device driver.

- The operating system begins to perform slowly or stalls for extended periods of time, or the operating system simply does not seem to be working correctly. If starting in safe mode corrects the problem, the issue is with something that loads normally but does not load in safe mode.

Note If a computer fails shortly after installing a new device or application, the new component is usually the source of the problem. However, there is a chance that the newly installed component is not causing the problem and that something else went wrong at about the same time. If the problem persists after the newly installed component has been removed, look at other troubleshooting options.

Boot Logging

When you select the Enable Boot Logging option from the Advanced Options menu, the computer starts normally and records boot-logging information in a file named **Ntbtlog.txt**. This log file contains a listing of all the drivers and services that the computer attempts to load during startup and is useful when trying to determine which service or driver is causing the computer to fail. Figure 2-11 displays a sample boot log file.

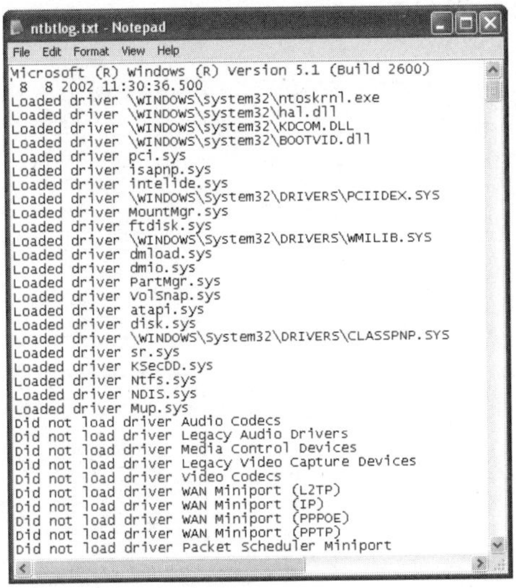

Figure 2-11   Use the boot log file (Ntbtlog.txt) to isolate startup problems.

> **Note**   Boot logging is enabled automatically when you start the computer with any of the safe mode boot options.

Last Known Good Configuration

The **Last Known Good Configuration** holds the configuration settings that existed the last time that a user successfully logged on to the computer. This option is useful if you have added or reconfigured a device driver that subsequently has caused the computer to fail. Using Last Known Good Configuration may allow you to start the computer so that you can try again with a different configuration or driver.

When starting by using the Last Known Good Configuration, you lose all system-setting changes that have been made since the last successful boot. In some situations, this means you may have to reconfigure the computer to some degree. You should consider troubleshooting by using safe mode before using the Last Known Good Configuration option to avoid this issue.

> **Note**   Last Known Good Configuration does not solve problems associated with drivers or files that are missing or have become corrupt. It is useful only in situations where drivers have been added or reconfigured since the last successful boot.

Using Recovery Console

Recovery Console is a command-line utility that gives you access to the hard disks when the operating system will not boot. You can use Recovery Console to access all partitions on a drive, regardless of the file system.

You can use the Recovery Console to perform the following tasks:

- Copy files between hard disks and from a floppy disk to a hard disk (but not from hard disk to a floppy disk), which allows you to replace or remove items that may be affecting the boot process or retrieve user data from an unsalvageable computer

- Control the startup state of services, which allows you to disable a service that could potentially be causing the operating system to crash

- Add, remove, and format partitions on the hard disk

- Repair the MBR or boot sector of a hard disk or volume

- Restore the Registry

Accessing the Recovery Console

You can permanently install the Recovery Console on a computer and make it accessible from the Boot menu. You can also access it at any time, without having installed it, by starting from the Windows XP installation CD.

To install the Recovery Console on a computer, access the Windows XP installation files (on the installation CD or at a network installation point) and execute the following command:

```
winnt32 /cmdcons
```

Windows XP Setup starts and installs the Recovery Console. After installation, the Recovery Console is accessible from a startup menu when the operating system is starting.

To access the Recovery Console on a computer in which Recovery Console is *not* installed, follow these steps:

1. Start the computer by using the Windows XP Professional CD.

2. When the text mode portion of Setup begins, follow the initial prompts. At the Welcome To Setup screen, press the R key to repair the Windows XP installation.

3. Enter the number that corresponds to the Windows XP installation that you want to repair (this is required even if only a single installation of Windows XP is on the computer).

4. When prompted, enter the local administrator's password.

Table 2-6 shows the commands that are available in the Recovery Console and provides brief descriptions of each.

Table 2-6 Recovery Console Command Descriptions

Command	Description
ATTRIB	Changes attributes on one file or directory (wildcards not supported)
BATCH	Executes commands specified in a text file
BOOTCFG	Scans hard disks to locate Windows installations and modifies or re-creates Boot.ini accordingly
CD	Displays the name of the current directory or switches to a new directory
CHDIR	Same as the CD command
CHKDSK	Checks a disk and displays a status report
CLS	Clears the screen
COPY	Copies a single file to another location (wildcards not supported)
DEL (also DELETE)	Deletes one file (wildcards not supported)
DIR	Displays a list of files and subdirectories in a directory
DISABLE	Disables a Windows system service or driver
DISKPART	Manages partitions on a hard disk, including adding and deleting partitions
ENABLE	Enables a Windows system service or driver
EXIT	Quits the Recovery Console and restarts the computer
EXPAND	Expands a compressed file
FIXBOOT	Writes a new boot sector to the system partition
FIXMBR	Repairs the MBR of the system partition
FORMAT	Formats a disk for use with Windows XP
HELP	Displays a list of available commands
LISTSVC	Lists all available services and drivers on the computer

Table 2-6   Recovery Console Command Descriptions

Command	Description
LOGON	Lists the detected installations of Windows XP and prompts for administrator logon
MAP	Displays drive letter to physical device mappings
MAP ARC	Displays the Address Resolution Client (ARC) path instead of the Windows XP device path for physical device mappings
MD	Creates a directory
MKDIR	Same as MD command
MORE	Displays a text file to the screen
RD	Removes a directory
REN	Renames a single file (wildcards not supported)
RENAME	Same as REN command
RMDIR	Same as RD command
SET	Used to set Recovery Console environment variables
SYSTEM_ROOT	Sets the current directory to system_root
TYPE	Displays a test file to the screen (same as MORE command)

Practice: Start the Recovery Console by Using the Windows XP CD

1. Start the computer by using the Windows XP installation CD.

2. When the text mode portion of Setup begins, follow the initial prompts. At the Welcome To Setup screen, press the R key to repair the Windows XP installation.

3. Enter the number that corresponds to the Windows XP installation that you want to repair and then press ENTER. Assuming that you are only running one Windows XP installation on your computer, you should choose 1.

4. When prompted, enter the local administrator's password.

5. At the Windows prompt, type **help** and then press ENTER to display a list of available commands. If your display does not show all the commands, you can press ENTER to scroll the list one entry at a time or press the spacebar to scroll a page at a time.

6. Type **dir** and then press ENTER to display the files in the current directory (the Windows directory). You probably need to scroll the list to see all of the files.

7. Type **exit** to exit the Recovery Console and restart the computer.

Lesson Review

The following questions are intended to reinforce key information presented in this lesson. If you are unable to answer a question, review the lesson materials and try the question again. You can find answers to the questions in the "Questions and Answers" section at the end of this chapter.

1. You believe that you have installed a faulty device driver and want to start up Windows XP to remove it. What mode should you start in to accomplish this?

_____

_____

2. A user reports to you that his computer running Windows XP Professional displays a series of errors on startup, stating that certain drivers are not loading. How could you have the user start the computer and easily send you a record of the startup process so that you can identify the problem drivers?

_____

_____

3. Which of the following advanced boot options loads only the basic devices and drivers required to start the computer and access the network?

   A. Safe Mode

   B. Safe Mode With Networking

   C. Last Known Good Configuration

   D. Safe Mode With Command Prompt

_____

_____

Lesson Summary

- Because safe mode loads only essential driver and service items, it is a useful tool for troubleshooting and resolving problems with faulty services, device drivers, and application programs that are automatically loaded at startup. From safe mode, you can perform reconfigurations that will enable you to make appropriate changes and then restart the computer normally.

- The Last Known Good Configuration restores the configuration settings that existed the last time that a user successfully logged onto the computer. This option is useful if you have added or reconfigured a device driver that subsequently has caused the computer to fail.

- The Recovery Console is a command-line utility that gives you access to the hard disks when the operating system will not start. The Recovery Console can access all volumes on the drive, regardless of the file system type. As the administrator of a Windows XP computer, you should be familiar with the Recovery Console and how you can use it to correct operating system problems.

Case Scenario Exercises

Scenario 2.1

You have been given a computer with the following hardware installed:

- 233-MHz Pentium II processor
- 64 MB of RAM
- 4-GB hard disk, 500 MB free
- 48x CD-ROM drive
- Floppy drive, mouse, keyboard
- SVGA monitor and video card
- 10-Mbps Ethernet network card

You will reformat the hard disk and install Windows XP Professional. What additional hardware do you need to install onto the computer prior to installing Windows XP?

_____

_____

_____

Scenario 2.2

You install a new device into a Windows XP computer and restart the computer because the device installation procedure prompted you to do so. When the computer restarts, you can log on, but the computer stops responding shortly thereafter. You suspect that the newly installed device is causing the problem, and you want to remove it. How do you accomplish this?

_____

_____

_____

Scenario 2.3

You are helping a user who is trying to perform an automatic installation of Windows XP on a network that has a RIS server. The RIS server contains the CD-based image and several other images that have been prepared. None of your clients' computers contain PXE-compliant network cards. What do you have to do to enable these clients to connect to the RIS server?

_____

_____

_____

Troubleshooting Lab

One of your users is attempting to upgrade to Windows XP Professional on a computer that is currently running Windows 98. She tells you that she has inserted the Windows XP installation CD and that the Setup program started successfully. She chose the upgrade option and then Setup walked her through several initial steps, copied a number of files, and restarted the computer. When the computer restarted, the installation continued. However, during the installation process, she receives an error message with the following description:

```
INF File Textsetup.sif is corrupt or missing Status 14 SETUP CANNOT CONTINUE
```

Using your knowledge of the setup process and the Knowledge Base, determine what the problem could be and how you might solve it.

_____

_____

_____

_____

_____

_____

_____

_____

Chapter Summary

- Before installing Windows XP, you must ensure that the computer meets or exceeds the hardware requirements for the operating system. You should also make sure that all hardware devices are listed in Microsoft's Windows Catalog.

- Windows XP supports three types of installations: clean installations, upgrades, and multiple boot installations. Windows XP also supports three methods of installations: standard (attended), network, and automated.

- The Files and Settings Transfer Wizard and the USMT can both be used to transfer files and settings. The Files And Settings Transfer Wizard is intended for home and small business users and provides a simple wizard interface. USMT is intended for users on larger networks.

- The system partition holds the files that are necessary to start the computer. The boot partition holds the files necessary to start the operating system. Often, the boot and system partition are the same partition.

- Common reasons for a Windows XP installation failure include insufficient disk space, a BIOS-based virus scanner that is preventing Setup from running properly, incompatible or malfunctioning hardware, and problems with the installation CD (or accessing the installation files on the network).

- You can use the Windows Setup log files (Setupact.log and Setupapi.log) to view information about the setup process and help identify the cause of installation failures.

- Stop errors occur when the computer detects a condition from which it cannot recover. You can look up specific stop errors in the Knowledge Base.

- Troubleshooting upgrade problems follow the same procedure as troubleshooting installation problems. However, there are many actions that you should take before performing an upgrade to ensure that the process goes as smoothly as possible. The most important of these actions are to make sure that a computer meets the minimum hardware requirements, that the software and hardware are compatible, that the data on the computer is backed up, and that all programs (especially antivirus software) are stopped.

- You can use the Microsoft Update site to scan a computer and display available high priority, optional software, and optional hardware updates.

- Automatic Updates is a Windows XP feature that downloads and installs critical updates automatically. Although you can specify that Automatic Updates prompt users before downloading or installing, Microsoft recommends that you configure Automatic Updates to download and install automatically according to a preset schedule.

- Service packs are collections of updates (and sometimes new features) that Microsoft has tested to ensure that they work together correctly. Microsoft occasionally issues new service packs for its products.

- The Safe Mode and Last Known Good Configuration options are two of the most useful tools to try first when troubleshooting Windows startup. Enabling Boot Logging is also useful typically when you are having trouble locating the source of the problem.

- The Recovery Console is a command-line utility that gives you access to the hard disks when the operating system does not start. The Recovery Console can access all volumes on the drive, regardless of the file system type. As the administrator of a Windows XP computer, you should be familiar with the Recovery Console and how you can use it to correct operating system problems.

Exam Highlights

Before taking the exam, review the key topics and terms that are presented in this chapter. You need to know this information.

Key Points

- You should memorize the basic hardware requirements for running Windows XP. A 233-MHz processor, 64 MB of RAM, and a 2-GB hard disk with 1.5 GB of free space are required.

- For the exam, know the features that Windows XP Home Edition does not support. In particular, know that a computer running Windows XP Home Edition cannot join a domain, does not support file level security, and does not support file encryption.

- The *only* reason to use FAT32 on a computer running Windows XP is if the computer is also configured to run an operating system that cannot interpret NTFS. If a computer runs only Windows XP, you should *always* use the NTFS format.

- A standard answer file is used to provide the common configuration settings for all computers that are affected during an unattended installation. A UDF provides the unique settings that each computer needs to distinguish it from other computers.

- You should understand the types of settings that you can change in the BIOS, particularly those that control the integrated components on the computer. Often, when an integrated device is not available in Windows, it is because the device is disabled.

- Enabling Automatic Updates and configuring it to download and install updates automatically according to a preset schedule is the recommended way to handle critical updates for Windows XP.

Key Terms

Boot partition   The disk partition that possesses the system files required to load the operating system into memory.

Files And Settings Transfer Wizard   One of two methods used by administrators to transfer user configuration settings and files from systems running Windows 95 or later to a clean Windows XP installation. The other method is the USMT.

Last Known Good Configuration   The configuration settings that existed the last time that the computer started successfully.

NTFS   The native file management system for Windows XP. However, Windows XP is also capable of using FAT and FAT32 file systems to maintain compatibility with previous versions of Windows.

Recovery Console   A command-line utility that gives you access to the hard disks and many command-line utilities when the operating system will not start. The Recovery Console can access all volumes on the drive, regardless of the file system type. You can use the Recovery Console to perform several operating system troubleshooting tasks.

Safe mode   An alternative startup mode that loads a minimal set of device drivers (keyboard, mouse, and standard mode VGA drivers) that are activated to start the computer.

System partition   Contains the hardware-specific files that are required to load and start Windows XP. Normally the same partition as the boot partition.

User State Migration Tool (USMT)   Allows administrators to transfer user configuration settings and files from systems running Windows 95 or later to a clean Windows XP installation.

Questions and Answers

Lesson 1 Review

Page 2-26 **1.** What are the minimum requirements for installing Windows XP?

Windows XP requires a 233-MHz Pentium-compatible processor, 64 MB of RAM, 800 x 600 SVGA display capabilities, a CD-ROM or DVD-ROM, and a 2-GB disk with 1.5 GB free.

2. A Windows XP Professional volume that is formatted with FAT32 cannot support which of the following? (Choose all that apply.)

   A. Disk quotas

   B. Disk compression

   C. File encryption

   D. Drives larger than 2 GB

Answers A, B, and C are correct. FAT32 does not support disk quotas, disk compression, or file encryption. Answer D is incorrect because FAT32 does support drives larger than 2 GB.

3. What are the two files that are created by Setup Manager that you can use to automate the Windows XP installation process? (Choose two.)

   A. Standard answer files

   B. Remote installation files

   C. Uniqueness database files

   D. System information files

Answers A and C are correct. Setup Manager creates standard answer files and UDFs. Answer B is incorrect because this is not a valid type of file. Answer D is incorrect because System Information files are reports generated by the System Information utility.

4. From which of the following versions of Windows can you upgrade directly to Windows XP Professional?

   A. Windows 95 OSR2

   B. Windows 98

C. Windows NT 4.0 Workstation (with Service Pack 3)

D. Windows NT 4.0 Workstation (with Service Pack 5)

E. Windows 2000 Professional

Answers B, D, and E are correct. Each of these versions of Windows can be upgraded to Windows XP Professional directly. Answer A is incorrect because you must first upgrade Windows 95 to Windows 98 and then upgrade to Windows XP. Answer C is incorrect because you must first apply Windows NT 4.0 Service Pack 5 before you can upgrade to Windows XP.

5. List the tools that are available for copying files and settings from an old computer running a previous version of Windows to a new computer running Windows XP. What are the differences between the tools?

The Files And Settings Transfer Wizard and the USMT can both be used to transfer files and settings. The Files And Settings Transfer Wizard is intended for home and small business users and provides a simple wizard interface. USMT is intended for users on larger networks.

Lesson 2 Review

Page 2-33 1. A user calls and tells you that she is trying to install Windows XP Professional by using the installation CD-ROM. However, she cannot get the computer to start using the CD-ROM. What steps should you take?

The first action you should take is to check the computer's BIOS settings to verify that the CD-ROM drive is configured as a bootable device and that it is configured to boot before the hard drive. If the user still cannot boot using the CD, you should verify that the CD-ROM drive is working and that she has a working installation CD. You should also clean the installation CD.

2. You are helping a user perform a remote installation from a RIS server on his notebook computer. He has a boot disk that his administrator told him will force the computer to boot from the network and start the installation. However, when he tries to start the computer by using the boot disk, he receives an error stating that a supported network card could not be found. You verify that the user's network adapter is functional by installing it on another computer and connecting to the network. What is likely to be the problem?

The boot disk probably does not have drivers for the user's network adapter. To solve this problem, the best course of action is to use a PXE-compliant network adapter in the computer and start the computer from the network.

Lesson 3 Review

Page 2-43 **1.** List the types of updates that are available from the Microsoft Update site and explain the differences between them.

The Microsoft Update site provides access to high priority, software optional, and hardware optional updates. High priority updates include patches that fix problems that compromise the security or stability of a computer, as well as service packs. Software optional updates are less-critical operating system updates. Hardware optional updates include new hardware drivers that have been submitted for certification to Microsoft from hardware vendors after the release of Windows XP.

2. What is the recommended way to configure the Automatic Updates feature in Windows XP?

Microsoft recommends that you configure Automatic Updates to download and install updates automatically according to a preset schedule.

3. How many days will Windows XP function if you do not activate Windows or are not part of a volume licensing agreement?

   A. 10 days

   B. 14 days

   C. 30 days

   D. 60 days

   E. 120 days

Answer C is correct. Windows will function normally for 30 days following installation. If you do not activate Windows within 30 days of installation, you cannot start Windows until you activate it.

Lesson 4 Review

Page 2-55 **1.** You believe that you have installed a faulty device driver and want to start up Windows XP to remove it. What mode should you start in to accomplish this?

You should start the computer in safe mode so that the driver is not loaded. You should then be able to remove the driver and restart Windows normally.

2. A user reports to you that his computer running Windows XP Professional displays a series of errors on startup, stating that certain drivers are not loading. How could you have the user start the computer and easily send you a record of the startup process so that you can identify the problem drivers?

Have the user start the computer using the Enable Boot Logging option to create a log of the drivers that load during startup. The user should then start the computer in safe mode, locate the log file (named ntbtlog.txt) in the root directory of the system partition, and send you a copy of the file.

3. Which of the following advanced boot options loads only the basic devices and drivers required to start the computer and access the network?

   A. Safe Mode

   B. Safe Mode With Networking

   C. Last Known Good Configuration

   D. Safe Mode With Command Prompt

Answer B is correct. The Safe Mode With Networking option loads basic devices and drivers required to start the computer and access the network. Answer A is incorrect because the Safe Mode option does not support network access. Answer C is incorrect because the Last Known Good Configuration option starts Windows normally using the configuration that was in effect the last time the user successfully logged on. Answer D is incorrect because this option does not support network access.

Case Scenario Exercises: Scenario 2.1

Page 2-56 You have been given a computer with the following hardware installed:

- 233-MHz Pentium II processor
- 64 MB of RAM
- 4-GB hard disk, 500 MB free
- 48x CD-ROM drive
- Floppy drive, mouse, keyboard
- SVGA monitor and video card
- 10-Mbps Ethernet network card

You will reformat the hard disk and install Windows XP Professional. What additional hardware do you need to install onto the computer prior to installing Windows XP?

If you were to stick strictly to the stated hardware requirements, you do not need to add any additional hardware to the computer. However, 128 MB of RAM is recommended for adequate performance, so you may consider adding an additional 64 MB of RAM. In addition, the hardware described is low on available disk space. However, the overall size of the hard disk is adequate for a Windows XP Professional installation. Because you will be formatting the hard disk and installing from the beginning, the lack of available disk space will not be a problem.

Case Scenario Exercises: Scenario 2.2

Page 2-56 You install a new device into a Windows XP computer and restart the computer because the device installation procedure prompted you to do so. When the computer restarts, you can log on, but the computer stops responding shortly thereafter. You suspect that the newly installed device is causing the problem, and you want to remove it. How do you accomplish this?

> Start the computer in safe mode, and disable or remove the device that was just installed. Using the Last Known Good Configuration is not an option in this scenario because when you logged on, Windows updated the Last Known Good control set to reflect the newly installed device that is now causing the computer to fail.

Case Scenario Exercises: Scenario 2.3

Page 2-57 You are helping a user who is trying to perform an automatic installation of Windows XP on a network that has a RIS server. The RIS server contains the CD-based image and several other images that have been prepared. None of your client computers contain PXE-compliant network cards. What do you have to do to enable these clients to connect to the RIS server?

> Client computers that do not contain PXE-compliant network cards do not have the capability to automatically connect to a RIS server at startup. Provided that the client computer contains a network adapter card that is supported by RIS (most PCI network cards are supported), you can ask an administrator to create a RIS boot disk to solve the problem. You can use this floppy disk to boot the computer and connect to a RIS server.

Troubleshooting Lab

Page 2-57 Using your knowledge of the setup process and the Knowledge Base, determine what the problem could be and how you might solve it.

> Because Setup fails when trying to copy an installation file, it is a good guess that something may be wrong with the installation CD or the CD-ROM drive. You should verify that both are working properly. One great way to find information when you have a specific error message like this is to enter the actual text of the error message as keywords into the Knowledge Base. In this case, the search should return only one article (plus a link to the Windows XP Support Center). The article, which is titled "How to Troubleshoot Windows XP Problems During Installation When You Upgrade from Windows 98 or Windows ME," discusses possible causes of the error and gives proposed solutions. The link to the article is *http://support.microsoft.com/ default.aspx?scid=kb;en-us;310064.*

3 Supporting Local Users and Groups

Exam Objectives in this Chapter:

- Configure the user environment

    - Configure and troubleshoot Fast User Switching

- Configure and troubleshoot local user and group accounts

    - Answer end-user questions related to user accounts

    - Configure and troubleshoot local user accounts

    - Answer end-user questions related to local group accounts

    - Configure and troubleshoot local group accounts

- Troubleshoot system startup and user logon problems

    - Answer end-user questions related to user logon issues

    - Troubleshoot local user logon issues

    - Troubleshoot domain user logon issues

- Troubleshoot security settings and local security policy

    - Answer end-user questions related to security settings

    - Identify end-user issues caused by local security policies such as Local Security Settings and Security Configuration and Analysis

    - Identify end-user issues caused by network security policies such as Resultant Set of Policy (RSoP) and Group Policy

Why This Chapter Matters

As a desktop support technician (DST), you will be responsible for troubleshooting logon and resource access problems that are associated with local user accounts and security groups. This is particularly important for home and small network users because local accounts provide the primary means for securing resources on a computer in a workgroup setting. In a domain setting, you will not be responsible for creating and managing user accounts and groups, but you should understand how they work because you may be called on to help troubleshoot domain logon and resource access. This chapter covers supporting and troubleshooting local user accounts and security groups. It also covers troubleshooting common local and domain logon problems. Finally, this chapter covers working with local security settings and security policy on a computer running Microsoft Windows XP.

Lessons in this Chapter:

Before You Begin

Before you begin this chapter, you should have a basic familiarity with working in a Windows-based operating system. To complete the practices in this chapter, you must have a computer running Microsoft Windows XP Professional.

Lesson 1: Supporting Local User Accounts and Groups

A user account is a collection of settings that define the actions that a user can perform after the user has logged on to Windows XP. Windows controls access to system resources based on the permissions and user rights that are associated with each user account. User rights are very different from permissions. User rights pertain to a user's ability to perform specific functions on a computer. Permissions control a user's ability to access resources such as files, folders, and printers. Local user accounts control access to resources on the local computer, and domain user accounts control access to resources on a network running Microsoft Active Directory directory service. You can use security groups (both at the local and domain level) to organize users according to common access needs. As a DST, you are responsible for creating, configuring, and troubleshooting local user accounts and local security groups in a workgroup setting. In a domain setting, you are not responsible for creating and managing user accounts or groups, but you might be called on to help troubleshoot logon problems for domain users.

After this lesson, you will be able to

- Explain the difference between local and domain accounts.
- Identify the built-in user accounts that are available in Windows XP Professional.
- Create and modify a user account in Windows XP Professional.
- Explain the use of groups.
- Create and add members to a group in Windows XP Professional.
- Explain the limitations of user accounts in Windows XP Home Edition.
- Configure Fast User Switching.

Estimated lesson time: 45 minutes

Understanding Logon

As you learned in Chapter 1, "Introduction to Desktop Support," a computer running Windows XP Professional can be a member of either a workgroup or a domain. (Microsoft Windows XP Home Edition does not support domain membership.) Even if you have a single computer running in isolation, it is still a member of a workgroup. Computers in a workgroup rely on local security databases that are stored on each individual computer. Computers in a domain rely on a security database that is part of Active Directory.

When you log on to a computer that is in a workgroup, you log on locally to that computer. This means that the user name and password that you enter are checked against the local accounts database of the computer on which you are working. If you provide proper credentials, you gain access to the Windows desktop and any local resources that you have permission to use.

When you log on to a computer that is a member of a domain, you have two choices presented to you at the logon screen. You can log on to the local computer, or you can log on to the domain. If you log on to the domain, your credentials are checked against a list of users that are defined in Active Directory. These credentials control your access to resources both on the local computer and on the network. Users in a domain environment should almost always log on to the domain rather than to the local computer, making local user accounts less important in a domain than they are in a workgroup. However, the ability to log on locally is useful for troubleshooting logon problems because it bypasses Active Directory.

Note This lesson focuses on features that are provided by Windows XP Professional. Windows XP Home Edition provides only a subset of these features. At the end of the lesson, you will find detailed information about the differences between Windows XP Professional and Windows XP Home Edition.

You will use **local user accounts** for the following purposes:

- To gain initial access to the computer
- To control access to local computer resources
- To control access to network resources in a workgroup environment

In Windows XP Professional, you can create groups by using one of the following tools:

- **User Accounts tool**   The User Accounts tool is available in Control Panel. This tool provides a simple interface for creating user accounts and a limited set of options for managing accounts, such as the ability to change passwords and change the basic account type.

- **Local Users And Groups tool**   The Local Users And Groups tool, which is shown in Figure 3-1, can be accessed through the Administrative Tools folder. This tool provides a much richer environment for creating and managing users than does the User Accounts tool. You can use the Local Users And Groups tool to perform all actions allowed by the User Accounts tool, as well as a number of additional actions. For this reason, this lesson focuses on using the Local Users And Groups tool.

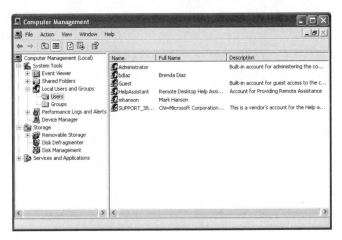

Figure 3-1   Use the Local Users And Groups tool to manage accounts.

Default User Accounts

When you install Windows XP Professional, the setup program creates several initial user accounts automatically. These built-in user accounts are as follows:

- **Administrator**   The local Administrator account is arguably the most important user account on a computer. This account is a member of the Administrators group and has full access to the computer. You should use the Administrator account to manage a computer; it is not for daily use. If you find that a user is using the Administrator account regularly, encourage the user to create a separate account for regular use.

> **Tip**   The initial password for the Administrator account is assigned during the installation of Windows XP Professional. If you log on to a computer running Windows XP for the first time and do not recall being asked to assign a password during installation, you may have created a blank password by accident. If you did assign a password and it is not being recognized at first logon, you may be entering the password in the incorrect case. Windows XP passwords are case sensitive.

- **Guest**   The Guest account has limited privileges on a computer and is used to provide access to users who do not have a user account on the computer. Although the Guest account can be useful for providing limited access to a computer, the account does present security problems because, by design, the Guest account allows anyone to log on to the computer. For a more secure environment, disable the Guest account and create a normal user account for anyone who needs to use the computer.

- **HelpAssistant** The HelpAssistant account is not available for standard logon. Instead, this account is used to authenticate users who connect by using Remote Assistance. Windows enables this account automatically when a user creates a remote assistance invitation and disables the account automatically when all invitations have expired. You will learn more about Remote Assistance in Chapter 10, "Supporting Network Connectivity."

- **SUPPORT_*xxxxx*** The SUPPORT_*xxxxx* account (where *xxxxx* is a random number generated during Windows setup) is used by Microsoft when providing remote support through the Help And Support Service. It is not available for logon or general use.

Although you cannot delete any of the built-in user accounts, you can rename or disable them. To rename a user account, in the Computer Management console, right-click the account and then select Rename. You will learn more about disabling accounts later in this lesson.

Creating User Accounts

Each user in an organization should have a unique user account, which allows Windows to control what each user can access and allows an administrator to monitor users' access to resources by using the auditing features in Windows XP. Each user should have a unique user account. You should encourage users not to share accounts because it is more difficult to secure resources according the needs of individual users when users share accounts.

To create a local user account, you must log on to a computer by using the built-in Administrator account or by using any user account that is a member of the Administrators or Power Users groups.

▶   **Creating User Accounts in Windows XP Professional**

To create user accounts in Windows XP Professional, follow these steps:

1. From the Start menu, select Control Panel. (It is assumed that Control Panel is in Category View.)

2. In Control Panel, select Performance And Maintenance.

3. In the Performance And Maintenance window, select Administrative Tools.

4. In the Administrative Tools window, double-click Computer Management.

Tip There is a shorter way to open the Computer Management console than by going through Control Panel. Just right-click the My Computer icon and then select Manage.

5. In the Computer Management console, expand the System Tools node and then expand the Local Users And Groups node.

6. Under the Local Users And Groups node, right-click the Users folder and select New User.

7. In the New User dialog box, enter the appropriate information, as shown in Figure 3-2.

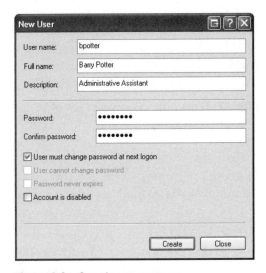

Figure 3-2 Creating a new user

8. Click Create when finished. An entry for the new user will appear in the Users folder.

When you create a user, you can supply the following information:

■ **User Name** The user name is the name that the user will enter to log on to the computer. You must specify a user name for each user. When you enter the user name, Windows XP preserves the case, but user names are not case sensitive. User names can be up to 20 characters in length, cannot consist entirely of spaces or periods, and must be unique in the local accounts database. User names cannot contain the following characters: * / \ [ ] : ; = , + ? < > ".

- **Full Name**   You can also enter the user's complete name. This is optional information that helps to identify the user more clearly. The full name does not have any functional relationship to the logon user name.

- **Description**   The description is also optional and is used for informational purposes only. You could enter a user's title, department, or any other information that you think is appropriate.

- **Password**   Passwords can be up to 128 characters in length and are case sensitive. You must confirm the entry of the password to ensure that no typing errors were made in the initial password entry. For more information about passwords, see the Real World sidebar, "Creating Strong Passwords."

- **User Must Change Password At Next Logon**   This option, which is selected by default, configures Windows XP to prompt users to change the password the next time that they log on. It is a good idea to specify this setting for new user accounts. You can assign all user accounts the same initial password and then have users change their password to something more appropriate for them.

- **User Cannot Change Password**   This option prevents users from ever changing their passwords. This option is not selected by default and is rarely used because it is a good security practice to have users change their passwords regularly. However, sometimes you might want the administrator to be in control of the passwords, such as for the Guest account or for other accounts that could be shared by multiple users. This option is not available if the User Must Change Password At Next Logon option is selected.

- **Password Never Expires**   This option overrides any password expiration policies that are configured by using Local Security Policy or Group Policy. For more information, see Lesson 3, "Supporting Security Settings and Local Security Policy." This option is not available if the User Must Change Password At Next Logon option is selected.

- **Account Is Disabled**   This option prevents the account from being used for logon purposes. If a user tries to log on as a disabled account, that user will receive an error message and is not granted access. For security purposes, you may choose to leave all new user accounts disabled until the first time the user needs access. This is especially true if you assign all new users the same password (that password will be commonly known in your organization).

Real World Creating Strong Passwords

Weak passwords are one of the big security risks in most environments. For this reason, you should encourage users to select and use strong passwords, even if they do not really want to. The following list shows why common password selections are considered weak:

- Using no password at all is not a good practice because it is then easy for other users to just walk up to an unsecured computer and log on.

- Using a real name, user name, or company name makes for an easy-to-guess password. Also avoid using common passwords such as "letmein" or "password."

- Using a common dictionary word makes you vulnerable to automated programs that are designed to guess passwords.

- Using any password that you write down or that you share with someone else is not secure.

On the other hand, you can use the following guidelines to create strong passwords:

- Passwords should be at least eight characters in length; longer is better.

- Passwords should use a combination of lowercase and uppercase letters, numbers, and symbols (for example, ` ~ ! @ # $ % ^ & * ( ) _ + - = { } | [ ] \ : " ; ' < > ? , . / or a space character).

- Passwords should be changed regularly.

An example of a strong password using these guidelines is X2#hg&5T.

If users find that complex passwords are difficult to remember, tell them that Windows XP allows the use of passphrases instead of passwords. For example, a perfectly valid passphrase in Windows XP is "My grandmother enjoys gardening 3 times each week." Another technique is to join together simple words with numbers and symbols. An example of a password that uses this technique is "2roosters+2hens=4chicks" (bad math, but an easy-to-remember password).

Managing User Accounts

During the creation of a user account, you can configure only a subset of the available account properties. After you create an account, you can configure several more properties by right-clicking the user account in the Local Users And Groups tool and then selecting Properties.

The General tab of the Properties dialog box for a user account, shown in Figure 3-3, allows you to reconfigure information that you provided when you created the account. The General tab also provides the option to disable an account, which is a useful security measure if the user has left the organization or will be out of the office for a long time.

The Member Of tab in the user account's Properties dialog box shows the groups that the user account is a member of. You will learn more about groups in the section "Supporting Groups," later in this lesson.

Figure 3-3   Use the General tab of a user account's Properties dialog box to modify basic account properties.

The Profile tab, shown in Figure 3-4, allows you to configure user profiles and the path to the user's home folder. These options allow administrators to customize the user's working environment, if necessary.

Figure 3-4   Use the Profile tab of the user account's Properties dialog box to specify a user profile and home folder.

You will learn more about using user profiles in the section "User Profiles," later in this lesson. Home folders are shared folders on a network server in which users can store files. In a networked environment, using centralized network storage for user documents instead of storing documents on each local computer can make security and backups easier to manage. As a DST, you will not be asked to configure home folders in a domain-based environment. However, you might need to configure home folders for users in a workgroup.

In addition to configuring user account settings by using the user account's Properties dialog box, you can also perform several important user-management functions by right-clicking a user account in the Local Users And Groups window:

- **Set Password**   Use this option to reset a user's password. You do not need to know the existing password to change it.

- **Delete**   Use this to option to delete user accounts if they are no longer necessary. Note that after you delete an account, you cannot recover it. For this reason, it is usually better to disable accounts than to delete them.

- **Rename**   Use this option to rename a user account if someone leaves an organization and someone else takes over that user's job responsibilities. You can rename the existing user account and change the password (for security reasons); you do not have to create a new account for the new user.

Supporting Groups

Groups simplify the assignment of permissions and user rights to user accounts. You can assign permissions and user rights to a group and then include users in that group instead of assigning the permissions and rights to each individual user account. For example, assume that there are 20 users who all need access to one particular printer. You could handle this task in one of two ways:

- You could assign access to the printer to each of those 20 user accounts individually. This method is time-consuming and introduces a greater possibility of error with each additional user account that you configure.

- You could create a single group, make the 20 user accounts members of that group, and then assign access to the printer to the group. All users who are members of a group automatically receive permissions that are assigned to the group. This method simplifies administrative tasks. If an additional user account needs access to the printer, you can simply add that user account to the group. If a user no longer needs access, you can remove the user account from the group.

Default Group Accounts

Windows XP Professional includes several built-in groups:

- **Administrators Group**   Has full control over the computer and can perform all management functions. The Administrator user account is a member of this group by default.

- **Backup Operators Group**   Backs up and restores all files on the computer. When using the backup utility, backup operators have access to the entire file system, even if they do not normally have permission to access each of the files. This group has no members by default.

- **Guests Group**   Has very limited access to the computer. In addition, members of this group cannot maintain individual user profile information—all members of the Guests group share the same profile. The Guest user account is a member of this group by default.

- **Network Configuration Operators Group**   Manages some aspects of the network configuration of the computer. Tasks that members of this group can perform include modifying Transmission Control Protocol/Internet Protocol (TCP/IP) properties, renaming local area network (LAN) connections, enabling/disabling LAN connections, and issuing Ipconfig release and renew commands. This group has no members by default.

- **Power Users Group**   Performs many management tasks on the computer, but does not have the full administrative privileges of the Administrator account. For example, Power Users can create user accounts and groups (and manage the user accounts and groups that they create), but they cannot manage objects that are created by members of the Administrators group. Also, Power Users do not have access to files and folders unless they are granted permissions. This group has no members by default.

- **Remote Desktop Users Group**   Grants the right to log on to the computer from a remote computer, which is required for Remote Desktop access. The group has no members by default.

- **Replicator Group**   Facilitates directory and file replication in domain environments. This group has no members by default.

- **Users Group**   Has limited permissions by default. You can add or remove user accounts from this group as necessary. All user accounts on a computer (except for the Guest account) are members of this group by default.

- **HelpServicesGroup**   Uses certain helper applications and diagnoses computer problems. By default, the member of this group is an account associated with Microsoft support applications, such as Remote Assistance, and you should not add regular users to this group. The HelpServicesGroup has no explicit User Privileges by default. The SUPPORT user account is a member of this group by default.

When a Windows XP computer joins a domain, Windows automatically adds several domain-based groups to local groups. These new memberships are as follows:

- The domain group Domain Admins is added to the local Administrators group, allowing the administrators of the domain to have administrative control over the computers that join the domain.

- The domain group Domain Guests is added to the local Guests group.

- The domain group Domain Users is added to the local Users group.

Domain Admins, Domain Guests, and Domain Users are predefined groups that exist on Windows domain controllers only. These group membership additions are not permanent and can be removed after the computer has joined the domain. The automatic addition of these domain-based groups allows domain administrators to configure access to resources that are connected to the local computer. For example, a Windows XP Professional computer might have a shared printer to which all users in the domain should have access. By default, the local Users group has access to the printer. After the Domain Users group is made a member of the local Users group, Domain Users can also access the printer without requiring any additional configuration.

Special Groups

Special groups are also built into Windows XP. The operating system classifies users based on different properties and places them into special groups accordingly. Special group membership is automatic; you cannot manage the membership of special groups with any Windows XP utility. You have access to special groups only when assigning user rights and permissions; you cannot access special groups through the Local Users And Groups tool.

Windows XP Professional includes the following special groups:

- **Everyone group**   Includes all users who can access the computer in any way, including the Guest account

- **Authenticated Users group**   Includes all users who have authenticated to a trusted domain

- **Interactive group**   Includes the user who is currently logged on locally to the computer

- **Network group**   Includes users who are currently accessing the computer through a connection over the network

When a user logs on locally to a computer running Windows XP, Windows makes that user a member of the Everyone and Interactive groups (and the Authenticated Users group if the user has authenticated to a domain from the computer). If the user connects to the computer over the network with a valid user name and password, Windows makes that user a member of the Everyone, Network, and (potentially) Authenticated Users groups.

If you want a user to have permission to access a certain resource, such as a printer, only when logged on locally, you assign access to the Interactive special group. Conversely, if you want a user to have access to a certain resource only when connecting through the network, you assign access to the Network special group.

The Everyone and Authenticated Users groups allow you to differentiate between users who have logged on to a domain and users who have logged on using an account in the local accounts database of a computer running Windows XP. Domain accounts are more secure than local accounts because the administrators of the domain create and manage domain accounts, whereas anyone who has local administrative privileges on a particular computer can manipulate local accounts. For resources that require higher security, you should assign access to the Authenticated Users group, not to the Everyone group.

▶ **Creating Groups**

To create a group, you must be logged in as a member of the Administrators or Power Users groups.

To create a group, follow these steps:

1. In the Computer Management console, expand the System Tools node and then expand the Local Users And Groups node.

2. Right-click the Groups folder, and select New Group.

3. Enter the group name and description as well as the group members, as illustrated in Figure 3-5. Group names can be up to 256 characters long.

Figure 3-5 Type a name and description for the new group; then add members.

4. Click Create when finished. The new group appears in the Groups folder.

> **Note** Members of the Power Users group can manage only the groups that they create. They cannot manage groups that are created by the Administrators group, and they cannot manipulate the membership of the default group accounts.

Adding User Accounts to Groups

You can modify group membership at the time you create the group or afterward. After creating a group, you can add user accounts to the group in the following ways:

- Open the Properties dialog box for a user and add the group on the Member Of tab.

- Open the Properties dialog box of a group and add members on the General tab.

> **Tip** To select multiple users simultaneously, select the first user, and then press and hold either the SHIFT or CTRL key. The SHIFT key allows you to select an entire range of users. The CTRL key allows you to add individual users to the selection. After you have selected users, right-click any of the selected users and select Properties to modify settings common to the users, such as group membership.

Security Identifiers (SIDs)

User accounts and groups are considered **security principals**, meaning that you can grant them access to resources on a computer. Windows assigns each security principal a unique **security identifier (SID)** when you create the user account.

Although you manage user accounts and groups by name, Windows tracks these objects by using the SIDs. It is more efficient for the operating system to use the SID to identify a user (instead of the user name or full name) because those names may change.

Keep the following items in mind concerning SIDs:

- When you rename a user or group account, the SID does not change, and all rights and permissions are preserved.

- If you delete a user or group account, all security assignments that are associated with the account are also deleted. Windows does not reuse the SID that was assigned to the account. If you create a new account by using the same user name, the new account will not receive the same security assignment as the previous account. Even if the accounts share the same name, they do not share the same SID.

Understanding the Limitations of Windows XP Home Edition

So far, this discussion has focused on supporting users and groups in Windows XP Professional. Although you can create user accounts in Windows XP Home Edition, you cannot create groups or perform as much user-account management as you can in Windows XP Professional.

When supporting Windows XP Home Edition, you should be aware of the following limitations:

- Windows XP Home Edition does not support the creation of local groups.

- The Local Users And Groups tool is not available in Windows XP Home Edition. Instead, you must create and manage users through the User Accounts tool in Control Panel. You are limited to creating and deleting accounts, changing passwords, and several other minor activities.

- Windows XP Home Edition supports only two types of accounts: Computer Administrator, which works much like the Administrators group in Windows XP Professional; and Limited, which restricts access to certain resources.

- Windows XP Home Edition does not have an account named Administrator. Following setup, Windows allows you to create one or more user accounts. Each of the accounts you create at this point is made a Computer Administrator account, although you can change any of the accounts to a Limited account if you choose.

- Computers running Windows XP Home Edition cannot join a domain.

User Profiles

Each user account in Windows XP Professional and Windows XP Home Edition has an associated user profile that stores user-specific configuration settings, such as a customized desktop or personalized application settings. Understanding how user profiles function and how to control them allows you to manage the user's desktop environment effectively.

Windows XP supports the following types of user profiles:

- **Local**   A local user profile is available only on the computer on which it was created. A unique local user profile is created and stored on each computer to which a user logs on. Both Windows XP Professional and Windows XP Home Edition support local user profiles.

- **Roaming**   Roaming profiles are stored in a shared folder on a network server and are accessible from any location in the network. Only Windows XP Professional supports roaming user profiles.

- **Mandatory**   Mandatory user profiles are roaming user profiles that users cannot make permanent changes to. Mandatory profiles are used to enforce configuration settings. Only Windows XP Professional supports roaming user profiles.

As a DST, you will mostly be concerned with local user profiles. You should understand where Windows stores local profiles and the type of information found in a local profile. If you are working in a corporate environment, you may also encounter roaming and mandatory profiles. However, you will not have to create or configure them.

Local Profile Storage

Windows stores local user profiles in the Documents And Settings folder hierarchy on the system_root drive. When a user first logs on to a computer running Windows XP, Windows creates a folder in Documents And Settings that matches the user's user name. Figure 3-6 shows a Documents And Settings folder, which includes several user profile folders.

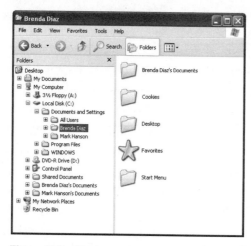

Figure 3-6 Windows stores user profile folders in the Documents And Settings folder.

Within each user profile, several files and folders contain configuration information and data, including the following:

- **Application Data**   Contains application configuration information. Applications that are designed for Windows XP can take advantage of this folder to store user-specific configuration settings. This folder is hidden by default.

- **Cookies**   Contains cookie files, which websites usually create to store user information and preferences on the local computer. When you return to a site, the cookie files allow the site to provide you with customized content and track your activity within the site.

- **Desktop**   Contains files, folders, and shortcuts that have been placed on the Windows XP desktop.

- **Favorites**   Stores shortcuts to locations that a user has added to the Favorites list in Windows Explorer or Internet Explorer.

- **Local Settings**   Holds application data, history, and temporary files (including temporary Internet files). This folder is hidden.

- **My Documents**   Stores documents and other user data. My Documents is easily accessible from the Start menu.

- **My Recent Documents**   Contains shortcuts to recently accessed documents and folders. You can also access My Recent Documents from the Start Menu. This folder is hidden.

- **NetHood**   Holds shortcuts created by the Add Network Place option in My Network Places. This folder is hidden.

- **PrintHood**   Contains shortcuts to printer folder items. This folder is hidden.

- **Send To** Contains shortcuts to document-handling utilities, such as e-mail applications. These shortcuts are displayed on the Send To option on the Action menu for files and folders. This folder is hidden.

- **Start Menu** Holds the shortcuts to programs that are displayed in the Start menu. One way to modify the Start menu is to add or delete folders and shortcuts to the Start Menu folder within a user's profile folder.

- **Templates** Contains template items that are created by user applications and are used by those applications when a user creates a new document. This folder is hidden.

- **NTUSER.DAT** The user-specific portion of the Registry. This file contains configuration changes made to Windows Explorer and the taskbar, as well as user-specific Control Panel and Accessories settings. These settings are visible under HKEY_CURRENT_USER in the Registry.

- **NTUSER.DAT.LOG** A log file used as part of the process of committing changes to NTUSER.DAT and also in the recovery of NTUSER.DAT if the computer crashes.

Built-In User Profiles

Windows stores user profiles locally by default. A local user profile is available only on the computer on which it was created. Windows creates two built-in local user profiles during installation:

- **Default User profile** Windows uses the Default User profile as a template to create all new profiles on the computer. When a new user logs on, the user receives a copy of the Default User profile as his or her own personal user profile. You can customize the Default User profile to control which options and settings a new user will receive. Modifications to the Default User profile affect only the profiles of new users—existing personal profiles are not affected. The Default User profile is stored in the \Documents And Settings\Default User folder, which is hidden. To view and work with this folder, you must set the Folder Options in Windows Explorer to include hidden files and folders.

- **All Users profile** The All Users profile contains settings that apply to every user who logs on to the computer. Windows merges the settings in All Users with the current user's profile for the duration of the logon session, but the settings are not made a permanent part of the user's profile. You can modify the All Users profile to contain settings that all users logging on to the computer should have. For example, many applications create shortcuts in the Start menu or desktop of the

All Users profile during installation. This ensures that all users who log on to the computer have easy access to those applications. As an administrator, you can directly edit the All Users profile to add and remove items as necessary. The All Users profile is stored in the \Documents And Settings\All Users folder. The folder contains only a subset of the folders contained in other profiles on the computer, because it is concerned only with settings that could apply to everyone.

Using Multiple Profiles for the Same User Account

If a computer running Windows XP Professional is a member of a Windows domain, there is the potential for two users with the same user account name to log on to the same computer. An example of this might involve the local Administrator account (stored in the local accounts database of the Windows XP computer) and the domain Administrator account (stored in the Active Directory database on the domain controllers). The local account and the domain account are discrete entities, each maintaining a different user profile.

Windows XP does not allow two user accounts with the same name to share the same profile folder (for example, C:\Documents And Settings\Administrator). If Windows were to allow this to occur, the profile of one user would overwrite the profile of the other. Instead, Windows creates the profile of the first user to log on using the user name of the user in \Documents And Settings\%*username*%. Windows stores subsequent user accounts with the same name using the path \Documents And Settings\%*username*%.x. The folder extension (*x*) varies as follows:

- If the additional user to log on with the same user name is a domain account, Windows creates the folder extension using the name of the domain.

- If the additional user to log on with the same user name is a local account, Windows creates the folder extension using the name of the computer.

For example, if the local Administrator logs on first and the domain Administrator logs on second, Windows stores the local Administrator's profile in the Administrator folder, and the domain Administrator's profile is stored in a folder named Administrator.<*domain_name*>.

Multiple user profiles are an issue only when the computer is a member of a domain because domain membership enables both local and domain accounts to log on. In a workgroup environment, Windows XP relies solely on the local accounts database, and you cannot create two user accounts of the same name on the same computer.

Fast User Switching

Fast User Switching is a feature introduced with Windows XP that allows multiple local user accounts to log on to a computer simultaneously. When you enable Fast User Switching, users can switch sessions without logging off or closing programs.

Although Fast User Switching is a useful tool on computers with multiple users, you should use it with care. When a user leaves programs running to switch to another user account, those programs still consume computer resources. If several users remain logged on with programs running, the performance of the computer will decline noticeably.

> **Exam Tip**   If a user, especially a home user, complains to you about a computer seeming to run slowly, be sure to ask whether the computer has Fast User Switching enabled.

Fast User Switching is enabled by default in Windows XP Home Edition and Windows XP Professional on computers with more than 64 megabytes (MB) of RAM. However, Fast User Switching is not available on computers running Windows XP Professional that are members of a domain.

To enable Fast User Switching, follow these steps:

1. Log on to the computer with a user account that has administrative privileges.

2. From the Start menu, select Control Panel. (It is assumed that Control Panel is in Category View.)

3. In Control Panel, select User Accounts.

4. In the User Accounts window, select User Accounts.

5. In the User Accounts dialog box, select Change The Way Users Log On Or Off.

6. Select Use Fast User Switching and then click Apply Options.

When a user initiates the Switch User option, the computer returns to the Welcome screen. The current user's session remains active, and another user can then log on and use the computer. You can initiate the Switch User command using one of the following options:

- Click Start, click Log Off, and then click Switch User.

- Press CTRL+ALT+DELETE to open Task Manager. From the Shut Down menu, click Switch User.

- Hold down the WINDOWS key, and then press the L key.

Practice: Work with Local User Accounts and Groups

In this practice, you will create a new local user account and then modify the account using the Computer Management console in Windows XP Professional. You will also create a new local group and then add user accounts to it.

Exercise 1: Create a User Account

1. From the Start menu, select Control Panel. (It is assumed that Control Panel is in Category View.)

2. In Control Panel, select Performance And Maintenance.

3. In the Performance And Maintenance window, select Administrative Tools.

4. In the Administrative Tools window, select Computer Management.

5. In the Computer Management console, expand the System Tools node and then expand the Local Users And Groups node.

6. Under the Local Users And Groups node, right-click the Users folder and select New User.

7. In the New User dialog box, type a user name. Optionally, you can also enter a full name, description, and password.

8. Click Create.

9. Click Close to exit the New User dialog box.

Exercise 2: Modify an Existing User Account

1. From the Start menu, select Control Panel. (It is assumed that Control Panel is in Category View.)

2. In Control Panel, select Performance And Maintenance.

3. In the Performance And Maintenance window, select Administrative Tools.

4. In the Administrative Tools window, select Computer Management.

5. In the Computer Management console, expand the System Tools node and then expand the Local Users And Groups node.

6. Under the Local Users And Groups node, select the Users folder.

7. Right-click the user account you created in the previous exercise and select Properties.

8. In the user account's Properties dialog box, on the General tab, change the full name and description of the user.

9. On the Member Of tab, click Add.

10. In the Select Groups dialog box, click Advanced.

11. Click Find Now.

12. In the list of groups, select Power Users and click OK. Click OK again to close the Select Groups dialog box.

13. Click OK to close the user account's Properties dialog box.

Exercise 3: Create a Group Account and Add User Accounts

1. From the Start menu, select Control Panel. (It is assumed that Control Panel is in Category View.)

2. In Control Panel, select Performance And Maintenance.

3. In the Performance And Maintenance window, select Administrative Tools.

4. In the Administrative Tools window, select Computer Management.

5. In the Computer Management console, expand the System Tools node and then expand the Local Users And Groups node.

6. Under the Local Users And Groups node, right-click the Groups folder and select New Group.

7. In the New Group dialog box, type a name for the group. Optionally, you can also type a description.

8. Click Add.

9. In the Select Groups dialog box, click Advanced.

10. Click Find Now.

11. In the list of groups, select the user account you created in Exercise 1 and click OK. Click OK again to close the Select Groups dialog box.

12. Click Create to create the new group. Click Close to close the New Group dialog box.

Lesson Review

The following questions are intended to reinforce key information presented in this lesson. If you are unable to answer a question, review the lesson materials and try the question again. You can find answers to the questions in the "Questions and Answers" section at the end of this chapter.

1. What utilities can you use to create user accounts on a Windows XP Professional computer?

_____

_____

2. What important limitations should you be aware of when supporting Windows XP Home Edition?

_____

_____

3. List the default user accounts in Windows XP Professional.

_____

_____

Lesson Summary

- User accounts allow users to log on to a computer or to a domain, and subsequently gain access to local and network resources.

- Group accounts simplify the assignment of security features by allowing you to assign access to groups and then include users in those groups.

- Domain Admins, Domain Guests, and Domain Users are predefined groups that exist on Windows domain controllers only. These domain-based groups are made members of local groups automatically when a computer joins a domain.

- Windows XP Home Edition does not support the use of groups, support the ability to join a domain, or include the Local Users And Groups tool.

- Fast User Switching is a feature introduced with Windows XP that allows multiple local user accounts to log on to a computer simultaneously. When Fast User Switching is enabled, users can switch sessions without logging off or closing programs.

Lesson 2: Troubleshooting User Logon

As a DST, you may be called for troubleshooting help when a user has problems logging on to a computer or a domain. Although many logon problems are caused by underlying problems with network connectivity (which you learn more about in Chapter 10, "Supporting Network Connectivity"), there are a number of other logon-related problems you should understand how to resolve.

After this lesson, you will be able to

- Troubleshoot common password problems.
- Troubleshoot domain-related logon problems.
- Troubleshoot profile-related logon problems.

Estimated lesson time: 20 minutes

Troubleshooting Password Problems

Password problems are the second-most common type of logon problem, following problems with network connectivity. If users see the error message, "Unknown Username Or Bad Password," they probably are not logging on correctly. The common causes of this error message are the following:

- The user is mistyping the user name or password or both.
- The user has the CAPS LOCK key engaged.

Have the user make sure that the correct information is being typed and that the CAPS LOCK key is not engaged. If this fails to resolve the issue and the user is trying to log on to a domain, have the user contact an administrator.

 Exam Tip   The two most common reasons why a user receives the "Unknown Username Or Bad Password" error message are that the user is typing the wrong credentials or that the CAPS LOCK key is engaged.

Resolving Lost Passwords for Local User Accounts

Users who are not connected to a domain and are trying to log on to a local computer can often use a different account with administrative privileges to log on to the computer and then reset their own password. However, if users reset their own passwords, the following information is lost:

- E-mail that is encrypted with the user's public key
- Internet passwords that are saved on the computer
- Files that the user has encrypted

To reset a local user account password, the user must log on to the computer with a different account, such as a local Administrator account. To reset a local user account password, follow these steps:

1. From the Start menu, select Control Panel. (It is assumed that Control Panel is in Category View.)
2. In Control Panel, select Performance And Maintenance.
3. In the Performance And Maintenance window, select Administrative Tools.
4. In the Administrative Tools window, select Computer Management.
5. In the Computer Management console, expand the Local Users And Groups node and then select the Users folder.
6. Right-click the user account and then select Set Password.
7. Read the warning message and then click Proceed.
8. In the New Password and Confirm New Password boxes, type the new password and then click OK.

Creating a Password Reset Disk

The password reset disk is a removable disk that contains encrypted password information and allows users to change their passwords without knowing the old passwords. As standard practice, you should encourage users to create a password reset disk and keep it in a secure location.

To create a password reset disk for a domain-based user account, follow these steps:

1. Press CTRL+ALT+DEL and then click Change Password.
2. In the User Name box, type the user name of the account for which you want to create a password reset disk.
3. In the Log On To box, click ComputerName, where ComputerName is your assigned computer name, and then click Backup.
4. Follow the steps in the Forgotten Password Wizard until the procedure is complete. Store the password reset disk in a secure place.

To create a password reset disk for a local user account, follow these steps:

1. From the Start menu, select Control Panel. (It is assumed that Control Panel is in Category View.)

2. In Control Panel, select User Accounts.

3. In the User Accounts window, select User Accounts.

4. If you are logged on using an Administrator account, click the account name and then, from the Related Tasks list, select Prevent A Forgotten Password. If you are logged on using a Limited account, the Prevent A Forgotten Password option is located on the main page of the User Accounts window (you do not have to click the account name first).

5. Follow the steps in the Forgotten Password Wizard until the procedure is complete. Store the password reset disk in a secure place.

Users cannot change their password and create a password reset disk at the same time. If a user types a new password in the New Password and Confirm New Password boxes before the user clicks Backup, the new password information is not saved. When the wizard prompts a user for his current user account password, the user must type the old password.

Users can change their password any time after they create a password reset disk. They do not have to create a new password reset disk if they change their password or if the password is reset manually.

When logging on, if a user forgets the password and has previously created a password reset disk, the user is presented with an option to reset his password by using the password reset disk. Select the option on the logon screen to launch the Password Reset Wizard. The Password Reset Wizard asks users to create a new password and hint. Log on with the new password and then return the password reset disk to its safe storage place. The user does not need to make a new password reset disk.

Troubleshooting Domain Logon Problems

When users log on to a domain, they must authenticate with the domain controller that contains their user account. Some corporate infrastructures are large and contain many domains. In this scenario, a user might have to choose which domain to log on to from a drop-down list on the logon screen. If users do not know which domain the user account is on, they cannot log on to the computer.

The Windows Log On dialog box does not show a list of available domains by default. The user can click the Options button in the Windows Log On dialog box and then select the correct domain name from the Log On To list box.

Exam Tip   The most common reasons for a failed logon for a domain user are network connectivity issues and attempting to log on to the wrong domain.

Resolving Problems with Cached Credentials

When users join a domain, there may be times when they must log on to their computers, but the computers cannot contact the domain controller to validate the logon. In this scenario, users can log on to their computers by using cached credentials, which are copies of the security credentials that were last used to access the domain.

Common issues when working with cached credentials are as follows:

- The user has installed Windows XP, but has not installed a service pack and cannot log on using cached credentials. This is a known issue; the user must install Service Pack 1 (SP1) or later to resolve the issue.

- After logging on with cached credentials and connecting to a network from home, the user cannot connect to resources on a mapped drive. The user cannot access the resources because the user has not received a current access token from the domain. To resolve this issue, the user should create a new map to a network resource. This process will reissue an access token to the remote computer.

Troubleshooting Missing Domain Controller Issues

A domain user might experience an error message during logon stating that a domain controller could not be located to perform the logon. This commonly occurs when a user is logging on to a computer on the domain for the first time, but the domain controller is not currently available or the computer is not connected to the domain. See Chapter 10 for information about troubleshooting network connections. If network connections are working properly for the computer, the user should contact an administrator for further assistance.

Troubleshooting Profile-Related Problems

Problems related to user profiles usually appear during the logon process. You can resolve some of these problems by starting the computer in safe mode. For example, if an application that is set to launch at startup becomes a problem, standard safe mode troubleshooting procedures can detect and correct this issue.

If starting in safe mode does not resolve the problem, or if you cannot locate the cause of the problem by using standard safe mode troubleshooting procedures, you should consider troubleshooting the user profile. The first step of troubleshooting the user profile is to determine whether the user profile is the issue. For local profiles, consider the following:

- Can another user log on to the same computer with a different user account? Does the other user experience the problem? If not, the problem is definitely a user-profile problem.

- If no other user accounts can access the computer, try to create a new user account. Then log off the computer and log on again as the new user account. This forces the creation of a new local profile from the default user profile. Does the issue go away? If so, this is a user-profile issue.

- If either of the preceding steps fails to solve the problem, troubleshoot the All Users profile.

For roaming profiles, consider the following:

- If the user attempts to log on to another computer, does the issue go away? If so, the issue is most likely with the All Users profile on the afflicted computer.

- If the user cannot log on to another computer, see whether another user can log on to the afflicted computer. Does the problem persist? If so, the problem is most likely with the All Users profile.

If you isolate a profile as the problem, try some or all of the following:

- Examine the amount of space that is available on the volume. If it is extremely low, instruct the user to create some free space.

- If you suspect the problem is within a certain profile subfolder, back up the contents of that folder and then delete its contents.

- Ensure that the user's account has sufficient permissions to access the profile folder.

- Restore the profile to previous settings using System Restore, following the steps outlined in Knowledge Base article 306084, "How to Restore the Operating System to a Previous State in Windows XP."

- If the preceding efforts fail, the user profile is probably corrupt and you must create a new profile. To create a new profile, you must log on to the computer as a user with administrative rights. After logging on, delete the old profile and then log on to the computer with the user's account. Windows will create a new profile when the user logs on.

Lesson Review

The following questions are intended to reinforce key information presented in this lesson. If you are unable to answer a question, review the lesson materials and try the question again. You can find answers to the questions in the "Questions and Answers" section at the end of this chapter.

1. A user complains that when he tries to log on, he receives the error message "Unknown Username Or Bad Password." What are the common causes of this problem?

_____

_____

2. When a local user must reset a password, what information is lost?

_____

_____

Lesson Summary

- Problems with passwords are the second-most common type of logon problem (following problems with network connectivity). If users see the error message "Unknown Username Or Bad Password," make sure that the user is typing the information correctly and that the CAPS LOCK key is not engaged.

- Users who are not connected to a domain and are trying to log on to a local computer can often use a different account with administrative privileges to log on to the computer and then reset their own password.

- The password reset disk is a removable disk that contains encrypted password information. The password reset disk allows users to change their password without knowing the old password.

- When troubleshooting domain logon problems, check network connectivity and make sure that the user is selecting the correct domain to which to log on.

- You can resolve many profile-related problems by starting a computer in safe mode. For more serious problems, you may have to delete a profile and let Windows re-create the profile the next time the user logs on.

Lesson 3: Supporting Security Settings and Local Security Policy

A security policy is a combination of security settings that affect the security on a computer. Computers that are members of a workgroup are subject only to Local Security Policy—settings that are applied to the computer when a user logs on. Computers that are members of a domain are subject to both Local Security Policy and Group Policy. As a DST, you must be able to configure, manage, and troubleshoot Local Security Policy. You should also understand how Group Policy affects a computer in a domain, but you will usually not be called upon to configure or troubleshoot Group Policy.

After this lesson, you will be able to

- Explain how Local Security Policy affects a computer running Windows XP.
- Identify the Resultant Set of Policy (RSoP) that is in effect on a computer.
- Use the Local Security Policy tool to change security settings.
- Identify the important security settings that are available through Local Security Policy.

Estimated lesson time: 30 minutes

Understanding Local Security Policy

As the name suggests, Local Security Policy applies only to the local computer. Using Local Security Policy, you can control the following:

- Who accesses the computer

- Which resources users are authorized to use on their computers

- Whether a user's or group's actions are audited (recorded in the Windows Event Log)

If you want to use Local Security Policy to control the computers in a workgroup, you must configure Local Security Policy on each computer in the workgroup.

Administrators manage Windows security in a domain environment using Group Policy, which enables the enforcement of security policies across all users in a specific site or domain. In an Active Directory environment, administrators can apply Group Policy to domains, sites, or organizational units (OUs), each of which is a type of container that is used to group user and computer accounts in the domain.

> **Note**   For more information about Active Directory structure, see "Active Directory Collection" at *http://www.microsoft.com/resources/documentation/WindowsServ/2003/all/techref/en-us/Default.asp?url=/resources/documentation/windowsServ/2003/all/techref/en-us/W2K3TR_ad_over.asp*.

Order of Policy Application

For computers that are members of a domain, both Local Security Policy and Group Policy are often used. As a result, policies can come from more than one source and are applied in the following order:

1. Local Security Policy is applied to the computer.

2. Group Policy settings are applied for the Active Directory site of which the computer is a member. Policy settings that are configured at this level override Local Security Policy.

3. Group Policy settings are applied for the Active Directory domain of which the computer is a member. Policy settings configured at this level override settings made at the previous levels.

4. Group Policy settings configured for the Active Directory OU of which the computer is a member are applied. Policy settings configured at this level override settings made at the previous levels.

Resultant Set of Policy (RSoP)

A single computer can be affected by Local Security Policy and any number of Group Polices at different levels. Policy settings are cumulative, so all settings contribute to effective policy. The effective policy is called the **Resultant Set of Policy (RSoP)**.

> **Note**   On computers with Windows XP Service Pack 2 installed, Windows Firewall is enabled by default for all network connections. Windows Firewall blocks unsolicited incoming traffic. This means that although you can use RSoP if you are sitting at the computer on which you need to check policy settings, you cannot use RSoP remotely to check the policy settings of a target computer running Windows Firewall in its default configuration. If you are unable to use RSoP to check settings on a remote computer, you will need to unblock specific ports in Windows Firewall or contact a network administrator for help. You can learn more about unblocking the proper ports by reading "Managing Windows XP Service Pack 2 Features Using Group Policy" at *http://www.microsoft.com/technet/prodtechnol/winxppro/maintain/mangxpsp2/mngdepgp.mspx*.

You can view the RSoP for a computer by using the command-line tool Gpresult.exe. To display RSoP, open the command prompt on a computer running Windows XP and type **gpresult**. Windows calculates the RSoP for the computer and displays the results, as shown in Figure 3-7.

> **See Also**   To learn more about the gpresult tool and for a list of options you can use with it, type **gpresult /?** at the command prompt.

Figure 3-7   The gpresult tool displays the RSoP for a computer running Windows XP.

The Help And Support Center also includes a tool that shows effective Group Policy settings for the current user. If you are troubleshooting policy settings for a user from a remote location, you can have the user use this tool to export the information to a file. The user can then e-mail the file to you or to an administrator.

To access the Group Policy tool, follow these steps:

1. From the Start menu, select Help And Support.

2. In the right pane of the Help And Support Center window, select Use Tools To View Your Computer Information And Diagnose Problems.

3. In the left pane, from the Tools list, select Advanced System Information.

4. In the right pane, select View Group Policy Settings Applied.

5. Scroll to the bottom of the report that is displayed and select Save This Report To An .Htm File.

6. In the Explorer User Prompt dialog box, type a path and name for the file and then click OK.

Configuring Local Security Policy

You can access the Local Security Policy tool, shown in Figure 3-8, from the Administrative Tools window on a computer running Windows XP Professional. The Local Security Policy tool is not available on computers running Windows XP Home Edition.

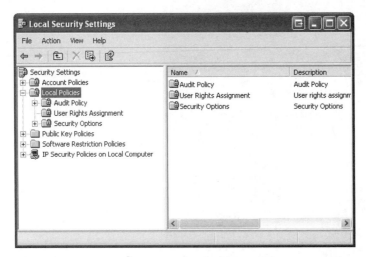

Figure 3-8   Local Security Policy administrative utility

> **Note**   Notice that after you launch the Local Security Policy utility, the window is named Local Security Settings. These settings are a subset of the Local Security Policy and can also be modified through the Group Policy utility.

The Local Security Policy settings that you should be concerned with as a DST are as follows:

■ Account Policies. These include the following:

❏ Password Policy, which controls settings such as the minimum and maximum password age, minimum password length, and whether passwords must be complex

❏ Account Lockout Policy, which controls whether user accounts are locked out after a preconfigured number of failed logon attempts

■ Local Policies. These include the following:

   ❑ Audit Policy, which controls whether various user activities are logged to the Windows Event Log

   ❑ User Rights Assignment, which controls settings that give users the ability to perform particular operating system tasks, such as backing up the computer, changing the time, or shutting down the computer

   ❑ Security Options, which control a number of important security settings regarding access to the computer and resources

Specific settings that are important to DSTs are cited in this section.

Password Policy

Password Policy allows you to increase the effectiveness of users' passwords. By default, users are not required to have passwords, and little control is placed on password usage. Password policies allow you to configure the following settings:

■ **Enforce Password History**   Specifies the number of passwords that Windows XP tracks for each user. When a user attempts to change a password, the user is not permitted to repeat the passwords that Windows is tracking. A setting of 0 effectively disables this option—all passwords, even the current password, could be used.

■ **Maximum Password Age**   Causes passwords to expire after the specified number of days. When the password expires, the user is prompted to change it. This setting ensures that even when passwords are discovered by unauthorized users, they will be changed periodically to increase security.

■ **Minimum Password Age**   Prevents a user from changing a password for the specified number of days.

■ **Minimum Password Length**   Specifies the minimum number of characters that a password must contain. The longer the password, the more difficult it is to guess and the more secure it is.

■ **Passwords Must Meet Complexity Requirements**   Forces users to configure passwords that support a password filter that you install on domain controllers. Password filters enforce more secure password policies. For example, Microsoft provides a filter that forces passwords to be at least six characters long, does not permit the password to contain the user name or parts of the full name, and requires the use of at least three of the following: lowercase letters, uppercase letters, numbers, and symbols.

■ **Store Password Using Reversible Encryption For All Users In The Domain**   Allows passwords to be recovered from the password database in case of emergency. Normally, passwords are stored in an encrypted format that cannot be reversed. Microsoft does not recommend this option. If someone were to break in to the domain, it would then be a simple matter to extract all the user passwords. The option applies in an Active Directory domain environment only.

Account Lockout Policy

Account Lockout Policy allows you configure the computer to stop responding to logon requests from a user who has a valid logon name but who keeps entering the incorrect password. This is called an *invalid logon attempt*. Generally, too many invalid logon attempts in a short period of time indicates that someone is try to guess the password and break in using that account.

You can configure the following Account Lockout Policy settings:

- **Account Lockout Duration**   Controls how long the account will be locked out. Setting this value to 0 locks the account indefinitely until an administrator manually unlocks it. The default setting for this value is 30 minutes.

- **Account Lockout Threshold**   Controls how many invalid logon attempts will trigger account lockout. Setting this value to 0 disables account lockout. The default value for this setting is 0 (account lockout features are disabled by default, providing for an infinite number of incorrect logon attempts).

- **Reset Account Lockout Counter After**   Enables you to configure the number of minutes that have to pass before the account lockout count is reset to 0. For example, if this option were set to 15 minutes, the account lockout threshold would have to be reached within a 15-minute time frame. If not, the counter would be reset. The default setting for this value is 5 minutes.

When Account Lockout Policy locks an account, an event is placed in the Windows System log, viewable through Event Viewer (which is available in the Administrative Tools folder in Control Panel). You can unlock the account by accessing the properties of the user account in Local Users And Groups or by waiting the number of minutes specified in the account lockout duration.

Audit Policy

Windows XP's auditing functionality allows you to monitor user and operating system activities on a computer. You can then use this information to detect intruders and other undesirable activity. Understanding how to implement and manage auditing is an important part of overall security policy.

Auditing consists of two major components:

- **Audit Policy**   Defines the types of events that will be monitored and added to the security logs. The system administrator controls Audit Policy.

- **Audit entries**   The individual entries added to the Windows security log when an audited event occurs. You can view entries in the security log using Event Viewer.

Choosing Events to Audit   You can audit many types of events. You must determine which events to audit based on the specific security needs that are associated with the computer that you are configuring. Events that you can audit are displayed in Table 3-1.

Table 3-1   Auditable Events

Auditable Event	Activated When
Account Logon Event	A domain controller receives a logon request, or a connection attempt is made to a domain resource.
Account Management	A user or group account is created, modified, or deleted.
Directory Service Access	An Active Directory object is accessed.
Logon Event	A user logs on to or logs off of a local computer.
Object Access	An object—such as a file, folder, or printer—is accessed.
Policy Change	A policy affecting security settings, user rights, or auditing is modified.
Privilege Use	A user right is exercised to perform some type of action, such as changing the system time.
Process Tracking	An application executes an action. Generally, this option is used only by programmers who need to track program execution.
System Event	A computer is shut down or rebooted, or various events occur that affect security.

Auditing impairs overall system performance, so be careful when choosing events to be audited. The more events that you audit, the greater the impact on overall system performance, and the larger and more difficult the security logs will be to analyze. Minimize the events to be audited, but make sure that you are auditing enough to meet your security needs. Typically, you will enable auditing when you suspect that there is a security problem and want to verify your suspicion, or when you have particularly sensitive files or computers to protect. Table 3-2 provides several suggestions about events to audit.

Table 3-2   Potential Events to Audit and Reasons to Audit Them

Action to Audit	Choose This Auditable Event
Shutting down and restarting the computer, potentially indicating an unauthorized reconfiguration or break-in attempt	System Events

Table 3-2   Potential Events to Audit and Reasons to Audit Them

Action to Audit	Choose This Auditable Event
Users logging on at odd hours or logging on to computers that they would not normally log on to, indicating a potential break-in or theft	Logon Events (and Account Logon Events in domain environment)
Users unsuccessfully attempting to log on, indicating a potential break-in attempt	Logon Events (and Account Logon Events in domain environment)
Changes to user and group accounts, potentially indicating that an administrative-level user is making unauthorized changes or providing someone with unauthorized access	Account Management
Printer usage, looks for excessive or unauthorized access	Object Access
Access to particular files and folders, looking for access by unauthorized users or for odd access patterns that could indicate a potential sabotage or theft incident	Object Access

Auditing File, Folder, and Printer Access   It is not practical for Windows XP to enable auditing automatically on every file, folder, and printer on the computer when object access auditing is enabled. It would create unnecessary overhead and significantly affect computer performance. Therefore, when you configure Audit Policy for file, folder, and printer access, you need to take additional steps. In addition to configuring the Audit Policy, you must also enable auditing on the object that you want to audit. For files and folders to be audited, they must exist on an NTFS partition.

To configure auditing on a file or folder, follow these steps:

1. In Windows Explorer, right-click the file or folder to be audited and select the Properties option.

2. On the Security tab, click Advanced.

3. On the Auditing tab, click Add. The Select User Or Group dialog box is displayed.

4. Add the users or groups whose access you want to audit and then click OK (if you want to audit all access, choose the group Everyone).

5. Configure the type of access that you want to audit. Click OK to exit.

6. The Auditing tab is displayed again. Verify that you have configured auditing the way that you intended and click OK.

To configure auditing for a printer, complete the following steps:

1. In the Printer folder, right-click the printer to be audited and select the Properties option.

2. On the Security tab, click Advanced.

3. On the Auditing tab, click Add. The Select User Or Group dialog box is displayed.

4. Select the users or groups whose access you want to audit and then click OK. The Auditing Entry dialog box is displayed.

5. Configure the type of access that you want to audit. In this case, we chose to audit successful printing events, permitting us to monitor printer usage. Click OK when complete.

6. The Auditing tab is displayed again. Verify that you have configured auditing the way that you intended and then click OK.

Viewing Audit Entries in the Security Log   For auditing to be a useful security tool, you must review and archive the Security Log regularly. You can view the Security Log by using the Event Viewer.

Figure 3-9 shows the Security Log on a typical Windows XP computer. Notice that both success and failure entries are stored in the same log.

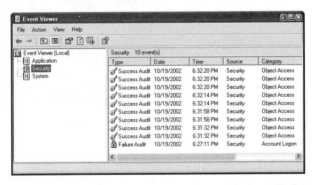

Figure 3-9   Use Event Viewer to view the Windows XP Security Log.

Figure 3-10 shows a failed audit entry—in this case, a failed logon attempt. The event properties contain the date and time that the event occurred, the user name that was used, and the computer on which the event occurred. Other types of audit entries will contain different information but at a similar level of detail.

Figure 3-10   Viewing a failed audit entry

User Rights Assignment

A User Rights Assignment gives the user the ability to perform a particular task, such as to back up the computer, change the time, or shut down the computer. User rights are very different from permissions. User rights pertain to a user's ability to perform specific functions on a computer. Permissions control a user's ability to access resources such as files, folders, and printers.

There are many user rights that you can assign. The following are several of the more commonly used options:

- **Access This Computer From The Network**   Allows users to connect to the computer through the network. This is enabled for Everyone by default. If you remove Everyone from this setting, no one could connect to any shares on this computer, including home folders and roaming profile folders.

- **Add Workstations To Domain**   Allows users to join computers with the domain.

- **Back Up Files And Directories**   Allows users to bypass file system security and back up all files and folders on the computer. There is a corresponding user right called Restore Files And Directories, which gives users the ability to perform file and folder restores.

- **Change The System Time**   Allows users to change the time, date, and time zone on a computer. Some functions are time-dependent, such as logon time restrictions, and you may not want general users to be able to change the time and interfere with such operations.

- **Log On Locally**   Allows users to log on directly to a computer. To clarify, it means that the user can sit in front of the computer, do a CTRL+ALT+DELETE, and log on. The other method of connecting to a computer is through the network, which is controlled through the Access This Computer From The Network user right.

- **Shut Down The Computer**   Allows users to shut down the computer. Computer shutdown interferes with the users' ability to access a server's resources. Also, shutting down and restarting the computer is required to activate certain critical reconfiguration options. The right to shut down the computer should be severely limited on machines that are functioning as servers, but can be granted as necessary on workstations.

- **Take Ownership Of Files Or Other Objects**   Allows users to take ownership of any resource on the computer. If a user owns a resource, that user has the ability to assign permissions to it. You need to be careful in assigning this right because it allows users access to every resource on the computer. By default, only administrators can take ownership, which is required for them to fully manage the resources on the computer.

Security Options

Security options apply to the entire system rather than to a particular user. All users on the computer will be affected by security options. You can configure options such as prompting users to change their passwords a certain number of days before they expire and displaying a message to the users at logon.

There are many security options available. Important settings include the following:

- **Shutdown: Allow System To Be Shut Down Without Having To Log On**   Allows users to perform a shutdown without having to be authenticated to the computer. Users perform this action by pressing CTRL+ALT+DELETE and selecting the Shutdown option at the Log On To Windows dialog box. This option is disabled by default.

■ **Microsoft Network Server: Amount Of Idle Time Required Before Suspending A Session**   Defines how long, in minutes, a connection to this computer can be idle before it is disconnected. If a user connects to a server but then does not use the connection for a while, it takes up resources on the server. By default, the computer automatically drops idle connections after 15 minutes.

■ **Network Security: Force Logoff When Logon Hours Expire**   Works in conjunction with the logon hours that are defined for user accounts. This setting controls whether users will be automatically disconnected when their logon hours expire. If this option is disabled, it means that users can stay logged on after their logon hours expire if they are already logged on, but they cannot establish a new session.

■ **Interactive Logon: Do Not Require CTRL+ALT+DELETE**   Allows you to control whether the user has to press that keystroke combination when logging on. This is an important security feature of Windows XP because the CTRL+ALT+DELETE sequence suspends processing during logon and prevents applications from running that may be trying to capture a user's credentials.

■ **Interactive Logon: Do Not Display Last User Name**   Causes the computer to not display the name of the last user who logged on using the Log On To Windows dialog box. If someone is trying to break into the computer, that person needs a user name and password; and if a valid user name is displayed when CTRL+ALT+DELETE is entered, the user already has half of the needed information.

■ **Interactive Logon: Message Text/Title For Users Attempting To Log On**   Displays a dialog box when a user uses CTRL+ALT+DELETE to log on. The message is generally used to warn users that unauthorized access to the computer is prohibited for legal reasons, but you can use it for general communication if you need to.

■ **Interactive Logon: Prompt User To Change Password Before Expiration**   Causes the computer to start prompting users for a new password a specific number of days before their password actually expires. This is an important option because if a user's password expires, the user may not be able to log on to change it, and the network administrator will have to change the user's password manually.

Lesson Review

The following questions are intended to reinforce key information presented in this lesson. If you are unable to answer a question, review the lesson materials and try the question again. You can find answers to the questions in the "Questions and Answers" section at the end of this chapter.

1. Which Password Policy setting permits you to specify the number of passwords that Windows XP keeps track of for each user so that, when a user attempts to change a password, the user cannot reuse any password the computer is keeping track of?

    A. Enforce Password History

    B. Maximum Password Numbers

    C. Minimum Password Numbers

    D. Password Must Meet Complexity

2. What is the primary disadvantage associated with auditing? Under what circumstances should you use auditing?

_____

_____

Lesson Summary

- Local Security Policy enables the administrator to do such things as set minimum password lengths, set account lockout policies to protect against break-ins, and control who can access the computer through the network.

- Password Policy enables you to increase the effectiveness of users' passwords. By default, users are not required to have passwords, and little control is placed on password usage.

- Account Lockout Policy enables you to configure the computer to stop responding to logon requests from a user who has a valid logon name but who keeps entering an incorrect password. Generally, too many invalid logon attempts in a short time indicate that someone is trying to guess the password and break in using that account.

- Windows XP's auditing functionality enables you to monitor user and operating system activities on a computer. You can then use this information to detect intruders and other undesirable activity. Understanding how to implement and manage auditing is an important part of overall security policy.

- A User Rights Assignment gives the user the ability to perform a particular task, such as backing up the computer, changing the time, or shutting down the computer. User rights are very different from permissions. User rights pertain to a user's ability to perform specific functions on a computer. Permissions control a user's ability to access resources such as files, folders, and printers.

Case Scenario Exercises

Scenario 3.1

A user calls you and reports that he has mistakenly deleted a user account from a local computer. He re-created the user account before restarting or logging off, and he cannot access any of the files he once had access to. How would you help this caller so that he can access all his old files?

_____

_____

_____

Scenario 3.2

A user calls and tells you that she created a Limited user account for her son on her home computer that is running Windows XP Professional. Her son created a password for his account, but now cannot remember the correct password. How can you help this user?

_____

_____

_____

Troubleshooting Lab

You are working as a DST for a large company with a corporate network. A user calls and tells you that he has been on vacation for the last two weeks. When he tries to log on to the network, he sees only the default Windows XP desktop with just the Recycle Bin. All his desktop icons are gone and his Start menu is completely changed. He also cannot find any of his files in his My Documents folder. He has tried logging on from several different computers using his domain user name and password, but has the same problem no matter what computer he tries to log on to. Normally, the user can log on to any computer and can access his desktop environment and folders. Other users on the network are not reporting this problem. What do you suspect is the problem?

_____

_____

_____

Chapter Summary

- User accounts allow users to log on to a computer or to a domain and subsequently gain access to local and network resources.

- Group accounts simplify the assignment of security features by enabling you to assign access to groups and then include users in those groups.

- Domain Admins, Domain Guests, and Domain Users are predefined groups that exist on Windows domain controllers only. These domain-based groups are made members of local groups automatically when a computer joins a domain.

- Windows XP Home Edition does not support the use of groups or the ability to join a domain, or include the Local Users And Groups tool.

- Fast User Switching is a feature introduced with Windows XP that allows multiple local user accounts to log on to a computer simultaneously. When Fast User Switching is enabled, users can switch sessions without logging off or closing programs.

- Password problems are the second most common type of logon problem (following problems with network connectivity). If users see the error message "Unknown Username Or Bad Password," make sure that the user is typing the information correctly and that the CAPS LOCK key is not engaged.

- Users who are not connected to a domain and are trying to log on to a local computer can often use a different account with administrative privileges to log on to the computer and then reset their own password.

- The password reset disk is a removable disk that contains encrypted password information. The password reset disk allows users to change their password without knowing the old password.

- When troubleshooting domain logon problems, check network connectivity and make sure that the user is selecting the correct domain to which to log on.

- You can resolve many profile-related problems by starting a computer in safe mode. For more serious problems, you may have to delete a profile and let Windows re-create the profile the next time the user logs on.

- Local Security Policy enables the administrator to do such things as set minimum password lengths, set account lockout policies to protect against break-ins, and control who can access the computer through the network.

- Password Policy enables you to increase the effectiveness of users' passwords. By default, users are not required to have passwords, and little control is placed on password usage.

- Account Lockout Policy enables you to configure the computer to stop responding to logon requests from a user who has a valid logon name but who keeps entering an incorrect password. Generally, too many invalid logon attempts in a short time indicate that someone is trying to guess the password and break in using that account.

- Windows XP's auditing functionality enables you to monitor user and operating system activities on a computer. You can then use this information to detect intruders and other undesirable activity. Understanding how to implement and manage auditing is an important part of overall security policy.

- A User Rights Assignment gives the user the ability to perform a particular task, such as backing up the computer, changing the time, or shutting down the computer. User rights are very different from permissions. User rights pertain to a user's ability to perform specific functions on a computer. Permissions control a user's ability to access resources such as files, folders, and printers.

Exam Highlights

Before taking the exam, review the key topics and terms that are presented in this chapter. You need to know this information.

Key Points

- If a user, especially a home user, complains to you about a computer seeming to run slowly, be sure to ask whether the computer has Fast User Switching enabled.

- The two most common reasons why a user receives the Unknown Username Or Bad Password error message are that the user is typing the wrong credentials or that the CAPS LOCK key is engaged.

- The most common reasons for a failed logon for a domain user are network connectivity issues and attempting to log on to the wrong domain.

Key Terms

domain group   A type of group created on the domain controllers that can be granted rights and permissions on any computer in the domain.

domain user account   A type of account created using the Active Directory Users And Computers utility on domain controllers and stored in the Active Directory database.

group   A type of account that is created in Windows XP Professional that can be granted rights and permissions to a local computer only.

Local Security Policy   A set of policies set by the administrator to secure or monitor a computer.

local user account   A type of user account created on a local computer.

Password policy   A policy in which the length, reuse, and complexity of a password can be set.

security identifier (SID)   A unique identifier assigned at the time an account is created.

User Rights Assignment   A feature that gives the user the ability to perform a particular task.

Questions and Answers

Lesson 1 Review

Page 3-24 **1.** What utilities can you use to create user accounts on a Windows XP Professional computer?

You can use the User Accounts tool, which is located in Control Panel, or you can use the Local Users And Groups tool, which is located in the Computer Management console.

2. What important limitations should you be aware of when supporting Windows XP Home Edition?

You cannot create groups in Windows XP Home Edition. Also, Windows XP Home Edition does not include the Local Users And Groups tool. Instead, you must use the User Accounts tool. Also, computers running Windows XP Home Edition cannot join a domain.

3. List the default user accounts in Windows XP Professional.

The default user accounts in Windows XP Professional are Administrator, Guest, HelpAssistant, and SUPPORT_*xxxxx*.

Lesson 2 Review

Page 3-30 **1.** A user complains that when he tries to log on, he receives the error message "Unknown Username Or Bad Password." What are the common causes of this problem?

The two most common causes of password problems are that the user is mistyping the user name or password, or that the CAPS LOCK key is engaged.

2. When a local user must reset a password, what information is lost?

When a user resets a password, the user loses access to e-mail and files that the user has encrypted, as well as Internet passwords that are saved on the computer.

Lesson 3 Review

Page 3-42 **1.** Which Password Policy setting permits you to specify the number of passwords that Windows XP keeps track of for each user so that when a user attempts to change a password, the user cannot reuse any of the passwords that the computer is keeping track of?

   A. Enforce Password History

   B. Maximum Password Numbers

C. Minimum Password Numbers

D. Password Must Meet Complexity

Answer A is correct. The Enforce Password History setting ensures that users cannot reuse a password within the period that Windows tracks passwords. Answers B and C are incorrect because these settings are invalid. Answer D is incorrect because this setting forces users to create passwords that meet complexity requirements.

2. What is the primary disavantage associated with auditing? Under what circumstances should you use auditing?

Auditing consumes system resources. If you audit too many events on a computer, the performance of the computer will suffer. You should typically enable auditing when you suspect that there is a security problem or when you have a particularly sensitive resource that you want to protect.

Case Scenario Exercises: Exercise 3.1

Page 3-44 A user calls you and reports that he has mistakenly deleted a user account from a local computer. He re-created the user account before restarting or logging off, and he cannot access any of the files he once had access to. How would you help this caller so that he can access all his old files?

To assist this caller, you must explain to him that after he deletes a user account and re-creates it, even using the same name, the SID is no longer associated with the files he needs to access. The administrator on that computer must now assign the new user account permissions to all files and folders that this user needs access to.

Case Scenario Exercises: Exercise 3.2

Page 3-44 A user calls and tells you that she created a Limited user account for her son on her home computer, which is running Windows XP Professional. Her son created a password for his account, but now cannot remember the correct password. How can you help this user?

The user must log on using a Computer Administrator account and reset her son's password using the User Accounts tool in Control Panel. You should warn her that her son will lose access to e-mail or files that he has encrypted and Internet passwords saved on the computer.

Troubleshooting Lab

Page 3-44 You are working as a DST for a large company with a corporate network. A user calls and tells you that he has been on vacation for the last two weeks. When he tries to log on to the network, he sees only the default Windows XP desktop with just the Recycle Bin. All his desktop icons are gone and his Start menu is completely changed. He also cannot find any of his files in his My Documents folder. He has tried logging on from several different computers using his domain user name and password, but has the same problem no matter what computer he tries to log on to. Normally, the user can log on to any computer and can access his desktop environment and folders. Other users on the network are not reporting this problem. What do you suspect is the problem?

Because the user says that he normally can log on to any computer and access his information, the corporate network is using roaming profiles. However, the user is seeing the Windows XP default profile when logging on to the domain. This likely means that the user's roaming profile is corrupted and that Windows is attempting to correct the problem by creating a new profile for him based on the Default User profile. You should tell the user to report the problem to an administrator because an administrator can probably restore the user's profile from before it became corrupt.

4 Supporting the Windows Desktop

Exam Objectives in this Chapter:

- Configure the user environment
    - ❑ Answer end-user questions related to configuring the desktop and user environment
    - ❑ Configure and troubleshoot task and toolbar settings
    - ❑ Configure and troubleshoot accessibility options
- Configure support for multiple languages or multiple locations
    - ❑ Answer end-user questions related to regional settings
    - ❑ Configure and troubleshoot regional settings
    - ❑ Answer end-user questions related to language settings
    - ❑ Configure and troubleshoot language settings

Why This Chapter Matters

The Microsoft Windows XP desktop environment provides a user interface that is easily customized. Appropriate configuration of the desktop enhances a user's experience with the operating system and can increase productivity. As a desktop support technician (DST), it is important that you understand the options that are available for desktop configuration and management. The requirement for multiple-language support is also increasing in today's multinational corporate environment. Users often need to create, view, and edit documents in multiple languages. You should understand the multilingual features that Windows XP offers and be able to configure and troubleshoot those features.

Lessons in this Chapter:

Before You Begin

Before you begin this chapter, you should have a basic familiarity with the Windows XP interface. You should also have a computer running Windows XP on which you can experiment with changing various settings.

Lesson 1: Troubleshooting the Windows Taskbar and Start Menu

The **taskbar** and the **Start menu** are two of the primary connections between the user and the Windows desktop. The taskbar displays files and programs that are currently open and running. The taskbar also allows the user to switch easily between open files and applications, group items, and to open the most-often-used programs quickly. The notification area to the right of the taskbar displays the system clock and programs that are running in the background. The Start menu provides access to the available programs, network places, connections, help and support files, recent documents, and more.

After this lesson, you will be able to

- Identify the types of questions that relate to the Start menu and taskbar.
- Troubleshoot and customize the notification area.
- Troubleshoot and customize the taskbar.
- Troubleshoot and customize the Start menu.
- Configure and troubleshoot accessibility options.

Estimated lesson time: 50 minutes

Common Start Menu and Taskbar Requests

Because of the amount of time the end user spends using these two components, you may receive several configuration (or troubleshooting) calls, including the following:

- The taskbar is always disappearing, and I want that to stop. I also want to be able to move the taskbar to another area of the screen.

- One of my colleagues has an icon next to his Start menu that he uses to open our accounting program. I do not have any icons there. How do I create one of them so that I do not always have to locate the program on the Start menu or place a shortcut on the desktop?

- I do not have enough room on my taskbar to show all my open programs, and I have to scroll to see the additional programs. Is there some way of grouping the programs together?

- Can I remove or hide the icons for my antivirus software, my pop-up stopper program, and other programs that run in the background? If I remove them, do they stop running?

- There are a lot of icons in the notification area that I do not think I need. How can I get rid of them? I do not think they should be running in the background, and I do not even know what some of them are.

- There are many programs in my Start menu that I do not need, and there are some that I need that are not there. Can you fix that for me?

- I want to be able to open My Network Places, open Control Panel, and access System Administrative Tools from the Start menu, but I do not want my recent documents to be listed. I also do not want to see the My Music or My Pictures folder or any other folders that are not work-related.

To answer questions like these, you must understand the options that are available and how to access and configure them. By the time you reach the end of this lesson, you will be able to resolve all of these issues and more.

Troubleshooting the Notification Area

The **notification area** shows the time, volume control, and icons for programs that start and run automatically. These program icons can be for antivirus programs, music programs, CD-burning programs, or third-party programs that have been downloaded or purchased. If an item is in the notification area, its program is running in the background, making it quickly available when needed. The notification area also shows icons for network connections, and it can show whether the connections are enabled or disabled.

In this section, you will learn to configure and troubleshoot the notification area. Troubleshooting can also include cleaning up the area by removing unnecessary programs. After completing this section, you will be able to do the following:

- Add items to the notification area if the program supports it
- Hide inactive icons so that the notification area does not take up too much room on the taskbar
- Remove icons and close running programs temporarily
- Remove icons and close running programs permanently

Adding Items to the Notification Area

You can add an icon to the notification area only if the program supports that feature in its preferences or configuration options, and many times icons are added by default when a new program is installed. You can also add icons that indicate when network connections are active, including local area networks (LANs), wireless connections, and dial-up connections to the Internet.

If a user requests that you add an icon to the notification area for an application such as an antivirus program, open the program and browse through the available options and preferences. If an option to show the program in the notification area is available, it should look similar to the one shown in Figure 4-1.

Figure 4-1   Microsoft OneNote offers the option to remove the icon from the tray.

Note   When you remove an item from the notification area, it does not necessarily disable the program; it might only remove the icon. Check the instructions for an application to make sure.

If a user requests that you add an icon to the notification area for any network or Internet connection on a computer running Windows XP, follow these steps:

1. From the Start menu, select Connect To, and then select Show All Connections. If the Connect To option is not available on the Start menu, open Control Panel, select Network And Internet Connections, and then select Network Connections.

2. Right-click the connection that you want to show in the notification area, and then click Properties.

3. On the General tab of the connection's Properties dialog box, select the Show Icon In Notification Area When Connected check box, and then click OK.

Figure 4-2 shows a notification area that has three active network connections. One is a wireless connection, one is a dial-up Internet connection, and one is a connection to a LAN. It also shows antivirus software and Instant Messenger icons.

Figure 4-2   The notification area shows active programs and connections.

Hiding Inactive Icons

If the computer has several programs that start automatically when Windows loads, and there are multiple icons in the notification area (as shown in Figure 4-2), the end user might complain that the notification area is taking up too much space on the task-bar. If this happens, enable the Hide Inactive Icons feature, and Windows will hide the icons for programs that are inactive but are still running in the background. To hide inactive icons, follow these steps:

1. Right-click an empty area of the taskbar and choose Properties.

2. On the taskbar tab, select the Hide Inactive Icons check box, and then click OK.

The inactive icons are hidden behind the arrow. Figure 4-3 shows a notification area configured with hidden icons. Compare the view in Figure 4-3 with the view in Figure 4-2; both views show the same notification area.

Figure 4-3   Hidden icons in the notification area are accessed by clicking the arrow.

Exam Tip   Remember that items in the notification area might be hidden behind the arrow. You (or the user) might not see them, but that does not mean they are not there. Check there before you access the program's preferences or restart the program.

Removing Icons and Temporarily Closing Background Programs

To close a program and remove an item from the notification area temporarily so that you can free up resources, disable the program, or briefly unclutter the notification area, right-click the icon and look at the choices. Figure 4-4 shows the choices for MSN Messenger 6.1, a program that a home user might have installed.

Figure 4-4   Click Exit to close this program and remove the icon from the notification area.

The choices for removing the icon and editing the program differ depending on the application or connection. Common options include the following:

- Exit
- Disable
- Close
- End
- Preferences (locate the Exit command in the dialog box)

Removing icons from the notification area in this manner is not permanent; this action removes an icon only until the program is started again or you restart the computer. Removing items permanently requires a little more work.

Removing Icons and Permanently Closing Programs That Are Running

A cluttered notification area is a good indicator that too many programs are starting when you start Windows. Having too many programs running can cause many common problems, including a slower-than-necessary startup process, an unstable system, or a computer that displays slow response times when accessing applications or performing calculations. When a user complains that the system exhibits these systems, check the notification area first.

Even if the computer seems to be running smoothly, you should remove items from a computer's notification area if the applications are never used. There is no reason to allow unused programs to start each time Windows does; this only drains necessary system resources.

If you decide to remove programs from the notification area permanently, follow these steps:

1. Click Start and then click Run.

2. In the Run dialog box, type **msconfig.exe** and click OK.

3. In the System Configuration Utility dialog box, click the Startup tab.

4. Scroll through the list, as shown in Figure 4-5, and clear the check box of any third-party item you do not want to start automatically when Windows does.

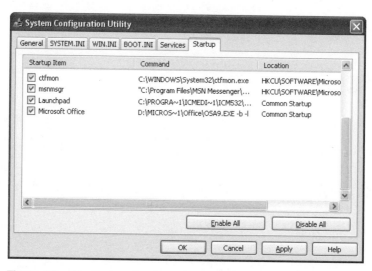

Figure 4-5 The System Configuration Utility dialog box offers lots of information.

5. Restart the computer, and, when prompted by the System Configuration Utility, verify that you understand that changes have been made.

Caution   Be careful when selecting programs to not start with Windows by using the msconfig.exe tool. Many of the programs listed in the System Configuration Utility dialog box are vital to Windows and to applications that the user might need. If you are not absolutely sure what a program does or whether it is safe to remove, you should err on the side of caution and leave it running. If you suspect that such a program is causing problems at startup, disable only that program and restart Windows to test the theory. You can also discover the purpose of many programs by searching the Internet. Many different websites provide details about programs commonly found in the Windows startup routine.

Real World   Users May Not Know What to Call Things

Part of your job as a DST is learning to listen to users. Remember that users are not trained and often do not know the proper terminology to use. For example, you may know what the notification area is, but it is not a name that is posted anywhere obvious or that just suggests itself. If a user is trying to explain something to you, feel free to let the user know the proper terminology, but try not to make it sound like something he or she should have known.

If you are explaining something to a user, use the proper terminology so that the user has the chance to hear it, but be prepared to help him or her navigate the first couple of times. Users are often embarrassed to speak up and tell you that they do not know what something is. Use landmarks that everyone understands to help guide the way. For example, you might tell a user, "Look in the notification area; it is on the bottom right where the clock and all the other icons are."

Locking and Unlocking the Taskbar

By default, the taskbar's position on the desktop is locked, which means that the user cannot move it to any other location and cannot resize it. When the taskbar is locked, users also cannot move or resize the toolbars that are displayed on the taskbar. If a user wants to unlock the taskbar, the procedure is easy: right-click an empty area of the taskbar and clear the Lock The Taskbar command (the command toggles on and off; the current setting is indicated by a check mark next to the command). Remember to lock the taskbar again when you get things the way the user wants them. When locked, the taskbar is protected from accidental changes, and you gain a little extra room because the toolbar handles are not displayed.

> **Note** If a toolbar is enabled and the taskbar is locked, there will be no handle (the rows of dotted lines) in front of the toolbar area. If a toolbar is enabled and the taskbar is unlocked, the handle is visible, as shown in the figures in this chapter. You can reposition a toolbar or even move it off the taskbar entirely by dragging the handle when the taskbar is unlocked.

Grouping Similar Items and Enabling Quick Launch

Two additional ways to enhance the taskbar are by enabling the Group Similar Taskbar Buttons options and by enabling the Quick Launch toolbar. (Both of these settings are available options in the Taskbar And Start Menu Properties dialog box.) Grouping similar taskbar buttons saves room on the taskbar by grouping similar entries (for example, all open Microsoft Word documents) together. Turning on the Quick Launch toolbar allows you to add icons to the Quick Launch area of the taskbar for any program that a user accesses often.

Grouping Similar Taskbar Buttons

As a DST, you will work with users of all levels. Some users are just learning how to use e-mail, some work with a single program and one or two files most of the day, and others work with multiple programs and have multiple open files. Users who multitask among multiple programs and have several open files probably have a crowded taskbar and might ask you about their options for organizing the files and programs shown on the taskbar.

Figure 4-6 shows a crowded taskbar, and Figure 4-7 shows the same taskbar with the grouping option enabled. Both taskbars include Microsoft Outlook Express, three open Windows Explorer folders, three open Microsoft Excel worksheets, two open graphics in Microsoft Paint, and three open Word documents. In Figure 4-6, you cannot see some of these open files without using the arrow on the taskbar.

Figure 4-6 A crowded taskbar might make the taskbar seem disorganized.

Figure 4-7 A crowded taskbar might seem better organized with grouping enabled.

If the user wants you to configure his or her computer to use these grouping options, open the Taskbar And Start Menu Properties dialog box, as discussed earlier. On the Taskbar tab, select the Group Similar Taskbar Buttons check box and click OK.

Enabling Quick Launch

Quick Launch is the area of the taskbar directly to the right of the Start menu that contains icons for programs that a user needs to launch frequently. If you enable Quick Launch right after installing Windows XP, three icons are available by default: e-mail, launch Internet Explorer browser, and show desktop, as shown in Figure 4-8. Clicking the respective icons opens these programs. You can also customize the Quick Launch area to include whichever programs you access most often, and you can even resize the toolbar if the taskbar is unlocked. (Figure 4-9 shows a customized Quick Launch area.) Some programs also add icons to the Quick Launch area automatically during the program's installation, so what you see when you first enable Quick Launch can vary.

Figure 4-8   Quick Launch is shown here with the taskbar unlocked.

If a user contacts you and wants to use Quick Launch, or asks you to add or remove program icons from it, follow these steps:

1. Right-click an empty area of the taskbar and choose Properties.

2. In the Taskbar And Start Menu dialog box, click the Taskbar tab.

3. Select the Show Quick Launch check box, and then click OK.

4. To remove any item from the Quick Launch area, right-click the icon and select Delete. Click Yes in the Confirm File Delete dialog box. (You are not deleting the program; you are removing only the shortcut from the Quick Launch area.)

5. To add a shortcut for any item to the Quick Launch area, locate the program (or folder or file) in Windows Explorer, the Start menu, or the All Programs list; right-click it; drag the program to the Quick Launch area; and then choose Create Shortcuts Here. If this option is not available, choose Copy Here. A new icon will be added to the Quick Launch area.

Tip   The quickest way to get things onto your Quick Launch toolbar is to drag them there. Use your right mouse button to drag any shortcut from the Start menu (or the desktop or any folder) to the Quick Launch area. When you let go of the mouse button, a menu pops up asking whether you want to copy or move the shortcut. Choose Copy to add the item to Quick Launch and also leave a copy in its original location. You might move items to the Quick Launch bar if, for example, you are cleaning shortcuts off of a cluttered desktop.

Figure 4-9 shows a personalized Quick Launch area with icons (from left to right) for Microsoft Outlook, Microsoft Internet Explorer, Microsoft Photo Editor, MSN Messenger 6.1, Help And Support, Backup, and Control Panel. Depending on the user's needs and preferences, you might be called on to create a Quick Launch area like this one.

Figure 4-9   A personalized and resized Quick Launch area is shown here with the taskbar unlocked.

Troubleshooting a Locked, Hidden, or Missing Taskbar

If an end user contacts you about a locked, hidden, or missing taskbar, carrying out the repair is most likely a simple procedure; this taskbar issue is also a surprisingly common complaint. Most of the time, the Start Menu And Taskbar Properties dialog box simply has the Lock The Taskbar, Auto-Hide The Taskbar, or Keep The Taskbar On Top Of Other Windows check box selected. Clearing the check box solves the problem immediately.

- **Lock The Taskbar**   When this check box is selected, the user cannot move or resize the taskbar by dragging. The user might complain that the taskbar is "locked."

- **Auto-Hide The Taskbar**   When this check box is selected, the taskbar is hidden until the user moves his or her mouse over the area where the taskbar should be. The user might complain that the taskbar is "missing" or "malfunctioning."

- **Keep The Taskbar On Top Of Other Windows**   When this check box is selected, the taskbar stays on top of all other running applications. The user might complain that the taskbar is "always in the way."

The user might also complain that the taskbar is too large or in the wrong area of the desktop. When this happens, inform the user that he or she can drag the top of the taskbar (when the mouse pointer becomes a two-headed arrow) to resize it. Move the taskbar to another area of the screen by dragging it there.

Advanced Troubleshooting

If you cannot solve a taskbar problem by using the preceding techniques, the problem is more advanced. Table 4-1 lists some known issues with the taskbar and the Microsoft Knowledge Base article number and brief solution.

Table 4-1   Advanced Taskbar Problems and Solutions

Problem	Knowledge Base Article Number and Brief Solution
The taskbar is missing when you log on to Windows.	Article 318027,"Taskbar Is Missing When You Log On to Windows." This behavior can occur if the Windows settings for a particular user account are corrupted. The solution involves checking for bad drivers, followed by creating a new user account, followed by performing an in-place repair of the operating system.
The taskbar stops responding intermittently.	Article 314228, "The Windows XP Taskbar May Stop Responding for Some Time." This is caused if the Language Bar is minimized and a Windows-based program is busy. Installing the latest service pack solves this problem.
After moving the taskbar from the bottom of the screen to the right side, the background picture is not displayed correctly.	Article 303137, "Background Picture Is Not Displayed Correctly After You Move the Taskbar." Microsoft has confirmed that this is a problem. To solve this problem, click once on an empty area of the desktop, and then press F5 to refresh the background.
A part of the ToolTips or a message from the status area remains behind or is partially displayed on the status area of the taskbar after it should be gone.	Article 307499, "ToolTips and Messages from the Status Area of the Taskbar May Remain." To resolve this behavior, right-click another location that does not contain the leftover message, click the displayed message, move the mouse pointer over the icon, or resize the taskbar.

Configuring Toolbars on the Windows Taskbar

Adding one of the built-in toolbars to the Windows taskbar typically adds a few shortcuts that allow a user to quickly access certain components. For example, adding the Desktop toolbar allows a user to easily access items on the desktop by clicking the shortcut to them on the taskbar. Adding the Links toolbar allows a user to quickly access Internet sites stored in their Links folder (in Internet Explorer Favorites) without first opening Internet Explorer.

You can add toolbars to the taskbar by right-clicking any open space on the taskbar, pointing to Toolbars, and making the appropriate selection from the choices available. Some choices you can add include the following:

- Address
- Windows Media Player
- Links

- Language Bar
- Desktop
- Quick Launch
- New Toolbar

If users often need access to any of these items, show them how to add the appropriate toolbar.

Troubleshooting the Start Menu

Usually, service calls regarding the Start menu involve what does or does not appear on the menu. One user might need access to My Network Connections, My Recent Documents, Internet, E-mail, and the company's accounting program. A user in a graphics department might need access to My Pictures, Printers And Faxes, My Music, and his or her favorite graphics program. When you are queried to personalize the Start menu, the combinations of ways in which the service call comes in are numerous. Figure 4-10 shows an example of a personalized Start menu.

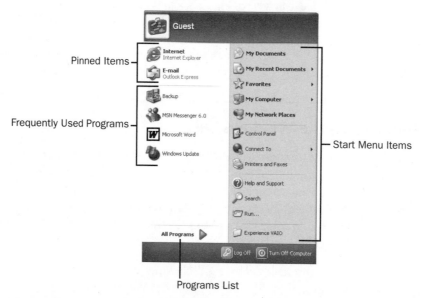

Figure 4-10   A customized Start menu offers personalized access to programs.

Two types of Start menus are available in Windows XP: the Start menu and the Classic Start menu. In this section, you learn about the Start menu and how to resolve the most basic troubleshooting calls. The tasks include adding or removing programs or Start menu items, permanently pinning items to the Start menu, and reordering the All Programs list. The Classic Start menu is discussed briefly in the next section.

Adding or Removing Items in the All Programs List

How to add and remove items from the All Programs list on the Start menu is a common request from end users. You can add a program in many ways, but you learn the easiest way here. Removing a program is the simpler of the two tasks.

To add an item to the All Programs list, follow these steps:

1. Right-click the Start menu and choose Open All Users.

2. Click File, point to New, and click Shortcut.

3. In the Create Shortcut dialog box, click Browse.

4. Locate the local or network program, file, folder, computer, or Internet address to create a shortcut for, and then click OK.

5. Click Next. On the Select A Title For The Program page, type a name for the shortcut and click Finish.

6. Close the Documents And Settings\All Users\Start Menu window.

To see the new addition, click Start, point to All Programs, and look toward the top of the All Programs list. You can now move that item by dragging it to any other area of the All Programs list, the Frequently Used Programs area of the Start menu, or the pinned items list. You can also add a shortcut for an item to the Start menu by dragging the item's icon to a position on the Start menu.

To remove an item from the All Programs list, simply right-click it and choose Delete. Click Yes when prompted to verify this action.

> **Note**   You can reorder items on the All Programs list by dragging and dropping, or you can order them alphabetically by right-clicking any entry and choosing Sort By Name.

Adding or Removing Items on the Start Menu

End users often initiate a service call because a colleague has something on his Start menu that the user does not, or there are items on the Start menu that a user simply does not need. Users might call to say that sometimes the program that they want is in the frequently used area of the Start menu and sometimes it is not, and they want it to always be available. Start menu items can include just about anything, such as frequently accessed programs; pinned items; and operating system components such as Control Panel, My Network Places, Help And Support, Search, Run, and similar items.

Windows adds items to the frequently used programs area as a user opens them. Windows then moves the items up or down the list automatically depending on how often a user opens them. When a computer is new and there are no items in this list, Windows adds programs to the list the first time a user opens them. As users continue to open programs, Windows orders the list automatically by how frequently the programs are opened. If a user does not need specific items that appear on the list, you can remove items by right-clicking and choosing Remove From This List. In addition, you can remove all items and even disable the frequently used programs list altogether from the Customize Start Menu dialog box by following these steps:

1. Right-click the Start button and select Properties.

2. In the Taskbar And Start Menu Properties dialog box, verify that Start Menu is selected and click Customize.

3. In the Customize Start Menu dialog box, in the Programs section, click Clear List to clear all items from the frequently used programs area of the Start menu.

4. To increase or decrease the number of programs shown, change the value for Number Of Programs On Start Menu by using the arrows. Zero disables the Start menu. Figure 4-11 shows an example of the Customize Start Menu dialog box. Click OK and click OK again to apply the changes.

Figure 4-11 The Customize Start Menu dialog box offers many ways to personalize the Start menu.

You can pin or unpin an item on the Start menu by right-clicking the item in the Start menu or All Programs list and then choosing Pin To Start Menu. Pinning an item to the Start menu places it in the upper-left corner of the Start menu with other pinned items such as Internet and E-Mail, allowing for easier access. This option is also available for items in the frequently used items area.

Finally, if a user asks you to add or remove an operating system component such as Favorites, Control Panel, Run, My Documents, or My Pictures to or from the Start menu or to configure how it is displayed, follow these steps:

1. Right-click Start and choose Properties.

2. In the Taskbar And Start Menu Properties dialog box, verify that Start Menu is selected and click Customize.

3. In the Customize Start Menu dialog box, click the Advanced tab.

4. In the Start Menu Items window, scroll through the options. Selecting an item will show it on the Start menu. Other choices for an item include the following:

   ❏ **Display As A Link**   The item is displayed on the Start menu.

   ❏ **Display As A Menu**   The item is displayed, and a menu is available that contains the objects in that folder.

   ❏ **Don't Display This Item**   The item is not displayed.

5. In the Recent Documents area, click Clear List to clear the list of recently opened documents, or clear List My Most Recently Opened Documents to prevent items from being shown. Click OK twice to apply the changes and exit.

> **Note**   Remember, if the troubleshooting call goes beyond these basic configuration issues, visit the Knowledge Base for help.

Troubleshooting the Classic Start Menu

The Classic Start menu is another option for users. If, after an upgrade, users complain that the Start menu is too complicated or that they want it to look more like their old Microsoft Windows 98 or Windows 2000 computer did, this is the menu to use. Troubleshooting the Classic Start menu is similar to troubleshooting the Start menu, as discussed earlier, except for the minor differences in the Customize dialog box. Figure 4-12 shows the Customize Classic Start Menu dialog box.

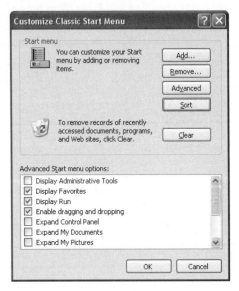

Figure 4-12   Customizing the Classic Start menu is also achieved through a dialog box.

In the Customize Classic Start Menu dialog box, you can perform the following actions:

- Click Add to add any item to the Start menu.

- Click Remove to remove any item from the Start menu.

- Click Advanced to start Windows Explorer to add or remove items from the Start menu.

- Click Clear to remove records of recently accessed documents, programs, and websites.

- Click any item in the Advanced Start Menu Options list to show that item.

- Click Sort to organize the items on the Start menu in alphabetical order.

Supporting Accessibility Options

Windows XP provides a number of features to help users with disabilities to use their computers more effectively. You can configure accessibility options by selecting Accessibility Options in the Control Panel window. Following are the accessibility options in Windows XP:

- **StickyKeys**   Allows a user to use key combinations (such as CTRL+ESC) by pressing one key at a time instead of having to press the keys simultaneously. StickyKeys works for the CTRL, ALT, and DEL keys, as well as for the Windows logo key. When a user presses one of these keys, Windows registers the key as "pressed" until the user completes the key combination. You can also enable a keyboard shortcut for StickyKeys, in which case the feature is activated when a user presses the SHIFT key five times in a row.

- **FilterKeys** Causes Windows to ignore repeated keystrokes, which is useful for people who have involuntary hand movements that cause them to press keys in rapid succession or hold a key longer than they intend to. There is also a keyboard shortcut for FilterKeys: the user holds down the right SHIFT key for eight seconds.

- **ToggleKeys** Causes Windows to play a sound when a user presses the CAPS LOCK, NUM LOCK, or SCROLL LOCK keys. The keyboard shortcut for ToggleKeys is to hold down the NUM LOCK key for five seconds.

- **SoundSentry** Causes Windows to generate visual warnings when the system makes a sound, which is useful for people who are deaf. You can have Windows flash the caption bar at the top of a window or dialog box, flash the active window itself, or flash the entire desktop.

- **ShowSounds** Causes Windows to display an icon or a text note on the screen to indicate the particular sound that Windows makes.

- **High Contrast** Uses a visual scheme that is easier for the visually impaired to see than the standard Windows desktop color scheme. You can choose from a wide variety of black-and-white and color high contrast schemes.

- **MouseKeys** Allows a user to use the numeric keypad on the keyboard to control pointer movements instead of (or in addition to) using a mouse. There is a keyboard shortcut available for activating MouseKeys: the user must simultaneously press the left ALT key, the left SHIFT key, and the NUM LOCK key.

- **SerialKeys** Allows a user to use an alternative input device attached to one of the computer's serial ports instead of using a standard keyboard and mouse.

In addition to configuring these options individually by using the Accessibility Options dialog box that is accessible from Control Panel, Windows XP also provides an Accessibility Wizard that helps users configure accessibility options to suit their particular needs. Access the wizard in the All Programs/Accessories folder on the Start menu.

You really will not be called upon to do much troubleshooting of accessibility options. Instead, most users will need help enabling and configuring the options and deciding whether to use the keyboard shortcuts. However, you may occasionally get calls from users who do not use accessibility options and are surprised when Windows turns the features on after they press the right keyboard shortcut accidentally.

In addition to the accessibility options mentioned previously, Windows XP also includes three accessibility accessories, all of which you can find in the Accessories folder on the Start menu:

- **Narrator** This program works with some applications and can read text aloud from the screen using a synthesized voice.

- **Magnifier**   This tool presents an enlarged version of the area directly surrounding the pointer in a separate window, making interface elements and text easier to see for the visually impaired.

- **On-Screen Keyboard**   This tool opens a software-based keyboard in an on-screen window. Users can press the keys on the keyboard by clicking them with their mouse or other pointing device.

Practice: Support the Windows Taskbar and Start Menu

In this practice, you will configure an icon so that it is always hidden in the notification area, configure an application to start with Windows, add a shortcut to the Quick Launch toolbar, and then add the Network Connections folder to the Start menu.

Exercise 1: Configure the Notification Area

1. Right-click any open area on the taskbar and select Task Manager.

2. Minimize the Task Manager window.

3. Observe the CPU Usage icon in the notification area.

4. Right-click any empty spot on the taskbar or in the notification area, and select Properties.

5. In the Taskbar And Start Menu Properties dialog box, in the Notification Area section, click Customize.

6. In the Customize Notifications dialog box, select Current Items, and click Hide When Inactive to the right of CPU Usage in the Behavior column.

7. From the Behavior drop-down list, select Always Hide, and click OK.

8. In the Taskbar And Start Menu Properties dialog box, click OK.

9. Notice that the Task Manager icon is no longer visible in the notification area.

10. To reset the default settings for the notification area, right-click any empty spot on the taskbar or in the notification area and select Properties.

11. In the Taskbar And Start Menu Properties dialog box, in the Notification section, click Customize.

12. In the Customize Notifications dialog box, click Restore Defaults and click OK.

13. In the Taskbar And Start Menu Properties dialog box, click OK.

Exercise 2: Configure Startup Applications

1. From the Start menu, select All Programs, right-click the Startup folder, and choose Open All Users.

2. In the Startup folder, choose New on the File menu, and then choose Shortcut.

3. In the Create Shortcut dialog box, type **notepad.exe** and click Next.

4. In the Select A Title For The Program dialog box, type **Notepad** and click Finish.

5. Log off Windows and log back on. Notepad should run as soon as you log on because a shortcut for it is now in the Startup folder.

Exercise 3: Add a Shortcut to the Quick Launch Toolbar

1. Right-click any open area on the taskbar and choose Properties.

2. In the Taskbar And Start Menu Properties dialog box, in the Taskbar Appearance section, select the Show Quick Launch check box and click OK.

3. On the Start menu, point to All Programs, right-click the Accessories folder, and choose Open All Users.

4. Drag the Notepad icon from the Accessories window to a position on the Quick Launch toolbar.

5. Click the Notepad icon on the Quick Launch toolbar to open Notepad. Close Notepad when you are done.

6. To delete the Notepad shortcut from the Quick Launch toolbar, right-click the icon and choose Delete.

Exercise 4: Add the Network Connections Folder to the Start Menu

1. Right-click the Start menu and choose Properties.

2. In the Taskbar And Start Menu Properties dialog box, on the Start Menu tab, click Customize.

3. In the Customize Start Menu dialog box, on the Advanced tab, in the Start Menu Items list, locate Network Connections and select Link To Network Connections Folder.

4. Click OK.

5. In the Taskbar And Start Menu Properties dialog box, click OK.

6. Verify that the item was successfully added to the Start menu.

Lesson Review

The following questions are intended to reinforce key information presented in this lesson. If you are unable to answer a question, review the lesson materials and try the question again. You can find answers to the questions in the "Questions and Answers" section at the end of this chapter.

1. Match the end-user request on the left with the solution on the right.

1. The Taskbar is always disappearing, and I want that to stop. I also want to be able to move the taskbar to another area of the screen.	A. Open the Taskbar And Start Menu Properties dialog box. On the Taskbar tab, select the Group Similar Taskbar Buttons check box.
2. John, my colleague down the hall, has an icon next to his Start menu that he uses to open our accounting program. I do not have any icons there. How do I create one of these icons so that I do not always have to locate the program in the Start menu or place a shortcut on the desktop?	B. Open the Taskbar And Start Menu Properties dialog box. On the Taskbar tab, select the Show Quick Launch check box. Then, on the Start menu, locate the program to display in the Quick Launch area, right-click it, and drag it there. Select Copy Here.
3. I do not have enough room on my taskbar to show all my open programs, and I have to scroll to see the additional programs. Is there some way of grouping the programs?	C. Open the Taskbar And Start Menu Properties dialog box. On the Taskbar tab, clear the Auto-Hide The Taskbar check box. Then verify that the Lock The Taskbar check box is cleared. Instruct the user to move the taskbar by dragging.
4. Can I remove or hide the icons for my anti-virus software, my pop-up stopper program, and other programs that run in the background? If I remove them, do they stop running?	D. Notification area icons can be removed by setting preferences in the program's configuration choices. If you right-click an item in the notification area and its shortcut menu lets you choose Exit or Close, the program will stop running when you choose the appropriate option.
5. In my notification area there are a lot of icons that I do not think I need. How can I get rid of them? I do not think they should be running in the background, and I do not even know what some of them are.	E. Open the Taskbar And Start Menu Properties dialog box. On the Start Menu tab, click Customize. In the Customize Start Menu (or Customize Classic Start Menu) dialog box, make the appropriate changes.

6. On my Start menu there are lots of programs that I do not need and some that I need but are not there. Can you fix that for me?

F. Click Start, and click Run. At the Run line, type **msconfig.exe** and click OK. On the Startup tab, clear the check boxes for the items that you do not want to start when the computer boots.

7. I want to be able to open My Network Places, open Control Panel, and access System Administrative Tools from the Start Menu, but I do not want my recent documents to be listed. I also do not want to see My Music, My Pictures, or any of that other stuff that is not work-related.

G. Open the Taskbar And Start Menu Properties dialog box. On the Start Menu tab, select Classic Start Menu and click Customize. Use the Add and Remove buttons to customize the menu. Apply the changes. If desired, select Start Menu to return to the default Start Menu look.

2. You want to have as few items as possible on the taskbar. Which of the following items can you easily remove from the taskbar? (Choose all that apply.)

    A. Start button

    B. System clock

    C. Notification area

    D. Quick Launch items

    E. Inactive icons in the notification area

Lesson Summary

■   To resolve problems involving the taskbar, use the Taskbar And Start Menu Properties dialog box. On the Taskbar tab, you can lock or hide the taskbar, group similar items, show Quick Launch, hide inactive icons, and keep the taskbar on top of other windows.

■   To resolve problems involving the Start menu, use the Taskbar And Start Menu Properties dialog box. On the Start menu tab, click Customize to define what should and should not appear on the taskbar, clear the taskbar of recently used programs or documents, and more.

Lesson 2: Supporting Multiple Languages

Regional and language options, available from Control Panel, define the standards and formats that the computer uses to perform calculations; provide information such as date and time; and display the correct format for currency, numbers, dates, and other units. These settings also define a user's location, which enables help services to provide local information such as news and weather. Language options define the input languages (one computer can accept input in many different languages); therefore, the computer must be configured with the proper settings. As a DST, you should be able to configure support for multiple languages or multiple locations.

After this lesson, you will be able to

- Configure the correct currency, date, and time for a user.
- Configure input languages.
- Troubleshoot language-related problems.

Estimated lesson time: 20 minutes

Understanding Regional and Language Settings

You will perform almost all regional and language configuration and troubleshooting tasks in Control Panel by selecting Date, Time, Language, And Regional Options and then selecting Regional And Language Options. Figure 4-13 shows the Regional And Language Options dialog box.

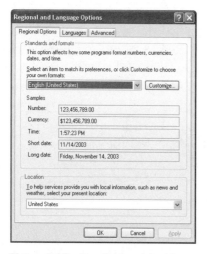

Figure 4-13   The Regional And Language Options dialog box offers a place to select available languages and customize formatting.

As a DST, you might be asked to help users configure and troubleshoot these settings. In many instances, users need to add a region or an input language because they travel, work, or live in two different countries or regions; an input language needs to be added because users who share a computer speak different languages; or a currency, time, and date need to be changed temporarily on a user's laptop while he or she is on a business trip. You will learn how to perform these tasks in the next few sections.

Configuring Correct Currency, Time, and Date

When a user requests a change to the currency, time, or date standards and formats on a computer, you make those changes in the Regional And Language Options dialog box on the Regional Options tab. Changing the standard and format is as simple as clicking the drop-down list in the Standards And Formats area and selecting a new option. In Figure 4-14, English (United States) is no longer selected; French (France) is. Notice that the date is written in French, that the currency has changed, and that the date, January 12, 2004, is written 12/01/2004, which is different from the English version, which is 1/12/2004.

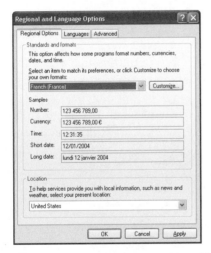

Figure 4-14   Changing standard and format options changes the currency, date, language, and more.

To make changes and to access the other regional and language options, follow these steps:

1. From the Start menu, select Control Panel.

2. In Control Panel, select Date, Time, Language, And Regional Options, and then select Regional And Language Options.

3. In the Regional And Language Options dialog box, on the Regional Options tab, in the Standards And Formats section, click the drop-down list to view the additional choices. Select one of these choices.

4. In the Location section, choose a country or region from the list to change the default location.

5. To further customize the settings, click Customize.

6. When finished, click OK in each open dialog box to exit.

Customizing Regional Options

If a user requests a specific change to the default settings—such as changing the currency symbol, the time or date format, or the system of measurement—but wants to keep other default settings intact, click Customize, as shown in Figure 4-13, and make the appropriate changes. Each option has a drop-down list, and selecting a different option requires only selecting it from the list.

Configuring Input Languages

The **input language** that is configured for the computer tells Windows how to react when a user types text using the keyboard. A user might want you to add a language if he or she works or travels between two or more countries that use different languages and he or she needs to work in those languages or perform calculations with the currencies in those countries. With multiple languages configured, the user can toggle between them as needed. In addition, users might want to change language settings even if they do not travel because they do work with an international group or conduct business with other countries.

To add (or remove) an input language, follow these steps:

1. From the Start menu, select Control Panel.

2. In Control Panel, select Date, Time, Language, And Regional Options, and then select Regional And Language Options.

3. In the Regional And Language Options dialog box, select the Languages tab, and then click Details.

4. In the Text Services And Input Languages dialog box, click Add to add a language.

5. In the Add Input Language dialog box, select the language you want to add. To choose a specific keyboard layout, select the Keyboard Layout/IME check box and choose the appropriate layout. To add a keyboard layout or input method editor (IME), you need to have installed it on your computer first. Click OK.

6. In the Text Services And Input Languages dialog box, select which language should be the default language from the Default Input Language drop-down list and click OK.

Figure 4-15 shows two available languages, English (United States)—US and Italian (Italy)—Italian. The user can now switch between these languages easily by using the Language Bar (located on the taskbar).

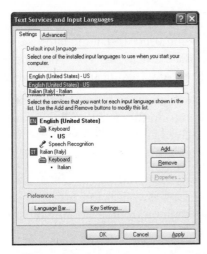

Figure 4-15   Two languages are now available for the user.

Troubleshooting Language-Related Problems

When users have multiple languages configured, language-related problems will probably occur. One of the more common issues occurs when a user who has multiple languages configured accidentally changes the default language in use by unintentionally hitting the key combination that switches between them. By default, pressing left ALT+SHIFT switches between languages. Users who accidentally use that combination might suddenly find themselves with a keyboard that does not act as it is supposed to, and they will not have any explanation for why it happened. You have to use the Language Bar to switch back to the default language, and you might want to disable this feature while you are at the computer.

Exam Tip   Consider regional settings as a possibility when keyboard errors are reported or when users report that symbols do not look correct.

The following are some other common language-related problems that you should know:

- If a user complains that, while using the On-Screen Keyboard accessibility tool, most keys on the screen do not blink when he or she presses a key on the physical keyboard, inform the user that this behavior is intended and correct. (See Knowledge Base article 294519, "On-Screen Keyboard May Not Indicate External Keyboard Activity.")

- If after installing a new IME as the default keyboard layout, the user complains that the previous keyboard layout is still being used, install the latest service pack to resolve the problem. (See Knowledge Base article 318388, "The Original Keyboard Layout Is Used After You Configure a New Default Input Method Editor.")

- If a user complains that after choosing a new language he or she cannot view the menus and dialog boxes in that language, inform the user that the Windows Multilingual User Interface Pack must be purchased and installed for these items to be changed. (See Microsoft Help And Support Center.)

Less-common and more-complex problems are covered in various articles in the Knowledge Base. Remember to search there for answers if the problem cannot be resolved through general reconfiguration and common troubleshooting techniques.

Practice: Configure Language Settings

In this practice, you will assign a different input language and disable the ALT+SHIFT language toggle keyboard shortcut.

Exercise 1: Assign Russian as the Input Language

1. From the Start menu, choose Control Panel.

2. In Control Panel, select Date, Time, Language, And Regional Options.

3. In the Date, Time, Language, And Regional Options window, select Regional and Language Options.

4. In the Regional And Language Options dialog box, on the Languages tab, in the Text Services And Input Languages section, click Details.

5. In the Text Services And Input Languages dialog box, in the Installed Services section, click Add.

6. In the Add Input Language dialog box, in the Input Language drop-down list, select Russian. Click OK.

7. In the Text Services And Input Languages dialog box, click OK.

8. In the Regional And Language Options dialog box, click OK.

9. From the Start menu, choose All Programs, Accessories, and then choose Notepad.

10. In the Untitled—Notepad window, type some random letters. Press the left ALT+SHIFT keys, and type some more random characters. Notice that the input language is toggled.

11. Close Notepad.

Exercise 2: Disable the ALT+SHIFT Language Toggle Option

1. From the Start menu, choose Control Panel.

2. In Control Panel, select Date, Time, Language, And Regional Options.

3. In the Date, Time, Language, And Regional Options window, select Regional and Language Options.

4. In the Regional And Language Options dialog box, on the Languages tab, in the Text Services And Input Languages section, click Details.

5. In the Text Services And Input Languages dialog box, in the Preferences section, click Key Settings.

6. In the Advanced Key Settings dialog box, click Change Key Sequence.

7. In the Change Key Sequence dialog box, clear the Switch Input Languages check box, and click OK.

8. In the Advanced Key Settings dialog box, click OK.

9. In the Text Services And Input Languages dialog box, click OK.

10. In the Regional And Language Options dialog box, click OK.

Lesson Review

The following questions are intended to reinforce key information presented in this lesson. If you are unable to answer a question, review the lesson materials and try the question again. You can find answers to the questions in the "Questions and Answers" section at the end of this chapter.

1. You receive a call from a user who creates blueprints for clients all over the world, and he uses the metric system instead of the U.S. system of measurement. The user's regional settings are configured to use the English (United States) standard. Which of the following is the best option for changing the default system of measurement on the user's computer from U.S. to metric?

   A. Change the default regional options for standards and formats to English (Canada). Canada is the nearest country that uses the metric system.

   B. Change the default regional options for standards and formats to English (United Kingdom). The United Kingdom uses the metric system, and many of your clients live there.

   C. Keep the English (United States) setting, but customize the measurement system to use the metric system. Do not make any other changes.

   D. Install a metric keyboard.

2. A user has multiple languages configured on her laptop and often needs access to the Language Bar. However, she does not want the Language Bar to be open continuously, taking up space on the taskbar. What can you tell the user to do? (Select the best answer.)

   A. In Regional And Language Options, remove and reinstall the languages each time she needs them.

   B. In the Text Services And Input Languages dialog box, select the Turn Off Advanced Text Services check box.

   C. Add the Language Bar to the taskbar only when it is needed by right-clicking the taskbar, pointing to Toolbars, and choosing Language Bar.

   D. None of the above. When multiple languages are configured, the Language Bar is always on the taskbar.

Lesson Summary

- To allow a user to work in different languages on one computer, make changes in the Regional And Language Options dialog box. There, you can select and configure options for currency, time, and dates and select input languages.

- When troubleshooting language-related problems, the most common problem is that a user has unknowingly switched to another language and is having problems with keyboard function.

Case Scenario Exercises

Scenario 4.1

A user reports to you that she can no longer locate her messaging program. When you ask her to explain the problem in more detail, you discover that she believed the icon was taking up too much space "in the area of the taskbar where the clock is," so she removed it by right-clicking and choosing Exit. Now she cannot find it and is afraid she has deleted it from her computer. What is the problem, and how do you help her resolve it?

_____

_____

_____

_____

_____

Scenario 4.2

After an upgrade from Microsoft Windows 2000 Professional to Windows XP Professional, a user reports that he finds the new Start menu and taskbar in Windows XP too confusing and prefers the interface used in Windows 2000 Professional. What can you do to make this user more comfortable with the new operating system?

_____

_____

_____

_____

_____

_____

_____

Troubleshooting Lab

A user tells you that he recently installed some new software that added an icon to the Quick Launch area of his taskbar. However, the Quick Launch bar is not big enough to display the additional icon, and he has to press a button with two "right arrows" to access the additional icon. He wants to enlarge the Quick Launch bar but cannot seem to do so by dragging its right edge. In fact, he says he cannot even see the right edge. What should you tell the customer?

_____

_____

_____

_____

Chapter Summary

- To resolve problems involving the taskbar, use the Taskbar And Start Menu Properties dialog box. On the Taskbar tab, you can lock or hide the taskbar, group similar items, show Quick Launch, hide inactive icons, and keep the taskbar on top of other windows.

- To resolve problems involving the Start menu, use the Taskbar And Start Menu Properties dialog box. On the Start menu tab, click Customize to define what should and should not appear on the taskbar, clear the taskbar of recently used programs or documents, and more.

- To allow a user to work in different languages on one computer, make changes in the Regional And Language Options dialog box. There, you can select and configure options for currency, time, and dates and select input languages.

- When troubleshooting language-related problems, the most common problem is that a user has unknowingly switched to another language and is having problems with keyboard function.

Exam Highlights

Before taking the exam, review the key topics and terms that are presented in this chapter. You need to know this information.

Key Points

■ Remember that items in the notification area might be hidden behind the arrow. You (or the user) might not see them, but that does not mean they are not there. Check there before you access the program's preferences or restart the program.

■ Consider regional settings as a possibility when keyboard errors are reported or when users report that symbols do not look correct.

Key Terms

input language   Tells Windows how to react when a user types text using the keyboard.

notification area   Displays the system clock and programs that are running in the background.

Start menu   Provides access to the available programs, network places, connections, help and support files, recent documents, and more.

taskbar   Displays files and programs that are currently open and running in Windows XP.

Questions and Answers

Lesson 1 Review

Page 4-20

1. Match the end-user request on the left with the solution on the right.

1. C. 2. B. 3. A. 4. D. 5. F. 6. G. 7. E.

2. You want to have as few items as possible on the taskbar. Which of the following items can you easily remove from the taskbar? (Choose all that apply.)

A. Start button

B. System clock

C. Notification area

D. Quick Launch items

E. Inactive icons in the notification area

Answers B, D, and E are correct. All of these items can be easily removed using the Taskbar And Start Menu Properties dialog box. Answer A is not correct because the Start button cannot be removed, and C is incorrect because, even though you can remove everything from the notification area, the tray itself is still visible on the taskbar.

Lesson 2 Review

Page 4-27

1. You receive a call from a user who creates blueprints for clients all over the world, and he uses the metric system instead of the U.S. system of measurement. The user's regional settings are configured to use the English (United States) standard. Which of the following is the best option for changing the default system of measurement on the user's computer from U.S. to metric?

A. Change the default regional options for standards and formats to English (Canada). Canada is the nearest country that uses the metric system.

B. Change the default regional options for standards and formats to English (United Kingdom). The United Kingdom uses the metric system, and many of your clients live there.

C. Keep the English (United States) setting, but customize the measurement system to use the metric system. Do not make any other changes.

D. Install a metric keyboard.

Answer C is correct because changing the measurement system is a customization option. No other changes are necessary. Answers A and B are incorrect because changing the default standards and formats also changes currency, time, date, and similar settings. Answer D is incorrect because there is no metric keyboard.

2. A user has multiple languages configured on her laptop and often needs access to the Language Bar. However, she does not want the Language Bar to be open continuously, taking up space on the taskbar. What can you tell the user to do? (Select the best answer.)

   A. In Regional And Language Options, remove and reinstall the languages each time she needs them.

   B. In the Text Services And Input Languages dialog box, select the Turn Off Advanced Text Services check box.

   C. Add the Language Bar to the taskbar only when it is needed by right-clicking the taskbar, pointing to Toolbars, and choosing Language Bar.

   D. None of the above. When multiple languages are configured, the Language Bar is always on the taskbar.

   Answer C is correct. The Language Bar, like other toolbars, can be added and removed from the taskbar as needed. Answer A is too drastic, and although the solution would work, this is not the best answer. Answer B does not have anything to do with the taskbar, and D is incorrect because C is the right answer.

Case Scenario Exercises: Scenario 4.1

Page 4-29

A user reports to you that she can no longer locate her messaging program. When you ask her to explain the problem in more detail, you discover that she believed the icon was taking up too much space "in the area of the taskbar where the clock is," so she removed it by right-clicking and choosing Exit. Now she cannot find it and is afraid she has deleted it from her computer. What is the problem, and how do you help her resolve it?

   The problem is most likely that the customer has just closed the program temporarily. Exiting a program from the notification area typically only closes the program. The customer can probably start the program again or restart her computer to have Windows start the program automatically.

Case Scenario Exercises: Scenario 4.2

Page 4-29

After an upgrade from Microsoft Windows 2000 Professional to Windows XP Professional, a user reports that he finds the new Start menu and taskbar in Windows XP too confusing and prefers the interface used in Windows 2000 Professional. What can you do to make this user more comfortable with the new operating system?

   There are a number of ways to make Windows XP behave more like its predecessor. To start with, the user can change the Start menu type to the Classic Start menu, which is similar to the Start menu used in previous versions of Windows. The user can also disable the feature that automatically hides inactive icons in the notification area.

Troubleshooting Lab

Page
4-30

A user tells you that he recently installed some new software that added an icon to the Quick Launch area of his taskbar. However, the Quick Launch bar is not big enough to display the additional icon, and he has to press a button with two "right arrows" to access the additional icon. He wants to enlarge the Quick Launch bar but cannot seem to do so by dragging its right edge. In fact, he says he cannot even see the right edge. What should you tell the customer?

It is likely that the customer's taskbar is locked. You should have the customer right-click any open area of the taskbar and select Lock The Taskbar (a check mark next to the command indicates its current state). After the taskbar is unlocked, the user should be able to drag the right edge of the Quick Launch toolbar to resize it. After the customer has configured the taskbar, you should encourage him to lock the taskbar again so that he cannot make any accidental changes.

5 Supporting Windows XP File and Folder Access

Exam Objectives in this Chapter:

- Monitor, manage, and troubleshoot access to files and folders
    - Answer end-user questions related to managing and troubleshooting access to files and folders
    - Monitor, manage, and troubleshoot NTFS file permissions
    - Manage and troubleshoot Simple File Sharing
    - Manage and troubleshoot file encryption
- Manage and troubleshoot access to shared folders
    - Answer end-user questions related to managing and troubleshooting access to shared folders
    - Create shared folders
    - Configure access permission for shared folders on NTFS partitions
    - Troubleshoot and interpret Access Denied messages
- Manage and troubleshoot access to and synchronization of offline files
    - Answer end-user questions related to configuring and synchronizing offline files
    - Configure and troubleshoot offline files
    - Configure and troubleshoot offline file synchronization

Why This Chapter Matters

Files, folders, and printers are the most commonly accessed resources on a computer or on a network. As a desktop support technician (DST), you must understand how Microsoft Windows XP controls these resources. You must also understand how you can secure and share resources with multiple users on the same computer and with other users on a network. This chapter focuses on supporting file and folder access in Windows XP. You will learn more about supporting printers in Chapter 9, "Managing Local and Network Printers." As a DST, you must understand the tools that Windows XP offers for managing files and folders and how to secure access to these resources.

Lessons in this Chapter:

Before You Begin

Before you begin this chapter, you should have experience working in a Windows operating system and have a basic familiarity with the Windows XP interface. You should also have a computer running Windows XP on which you can experiment with changing various settings.

Lesson 1: Managing Files and Folders

A file is a collection of data that has a name, which is called a file name. Windows supports file names up to 256 characters and appends each file name with a three-letter file extension (such as .txt or .doc) to indicate the file type. You use folders to group files. Windows allows you to configure a number of file options that govern how Windows displays and allows access to all files and folders collectively.

Files and folders also have certain attributes that control how Windows displays or allows access to the individual objects. File compression is a file attribute that increases the amount of available disk space, giving users the ability to store more data on a hard disk. File encryption is a file attribute that allows you to protect files and folders by making them unreadable by anyone except users to whom you provide access. Disk quotas allow the administrator to control how much disk space is being consumed by any particular user and to prevent a user from filling up a hard disk and causing system problems. As a DST, it is your responsibility to understand how files and folders work on a computer running Windows XP.

After this lesson, you will be able to

- Identify the types of files and folders in Windows XP.
- Identify common file and folder attributes.
- Configure folder options in Windows XP.
- Compress files and folders.
- Encrypt files and folders.
- Manage disk space using disk quotas.
- Troubleshoot folder access.

Estimated lesson time: 60 minutes

Understanding File and Folder Types

Windows XP provides access to the following types of files and folders:

- **Local**   Files and folders that are stored on the local computer.
- **Shared**   Files and folders that are shared between users. These files and folders can be shared from another computer or over the network.
- **Offline**   Files and folders from network shares that are available when you are not connected to the network. Offline files are available only in Windows XP Professional, not in Windows XP Home Edition. When you enable a shared file or folder for offline use, Microsoft Windows caches a copy of that file or folder on the

hard disk of your local computer so that while you are disconnected from the network, you can work with the local copy exactly as if it were the original. When you reconnect to the network, Windows synchronizes your cached files with the remote counterpart, so that the file or folder is current on both your local computer and the remote network share. You will learn more about offline files in Lesson 5, "Supporting Offline Files."

Understanding File Name Extensions

A file name extension is a set of characters at the end of a file name that describes the type of information that is stored in the file. For example, in the file name winword.exe, the .exe extension indicates that it is an executable file.

A file name extension can also indicate which application is associated with the file. For example, in the file name mydocument.doc, .doc is the extension that indicates that it is a Microsoft Word file.

When you access a file, Windows XP compares the file name extension to a list of installed applications so that it can launch the appropriate application for viewing that file. This process of matching an extension to an application is referred to as file association. File association determines which application will run or open the file by default.

Table 5-1 shows some common file type associations. In the far right column, additional programs are listed that can be used to open the same file. This is by no means a complete list of file types; it contains only a few of the hundreds of available file types. Users might ask you to change the program that is used to open a specific file type because they prefer one program to another or because company policy requires them to use a specific program.

Table 5-1 Common File Type Associations

File Extension	Common Default Programs	Alternate Programs
.avi	Microsoft Windows Media Player	Third-party media tools
.bmp	Paint	Microsoft Photo Editor, third-party graphics programs, Internet Explorer
.doc	Word	WordPad, Notepad, or third-party word processing programs
.gif, .jpg, .jpeg, .tiff	Paint, Windows Picture And Fax Viewer	Third-party graphics programs, Internet Explorer

Table 5-1   Common File Type Associations

File Extension	Common Default Programs	Alternate Programs
.htm, .html	Internet Explorer, Notepad	WordPad, Microsoft FrontPage, third-party Web browsers
.mp3, .wav	Windows Media Player	Third-party media tools
.txt	Notepad	WordPad, Internet Explorer, Word
.xls	Microsoft Excel	Third-party database applications

Changing the Default Way That a File Type Opens

If a user requests that a specific type of file should open with a specific program every time that file type is encountered, you need to change the details for that particular file extension to create a permanent default for that file type. For instance, if a user requests that all .gif files always open with Windows Picture And Fax Viewer, you can configure it by following these steps:

1. From the Start menu, select Control Panel.

2. In Control Panel, select Appearance And Themes.

3. In the Appearance And Themes window, select Folder Options.

4. On the File Types tab of the Folder Options dialog box, scroll down and select GIF.

5. In the Details For 'GIF' Extension area, next to Opens With: *<program name>*, click Change.

6. In the Open With dialog box, shown in Figure 5-1, click Windows Picture And Fax Viewer, and then click OK.

7. Click Close in the Folder Options dialog box.

Figure 5-1 The Open With dialog box offers personalization options for the user.

From this point on, or until this new default configuration is changed manually, all .gif files will open by using Windows Picture And Fax Viewer. You can use this same procedure to change any file type and the program it opens with.

Changing the Way That a File Type Opens One Time

If a user wants the file to open with a different program only one time, it is as simple as right-clicking. Suppose a user who has never edited a picture has one that she wants to brighten using the tools in Photo Editor, but all her graphics files open in the Windows Picture And Fax Viewer by default. You can instruct her to open the picture in another program easily by following these steps:

1. Browse to the file by using Windows Explorer or My Computer; or by opening My Documents, My Pictures, or another folder that contains the file.

2. Right-click the file, point to Open With, and then select the program from the list. The file opens in the designated program.

Note The Open With dialog box includes the Always Use The Selected Program To Open This Kind Of File check box. If you select this check box, the program will always open with this type of file. Do not select this check box if you do not want to make this program the default program.

Understanding File and Folder Attributes

You can define the following attributes (settings for files and folders) in Windows XP:

- **Read-Only**   File that can only be read; it cannot be changed or deleted.

- **Hidden**   File that is hidden from view, which protects the resource from unintended access. Windows XP hides critical system files and folders to protect them from deletion or modification. You can view hidden files and folders by selecting the option to show hidden files and folders in the Folder Options dialog box on the View tab.

- **Ready For Archiving**   File that has not been backed up recently. When a backup utility backs up a resource, it marks the resource as archived. If the resource changes in any way, the archived flag is removed.

In addition to the Hidden file attribute, Windows XP displays a warning message when the following critical files are accessed:

- **System Volume**   The entire system volume is protected from access by users with limited rights.

- **Program Files**   This folder contains the majority of application-specific files on the computer and is therefore protected.

- **Windows**   The system folder contains the operating system and is protected.

> **Note**   Any user can access hidden resources and protected folders by taking the appropriate steps if the user is not blocked by a Local or Group Policy.

Configuring Folder Options

You can use folder options to resolve many types of service calls and requests from end users. You can access folder options from Control Panel or from the Tools menu in Windows Explorer. Following are brief descriptions of the four available tabs in the Folder Options dialog box and some common tasks that you can perform by using them:

- **General tab**   Use the options on this tab to change how folders look and how they open. You can configure Windows to use Windows classic folders for a pre–Windows XP look and feel, and opening a folder inside another folder can be configured to appear in different ways. You can configure folders so that the new folder opens either in the same window or in a different one. You can also configure folders to open with a single- or double-click.

- **View tab**   Use the options on this tab to apply folder views system-wide (Details, Tiles, Icons, and so on) or to reset the folder views to their default. Configure advanced settings to remember (or not remember) each folder's view settings, to show (or not show) pop-up descriptions of folder and desktop items, to use (or not use) Simple File Sharing, to automatically search for network folders and printers, and more.

- **File Types tab**   Use the options on this tab to view, add, or reconfigure which types of files open with which particular program. When an end user requests that a specific file open with a specific program, make that change here.

- **Offline files**   You can enable and configure offline files here. When offline files are enabled, a user can work on network files even if he or she is not connected to the network. (Offline files are covered in Lesson 5.)

Supporting File Compression

File compression reduces the amount of disk space that is required to store files and increases the amount of information that you can place on a single volume. This is useful on a volume that is running low on available disk space. Windows XP Professional supports file compression on NTFS volumes only. (For more information on NTFS and file systems, see Chapter 2, "Installing Windows XP.")

You can enable compression for an entire NTFS volume, for one or more folders, or for individual files. Each file and folder has its own compression attribute that you can control on an individual basis.

Windows provides compression entirely through NTFS, and after a file or folder is compressed, that compression is transparent to applications and users. The NTFS compression filter automatically decompresses files into memory when you open them and compresses any files again when they are saved to the disk.

To enable compression of a volume, folder, or file on an NTFS partition, follow these steps:

1. In Windows Explorer, right-click the volume, folder, or file that you want to compress, and then select the Properties option from the action menu.

2. In the Properties dialog box for the volume, folder, or file, on the General tab, click Advanced.

3. In the Advanced Attributes dialog box, shown in Figure 5-2, select the Compress Contents To Save Disk Space option, and then click OK.

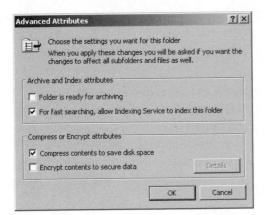

Figure 5-2   Use the Advanced Attributes dialog box to enable compression for a folder.

4. If you have selected a folder that contains files and subfolders, you will be prompted to apply compression—either to the folder only or to the files and sub-folders, as shown in Figure 5-3. Select the appropriate response and click OK.

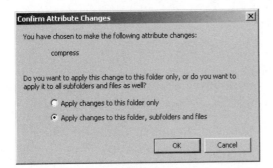

Figure 5-3   Choose the scope of compression.

Moving and Copying Compressed Files and Folders

When you move and copy compressed files and folders in Windows, those files and folders are affected in the following manner:

- When you move files and folders within the same NTFS volume, the compression attribute remains the same in the new location. For example, if files were com-pressed in the original location, they will remain compressed in the new location, even if the new parent folder is not compressed.

- When you copy files and folders within the same volume, the compression attribute is lost, and the files will take on the compression attribute of the new par-ent folder.

- When you move or copy files and folders to a different volume, the files and fold-ers take on the compression attribute of the new parent folder.

■ When you move or copy files or folders to a volume that is formatted with FAT or FAT32, compression is lost because these file systems do not support compression.

Compressed (Zipped) Folders

Windows XP contains a new feature called **compressed (zipped) folders**. You can create these folders on any FAT, FAT32, or NTFS volume, including floppy disks, and any files copied into the folders will be compressed. Compressed (zipped) folders are compatible with other programs that create zipped files, so you can easily share the compressed folders with other users, even if those users are not running Windows XP Professional or using a drive formatted with NTFS.

To create a compressed (zipped) folder, follow these steps:

1. Open Windows Explorer.

2. From the File menu, select New, and then select Compressed (Zipped) Folder.

A zipped folder is represented by a folder icon with a zipper on it, so it is easily differentiated from nonzipped folders. After you have created a zipped folder, you can drag files into the folder to compress them.

Supporting File Encryption

In Windows XP Professional, you can protect files and folders by using the Encrypting File System (EFS). EFS is not available in Windows XP Home Edition.

EFS encodes your files so that even if a person can obtain the file, he cannot read it. The files can be read-only when you log on to the computer by using your user account and password. Windows uses your user account's public key to create a file encryption key that can be decrypted only by your personal encryption certificate, which is generated from your user account's private key.

There are two restrictions when implementing EFS:

■ You cannot use EFS on storage volumes that are not formatted with NTFS.

■ You cannot use EFS to encrypt a file that has been compressed by using NTFS compression.

Although NTFS manages access to file system resources in Windows or on an internal network, when you have a dual-boot configuration, NTFS permissions can be circumvented by the second operating system. This issue is especially pertinent to portable computers because they can easily be moved or stolen, which would enable a second installation of Windows to be installed as a dual boot. The protected NTFS files would then be accessible on the second installation of Windows. EFS addresses this security issue by requiring you to enter your user account and password information before it will encrypt a file. In a dual-boot environment, the EFS-protected files would still be inaccessible.

When an unauthorized user attempts to access an EFS-encrypted resource, the user receives an "Access Denied" message. This message is similar to what a user experiences when he attempts to access an NTFS resource that he does not have permission to access.

Determining Whether a File or Folder Is Encrypted

As a DST, you may receive calls from users who are attempting to access encrypted data, and they may not understand why they cannot access certain files. To recommend an appropriate solution, you must determine whether their files are encrypted or whether they have the proper NTFS permissions.

Windows XP displays the names of encrypted files in green by default, but you can change this setting. To verify that a folder or file is encrypted:

1. Right-click the file or folder, and then click Properties.

2. On the General tab, click Advanced.

3. If the Encrypt Contents To Secure Data check box is selected, the file or folder is encrypted.

Enabling and Disabling File Encryption

In Windows XP, you can use Windows Explorer to encrypt or disable encryption on individual files or folders.

To encrypt a file or folder:

1. In Windows Explorer, right-click the file or folder, and then select Properties.

2. On the General tab, click Advanced.

3. In the Advanced Attributes dialog box, select Encrypt Contents To Secure Data.

4. Click OK twice.

If the file or folder contains any files or subfolders, the operating system displays a confirmation message that asks if you want to apply the changes to the folder only, or also to subfolders and files. If you select the Apply Changes To This Folder Only option, Windows does not encrypt any of the files that are in the folder. However, any new files that you create in the folder, including files that you copy or move to the folder, will be encrypted.

If you receive an error message when you attempt to encrypt or access an encrypted file or folder, it might indicate that EFS has been disabled on your computer by local or group policy.

EFS Recovery Agents

An EFS recovery agent is a user account that is explicitly granted rights to recover encrypted data. The purpose of a recovery agent is to allow a company to recover encrypted files on a company resource at any time if the user that encrypted the files cannot (or is not available to) decrypt them.

To grant a user account recovery agent rights, an administrator must first generate a recovery agent certificate, which grants permission to the user account to access encrypted resources. After the recovery agent rights are granted, the certificate should be removed from the computer or domain and then stored in a safe place.

You must create a recovery agent certificate before a resource is encrypted to allow the user account to access this resource. Files and folders that are encrypted before a recovery agent certificate has been created cannot be accessed by that recovery agent certificate.

If a computer is not part of a domain, there is no default recovery agent and you should create one. To create a data recovery agent, you must first create a data recovery certificate and then designate a user to be the data recovery agent.

To generate a recovery agent certificate, follow these steps:

1. Log on using a user account with administrator privileges.

2. Open a command prompt, and type **cipher /r:** *filename*, where *filename* is the name of the recovery agent certificate.

3. When prompted, type a password that will be used to protect the recovery agent certificate.

When you create the recovery agent certificate, it creates both a .pfx file and a .cer file with the file name that you specify. You can designate any user account as a data recovery agent, but do not designate the account that encrypts the files as a recovery agent. Doing so provides little or no protection of the files. If the current user profile is damaged or deleted, you will lose all the keys that allow decryption of the files.

To designate an EFS recovery agent, follow these steps:

1. Log on using the user account that you want to designate as an EFS recovery agent. This can be the Administrator account, or you may want to create a special account just for this purpose. If you create a special account, make sure that you make the account a member of the Local Administrators group.

2. Click Start, click Run, type **certmgr.msc**, and then click OK.

3. In Certificates, under Certificates—Current User, expand Personal, and then click Certificates.

4. On the Action menu, click All Tasks, click Import to launch the Certificate Import Wizard, and then click Next.

5. On the File To Import page, enter the path and file name of the encryption certificate (a .pfx file) that you exported, and then click Next. If you click Browse, in the Files Of Type box, you must select Personal Information Exchange to see .pfx files, and then click Next.

6. Enter the password for this certificate, select Mark This Key As Exportable, and then click Next.

7. Select Automatically Select The Certificate Store Based On The Type Of Certificate, click Next, and then click Finish.

8. Click Start, click Run, type **secpol.msc**, and then click OK.

9. In Local Security Settings, under Security Settings, expand Public Key Policies, and then click Encrypting File System.

10. On the Action menu, click Add Data Recovery Agent, and then click Next.

11. On the Select Recovery Agents page, click Browse Folders, and then navigate to the folder that contains the .cer file that you created.

12. Select the file, and then click Open. The Select Recovery Agents page now shows the new agent as USER_UNKNOWN. This is normal because the name is not stored in the file.

13. Click Next, and then click Finish.

The current user is now the recovery agent for all encrypted files on this computer.

Caution   All encrypted files and folders will be inaccessible if you reinstall the operating system. For this reason, make a copy of your personal encryption certificate and (if possible) the recovery agent certificate on a disk. Store the disk in a safe place. For more information about EFS best practices, see Microsoft Knowledge Base article 223316, "Best Practices for the Encrypting File System."

Managing Disk Space by Using Disk Quotas

Disk quotas allow you to track and control disk space usage. You can enable disk quotas strictly for the purpose of monitoring how much disk space each user is consuming, or you can take the additional step to create and enforce quota limits. You must manage disk quotas on a user-by-user basis; you cannot assign disk quotas to groups.

Disk quotas are available only on NTFS volumes and only in Windows XP Professional. You must configure disk quotas at the root of the volume (for example, on an entire partition). Disk quotas apply to the entire volume; you cannot configure disk quotas on a folder-by-folder basis. If you enable disk quotas on a volume that contains multiple shared folders, the total amount of disk space users can consume in all shared folders on the volume cannot exceed their quota limit for that volume. (You will learn more about sharing in Lesson 3, "Supporting Shared Folders.")

Windows calculates the amount of disk space that a user is consuming by adding up the space consumed by all the files where the user is listed as the owner. By default, the owner of a file is the user who created it. If quota limits are enforced, the amount of disk space shown as available in applications (such as Windows Explorer) will be the remaining space in the quota assigned to the user, not the total space available on the volume. When a user reaches his or her quota limit, the user must delete files to make space, ask another user to take ownership of some files, or ask an administrator to increase the quota. Also, compressed files are charged to the owner's disk quota using the uncompressed file size. If a user is approaching the quota limit, you cannot increase the user's available disk space simply by compressing files.

To configure disk quotas and enforce quota limits for all users, follow these steps:

1. In Windows Explorer, right-click the volume (C, D, and so on) that you want to enforce quota limits on, and then select Properties.

2. Select the Quota tab, as shown in Figure 5-4. If the Quota tab does not exist, either you did not select the root of the volume, the volume is not formatted with NTFS, or you are not a member of the Administrators group.

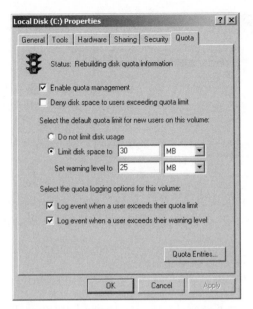

Figure 5-4   Enable disk quota management before you assign specific quotas to user accounts.

3. Select the Enable Quota Management check box.

4. If you want to limit the disk space provided to users, select the Deny Disk Space To Users Exceeding Quota Limit check box. If you just want to use disk quotas to monitor disk usage for users, do not select this option.

5. Select the Limit Disk Space To option, and configure the default quota limit and warning level. You can also select whether Windows adds an event to the Windows Event Log when users exceed their quota or their warning level.

6. Click OK to enable disk quotas. There will be a short delay while Windows XP Professional scans the volume and builds the quota information.

If you click Quota Entries on the Quota tab, you can view the amount of space used, quota limit, and warning level for each user. The Quota Entries window is shown in Figure 5-5. New users on the volume receive the default quota limit. Quota limits can be modified on a per-user basis, including the ability to assign no quota limit to particular users.

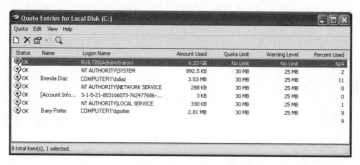

Figure 5-5   Use the Quota Entries dialog box to view quota information for users.

Users do not receive a message when they exceed their warning level or when they reach their quota limit. The drive simply acts as if it is full when the quota limit is reached.

The following are additional points concerning disk quotas:

■ By default, members of the Administrators group are not subject to disk quotas when they are enabled. However, you can enable quota limits for all users except the built-in Administrator account.

■ The user who installs a software program owns all files that are associated with that program. Make sure that the amount of space used by applications that the user may install is included in the user's quota limit.

■ You cannot delete a quota entry for a user who owns files and folders on the volume. You must either delete, take ownership of, or move the files and folders before you can delete the quota entry.

Troubleshooting Folder Access

Although there are many issues that can occur when managing files and folders, most issues occur when users try to access and configure files and folders that are corrupt or have been encrypted.

When troubleshooting management of files and folders, you can begin to develop a general idea of the problem and possible solutions by asking your user the following questions:

■ What were you trying to do when the error occurred?

■ Whose resources are you working with?

■ Where are these resources located?

■ When were the resources created?

■ How were the resources created?

■ How are you accessing the resources?

Troubleshooting Folder View Settings

When a user requests help regarding how folders are viewed, how windows open, and what can and cannot be seen inside a folder, check the configured folder options first. There, you can discover the cause of many common problems and resolve them easily.

Before starting any troubleshooting in the Folder Options dialog box, ask the user if she has made any changes there already. If she tells you that she has made changes to the folder options but cannot remember what the changes were, use the Restore Defaults button on the General tab and the View tab to restore the defaults. Many times this solves the problem. Table 5-2 shows some other common problems and their resolutions, all of which are available in the Folder Options dialog box.

Table 5-2   Common Folder View Issues and Their Solutions

Common Problem	Solution
A user reports that each time he opens a folder or clicks an icon in Control Panel, it opens a separate window. Sometimes he has 15 open windows on his desktop, and he finds it quite annoying. He wants you to change this behavior.	In the Folder Options dialog box, on the General tab, in the Browse Folders area, select Open Each Folder In The Same Window.
A user reports that she needs to view encrypted and compressed folders in a different color when using Windows Explorer to locate them. She wants to know how to do this.	In the Folder Options dialog box, on the View tab, select the Show Encrypted Or Compressed NTFS Files In Color check box.
A user reports that his coworkers often see new folders and printers in My Network Places, but he never does. He has to search for and add them manually. He wants you to resolve this problem.	In the Folder Options dialog box, on the View tab, select the Automatically Search For Network Folders And Printers check box.
Your CEO wants to be able to view and access protected system files and hidden files and folders. How do you allow this?	In the Folder Options dialog box, on the View tab, select the Show Hidden Files And Folders check box and clear the Hide Protected Operating System Files (Recommended) check box.
A user who has recently upgraded from Microsoft Windows 98 to Windows XP does not like the "Web" look that is associated with the folders and the interface. What can you do to make the user more comfortable?	In the Folder Options dialog box, on the General tab, click Use Windows Classic Folders.

Exam Tip   Review all the folder options that are available before you take the exam, but particularly remember those listed in Table 5-2.

Troubleshooting Compression Issues

Compression issues are usually related to disk space issues, moving files, and conflicts with open files. To troubleshoot compression issues, remember the following:

- You cannot use file encryption on compressed resources.

- You cannot compress open files that are currently being accessed by applications or the operating system.

- When you uncompress compressed resources, the resulting files might exceed the available space on the storage volume. This problem can also occur when you move a compressed resource to another volume and compression is lost. To resolve this issue, you must increase the amount of empty drive space or move portions of the compressed data separately.

- You should not compress high-performance areas of a volume, such as system folders, databases, and video game directories. If the user has compressed the entire volume, recommend that the user undo the compression and then recompress files and folders on a case-by-case basis.

- You can enable color coding of compressed and encrypted files for easy identification.

Troubleshooting Encryption Issues

Issues with EFS are generally caused by conflicts with domain policies, lost certificates, or operating system reinstallations. To troubleshoot EFS issues, remember the following:

- You cannot encrypt compressed resources, nor can you compress encrypted resources.

- Only the user who encrypted the resource or a user account equipped with a recovery agent certificate at the time the resource was encrypted can access the resource. If you can obtain a copy of one of the certificates, you can reestablish access; otherwise, the resource is lost.

Troubleshooting Corrupted Files

Occasionally, files can become corrupted. Corruption can occur when a user shuts down a computer or application unexpectedly, when file system problems occur, or even due to malicious activities such as viruses. To verify that files are not corrupt, do the following:

- Run Chkdsk on the volume to verify its integrity. (You can learn more about this utility in Chapter 8, "Supporting Storage Devices in Windows XP.")

- Try to copy or move the affected resources to another location or volume.

- Attempt to access the resource with an application, such as Notepad.

- Check for viruses with a third-party virus scanner.

Practice: Manage Files and Folders

In this practice, you will configure folder options and file extensions. You will also compress a folder and encrypt a folder.

Exercise 1: Configure Folder Options

1. From the Start Menu, select Control Panel.

2. In Control Panel, select Appearance And Themes.

3. In the Appearance And Themes window, select Folder Options.

4. In the Folder Options dialog box, on the General tab, in the Tasks section, select Use Windows Classic Folders.

5. In the Browse Folders section, select Open Each Folder In The Same Window.

6. In the Click Items As Follows section, select Single-Click To Open An Item (Point To Select).

7. On the View tab, in the Advanced Settings list, under Files And Folders, clear the Hide Extensions For Known File Types check box.

8. In the Advanced Settings list, under Hidden Files And Folders, select Show Hidden Files And Folders. Click OK.

9. In Control Panel, select Folder Options. On the General tab, click Restore Defaults. On the View tab, click Restore Defaults. Click OK.

Exercise 2: Configure File Extensions

1. From the Start menu, select Control Panel.

2. In Control Panel, select Appearance And Themes.

3. In the Appearance And Themes window, select Folder Options.

4. In the Folder Options dialog box, on the File Types tab, in the Registered File Types list, in the Extensions column, select TXT. In the Details For 'TXT' Extension section, click Change.

5. In the Open With dialog box, under Recommended Programs, select WordPad. Click OK.

6. Close the Folder Options dialog box, and then close Control Panel.

7. Right-click any open space on the desktop, point to New, and then select Text Document.

8. Double-click the new text document to see that it opens in WordPad instead of Notepad.

9. From the Start menu, choose Control Panel. Select Appearance And Themes, and then select Folder Options.

10. In the Folder Options dialog box, on the File Types tab, in the Registered File Types list, in the Extensions column, select TXT.

11. In the Details For 'TXT' Extension section, select Restore.

12. In the Folder Options dialog box, click Close.

Exercise 3: Compress a Folder

> **Note**   This practice requires that you have a computer running Windows XP Professional and that you have a volume formatted by using NTFS. If you do not already have a particular folder that you want to compress, create a new folder and populate it with blank text files.

1. In Windows Explorer, locate the folder that you want to compress.

2. Right-click the folder and select Properties.

3. In the Properties dialog box for the folder, on the General tab, click Advanced.

4. In the Advanced Attributes dialog box, select Compress Contents To Save Disk Space, and then click OK.

5. In the Compression Properties dialog box, click OK.

Exercise 4: Encrypt a Folder

> **Note**   This practice requires that you have a computer running Windows XP Professional and that you have a volume formatted by using NTFS. If you do not already have a particular folder you want to encrypt, create a new folder and populate it with blank text files. Note that you cannot encrypt a folder that is compressed (such as the folder you compressed in the previous exercise). If you are encrypting a folder with important contents, make sure that you follow the instructions in this chapter to designate an EFS recovery agent before encrypting the folder.

1. In Windows Explorer, locate the folder that you want to encrypt.

2. Right-click the folder and select Properties.

3. In the Properties dialog box for the folder, on the General tab, click Advanced.

4. In the Advanced Attributes dialog box, select Encrypt Contents To Secure Data, and then click OK.

5. In the Encryption Properties dialog box, click OK.

Lesson Review

The following questions are intended to reinforce key information presented in this lesson. If you are unable to answer a question, review the lesson materials and try the question again. You can find answers to the questions in the "Questions and Answers" section at the end of this chapter.

1. There are many ways to access the Folder Options dialog box. Which of the following are valid examples? (Choose all that apply.)

   A. In Windows Explorer, click Tools, and click Folder Options.

   B. In the My Documents folder, click Tools, and click Folder Options.

   C. In Control Panel, open Folder Options.

   D. In My Computer, click Tools, and click Folder Options.

   E. From the All Programs list, under Accessories, click Folder Options.

2. Which of the following allows you to open a file with an unknown file type? (Choose two.)

   A. Install the application used to create the file, and then open the file in that program.

   B. Register the file type in the Folder Options dialog box, and associate it with a program already installed on the computer that has the capability to open the file.

   C. Use the Web to determine which programs can be used to open the file.

   D. Register the file type and allow Windows to choose a program to open the file with.

3. One of your users has a computer running Windows XP Professional at her office and a portable computer running Windows XP Home Edition. She copies the contents of an encrypted folder to her portable computer, which she then takes home with her. At home, her son often needs to use her computer, so she configured a separate user account for him. She calls you to say that her son can access the contents of the encrypted folder even when logging on using his own account. What should you tell her?

_____

_____

_____

_____

Lesson Summary

- Windows XP provides access to local, shared, and offline files.

- A file name extension is a set of characters at the end of a file name that describes the type of information that is stored in the file. A file name extension can also indicate which application is associated with the file.

- File compression reduces the amount of disk space that is required to store files and increases the amount of information that you can place on a single volume. This is useful on a volume that is running low on available disk space. Windows XP Professional supports file compression on NTFS volumes only. Windows XP Home Edition does not support file compression.

- In Windows XP Professional, you can protect files and folders by using EFS. (EFS is not available in Windows XP Home Edition.) EFS encodes your files so that even if a person obtains the file, he cannot read it.

- Disk quotas allow you to track and control disk space usage. You can enable disk quotas strictly for the purpose of monitoring how much disk space each user is consuming, or you can take the additional step to configure and enforce quota limits.

Lesson 2: Supporting NTFS Permissions

As an administrator, you must give users appropriate access to files and folders while still protecting the computer as much as possible. You do this through the proper assignment of NTFS permissions. As the name suggests, NTFS permissions are available only on volumes that are formatted with NTFS. NTFS permissions allow you to control which user accounts and groups can access files and folders and specifically which actions the users can perform. NTFS permissions are in effect when users log on locally to the computer and when they connect to a resource across the network. As a DST, you must understand how NTFS permissions work and how to properly assign them to user accounts and groups.

After this lesson, you will be able to

- Identify basic file and folder permissions.
- Identify the default permissions on an NTFS volume.
- Configure advanced file and folder permissions.
- Calculate effective NTFS permissions.
- Control NTFS permission inheritance.
- Explain the effect on NTFS permissions when you move or copy files.
- Explain the concept of file ownership.
- Troubleshoot NTFS permissions.

Estimated lesson time: 40 minutes

Basic File and Folder Permissions

Every file and folder on an NTFS volume has a discretionary access control list (DACL) associated with it. The DACL contains the user accounts and groups that have been granted permissions to a resource and the specific permissions that have been granted. Each entry in the DACL is called an access control entry (ACE). A user account or a group that the user account is a member of must be listed as an ACE in the DACL for the user account to gain access to a resource. Otherwise, access is denied.

You will generally control file security by using basic folder permissions. Basic permissions allow users to perform the tasks that are most commonly required. Table 5-3 lists the six basic NTFS folder permissions.

Table 5-3   Basic NTFS Folder Permissions

Permission	Tasks Allowed
List Folder Contents	User can view the names of files and subfolders in the folder, but this permission does not allow any access to the files and folders.
Read	User can see the files and subfolders of the folder and view the properties of the folder, including permissions, ownership, and folder attributes.
Write	User can create new files and subfolders within the folder, change folder attributes, and view permissions and folder ownership.
Read & Execute	User can perform all actions that are allowed by the Read and List Folder Contents permissions and traverse folders (move through the folder to reach other files and folders that are further down in the hierarchy).
Modify	User can perform all actions that are allowed by the Write and Read & Execute permissions and delete the folder.
Full Control	User can perform all actions that are allowed by the other basic permissions, assign permissions to other users, take ownership of the folder, and delete subfolders and files.

By default, a file's DACL inherits the same entries as that of the parent folder. However, you can control permissions on individual files if necessary. Although file and folder permissions are similar to each other, there are some small differences. Table 5-4 lists the five basic NTFS file permissions.

Table 5-4   Basic NTFS File Permissions

Permission	Tasks Allowed
Read	User can read the contents of the file and view the properties of the file, including permissions, ownership, and file attributes.
Write	User can overwrite the file entirely (but not modify its contents), change file attributes, and view permissions and file ownership.
Read & Execute	User can perform all actions that are allowed by the Read permission and run application programs.

Table 5-4   **Basic NTFS File Permissions**

Permission	Tasks Allowed
Modify	User can perform all actions that are allowed by the Write and Read & Execute permissions and modify the contents of the file and delete the file.
Full Control	User can perform all actions that are allowed by the other basic permissions, assign permissions to other users, and take ownership of the file.

Viewing NTFS Permission Assignments

You can view NTFS permissions on the Security tab of the Properties dialog box of any file or folder on an NTFS volume. If the Security tab is not visible, first verify that you are working on an NTFS volume. If the volume is formatted with NTFS and you still do not see the Security tab, the computer most likely has Simple File Sharing enabled (you will learn more about Simple File Sharing in Lesson 4, "Supporting Simple File Sharing"). You must disable Simple File Sharing to access the Security tab.

To view the NTFS permissions assignments of any file or folder, follow these steps:

1. In My Computer, locate the file or folder for which you want to view the NTFS permissions.

2. Right-click the file or folder and select Properties from the action menu.

3. Select the Security tab. Figure 5-6 shows the Security tab on the Properties dialog box of a folder named Data.

Figure 5-6   Use the Security tab of a folder's Properties dialog box to assign NTFS permissions.

Objects gain permissions in one of two ways: a user specifically assigns permissions or the object inherits permissions from the parent folder.

> **Note**   When you are viewing permission assignments, Windows usually identifies a user account or group by name. However, if Windows cannot resolve the name, it displays the Security Identifier (SID) for the object instead. Windows can display the SID when the security principal is a domain account and the computer is disconnected from the network.

Understanding Default Permissions on an NTFS Volume

When an NTFS volume is created, there are a series of default permission assignments. These assignments are listed in Table 5-5.

> **Note**   The default NTFS permission assignment in previous versions of Windows was to assign the Full Control permission to the group Everyone. This permission allows a significant level of access to all users. Windows XP Professional takes a more protective approach and assigns a much more limited set of permissions.

Table 5-5   Default Permissions at the Root of an NTFS Volume

Group or User Name	Permission Assigned
Administrators	Full Control to the root, subfolders, and files
CREATOR OWNER	Full Control to subfolders and files only
Everyone	Read & Execute to the root only
SYSTEM	Full Control to the root, subfolders, and files
Users	Read & Execute to the root, subfolders, and files Create Folders/Append Data to the root and subfolders Create Files/Write Data to subfolders only

You can add, edit, and remove NTFS permission assignments from the Security tab in the Properties dialog box of the file or folder.

To add basic file and folder permission assignments, follow these steps:

1. On the Security tab of the file or folder's Properties dialog box, click Add.

2. In the Select Users Or Groups dialog box, enter the name of the object to be selected, as shown in Figure 5-7, and click OK. If you are unsure of the name of the object, click Advanced, select the object type and location, and click Find Now.

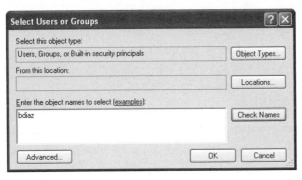

Figure 5-7   Add user accounts or groups by using the Select Users Or Groups dialog box.

3. The default permissions assignments are Read & Execute and List Folder Contents (Folders Only). Modify the permissions as necessary by selecting or clearing the individual permission boxes and click OK or Apply.

When you assign permissions, the generally recommended rule is that you grant the user the lowest level of permission that is required to access the resource in the appropriate fashion. Granting Everyone the Full Control permission will always provide access and allow users to perform any task that they need to. However, granting the Everyone group Full Control can potentially give some users too much power, and a user can accidentally (or purposefully) change or delete files and folders, and even modify permission assignments. These actions can result in application program failures and data loss.

Exam Tip   When you grant permissions, grant users the minimum permissions that they need to get their job done.

Understanding Allow and Deny Permission Assignments

For each permission, you can choose one of two states: allow or deny. In most cases, you will allow specific permissions, which provide the user with the ability to perform the specified function. If a user is not allowed a particular permission, the user cannot perform that function. If a user is not allowed any permissions at all, the user cannot access the resource.

Deny permissions, which prevent a user from performing the specified function, are used in only special circumstances. An example of deny permission usage is as follows: if a user is a member of one or more groups that have been granted permission to access a resource, but you do not want that particular user to access the resource, you can assign deny permissions to that user. The deny permission overrides the allow permission that is assigned to the group, and the user is prevented from accessing the resource. Combining different types of permissions is discussed in more detail in the section titled "Calculating Effective NTFS Permissions" later in this chapter.

Basic Permission Relationships

When selecting basic permissions, additional permissions are automatically selected in some cases. This situation occurs when the selected permission includes the actions of another permission. Table 5-6 describes these permission relationships.

Table 5-6 Permission Relationships

Selecting This Permission	Automatically Includes These Permissions
Read & Execute	List Folder Contents (Folders Only) and Read
Modify	Read & Execute, List Folder Contents (Folders Only), Read, and Write
Full Control	Modify, Read & Execute, List Folder Contents (Folders Only), Read, and Write

Advanced File and Folder Permissions

Although you can manage most permissions assignments by using basic file and folder permissions, sometimes you need to work with advanced permissions. Advanced permissions allow you to assign specific and potentially unusual levels of permission. An example of an advanced permission assignment is granting a user the ability to read the attributes (properties) of a file without being able to open the actual file.

To add advanced permission assignments, follow these steps:

1. In the Security tab of the file or folder's Properties dialog box, click Advanced. The Advanced Security Settings dialog box appears, as shown in Figure 5-8.

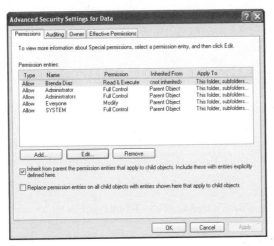

Figure 5-8   Use the Advanced Security Settings dialog box to configure advanced permissions.

2. Click Add. Select the appropriate users and groups, and then click OK to continue.

3. The Permission Entry dialog box appears next. Notice that there is no default permissions assignment.

4. Modify the permissions as necessary and click OK. You will return to the Advanced Security Settings dialog box.

5. Click OK again to return to the Security tab.

Note   If you highlight users or groups in the Security tab and they have no basic permissions assigned to them, they have an advanced permissions assignment.

Calculating Effective NTFS Permissions

A user can receive NTFS permissions from multiple sources. You can assign permissions directly to a user, permissions can be inherited from a parent folder, or a user might receive permissions based on group membership. **Effective NTFS permissions** are the permission levels that a user actually has after combining the permissions from all sources.

The rules for calculating effective permissions are as follows:

■ Allow permissions from all sources are combined, and the user receives the highest possible level of permission.

■ Deny permissions override allow permissions.

■ If a user has not been assigned any permission from any sources, access is denied.

The following sections provide several examples of effective permission calculations. In all cases, we are looking at permissions for the user JSmith, who is a member of the Managers, IT, and Everyone groups.

Calculating Allow Permissions

When calculating effective permissions, allow permissions from all sources are combined, and the user receives the highest possible level of permission. However, if the user has not been assigned permissions from any sources, access is denied. Table 5-7 illustrates several examples of combining allow permissions and the resulting effective permissions.

Table 5-7   Calculating Effective Permissions, Allow Permissions Only

Example Number	User or Group	Allow Permissions Assigned to User or Group	JSmith's Effective Permission
1	JSmith (user)	(None assigned)	Modify
	Managers (group)	Modify	
	IT (group)	Write	
	Everyone (group)	Read	
2	JSmith (user)	Read	Full Control
	Managers (group)	Full Control	
	IT (group)	(None assigned)	
	Everyone (group)	Write	
3	JSmith (user)	(None assigned)	Access Denied
	Managers (group)	(None assigned)	
	IT (group)	(None assigned)	
	Everyone (group)	(None assigned)	

The effective permission calculations in Table 5-7 are as follows:

- **Example 1**   Modify is the highest level of permission assigned to the user or any group the user is a member of, and is therefore the effective permission.

- **Example 2**   Full Control is the highest level of permission assigned to the user or any group the user is a member of, and is therefore the effective permission.

- **Example 3**   No permissions have been assigned to the user or any group the user is a member of. The user cannot access the resource.

These types of calculations are fairly simple and are most likely the types of calculations that you will need to perform.

Determining the Effect of Deny Permissions

Deny permissions override allow permissions. If a deny permission has been assigned to the user or to any group that the user is a member of, that permission is denied. When the permission is denied, any related permission will also be denied (refer to Table 5-6 for permission relationships). Table 5-8 provides two examples of the way effective permissions are calculated when deny permissions are involved.

Table 5-8   Calculating Effective Permissions When Deny Permissions Are Assigned

Example Number	User or Group	Allow Permissions Assigned to User or Group	JSmith's Effective Permission
1	JSmith (user) Managers (group) IT (group) Everyone (group)	Write–Allow Read–Deny (None assigned) Full Control–Allow	Write
2	JSmith (user) Managers (group) IT (group) Everyone (group)	Full Control–Deny Write–Allow (None assigned) Read–Allow	Access Denied

The following points demonstrate effective permission calculations for the scenarios outlined in Table 5-8:

- **Example 1**   The group Managers is denied the Read permission. The Full Control permission assigned to the group Everyone is also denied because Read is related to Full Control. The Write permission allowed to JSmith is allowed because it is not related to the Read permission. The effective permission is therefore Write.

- **Example 2**   JSmith is denied Full Control. The Write permission assigned to Managers and the Read permission assigned to Everyone are also denied because they are related to Full Control. Access is denied because no permissions have been allowed.

Calculation of effective permissions when deny permissions have been applied is difficult. Because it is easy to make a permissions assignment error when deny permissions are involved, it is recommended that you do not assign deny permissions except when you have no alternative.

Viewing Effective Permissions

Windows XP contains an Effective Permissions tab in Advanced Security Settings. This is a new feature that was not available in earlier versions of Windows.

To view the effective permissions for a user or group, follow these steps:

1. In the Security tab of the file or folder's Properties dialog box, click Advanced.

2. In the Advanced Security Settings dialog box, select the Effective Permissions tab.

3. Click Select, choose the user or group for whom you want to view effective permissions, and then click OK. The effective permissions are displayed, as illustrated in Figure 5-9.

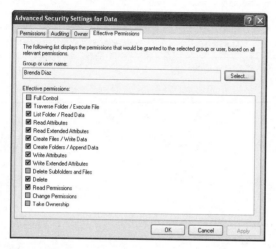

Figure 5-9   Windows XP can display the effective permissions for a user or group.

Controlling NTFS Permission Inheritance

By default, when you assign permissions to a parent folder, all files and folders in the parent folder inherit those permissions automatically. However, you can control inheritance at either the parent or child level.

To control permission inheritance on a per-user basis at the parent folder, follow these steps:

1. On the Security tab of the parent folder's Properties dialog box, click Advanced.

2. In the Advanced Security Settings dialog box for the parent folder, on the Permissions tab, select the user account or group for whom you want to control permissions inheritance, and then click Edit.

3. In the Permission Entry dialog box for the user account or group, shown in Figure 5-10, use the Apply Onto drop-down list to select one of the options listed in Table 5-9 and then click OK.

4. In the Advanced Security Settings dialog box, click OK.

5. In the Properties dialog box for the folder, click OK.

Figure 5-10   Control permission inheritance at the level of the parent folder.

Table 5-9   Controlling Inheritance from the Parent Folder

Permission	Tasks Allowed
This Folder Only	Grants permissions for the folder but none of the files or subfolders within it.
This Folder, Subfolders And Files	Grants permissions for the folder and allows those permissions to inherit to all files and subfolders within the folder. This is the default inheritance setting.
This Folder And Subfolders	Grants permissions for the folder and allows those permissions to inherit to subfolders only. Files do not inherit the permissions.
This Folder And Files	Grants permissions for the folder and allows those permissions to inherit to files only. Subfolders do not inherit the permissions.
Subfolders And Files Only	Does not grant permissions for the folder, but allows the permissions to be inherited by files and subfolders within the folder.
Subfolders Only	Does not grant permissions for the folder, but allows the permissions to inherit to subfolders within the folder only.
Files Only	Does not grant permissions for the folder, but allows the permissions to inherit to files within the subfolder only.

To block inheritance from a parent folder at the level of a child file or folder, follow these steps:

1. On the Security tab of the child file or folder's Properties dialog box, click Advanced.

2. Clear the Inherit From Parent The Permission Entries That Apply To Child Objects check box.

3. In the Security dialog box that opens, choose one of the following options:

   ❏ **Copy**   The permissions that the child object is inheriting are retained, but future inheritance from the parent folder is not allowed.

   ❏ **Remove**   The permissions that the child object is inheriting are removed, and future inheritance from the parent folder is not allowed.

   ❏ **Cancel**   The action is canceled without affecting any inherited permissions or affecting future inheritance.

4. In the Advanced Security Settings dialog box, click OK.

5. In the Properties dialog box for the child object, click OK.

Moving and Copying Files

When you move or copy files and folders on NTFS volumes, permissions can be affected. The following basic rules apply:

- When you copy files or folders to a new location, the objects do not retain permission assignments. The files or folders inherit permissions from the new parent folder.

- When you move files or folders within an NTFS volume, the objects retain permission assignments. However, inherited permissions are left behind. Permissions will be inherited from the new parent.

- When you move files or folders between NTFS volumes, the objects do not retain permission assignments. The file or folder inherits permissions from the new parent folder.

- When you move or copy files or folders to a FAT or FAT32 partition, all NTFS permission information is lost.

Exam Tip   When you move files or folders within an NTFS volume, permissions that have been directly assigned to the file or folder carry over to the new location. In all other cases, existing permissions are lost, and the object will inherit permissions from the new parent.

Understanding Ownership

By default, the owner of a file, folder, or printer is the user who created it. The owner of a resource has the ability to grant permissions and share the resource, thereby controlling access. Ownership guarantees the ability to perform these functions whether or not the owner has been granted any other level of permission.

Administrators are granted the user right to take ownership of any resource, which ensures that the administrators can always control access to all resources on the computer. Most likely, an administrator takes ownership in situations in which the current owner has left the organization and the administrator needs to gain control of the resource to manage it.

Users who are not administrators can take ownership if they have been granted the Take Ownership special permission, which is included with the Full Control file or folder permission and the Manage Printers printer permission. To view ownership and to take ownership of a file, folder, or printer, complete the following steps:

1. On the Security tab of a file or folder's Properties dialog box, access the Owner tab. You can view the current owner, as shown in Figure 5-11.

Figure 5-11   Use the Owner tab in the Advanced Security Settings dialog box to view and take ownership.

2. The Change Owner To section displays user accounts that have permission to take ownership of the object. If you are a member of the Administrators group, you have the option to change ownership to either your user account or the Administrators group.

3. Click OK.

Troubleshooting NTFS Permissions

You are working at your company's help desk supporting users who call in with problems. You have just finished resolving a logon problem call from a user who could not log on by using her user name and password. You determined that she needed to log on by using her domain credentials instead of her local user account credentials. The user has now called back and the call is forwarded to you for resolution. She tells you that she can log on without a problem; however, she cannot access some files on her local computer that she created while working from home. These files are necessary for a presentation that she is giving in one hour, and she has no time to create the information again. What can you do to help this user?

One of the biggest challenges that users encounter with permissions is knowing what the current permissions are. Whenever you work with permissions, you must take the following items into account:

- Permissions are inherited from above in the folder hierarchy.

- Permissions are cumulative, except for the deny permission.

- Permissions are assigned to users and groups.

- Windows XP computers that are members of a domain have two lists of users and groups: the local user accounts and the domain user accounts.

- The user who creates a new file or folder becomes the CREATOR OWNER who has Full Control of that object.

To resolve the caller's problem, you must determine the assigned permissions that are on the files, usually by examining the Security tab in the file's Properties dialog box. After you determine the permissions, you need to assign the appropriate permissions based on the user's needs.

Based on this caller's symptoms, you should suspect that when the user logged on to the local computer, she accessed those files using a local user account. Now that she is logging on to a domain, her domain user account does not have the necessary permissions to access the files. She should log on to the computer locally (or have an administrator do so) and grant her domain user account the permissions necessary to access the files.

Practice: Configure NTFS Permissions

In this practice, you will identify the NTFS permissions assigned to a folder, assign NTFS permissions to a user, and view the effective permissions for a user.

Exercise 1: Identify the NTFS Permissions That Are Assigned to a Folder

1. Log on to Windows XP using an account with administrator privileges.

2. From the Start menu, right-click My Documents and select Properties.

3. In the My Documents Properties dialog box, select the Security tab.

4. List the user accounts and groups that are assigned permissions to the My Documents folder, and list the specific basic permissions assigned to each account.

Exercise 2: Assign NTFS Permissions to a User Account

1. Log on to Windows XP using an account with administrator privileges.

2. From the Start menu, right-click My Documents and select Properties.

3. In the My Documents Properties dialog box, on the Security tab, click Add.

4. In the Select Users Or Groups dialog box, in the Enter The Object Names To Select window, type **Guest** and click OK.

5. In the My Documents Properties dialog box, on the Security tab, in the Group Or User Names window, select the Guest account.

6. In the Permissions For Guest window, clear the Allow check boxes for all except the Read permission.

7. Click Apply. The Guest account now has Read permissions on the My Documents folder. Do not yet close the My Documents Properties dialog box.

Exercise 3: View the Effective Permissions for a User

1. In the My Documents Properties dialog box, click Advanced.

2. In the Advanced Security Settings For My Documents dialog box, on the Effective Permissions tab, click Select.

3. In the Select User Or Group dialog box, in the Enter The Object Name To Select window, type **Guest** and click OK.

4. In the Advanced Security Settings For My Documents dialog box, in the Effective Permissions window, note the effective permissions for the Guest account. Click OK.

5. In the My Documents Properties dialog box, in the Group Or User Names window, select the Guest account and click Remove. Click OK.

Lesson Review

The following questions are intended to reinforce key information presented in this lesson. If you are unable to answer a question, review the lesson materials and try the question again. You can find answers to the questions in the "Questions and Answers" section at the end of this chapter.

1. List the basic folder and file permissions.

   _____

   _____

2. A user wants to configure NTFS permissions on a folder that contains personal information. Following your instructions, the user opens the Properties dialog box for the folder in Windows XP but does not see a Security tab. What might this situation indicate?

   _____

   _____

3. You are moving a folder named Old to a folder named New on the same volume. The volume is formatted using NTFS. Which of the following is true?

   A. The permissions on the folder named Old remain intact.

   B. The folder named Old inherits the permissions of the folder named New.

   C. All permissions on the folder named Old are lost.

   D. The permissions on the folder named Old revert to the default permissions for a new folder.

Lesson Summary

- Every file and folder on an NTFS volume has a discretionary access control list (DACL) associated with it. The DACL contains the user accounts and groups that have been assigned permissions to a resource and the permissions that have been granted. Each entry in the DACL is called an access control entry (ACE). A user account or a group that the user account is a member of must be listed as an ACE in the DACL for the user account to gain access to a resource.

- Basic file and folder permissions include the following: List Folder Contents, Read, Write, Read & Execute, Modify, and Full Control.

- When assigning permissions, you should grant the user the lowest level of permission required to access the resources in the appropriate fashion.

- For each permission, you can choose one of two states: allow or deny. In most cases, you will allow specific permissions, which will provide the user with the ability to perform the specified function. When you deny a permission, that denial overrides any allowances of the same permission that may come from other sources.

- When you calculate effective NTFS permissions, you should combine all allowed permissions. A denied permission always overrides an allowed permission.

Lesson 3: Supporting Shared Folders

Shared folders provide users with access to resources across the network. As a DST, you must understand how to share folders, how to manage shared folders, and how to troubleshoot shared folder access issues if the need arises. This lesson covers sharing folders on a computer running Windows XP Professional on which Simple File Sharing is disabled. (You will learn more about Simple File Sharing in Lesson 4.)

After this lesson, you will be able to

- Identify basic file and folder permissions.
- Configure shared folders.
- Control access to shared folders.
- Monitor the shared folders on a computer running Windows XP.
- Troubleshoot access to shared folders.

Estimated lesson time: 40 minutes

Configuring Shared Folders

The first step of providing network access to file and folder resources is to create shared folders. After you create a shared folder, network users with the appropriate permissions can connect to the folder and access resources. When a shared folder is no longer needed, you should disable the share so that it is no longer accessible from the network.

To create shared folders on a computer running Windows XP Professional, you must be a member of the Administrators or Power Users groups. Also, users who are granted the Create Permanent Shared Objects user right are also allowed to share folders. You can share only folders; you cannot share individual files. If you need to provide users network access to files, you must share the folder that contains the files.

To create a shared folder on a computer running Windows XP Professional on which Simple File Sharing is disabled, follow these steps:

1. In Windows Explorer, right-click the folder to be shared and select Sharing And Security.

2. In the Properties dialog box of the folder, on the Sharing tab, select the Share This Folder check box, as shown in Figure 5-12. By default, Windows assigns a Share Name that is the same as the name of the folder. You can change the name if you want and optionally enter a description that helps users further identify the contents of the folder. Click OK.

Figure 5-12   Share a folder by using the Sharing tab of a folder's Properties dialog box.

After you share a folder, the folder's icon will change to the shared folder icon (a folder with a hand beneath it). The shared folder icon is visible only to users who have permission to share folders. Users who do not have permission to share folders do not see this visual indicator and therefore are not aware of which folders have been shared.

> **Note**   You can also create shared folders by using Computer Management, which is discussed in the section titled "Managing Shared Folders in Computer Management" later in this chapter, and by using the NET SHARE command-line utility. For help using Netshare, execute **NET SHARE /?** from a command prompt.

Setting User Limits on Shared Folders

By default, the User Limit option on the Sharing tab of a shared folder's Properties dialog box is set to the maximum allowed, which indicates that the number of users who can connect to the share is limited only by the number of connections the computer allows. Computers running Windows XP Professional are limited to 10 simultaneous connections. There are some cases in which you may want to limit the number of users who can connect to a shared folder, including the following:

- **Licensing limits on software**   If you purchase a limited number of user licenses for a particular software program, limiting the number of users who can connect to the share and therefore run the program can help you stay within your licensing limits.

- **Performance considerations**   If an application program's performance degrades significantly with many users accessing it simultaneously, you can limit the number of users who can connect to the share to keep performance at an acceptable level.

Sharing an Existing Shared Folder with Another Name

You can share the same folder multiple times with different share names and different permissions assignments. This sharing is useful if diverse groups of users would recognize the same data more intuitively under different share names or if different users require different levels of share permissions for the same folder.

Existing shared folders have a New Share button at the bottom of the Sharing tab, as shown in Figure 5-13. This button enables you to share the folder again with a different name and a unique set of properties.

Figure 5-13   After a folder is shared, a New Share button is added that lets you create additional shares.

When you click New Share, you simply enter a name and comment, configure user limits, modify the permissions if necessary, and click OK to create the new share.

After you create an additional share, you can choose which share you want to modify by selecting it from the Share Name drop-down list on the shared folder's Properties dialog box, as shown in Figure 5-14. Also notice the addition of the Remove Share button at the bottom of the Sharing tab, which you can use to remove a selected share. When only one share name remains for a shared folder, the Remove Share button is not present. To remove the last share name, you must stop sharing the folder entirely.

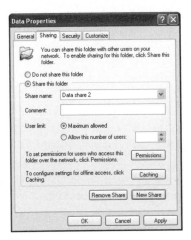

Figure 5-14   After creating additional shares, the Sharing tab changes so that you can select and modify each share.

Changing the Share Name of a Shared Folder

You cannot modify the share name of a shared folder. However, you can effectively change the share name by creating a new share name by using one of the following methods:

■ Stop sharing the folder and then share it again with the new name.

■ Use the New Share button to share the folder again with the new name. Click the Share Name drop-down list and select the old name. Click Remove Share to remove the old name.

If the share has been in existence for some time and users are already using it, you may want to share the folder again with the new name and also leave the old name in place. When you are sure that no one is connecting to the old share name any more, you can remove it.

Hidden Shares

Using a dollar sign ($) at the end of a share name creates a hidden share, which prevents users who are browsing the network from seeing the share. Users have to know the name and location of the share to connect to it. The $ is part of the share name and needs to be specified in the path.

For example, if you share the folder C:\Private with the share name Private$ on a computer named Computer1, the user has to use the following path to access the shared folder:

```
\\Computer1\Private$
```

Figure 5-15 illustrates a user connecting to a hidden share by using the Run option from the Start menu.

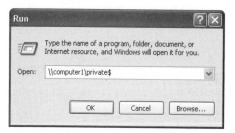

Figure 5-15   Users must know the exact name of a hidden share to connect to it.

Removing Shared Folders

When network access to a shared folder is no longer needed, you can stop sharing the folder. When you stop sharing a folder, it does not affect the folder's contents; it affects only users' ability to connect to the folder across the network.

To stop sharing a folder, select the Do Not Share This Folder option on the Sharing tab of the shared folder's Properties dialog box, and then click the OK button to continue.

Caution   If any users are connected to the shared folder when you attempt to stop sharing it, you will receive a warning message. Pay careful attention to this warning. If a user is working with files in this folder and you take the share privilege away from that user, data can be lost. If you receive this message, use the Computer Management utility to determine who is connected to the share and then contact that person before you take further action.

Additional Shared Folder Characteristics

Some general characteristics of shared folders to be aware of include the following:

- By default, the share name is the same as the name of the folder. However, you can change the share name to anything that you think is appropriate.

- Use intuitive share names and include comments that will help users identify the share's contents.

- Do not use spaces in share names if you are working with computers running Microsoft Windows 95, Windows 98, or Windows 3.*x* clients on the network. Share names with spaces do not display appropriately when those types of clients are browsing for network resources.

- Computers running Microsoft Windows NT, Microsoft Windows 2000, and Windows XP can recognize 80-character share names; Windows 95 and Windows 98 can recognize 12-character share names; and previous versions of Windows and MS-DOS can recognize only share names that follow the 8.3 naming convention. If you have client computers running previous versions of Windows that support only shorter names, consider using a naming convention that all the operating systems on the network support.

- When you copy a shared folder, the shared folder configuration does not copy with it. The new folder will not be shared.

- When you move or rename a shared folder, sharing configuration is lost. You will need to share the folder again after a move or rename operation.

Controlling Access to Shared Folders

You have just helped a caller create a shared folder on a volume that is formatted by using NTFS. Now, you need to grant both shared and NTFS permissions so that only selected users have access to the share. You gather information from the user who called with the problem, and now you must assist him with setting permissions.

To grant permissions so that only selected users can access the files, you must know how to control access to shared folders by using permissions. You can protect shared folders by using **shared folder permissions** or through a combination of shared folder and NTFS permissions. You must understand how shared folder permissions and NTFS permissions interact to ensure that users have the proper level of access to application programs and data on the network.

Shared folder permissions are in effect only when a user connects to the shared folder across the network; they have no effect when the user is accessing a resource when the user is logged on locally to the computer. This is in contrast with NTFS permissions, which are in effect both when the user logs on locally and when the user accesses the resource across the network.

Shared Folder Permissions

Shared folder permissions are simple. Unlike NTFS permissions, there is no differentiation between basic and advanced permissions. Shared folder permissions are described in Table 5-10.

Table 5-10 Shared Folder Permissions

Permission	Allows These Actions
Read	User can view file and folder names, execute applications, open and read data files, view file and folder attributes, and navigate the folder hierarchy from the level of the shared folder down.
Change	User can perform all actions that are allowed by the Read permission and create and delete files and folders, edit files, and change file and folder attributes.
Full Control	User can perform all actions that are allowed by the Change permission, modify permission assignments, and take ownership.

You grant shared folder permissions on the folder that is shared. Shared permissions are automatically inherited by all files and folders contained in the shared folder, and you cannot disable share permission inheritance—all files and folders within the shared folder have the same level of share permissions. If you need varying levels of permissions to files within a shared folder, you have to use a combination of shared folder and NTFS permissions.

Shared folder permissions are in effect only when users connect to the shared folder across the network. If a user logs on to a computer locally, the only permissions that take effect are NTFS permissions.

Viewing Shared Folder Permissions

You can view shared folder permissions on the Sharing tab in the Properties dialog box of a shared folder. To view shared folder permissions, follow these steps:

1. In Windows Explorer, locate the folder for which you want to view shared folder permissions.

2. Right-click the folder, and then select Sharing And Security.

3. Click the Permissions button to view the Share Permissions dialog box, shown in Figure 5-16. In this case, we are viewing the share permissions of a folder called Data.

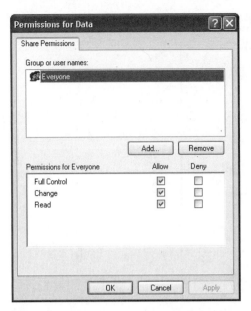

Figure 5-16 Configure share permissions using the Share Permissions dialog box.

Notice the shared folder permissions assignment in Figure 5-16. The group Everyone has been allowed the Full Control permission. This is the default shared folder permission assigned to all shared folders.

Modifying Shared Folder Permissions

You can add, edit, and remove shared folder permissions from the Share Permissions dialog box.

To add shared folder permission assignments, follow these steps:

1. In the Sharing tab of the folder's Properties dialog box, click Permissions.

2. In the Share Permissions dialog box, click Add.

3. Select the user accounts or groups to which you want to assign permissions and click OK. You are returned to the Share Permissions dialog box.

4. The default permissions assignment is Read, as shown in Figure 5-17. Modify the permissions as necessary and click OK or Apply.

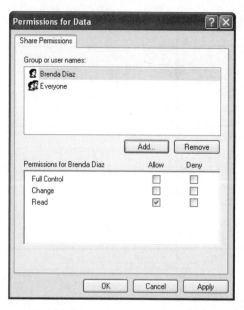

Figure 5-17 Add user accounts or groups to the Share Permissions list and then assign specific permissions.

Calculating Effective Shared Folder Permissions

The rules for calculating effective shared folder permissions are the same as those used for NTFS permissions:

- Allow permissions from all sources are combined, and the user will receive the highest possible level of permission allowed.

- Deny permissions override allow permissions.

- If a user has not been assigned any permission from any sources, access is denied.

> **Note** Shared folder permissions are the only way to control network access to resources on non-NTFS volumes. FAT and FAT32 systems do not have any local file and folder security features. When determining effective permissions on FAT or FAT32 volumes, you calculate only effective shared folder permissions.

Calculating Effective Permissions of Shared Folders on NTFS Volumes

When users connect to shared folders that are located on NTFS volumes, share permissions and NTFS permissions will combine to control the actions that a user can perform. Determining effective permissions can be somewhat difficult when both NTFS and shared permissions are involved.

Calculating effective permissions for resources within a shared folder on an NTFS partition is a three-step process:

1. Calculate the NTFS effective permissions for the user.

2. Calculate the shared folder effective permissions for the user.

3. Analyze the results of Steps 1 and 2, and select the result that is the more restrictive of the two. This will be the user's effective permission for the shared folder.

Table 5-11 illustrates effective permissions calculations for shared folders on NTFS partitions. In these examples, the user JSmith is a member of the groups Managers, IT, and Everyone. For simplicity, all permissions specified are allow permissions.

Table 5-11   Calculating Effective Permissions for Shared Folders on NTFS Partitions

Example Number	User or Group	Share Permissions Allowed	NTFS Permissions Allowed	Effective Permissions
1	JSmith (user)	(None assigned)	(None assigned)	Read
	Managers (group)	(None assigned)	(None assigned)	
	IT (group)	(None assigned)	(None assigned)	
	Everyone (group)	Full Control	Read	
2	JSmith (user)	(None assigned)	(None assigned)	Read
	Managers (group)	(None assigned)	(None assigned)	
	IT (group)	(None assigned)	Write	
	Everyone (group)	Read	Full Control	
3	JSmith (user)	(None assigned)	(None assigned)	Modify
	Managers (group)	(None assigned)	Modify	
	IT (group)	(None assigned)	Read	
	Everyone (group)	Full Control	(None assigned)	
4	JSmith (user)	(None assigned)	(None assigned)	Access Denied
	Managers (group)	(None assigned)	(None assigned)	
	IT (group)	(None assigned)	(None assigned)	
	Everyone (group)	Full Control	(None assigned)	
5	JSmith (user)	(None assigned)	Full Control	Full Control
	Managers (group)	Full Control	Read	
	IT (group)	(None assigned)	(None assigned)	
	Everyone (group)	Read	(None assigned)	
6	JSmith (user)	(None assigned)	(None assigned)	Access Denied
	Managers (group)	(None assigned)	(None assigned)	
	IT (group)	(None assigned)	(None assigned)	
	Everyone (group)	(None assigned)	Full Control	

The effective permission calculations in Table 5-11 are as follows:

- **Example 1** The user's effective share permission is Full Control, and the effective NTFS permission is Read. The more restrictive of those two permissions is Read, so it is the effective permission. Even if the share permissions allow Full Control, the NTFS permissions further limit access to the resource.

- **Example 2** The user's effective share permission is Read, and the effective NTFS permission is Full Control. The more restrictive of those two permissions is Read, so it is the effective permission. Even if the NTFS permission is Full Control, the user never has more permission than the share permissions allow.

- **Example 3** The user's effective share permission is Full Control, and the effective NTFS permission to the resource is Modify (Read and Modify combine to allow the user the maximum level). The more restrictive of the two is Modify, so it is the effective permission. Even if the share permissions allow Full Control, the NTFS permissions further limit access to the resource.

- **Example 4** The user's effective share permission is Full Control, and the effective NTFS permission is None. The more restrictive of the two permissions is None, so it is the effective permission and access will be denied. A user must be assigned permissions to gain access to a resource.

- **Example 5** The user's effective share permission is Full Control (Read and Full Control combine to give the user the maximum level), and the effective NTFS permission is Full Control (Read and Full Control combine to allow the user the maximum level). Both permissions are equal (neither is more restrictive), and the effective permission is Full Control.

- **Example 6** The user's effective share permission is None, and the effective NTFS permission is Full Control. The more restrictive of the two permissions is None, so it is the effective permission and access is denied.

You can assign different levels of NTFS permissions to file and folder resources within the same shared folder, giving users varying levels of permissions in different areas. You may need to do multiple calculations to get a full picture of the actions that a user can perform within a single shared folder.

Real World   Share Permissions on Large Networks

If you are working on home and small business networks, you are likely to find that either Simple File Sharing or share permissions are used to control access to files and folders on the network. Even when drives are formatted with the NTFS file system, most people on small networks just do not use NTFS permissions.

On large company networks, you find just the opposite. Administrators typically rely on NTFS permissions and leave the default share permissions (where Everyone has full access) in place because NTFS permissions do a much better job of securing data. Because of the way that shared permissions and NTFS permissions interact, NTFS permissions secure data for both local and network access. Adding shared permissions is really unnecessary and in fact complicates the permissions that administrators must deal with. The exception to this is on computers running earlier versions of Windows (for example, Windows 98 or Windows Me) that do not support the NTFS file system; these systems must use shared permissions if their data is to be shared on the network.

Here are some rules to follow when you are working with different kinds of networks. If you are working on a home network, users are probably using Simple File Sharing. If you are working on a small business network, users might be using Simple File Sharing or shared permissions. If all the computers on the network are running Windows 2000 or Windows XP, you might suggest moving over to the security of NTFS permissions and not worry about share permissions. If you are working on a large network, NTFS permissions are probably used, and shared permissions probably are not used. Make sure that you understand the policies of the network before you make any changes.

Administrative Shares

Several built-in **administrative shares** exist on all Windows XP computers. These shares are created automatically and cannot be unshared through conventional shared folder administration. The names of these shares all end in $, which means that they are hidden shares and cannot be viewed when users are browsing for shared folder resources.

The root of each volume is shared as drive_letter$ (that is, C$, D$, E$, and so on). Members of the Administrators and Power Users groups can connect to these shares to gain access to the entire volume. Because the shares are hidden, you must specify the path used to connect to them. For example, to connect to the root of the C drive on a server named Computer1, from the Start menu, select Run, and then type **\\Computer1\C$** in the Run dialog box.

The following are additional administrative shares:

- **Admin$**   The Windows SystemRoot folder is shared as Admin$. This share allows administrators to connect to the SystemRoot for maintenance purposes without specifically knowing the name of the folder in which Windows is installed.

- **Print$**   The SystemRoot\System32\spool\drivers folder is shared as Print$ when the first printer is shared. Client computers automatically connect to this folder to download print device drivers when connecting to shared printers.

- **IPC$**   IPC$ is the share that is used when connections are established to the computer but not to any particular shared resource. For example, if you connect to a computer by using Computer Management to manage the computer, you are not connecting to a particular shared folder. Instead, you are connecting to the IPC$ share. Interprocess communication (IPC) is a term used to describe connections between applications that are running on different computers across the network.

Managing Shared Folders in Computer Management

You can fully manage shared folders in the **Computer Management** utility. Available shared folder management options are as follows:

- View a list of all folders that are currently shared

- Create additional shared folders

- View and edit the properties of shared folders

- Remove shared folders

- View users connected to shared folders

- Remotely manage shared folders on other computers

Viewing a List of Shared Folders in Computer Management

You can view all folders that are currently shared in a single location within Computer Management. To view shared folders, follow these steps:

1. Start Computer Management, either by right-clicking My Computer and selecting Manage, or from the Administrative Tools folder in Control Panel.

2. Expand the System Tools node.

3. Under the System Tools node, expand the Shared Folders node, and then select the Shares folder. Shared folders are displayed in the details pane, as shown in Figure 5-18.

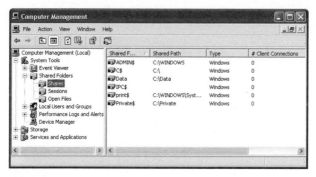

Figure 5-18   View shared folders in Computer Management.

Creating New Shared Folders in Computer Management

You can easily share folders by using Computer Management. To share a folder, complete the following steps:

1. In Computer Management, right-click the Shares folder (in the Shared Folders node) and select New File Share.

2. In the Create Shared Folder dialog box, type the path to be shared, the share name, and the share description. Click Next to continue.

3. If the folder to be shared does not exist, Windows opens a dialog box asking whether or not you want to create the folder. Click Yes to create the folder and continue.

4. In the Create Shared Folder dialog box, select the appropriate permissions option and click Finish to create the shared folder.

Viewing and Editing the Properties of Shared Folders in Computer Management

You can view and edit the properties of any shared folder through Computer Management by right-clicking the shared folder and selecting Properties. Figure 5-19 shows the Properties dialog box of a shared folder named Public. Notice the Security tab; you can also manage the NTFS permissions of the folder.

Figure 5-19   Use Computer Management to modify the properties of a shared folder.

Managing Users That Are Connected to Shared Folders

To view the users that are connected to the server, expand the Shared Folders node in Computer Management and then select the Sessions folder. Occasionally, you may need to disconnect users from the computer so that you can perform maintenance tasks on hardware or software. To disconnect users from the server, do one of the following:

■ To disconnect a single user, right-click the user name in the Sessions folder and then select the Close Session option from the action menu.

■ To disconnect all users from the server, right-click the Sessions folder and then select the Disconnect All Sessions option from the action menu.

To view users who have shared files and folders open, select the Open Files option under the Shared Folders entry, as illustrated in Figure 5-20. The details pane displays the files and folders that are currently in use on the server. This information is valuable if you are trying to work with a shared folder or file and need to know who is currently accessing the resource so that you can ask that person to disconnect.

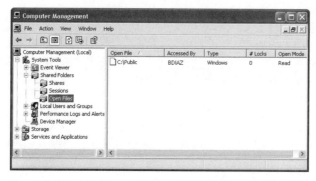

Figure 5-20   View open files and folders by using Computer Management.

Troubleshooting Access to Shared Folders in Windows XP

When you troubleshoot access to shared folders, you must examine several issues. Most of the time, you should check share permissions first. If the share permissions are not granted so that the user has at least the Read permission, the user cannot access the resource. If the folder is on an NTFS volume, examine the security settings to ensure that the user has proper permissions. Finally, determine if the share is available. (Has someone disabled sharing on the folder, or is the computer that is sharing the resource still available on the network?)

Practice: Share a Folder

> **Note**   These practices require that you have a computer running Windows XP Professional and that you have a volume formatted using NTFS. You must also have disabled Simple File Sharing.

1. Log on to Windows XP using an account with administrator privileges.
2. From the Start menu, select My Documents.
3. In My Documents, from the File menu, point to New and select Folder.
4. Type **Documents For Administrators** for the name of the folder and press ENTER.
5. Right-click the new folder and select Sharing And Security.
6. In the Documents For Administrators Properties dialog box, on the Sharing tab, select Share This Folder. Click Permissions.
7. In the Permissions For Documents For Administrators dialog box, ensure that Everyone is selected in the Group Or User Names window. Click Remove and then click Add.

8. In the Select Users Or Groups dialog box, click Advanced.

9. In the second Select Users Or Groups dialog box, click Find Now.

10. In the search pane, select Administrators and click OK. (Make sure that you select the Administrators group and not the Administrator user.)

11. In the first Select Users Or Groups dialog box, click OK.

12. In the Permissions For Documents For Administrators dialog box, under Permissions For Administrators, select the Change check box in the Allow column, and then click OK.

13. In the Documents For Administrators Properties dialog box, click OK.

Lesson Review

The following questions are intended to reinforce key information presented in this lesson. If you are unable to answer a question, review the lesson materials and try the question again. You can find answers to the questions in the "Questions and Answers" section at the end of this chapter.

1. Which of the following built-in groups in Windows XP Professional have the permissions to create shared folders by default? (Choose all that apply.)

    A. Administrators

    B. Backup Operators

    C. Power Users

    D. Users

2. One of your users is a sales executive with a folder on her computer named Customers, and she wants to share the folder with other sales executives on the network. She understands that she can secure the folder by assigning permission to access the folder to only the appropriate users. However, she prefers that other users on the network not even see the folder when they browse My Network Places on their computers. What would you name the share for this folder so that it is hidden?

    A. Customers#

    B. #Customers

    C. Customers$

    D. $Customers

Lesson Summary

- To create shared folders on a computer running Windows XP Professional, you must be a member of the Administrators or Power Users groups. Also, users that are granted the Create Permanent Shared Objects user right can share folders.

- Using a $ at the end of a share name creates a hidden share, which prevents users who are browsing the network from seeing the share. Users have to know the name and location of the share to connect to it.

- You can share the same folder multiple times with different share names and different permissions assignments. This feature is useful if diverse groups of users would recognize the same data more intuitively under different share names or if different users require different levels of share permissions for the same folder.

- You can protect shared folders through shared folder permissions or through a combination of shared folder and NTFS permissions. When shared and NTFS permissions are applied, the cumulative permissions of both are determined, and the most restrictive of those create the user's effective permission.

Lesson 4: Supporting Simple File Sharing

Simple File Sharing, as its name implies, is a simplified sharing model that allows users to easily share folders and files with other local users on the same computer or with users in a workgroup without configuring NTFS permissions and standard shared folders. Simple File Sharing is the only option on computers running Windows XP Home Edition. On computers running Windows XP Professional that are members of a workgroup, you can use Simple File Sharing, or you can disable Simple File Sharing and use NTFS permissions and shared folders. On computers running Windows XP Professional that are members of a domain, Simple File Sharing is not available. As a DST, you will encounter Simple File Sharing on home computers and on small networks.

After this lesson, you will be able to

- Share folders using Simple File Sharing.
- Troubleshoot Simple File Sharing.

Estimated lesson time: 15 minutes

Understanding Simple File Sharing

When you create a home office network with Windows XP, Simple File Sharing is enabled by default. This is exactly what it sounds like: a simple way for home users to share files on a network. When Simple File Sharing is enabled, users can share files easily and in just one step.

With Simple File Sharing, users can do the following:

- Share folders with everyone on the network
- Allow users who access the folder to view the files, edit the files, or both
- Make folders in his or her user profile private

Simple File Sharing does not permit users to do the following:

- Prevent specific users and groups from accessing folders
- Assign folder permissions to specific users and groups
- View the Security tab of a shared folder's Properties dialog box

Enabling and Disabling Simple File Sharing

To enable or disable Simple File Sharing or to see whether Simple File Sharing is in use, follow these steps:

1. From the Start menu, select Control Panel.

2. In Control Panel, select Appearance And Themes and then select Folder Options.

3. Select the View tab, and under Advanced Settings, scroll down the list of choices to the last option.

4. Simple File Sharing is enabled if the Use Simple File Sharing (Recommended) check box is selected. To disable it, clear the check box. For the purposes of this section, verify that it is selected. Click OK.

Sharing a File on the Network

After you have verified that Simple File Sharing is enabled, sharing a folder on the network is easy. Just follow these steps:

1. Using Windows Explorer, locate the folder you want to share, right-click it, and choose Sharing And Security.

2. In the Properties dialog box, select the Share This Folder On The Network check box, which is shown in Figure 5-21. Notice that a share name is automatically assigned. This is the name that the users will see when they browse the network for this shared folder. Change the name if desired; if the share must be readable to earlier operating systems such as MS-DOS and Windows 3.1, the share name must be 12 characters or fewer.

Figure 5-21   Share a file in one step when Simple File Sharing is enabled.

3. To allow others to make changes to the files in the shared folder, select the Allow Network Users To Change My Files check box and then click OK.

When sharing a folder on a network in this manner, you give permission for everyone on the network to access and read the files in the folder. With Simple File Sharing, you cannot choose who can and cannot access a folder. When you also choose to allow users to make changes to the files in the shared folder, you allow them to write to (or make changes to) those files.

> **Exam Tip**   Remember the limitations of Simple File Sharing when you are exploring a situation on the exam. Simple File Sharing is really an all-or-none proposition; the object is shared with everyone on the network or not shared at all.

Sharing a File with Other Users on the Same Computer

The Sharing tab of a folder's Properties dialog box also provides an option for sharing a folder with other users on the same computer. Such a share is called a local share. In the Local Sharing And Security dialog box, click the Shared Documents link (you can also open the Shared Documents folder from the My Computer window). Share a folder with other users on the same computer by dragging the folder to the Shared Documents folder. Anyone who is logged on to the workgroup or the local computer can access the Shared Documents folder. The folder is stored in the C:\Documents And Settings\All Users\Documents folder, as shown in Figure 5-22. Sharing a folder in this manner works only for workgroups, however—not domains.

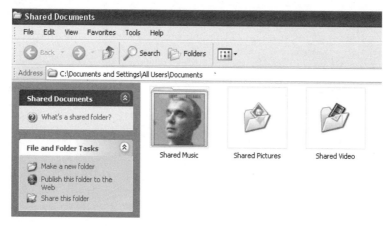

Figure 5-22   You can use the Shared Documents folder to share files on a computer or in a workgroup.

Making a Folder Private

You can also use the Sharing tab of a folder's Properties dialog box to make a folder private. When you make a folder private, only the owner of the folder can access its contents. You can make folders private only if they are in the user's personal user profile (and only if the disk is formatted with NTFS). As you learned in Chapter 3, "Supporting Local Users and Groups," a user profile defines customized desktop environments. Personal user profile folders include My Documents and its subfolders Desktop, Start Menu, Cookies, and Favorites.

Note   Simple File Sharing works on volumes formatted to use the FAT or NTFS file system. However, you can make a folder private only if the volume is formatted with NTFS.

Troubleshooting Simple File Sharing

There are only a few problems that you will run into when troubleshooting shares that are configured with Simple File Sharing, and they deal with user access to the shared resource. Assuming that all network connections are functional, all computers and hubs are working properly, and Simple File Sharing is in use, Table 5-12 details some common problems and their solutions.

Table 5-12   Troubleshooting Simple File Sharing

Scenario/Report	Cause/Solution
A Windows Me user reports that he cannot access a shared folder.	If the share name is longer than 12 characters, computers running Microsoft Windows 98 SE, Windows Me, Windows NT 4.0, or earlier Microsoft operating systems cannot access the folder. Rename the share.
An owner of a file reports that users can access the file but cannot make changes. The owner wants users to be able to make changes.	On the Sharing tab of the shared folder, select the Allow Network Users To Change My Files check box.
The owner of a file dragged the file to the Shared Documents folder and logged off the computer. When others log on, no one can access or even view the Shared Documents folders.	Users are logging on to a domain. Users must log on to the workgroup to access the file.
A user wants to share a file and assign specific permissions from the Security tab. However, the Security tab is not available.	With Simple File Sharing, the Security tab is not available. This is by design.

Practice: Work with Simple File Sharing

In this practice, you will share a document locally by using the Shared Documents folder and make a folder private. You will also share a document on the network using Simple File Sharing.

Note   These practices require that you enable Simple File Sharing on your computer. Exercise 2 requires that you have a volume formatted with NTFS.

Exercise 1: Share a Document by Using the Shared Documents Folder

1. Right-click the desktop, point to New, and select Text Document. Type **Shared Document** for the name of the document and then press ENTER.

2. Right-click Shared Document on the desktop and then select Cut.

3. From the Start menu, select My Computer.

4. In the My Computer window, open the Shared Documents folder.

5. In the Shared Documents folder, from the Edit menu, select Paste.

Exercise 2: Make a Folder Private

1. From the Start menu, select My Documents.

2. In My Documents, on the File Menu, select New, and then select Folder. Type **Private** for the name of the new folder.

3. Right-click the Private folder and select Properties.

4. In the Private Properties dialog box, on the Sharing tab, in the Local Sharing And Security section, select the Make This Folder Private check box. Click OK.

Exercise 3: Share Folders in a Workgroup by Using Simple File Sharing

1. Log on to Windows XP using an account with administrator privileges.

2. From the Start menu, select My Documents.

3. In My Documents, from the File menu, point to New and then select Folder.

4. Type **Documents for Network** as the name of the folder and then press ENTER.

5. Right-click the new folder, and select Sharing And Security.

6. In the Documents For Network Properties dialog box, on the Sharing tab, in the Network Sharing And Security section, select the Share This Folder On The Network check box. Also select the Allow Network Users To Change My Files check box and then click OK.

7. If you see a Sharing message box, click Yes.

Lesson Review

The following question is intended to reinforce key information presented in this lesson. If you are unable to answer the question, review the lesson materials and try the question again. You can find the answer to the question in the "Questions and Answers" section at the end of this chapter.

1. You receive a call from a user who manages a small business network. The business has 10 computers on a network, all running Windows XP Professional and all members of the same workgroup. One of the computers has several folders on it that the manager shares on the network, but there are certain folders that the manager does not want anyone else to access—not even other users on the same computer. The manager right-clicks the folder and selects Properties. You ask her to switch to the Sharing tab and select the Make This Folder Private check box. She says the option is there, but she cannot select it. The option is dimmed. What is the likely problem?

_____

_____

_____

_____

Lesson Summary

- Simple File Sharing is a simplified sharing model that allows users to easily share folders and files with other local users on the same computer or with users in a workgroup without having to worry about configuring NTFS permissions and standard shared folders.

- Windows XP Home Edition supports only Simple File Sharing. Windows XP Professional supports Simple File Sharing in a workgroup setting, but not when a computer is a member of a domain.

- By using Simple File Sharing, you can share folders and files with other local users on the same computer by placing the folders and files in the Shared Documents folder. You can share folders with network users using the Sharing tab of a folder's Properties dialog box.

- On volumes that are formatted with NTFS, you can also make folders private, which prevents access by other users on the same computer and users on the network.

Lesson 5: Supporting Offline Files

Offline files, which increase the availability of network files and folders, are used primarily by users of portable computers. When files and folders on network servers are made available offline, users will continue to have access to those resources even when they are not connected to the network. As a DST, you must be aware of the procedures for making files available offline and for synchronizing offline content between the client and the server.

After this lesson, you will be able to

- Enable offline files.
- Configure files for offline use.
- Synchronize offline files.

Estimated lesson time: 20 minutes

Configuring Offline Files on the Server

To use offline files, the following conditions must be met:

1. The shared folder must be made available offline. Windows configures all shared folders to be available offline by default.

2. You must configure the client computer to use the shared folder as an offline resource.

Offline files are available by default on all shared folders. To access the Offline Files configuration options for a shared folder on the computer that is sharing the folder, complete the following steps:

1. In Windows Explorer, right-click the shared folder that you want to make available offline, and then select the Sharing option from the action menu.

2. Click Caching.

3. In the Caching Settings dialog box, shown in Figure 5-23, in the Setting drop menu, select one of the following options and then click OK:

   - **Manual Caching For Documents (default setting)**   Recommended for folders containing user documents. Users are required to manually specify which documents will be cached. The server versions of the files are always opened unless the user is working offline.

   - **Automatic Caching For Documents**   Also recommended for folders containing user documents. Documents that a user accesses are automatically cached. Files that the user does not access are not cached. The server versions of the files are always opened unless the user is working offline.

❑ **Automatic Caching For Programs**   This option is recommended for application programs or read-only data. Files are automatically cached on the client, but changes cannot be copied back to the network. This effectively provides read-only caching.

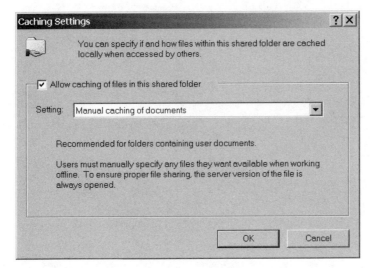

Figure 5-23   On the computer sharing the file, configure the caching (offline file) settings.

4. If you do not want the files to be available for offline use, clear the Allow Caching Of Files In This Shared Folder check box.

5. After you have made the desired settings, click OK.

Configuring Offline Files on the Client

Configuring the client for offline files is a two-part process:

1. You must enable the Offline Files feature. After you perform this action, automatic caching of documents or programs will be supported immediately.

2. For shared folders configured for manual caching, you then must configure the shared folder(s) that you want to have available offline.

To enable the Offline File feature on the client, follow these steps:

1. From the Start menu, select Control Panel.

2. In Control Panel, select Appearance And Themes.

3. In the Appearance And Themes window, select Folder Options.

4. In the Folder Options dialog box, on the Offline Files tab (shown in Figure 5-24), select the Enable Offline Files check box and then click OK.

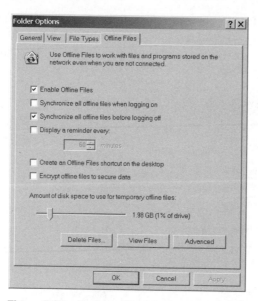

Figure 5-24   Enable offline files on the client.

> **Note**   You must disable Fast User Switching before configuring offline files.

To make a specific file or folder available offline and enable automatic synchronization with the network, follow these steps:

1. Right-click the shared folder or file that you want to make available offline, and then select the Make Available Offline option.

2. In the Offline Files Wizard's Welcome page, click Next.

3. Select the Automatically Synchronize The Offline Files When I Log On And Log Off My Computer check box, as shown in Figure 5-25, and click Next.

Figure 5-25   Enable automatic synchronization of offline files.

4. Optionally, you can enable reminders and create a shortcut to the Offline Files folder on your desktop, as displayed in Figure 5-26. Click Finish. The files will be synchronized to your computer.

Figure 5-26   Enable reminder balloons for offline files.

Files with extensions that are associated with certain database applications initially cannot be cached. By default, the following file types cannot be cached:

*.slm; *.mdb; *.ldb; *.mdw; *.mde; *.pst; *.db

Accessing Offline Files

When you make network resources available offline, Windows automatically copies them to the computer's local hard disk drive, along with a reference to the original network path. Windows stores offline files and information about the files in a database in the SystemRoot\CSC folder. (CSC is an acronym for client-side caching, which is another name for offline files.) The database emulates the network resource when it is offline.

When a user works offline, she continues to access offline resources as if she were connected to the network, but she is actually using the local copy of the file. When the network share becomes available again, the client will switch from the local offline files to the live files automatically, provided that the following conditions are met:

■ The user does not have any files currently open from that network share.

■ Synchronization is not required for any offline files in the share.

■ The user is not connecting to the network over a slow link.

If any of these conditions are not met, the user will continue to work with the offline version of the share until all files are closed and synchronization occurs.

> **Note**   Users have the same permissions to the locally stored versions of offline files as they do to the original network versions.

Synchronizing Offline Files

By default, synchronization of offline files is configured to happen at logoff when offline files are initially made available on the client. You can reconfigure or manually launch synchronization by using Synchronization Manager. You can access Synchronization Manager in the following ways:

- From the Start menu, select All Programs, Accessories, and then Synchronize.

- From the Tools menu in Windows Explorer, select Synchronize.

Figure 5-27 shows Synchronization Manager. You can force synchronization of any offline item by selecting the item and clicking Synchronize.

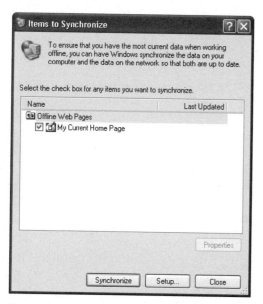

Figure 5-27   Choose an item to synchronize manually.

Clicking Setup in the Items To Synchronize dialog box opens the Synchronization Settings dialog box, depicted in Figure 5-28. You can configure synchronization to run at logon, logoff, or after a certain amount of idle time has passed. You can also schedule it to run whenever you choose. You can control these configuration options separately for each network connection. For example, you can configure different synchronization settings for a dial-up connection and for a local area network (LAN) connection. This can be useful for users who travel because you can limit the amount of synchronization that occurs over a slow dial-up link.

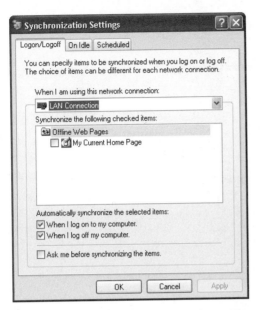

Figure 5-28   Configure synchronization settings.

Notice the Ask Me Before Synchronizing The Items option at the bottom of the figure. This is another way that you can give the user control over file synchronization.

Troubleshooting Offline File Access and Synchronization Issues

Resolving issues with offline file access and synchronization typically involves determining whether there is a connectivity problem between the computer and the server or with the user account that is currently logged on. To resolve connectivity problems between the local computer and the server where the original files are stored, refer to Chapter 10, "Supporting Network Connectivity." If the user has logged on by using an account that is different from the account that was used to create the offline files, no synchronization occurs. The offline files are not accessible to the user until the user has logged on with the proper credentials.

File Conflicts

Normally, the network version of a file is modified only when the user is working online. If the user is working offline, the local versions are modified and then uploaded to the server during synchronization. If Synchronization Manager detects that the network version of the file has been modified while a user was offline, the user is given the following options:

- **Keep Both Versions** Saves the local version to the network with a different name, that is, file name (*username* vX).doc

- **Keep Only The Version On My Computer** Saves the local version to the network

- **Keep Only The Network Version** Copies the network version to the local offline file cache

Be careful when making shared data files available offline. If many users are sharing the same offline file and they all have the ability to make modifications to it, issues can arise when the files are synchronized to the network.

Deleting Offline Files and Folders from the Cache

When files are deleted normally from a network share, they will be removed from the offline files folder (SystemRoot\CSC) as well. However, if you want to delete the offline versions of files and folders without deleting the network versions, you can follow these steps:

1. Open the Folder Options dialog box.

2. In the Offline Files tab, select View Files.

3. Select the files to be deleted.

4. From the File menu, select Delete.

If you manually delete cached files in this manner, Windows does not automatically cache the files again; you have to reselect them for caching.

Caution Do not delete offline files directly from the %SystemRoot%\CSC folder because deleting them can cause the synchronization process to cache the files again automatically.

In some cases, you might need to reinitialize the cache to relieve synchronization errors. To do that, follow these steps:

1. Open the Folder Options dialog box.

2. Select the Offline Files tab.

3. Press CTRL+SHIFT and then click Delete Files.

4. Restart the computer.

You must restart to complete the initialization of the cache. All offline files are permanently removed from the computer during this process, and they cannot be recovered.

Lesson Review

The following questions are intended to reinforce key information presented in this lesson. If you are unable to answer a question, review the lesson materials and try the question again. You can find answers to the questions in the "Questions and Answers" section at the end of this chapter.

1. List the caching options that are available when you make a shared folder available offline on the computer sharing the file.

_____

_____

2. List the steps that you must take to use offline files on a client computer.

_____

_____

3. When does Windows synchronize offline files by default? (Choose all that apply.)

   A. At logon

   B. At logoff

   C. During idle time on the computer

   D. Only when you initiate synchronization manually

Lesson Summary

- When files and folders on network servers are made available offline, users will continue to have access to those resources even when they are not connected to the network.

- All shared folders are available offline by default, though you can control the caching settings available or disable offline access.

- You must enable the Offline Files feature before you can select network shares to make available offline on the client computer. After the feature is enabled, you can select a shared folder on the network and make it available offline.

- Offline files are synchronized at logon and logoff by default, although you can also initiate a manual synchronization.

Case Scenario Exercises

Scenario 5.1

A user has a user home folder on a server named DATA. The administrator has assigned the user a 100-MB disk quota on the volume that contains the home folder. The user notices in My Computer that he is running low on disk space in his home folder. In an attempt to recover some space, he compresses all files in the home folder. However, after the compression, he does not notice an increase in available disk space. Why is this the case?

_____

_____

_____

_____

Scenario 5.2

A user in a small office with three employees has just purchased a new computer running Windows XP and has configured a network by using a four-port hub. She connected her three existing computers running Windows 98 and her new computer running Windows XP, and then she used the Network Setup Wizard on the computer running Windows XP to create the network. She reports that she made no other changes. After sharing a few folders, she reports that everyone on the network can view and make changes to her shared files. She wants the users on her network to be able to view the files only, not edit or change them. What should you tell the owner to do? (Choose all that apply.)

A. Disable Simple File Sharing.

B. Convert the file system of the Windows XP computer to NTFS.

C. Clear the Allow Users To Change My Files check box on the Sharing tab of each shared folder.

D. Drag the shared folders to the Shared Documents folder.

E. Upgrade all the computers to Windows XP.

Troubleshooting Lab

A user named Brenda is attempting to access a file in a shared folder on the network. Brenda is a member of the Sales group and the Managers group. Permissions are configured in the following manner:

- **NTFS Permissions**   Brenda's user account is assigned the Modify permission on the folder. The Sales group is assigned the Modify permission. The Managers group is assigned the Full Control permission.

- **Shared Permissions**   Brenda's user account is assigned the Change permission on the shared folder. The Sales group is assigned the Full Control permission on the shared folder. The Managers group is assigned the Read permission on the shared folder.

What are Brenda's effective permissions?

A. Modify

B. Read

C. Change

D. Full Control

Chapter Summary

- Windows XP provides access to local, shared, and offline files.

- A file name extension is a set of characters at the end of a file name that describes the type of information that is stored in the file. A file name extension can also indicate which application is associated with the file.

- File compression reduces the amount of disk space required for the storage of files and increases the amount of information that you can place on a single volume. This is useful on a volume that is running low on available disk space. Windows XP Professional supports file compression on NTFS volumes only. (Windows XP Home Edition does not support file compression.)

- In Windows XP Professional, you can protect files and folders by using the Encrypting File System (EFS). (EFS is not available in Windows XP Home Edition.) EFS encodes your files so that even if a person can obtain the file, he cannot read it.

- Disk quotas allow you to track and control disk space usage. You can enable disk quotas strictly for the purpose of monitoring how much disk space each user is consuming, or you can take the additional step to configure and enforce quota limits.

- Every file and folder on an NTFS volume has a discretionary access control list (DACL) associated with it. The DACL contains the user accounts and groups that have been assigned permissions to a resource and the permissions that have been granted. Each entry in the DACL is called an access control entry (ACE). A user account or a group that the user account is a member of must be listed as an ACE in the DACL for the user account to gain access to a resource.

- Basic file and folder permissions include the following: List Folder Contents, Read, Write, Read & Execute, Modify, and Full Control.

- When assigning permissions, you should grant the user the lowest level of permission required to access the resources in the appropriate fashion.

- For each permission, you can choose one of two states: allow or deny. In most cases, you will allow specific permissions, which provide the user with the ability to perform the specified function. When you deny a permission, that denial overrides any allowances of the same permission that may come from other sources.

- When you calculate effective NTFS permissions, you should combine all allowed permissions. A denied permission always overrides an allowed permission.

- To create shared folders on a computer running Windows XP Professional, you must be a member of the Administrators or Power Users groups. Also, users granted the Create Permanent Shared Objects user right can share folders.

- Using a $ at the end of a share name creates a hidden share, which prevents users who are browsing the network from seeing the share. Users have to know the name and location of the share to connect to it.

- You can share the same folder multiple times with different share names and different permissions assignments. This sharing is useful if diverse groups of users would recognize the same data more intuitively under different share names or if different users require different levels of share permissions for the same folder.

- You can protect shared folders by using shared folder permissions or by using a combination of shared folder and NTFS permissions. When shared and NTFS permissions are applied, the cumulative permissions of both are determined, and the most restrictive of those permissions create the user's effective permission.

- Simple File Sharing is a simplified sharing model that allows users to easily share folders and files with other local users on the same computer or with users in a workgroup without having to worry about configuring NTFS permissions and standard shared folders.

- Windows XP Home Edition supports only Simple File Sharing. Windows XP Professional supports Simple File Sharing in a workgroup setting, but not when a computer is a member of a domain.

- By using Simple File Sharing, you can share folders and files with other local users on the same computer by placing the folders and files in the Shared Documents folder. You can share folders with network users by using the Sharing tab of a folder's Properties dialog box.

- On volumes that are formatted with NTFS, you can also make folders private, which prevents access by other users on the same computer and users on the network.

- When files and folders on network servers are made available offline, users will continue to have access to those resources even when they are not connected to the network.

- All shared folders are available offline by default, although you can control the caching settings available or disable offline access.

- You must enable the Offline Files feature before you can select network shares to make available offline on the client computer. After the feature is enabled, you can select a shared folder on the network and make it available offline.

- Offline files are synchronized at logon and logoff by default, though you can also initiate a manual synchronization.

Exam Highlights

Before taking the exam, review the key points and terms that are presented in this chapter. You need to know this information.

Key Points

- When you assign permissions, grant users the minimum permissions that they need to get their job done.

- When you move files or folders within an NTFS volume, permissions that have been directly assigned to the file or folder carry over to the new location. In all other cases, existing permissions are lost and the object will inherit permissions from the new parent.

- Remember the limitations of Simple File Sharing when you explore a situation on the exam. Simple File Sharing is really an all-or-none proposition; the object is shared with everyone on the network or not shared at all.

Key Terms

disk quotas   Quotas that allow you to control the amount of disk space that any individual user can occupy.

effective permissions   The permissions level that a user actually has, taking all permission sources into account.

hidden share   A method of preventing users who are browsing the network from viewing the share. If you append the dollar sign ($) to a share name, it becomes hidden.

offline files   Files and folders that are available to a user when the user is no longer connected to the network share.

owner   The user who created a file, folder, or printer.

Shared Documents folder   The folder used in Simple File Sharing that contains all shared files and folders.

shared folders   Folders made accessible to users on the network.

Simple File Sharing   A type of sharing that is used when a Windows XP computer has not joined a domain or is running Windows XP Home Edition.

Questions and Answers

Lesson 1 Review

Page
5-21

1. There are many ways to access the Folder Options dialog box. Which of the following are valid examples? (Choose all that apply.)

    A. In Windows Explorer, click Tools, and click Folder Options.

    B. In the My Documents folder, click Tools, and click Folder Options.

    C. In Control Panel, open Folder Options.

    D. In My Computer, click Tools, and click Folder Options.

    E. From the All Programs list, under Accessories, click Folder Options.

    Answers A, B, C, and D all offer ways to open folder options. Answer E does not.

2. Which of the following allows you to open a file with an unknown file type? (Choose two.)

    A. Install the application used to create the file, and then open the file in that program.

    B. Register the file type in the Folder Options dialog box, and associate it with a program already installed on the computer that has the capability to open the file.

    C. Use the Web to determine which programs can be used to open the file.

    D. Register the file type and allow Windows to choose a program to open the file with.

    Answers A and B are correct. Answer A is correct because installing the application used to create the file allows a user to open that file. Answer B is correct because the file type is registered and a program is available to open the file. Answer C is incorrect because a compatible program must be installed or available, and simply knowing what programs can be used to open the file is not enough. Answer D is incorrect because Windows cannot automatically select a program; it is done manually.

3. One of your users has a computer running Windows XP Professional at her office and a portable computer running Windows XP Home Edition. She copies the contents of an encrypted folder to her portable computer, which she then takes home with her. At home, her son often needs to use her computer, so she configured a separate user account for him. She calls you to say that her son can access the contents of the encrypted folder even when logging on using his own account. What should you tell her?

Windows XP Home Edition does not support file encryption. When the user copied the encrypted folder to the portable computer, file encryption on the folder was lost. The user has to upgrade her portable computer to Windows XP Professional if she needs to maintain file encryption.

Lesson 2 Review

Page 5-38

1. List the basic folder and file permissions.

The basic NTFS folder and file permissions are List Folder Contents, Read, Write, Read & Execute, Modify, and Full Control.

2. A user wants to configure NTFS permissions on a folder that contains personal information. Following your instructions, the user opens the Properties dialog box for the folder in Windows XP but does not see a Security tab. What might this situation indicate?

The absence of the Security tab might indicate that the user is running Windows XP Home Edition (which does not support NTFS permissions) or that the volume is not formatted with NTFS.

3. You are moving a folder named Old to a folder named New on the same volume. The volume is formatted using NTFS. Which of the following is true?

A. The permissions on the folder named Old remain intact.

B. The folder named Old inherits the permissions of the folder named New.

C. All permissions on the folder named Old are lost.

D. The permissions on the folder named Old revert to the default permissions for a new folder.

Answer A is correct. When you move files and folders to a new location on the same volume, all NTFS permissions are retained. When you copy files and folders within the same volume, the objects inherit the permissions of the folder to which you are copying. When you move or copy files and folders to a different NTFS volume, the objects inherit the permissions of the folder to which you are copying. When you move or copy files and folders to a volume that is not formatted with NTFS, permissions are lost. Answers B, C, and D are not correct because the permissions remain intact.

Lesson 3 Review

Page 5-56

1. Which of the following built-in groups in Windows XP Professional have the permissions to create shared folders by default? (Choose all that apply.)

A. Administrators

B. Backup Operators

C. Power Users

D. Users

Answers A and C are correct. Members of the Administrators and Power Users groups have the permission to create shared folders by default. Answers B and D are not correct because these groups do not have the permission to create shared folders by default.

2. One of your users is a sales executive with a folder on her computer named Customers, and she wants to share the folder with other sales executives on the network. She understands that she can secure the folder by assigning permission to access the folder to only the appropriate users. However, she prefers that other users on the network not even see the folder when they browse My Network Places on their computers. What would you name the share for this folder so that it is hidden?

   A. Customers#

   B. #Customers

   C. Customers$

   D. $Customers

Answer C is correct. To create a hidden share, you must add a dollar sign to the end of the share name. Answers A and B are not correct because using the pound sign does not create a hidden share. Answer D is not correct because you must add the dollar sign to the end of the share name, not the beginning.

Lesson 4 Review

Page
5-63

1. You receive a call from a user who manages a small business network. The business has 10 computers on a network, all running Windows XP Professional and all members of the same workgroup. One of the computers has several folders on it that the manager shares on the network, but there are certain folders that the manager does not want anyone else to access—not even other users on the same computer. The manager right-clicks the folder and selects Properties. You ask her to switch to the Sharing tab and select the Make This Folder Private check box. She says the option is there, but she cannot select it. The option is dimmed. What is the likely problem?

The Make This Folder Private checkbox is available only on volumes formatted with NTFS. It is likely that the manager's computer has a volume formatted with the FAT file system.

Lesson 5 Review

Page
5-71

1. List the caching options that are available when you make a shared folder available offline on the computer sharing the file.

The available caching options are Manual Caching For Documents (the default setting), Automatic Caching For Documents, and Automatic Caching For Programs.

2. List the steps that you must take to use offline files on a client computer.

First, you must enable the Offline Files feature using the Offline Files tab in the Folder Options dialog box. Next, you must access the shared network folder and make it available offline.

3. When does Windows synchronize offline files by default? (Choose all that apply.)

   A. At logon

   B. At logoff

   C. During idle time on the computer

   D. Only when you initiate synchronization manually

Answers A and B are correct. Windows synchronizes offline files at logon and logoff by default. Answer C is not correct because files are not synchronized during idle time by default. Answer D is not correct because files are synchronized automatically at logon and logoff.

Case Scenario Exercises: Scenario 5.1

Page
5-72

A user has a user home folder on a server named DATA. The administrator has assigned the user a 100-MB disk quota on the volume that contains the home folder. The user notices in My Computer that he is running low on disk space in his home folder. In an attempt to recover some space, he compresses all files in the home folder. However, after the compression, he does not notice an increase in available disk space. Why is this the case?

Compressed files are charged to the quota as their uncompressed size, so the user will not see a difference in the available disk space after he has compressed his files. The user will need to request an increase in his disk quota, delete or move some files, or have another user take ownership of some of the files before he will see an increase in available disk space.

Case Scenario Exercises: Scenario 5.2

Page
5-72

A user in a small office with three employees has just purchased a new computer running Windows XP and has configured a network by using a four-port hub. She connected her three existing computers running Windows 98 and her new computer running Windows XP, and then she used the Network Setup Wizard on the computer running Windows XP to create the network. She reports that she made no other changes. After sharing a few folders, she reports that everyone on the network can view and make changes to her shared files. She wants the users on her network to be able to view the files only, not edit or change them. What should you tell the owner to do? (Choose all that apply.)

   A. Disable Simple File Sharing.

   B. Convert the file system of the Windows XP computer to NTFS.

   C. Clear the Allow Users To Change My Files check box on the Sharing tab of each shared folder.

D. Drag the shared folders to the Shared Documents folder.

E. Upgrade all the computers to Windows XP.

Answer C is the only correct answer because, by default, new networks that are created by using the Network Setup Wizard use Simple File Sharing. Clearing this option from the shared folders solves the problem. Answer A is incorrect because, although disabling Simple File Sharing allows the user to configure other options, disabling it does not solve the problem at hand. Answer B is incorrect because Simple File Sharing works with both FAT and NTFS. Answer D is incorrect because this technique is used to share folders with other users of the same computer. Answer E is incorrect because the computers do not need to be running Windows XP to participate in and follow the rules of a network.

Troubleshooting Lab

Page
5-73

What are Brenda's effective permissions?

A. Modify

B. Read

C. Change

D. Full Control

Answer D is correct. Brenda's effective permission is Full Control. Share permissions are combined, and the least-restrictive combination is the effective share permission, resulting in a Full Control permission. Next, NTFS permissions are combined, and the least-restrictive combination is the effective NTFS permission, resulting in another Full Control permission. Finally, effective share and effective NTFS permissions are combined, and the most restrictive of the two is applied. Because Brenda has Full Control on both the effective share and effective NTFS permissions, her overall effective permission is Full Control.

6 Installing and Managing Hardware

Exam Objectives in this Chapter:

- Configure and troubleshoot input/output (I/O) devices
- Configure and troubleshoot hardware profiles

Why This Chapter Matters

Problems with the installation, configuration, and maintenance of hardware devices account for a significant number of the issues that you will face as a desktop support technician (DST). Supporting and troubleshooting hardware means installing and configuring devices, keeping device drivers updated to ensure optimal operation, troubleshooting hardware issues, and removing devices when they are no longer connected to the computer.

Lessons in this Chapter:

Before You Begin

Before you begin this chapter, you should have a basic familiarity with working in a Microsoft Windows–based operating system and with the types of hardware that are typically used on a computer running Windows XP. You should also have a computer running Windows XP Professional.

Lesson 1: Installing Hardware

Installing new hardware on a computer is typically a three-step process. First, you must physically connect the hardware device to the computer. Second, you must install the device in Windows, which usually means installing hardware drivers and any other software that is used to control the device. Third, you must test the device to ensure that it works as you expect. This lesson focuses on installing hardware in Windows XP.

After this lesson, you will be able to

- Explain how hardware is installed in Windows XP.
- Add a hardware device to Windows XP.
- Work with hardware drivers in Windows XP.

Estimated lesson time: 20 minutes

Installing Hardware in Windows XP

It is easier to install hardware in Windows XP than in any previous version of Windows. Support for Plug and Play devices that largely configure themselves and the inclusion of more hardware drivers than ever before with Windows XP means that users are more comfortable installing hardware themselves. However, there are still many details that must be done correctly, and often users will call on you to help them install and configure new hardware.

To install any new hardware, you must perform the following general steps:

1. Connect the device to the computer. Sometimes, this means opening the computer case and adding new memory or an expansion card. Other times, it simply means plugging a new device into an external port and turning the device on.

2. Install the device drivers and other software in Windows so that the operating system can recognize and communicate with the device. Windows XP may already have the necessary drivers, or you may need to supply them.

3. Test the new device to make sure that it works properly and that it does not interfere with other devices on the computer.

Note Although the previous steps are accurate most of the time, you will occasionally encounter a device that requires a different method. For example, some devices require that you first install the drivers and software for the device and *then* connect the device to the computer. You should always read the manufacturer's instructions before installing a hardware device. If you are troubleshooting a device for a user, ask the user to locate the instructions and tell you how he or she installed the device.

Understanding Plug and Play Devices

Plug and Play is a set of specifications that is used to design and build devices that install with little or no user intervention. Windows XP Professional contains comprehensive Plug and Play support, but it relies on the hardware, device drivers, and the basic input/output system (BIOS) to provide full functionality.

Installing Plug and Play devices is usually straightforward. When the device is connected to the computer, Windows XP detects it, installs any necessary drivers, and automatically configures the device. Windows makes sure that there are no resource conflicts between the new device and other Plug and Play devices on the computer.

Note Windows XP Plug and Play support works optimally on computers that use the Advanced Configuration and Power Interface (ACPI), which is discussed in detail in Chapter 7, "Supporting Display Devices, I/O Devices, and ACPI." Windows supports the use of Plug and Play devices on older computers that use Advanced Power Management (APM) or Plug and Play BIOS, but a computer must have ACPI to support the full scope of Plug and Play features.

The level of Plug and Play support for any device depends on both the device and the device drivers. If the device supports Plug and Play but the driver does not (or vice versa), the device presents itself as a non–Plug and Play device to the operating system. This can result in a loss of functionality.

If you connect a new hardware device to a computer running Windows XP Professional and the device is not automatically recognized, the device is most likely to be one of two types:

- **A Plug and Play device that Windows does not recognize automatically** Windows XP does not recognize some Plug and Play devices until you either restart the computer or run the Add Hardware Wizard (discussed in the next section).

- **A Non–Plug and Play device**   Non–Plug and Play devices do not contain Plug and Play functionality at all. If you install a non–Plug and Play device, you must run the Add Hardware Wizard and manually install the device driver. It is your responsibility to ensure that the hardware resource settings for non–Plug and Play devices do not conflict with any other devices on the computer. Windows XP does not configure non–Plug and Play devices automatically.

Installing Hardware by Using the Add Hardware Wizard

The vast majority of devices that you, as a DST supporting Windows XP, will encounter are likely to be Plug and Play devices, which makes your job a lot easier. However, if you are supporting computers with older devices or older computers that have been upgraded to Windows XP, you may run into non–Plug and Play devices that require a little more effort to install than simply connecting the device.

You can use the Add Hardware Wizard to install and configure non–Plug and Play devices and Plug and Play devices that have been recently connected to the system, but were not automatically detected. You can also use the Add Hardware Wizard to access Windows XP troubleshooting tools for all installed hardware.

Exam Tip   For the exam, remember that you must use the Add Hardware Wizard for all non–Plug and Play devices. You can use the Add Hardware Wizard or restart the computer for Plug and Play devices that Windows does not recognize automatically.

▶   **Adding a Device by Using the Add Hardware Wizard**

To install a new device by using the Add Hardware Wizard, follow these steps:

1. From the Start menu, select Control Panel.
   (It is assumed that Control Panel is in Category View).

2. In the Control Panel window, select Printers And Other Hardware.

3. In the Printers And Other Hardware window, from the See Also list, select Add Hardware to start the Add Hardware Wizard. After reading the Welcome To The Add Hardware Wizard page, click Next.

4. The wizard searches the system for new devices and then asks whether the new hardware is attached to the computer, as shown in Figure 6-1. Select Yes, I Have Already Connected The Hardware, and then click Next.

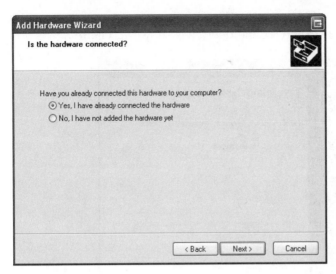

Figure 6-1   You can specify whether you have already connected the hardware device.

5. The Add Hardware Wizard displays a list of the hardware it detected, as shown in Figure 6-2. Scroll down the list to see whether you can locate the device that you want to install.

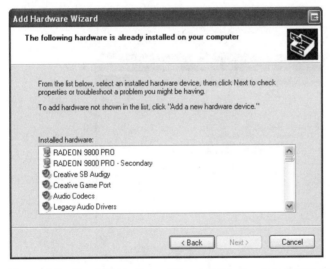

Figure 6-2   The Add Hardware Wizard displays a list of detected hardware.

6. If you find the device in the list, select the device and click Next. Windows displays the current status of the device, as shown in Figure 6-3.

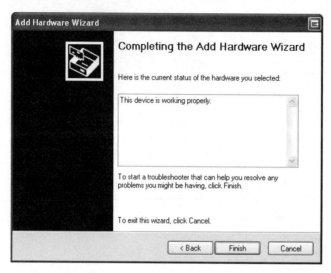

Figure 6-3   If Add Hardware Wizard detects a device, it displays the device's status.

7. If your device is not listed in the Installed Hardware window in Step 6 (see Figure 6-2), scroll to the bottom of the list and choose Add A New Hardware Device, as shown in Figure 6-4. Click Next.

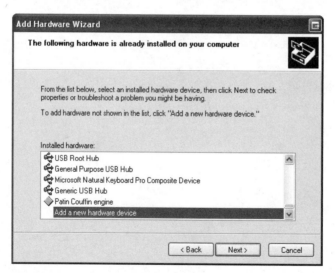

Figure 6-4   Use the Add A New Hardware Device option if the device is not detected.

8. The wizard offers to help you install other hardware, as shown in Figure 6-5. You can choose one of two options:

❑ You can have the wizard search for and install the hardware device automatically. If you choose this option and the wizard finds the appropriate device and drivers, the installation finishes. If the wizard fails to find any new hardware, it informs you that the detection has failed and prompts you to choose the device from a list.

❑ You may also skip the automatic detection and install the device manually by selecting the device from a list. The remainder of this procedure assumes that you are choosing the device from this list.

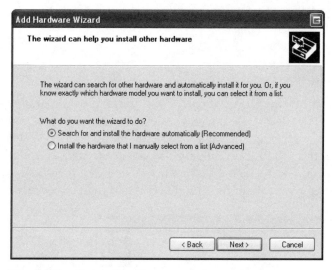

Figure 6-5   Choose whether to perform an automatic search or to select a device manually.

9. Whether you choose from the outset to select a device from a list of available hardware devices or whether you are forced to choose from the list because the Add Hardware Wizard cannot detect a new device, the process from this point is the same. The wizard displays a page with a list of device types from which you can choose, as shown in Figure 6-6. Select the correct category for your type of hardware and then click Next.

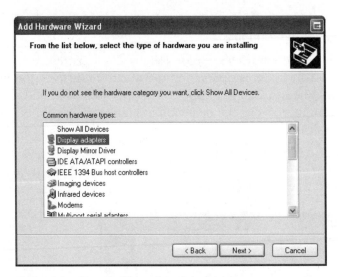

Figure 6-6   Choose from a list of device types.

10. Next, the Add Hardware Wizard displays a list of hardware manufacturers for the chosen device type in a column on the left and the different models that the selected manufacturer offers on the right, as shown in Figure 6-7. When you select a manufacturer from the list on the left, the list on the right is updated to include only the drivers that are available for that manufacturer's devices. If the device you are trying to install appears in this list, select it and then click Next to continue.

Figure 6-7   Choose the manufacturer and model of the device.

11. If the Add Hardware Wizard cannot locate the installation files, you are prompted for the location of the necessary drivers. If the device you are installing does not appear anywhere in the list, you must click the Have Disk button and provide the path to the drivers.

> **Note** It is a good idea to install the latest version of any device driver. The drivers that ship with Windows XP are current as of the release date of the installation CD. Microsoft also updates the Driver.cab file with new drivers each time they release a new service pack. If the device you are installing comes with a newer Windows XP-compatible driver, click the Have Disk option and install the new driver, rather than use the driver from the Windows XP installation CD.

12. When the installation and configuration processes are complete, the wizard displays the Completion page. If prompted, click Finish and restart your computer.

> **Tip** In some cases, Windows XP prompts you to restart the computer after a configuration change. It is not always necessary to restart immediately. If you are in the process of making several changes that will require restarting, you can try performing all the changes and then restarting only once.

Practice: Run the Add Hardware Wizard

In this practice, you will manually install the software for a printer that is not actually connected to your computer. This practice assumes that you do not already have a hardware device connected to a parallel port named LPT2 on your computer. Do not worry if you do not have an LPT2 port; the exercise will work anyway.

1. From the Start menu, select Control Panel.
(It is assumed that Control Panel is in Category View).

2. In the Control Panel window, select Printers And Other Hardware.

3. In the Printers And Other Hardware window, in the See Also section, select Add Hardware.

4. On the Welcome To The Add Hardware Wizard page of the Add Hardware Wizard, click Next.

5. The Add Hardware Wizard searches for any new Plug and Play devices, and then displays the Is The Hardware Connected page. Select Yes, I Have Already Connected The Hardware, and then click Next.

6. In the list of installed hardware, scroll to the bottom and select Add A New Hardware Device. Click Next.

7. Select Install The Hardware That I Manually Select From A List (Advanced) and click Next.

8. In the list of common hardware types, select Printers and then click Next.

9. On the Select A Printer Port page, from the Use The Following Port drop-down list, select LPT2: (Printer Port), and then click Next.

10. On the Install Printer Software page, from the Manufacturer list, select Alps. From the Printers list, select Alps MD-1000 (MS). Click Next.

11. On the Name Your Printer page, click Next.

12. On the Print Test Page page, select No and then click Next.

13. If you are using Windows XP Professional and you have Simple File Sharing disabled, you next will see a page asking whether you want to share the new printer. Select Do Not Share This Printer, and then click Next.

14. Click Finish to exit the Add Hardware Wizard.

Lesson Review

The following questions are intended to reinforce key information presented in this lesson. If you are unable to answer a question, review the lesson materials and try the question again. You can find answers to the questions in the "Questions and Answers" section at the end of this chapter.

1. Which Windows feature is the primary tool for installing and removing devices in Windows XP?

   A. Add Hardware Wizard

   B. Device Manager

   C. Ipconfig

   D. Event Viewer

2. What are the three general steps for installing a new hardware device in Windows XP?

   _____

   _____

Lesson Summary

- Plug and Play operation is supported in Windows XP, greatly simplifying the installation of devices that support that technology.

- Windows XP does not detect some Plug and Play devices automatically when they are connected. You must restart the computer or use the Add Hardware Wizard to initiate the detection and installation.

- Windows XP does not automatically detect and configure non–Plug and Play devices. You must use the Add Hardware Wizard to install non–Plug and Play devices. Often, you must also manually configure hardware resources for non–Plug and Play devices, as well.

Lesson 2: Supporting and Troubleshooting Hardware

Windows XP provides many tools for managing and troubleshooting a computer. The key tools that are used for troubleshooting hardware problems include the System Information and Device Manager utilities, and various Windows troubleshooters that can help walk you through the troubleshooting process.

After this lesson, you will be able to

- Use the System Information tool to view configuration information.
- Use Device Manager to manage hardware devices.
- Use Windows troubleshooters to help determine the cause of, and solution for a problem.
- Explain general hardware troubleshooting procedures.

Estimated lesson time: 15 minutes

Using the System Information Tool

System Information allows you to view a vast amount of Windows XP configuration information. The majority of this information is available in other utilities, but System Information consolidates it into a single source. You can easily document a system's current configuration by printing the information that is in System Information or by saving the information to a file.

You can launch System Information in two ways:

- From the Start menu, select All Programs, Accessories, System Tools, and then System Information.
- In the Run dialog box, type **msinfo32.exe**.

When you first open the System Information window, you might experience a delay while the utility scans your system for the most current configuration information. After the scan is complete, a System Summary (as shown in Figure 6-8) displays general information about the system, including the operating system version, computer name, processor type, BIOS version, and memory statistics.

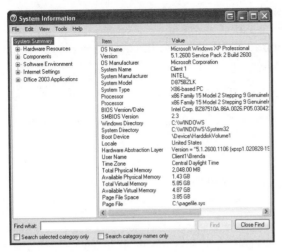

Figure 6-8   System Information provides a detailed summary of a system.

In addition to viewing the System Summary, you can also find more detailed information in the following categories:

- **Hardware Resources**   Expanding the Hardware Resources node displays resources that are in use, including interrupt requests (IRQs), I/O addresses, direct memory access (DMA), and memory addresses. You can also view conflicts and shared resources. System Information allows you only to view this information; to change resource assignments, you must use Device Manager.

- **Components**   Expanding the Components node displays a summary of the hardware components that are on the system and their associated settings.

- **Software Environment**   Expanding the Software Environment node displays device driver status, environment variables, processes that are currently running, service status, and programs that load automatically at startup.

- **Internet Settings**   Expanding the Internet Settings node displays many configuration settings that are related to Microsoft Internet Explorer. Other available information includes cipher strength, cached objects, and security configuration information.

Saving System Information

You can save the report that is displayed by System Information. Saving a report provides a way to document a system's condition at a specific point, which often is useful in troubleshooting. Also, if you have previously saved a baseline configuration of the system (a snapshot of the system when it is performing properly), you can compare the baseline information with the information at the point at which the system experiences problems and potentially determine what changes have occurred to the system that could contribute to the problem.

You can save System Information to a file in two ways:

- The Save command on the File menu saves the information to a System Information file (.nfo). Only the System Information utility can read these files. You can open, view, and print them at any time.

- The Export command on the File menu saves information to a text file, which you can then view or print from any text editor.

> **Note**   Extracting the volume of information from the system that is required to create either an .nfo or .txt file in System Information takes several minutes and may consume a noticeable amount of system resources during the export process.

Using the System Information Tools Menu

The Tools menu in System Information provides shortcuts to many other system and troubleshooting utilities. Table 6-1 lists these tools and alternate methods of accessing the tools.

Table 6-1   Tools Available through System Information

Tool	Use	Alternate Method of Accessing the Tool
Net Diagnostics	Gathers information about your computer to help troubleshoot network-related problems. For more information, see Chapter 10, "Supporting Network Connectivity."	From the Start menu, select Help And Support. In the Pick A Task section of the Help And Support Center window, select Use Tools To View Your Computer Information And Diagnose Problems. From the list of tools, select Network Diagnostics.
System Restore	Creates restore points by saving Windows configuration information. You can revert to a previous restore point to restore important configurations.	On the Start menu, select All Programs, then Accessories, then System Tools, and then System Restore.

Table 6-1 Tools Available through System Information

File Signature Verification Utility	Scans hardware drivers on a computer and displays any unsigned drivers. See Lesson 3, "Supporting and Troubleshooting Device Drivers."	Type **sigverif.exe** at the command prompt or in the Run dialog box.
DirectX Diagnostic Tool	Displays information about and lets you troubleshoot the DirectX graphics engine.	Type **dxdiag.exe** at the command prompt or in the Run dialog box.
Dr. Watson	Traps program faults so that you can troubleshoot program errors.	Type **drwtsn32.exe** at the command prompt or in the Run dialog box.

See Also   For detailed information about using Dr. Watson to troubleshoot program errors, see the Microsoft Knowledge Base article 308538, "Description of the Dr. Watson for Windows (Drwtsn32.exe) Tool."

Using Device Manager

Device Manager, as shown in Figure 6-9, displays all installed devices and provides an environment for managing those devices. Device manager allows you to perform the following types of tasks:

- View current device settings
    - View the names of the device driver files
    - Reconfigure devices
- Update device drivers
    - Scan for hardware changes
    - Remove devices
    - Enable or disable devices
    - Troubleshoot devices

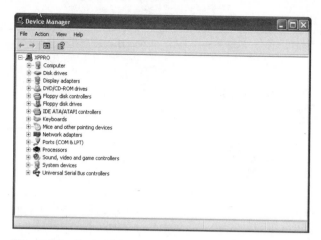

Figure 6-9 Device Manager provides a central interface for managing hardware devices.

You can access Device Manager in the following ways:

- In Control Panel, select Performance And Maintenance, select the System tool, and then, on the Hardware tab of the System Properties dialog box, click the Device Manager button.

- Right-click My Computer and then select Properties. On the Hardware tab of the System Properties dialog box, click the Device Manager button

- Right-click My Computer and then select Manage. Expand the System Tools node and then select Device Manager.

Changing Views in Device Manager

You can change the view in Device Manager by selecting a command from the View menu. Device Manager offers the following views:

- **Devices By Type**   This is the default view. Devices are organized by device type such as display adapters, keyboards, modems, and network adapters.

- **Devices By Connection**   This view organizes devices by how they are connected to the computer. This is useful if you want to see all the devices that are connected to a Peripheral Component Interconnect (PCI) bus or see how devices are linked in a universal serial bus (USB) chain.

- **Resources By Type** This view is organized by the four major resource types: DMA channels, I/O port addresses, IRQs, and memory addresses. Expanding a resource type displays devices that are using that resource and details on resource allocation.

- **Resources By Connection** This view is also organized according to the four major resource types. Within each resource type, devices are organized by the way they are connected.

Device Manager hides some devices by default. For example, Device Manager hides printers because you typically manage them by using the Printers And Faxes folder. Device Manager also hides many non–Plug and Play devices that you normally would not need to configure and devices that were connected to the computer at one time but are not currently connected. To view hidden devices in Device Manager, from the View menu, select Show Hidden Devices.

Identifying Devices in Device Manager

The icon that Device Manager displays next to each device indicates the device's type. When a device is working normally, a standard icon appears. However, when a specific condition exists for a device (such as being disabled), Device Manager overlays the device's icon with a symbol. Device Manager uses the following symbols on device icons to denote particular conditions:

- **Yellow exclamation point** Indicates a problem with a device. This could mean that the device has a resource conflict or that Windows is unable to locate the device.

- **Red "X"** Indicates that the device is disabled.

- **Blue lowercase "i"** Indicates that the device has been configured manually. This icon is viewable only in the Resources By Type and Resources By Connection views.

- **Yellow question mark** Indicates that Windows recognizes that a device is present, but cannot determine the correct device type. This usually means that drivers have not yet been installed for the device.

Viewing and Modifying Device Properties

In Device Manager, you can access the Properties dialog box of any device either by double-clicking the device or by right-clicking the device and selecting Properties. Figure 6-10 shows the Properties dialog box of a typical network adapter. The tabs available in a device's Properties dialog box vary depending on the device being examined.

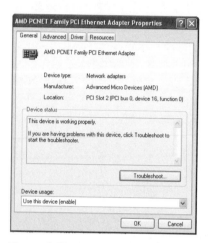

Figure 6-10   A device's Properties dialog box provides tools for configuring the device.

The standard tabs that you encounter on the Properties dialog boxes for hardware devices include the following:

- **General tab**   The General tab shows basic information about the device, such as device type and manufacturer. The Device Status section lets you know that the device is working properly and provides access to the Windows Troubleshooter for the device. You can also enable or disable the device from this tab.

- **Driver tab**   The Driver tab shows details about the driver currently installed for the device and provides tools for managing the driver. Drivers are discussed in Lesson 3, "Supporting and Troubleshooting Device Drivers."

- **Resources tab**   The Resources tab shows the system resources used by the device. Managing resources is discussed in the section, "Resource Assignments."

- **Device-specific tabs**   Most devices also feature tabs for viewing and configuring device-specific settings. The options available on these tabs vary widely with the type of device that you are working with. The names of these tabs also vary with the type of device. For example, network adapters have a tab named Advanced (shown in Figure 6-10), whereas modems have a tab named Modem.

Resource Assignments

Windows XP Professional automatically handles the assignment of resources to Plug and Play devices, but you can manipulate resource assignments on some Plug and Play devices. Non–Plug and Play devices generally require that you manually configure resource assignments, including DMA channels, I/O port address, IRQs, and memory addresses.

The Resources tab, shown in Figure 6-11, lets you configure the hardware resources that are assigned to the device. The Conflicting Device List notifies you if any other devices are configured to use the same resources, thereby making it easier to troubleshoot resource conflicts.

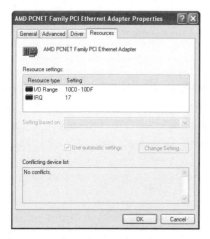

Figure 6-11   Managing resources by using the Resources tab.

Occasionally, you may run into situations in which two devices are requesting the same resource. To remedy the situation, you must use Device Manager to identify the conflict, determine what resources are currently available, and try to reconfigure one of the devices to eliminate the conflict.

Hardware manufacturers limit the settings that you can configure for each required resource. For example, a particular non–Plug and Play network card might permit you to configure only an IRQ value of 3 or 10. If both of those IRQ values were in use, you would need to reconfigure the device that is using either an IRQ value of 3 or 10 to free that resource and then assign it to the network card.

Device Manager's Resources By Type view (configurable from the View menu) is useful for determining which devices are using which resources and which resources are currently available. Figure 6-12 displays the Resources By Type view.

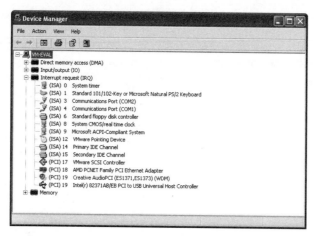

Figure 6-12   The Resources By Type view is useful for troubleshooting resource conflicts on non–Plug and Play devices.

Note   Plug and Play devices have a Use Automatic Settings option, which allows Windows XP to determine the resource assignments for the device. Unless you have a compelling reason to do otherwise, you should always choose Use Automatic Settings if the option is available. This allows the operating system to ensure that resource assignments do not conflict.

Scanning for Hardware Changes

Windows XP detects and installs most Plug and Play devices without requiring any configuration by the user. Windows might not automatically detect some Plug and Play devices. Although you can force Windows to detect such devices by restarting Windows or by running the Add Hardware Wizard, you can also initiate the detection process by right-clicking the computer name in Device Manager and selecting Scan For Hardware Changes. Scanning for hardware changes in Device Manager is equivalent to the hardware search performed by the Add Hardware Wizard.

Removing and Disabling Devices

You can remove a device in Device Manager by right-clicking the device and then selecting Uninstall. If you remove a Plug and Play device from Windows by using Device Manager, but do not physically disconnect the device from the computer, Windows will automatically detect and install the device again the next time you restart the computer. If you want to leave a Plug and Play device connected to the computer, but do not want it to be initialized, disable the device instead of removing it.

You disable a device in Device Manager by right-clicking the device and then selecting Disable. Device Manager overlays a red "X" on the device icon to indicate a disabled state. Disabling a device makes the device temporarily unavailable. The device driver and all configuration information are still present; the device is simply not activated. A disabled device does not consume any system resources. If two devices in a system are experiencing a resource conflict, disabling one of the devices will resolve the conflict. However, if both devices are required and should not be disabled, you will need to take further action to remove the conflict so that both devices can be accessible simultaneously.

Right-click a disabled device in Device Manager and then select Enable to enable the device. You can also enable and disable devices using the General tab of the Properties dialog box for a device.

Safely Removing Hot-Plugged Devices

A hot-plugged device is one that you can connect or disconnect while a computer is running. Most PC Card (PCMCIA), USB, and FireWire (IEEE 1394) devices fall into this category.

Some hot-plugged devices require the extra step of stopping the device in Windows before you can safely disconnect it from the computer. If any connected devices require safe removal, the Safely Remove Hardware icon appears in the notification area of the taskbar, as shown in Figure 6-13. Double-click this icon to open the Safely Remove Hardware dialog box. Select the device you want to disconnect and then click Stop. Windows notifies you when it is safe to disconnect the device.

The practice of disconnecting a device that requires safe removal without first stopping the device is referred to as a surprise removal. If the device is being accessed in any way when it is disconnected, Windows may react unpredictably. If the device is a hard disk with write caching enabled, for example, data in the cache that has not yet been saved to disk will be lost.

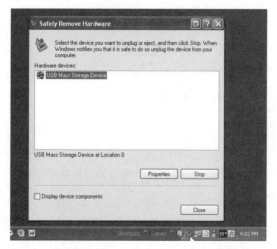

Figure 6-13   Use the Safely Remove Hardware dialog box to stop a device before disconnecting it.

Using Windows Troubleshooters

Windows Troubleshooters are special types of help files available in the Windows XP Help And Support Center. Troubleshooters help you pinpoint problems and identify solutions by asking a series of questions and then providing you with detailed troubleshooting information based on your responses to those questions.

Troubleshooters provide support for hardware and software issues. When troubleshooting problems with a specific device, the easiest way to access an appropriate troubleshooter is to click the Troubleshoot button on the General tab of the device's Properties dialog box in Device Manager. Figure 6-14 displays a generic hardware troubleshooter.

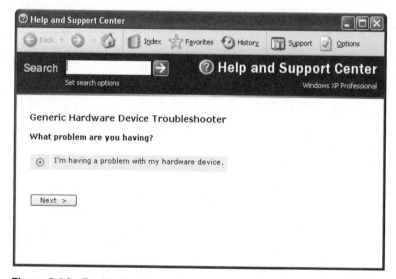

Figure 6-14   Troubleshooters walk you through the potential solutions to a problem.

In addition to using troubleshooters yourself to help solve problems, you should also teach users how to access them. Often, users can identify and solve minor problems themselves with pointers in the right direction.

Access the full list of troubleshooters by following these steps:

1. From the Start menu, select Help And Support.

2. In the Help And Support Center window, select the Fixing A Problem link.

3. In the Fixing A Problem section, select Troubleshooting Problems.

4. In the Troubleshooting Problems list, select List Of Troubleshooters.

Tip You can use the troubleshooting wizards to practice and enhance your troubleshooting skills and to look for answers to common problems. The troubleshooters work through the problem-solving process as you should, suggesting obvious solutions first and then moving on to more complex ones. Take the time to work through the available troubleshooters, and you can learn a lot about troubleshooting hardware in Windows XP.

Troubleshooting General Hardware Problems

You can use Device Manager to identify devices that are not functioning correctly, either because the device is not properly configured or because it has become inoperable. You may receive an error when the system starts that sends you to Device Manager to troubleshoot the problem, or you may simply notice a loss of functionality. When you open Device Manager, devices that are experiencing problems are identified with either a yellow exclamation point or a red "X" icon.

If a device is not functioning, consider the following:

- Verify that the device is plugged in and turned on.

- Verify that the device is on the Hardware Compatibility List (HCL).

- If the device has been functioning for a time and suddenly stops functioning, determine whether there have been any configuration changes to the system. If changes have occurred, look for potential conflicts associated with new hardware or software. If there have not been any configuration changes (hardware or software), most likely the device drivers have become corrupted and need to be updated, or else the device is physically damaged in some way and needs to be repaired or replaced.

- Make sure that you are using the latest version of the device drivers. You can use the Drivers tab in the device properties to update device drivers to the most current version. You will learn more about working with drivers in Lesson 3, "Supporting and Troubleshooting Device Drivers."

- Consider shutting Windows down and turning off the computer. This action causes all hardware to reinitialize and all device drivers to reload, potentially eliminating a transient problem.

- In some cases, you may need to update the firmware on a device. (Firmware is a set of software instructions written onto read-only memory [ROM] on a device.) If there is a firmware update for the device, attempt to apply it to see whether the problem is corrected.

- Move the device to another slot or port on the system to determine whether the slot or port is malfunctioning.

- If you suspect a physical device malfunction, install a known good replacement for the device that is configured in the same fashion and determine whether the replacement device functions. If it does, the original device is most likely damaged and needs to be replaced.

- If you have installed a device driver that is causing the system to crash, attempt to boot into Safe Mode and update or remove the driver. If you are unable to boot into Safe Mode, try the Last Known Good Configuration. If both of these methods fail, use the Recovery Console. The Recovery Console's Disable command will disable a driver, enabling the system to boot properly so that the driver can be updated or removed.

Practice: Troubleshoot Hardware Problems

In this practice, you will disable and re-enable a hardware device. You will also use the System Information tool to determine information about your computer.

Exercise 1: Disable and Re-enable a Device

> **Note**   The information and procedures in this chapter are based on a default installation of Windows XP Professional. Some of the information and procedures may change if you have installed Windows XP Service Pack 2. For more information, see Appendix A, "Windows XP Service Pack 2."

1. Log on to Windows XP using an account with administrator privileges.

2. From the Start menu, select Control Panel. (It is assumed that Control Panel is in Category View).

3. In Control Panel, select Performance And Maintenance.

4. In the Performance And Maintenance window, select System.

5. On the Hardware tab, select Device Manager.

6. Expand Ports (COM & LPT), right-click the parallel port [almost always named Printer Port (LPT1)], and choose Properties.

7. On the General tab of the Printer Port (LPT1) Properties dialog box, from the Device Usage drop-down list, select Do Not Use This Device (Disable). Click OK.

8. In the Device Manager window, note that the icon for Printer Port (LPT1) has a red "X" on it, indicating that the device is disabled. Right-click the Printer Port (LPT1) and choose Properties.

9. On the General tab of the Printer Port (LPT1) Properties dialog box, from the Device Usage drop-down list, select Use This Device (Enable). Click OK.

10. Close all open dialog boxes.

Exercise 2: Use System Information to Find Information about Your Computer

1. Log on to Windows XP.

2. On the Start menu, choose Run. In the Run dialog box, in the Open text box, type **msinfo32** and press ENTER.

3. In the System Information window, under System Summary, note the processor and the total physical memory on your computer.

4. Expand the Components node and click the Display component. Note the information and settings for your display adapter.

5. From the File menu, select Save.

6. In the File Name box, type **My System**. Select a location to which to save the file and then click Save.

7. Close the System Information window.

Lesson Review

The following questions are intended to reinforce key information presented in this lesson. If you are unable to answer a question, review the lesson materials and try the question again. You can find answers to the questions in the "Questions and Answers" section at the end of this chapter.

1. Which Windows XP Professional tool would you use to check for resource conflicts, and what indications does the tool give when it detects such a conflict?

   _____

   _____

2. Which Windows XP utility can you use to both remove and disable devices?

   A. Add Hardware Wizard

   B. Task Manager

   C. Device Manager

   D. Administrative Tools

Lesson Summary

- System Information displays configuration information about a computer. Most of this information is available in other utilities, but System Information consolidates it into a single source. You can document the system's current configuration by printing the System Information report or by saving the report to a file.

- Device Manager is the primary tool used for managing and troubleshooting hardware devices. Device Manager provides a central location to view the status hardware devices, enable and disable devices, change hardware settings, and troubleshoot hardware problems.

- Troubleshooters are special types of help files that pinpoint problems and identify solutions by asking you a series of questions.

Lesson 3: Supporting and Troubleshooting Device Drivers

Hardware drivers are software that governs the interactions between Windows and a hardware device. As a DST, part of your job will be to ensure that drivers are reliable and up-to-date. Device Manager provides a simple method of viewing and updating drivers for any device in the system. Windows XP also supports driver signing, which provides a method to verify that Microsoft has tested the designated device drivers for reliability.

After this lesson, you will be able to

- ■ Explain the use of the Driver.cab file.
- ■ Update drivers for a device.
- ■ Work with hardware drivers in Windows XP.

Estimated lesson time: 20 minutes

Understanding the Driver.cab File

Drivers that ship with Windows XP are stored on the installation CD in a single cabinet file called Driver.cab. Windows XP Setup copies this file to the %SystemRoot%\Driver Cache\I386 folder on the local hard disk during installation. Windows uses this file during and after installation to install drivers when new hardware is detected. This process helps by ensuring that users do not have to provide the installation CD whenever drivers are installed. All drivers in the Driver.cab file are digitally signed.

Note   %SystemRoot% refers to the directory in which Windows XP is installed. In various documentation and literature, you will see this directory referred to as "%SystemRoot%," "system_root," and "systemroot."

Updating Drivers

It is important to keep device drivers updated for all devices in a system. Using up-to-date drivers ensures optimum functionality and reduces the chance of an outdated device driver causing problems.

The Driver tab of a device's Properties dialog box (shown in Figure 6-15) displays basic information about the device driver (for example, the date of the driver and version number). You can also perform the following actions on the Driver tab:

- ■ View the names of the actual driver files by clicking Driver Details.

■ Update a device driver to a more recent version by selecting Update Driver. Windows prompts you for the location of the newer version of the driver. You can obtain new drivers from the device's manufacturer. You can also use the Update Driver option to reinstall drivers for a device that has ceased to function correctly because of a driver problem. If updating the drivers does not successfully restore device functionality, consider removing the device by using Device Manager and then restarting the computer. If the device supports Plug and Play, Windows will recognize the device when the computer restarts. Non–Plug and Play devices require manual reinstallation.

■ Revert to a previous version of a driver by selecting Roll Back Driver. This feature restores the last device driver that was functioning before the current driver was installed. Windows supports driver rollback for all devices *except* printers. In addition, driver rollback is available only on devices that have had new drivers installed. When a driver is updated, the previous version is stored in the %system_root%\system32\reinstallbackups folder.

■ Remove the device from the computer by selecting Uninstall.

Figure 6-15   Use the Driver tab of a device's Properties dialog box to view driver details.

Exam Tip   You should consider rolling back a driver when you are sure that a new driver is causing a problem and you do not want to affect other system configurations or drivers with a tool such as System Restore.

Driver Signing

Often, hardware drivers can cause a computer running Windows XP to become unstable or to fail entirely. Windows XP implements **driver signing** as a method to avoid such issues. Driver signing allows Windows XP to identify drivers that have passed all

Windows Hardware Quality Labs (WHQL) tests and that have not been altered or over-written by any program's installation process.

Configuring How Windows Reacts to Unsigned Drivers

You can configure how Windows XP handles unsigned drivers by using the System Properties dialog box. On the Hardware tab, select the Driver Signing option to open the Driver Signing Options dialog box, as shown in Figure 6-16. You can control the way that Windows reacts if you attempt to load a driver that Microsoft has not signed. You can choose from the following options:

- **Ignore**   Checks for digital signatures in the background, logs the installation of unsigned drivers, and permits the installation of unsigned drivers. Windows warns users only when an attempt is made to replace a signed driver with an unsigned driver.

- **Warn**   Warns the user that a driver has not been signed and then allows the user to determine whether the driver should be installed. This is the default setting.

- **Block**   Prevents all unsigned drivers from being installed.

- **Make This Action The System Default**   Specifies that the signature verification setting applies to all users who log on to the computer. When you disable this option, the selected settings apply only to the user that is currently logged on. Only users that are members of the local Administrators group can configure this option.

Figure 6-16   You can allow or block the installation of unsigned drivers, or have Windows prompt the user.

Using the File Signature Verification Utility

The **File Signature Verification utility (Sigverif.exe)** scans a computer running Windows XP and notifies you if there are any unsigned drivers on the computer. You can start the utility by typing **sigverif.exe** at the command prompt or in the Run dialog box. After the File Signature Verification utility scans your computer, the utility displays the results in a window similar to the one shown in Figure 6-17. Note that you cannot use the utility to remove or modify unsigned drivers; the utility scans only for unsigned drivers and shows you their location.

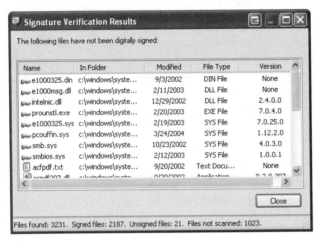

Figure 6-17   The File Signature Verification utility scans a system for unsigned drivers.

The File Signature Verification utility also writes the results of the scan to a log file named Segverif.txt, which is found in the %system_root% folder. You can change this log file's name and location, as well as configure advanced search options by clicking the Advanced button on the File Signature Verification dialog box.

Practice: Work with Hardware Drivers

In this practice, you will verify the details of a hardware driver, configure settings for unsigned drivers, and use the File Signature Verification utility to scan your computer for unsigned drivers.

Exercise 1: Verify Hardware Driver Details

1. From the Start menu, select Control Panel. (It is assumed that Control Panel is in Category View).

2. In Control Panel, select Performance And Maintenance.

3. In the Performance And Maintenance window, select System.

4. In the System Properties dialog box, on the Hardware tab, click the Device Manager button.

5. In the Device Manager window, expand the Display Adapters node by clicking the plus sign (+) next to it.

6. Under the Display Adapters node, you should see an icon representing the display adapter on your computer. Double-click the icon to open the Properties dialog box for your display adapter.

7. In the Properties dialog box for your display adapter, select the Driver tab.

8. The Driver tab shows the provider, date, version, and signer of the drivers for the selected hardware device. Click the Driver Details button.

9. The Driver File Details dialog box shows the specific files that make up the hardware drivers for your device. Click OK to close the Driver File Details dialog box.

10. Click OK to close the Properties dialog box for your display adapter, close the Device Manager window, and then click OK again to close the System Properties dialog box.

Exercise 2: Configure Settings for Driver Signatures

1. From the Start menu, select Control Panel. (It is assumed that Control Panel is in Category View).

2. In Control Panel, select Performance And Maintenance.

3. In the Performance And Maintenance window, select System.

4. In the System Properties dialog box, on the Hardware tab, click the Driver Signing button.

5. In the Driver Signing Options dialog box, ensure that the Warn option is selected so that you are prompted whenever Windows detects drivers that have not been digitally signed.

6. Click OK to close the Driver Signing Options dialog box. Click OK again to close the System Properties dialog box.

Exercise 3: Use the File Signature Verification Tool to Scan for Unsigned Drivers

1. From the Start menu, select Run.

2. In the Run dialog box, type **sigverif.exe** and click OK.

3. In the File Signature Verification dialog box, click Start.

4. The File Signature Verification utility scans your system for unsigned drivers, a process that can take a few seconds to a few minutes. When the scan is finished, a list of unsigned drivers is displayed.

5. Click Close to exit the Signature Verification Results window. Click Close again to exit the File Signature Verification dialog box.

Lesson Review

The following questions are intended to reinforce key information presented in this lesson. If you are unable to answer a question, review the lesson materials and try the question again. You can find answers to the questions in the "Questions and Answers" section at the end of this chapter.

1. You suspect that a user has installed device drivers that are causing compatibility issues with an installation of Windows XP. What utility would you use to identify all unsigned drivers and what would you set to provide a warning to the user if the system detects that an unsigned driver is being installed?

_____

_____

2. A user complains to you that he recently downloaded and installed the newest drivers for his video card. Since then, his computer occasionally restarts spontaneously. The customer did not make any other changes to his computer before the problem started. What would you recommend?

_____

_____

Lesson Summary

- You can view the details for a driver by using the related hardware device's Properties dialog box in Device Manager.

- Windows XP offers the capability to roll back a driver to a previous version if a new driver causes instability in a system.

- Digitally signed drivers indicate that a driver has passed quality testing at Microsoft and has not been altered since testing. You can configure Windows to ignore or accept unsigned drivers, or to notify you if an unsigned driver is about to be installed.

- You can use the File Signature Verification utility to scan a system for unsigned drivers.

Lesson 4: Supporting Hardware Profiles

A hardware profile is a collection of configuration information about the hardware that is installed on your computer. Within a profile, you can enable or disable each piece of hardware (such as networking adapters, ports, monitors, and so on) or provide specific configuration information. You can have many hardware profiles on a computer and switch between different profiles when booting into Windows XP. As a DST, you may decide to configure additional hardware profiles for users who need them or be asked to troubleshoot hardware on a computer that has multiple hardware profiles.

After this lesson, you will be able to

- Create a hardware profile.
- Manage profiles in Windows XP.
- Configure hardware devices within a profile.

Estimated lesson time: 20 minutes

Creating a Hardware Profile

Hardware profiles provide a way to configure a single computer for different situations. Within a profile, you can enable or disable specific hardware devices and configure those devices differently. As an example, assume that you have a user with a portable computer. When the user is at home, the computer is connected to an external monitor, keyboard, mouse, and printer. When the user takes the computer away from home, none of these devices is connected. You could set the user's computer up with two hardware profiles: one in which those devices were enabled, and one in which they were disabled. Whenever the computer starts, the user would choose the hardware profile to use, preventing the user from having to make configuration changes or be notified of missing devices.

By default, one hardware profile is created during the installation of Windows XP: Profile 1. To create an additional hardware profile, perform the following steps:

1. From the Start menu, select Control Panel. (It is assumed that Control Panel is in Category View).

2. In Control Panel, select Performance And Maintenance.

3. In the Performance And Maintenance window, select System.

4. In the System Properties dialog box, on the Hardware tab, click Hardware Profiles.

5. In the Hardware Profiles dialog box, as shown in Figure 6-18, select Profile 1 (Current) and then click Copy. You cannot create a new profile directly; you must copy an existing profile and then modify the copy.

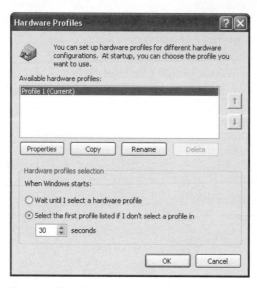

Figure 6-18   Copy and modify an existing hardware profile.

6. In the Copy Profile dialog box, type a name for the new profile and then click OK.

7. In the Hardware Profiles dialog box, select the new profile you just named and then click Properties.

8. In the Properties dialog box for the profile, shown in Figure 6-19, you can configure two options:

❑ Select This Is A Portable Computer if the computer is a portable computer that uses a docking station (and if that docking station is one that Windows XP supports). When a supported docking station is used, Windows XP can determine whether a portable computer is docked or undocked and then apply the correct profile automatically. If you do not use a docking station (or just prefer to set up and control your own profiles), leave this option deselected.

❑ Select Always Include This Profile As An Option When Windows Starts if you want the profile to appear on the boot menu as a selectable profile.

Figure 6-19   Configure properties for the hardware profile.

9. In the Properties dialog box for the profile, click OK to return to the Hardware Profiles dialog box.

10. Click OK to return to the System Properties dialog box and then click OK again to return to Windows.

Managing Hardware Profiles

After you have created a profile, you can control generally how Windows XP treats profiles by using the Hardware Profiles dialog box shown in Figure 6-20. (Open the System Properties dialog box, switch to the Hardware tab, and then click Hardware Profiles to access the dialog box.)

First, you can specify how Windows uses hardware profiles during startup. You have the following options:

■ Have Windows wait until you select a hardware profile before it continues booting.

■ Have Windows automatically select the first hardware profile on the list and continue booting after a specified amount of time. If you select this option, you can specify how long Windows should wait before going on without you. The default is 30 seconds.

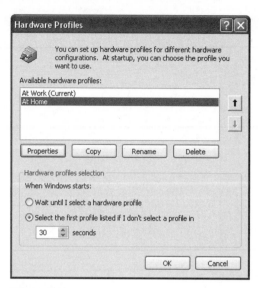

Figure 6-20   Manage hardware profiles using the Hardware Profiles dialog box.

You can also specify the order in which hardware profiles appear on the list during startup. The order is important, mostly because it is the first profile on the list that Windows will boot if you configure Windows to select a profile automatically. Select any profile on the list and use the up or down buttons on the right to move the profile around.

Configuring Hardware Settings for a Profile

After you have created the necessary profiles and configured Windows to display and start them the correct way, the next step is to configure hardware settings for each profile. To configure hardware for a profile, you must start the computer by using that profile. After you have started Windows by using a profile, use Device Manager to enable, disable, and configure individual devices. The settings you make will affect the currently loaded profile.

The only tricky part of setting up hardware devices in profiles is actually remembering which profile you are currently using because neither Device Manager nor a device's Properties dialog box provides information on the current profile. You can always switch back to the System Properties dialog box and open the Hardware Profiles window to determine your current profile.

Selecting a Profile During Startup

After you create and configure hardware profiles, using them is easy. Whenever you start your computer, Windows displays a menu early in the boot process that looks like the one in Figure 6-21.

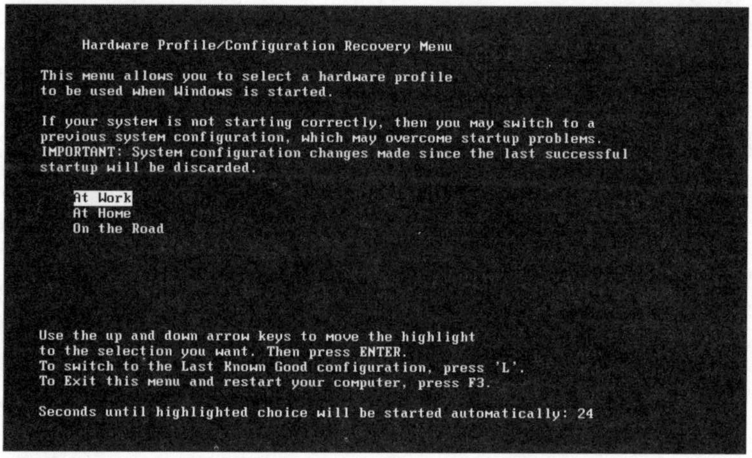

```
        Hardware Profile/Configuration Recovery Menu

    This menu allows you to select a hardware profile
    to be used when Windows is started.

    If your system is not starting correctly, then you may switch to a
    previous system configuration, which may overcome startup problems.
    IMPORTANT: System configuration changes made since the last successful
    startup will be discarded.

        At Work
        At Home
        On the Road




    Use the up and down arrow keys to move the highlight
    to the selection you want. Then press ENTER.
    To switch to the Last Known Good configuration, press 'L'.
    To Exit this menu and restart your computer, press F3.

    Seconds until highlighted choice will be started automatically: 24
```

Figure 6-21 Choose a hardware profile during Windows startup.

By default, if you do not select a profile within 30 seconds, Windows loads the first profile on the list. If you configured Windows not to start a profile automatically, you will not see the timer at the bottom of the screen. Use the arrow keys to select a profile and press ENTER to start the computer.

Lesson Review

The following question is intended to reinforce key information presented in this lesson. If you are unable to answer the question, review the lesson materials and try the question again. You can find answers to the question in the "Questions and Answers" section at the end of this chapter.

1. You are helping a user who has recently configured a second hardware profile on her computer. She tells you that by following a friend's instructions, she copied an existing profile and then renamed it. She then restarted her computer so that she could configure her hardware for the new profile, but Windows did not display a menu that allowed her to select the new profile. What do you suspect is the problem?

_____

_____

Lesson Summary

- A hardware profile is a collection of configuration information about the hardware on your computer. Within a profile, you can enable or disable each piece of hardware (such as networking adapters, ports, monitors, and so on) or provide specific configuration information.

- To create a hardware profile, you must copy and then modify an existing profile.

- To configure hardware devices for use with profiles, you must start Windows by using a particular profile and then use Device Manager to enable, disable, and configure devices within that profile.

Case Scenario Exercises

Scenario 6.1

You upgrade a computer running Windows 98 to Windows XP. After the installation, the sound card does not work. You check Device Manager: The sound card is installed, but it indicates an error condition. You decide to update the drivers to see whether that will resolve the problem. How do you update the sound card drivers?

_____

_____

Scenario 6. 2

A user is attempting to install a device driver for a new video card that she has obtained for her computer, which is running Windows XP. She is receiving an error message that says that unsigned drivers cannot be installed. The user has done some research and has located the Driver Signing option on the Hardware tab of the System Properties dialog box. However, the option to disable driver signing is not available to her. What must you do to enable the user to control driver signing on her computer?

_____

_____

Troubleshooting Lab

One of your customers uses a portable computer as her primary computer at work. She disconnects the computer from the company network and several peripheral devices so that she can take the computer home with her in the evenings.

The computer has two network adapters installed. One adapter allows her to connect the networking cable at the office so that she can share information with other computers and take advantage of the office's Internet access. The other adapter is a wireless networking card that allows the computer to communicate with a desktop computer at her home and share that desktop computer's Internet connection.

At the office, she connects her portable computer to an external monitor, keyboard, and mouse. At home, she uses the portable computer's display, keyboard, and mouse.

The customer would rather not be notified every time she starts her computer at home that hardware devices are missing. She also thinks that having Windows search for the missing devices when they are not connected is causing her not to be able to connect to certain resources on her home desktop computer—especially her printer. She has also noticed that the network connections at both the office and home seem to run slower when both network adapters are active. However, she would rather leave both adapters connected to the computer. What would be your solution?

Chapter Summary

- In Windows, you control the installation and removal of devices by using the Add Hardware Wizard in Control Panel. Windows XP also supports Plug and Play devices, which greatly simplifies installation and configuration.

- Device Manager is the primary tool for managing and troubleshooting hardware devices. Device Manager provides a central location to view the status of hardware devices, enable and disable devices, change hardware settings, and troubleshoot hardware issues.

- System Information displays configuration information about a computer. You can document a computer's current configuration by printing the information or by saving it to a file.

- Faulty hardware drivers can cause a computer running Windows XP to become unstable or to fail entirely. Driver signing allows Windows XP to identify drivers that have passed all WHQL tests.

- Windows Troubleshooters are special types of help files that allow you to pinpoint problems and identify solutions by asking a series of questions and then provide you with detailed troubleshooting information based on your responses.

- A hardware profile is a collection of configuration information about the hardware on your computer. Within a profile, each piece of hardware (such as networking adapters, ports, monitors, and so on) can be enabled, disabled, or given specific configuration information. You can have any number of hardware profiles on a computer and switch between different profiles when booting into Windows XP.

Exam Highlights

Before taking the exam, review the key topics and terms that are presented in this chapter. You need to know this information.

Key Points

- You should consider rolling back a driver when you are sure that a new driver is causing a problem and you do not want to affect other system configurations or drivers with a tool such as System Restore.

- You must use the Add Hardware Wizard for all non–Plug and Play devices. You can use the Add Hardware Wizard or restart the computer for some Plug and Play devices.

Key Terms

Device Manager   An administrative tool that you can use to manage the devices on your computer. Using Device Manager, you can view and change device properties, update device drivers, configure device settings, and uninstall devices.

Driver rollback   A feature in Windows XP that permits you to reinstall (roll back) a previously installed driver. The uninstalled drivers are stored in the system_root \system32\reinstallbackups folder.

Driver signing A process in which device drivers that have passed a series of tests by Microsoft are digitally signed, enabling the operating system to determine whether the drivers are acceptable for use.

File Signature Verification utility (Sigverif.exe) A utility that is used to scan a Windows XP system for unsigned files, providing a simple method to identify unsigned drivers.

Plug and Play A technology that enables the computer to automatically determine which hardware devices are installed on the computer and then to allocate system resources to those devices, as required, to configure and manage the devices.

System Information A utility that allows you to view the status of different components of a Windows XP system, including hardware devices.

Questions and Answers

Lesson 1 Review

Page 6-10 **1.** Which Windows feature is the primary tool for installing and removing devices in Windows XP?

    A. Add Hardware Wizard

    B. Device Manager

    C. Ipconfig

    D. Event Viewer

Answer A is correct. The Add Hardware Wizard is the primary tool used to install and remove devices in Windows XP. Answer B is incorrect because Device Manager is used to manage hardware devices, not to install them. Answer C is incorrect because Ipconfig is used to display network information. Answer D is incorrect because Event Viewer is used to view application and system event logs.

2. What are the three general steps for installing a new hardware device in Windows XP?

First, connect the new hardware device to the computer. Next, install the device in Windows. Windows installs Plug and Play devices automatically, but you must use the Add Hardware Wizard to install and configure non–Plug and Play devices. Finally, test the device to make sure that it works and does not interfere with other devices.

Lesson 2 Review

Page 6-25 **1.** Which Windows XP Professional tool would you use to check for resource conflicts, and what indications does the tool give when it detects such a conflict?

You will use Device Manager to check for resource conflicts. A yellow exclamation point indicates a problem with a device. A red "X" indicates that the device is disabled. A blue lowercase "i" indicates that the device has been manually configured.

2. Which Windows XP utility can you use to both remove and disable devices?

    A. Add Hardware Wizard

    B. Task Manager

    C. Device Manager

    D. Administrative Tools

Answer C is correct. You can use Device Manager to remove and disable devices. Answer A is incorrect because the Add Hardware Wizard cannot be used to disable devices. Answer B is incorrect because Task Manager is used to view running applications and processes. Answer D is incorrect because Administrative Tools is a folder that holds various administrative tools.

Lesson 3 Review

Page 6-32 **1.** You suspect that a user has installed device drivers that are causing compatibility issues with an installation of Windows XP. What utility would you use to identify all unsigned drivers and what would you set to provide a warning to the user if the system detects that an unsigned driver is being installed?

Use the Sigverif.exe utility to locate unsigned drivers. Driver signing is configured through the Hardware tab of the System tool in Control Panel.

2. A user complains to you that he recently downloaded and installed the newest drivers for his video card. Since then, his computer occasionally restarts spontaneously. The customer did not make any other changes to his computer before the problem started. What would you recommend?

The customer should use the driver rollback feature to revert to his previous driver. This is the simplest way to determine whether the new driver is causing the problem.

Lesson 4 Review

Page 6-37 **1.** You are helping a user who has recently configured a second hardware profile on her computer. She tells you that by following a friend's instructions, she copied an existing profile and then renamed it. She then restarted her computer so that she could configure her hardware for the new profile, but Windows did not display a menu that allowed her to select the new profile. What do you suspect is the problem?

The problem is most likely that the Always Include This Profile As An Option When Windows Starts option is not selected on the Properties dialog box for the profile.

Case Scenario Exercises: Scenario 6.1

Page 6-38 You upgrade a computer running Windows 98 to Windows XP. After the installation, the sound card does not work. You check Device Manager: The sound card is installed, but it indicates an error condition. You decide to update the drivers to see whether that will resolve the problem. How do you update the sound card drivers?

In Device Manager, access the Properties of the sound card. On the Driver tab, select Update Driver. The Upgrade Device Driver Wizard launches. When you are prompted to select a device driver, click Have Disk and provide the path to the Windows XP device drivers for the sound card. The path can be a folder on the floppy drive, any other drive on the system, or a location on the network. Make sure that the path that you specify contains the .inf file for the driver package, which describes how to install and configure the driver.

Case Scenario Exercises: Scenario 6.2

Page 6-38 A user is attempting to install a device driver for a new video card that she has obtained for her Windows XP computer. She is receiving an error message that says that unsigned drivers cannot be installed. The user has done some research and has located the Driver Signing option on the Hardware tab of the System Properties dialog box. However, the option to disable driver signing is not available to her. What must you do to enable the user to control driver signing on her computer?

> It is likely that an administrator has configured a system default for the computer so that Windows blocks unsigned drivers. For the user to be able to install the driver, she must be able to configure Windows to allow the installation of unsigned drivers. You must reconfigure the system default, remove the system default, or make the user a member of the Administrators group.

Troubleshooting Lab

Page 6-39 One of your customers uses a portable computer as her primary computer at work. She disconnects the computer from the company network and several peripheral devices so that she can take the computer home with her in the evenings.

The computer has two network adapters installed. One adapter allows her to connect the networking cable at the office so that she can share information with other computers and take advantage of the office's Internet access. The other adapter is a wireless networking card that allows the computer to communicate with a desktop computer at her home and share that desktop computer's Internet connection.

At the office, she connects her portable computer to an external monitor, keyboard, and mouse. At home, she uses the portable computer's display, keyboard, and mouse.

The customer would rather not be notified every time she starts her computer at home that hardware devices are missing. She also thinks that having Windows search for the missing devices when they are not connected is causing her not to be able to connect to certain resources on her home desktop computer—especially her printer. She has also noticed that the network connections at both the office and home seem to run slower when both network adapters are active. However, she would rather leave both adapters connected to the computer. What would be your solution?

> A great solution for this situation is to create two hardware profiles. You could name one At Work and one At Home (or whatever). For the At Work profile, you should leave all the hardware enabled except for the wireless network adapter. You should start the At Work profile and then use Device Manager to disable that device. For the At Home profile, you should use Device Manager to enable the wireless network adapter; then disable the other networking card and the external monitor, mouse, keyboard, and printer.

7 Supporting Display Devices, I/O Devices, and ACPI

Exam Objectives in this Chapter:

- Configure and troubleshoot display devices
  - ❏ Answer end-user questions related to configuring desktop display settings
  - ❏ Configure display devices and display settings
  - ❏ Troubleshoot display device settings
- Configure and troubleshoot Advanced Configuration and Power Interface (ACPI)
  - ❏ Answer end-user questions related to configuring ACPI settings
  - ❏ Configure and troubleshoot operating system power settings
  - ❏ Configure and troubleshoot system standby and hibernate settings
- Configure and troubleshoot I/O devices
  - ❏ Answer end-user questions related to configuring I/O devices
  - ❏ Configure and troubleshoot device settings
  - ❏ Configure and troubleshoot device drivers for I/O devices
  - ❏ Configure the user environment
  - ❏ Configure and troubleshoot pointing device settings

Why This Chapter Matters

In Chapter 6, "Installing and Managing Hardware," you learned the basics of supporting hardware in Microsoft Windows XP, including using Device Manager, working with hardware drivers, and using hardware profiles. This chapter looks specifically at configuring and troubleshooting three types of hardware: display devices, input/output (I/O) devices, and devices that support the **Advanced Configuration and Power Interface (ACPI)**.

Lessons in this Chapter:

Before You Begin

Before you begin this chapter, you should have a basic familiarity with working in a Windows-based operating system. You should understand the concepts of hardware installation, support, and troubleshooting presented in Chapter 6. You also need to have a computer running Windows XP Professional.

Lesson 1: Configuring and Troubleshooting Display Devices

Display devices include the display adapter (often referred to as a video card or graphics adapter) and the monitor. You can manage some of the properties of these individual components by using Device Manager, but you will perform the majority of display support and customization tasks by using the Display Properties dialog box available in Control Panel.

After this lesson, you will be able to

- Configure display settings in Windows XP.
- Configure multiple display configurations.
- Troubleshoot problems with display devices.

Estimated lesson time: 20 minutes

Configuring Display Settings in Windows XP

You will manage the majority of display settings in Windows XP by using the Display Properties dialog box. You can access this dialog box in one of the following ways:

- In Control Panel, select Appearance And Themes, and then select Display.

- Right-click any empty area on the Windows desktop and choose Properties.

The Display Properties dialog box contains a number of tabs that you can use to control various settings, including the screen saver and many qualities of the Windows desktop appearance.

You control settings that are specific to display configuration by using the Settings tab of the Display Properties dialog box, shown in Figure 7-1. The Settings tab allows you to configure screen resolution, color quality, and several other advanced display settings.

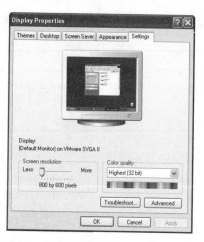

Figure 7-1   Use the Settings tab of the Display Properties dialog box to control display settings.

The resolution options that are available on a computer depend largely on the display adapter and monitor that is installed on the computer. With most configurations, you can change two settings:

- **Screen resolution**   Screen resolution governs the number of pixels that are displayed on the screen. Pixels are measured horizontally and vertically. Using a larger screen resolution means that more information (windows, dialog boxes, icons, and so on) can fit on the screen at a time, but it also means that the relative size of those elements appears smaller than at lower resolutions. To change the resolution, drag the Screen Resolution slider to the appropriate setting.

- **Color quality**   Color quality governs the number of colors used to display the Windows desktop and other on-screen elements. Common settings include Medium (16 bit), High (24 bit), and Highest (32 bit); but the exact settings that are available depend on your display adapter and monitor. Using a higher color quality setting improves how desktop elements look and does not really affect performance on most computers. So you typically should use the highest setting available. If a color setting is not available, it means that that the setting is not supported by your display hardware or the appropriate device drivers are not installed.

When you make a change to the screen resolution or color quality and then apply the new settings, Windows reconfigures the display (the screen may flicker and go blank momentarily) and then gives you 15 seconds to confirm the new settings. If you do not confirm the new settings, Windows reverts the resolution to the previous setting. Requiring a confirmation ensures that if you switch to a configuration that makes you unable to see the display, reversion is automatic.

Clicking the Advanced button on the Settings tab opens a Properties dialog box that lets you configure additional settings, including:

- The dots per inch (dpi) setting that Windows uses to display screen elements. The default dpi setting is Normal Size (96 dpi). Changing to a larger setting often helps users who have trouble seeing or clicking on window components such as title bars, scroll bars, close buttons, and so on.

- Whether Windows restarts or prompts you when you change display settings.

- The refresh rate that Windows uses to redraw the display. Typically, you should set the refresh rate to the highest setting that the video hardware can accommodate. Higher settings help reduce the flicker-effect on conventional displays.

- The level of hardware acceleration that Windows uses. By default, the Hardware Acceleration option is set to Full. If a computer is having display issues, reducing hardware acceleration can help you isolate and remedy the problem.

Note   In addition to the settings listed, you may see more tabs on the Properties dialog box that are particular to the video adapter installed on a computer. Video adapters that support 3D in particular often provide many additional settings for controlling advanced features for the adapter.

Exam Tip   If a user is experiencing intermittent display problems, such as garbled text, problems with the mouse pointer, or more severe problems, troubleshoot by reducing the level of hardware acceleration.

Supporting Multiple Displays

From time to time, users might require more than one monitor on a computer. Users that work with desktop publishing, Web design, or any graphic design programs frequently need to see more than can be displayed on a single monitor.

Windows XP allows you to configure up to ten monitors on a single computer. You can configure each monitor with a different screen resolution and color depth. The Windows XP desktop is spread across all monitors so that you can actually drag windows and dialog boxes from monitor to monitor. Multiple monitor support is especially useful in situations in which users need easy access to multiple applications simultaneously.

To support additional monitors, you must first install additional video adapters (often called secondary display adapters) onto a computer. Secondary display adapters must meet a particular set of criteria:

- They must be Peripheral Component Interconnect (PCI) or Accelerated Graphics Port (AGP) devices. Note that computers support only one AGP device, so additional devices would have to be PCI-based.

- They must be able to run in GUI mode or without using Video Graphics Adapter (VGA) resources (otherwise, the secondary display causes a resource conflict with the primary video adapter when the computer is starting up).

▶ **Adding an Additional Monitor to a Computer Running Windows XP**

To add an additional monitor to a computer, complete the following steps:

1. Verify that the primary display adapter works properly and that the correct driver is installed.

2. Install the additional video adapter and the appropriate drivers, and then plug in the additional monitor.

3. In Display Properties, select the Settings tab. Verify that the appropriate monitors are displayed.

4. Make sure that the physical configuration of your monitors matches the on-screen arrangement, as shown in Figure 7-2. You can control the placement of the secondary displays by dragging the monitor icons.

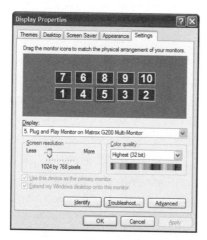

Figure 7-2   Configure the arrangement of monitors to match your physical setup.

5. Select the additional display by clicking the display or by choosing it from the Display drop-down list.

6. Select the Extend My Windows Desktop To This Monitor check box.

7. Configure the appropriate screen resolution and color quality for the new display.

8. Click Apply to enable the new display.

> **Tip**   On computers with multiple displays, it sometimes can be hard to tell which display is which. On the Settings tab of the Display Properties dialog box, notice that the displays are numbered. Right-click a display and choose Identify to have Windows display that number on the corresponding monitor.

Potential problems with multiple display configurations include the following:

■ If the computer has a motherboard with an on-board display adapter, you sometimes must configure that display adapter as the power-on self test (POST)/VGA-compatible primary display device.

■ You should not remove portable computers from a docking station while you are using multiple displays. Use the Display properties to disable the secondary display before removing the computer from its docking station. You could also create a hardware profile that does not use the additional display adapters and restart the computer using that profile before removing the computer from its docking station.

■ If Windows does recognize the secondary display, but nothing appears on the monitor, verify that the Extend My Windows Desktop Into This Monitor check box is selected in the Display Properties dialog box.

■ If you have any problems running a DOS application in a multiple monitor configuration, configure the DOS application to run full-screen. The application is then displayed on the POST display device.

■ Make sure that the display with the best DirectX support is the primary monitor. Only the primary monitor can run DirectX applications in full-screen mode and can fully accelerate DirectX graphics.

Troubleshooting Display Devices in Windows XP

You can view display adapter information, monitor properties, and driver information by using both Device Manager and the Display Properties dialog box. When a user experiences problems with display devices, you should first make sure that the appropriate drivers are installed. Also, try to set a different screen resolution or color depth to see if you can correct the problem until you can find an appropriate driver.

If Windows XP does not recognize a display adapter, try loading the basic VGA driver. If you cannot start Windows successfully because of the currently installed driver, you can use the advanced boot options. Enable VGA mode or safe mode to start the computer with basic VGA support (see Chapter 2, "Installing Windows XP," for more details). Many features are not available in these modes (including high-resolution rates and multiple-monitor support), but you may be able to at least get Windows to recognize the device while you search for the correct driver.

Hardware acceleration improves display performance but also has the potential to cause problems. Consider turning off hardware acceleration as part of your troubleshooting process.

Note   Windows XP Professional automatically uses a generic VGA display driver if the configured driver fails to load or initialize.

Practice: Configure Display Settings in Windows XP

In this practice, you will change the resolution and color depth of your display.

1. From the Start menu, select Control Panel.

2. In Control Panel, select Appearance And Themes.

3. In the Appearance And Themes window, select Display.

4. In the Display Properties dialog box, switch to the Settings tab.

5. In the Screen Resolution section, drag the slider to a different setting than the current configuration.

6. In the Color quality setting, select a different setting than the current configuration. Click Apply.

7. Your monitor should flicker as it adjusts to the new settings, and then Windows displays the Monitor Settings dialog box. Within 15 seconds, click Yes to save the new settings or click No to revert to your previous display settings. (If you do not click No within 15 seconds, Windows automatically reverts to the previous setting.)

8. Click OK to close the Display Properties dialog box.

Lesson Review

The following questions are intended to reinforce key information presented in this lesson. If you are unable to answer a question, review the lesson materials and try the question again. You can find answers to the questions in the "Questions and Answers" section at the end of this chapter.

1. How many monitors can you configure to work with Windows XP simultaneously?

_____

_____

_____

2. A user tells you that he has recently installed a new video adapter. He downloaded what he thought were the most recent drivers for the device from a website, but he came to realize that the drivers he downloaded were not from the manufacturer of the device. He was able to install the drivers, but when he restarted Windows, the display was garbled and he cannot adjust any settings. What should you tell the user to do?

_____

_____

_____

Lesson Summary

■ You can view display adapter and monitor properties and driver information through both Device Manager and the Display Properties dialog box. When you are experiencing problems with display devices, first always make sure that the appropriate drivers are installed. Also, try to set a different screen resolution or color depth to determine whether the problem can be corrected until an appropriate driver can be found.

■ The Windows XP Professional desktop can be spread across up to ten different monitors. Each monitor can have a different configuration, such as different screen resolution and color depth settings. This is useful when users must have easy access to multiple applications simultaneously. With multiple displays configured, each monitor can display a different application.

Lesson 2: Configuring and Troubleshooting I/O Devices

I/O devices extend the capabilities of the basic PC computer. Standard input devices associated with personal computers include the keyboard and mouse, although other devices exist. Standard output devices include monitors and printers. In addition, users routinely add many other types of peripheral equipment to their computers. As long as a computer has open expansion slots or other standard I/O connectors available, you can add compatible devices to the computer.

After this lesson, you will be able to

- Configure general I/O devices in Windows XP.
- Troubleshoot I/O devices.
- Troubleshoot additional devices, including PC cards, modems, universal serial bus (USB) devices, and infrared devices.

Estimated lesson time: 45 minutes

Configuring I/O Devices

You are providing telephone support at a help desk when a caller contacts you wanting to add several pieces of new hardware to her computer. While talking to the user, you determine that some of the hardware is completely new to the computer, and other pieces are upgrades to what she currently has installed. What can you do to help her get the hardware installed?

As a DST, you must be familiar with the operation of various types of I/O devices and the procedures used to troubleshoot them when they fail. Often, Windows XP identifies a class of hardware and installs generic drivers, which make only basic features available to the user. To take advantage of the advanced features that may be available with many devices, you must install the proper hardware drivers (and sometimes software applications bundled with the hardware).

Supporting Printers

You usually install printers directly by using the Add Printer Wizard, but you can also install them by using the Add Hardware Wizard. The installation and management of printers is discussed fully in Chapter 9, "Managing Local and Network Printers."

Supporting Scanners and Cameras

Windows XP detects most scanners and cameras automatically during the installation of Windows, if the hardware devices are connected to the computer. Windows usually detects and installs Plug and Play devices automatically when you connect them to the computer. If Windows does not detect and install an imaging device automatically, you must use the Add Hardware Wizard or the Scanners And Cameras tool in Control Panel to perform the installation. If a device does not support Plug and Play, the user must log on to Windows XP using an account with administrator privileges to complete the installation of the device.

You use the Scanners And Cameras tool in Control Panel to manage imaging devices. Configuration options vary depending on the device that is connected, but at a minimum you will be able to test the device to verify that it is functioning, set the rate at which data is transferred from the camera or scanner to the computer, and control color profiles. It is important to not set the data transfer rate higher than what the device supports. If the transfer rate is set too high, image transfer may fail.

> **Note**   Windows XP Professional supports Infrared Picture Transfer (IrTran-P), which is an image-transfer protocol that is used to send images by using infrared technology. Both the imaging device and the computer must support infrared data transfer for this option to be available.

Supporting Mouse Devices

Mouse devices are generally Plug and Play devices and are recognized when they are connected to the computer or, at the least, when Windows starts up. In some cases, though, you must install a mouse using the Add Hardware Wizard. Mouse devices connect to computers through a mouse (PS/2) port, serial port, or USB port. Wireless mouse devices are also available, although they usually communicate with a receiver that connects to the computer using a USB port.

The Mouse tool in Control Panel lets you configure mouse properties and other pointing device settings. You can update mouse drivers on the Hardware tab of the Mouse Properties dialog box, as well as through Device Manager.

The Buttons tab of the Mouse Properties dialog box, shown in Figure 7-3, lets you configure properties such as button configuration, double-click speed, and ClickLock functionality. Be careful not to set the double-click speed too fast for the user. If users cannot double-click at the selected speed, they will have difficulty navigating the operating system.

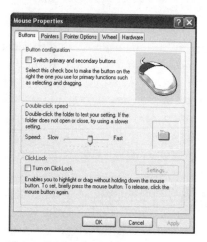

Figure 7-3 Configuring mouse settings with the Mouse tool.

The Pointers tab of the Mouse Properties dialog box, shown in Figure 7-4, allows you to customize the pointer scheme to reflect your preferences. Microsoft provides several pointer schemes with Windows XP, such as Hands, Dinosaur, Conductor, and Magnified. You can customize and save existing schemes under another name. You also can click Browse and point the computer to a pointer scheme configuration file to add schemes.

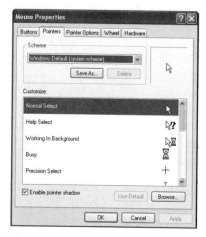

Figure 7-4 Use the Pointers tab to customize the pointer appearance.

The Pointer Options tab of the Mouse Properties dialog box, shown in Figure 7-5, lets you configure how fast the pointer on the screen moves in relation to movements of the mouse on the mouse pad. Selecting the Snap To option causes Windows to automatically place the pointer over the default button (such as OK or Apply) of new windows or dialog boxes. Although some users find that this feature increases productivity, many users who are not accustomed to the feature may experience unde-sirable results because it unexpectedly changes where the pointer is on the screen. This can be especially frustrating to users of portable computers, on which the pointer is sometimes hard to locate.

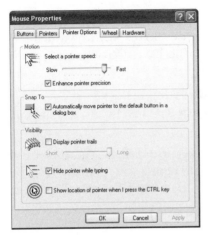

Figure 7-5   Use the Pointer Options tab to control the way the pointer behaves in different situations.

Note   Windows XP Professional supports the use of multiple pointing devices simulta-neously (such as a portable computer with an add-on mouse and a built-in touch pad).

Erratic mouse behavior is a fairly common hardware problem. If a user experiences mouse problems, use the following troubleshooting techniques:

- Verify that the mouse is securely connected to the computer.

- Clean the mouse ball and contacts.

- Replace the mouse driver because it may have become corrupted.

- Substitute a different mouse to see if the problem is eliminated. If so, replace the mouse.

Supporting Keyboards

Like mouse devices, keyboards are generally Plug and Play devices. Keyboards are usually connected to the computer through a PS/2 keyboard port or a USB port. Wire-less keyboards are also available, although (like wireless mouse devices) they typically communicate with a receiver that connects to the computer using a USB port.

You use the Keyboard tool in Control Panel to configure keyboard properties. You can manage device drivers through the Hardware tab of the Keyboard Properties and through Device Manager.

The Speed tab of the Keyboard Properties dialog box, shown in Figure 7-6, lets you configure the following options:

- **Repeat Delay**   Controls how long a user can hold a key down before Windows begins repeating the key press. For users who have difficulty using the keyboard, consider suggesting a longer repeat delay.

- **Repeat Rate**   Controls how fast Windows repeats a key press. Use the Click Here And Hold Down A Key To Test Repeat Rate text box to test the repeat delay and repeat rate settings.

- **Cursor Blink Rate**   Controls how fast the cursor blinks. The cursor is the blinking vertical line that indicates where you are typing text. In many word processing programs, the cursor is also referred to as the insertion point.

Figure 7-6   Configuring keyboard properties with the Keyboard tool.

Supporting Smart Card Readers

Smart cards are small, credit card–sized devices that are used to store information. Smart cards are generally used to store authentication credentials, such as public and private keys, and other forms of personal information. They are highly portable, allowing users to easily carry their credentials and other personal information with them.

A computer must have a smart card reader to access a smart card. The reader is generally a PS/2, USB, or Personal Computer Memory Card International Association (PCMCIA) device. Windows XP supports Plug and Play smart card readers that follow the Personal Computer/Smart Card (PC/SC) standards. A manufacturer may provide a device driver for its legacy smart card device, but Microsoft recommends using only Plug and Play smart card readers.

In addition to installing drivers for a smart card reader, you must enable the Smart Card service for Windows XP Professional to read smart cards. After you have installed and configured the smart card reader, make sure that the Smart Card service is started by using the Services tool in Computer Management.

Supporting Modems

Analog modems connect a computer to a remote device by using the Public Switched Telephone Network (PSTN). Modems are used to connect to the Internet through an Internet service provider (ISP) or to connect to a remote private network, such as a corporate network.

A modem can be either an internal or an external device. Internal modems connect to one of the computer's internal expansion slots. External modems connect to one of the computer's serial or USB ports.

You can manage modems through the Phone And Modem Options tool in Control Panel and through Device Manager. In Control Panel, select Printers And Other Hardware, then select Phone And Modem Options. In the Phone and Modem Options dialog box, on the Modems tab, double-click a modem to open a modem's Properties dialog box, as shown in Figure 7-7. The Properties dialog box allows you to control speaker volume for the modem or disable modem sound entirely. This is actually a common request from users who do not like hearing the modem sounds every time they connect to the Internet.

The Maximum Port Speed controls how quickly communications programs are permitted to send information to the modem. This is not the same as the modem's connection speed, which is negotiated when the modem dials out and establishes a connection. The maximum port speed is generally configured during installation and does not need to be reconfigured to match the modem's connection speed.

The Wait For Dial Tone Before Dialing check box is enabled by default. The telephone systems of some countries do not use a dial tone, in which case this option must be disabled or the modem will never dial.

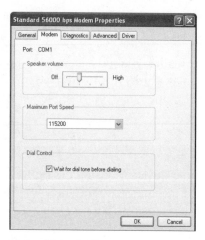

Figure 7-7   Configure general modem properties on the Modem tab.

The Diagnostics tab of the modem's Properties dialog box, shown in Figure 7-8, lets you query the modem to see if it can respond to standard modem commands. When you are troubleshooting, this is a useful way to determine whether the modem is initializing and functioning correctly.

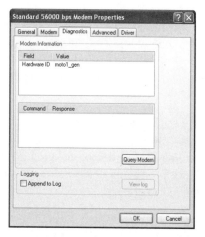

Figure 7-8   Troubleshoot modems using the Diagnostics tab of a modem's Properties dialog box.

During installation, Windows XP often installs a standard modem driver rather than the specific driver for the modem. This happens in cases where Windows cannot find a device-specific driver. The standard modem driver provides basic functionality but does not support advanced modem features. You can use this driver temporarily until you obtain the appropriate driver from the manufacturer.

USB Devices

Universal serial bus (USB) is a type of connection developed to provide a fast, flexible method of attaching up to 127 peripheral devices to a computer. USB provides a connection format designed to replace the computer's traditional serial-port and parallel-port connections. The term "universal" indicates that many kinds of devices can take advantage of USB. USB is fully Plug and Play–compliant.

The USB system comprises a single USB host and USB devices. The host is at the top of the USB hierarchy. In a Windows XP environment, the operating system and the hardware work together to form the USB host. Devices include hubs, which are connection points for other USB devices and nodes. Nodes are end devices such as printers, scanners, mouse devices, keyboards, and so on. Some nodes also function as hubs, allowing additional USB devices to be connected to them.

You can connect USB peripherals together by using connection hubs that allow the bus to branch out through additional port connections. A practical USB desktop connection scheme is presented in Figure 7-9. In this example, some of the peripheral devices are simply devices, whereas others serve as both devices and connection hubs. The computer provides a USB host connection that serves as the main USB connection.

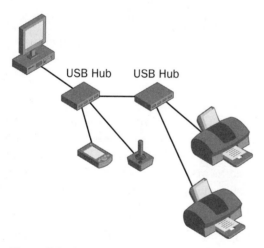

Figure 7-9   You can chain USB hubs and devices together to support up to 127 nodes.

A special hub, called the root hub, is an integral part of the host system (typically built into the motherboard) and provides one or more attachment points for USB devices (the ports available on the computer). The built-in USB ports on computers function as the root hub. USB provides for a total of up to five levels of devices. The root hub is at the first level. Regular hubs can form up to three additional levels, and nodes can function as the last level.

You can add or remove most USB devices from a computer while the computer is turned on. This practice is often referred to as hot-plugging the device. Plug and Play detects the presence (or absence) of the device and configures it for operation.

The USB interface provides power to the peripheral that is attached to it. The root hub provides power directly from the host computer to directly connected devices. Hubs also supply power to connected devices. Even if the interface supplies power to the USB devices, USB devices also can have their own power sources if necessary. Many devices, such as digital cameras and scanners, draw more power than a USB hub can provide.

> **Exam Tip**   Some USB hubs are self-powered, and some are not. Hubs that are not self-powered draw power from the hub to which they are connected or from the computer itself. If you find that a USB device that is connected to an unpowered USB hub is not working as expected, try replacing the unpowered USB hub with a self-powered hub.

Because you can add nearly any type of peripheral device to the PC through the USB port, the range of symptoms that are associated with USB devices include all the symptoms that are listed for peripheral devices in this chapter. Problems that are associated specifically with the USB technology occur in the following general areas:

- USB hardware device
- USB controller
- USB drivers

The first step in troubleshooting USB problems is to check the complementary metal oxide semiconductor (CMOS) setup screens to make sure that the USB function is enabled for the computer. If USB functionality is enabled in the basic input/output system (BIOS), check Device Manager next to make sure that the USB controller appears there. In Windows XP, the USB controller should be listed under the Universal Serial Bus Controllers entry (using the default Devices By Type view in Device Manager).

If the controller does not appear in Device Manager, or if a yellow warning icon appears next to the controller, the computer's BIOS may be outdated. Contact the BIOS manufacturer for an updated copy of the BIOS.

If the controller is present in Device Manager, right-click the USB controller and then select Properties. If there are any problems, a message should appear in the Device Status section on the General tab of the controller's Properties dialog box.

If the BIOS and controller settings appear to be correct, check the USB port drivers next. USB ports are listed in Device Manager as USB Root Hubs. Right-click a USB Root Hub entry and then select Properties. Use the Driver tab of the USB Root Hub Properties dialog box to update or roll back drivers if necessary.

When troubleshooting USB devices, you must be aware that the problem could be a result of general USB issues or be a problem with the device itself. Usually, but not always, general USB issues affect more than one device. If you suspect a problem with a specific device, uninstall the device by using Device Manager, disconnect the device from the computer, and then restart the computer. After the computer restarts, reconnect the device and let Plug and Play detect, install, and configure it again. If the device still does not function correctly, investigate the possibility that the device is damaged in some way or that you need to obtain updated drivers from Microsoft or the device manufacturer.

FireWire Port

Many newer media centers and high-end computers now come with FireWire ports (often called IEEE 1394 ports after the Institute of Electrical and Electronics Engineers standard that defines the technology). FireWire can transfer data at a rate of 400 or 800 Mbps. Firewire is used mainly for video transfer from digital movie cameras, but it will soon become a popular option for newer PDAs and handhelds, including cradles, chargers, and synchronizers.

When troubleshooting a device that connects by using a FireWire port, you can verify that the port is functional by plugging in another device (such as a digital camera). You should also ensure that the connection to and from the peripheral and the computer is solid and verify that the cable that connects the two is not worn or damaged.

Handheld Devices

Most handheld devices support either Infrared Data Association (IrDA) standards or connect to the computer through a serial or USB port. For handheld devices that use a port, some connect directly to the port, and some connect to a cradle, which in turn is connected to the port.

You will need to install software so that Windows XP can communicate correctly with the handheld device. For example, Palm-based personal digital assistants (PDAs) require you to install the Palm desktop software to allow the PDA to transfer data to and from a Windows-based PC. Handheld devices running Windows Mobile software, such as the Pocket PC, require that you install a program named ActiveSync on the computer.

> **See Also**   For more information on supporting handheld devices running Windows Mobile software, visit the Windows Mobile website at *http://www.microsoft.com/windowsmobile /default.mspx.*

Lesson Review

The following questions are intended to reinforce key information presented in this lesson. If you are unable to answer a question, review the lesson materials and try the question again. You can find answers to the questions in the "Questions and Answers" section at the end of this chapter.

1. What is the first step associated with troubleshooting USB problems?

   _____

   _____

2. You receive a call from a user who is having trouble installing a scanner on her computer running Windows XP. She disconnected her printer from the computer's parallel port and connected the scanner in its place. She then turned the scanner on and ran the Add Hardware Wizard. She thinks that Windows XP did detect the scanner, but she received a number of error messages and was unable to complete the installation. She downloaded the most recent drivers for the scanner from the manufacturer's website, which claimed that they support Windows XP, and tried the Add Hardware Wizard again, but got the same results. What is the likely problem?

   A. She must log on to the computer with administrator privileges to install hardware devices that are not Plug and Play.

   B. The scanner is not compatible with Windows XP.

   C. The parallel cable is damaged.

   D. The scanner is not working.

Lesson Summary

- I/O devices extend the capabilities of the basic PC. Standard input devices associated with personal computers included the keyboard and mouse, although other devices exist. Standard output devices include monitors and printers.

- Windows detects and installs most Plug and Play devices automatically. If a device does not support Plug and Play, a user must log on to Windows XP using an account with administrator privileges in order to complete the installation of the device.

■ Mouse devices and keyboards are generally Plug and Play devices and are recognized when they are connected to the computer or, at the least, when Windows starts up. In some cases, though, you must install a mouse or keyboard using the Add Hardware Wizard. Mouse devices typically connect to computers through a mouse (PS/2) port, serial port, or USB port on the computer or on the keyboard. Keyboards connect using a keyboard or USB port.

■ USB is an external serial bus developed to provide a fast, flexible method of attaching up to 127 peripheral devices to a computer. USB provides a connection format designed to replace the computer's traditional serial port and parallel port connections.

■ FireWire ports (often called IEEE 1394 ports) can transfer data at a rate of 400 or 800 Mbps.

Lesson 3: Configuring and Troubleshooting ACPI

Advanced Configuration and Power Interface (ACPI) lets computers running Windows XP use power more efficiently. Windows XP also supports the older Advanced Power Management (APM) standard for backward compatibility with older computers. In this lesson, you will learn about ACPI and APM, and how to configure power options in Windows XP.

After this lesson, you will be able to

- Explain the use of ACPI on a computer running Windows XP.
- Explain the use of APM on a computer running Windows XP.
- Configure power options.

Estimated lesson time: 15 minutes

Understanding ACPI

Advanced Configuration and Power Interface (ACPI) is a specification that controls power consumption in computers. With ACPI, a computer allows the operating system to control power management instead of controlling it through the BIOS. ACPI supports power management on desktop and portable computers. However, because portable computers are capable of running on batteries, power management is of greater concern, and more configuration options are available when a computer has a battery. Desktop computers connected to a universal power supply (UPS) also provide extended capabilities.

> **Note**   In addition to power management, ACPI also provides Plug and Play functionality in Windows XP.

On computers that support ACPI, Windows XP maintains a power policy that controls which devices to turn off (and when to turn them off) and also when to put the computer into a reduced power mode. Each device connected to the computer has different power management features for the different types of devices. For example, you can configure hard disks to power down after a certain period of time has elapsed, or network cards to request a low-power state when a network cable is not connected.

ACPI supports two important power modes: standby and hibernate. In standby mode, Windows takes devices offline but does not shut down the computer. When you activate the computer (usually by moving the mouse or by pressing a key on the keyboard), the computer automatically brings devices back online. Processing then continues normally.

In hibernate mode, Windows stores the current contents of memory to the hard disk, and the computer shuts down entirely. Windows does not close applications or log the current user off the computer. When you restart the computer, the computer returns to the same state it was in when it went into hibernation. By default, the user is prompted to enter a user name and password to regain access to the desktop.

To gain full ACPI support, a computer's BIOS must support ACPI. During the installation of Windows XP, the setup program detects the level of ACPI support that is provided by the computer and configures itself appropriately. If Windows XP is installed on a computer without ACPI support, only limited power management functionality is available.

> **Note**   If you perform an upgrade on the BIOS to enable ACPI on a computer that is already running Windows XP, you must reinstall the operating system to enable ACPI support.

To determine whether ACPI support is enabled on a computer running Windows XP, follow these steps:

1. Open Device Manager.

2. Expand the Computer node. If Advanced Configuration And Power Interface (ACPI) PC is listed, the operating system supports ACPI.

If a computer's BIOS claims to be ACPI-compliant, but support is not enabled in Windows XP, the BIOS actually may not be compliant. Contact the manufacturer to see if an update is available.

Understanding APM Support in Windows XP

Advanced Power Management (APM) was originally introduced in Windows 95. APM is designed to support battery status, suspend, resume, and automatic hibernation functions. Windows XP supports APM version 1.2 on computers with an APM-compatible BIOS. If APM support is enabled, it is detected and installed during Windows XP setup.

> **Note**   Microsoft provides a utility called Apmstat.exe, which you can use to determine the APM BIOS compatibility on a computer. Apmstat.exe is located in the Support\Tools folder of the Windows XP CD-ROM.

Configuring Power Schemes

You can access power management options by using the Power Options tool in Control Panel. On the Power Schemes tab of the Power Options Properties dialog box, shown in Figure 7-10, you can control the power-consumption behavior of the monitor and the hard disks, and when the computer enters standby. Portable computers and desktop computers with which you use a UPS offer separate options for when the computer is plugged in and when it is running on batteries.

Figure 7-10   Use the Power Schemes tab to configure basic power options.

When Windows XP is installed on a portable computer, several power schemes are available, such as Portable/Laptop, Presentation, and Max Battery. Each of these schemes has different default configurations for monitor and hard disk behavior. For example, Presentation never shuts down the monitor, even when running on batteries, whereas Max Battery shuts down both the monitor and hard disks after very brief periods of inactivity.

You can easily edit existing power schemes to reflect personal preferences. You can create new power schemes by selecting an existing power scheme, clicking the Save As button, and then saving it under a different name. You can then edit the new scheme as needed by simply configuring new options.

Real World   Configuring Power Options

On a portable computer running on battery power, it is a good idea to configure the computer to shut down the monitor and hard disks or enter standby after a period of time to help conserve battery power. On desktop computers (or on portable computers running on AC power), you can also configure these options, but you should be aware of potential problems.

Some display adapters respond unpredictably when turned off, and you often cannot restore the display by simply moving the mouse or pressing a key. Unfortunately, the only way to recover when a display does not restore is to reset the computer. Also, many users become confused when they come back to their computer to find a blank screen. Often, their solution is to turn the computer off or reset it.

Many computers also do not work well when they come out of standby or when the hard disk is powered down. Sometimes the computer will not come back at all, forcing you to reset the computer. Sometimes the computer will come out of standby, but running applications and open documents crash.

Your best bet is usually to disable such power options when a computer is plugged in by selecting the Never option on the Turn Off Monitor, Turn Off Hard Disks, System Standby, and System Hibernates drop-down lists.

You can view and modify the way that a computer works when a battery is close to running out of power by using the Alarms tab, shown in Figure 7-11. You can configure low battery and critical battery alarm levels and actions for each. Actions include sounding an alarm, displaying a message, forcing the computer into standby or shutting it down, and running a program (useful for custom programs that log problems or send status alerts).

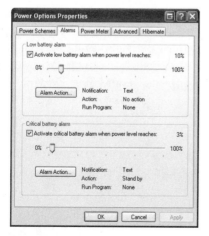

Figure 7-11   Configure the Alarms tab to alert you to low battery situations.

The Power Meter tab, shown in Figure 7-12, displays the current charge level and status of each battery in the computer. You can display the type of battery (NiCad, Lithium Ion, and so on) and the manufacturer by clicking the battery icon.

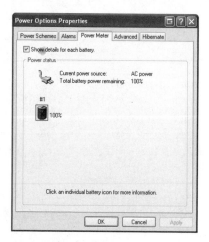

Figure 7-12 The Power Meter tab shows you the remaining battery power.

Figure 7-13 shows the Advanced tab, on which you can configure the following options:

- The Always Show Icon On The Taskbar option places a power icon in the System Tray for fast access to the Power Meter tab of Power Options.

- The Prompt For Password When Computer Resumes From Standby option configures Windows XP to prompt the user for logon credentials when the user restarts a computer that has gone on standby. Because standby does not log the user off the computer, this is an important security feature that should be enabled unless there is a compelling reason not to.

- The Power Buttons section has options that control system behavior when the power button or sleep button on a computer is pressed. If a computer does not feature a sleep button, the option is not shown. Also note that on some portable computers, closing the display usually activates the sleep function. If a computer supports it, you can choose the following options: Do Nothing, Ask Me What To Do, Standby, Hibernate (if the computer supports it), and Shut Down.

Figure 7-13   Configure advanced power options on the Advanced tab.

The Hibernate tab, shown in Figure 7-14, lets you enable hibernate support for a computer. After they are enabled, the hibernate options appear within the Power Options Properties and the Shutdown dialog boxes. If the Hibernate tab is not available, the computer does not support Hibernate mode.

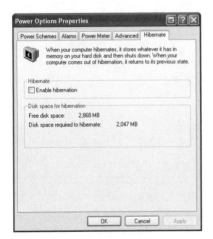

Figure 7-14   Configure hibernation in the Power Options Properties dialog box.

Tip   When hibernation is enabled, some computers show the Hibernate option in the Turn Off Computer dialog box, but some computers still show the Standby option. No matter which option Windows displays, you can access the other option by holding down the SHIFT key.

Practice: Set Power Options

In this practice, you will configure power options. This practice requires that you have a computer running Windows XP that supports ACPI.

1. From the Start menu, select Control Panel.

2. In Control Panel, select Performance and Maintenance.

3. In the Performance and Maintenance window, select Power Options.

4. In the Power Options Properties dialog box, on the Power Schemes tab, on the Turn Off Monitor drop-down list, select After 1 Min and click Apply.

5. Wait for one minute, without moving your mouse or pressing any keys. After one minute, your display should go blank.

6. Move your mouse back and forth. This should restore your display. Configure the Turn Off Monitor option the way it was previously configured and click Apply again.

7. On the Advanced Tab of the Power Options Properties dialog box, select the Prompt For Password When Computer Resumes From Standby check box. Click OK.

8. From the Start menu, select Turn Off Computer.

9. In the Turn Off Computer dialog box, click Standby. If the Hibernate option appears instead of the Standby option, hold the SHIFT key down to change to the Standby option.

10. Your display should go blank as Windows enters a low-power standby mode. Move your mouse back and forth a few times. The computer should come out of standby mode. If it does not, try pressing your spacebar instead.

11. Enter your user name and password to return to Windows.

Lesson Review

The following questions are intended to reinforce key information presented in this lesson. If you are unable to answer a question, review the lesson materials and try the question again. You can find answers to the questions in the "Questions and Answers" section at the end of this chapter.

1. One of your users has Windows XP Professional installed on his portable computer. He often carries the portable computer from office to office and must occasionally leave the computer unattended. The user wants to maximize the battery life on his computer yet still be able to resume work as quickly as possible. He does not want to shut the computer down because he prefers not to have to restart

applications whenever he comes back to the computer. What should you tell him to do?

   A. Use the Power Options in Control Panel to select the Max Battery power scheme.

   B. Use the Power Options in Control Panel to create a custom power scheme.

   C. Put the computer into standby mode when left unattended.

   D. Put the computer into hibernate mode when left unattended.

2. Which of the following standards does Windows XP use for Plug and Play support, as well as for supporting extended power options?

   A. APM

   B. ACPI

   C. USB

   D. BIOS

Lesson Summary

■ Windows XP Professional supports ACPI, which is a specification that controls power consumption in computers. With ACPI, the computer can pass power management responsibility to the operating system.

■ ACPI supports power management on desktop and portable computers. However, because portable computers are capable of running on batteries, power management is of greater concern, and more configuration options are available.

Case Scenario Exercises

Scenario 7.1

One of your users works from home using a computer running Windows XP Professional that supports ACPI. She tells you that her son often presses the power button on her computer and asks you if there is a way to disable the power button. What do you tell her?

_____

_____

_____

_____

Scenario 7.2

You are providing support for a user who recently purchased a new computer. The display adapter in the computer supports a number of advanced features, but the computer does not have the appropriate software installed to take advantage of these features. Your customer downloaded the new drivers and extra software from the manufacturer of the display adapter. He used the installation program that was part of the download to install the new drivers and software. Now, when he starts his computer, Windows seems to start normally, but just after startup, the customer sees an error message stating that the display settings have been restored to their default level. The user notes that the display settings seem to be a low resolution and color quality, but when he tries to open the Display Properties dialog box, the computer freezes. What do you tell him?

_____

_____

_____

_____

Troubleshooting Lab

In this lab, you will work within Device Manager to familiarize yourself with the devices that are attached to your own computer. Open Device Manager by following these steps:

1. Log on to Windows XP using an account with administrator privileges.

2. From the Start menu, select Control Panel.

3. In the Control Panel window, select Performance And Maintenance.

4. In the Performance And Maintenance window, select System.

5. On the Hardware tab, select Device Manager.

Using Device Manager, answer the following questions about your own computer:

1. What type of display adapter is installed in your computer and what version are the current drivers?

_____

_____

2. What type of monitor is installed in your computer? Does the monitor listed in Device Manager match the actual model monitor you use?

3. Using Device Manager, can you determine how many USB ports your computer has built in?

Chapter Summary

- Windows XP supports up to ten displays, and you can configure each display with different screen resolution and color depth settings. This is useful in situations when users must have easy access to multiple applications simultaneously.

- You can view display adapter and monitor properties and driver information through both Device Manager and Display Properties. When you are experiencing problems with display devices, first always make sure that the appropriate drivers are installed. Also, try to set a different screen resolution or color depth to determine whether the problem can be corrected until you locate an appropriate driver.

- I/O devices extend the capabilities of the basic PC. Standard input devices associated with personal computers include the keyboard and mouse, although other devices exist. Standard output devices include monitors and printers.

- Windows detects and installs most Plug and Play devices automatically. If a device does not support Plug and Play, a user must log on to Windows XP using an account with administrator privileges to complete the installation of the device.

- Windows XP Professional supports ACPI, which is a specification that controls power consumption in computers. With ACPI, the computer can pass power management responsibility to the operating system. ACPI supports power management on desktop and portable computers. However, because portable computers are capable of running on batteries, power management is of greater concern, and more configuration options are available.

Exam Highlights

Before taking the exam, review the key topics and terms that are presented in this chapter. You need to know this information.

Key Points

- Some USB hubs are self-powered, and some are not. Hubs that are not self-powered draw power from the hub to which they are connected or from the computer itself. If you find that a USB device connected to an unpowered USB hub is not working as expected, try replacing the unpowered USB hub with a self-powered hub.

■ If a user is experiencing intermittent display problems, such as garbled text, problems with the mouse pointer, or more severe problems, troubleshoot by reducing the level of hardware acceleration.

Key Terms

Advanced Configuration and Power Interface (ACPI)   An open industry specification that defines power management on a wide range of mobile, desktop, and server computers and peripherals. ACPI provides for the OnNow industry initiative that allows computer manufacturers to configure a computer that will start at the touch of a keyboard. ACPI design is essential to taking full advantage of power management and Plug and Play.

Advanced Power Management (APM)   An advanced Plug and Play that is designed to support battery status, suspend, resume, and autohibernate functions.

universal serial bus (USB)   An external serial bus developed to provide a fast, flexible method of attaching up to 127 peripheral devices to a computer.

Questions and Answers

Lesson 1 Review

Page
7-8

1. How many monitors can you configure to work with Windows XP simultaneously?

Windows XP supports up to ten monitors, each capable of using a different resolution and color quality.

2. A user tells you that he has recently installed a new video adapter. He down-loaded what he thought were the most recent drivers for the device from a web-site, but he came to realize that the drivers he downloaded were not from the manufacturer of the device. He was able to install the drivers, but when he restarted Windows, the display was garbled and he cannot adjust any settings. What should you tell the user to do?

You should tell the user to press the F8 key just before the operating system loads to access the Advanced Boot Options menu. He should select the Enable VGA Mode option so that Windows boots using standard VGA drivers. After Windows starts, the user should be able to remove the questionable drivers, download the appropriate drivers, and install them.

Lesson 2 Review

Page
7-20

1. What is the first step associated with troubleshooting USB problems?

The first step in troubleshooting USB problems is to check the CMOS setup screens to make sure that the USB function is enabled there.

2. You receive a call from a user who is having trouble installing a scanner on her computer running Windows XP. She disconnected her printer from the computer's parallel port and connected the scanner in its place. She then turned the scanner on and ran the Add Hardware Wizard. She thinks that Windows XP did detect the scanner, but she received a number of error messages and was unable to com-plete the installation. She downloaded the most recent drivers for the scanner from the manufacturer's website, which claimed that they support Windows XP, and tried the Add Hardware Wizard again, but got the same results. What is the likely problem?

A. She must log on to the computer with administrator privileges to install hard-ware devices that are not Plug and Play.

B. The scanner is not compatible with Windows XP.

C. The parallel cable is damaged.

D. The scanner is not working.

Answer A is correct. Windows XP installs Plug and Play devices automatically, so an adminis-trator does not need to be logged on to the computer. However, a user must have administra-tor privileges to install non–Plug and Play devices. Answer B is not correct because the downloaded drivers do support Windows XP. Answer C is not correct because if the parallel cable were damaged, the user would also have had problems with her printer. Answer D is not correct because the scanner is working; the Add Hardware Wizard was able to detect it.

Lesson 3 Review

Page
7-28

1. One of your users has Windows XP professional installed on his portable computer. He often carries the portable computer from office to office and must occasionally leave the computer unattended. The user wants to maximize the battery life on his computer yet still be able to resume work as quickly as possible. He does not want to shut the computer down because he prefers not to have to restart applications whenever he comes back to the computer. What should you tell him to do?

   A. Use the Power Options in Control Panel to select the Max Battery power scheme.

   B. Use the Power Options in Control Panel to create a custom power scheme.

   C. Put the computer into standby mode when left unattended.

   D. Put the computer into hibernate mode when left unattended.

   Answer D is correct. Hibernation mode restores all applications and windows to their previous state while extending battery life. Answers A and B are not correct because, until hibernation is enabled, power schemes can only turn off the monitor and hard disks and send the computer into standby mode. Answer C is not correct because, although standby mode restores applications and windows to their previous state, it does not extend battery life as much as hibernation mode.

2. Which of the following standards does Windows XP use for Plug and Play support, as well as for supporting extended power options?

   A. APM

   B. ACPI

   C. USB

   D. BIOS

   Answer B is correct. ACPI provides the Plug and Play specifications used by Windows XP. Answer A is not correct because APM is an older power standard used for backward compatibility. Answer C is not correct because USB is the standard used for a specific type of serial connection. Answer D is not correct because BIOS refers to the computer configuration stored in a permanent area of memory for starting and configuring hardware devices on a computer.

Case Scenario Exercises: Scenario 7.1

Page
7-29

One of your users works from home using a computer running Windows XP Professional that supports ACPI. She tells you that her son often presses the power button on her computer and asks you if there is a way to disable the power button. What do you tell her?

Assuming that the computer does support ACPI and that it is enabled, your customer can disable the power button. She should open the Power Options Properties dialog box, click the Advanced tab, and select Do Nothing from the When I Press The Power Button On My Computer drop-down list.

Case Scenario Exercises: Scenario 7.2

Page
7-30

You are providing support for a user who recently purchased a new computer. The display adapter in the computer supports a number of advanced features, but the computer does not have the appropriate software installed to take advantage of these features. Your customer downloaded the new drivers and extra software from the manufacturer of the display adapter. He used the installation program that was part of the download to install the new drivers and software. Now, when he starts his computer, Windows seems to start normally, but just after startup, the customer sees an error message stating that the display settings have been restored to their default level. The user notes that the display settings seem to be a low resolution and color quality, but when he tries to open the Display Properties dialog box, the computer freezes. What do you tell him?

This problem is most likely the result of a bad driver. You should try starting the computer into VGA mode or safe mode using the advanced options during startup. It is possible that once in one of these two modes, you can open the Display Properties dialog box and resolve the problem. You could try adjusting the hardware acceleration setting or look through some of the advanced settings provided by your display adapter. It is more likely, however, that you will need to use Device Manager to roll back the display adapter to the previous version.

Troubleshooting Lab

Page
7-30

1. What type of display adapter is installed in your computer and what version are the current drivers?

   In Device Manager, expand Display Adapters and note the name of the display adapter. Right-click the display adapter and then select Properties. Look for driver information on the Driver tab.

2. What type of monitor is installed in your computer? Does the monitor listed in Device Manager match the actual model monitor you use?

   In Device Manager, expand Monitors and note the name of the monitor. Windows installs standard monitor drivers when it cannot find specific drivers for your monitor.

3. Using Device Manager, can you determine how many USB ports your computer has built in?

   In Device Manager, expand Universal Serial Bus Controllers. Look for devices named USB Root Hub. Each USB Root Hub corresponds to a USB port on your computer.

8 Supporting Storage Devices in Windows XP

Exam Objectives in this Chapter:

- Configure and troubleshoot storage devices
    - ❑ Answer end user questions related to configuring hard disks and partitions or volumes
    - ❑ Manage and troubleshoot disk partitioning
    - ❑ Answer end user questions related to optical drives such as CD-ROM, CD-RW, DVD-ROM, and DVD+R

Why This Chapter Matters

A storage device is any device that is installed on a computer designed to store data. Microsoft Windows sorts storage devices into two categories: fixed storage devices and removable storage devices. Hard disks are considered to be fixed storage devices because the hard disk's media are not removable. Most other storage devices, including CD-ROM and DVD-ROM, are considered removable because you can remove either the device itself or the storage media that the device uses. This chapter covers the support and troubleshooting of hard disks and removable storage devices.

Lessons in this Chapter:

Before You Begin

Before you begin this chapter, you should have a basic familiarity with working in a Windows-based operating system and with the types of storage devices typically used on a computer running Microsoft Windows XP. You should also have a computer running Windows XP Professional.

Lesson 1: Supporting and Troubleshooting Hard Disks

Hard disks are fixed storage devices that are connected to a computer by Integrated Device Electronics (IDE) or Small Computer System Interface (SCSI) controllers. Portable hard disks are also available, and they can be connected with universal serial bus (USB) and Institute of Electrical and Electronics Engineers (IEEE) 1394 interfaces. However, because Windows typically treats portable hard disks as removable storage devices, this lesson focuses on fixed hard disks. As a desktop support technician (DST), you must understand how to configure and troubleshoot hard disks in Windows XP. You should also be able to use the tools that Windows XP provides for managing, maintaining, and troubleshooting hard disks.

After this lesson, you will be able to

- Explain the use of basic and dynamic disks.
- Manage hard disks by using the Disk Management utility.
- Use the hard disk maintenance tools that are available in Windows XP.

Estimated lesson time: 70 minutes

Understanding Basic and Dynamic Disks

Windows XP Professional supports two types of hard disk storage: **basic disks** and **dynamic disks**. Windows XP Home Edition supports only basic disks. You cannot use dynamic disks on portable computers, even if they are running Windows XP Professional.

> **Exam Tip** When taking the exam, pay close attention to the operating system in use and the type of computer. Remember that you can use dynamic disks only on nonportable computers that are running Windows XP Professional.

Basic Disks

Basic disks are the traditional type of storage that is available in earlier versions of Windows. Basic disks are also the default storage type in Windows XP, so all hard disks begin as basic disks. Windows XP recognizes all disks as basic by default, including all new installations and upgrades from previous versions of Windows. To use a dynamic disk, you must convert a basic disk to a dynamic disk.

On a basic disk, you must create one or more partitions (also called basic volumes). Partitions were covered in detail in Chapter 2, "Installing Windows XP," but a brief review is in order.

You must configure a basic disk with at least one partition. In fact, most computers that you will encounter have a single hard disk with one partition that takes up all the physical space on the disk. You can also divide a hard disk into multiple partitions for the purpose of organizing file storage or supporting multiple operating systems on a single computer. You can create the following three types of partitions on a basic hard disk:

- **Primary**   You can configure up to four primary partitions on a computer running a Windows operating system (three partitions if you also have an extended partition on the disk). You can configure any primary partition as the active, or bootable, drive, but only one primary partition is active at a time. Other primary drives are typically hidden from the operating system and are not assigned a drive letter.

- **Extended**   An extended partition provides a way to exceed the limit of four primary partitions. You cannot format an extended partition with any file system. Rather, extended partitions serve as a shell in which you can create any number of logical partitions.

- **Logical**   You can create any number of logical partitions inside an extended partition. Logical partitions are normally used for organizing files. All logical partitions are visible, no matter which operating system is started.

Microsoft introduced dynamic disks with Windows 2000, and Windows XP Professional supports dynamic disks. Instead of using partitions, you can divide dynamic disks into dynamic volumes, which support features that basic disks do not, such as the creation of more than four partitions per disk and volumes that span multiple hard disks.

You can extend partitions on dynamic disks, provided that contiguous disk space is available. However, partitions on basic disks cannot span multiple hard disks.

Windows stores partition information for basic disks in the partition table, which is not part of any operating system (it is an area of the drive that is accessible by all operating systems). Other configuration options, such as drive letter assignments, are controlled by the operating system and are stored in the Windows Registry.

Basic disks are generally sufficient for a computer with a single hard disk. Also, if a computer is configured to start multiple operating systems, you must use basic disks instead of dynamic disks.

Dynamic Disks

Windows XP Professional supports dynamic disks (dynamic disks are not supported in Windows XP Home Edition or on portable computers). Dynamic disks offer several advantages over basic disks:

- You can divide a dynamic disk into many volumes. The basic disk concept of primary and extended partitions does not exist when using dynamic disks.

- Windows stores configuration information for dynamic disks entirely on the disk. If there are multiple dynamic disks, Windows replicates information to all other disks so that each disk has a copy of the configuration information. This information is stored in the last 1 MB of the disk.

- You can extend dynamic volumes by using contiguous or noncontiguous disk space. Dynamic volumes can also be made up of areas of disk space on more than one disk.

Windows XP supports the following types of dynamic volumes:

- **Simple volumes** Contain disk space from a single disk and can be extended if necessary.

- **Spanned volumes** Contain disk space from 2 or more (up to a maximum of 32) disks. The amount of disk space from each disk can vary. You will most often use spanned volumes when a simple volume is running low on disk space and you need to extend the volume by using space on another hard disk. You can continue to extend spanned volumes to include areas from additional hard disks as necessary. When Windows writes data to a spanned volume, it writes data to the area on the first disk until the area is filled, then to the area on the second disk, and so on. There is no fault tolerance in spanned volumes. If any of the disks containing the spanned volume fail, you lose all data in the entire spanned volume.

- **Striped volumes** Contain disk space from 2 or more (up to a maximum of 32) disks. Unlike spanned volumes, striped volumes require that you use an identical amount of disk space from each disk. When Windows writes data to a striped volume, it divides the data into 64-KB chunks and writes to the disks in a fixed order. Thus, Windows will split a 128-KB file into two 64-KB chunks and then store each chunk on a separate disk. Striped volumes provide increased performance because it is faster to read or write two smaller pieces of a file on two drives than to read or write the entire file on a single drive. However, you cannot extend striped volumes and they provide no fault tolerance. If any of the disks that contain the striped volume fail, you lose all data on the volume. Striped volumes are also referred to as RAID 0.

Exam Tip Windows XP does not support fault-tolerant disk configurations. Spanned volumes simply allow you to use different amounts of disk space from multiple hard disks in a single volume. Striped volumes allow you to use an identical amount of disk space from multiple hard disks. The advantage of using striped volumes is that Windows can write information to the disk more quickly.

Managing Hard Disks with the Disk Management Tool

As a DST, managing hard disks on users' computers will be an important part of your job. You must be able to create volumes on hard disks and configure hard disks to suit users' needs. You use the Disk Management tool to create and manage volumes on fixed and removable disks. You access Disk Management from within the Computer Management window, as shown in Figure 8-1. You can also access Computer Management by using the Administrative Tools icon in Control Panel or by right-clicking My Computer and selecting Manage.

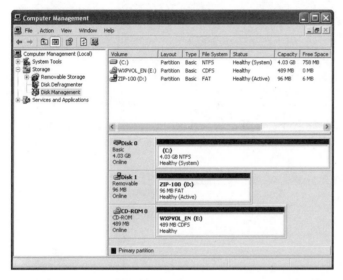

Figure 8-1   Use the Disk Management tool to manage fixed and removable storage.

Supporting Basic Disks

You make unallocated space on basic disks available to the operating system by creating a partition and then formatting that partition with the file system of your choice.

Creating a Primary Partition   To create a primary partition, follow these steps:

1. In Disk Management, right-click the unallocated space in which you want to create the primary partition, as shown in Figure 8-2, and then select New Partition.

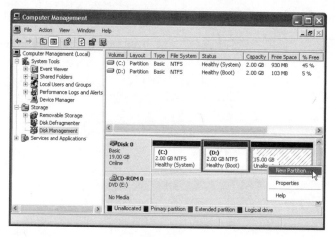

Figure 8-2   Creating a partition on a basic disk.

2. On the Welcome page for the New Partition Wizard, click Next.

3. On the Select Partition Type page, shown in Figure 8-3, choose Primary partition and click Next.

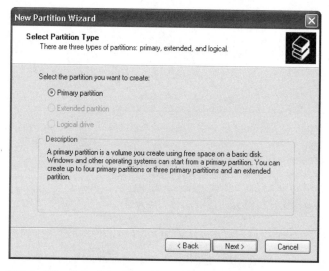

Figure 8-3   Selecting a partition type on a basic disk.

4. On the Specify Partition Size page, enter the amount of disk space in megabytes (MB) that you want to use for this partition and then click Next.

5. On the Assign Drive Letter Or Path page, choose an available drive letter or a path for a volume mount point and click Next.

6. On the Format Partition page, choose Format This Partition, select a file system, and then assign a volume label. Click Next.

7. On the Completion page, click Finish to create and format the partition. Be patient: Windows must perform a number of functions, which can take several minutes.

Creating Extended Partitions   To create an extended partition, follow these steps:

1. In Disk Management, right-click the unallocated space in which you want to create the extended partition and select New Partition.

2. On the Welcome page for the Create Partition Wizard, click Next.

3. On the Select Partition Type page, choose Extended Partition and click Next.

4. On the Specify Partition Size page, enter the amount of disk space in MB that you want to use for this partition and click Next.

5. On the Completion page, click Finish to create the extended partition.

You are not prompted to assign a drive letter or to format an extended partition because the extended partition serves only as a shell to contain logical partitions. You will format and assign drive letters to logical partitions.

Creating Logical Drives   To create a logical drive inside an extended partition, follow these steps:

1. In Disk Management, right-click the free space in the extended partition where you want to create the logical drive and select Create Logical Drive.

2. On the Welcome page for the Create Partition Wizard, click Next.

3. On the Select Partition Type page, choose Logical Drive and click Next.

4. On the Specify Partition Size page, enter the amount of disk space in MB that you want to use for this logical drive and click Next.

5. On the Assign Drive Letter Or Path page, choose an available drive letter and click Next.

6. On the Format Partition page, choose Format This Partition, select a file system, and then assign a volume label. Click Next.

7. On the completion page, click Finish to create and format the logical drive.

Figure 8-4 shows an extended partition on Disk 1, containing a 502-MB logical drive, and 612 MB of remaining free space.

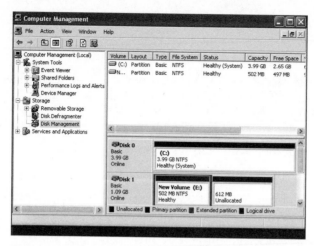

Figure 8-4   Viewing extended and logical partitions in Disk Management.

Formatting Volumes

Formatting a basic or dynamic volume with a file system prepares the volume to accept data. Unformatted volumes contain no file system and are not accessible by using Windows Explorer or any other application.

You can format volumes in the following ways:

- By using Disk Management and formatting the new volume as it is being created

- By using Disk Management, right-clicking an existing volume, and then selecting Format

- By using Windows Explorer, right-clicking the drive letter, and then selecting Format

- By using a command prompt, using the Format.exe command, and selecting the appropriate parameters

If you format an existing volume that contains data, all data is lost. Windows XP protects itself by preventing you from formatting the system and boot partition for the operating system by using any of the built-in Windows utilities.

Formatting options, shown in Figure 8-5, include the following:

- **Volume Label**   The character name for a volume of up to 11 characters. This is the name that is displayed in Disk Management and Windows Explorer. You should choose a label that describes the type of information that is stored on the volume, such as System for the volume that contains the operating system, or Documents for a volume that contains user documents.

- **File System**   Allows you choose from the FAT (for FAT16), FAT32, or NTFS file systems (see Chapter 2 for more information on file systems).

- **Allocation Unit Size**   Allows you change the default cluster size for any of the file systems. Microsoft recommends leaving this value at its default setting.

- **Perform A Quick Format**   Specifies that you want to format the drive without having Windows perform an exhaustive scan of the drive to check for bad sectors. Select this option only if you have previously performed a full format and are certain that the disk is not damaged.

- **Enable File And Folder Compression**   Specifies that all files placed on the disk will be compressed by default. Compression is always available on an NTFS volume, and you can enable or disable it at any time through the properties of the files and folders on the volume. File And Folder Compression is available only when you format a volume with NTFS.

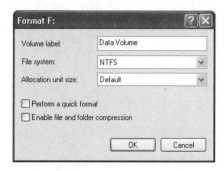

Figure 8-5   Formatting a partition using the Disk Management tool.

Assigning Drive Letters to Volumes

When you create a basic or dynamic volume, you assign it a drive letter such as C or D. The drive letter is used to access the volume through Windows Explorer and other applications. Floppy drives, CD-ROM and DVD drives, removable drives, and tape devices are also assigned drive letters.

To change the currently assigned drive letter for a volume, right-click the volume in Disk Management, select Change Drive Letter And Paths from the action menu, and then click Change. Note that you can change a volume only to a drive letter that is not already being used.

Note   Windows XP does not allow you to modify the drive letter for the system and boot partitions.

Using Volume Mount Points

Windows XP also allows you to mount a volume by using a path instead of assigning a drive letter. For example, you could create a folder named C:\Data. You could then assign the C:\Data path to a new volume labeled Data. When you open the C:\Data folder within Windows Explorer, you would actually see the information that is stored on the Data volume. This type of volume is referred to as a mounted volume, and the folder that the mounted volume is attached to is referred to as a volume mount point. You can create multiple volume mount points for a single volume. You can dismount and move a mounted volume to another volume mount point if necessary.

Mounted volumes provide a method of extending the perceived available space on an existing volume without extending the volume's actual size. Technically, a mounted volume is a separate volume, but in the user's eyes it appears to be an extension of an existing volume. Therefore, you can use mounted volumes to increase the amount of disk space that is available on a basic volume to include disk space on another hard disk (remember that you cannot actually extend a basic volume to include space on another disk). Also, mounted volumes provide a method for managing multiple volumes of information from the same drive letter.

Volume mount points are supported on NTFS volumes only. The volume that is being mounted can be formatted with any supported file system.

To add a mounted volume to an existing volume, follow these steps:

1. By using Windows Explorer, create a folder on an NTFS volume to serve as the volume mount point.

2. In Disk Management, locate the volume for which you want to modify the drive letter or path information.

3. Right-click the volume and select Change Drive Letter And Paths from the action menu.

4. In the Change Drive Letter And Paths For New Volume dialog box, click Add to create a new mounted volume.

5. In the Add New Drive Letter Or Path dialog box, choose Mount In The Following Empty NTFS Folder and enter the path to the volume mount point, as shown in Figure 8-6.

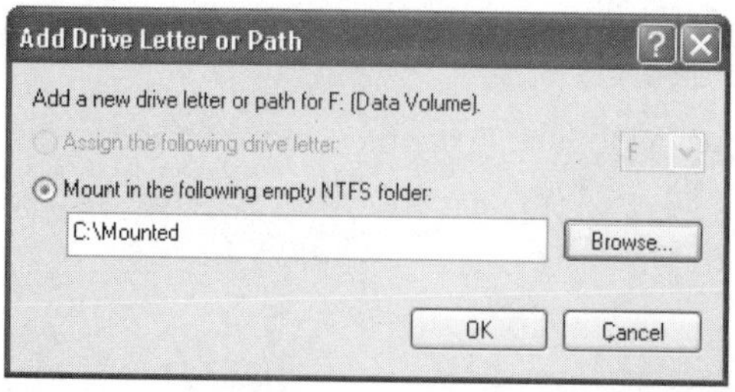

Figure 8-6   Mounting a volume into the C:\mounted folder.

6. Click OK and then click Close.

Mounted volume paths have a different icon in Windows Explorer, as shown in Figure 8-7, and are represented by the <JUNCTION> identifier when viewed at a command prompt, as shown in Figure 8-8.

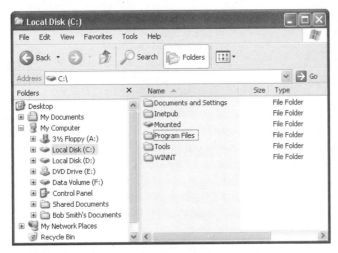

Figure 8-7   Viewing a volume mount point in Windows Explorer (C:\mounted).

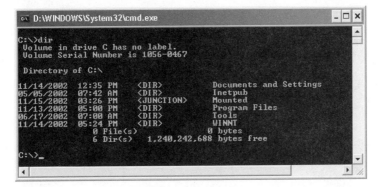

Figure 8-8   Viewing a volume mount point at a command prompt (C:\mounted).

The following list contains some additional information about drive letters and paths:

■ You cannot assign multiple drive letters to a single volume.

■ You cannot assign the same drive letter to multiple volumes on the same computer.

■ You can mount a volume into multiple paths simultaneously.

■ A volume can exist without a drive letter or mount path assigned; however, the volume will not be accessible by applications.

Converting a Basic Disk to a Dynamic Disk

All disks are basic disks by default. When you need to take advantage of the functionality that dynamic disks provide, you must convert the basic disks to dynamic disks (remember that this feature is available only in Windows XP Professional and that you cannot use dynamic disks on portable computers). You can convert a basic disk to a dynamic disk without losing existing data.

For the conversion to be successful, there must be at least 1 MB of free, unpartitioned space available on the basic disk. This 1 MB is necessary to store the dynamic disk database, which tracks the configuration of all dynamic disks in the computer. If Windows XP Professional created the existing partitions, it will have automatically reserved the 1 MB of space required for the conversion. If another operating system or a third-party utility program created the partitions prior to upgrading, there is a chance that no free space is available. In that case, you will probably have to repartition the drive so that 1 MB of space is reserved as blank space.

During the conversion, all primary and extended partitions become simple dynamic volumes, and the disk will join the local disk group and receive a copy of the dynamic disk database.

Caution Recall that after disks have been upgraded to dynamic disks, supporting multiple operating systems is no longer an option.

To convert a basic disk to a dynamic disk, follow these steps:

1. In Disk Management, right-click the basic disk that you want to convert and select Convert To Dynamic Disk, as shown in Figure 8-9. Make sure that you right-click the actual disk, not one of the partitions on the disk.

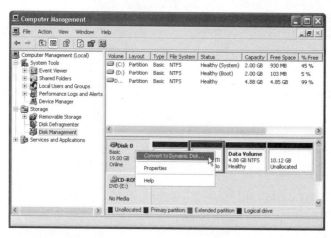

Figure 8-9 Use Disk Management to convert a basic disk to a dynamic disk.

2. In the Convert To Dynamic Disk dialog box, verify the disks that you want to convert and then click OK.

3. In the Disks To Convert dialog box, click Convert and then click Yes to confirm.

   Windows returns you to the Disk Management tool and begins the conversion.

> **Note**   If the disk contains the system or boot volume or any part of the paging file, you need to restart the computer before the conversion process is complete.

You can verify that Windows completed the conversion by viewing the disk type in Disk Management, as shown in Figure 8-10.

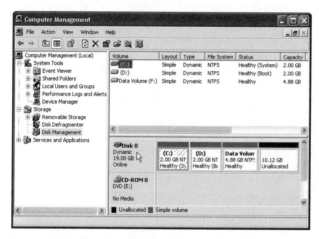

Figure 8-10   The dynamic disk type is displayed in Disk Management.

If you right-click the disk and do not see the Convert To Dynamic Disk option, one of the following conditions may exist:

■ The disk has already been converted to dynamic.

■ You have right-clicked a volume instead of the disk.

■ The disk is in a portable computer. Portable computers do not support dynamic disks.

■ There is not 1 MB of available space at the end of the disk to hold the dynamic disk database.

■ The disk is a removable disk, such as a Zip disk or a detachable USB disk device. Dynamic disks are not supported on removable disks.

■ The sector size on the disk is larger than 512 bytes. Windows XP Professional supports dynamic disks only on disks with a sector size of 512 bytes. The vast majority of hard disks use this sector size.

Reverting from a Dynamic Disk to a Basic Disk

To make a dynamic disk locally accessible by an operating system other than Windows XP Professional (for example, to allow a computer running Windows 98 to access the hard disk when you install the hard disk in that computer), you must convert the dynamic disk back to a basic disk. Data is not preserved when reverting to a basic disk; the downgrade process requires that all data be removed from the disk.

> **Note**   Whether a disk is dynamic or basic has no effect on whether clients running any operating system can connect to shared folders on that disk remotely over the network. Computers running previous versions of Windows cannot locally access a dynamic disk when you install the disk into the computer.

To revert from a dynamic disk back to a basic disk, follow these general steps:

1. Back up all files and folders on the entire disk.

2. In Disk Management, delete all the volumes from the disk.

3. Right-click the dynamic disk you want to convert and select Revert To Basic Disk.

4. Follow the onscreen instructions.

5. Create an appropriate partition scheme on the disk and format the newly created drives.

6. Restore data as necessary.

> **Exam Tip**   When you convert a basic disk to a dynamic disk, data on the disk is preserved. When you revert a dynamic disk to a basic disk, data on the disk is lost.

Creating a Simple Dynamic Volume

A simple dynamic volume contains space on a single disk. Although similar to a primary basic volume, there are no limits to how many simple volumes you can create on a single disk.

To create a simple volume, follow these steps:

1. In Disk Management, right-click the unallocated space on which you want to create the simple volume and then select Create Volume.

2. On the first page of the Create Volume Wizard, click Next.

3. On the Select Volume Type page, select Simple Volume and click Next.

4. On the Select Disks page, enter the desired size in MB and click Next.

5. On the Assign A Drive Letter Or Path page, select a drive letter or enter a path for a mounted volume, and then click Next.

6. On the Format Volume page, select the file system and enter a volume label. Click Next.

7. On the Completion page, click Finish to create the volume.

Creating a Striped Dynamic Volume

Striped volumes can contain from 2 to 32 disks. Data is written to and read from multiple disks simultaneously, increasing disk performance. Data is written (striped) in 64 KB blocks. Striped volumes do not provide any fault tolerance. If one or more of the disks in a striped volume fails, all data on the entire volume is lost. Striped volumes are also known as RAID 0.

To create a striped volume, complete the following steps:

1. In Disk Management, right-click the unallocated space on one of the disks on which you want to create the striped volume and select Create Volume.

2. On the first page of the Create Volume Wizard, click Next.

3. On the Select Volume Type page, select Striped Volume and click Next.

4. On the Select Disks page, select the disks to be included in the striped volume. Adjust the size of the striped volume accordingly and then click Next.

5. On the Assign A Drive Letter Or Path page, select a drive letter or enter a path for a mounted volume and then click Next.

6. On the Format Volume page, select the file system and enter a volume label. Click Next.

7. On the Completion page, click Finish to create the volume.

The amount of disk space that is consumed on each disk in the striped volume must be equal. The disk with the smallest amount of available space limits the maximum amount of space available on a striped volume. For example, assume that you have the following drive configuration on your computer:

- Disk 0—No space available

- Disk 1—2 GB available

- Disk 2—2 GB available

- Disk 3—1 GB available

If you attempt to create a striped volume with Disks 1, 2, and 3, the maximum volume size that you can create is 3 GB. Because Disk 3 has only 1 GB of space available, you are limited to using only 1 GB from each of the disks in the set. However, if you create a striped volume using only Disks 1 and 2, the maximum volume size you can create is 4 GB because both disks have 2 GB of available space.

Extending Volumes

Windows XP Professional supports extending volumes on both basic and dynamic disks, whereas Windows XP Home Edition supports extending volumes only on basic disks. You extend volumes on basic disks by using the DiskPart command-line utility. You can extend volumes on dynamic disks using either the Disk Management utility or the DiskPart command-line utility.

Extending Volumes on Basic Disks   You can extend primary partitions and logical drives on basic disks if the following conditions are met:

- The volume to be extended is formatted with NTFS.

- The volume is extended into contiguous, unallocated space (adjacent free space) that follows the existing volume (as opposed to coming before it).

- The volume is extended on the same hard disk. Volumes on basic disks cannot be extended to include disk space on another hard disk.

- The volume is not the system or boot volume. The system or boot volumes cannot be extended.

You extend volumes by running the DiskPart utility from the command line, selecting the appropriate volume, and then executing the following command:

```
extend [size=n] [noerr]
```

> **See Also**   For further information on the use of DiskPart, refer to the section entitled "Managing Disks from the Command Line" later in this chapter.

Extending Volumes on Dynamic Disks   You can extend a simple volume as long as it has been formatted with NTFS. You do this by attaching additional unallocated space from the same disk, or from a different disk, to an existing simple volume. Disk space that is used to extend a simple volume does not have to be contiguous. If the additional space comes from a different disk, the volume becomes a **spanned volume**. Spanned volumes can contain disk space from 2 to 32 disks.

If the volume is not formatted with NTFS, you must convert the volume to NTFS before you can extend it.

You extend simple volumes by using Disk Management or the DiskPart command-line utility. Perform extensions of simple volumes with DiskPart the same way that you perform extensions of basic volumes.

To extend a simple volume using Disk Management, follow these steps:

1. In Disk Management, right-click the simple volume that you want to extend and select Extend Volume.

2. On the first page of the Extend Volume Wizard, click Next.

3. On the Select Disks page, select the disk(s) that contain free space that you want to attach to this volume, enter the amount of space for each disk, and then click Next.

4. On the Completion page, click Finish to extend the volume.

Figure 8-11 shows the Select Disks page on a single-drive system. In this case, the maximum available space on the selected disk that you can use to extend the volume is 2048 MB.

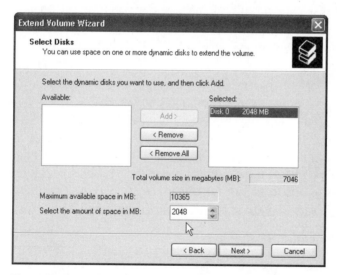

Figure 8-11   Extending a simple dynamic volume in Disk Management.

You are not prompted for any information concerning drive lettering or formatting because the added space assumes the same properties as the existing volume.

Moving Disks

If a computer fails but the hard disks are still functional, you can install the disks into another computer to ensure that the data is still accessible. However, you need to consider the following issues that are associated with moving disks:

- You cannot move dynamic disks to computers running Windows 95, Windows 98, Windows Millennium Edition (Windows Me), Windows NT 4.0 or earlier, or Windows XP Home Edition because these operating systems do not support dynamic disks. To move a disk to these operating systems, you must first convert it to a basic disk.

- When moving spanned or striped volumes, move all disks that are associated with the volume at the same time. If one disk is missing from a spanned or striped volume, none of the data on the entire volume is accessible.

- Windows XP Professional does not support volume sets or stripe sets that were created in Windows NT 4.0. You must back up the data, delete the volumes, install the disks into the Windows XP Professional computer, create new volumes, and then restore the data. Alternatively, you can install the disks into a computer running Windows 2000 (which does support Windows NT volume and stripe sets), convert the disks to dynamic disks (which converts volume sets to spanned volumes and stripe sets to striped volumes), and then install the disks into a computer running Windows XP Professional.

After moving disks, the disks appear in Disk Management on the new computer. Basic disks are immediately accessible. Dynamic disks initially appear as foreign disks and need to be imported before you can access them.

Importing Foreign Disks

All dynamic disks on a computer running Windows XP Professional are members of the same disk group. Each disk in the group contains the dynamic disk database for the entire group, stored in the 1-MB reserved disk area at the end of the disk. When you move a dynamic disk from one computer to another, Windows displays it as a foreign disk because it does not belong to the local disk group. You must import foreign disks, which merges the disk's information into the dynamic disk database on the new computer and places a copy of the database on the newly installed disk.

To import a foreign disk, follow these steps:

1. In Disk Management, right-click the disk that is marked Foreign and select Import Foreign Disks from the action menu.

2. Select the disk group that you want to import. (There may be more than one foreign disk group if you have moved multiple disks from different computers into the same computer running Windows XP Professional.)

3. In the Foreign Disk Volumes dialog box, review the information to ensure that the condition for the volumes in the disk group being imported is displayed as OK. If all the disks for a spanned or striped volume are not present, the condition is displayed as incomplete. You should resolve incomplete volume conditions before continuing with the import.

4. If you are satisfied with the information that is in the Foreign Disk Volumes dialog box, click OK to import the disks.

Removing Disks from the Dynamic Disk Database

If you remove a dynamic disk from a computer running Windows XP, Disk Management displays the disk as either Offline or Missing because the disk's configuration is still present in the dynamic disk database stored on the other disks on the computer. You can remove the missing disk's configuration from the dynamic disk database by right-clicking the disk and selecting Remove Disk.

Managing Disks Remotely

You can perform disk functions on a remote computer by connecting to that computer through Computer Management. To connect to a remote computer in Computer Management, follow these steps:

1. From the Start menu, right-click My Computer and select Manage to open the Computer Management window.

2. In the Computer Management window, right-click Computer Management and select Connect To Another Computer from the action menu, as shown in Figure 8-12.

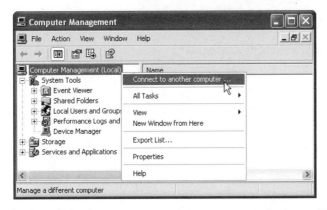

Figure 8-12   Connecting to another computer in Computer Management.

3. In the Select Computer dialog box, select the computer that you want to manage remotely and then click OK. Computer Management displays the remote computer's information, and you can manage the disks on that computer by using the Disk Management tool.

Managing Disks from the Command Line

You can use the Diskpart.exe command to execute disk-management tasks from a command prompt and to create scripts for automating those tasks that you need to perform frequently or on multiple computers.

Executing DiskPart from a command prompt opens the DiskPart command interpreter. When you are in the DiskPart command interpreter, the command prompt changes to DISKPART>. You can view available commands for the DiskPart tool by typing **commands** at the DiskPart command prompt, as shown in Figure 8-13. Note that you use the Exit command to close the DiskPart command interpreter and return to the normal command prompt.

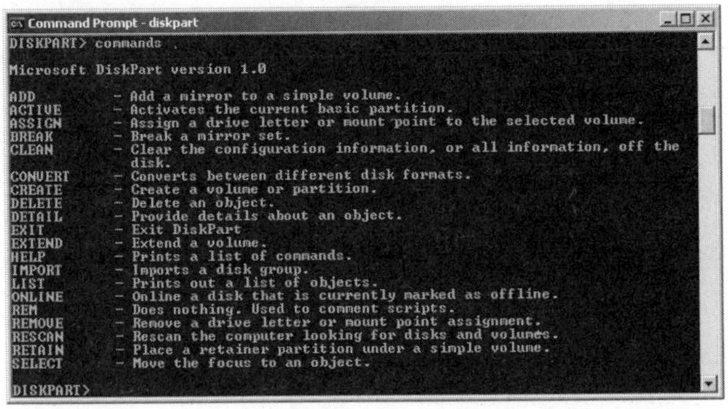

Figure 8-13 Viewing DiskPart command options.

One feature that is not available in DiskPart is the capability to format volumes. To format volumes, you must use the Format.exe command from the standard command prompt.

Maintaining Disks

The Windows XP Professional operating system includes several utilities for maintaining hard disks. This section covers the following utilities:

- Chkdsk.exe
- Disk Defragmenter
- Disk Cleanup

Performing Error Checking by Using Chkdsk.exe

In Windows XP, you perform error checking on hard disks by using the Chkdsk.exe command-line utility. Chkdsk verifies and repairs the integrity of the file system on a volume. If file system errors are detected on a volume, Chkdsk schedules itself to run automatically the next time Windows XP is started and fixes the errors. As a DST, you should encourage users to run Chkdsk periodically. You should also use Chkdsk as one of your initial troubleshooting steps when you suspect a hard disk problem.

You can run Chkdsk with or without additional parameters. When you simply type **chkdsk** at the command prompt with no additional parameters, Chkdsk analyzes the disk and generates a report, but does not repair errors. To fix errors, you must use one of the following additional parameters:

- **/f**   Locks a volume and fixes errors, scheduling a repair on the next restart if the volume contains files currently in use.

- **/r**   Locks a volume, locates bad sectors, and recovers readable information.

Chkdsk can take a long time to repair a volume. When a volume is being repaired, it is locked and inaccessible. If Chkdsk cannot lock the volume, it will offer to repair the volume at the next computer restart. The boot volume can never be locked while the computer is up and running, and you can repair it only by restarting the computer.

In addition to command-line Chkdsk, Windows also provides a graphical utility. To access the graphical version of Chkdsk, shown in Figure 8-14, right-click the volume letter in Windows Explorer, select the Tools tab and, in the Error-Checking section, click Check Now.

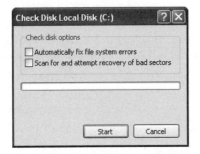

Figure 8-14   Using the graphical version of Chkdsk.

Real World   Autochk.exe and Chkntfs.exe

The Autochk.exe command-line utility is the version of Chkdsk that runs only when Windows XP starts. Autochk is used instead of Chkdsk in the following situations:

- When a file system error is detected and a volume needs repair
- When Chkdsk is run on the boot volume
- When Chkdsk cannot gain exclusive use of the volume

Normally, when Chkdsk is run on a volume other than the system or boot partition, it dismounts the volume, locks it, and proceeds. However, if Chkdsk cannot dismount the volume (normally because one or more files cannot be closed), you are prompted to run Autochk at next startup.

When Autochk runs, the computer can be unavailable for a significant time. The Chkntfs.exe command-line utility enables you to control which volumes will be checked by Autochk. If Autochk is scheduled to scan hard disks the next time the computer starts, you can use Chkntfs prior to restarting to perform the following tasks:

- Check the status of volumes
- Exclude dirty volumes from being checked by Autochk
- Cancel scheduled Autochk sessions

Using the Disk Defragmenter

Fragmented files and folders are stored in locations scattered throughout the disk rather than in one contiguous location. The more fragmented a file or folder is, the more reads it takes to access, and the more Windows performance suffers. Fragmentation generally occurs when files are frequently added and removed from the disk or when the disk begins to fill up. In both of these cases, it can be difficult for the operating system to locate a contiguous area of the disk to write to, and data can become fragmented.

Defragmentation refers to the process of rearranging the various pieces of files and folders on the disk into contiguous spaces, thereby improving performance. In Windows XP, you use the Disk Defragmenter tool to defragment hard disks. In addition to defragmenting the existing files and folders, Disk Defragmenter can also consolidate free space, making it less likely that a new file or folder will become fragmented in the near future.

You access Disk Defragmenter from the Start menu by selecting All Programs, Accessories, System Tools, and then Disk Defragmenter. This utility first performs an analysis of the selected volume and lets you know if the drive would benefit from being defragmented.

Figure 8-15 shows a Disk Defragmenter Analysis Report. In this case, the disk is significantly fragmented (23%) and would benefit from defragmentation.

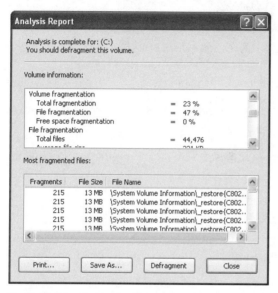

Figure 8-15   Viewing a Disk Defragmenter analysis report.

A defragmentation in process is shown in Figure 8-16. The Analysis display gives an indication of the amount and location of fragmented files. The Defragmentation display shows the progress that is being made as the defragmentation progresses.

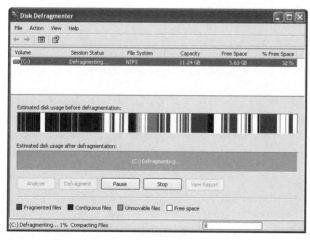

Figure 8-16   Viewing a defragmentation in process.

Windows XP also provides a command-line version of Disk Defragmenter, called Defrag.exe. Figure 8-17 shows the parameters available with Defrag.exe.

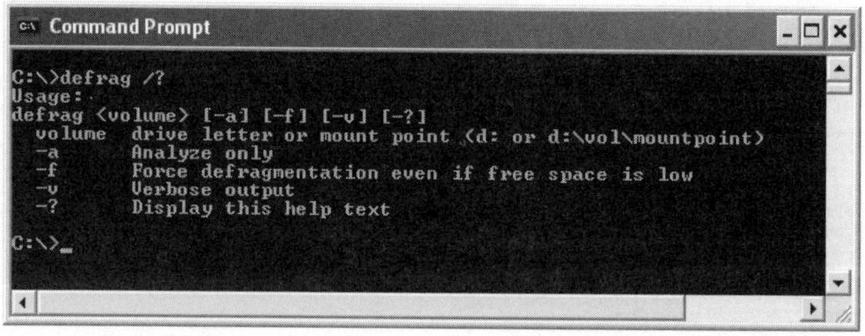

```
C:\>defrag /?
Usage:
defrag <volume> [-a] [-f] [-v] [-?]
   volume    drive letter or mount point (d: or d:\vol\mountpoint)
   -a        Analyze only
   -f        Force defragmentation even if free space is low
   -v        Verbose output
   -?        Display this help text

C:\>_
```

Figure 8-17   Viewing the Defrag.exe command-line parameters.

For optimal performance, you should perform disk defragmentation in the following circumstances:

- After you have deleted a large number of files, to defragment and consolidate disk space.

- Before you add a large number of files, to ensure that the newly added files occupy contiguous disk space.

- After installing application programs, to defragment and consolidate disk space. Application programs can use temporary files during installation. After these files are deleted, disk space allocation is no longer optimal.

- After installing Windows XP, to ensure optimal operating system performance.

Disk defragmentation is best performed during periods of low system activity. Prior to running Disk Defragmenter, consider deleting unnecessary files to free up disk space and to minimize the work that Disk Defragmenter has to do.

Disk Cleanup

If a computer is getting low on available hard disk space, you can delete certain types of files to create more available space. Users may not be aware of which files they can delete safely, so Windows includes the Disk Cleanup utility to help with this process.

You access the Disk Cleanup utility, shown in Figure 8-18, from the Start menu by selecting All Programs, Accessories, System Tools, and then Disk Cleanup. When you start Disk Cleanup, the utility calculates the amount of space that you can gain by deleting selected items. The following list describes the most common options in Disk Cleanup:

- **Downloaded Program Files**   Files that have been downloaded from the Internet and stored in the Downloaded Program Files folder on the hard disk.

- **Temporary Internet Files**   Copies of previously visited Web pages that are stored on the hard disk for faster access the next time you need to view the same Web pages.

- **Recycle Bin**   Files that have been deleted but not yet removed from the hard disk.

- **Temporary Files**   Files that are used for temporary workspace by any number of applications and that are usually stored in the TEMP folder. Temporary files are supposed to be deleted by the application that created them, but that does not always happen.

- **Temporary Offline Files**   Files that have been cached locally for use when the network is offline. You can remove them from the computer, but synchronize beforehand to ensure that all changes have been copied to the network.

- **Compress Old Files**   Compresses infrequently used files on NTFS partitions, which often saves a significant amount of disk space.

> **Tip**   The Disk Cleanup options list is built dynamically, based on the types of data present in the computer when the utility is started. Therefore, this example does not represent all the options you may encounter—only the most common ones.

To delete any of the listed items, you must select the item. As you select items for deletion, Disk Cleanup displays the total amount of disk space that you will gain. By default, only Downloaded Program Files, Temporary Internet Files, and Temporary Offline Files are selected for deletion.

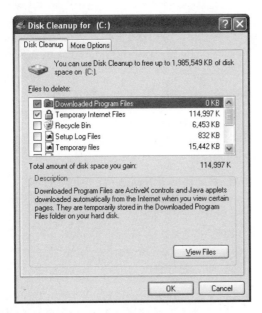

Figure 8-18   Using the Disk Cleanup utility to delete unnecessary files.

Troubleshooting Disks and Volumes

Disk Management displays the status of each disk and volume. If you refer to Figure 8-1, you notice that all disks are online and all volumes are showing the desired status of Healthy.

Disk status types are as follows:

- **Online**   Displayed by basic and dynamic disks. The disk is accessible. No user action is required.

- **Online (Errors)**   Displayed by dynamic disks only. The disk is accessible, but input/output (I/O) errors have been detected. If the I/O errors are intermittent, right-click the disk and select Reactivate Disk. This normally returns the disk to Online status.

- **Offline Or Missing**   Displayed by dynamic disks only. This disk is not accessible. Attempt to rescan the disks on the computer by selecting Rescan Disks from the Action menu in Disk Management. If the scan is unsuccessful, look for a physical reason for the drive failure (cables disconnected, no power to disk, failed disk). If you must replace a failed drive, first delete all volumes on the disk and then right-click the disk and select Remove Disk.

- **Foreign**   Displayed by dynamic disks only. The disk has been moved to this computer from another computer. Right-click the disk and select Import Foreign Disk. If you do not want to keep the information on the disk, you can select Convert To Basic Disk, and all information on the disk will be lost.

- **Unreadable**   Displayed by basic and dynamic disks. The disk is not accessible. Disks may show this status while they are initializing. If a disk continues to show this status, the disk may have failed entirely. Restart the computer to determine whether the disk will become accessible. If it is a dynamic disk, attempt to repair the disk by right-clicking it and selecting Rescan Disks.

- **Unrecognized**   The disk is an unknown type, and Windows XP cannot recognize it.

- **No Media**   This status is on drives with removable media, such as a CD-ROM drive, when the drive is empty.

Volume status types and the recommended action (if required) are as follows:

- **Healthy**   The volume is accessible and has no detected problems.

- **Healthy (At Risk)**   If the disk status is Online (Errors), the volumes will be accessible, but all volumes will display this status. Restoring the disk to Online will clear this status from the volume.

- **Initializing**   The volume is in the process of initializing. No action is required. Once the initialization is complete, the volume should show a status of Healthy.

Practice: Manage Hard Disks

In this practice, you will check the status of existing volumes on your computer using Disk Management and change the drive letter for a volume. You will use Disk Cleanup to delete unnecessary files from a volume and then defragment a volume using Disk Defragmenter.

Exercise 1: Check the Status of Existing Volumes

1. From the Start menu, right-click My Computer and then select Manage.

2. In the Computer Management window, select Disk Management.

3. After the Disk Management display initializes, record the description in the Status column for each volume on your computer.

Exercise 2: Change the Drive Letter for a Volume

1. From the Start menu, right-click My Computer and then select Manage.

2. In the Computer Management window, select Disk Management.

3. Right-click a volume in the Disk Management display and select Change Drive Letter And Paths.

4. In the Change Drive Letter And Paths dialog box, click Change.

5. In the Change Drive Letter Or Path dialog box, select a new drive letter from the Assign The Following Drive letter drop-down list and then click OK.

6. Click OK again to return to the Disk Management window.

Exercise 3: Run Disk Cleanup

1. From the Start menu, point to All Programs, Accessories, System Tools, and then select Disk Cleanup. Disk Cleanup often takes a few minutes to open because it first calculates how much space you can free up on the computer's disk drive.

2. In the Select Drive dialog box, select the volume to clean up from the drop-down list. Click OK.

3. In the Disk Cleanup dialog box, review the files to be deleted. Click OK when finished.

4. Click Yes to verify that you want to perform these actions.

Exercise 4: Defragment a Volume

1. Close all open programs.

2. Turn off screen savers and antivirus software.

3. From the Start menu, point to All Programs, Accessories, System Tools, and then select Disk Defragmenter.

4. Select a volume from the list and click Analyze. After several minutes, Disk Defragmenter shows you the analysis of the volume.

5. If the volume is significantly fragmented (more than 10 percent), click Defragment to begin the defragmenting process. Note that this process can take quite awhile (even a few hours), depending on the size of the volume and the amount of data it contains.

Lesson Review

The following questions are intended to reinforce key information presented in this lesson. If you are unable to answer a question, review the lesson materials and try the question again. You can find answers to the questions in the "Questions and Answers" section at the end of this chapter.

1. What is the process of rearranging files and folders into contiguous blocks called?

_____

_____

2. On what types of computers can you use dynamic disks?

_____

_____

3. What actions must you take to revert from a dynamic disk to a basic disk? What limitations does this process impose?

_____

_____

_____

Lesson Summary

■ Windows XP Professional provides the Disk Management utility to configure, manage, and monitor hard disks and volumes. Using this utility, you can accomplish tasks such as the creation and formatting of volumes, moving disks from one computer to another, and remote disk management. You can use additional disk utilities such as Disk Defragmenter and Chkdsk to ensure optimal disk performance.

- Windows XP Professional supports two types of disk storage: basic disks and dynamic disks. Windows XP Home Edition and portable computers support only basic disks.

- All disks are basic disks by default. When you need to take advantage of the functionality that dynamic disks provide, you must upgrade the basic disks to dynamic disks. (Remember that this feature is available only in Windows XP Professional and Windows 2000 Professional.) You can perform this operation with no loss of data.

- You must format a volume before it can accept data, and each volume can be formatted with only a single file system. Volumes are usually assigned drive letters, such as C or D, which are used to reference the volume from within the operating system and through applications.

- Mounted volumes provide a method of extending the perceived available space on an existing volume without extending the volume's size. Technically, a mounted volume is a separate volume, but in the user's eyes it appears to be an extension of an existing volume.

Lesson 2: Supporting and Troubleshooting Removable Media

Windows XP contains built-in support for both CD-ROM and DVD-ROM devices. Windows XP also supports a number of other removable media types, such as tape drives and memory storage. This lesson covers the monitoring and troubleshooting of removable media.

After this lesson, you will be able to

- Monitor and troubleshoot CD-ROM and DVD-ROM devices.
- Troubleshoot problems with other removable devices.

Estimated lesson time: 15 minutes

Monitoring and Troubleshooting CD-ROM and DVD Devices

Most CD-ROM and DVD-ROM devices are Plug and Play–compliant and therefore require little configuration. To view the status and configuration of these types of devices, access the device's Properties dialog box through Device Manager (see Chapter 6, "Installing and Managing Hardware," for detailed information on using Device Manager). The General tab of the device's Properties dialog box indicates whether the device is functioning properly within Windows. The Properties tab, shown in Figure 8-19, provides configuration options.

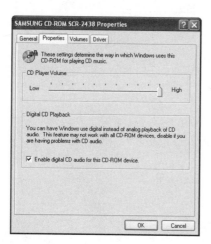

Figure 8-19   Configure CD-ROM and DVD-ROM devices using Device Manager.

If Device Manager indicates that the device is installed and functioning, yet the device does not appear to be working properly, there may be a physical problem with the device installation or the device itself may be faulty. If the disk tray does not eject properly or the power/usage light-emitting diode (LED) indicators are not illuminated, open the computer and verify that all connections have been properly established.

If a CD or DVD device appears to read data correctly but does not play back audio, there is most likely a device driver problem or additional required components are not currently configured. Always verify that the device is listed in the Windows Catalog. Also, make sure that the latest version of the device driver and associated software is installed.

To troubleshoot an audio playback problem, take the following additional steps:

- Verify that the sound card is properly configured and functional.
- Verify that the speakers are plugged in and turned on.
- Verify that the sound has not been muted.
- Verify that the audio cables connecting the CD/DVD to the sound card are properly connected.
- Make sure that the CD is clean.

If the CD device supports it, you can enable the digital CD playback feature in the drive's Properties dialog box in Device Manager. On the Properties tab, select the Enable Digital CD Audio For This CD-ROM Device check box. Digital CD playback requires that CD devices support Digital Audio Extraction (DAE), which older devices might not support. When digital CD playback is enabled, the CD-ROM drive does not have to be connected to the sound card, and audio output from the headphone jack on the CD-ROM drive is disabled.

Supporting and Troubleshooting Removable Media

Removable media consist of devices such as disks, tape, and optical media, which are stored either online in the form of information libraries or offline on a shelf or in a file drawer. These media are used primarily for backup of applications and data. They are also used to archive data that is not accessed frequently.

Previous versions of Windows (pre–Windows 2000) did not provide strong support for removable devices. Each application that required access to a removable device needed a custom solution for accessing and managing removable storage media. Windows XP centralizes the management of these devices with Removable Storage technology. Removable Storage allows the operating system to manage removable media centrally, and applications gain access to removable devices through the

Removable Storage interface. Devices with drivers that have been written to take advantage of Removable Storage are easily accessible and sharable by both the operating system and applications.

Understanding Removable Storage

Removable Storage uses the concept of media pools to organize removable media. Media pools group media by usage, allow media to be shared by multiple applications, control media access, and provide for tracking of media usage. Other concepts of removable storage include the following:

- **Media units**   The actual devices that store information, such as a CD-ROM, tape cartridge, or removable disk.

- **Media libraries**   Encompass both online libraries and offline media physical locations. Online libraries, which include robotic libraries and stand-alone drives, are data-storage devices that provide a method of reading and writing to media when necessary. Offline media physical locations are holding places for media units that are cataloged by Removable Storage, but are not currently immediately available through an online library.

- **Work queues**   Hold library requests until resources become available. For example, a robotic tape library has a fixed number of tape drives to access media. A request submitted to the library is held in a work queue until a tape drive becomes available and the requested tape is mounted.

- **Operator (administrator) requests**   Hold requests for offline media. The operator must make the media available before processing can continue. Other situations that generate operator requests include the failure of a device or a device needing to be cleaned when no cleaner cartridge is available. After a request is satisfied, the administrator must inform Removable Storage so that processing can continue.

> **Note**   Removable storage devices can contain primary partitions only, and those partitions cannot be marked as active.

Using the Removable Storage Utility

You perform initial installation, configuration, and troubleshooting of removable storage devices by using the Add Hardware Wizard and Device Manager, as described in Chapter 6. After being recognized by the operating system, removable storage devices are available for management through the Removable Storage utility. Access Removable Storage by expanding the Storage node in the Computer Management window.

Figure 8-20 shows the Removable Storage utility, launched on a computer with only a single CD-ROM drive. By using the Removable Storage utility, you can insert and eject removable media, control access to media, and manage the use of media by applications. Systems with standard, stand-alone, removable devices (such as a CD-ROM or DVD-ROM drive, Zip drive, or tape drive) do not require management and configuration by using Removable Storage. Removable Storage is required for computers with more complex configurations, which can include tape or optical disk libraries, especially if multiple applications will access those devices. You should always consult the documentation for the removable device to determine how it is best managed.

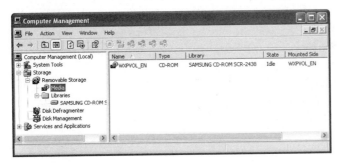

Figure 8-20   Using the Removable Storage utility.

Removable storage devices that require management through the Remote Storage utility are most likely attached to Windows servers in a network environment. Further discussion of Removable Storage management is beyond the scope of this text. For more information, see *http://www.microsoft.com* and search on "Removable Storage."

Lesson Review

The following questions are intended to reinforce key information presented in this lesson. If you are unable to answer a question, review the lesson materials and try the question again. You can find answers to the questions in the "Questions and Answers" section at the end of this chapter.

1. If Device Manager indicates that the CD-ROM is installed and functioning, yet the device does not appear to be functioning properly, what is indicated?

_____

_____

_____

Lesson Summary

■ You can adjust the settings for a CD-ROM or DVD-ROM device using the device's Properties dialog box in Device Manager.

- The Removable Storage utility is used to manage media devices such as disks, tape, and optical media, which are stored either online in the form of information libraries or offline on a shelf or in a file drawer.

Case Scenario Exercises

Scenario 8.1

One of the users for whom you provide support has two identical hard disks installed in her computer. She says that she has more than enough space on just one drive and has not stored anything on the second drive. The user has read about Windows XP Professional's support of disk striping and wants you to help her configure these two disks as a striped volume. Both disks are currently configured as basic disks and you know you must upgrade the disks to dynamic disks to support striping. You cannot upgrade one of the disks, however. What might prevent you from upgrading the disk, and how can you resolve the issue?

_____

_____

_____

_____

Scenario 8.2

You have a user who needs to increase the amount of free space available to Windows XP Professional. The current hard disk is a 20-GB drive with 1 GB of available free space and is formatted as FAT32.

You help the user complete the installation of an additional 40-GB hard disk. You configure the basic input/output system (BIOS) to recognize the newly installed drive, and Disk Management recognizes both drives.

The user does not want an additional drive letter assigned to the new hard disk space. She does want to retain the original drive and its contents. How can you configure this computer to meet the user's needs? What, if any, changes will she notice to the file system? What, if any, are the disadvantages of using volume mount points?

_____

_____

_____

_____

Troubleshooting Lab

You receive a call from a user who says that when he turned on his computer this morning, he could not access the F drive that he uses to store documents. He is not sure how the hard disks on the computer are configured, so you help him open the Disk Management tool. The customer reports the following configuration to you:

- Disk 0 is configured as a basic disk and contains one partition. The drive letter for the partition is C, and the partition is labeled as the System partition. Disk Management reports the disk as online and the C partition as healthy.

- Disk 1 is configured as a dynamic disk, but Disk Management reports the disk as missing.

What do you suspect is the problem? What would you suggest that the user do?

_____

_____

_____

_____

Chapter Summary

- Windows XP Professional provides the Disk Management utility to configure, manage, and monitor hard disks and volumes. Using this utility, you can accomplish tasks such as the creation and formatting of volumes, moving disks from one computer to another, and remote disk management. You can use additional disk utilities such as Disk Defragmenter and Chkdsk to ensure optimal disk performance.

- Windows XP Professional supports two types of disk storage: basic disks and dynamic disks. Windows XP Home Edition supports only basic disks. Portable computers also support only basic disks.

- All disks are basic disks by default. When you need to take advantage of the functionality that dynamic disks provide, you must upgrade the basic disks to dynamic disks. (Remember that this feature is available only in the Windows XP Professional version.) You can perform this operation with no loss of data.

- You must format a volume before it can accept data, and each volume can be formatted with only a single file system. Volumes are usually assigned drive letters, such as C or D, which are used to reference the volume from within the operating system and through applications.

- Mounted volumes provide a method of extending the perceived available space on an existing volume without extending the volume's size. Technically, a mounted volume is a separate volume, but in the user's eyes, it appears to be an extension of an existing volume.

Exam Highlights

Before taking the exam, review the key topics and terms that are presented in this chapter. You need to know this information.

Key Points

- When taking the exam, pay close attention to the operating system in use and the type of computer. Remember that you can only use dynamic disks on nonportable computers that are running Windows XP Professional.

- Windows XP does not support fault-tolerant disk configurations. Spanned volumes simply allow you to use different amounts of disk space from multiple hard disks in a single volume. Striped volumes allow you to use an identical amount of disk space from multiple hard disks. The advantage of using striped volumes is that Windows can read from and write to the disk more quickly.

- When you convert a basic disk to a dynamic disk, data on the disk is preserved. When you revert a dynamic disk to a basic disk, data on the disk is lost.

Key Terms

basic disk   A physical disk that can be accessed locally by MS-DOS and all Windows-based operating systems. Basic disks can contain up to four primary partitions or three primary partitions and an extended partition with multiple logical drives. If you want to create partitions that span multiple disks, you must first convert the basic disk to a dynamic disk using Disk Management or the DiskPart.exe command-line utility. Note that whether a disk is basic or dynamic has no bearing on whether computers running other operating systems can connect to shared folders on the disk.

Disk Management   The process of creating, managing, and monitoring disks in Windows XP. Also the name of the Windows XP utility used to perform these functions.

DiskPart.exe   A command-line utility used to manage the partitions on your hard disk volumes.

dynamic disk   A physical disk that can be accessed locally only by Windows 2000 and Windows XP. Dynamic disks provide features that basic disks do not, such as support for volumes that span multiple disks. Dynamic disks use a hidden database to track information about dynamic volumes on the disk and other dynamic disks in the computer. You convert basic disks to dynamic by using the Disk Management snap-in or the DiskPart command-line utility. When you convert a basic disk to a dynamic disk, all existing basic volumes become dynamic volumes. Note that whether a disk is basic or dynamic has no bearing on whether computers running other operating systems can connect to shared folders on the disk.

logical drive   A disk storage area that you create within an extended partition on a basic Master Boot Record (MBR) disk. Logical drives are similar to primary partitions, except that you can create an unlimited number of logical drives per disk. A logical drive can be formatted and assigned a drive letter.

partitioning   The process of dividing a physical disk into logical sections that function as if they are physically separate disks. After you create a partition, you must format it and assign it a drive letter before you can store data on it.

Questions and Answers

Lesson 1 Review

Page
8-28

1. What is the process of rearranging files and folders into contiguous blocks called?

Defragmenting. Windows XP includes the Disk Defragmenter utility to analyze and defragment disks.

2. On what types of computers can you use dynamic disks?

To use a dynamic disk, you must be running Windows XP Professional or Windows 2000 Professional. Windows XP Home Edition and portable computers do not support dynamic disks.

3. What actions must you take to revert from a dynamic disk to a basic disk? What limitations does this process impose?

By using Disk Management, you must delete all volumes on the disk. You must then right-click the disk and select Revert To Basic Disk. All data is lost when reverting a dynamic disk to a basic disk. You must repartition and reformat the basic disk following the conversion.

Lesson 2 Review

Page
8-33

1. If Device Manager indicates that the CD-ROM is installed and functioning, yet the device does not appear to be functioning properly, what is indicated?

The CD media may be defective, dirty, or not readable.

Case Scenario Exercises: Scenario 8.1

Page
8-34

One of the users for whom you provide support has two identical hard disks installed in her computer. She says that she has more than enough space on just one drive and has not stored anything on the second drive. The user has read about Windows XP Professional's support of disk striping and wants you to help her configure these two disks as a striped volume. Both disks are currently configured as basic disks and you know you must upgrade the disks to dynamic disks to support striping. You cannot upgrade one of the disks, however. What might prevent you from upgrading the disk, and how can you resolve the issue?

To convert from a basic disk to a dynamic disk, 1 MB of free, unpartitioned space must be available at the end of the disk. This 1 MB is necessary to store the database that tracks the configuration of all dynamic disks in the computer. If Windows XP created the existing partitions, it automatically reserved the 1 MB of space required for the conversion. If the partitions were created by another operating system or utility program, there is a good chance that no free space is available. To create the 1 MB of free space required, you can delete all partitions on the disk, re-create them through Disk Management, and restore the data.

Case Scenario Exercises: Scenario 8.2

Page
8-34

You have a user who needs to increase the amount of free space available to Windows XP Professional. The current hard disk is a 20-GB drive with 1 GB of available free space and is formatted as FAT32.

You help the user complete the installation of an additional 40-GB hard disk. You configure the basic input/output system (BIOS) to recognize the newly installed drive, and Disk Management recognizes both drives.

The user does not want an additional drive letter assigned to the new hard disk space. She does want to retain the original drive and its contents. How can you configure this computer to meet the user's needs? What, if any, changes will she notice to the file system? What, if any, are the disadvantages of using volume mount points?

To meet all your customer's needs, you first need to explain that the file system must be NTFS. Volume mount points are available only to NTFS partitions. To create a volume mount point, you must first convert the file system to NTFS, create a new folder on drive C, select the drive you want to add the volume mount point to from Disk Management, right-click and select Change Drive Letter And Paths For New Volumes, and choose Add Then Mount In This NTFS Folder from the Add New Drive Letter Of Path dialog box. To confirm that the volume mount point has been created, you can view the folder from Windows Explorer and note that the icon is different from the standard folder icons, or you can open a command prompt and then change to the parent folder of the volume mount point and type **dir**; it displays the folder as a <JUNCTION>. This solution allows you to increase the storage space available to Windows XP without assigning a drive letter to the new disk.

Troubleshooting Lab

Page
8-35

What do you suspect is the problem? What would you suggest that the user do?

Disk Management reports dynamic disks as either Offline or Missing when it cannot detect the disk. The cause of a missing dynamic disk can be an operating system error or a problem with the drive itself. You should first have the customer attempt to rescan the disks by selecting Rescan Disks from the Action menu of Disk Management. If that does not resolve the issue, he should next try restarting the computer. If Disk Management continues to report the disk as missing, you or he should check to make sure that the drive is properly connected in the computer. It is also possible that the drive has failed and must be replaced.

9 Managing Local and Network Printers

Exam Objectives in this Chapter:

- Connect to local and network print devices
    - Answer end-user questions related to printing locally
    - Configure and manage local printing
    - Answer end-user questions related to network-based printing
    - Connect to and manage printing to a network-based printer

Why This Chapter Matters

Users can connect a printer directly to a local computer and print documents from that computer, or they can share the local printer with other users on the network. A user on a network might also connect to a shared network printer that is attached to another computer on the network, or even attached directly to the network itself. Microsoft Windows XP offers many advanced options for implementing printers locally or on a network, including the capability to operate printers in groups so that print jobs from different network locations can be routed to an available printer for faster printing. As a desktop support technician (DST), you need to know how to install a local printer and share it on the network. You should also understand how to access a shared printer. You must understand how to control access to printers, configure printers, and manage documents that are waiting to be printed.

Lessons in this Chapter:

Before You Begin

Before you begin this chapter, you should be familiar with working in a Windows-based operating system and with basic printing tasks on a computer running Windows XP. You should also have a computer running Windows XP Professional.

Lesson 1: Supporting Printers

As a DST, being able to deal with printers is paramount. You should have a good understanding of how printers work in Windows XP and be able to help users install, configure, and troubleshoot printers.

After this lesson, you will be able to

- Explain the printing process in Windows XP.
- Install a local printer.
- Install a network printer.
- Configure printers in Windows XP.
- Manage print jobs.
- Troubleshoot printers.

Estimated lesson time: 60 minutes

Understanding Printer Terminology

To manage printers successfully, you must first understand the printing concepts and terminology that are used in a Microsoft environment. You must know the following terms:

- **Printer**   The physical device that performs the printing. This device is usually a **printer**, but it can also be a fax device or a plotter.

- **Logical printer**   The software configuration that is created in Windows XP and is represented by an icon in the Printers And Faxes window. The **logical printer** controls the printer's configuration and the way in which Windows sends documents to the printer.

Note   In previous versions of Windows, Microsoft made an important distinction between the terms "printer" and "print device." Prior to Windows XP, a "printer" was the software on the computer that controlled printing, and a "print device" was the actual hardware device. The two terms were not used interchangeably. In Windows XP, that terminology has changed. The Windows XP documentation generally defines the "printer" as "a device that puts text or images on paper or other print media" and the "logical printer" as the "collection of software components that interface between the operating system and the printer."

- **Printer driver**   The software driver that contains printer-specific information. The **printer driver** is used by the Graphical Device Interface (GDI) to render print jobs.

- **Print job** A document that Windows has prepared for printing. Print jobs wait in a printer's print queue until it is their turn to be printed. While a print job is waiting in the queue, users can manage or delete the print job.

- **Graphical Device Interface** A Windows component that creates print jobs by interpreting document information from an application and combining it with printer information that is obtained from the printer driver. This process is called *rendering*.

- **Print server** A computer or other network device that has a printer physically attached to it and shares that printer with the network. When a user's computer that is running Windows XP shares a locally attached printer with the network, the user's computer is referred to as the **print server**.

- **Print spooling** The process of saving a print job to the hard disk before sending it to the printer. The process increases user productivity because after the job has been spooled, the application is released, and the user can continue working while the printing process continues in the background. **Print spooling** also ensures that print jobs will be saved in the event of a computer, application, or printer failure. In addition, when a client is printing to a printer on the network, print spooling also manages the routing of the print job from the client to the appropriate print server.

- **Spool directory** The folder to which print documents are spooled. This is %System_root%\System32\Spool\Printers by default.

- **Print spooler** The Windows operating system service that controls the **print spooling** process. The file Winspool.drv is the client-side spooler, and Spoolsv.exe is the server-side spooler.

- **Print router** When a user prints to a network printer, the **print router** locates a remote print provider that can service the print job's protocol. The file Spoolss.exe contains the print router.

- **Remote print provider** A service that can forward jobs to remote print servers. The **remote print provider** exists on the client-side of the printing process ("remote" refers to the physical location of the printer).

- **Local print provider** A Windows service that receives print jobs, spools them to the hard disk, and keeps track of job information while the job is in the print queue. The **local print provider** exists on the server-side of the printing process ("local" refers to the physical location of the printer). The local print provider sends a print job through the **print processor** and **separator page processors** and then forwards the job to the appropriate *port monitor*. The local print provider is contained in the Localspl.dll file. You will learn more about local and remote print providers in the section "Understanding the Printing Process," later in this lesson.

- **Print processor**   Software that makes any necessary modifications to the print job, and then calls on the GDI to further render the job, if necessary. Windows XP includes Winprint as its only print processor. Winprint is included in the Localspl.dll file.

- **Printer pool**   A single logical printer configured for multiple printers. Printer pools allow you to divide the printing workload among several printers of the same manufacturer and model.

- **Separator page processor**   Software that adds separator pages between print jobs as required. A separator page is a page that indicates the name of the document and time of printing. Separator pages help users distinguish between different documents on printers in which multiple documents are routinely printed.

- **Port monitor**   Software that controls communication with the ports to which printers are attached. The local port monitor (included in Localspl.dll) controls parallel and serial ports where a printer might be attached. The standard port monitor controls communication with network printers using the Transmission Control Protocol/Internet Protocol (TCP/IP) protocol, such as Hewlett-Packard printers containing JetDirect network adapters. The Hypertext Transfer Protocol (HTTP) port monitor is used when Internet printing is enabled.

Understanding Print Job Formats

When a print job is created, the **print spooler** looks at the format of the print job to determine whether the print job requires further processing by the print processor. Print job formats include the following:

- **RAW**   Ready to be printed, no further processing required. Most non-Windows applications generate print jobs in RAW format.

- **RAW [FF appended]**   Same as the RAW format, except that it requires a form-feed character to be appended to the end of the print job before sending it to the printer. This format ensures that the last page of the job is ejected from the printer.

- **RAW [FF auto]**   Same as RAW format, but checks to see whether a form-feed character exists at the end of the print job. If not, a form-feed character is added.

- **EMF**   Enhanced Metafile (EMF) format is a device-independent print job format that can be created much more quickly than RAW format jobs. The application that requested printing is released faster, allowing the user more productive work time. Processing continues in the background. EMF documents are sent to the print processor and GDI for further rendering into RAW format prior to printing. Most Windows applications generate EMF format jobs.

- **TEXT**   American National Standards Institute (ANSI) text data. The print processor and GDI further process the data. The text is printed in the printer's default font.

EMF format print jobs are much smaller in size than RAW format print jobs. In Windows XP, print jobs that are created in EMF format are transmitted across the network as an EMF and further rendered on the print server. This conserves network bandwidth. In previous versions of Windows, jobs were fully rendered to RAW format prior to being sent across the network.

Understanding the Printing Process

The local printing process happens as follows:

1. The user prints from within an application.

2. The application contacts the GDI.

3. The GDI contacts the print driver for printer-specific information, renders the job, and delivers the job to the print spooler.

4. The client-side of the spooler contacts the server-side spooler.

5. The server-side spooler contacts the print router.

6. The print router sends the print job to the local print provider.

7. The local print provider polls the print processors to find one that can process the type of data that is contained in the print job and then sends the job to the appropriate print processor.

8. The print processor contacts the GDI to further render the job if required to make it print properly.

9. The print processor sends the job to the page separator processor, where a separator page is added if required.

10. The print job is then sent to the appropriate port monitor, which ultimately delivers the job to the printer.

In local printing, the client server and print server are the same computer. Printing processes differentiate between client-side and server-side components, regardless of whether printing is local or remote. This explains why you see the client-side spooler needing to contact the server-side spooler even during the local printing process.

The remote printing process is largely the same as the local printing process, except for the need to forward the print job across the network to the print server in the middle of the process. The following steps outline the remote printing process:

1. The user prints from within an application.

2. The application contacts the GDI.

3. The GDI contacts the print driver for printer-specific information, renders the job, and delivers the job to the print spooler.

4. The client-side of the spooler contacts the server-side spooler.

5. The server-side spooler contacts the print router.

6. The print router locates a remote print provider that can forward the job to the appropriate print server and transfers the job to the remote print provider.

7. The remote print provider forwards the job across the network to the remote print server, where the local print provider receives it.

8. The local print provider polls the print processors to find one that can process the type of data that is contained in the print job and sends the job to the appropriate print processor.

9. The print processor contacts the GDI to further render the job if required to make it print properly.

10. The print processor sends the job to the page separator processor, in which a separator page is added if required.

11. The job is then sent to the appropriate port monitor, which ultimately delivers the job to the printer.

The flowchart in Figure 9-1 illustrates the local and remote printing processes in Windows XP, with the differences between the processes highlighted for easy comparison.

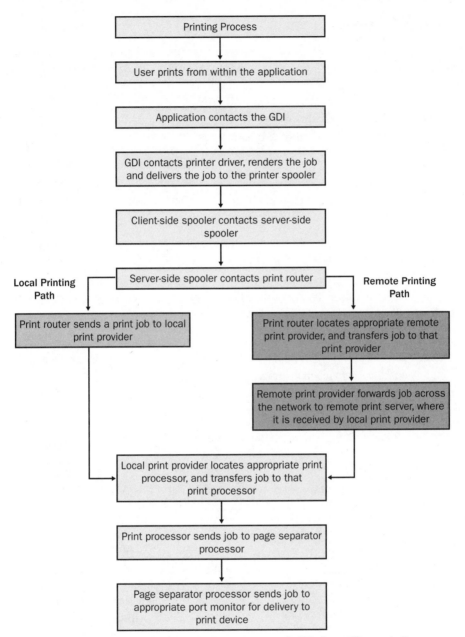

Figure 9-1   The local and remote printing processes in Windows XP are similar.

Installing Local Printers

Installing printers is a basic function that all administrators and most users should be able to perform. Many printers support automatic Plug and Play detection, and Windows automatically begins the installation process when the printers are first connected to the computer. Windows automatically installs drivers from the Drivers.cab file. Drivers.cab contains thousands of commonly used files, including print drivers. Drivers.cab is installed as part of the Windows XP Professional operating system installation.

If the printer is not Plug and Play–compliant, you must use the **Add Printer Wizard** to install it. The Add Printer Wizard is located in the Printers And Faxes folder, which is accessible from Control Panel or the Start menu.

To install a printer, a user running Windows XP Professional must be a member of the Administrators or Power Users groups and must have the Load And Unload Device Drivers user right assigned. A user running Windows XP Home Edition must have a Computer Administrator user account. For information on assigning user rights, refer to Chapter 3, "Supporting Local Users and Groups."

Exam Tip Users running Windows XP Professional must be members of the Administrators or Power Users groups to install a printer. Users running Windows XP Home Edition must have a Computer Administrator user account to install a printer.

To install a local printer, follow these steps:

1. From the Start menu, select Printers And Faxes.

2. In the Printers And Faxes window, double-click the Add Printer icon to start the Add Printer Wizard. On the Welcome page of the wizard, click Next.

3. On the Local Or Network Printer page, shown in Figure 9-2, select the Local Printer Attached To This Computer option. You can select the Automatically Detect And Install My Plug And Play Printer option if you have a Plug and Play printer that was not automatically detected when it was connected to the computer. Click Next to continue. If Windows detects a printer, Windows installs the printer automatically. If not, you need to select a printer manually.

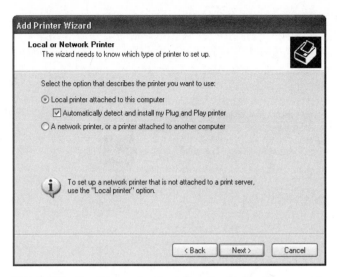

Figure 9-2   Configure a local printer attached to the computer.

4. On the Select A Printer Port page, shown in Figure 9-3, select one of the following ports that are available by default, and then click Next:

❑ LPT1-3, standard printer (parallel) ports.

❑ COM1-4, standard serial ports.

❑ FILE, which enables you to print to a file on the hard disk rather than directly to a printer. The file can then be forwarded to a printer when necessary.

Figure 9-3   Select a printer port.

5. On the Install Printer Software page, shown in Figure 9-4, select the printer's manufacturer and model. If your printer is not available in the list, or if you have a driver that is newer than the one that shipped with Windows, select the Have Disk option and provide Windows with the path to the printer driver. When you are finished, click Next.

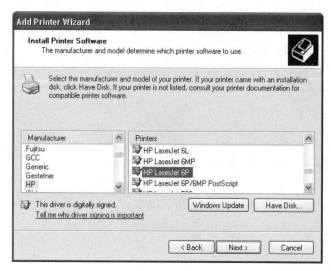

Figure 9-4   Select the printer to install or provide a driver disk.

6. On the Name Your Printer page, shown in Figure 9-5, choose a name that is descriptive of the type of printer. You should limit the name to 31 characters or fewer to maintain compatibility with older applications and previous versions of operating systems. Also, select whether or not you want this printer to be the default printer that is used, and then click Next.

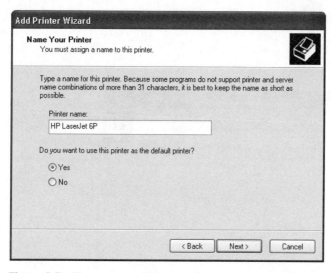

Figure 9-5   Name your printer and choose whether it should be the default printer.

7. On the Printer Sharing page shown in Figure 9-6, indicate whether you want this printer to be available to users on the network by sharing it or to be available only to users who use this computer. If you choose to share the printer, you are required to enter a share name, and then you will be given an opportunity to configure a location and description for the printer (you will learn more about sharing printers in Lesson 3, "Sharing a Printer"). Click Next.

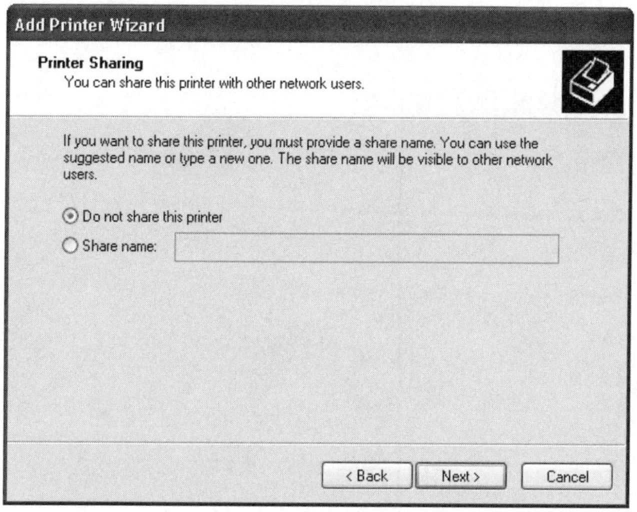

Add Printer Wizard

Printer Sharing
You can share this printer with other network users.

If you want to share this printer, you must provide a share name. You can use the suggested name or type a new one. The share name will be visible to other network users.

⦿ Do not share this printer
◯ Share name:

< Back   Next >   Cancel

Figure 9-6   Specify whether the printer should be shared.

8. On the Print Test Page page, shown in Figure 9-7, select Yes to print a test page, which is a single page of text and images that are designed to verify that the printer is functioning correctly and that the appropriate printer driver has been selected. Click Next.

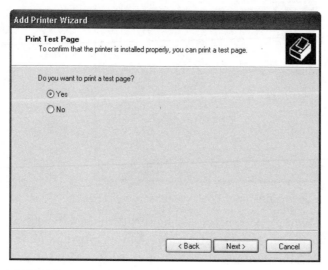

Figure 9-7   Specify whether to print a test page.

9. On the Add Printer Wizard Completion page, verify that you have selected the appropriate settings and then click Finish to install the printer.

Figure 9-8 shows the Printers And Faxes window with the newly installed printer.

Figure 9-8   You can view the new printer in the Printers And Faxes window.

Installing Network-Attached Printers

If the printer has a network card installed and is plugged directly into the network, you need to create a port for the printer on a computer running Windows XP so that you can use the Windows interface to control and share the printer. On the Select a Printer Port page (Step 4 of the instructions on installing a local printer), select the Create A New Port option and then create the appropriate connection to the printer. In most cases, this is what is called a standard TCP/IP printer port. When you define this type of port, you are providing Windows with the printer's Internet Protocol (IP) address so that Windows can establish a connection with the network printer. Figure 9-9 illustrates this process. You will learn more about using TCP/IP and IP addresses in Chapter 10, "Supporting Network Connectivity."

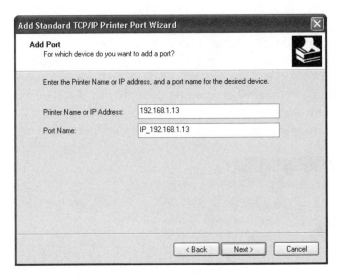

Figure 9-9   Create a TCP/IP printer port.

Troubleshooting Printer Driver Issues

Choosing the correct printer driver is critical for proper printer operation. If you choose an incorrect driver, one of two things is likely to happen: not all features of the printer will be available or the printer output will be incorrect.

If you choose a compatible but incorrect driver, you can use whatever features of the printer that the driver you selected allows. For example, if you chose an HP LaserJet 4 driver for use with an HP LaserJet 5si printer, you would get basic printer functionality, but the enhanced font and paper-handling capabilities of the LaserJet 5si would be unavailable because the driver does not support them.

If you choose an incompatible printer driver, the printer's output will be significantly affected and (in most cases) unrecognizable. A common symptom of an incompatible driver is that the printer will produce a given character or a line of characters on a page for a significant period of time (potentially hundreds or thousands of pages). If this condition occurs, turn off the printer to clear its memory, delete the print job from the print queue if it is still there, and then install an appropriate driver.

Note   If Windows XP does not support your printer and you do not have drivers from the manufacturer, try using the driver for a similar or older printer from the same manufacturer. You will often get partial functionality until you can get the appropriate drivers for the printer. You should also check the printer's user manual for compatibility with other printers that have a Windows XP driver.

Configuring Printers

After you have installed a printer, you have access to a number of options for configuring the printer. As a DST, you must understand what options are available and how to implement them because users are likely to ask you to help them set up printers and to help troubleshoot printing options when printing does not occur as they expect. You access some options for managing a printer by right-clicking the printer's icon in the Printers And Faxes window and selecting a command, as shown in Figure 9-10.

Figure 9-10   Select a command from a printer's shortcut menu.

Commands that you can perform from the printer's shortcut menu include the following:

- **Set As Default Printer**   Specifies this printer as the default printer for use in all programs. When a user prints and does not specify a printer, this is the printer that Windows uses. You can specify only one printer as the default at a given time.

- **Printing Preferences**   Enables the configuration of the default page orientation, page order, pages per sheet, and so on.

- **Pause Printing**   Stops print documents from being sent to the printer. When the printer is paused, there is a check mark next to this option in the action menu. To restart the printer, select the Pause Printing option again to clear the check mark. Pausing printing is useful when a number of documents are waiting to be printed and you need to make adjustments to or fix a problem with the printer configuration.

- **Sharing**   Allows the management of shared printer resources.

- **Use Printer Offline/Online**   Allows the printer to be used offline if the computer is not connected to the printer or the network, or if the user wants to hold all jobs locally for a period of time. When you bring the printer back online, all documents waiting in the local queue are printed.

- **Properties**   Provides access to the printer's Properties dialog box, from which you can configure a number of options, including many of the options that you can also access from a printer's shortcut menu. The options that are available in the Properties dialog box are covered in the next few sections.

Configuring General Properties

The General tab of a printer's Properties dialog box, shown in Figure 9-11, allows you to perform the following tasks:

- Change the name of the printer
- Configure the printer's location
- Enter a comment about the printer that helps to identify its use
- View the printer model and feature settings
- Configure printing preferences, such as portrait or landscape, and page order (front-to-back or back-to-front)
- Print a test page to verify printer functionality

Figure 9-11   Configure basic printer settings using the General tab of a printer's Properties dialog box.

Configuring Printer Ports

The Ports tab of a printer's Properties dialog box, shown in Figure 9-12, allows you to reconfigure the port to which the printer is connected. In addition, you can configure bidirectional support (if available) and use a printer pool. Bidirectional support enables Windows to receive setting and status information from the printer. Most modern printers and computers support bidirectional communication.

Figure 9-12   Configure printer port settings using the Ports tab of the printer's Properties dialog box.

Configuring Printer Pools

The Ports tab also allows you to enable a printer to use a printer pool. A **printer pool** allows you to associate two or more printers to a single logical printer. When documents enter the queue of a printer pool, Windows assigns the document to the first available printer, automatically distributing the printing load to all printers. This feature allows you to combine several lower-speed printers into a single, higher-speed logical printer. For example, if you have three printers that are each capable of printing 10 pages per minute, you can combine them into a printer pool and receive a total of 30 pages per minute from the pool.

Setting up a printer pool is often more efficient than setting up three separate logical printers and assigning a group of users to each of them. When using separate logical printers, there is always the chance that one printer is busy while the others sit idle. Creating a printer pool ensures that Windows distributes the printing load among all printers in the pool and that users receive their output more quickly. Also, if one of the printers fails, the others continue to process print documents, preventing interruptions of service.

Ideally, all printers in a printer pool should be the same make and model. You can create a printer pool using printers if all the printers support the same print driver, but you may lose any advanced print functionality supported by the different printers. If the printers do not support the same driver, the output on the printer(s) that does not support the installed driver might be problematic. For more information, see the section earlier in this chapter titled "Troubleshooting Printer Driver Issues."

To establish a printer pool, follow these steps:

1. Identify the printers that will be part of the printer pool and the ports that they are attached to.

2. Use the Add Printer Wizard to create a logical printer for one of the printers. The wizard permits you to assign only a single port to the printer. Assign a port that has one of the printers attached to it.

3. After creating the first logical printer, open the Properties dialog box for the logical printer and select the Ports tab.

4. Enable printer pooling.

5. Select each additional port that contains a printer that will be part of the pool.

When documents are sent to a printer pool, Windows does not notify users about which printer their document was printed to. Users must check all printers in the pool. For this reason, you should ensure that all the printers in a printer pool are in close proximity.

Configuring Advanced Printer Properties

The Advanced tab of a printer's Properties dialog box, shown in Figure 9-13, allows you to configure features associated with the way the printer handles documents. These features vary from printer to printer, depending on the features associated with the particular printer, but you should be aware of a few important settings:

- **Availability** By default, a printer is available 24 hours a day. You can limit the hours that a printer is available by selecting the Available From option on the Advanced tab and entering a time range.

- **Priority** The printer Priority option allows you to define a priority for this printer, ranging from 1 to 99 (the higher the number, the higher the printer's priority). Priority comes into effect only if you have multiple logical printers defined for a single printer. For example, you can create two logical printers, each printing to the same printer. You can name one logical printer HIGHPRIORITY and assign a priority of 99. You can name the other logical printer LOWPRIORITY and assign a priority of 1. Documents printed to the HIGHPRIORITY logical printer always take precedence over documents printed to the LOWPRIORITY logical printer.

> **Exam Tip** You can configure multiple logical printers for a single printer to control how the printer is used in different circumstances or by different users. You can also create a printer pool to configure multiple printers for a single logical printer.

- **Spooling** Select the Spool Print Documents So The Program Finishes Printing Faster to enable printer spooling. Select Print Directly To The Printer to disable spooling. If spooling is enabled, you need to decide whether you want the document to be spooled in its entirety before printing (the best option for remote printers) or to start printing immediately upon receiving the first page (the best option for local printers).

- **Hold Mismatched Documents** A mismatched document is a print document that requires a different type of paper than that which is currently installed in the printer. Selecting the Hold Mismatched Documents option causes the spooler to check the current printer setup against the document setup before sending the document to the printer. This prevents mismatched documents from blocking the queue. For example, many printers do not have envelope trays and require envelopes to be fed manually. If a user prints an envelope, someone must be at the printer to feed the envelope through so that the job can complete. If no one is at the printer to feed the envelope, the print queue is blocked until someone either feeds the envelope or deletes the print job.

- **Print Spooled Documents First**   When this option is disabled, the spooler determines which document to print next based only on the document's priority and the time the document arrived in the queue. Also, the spooler prints jobs that are completely spooled before jobs that are in the process of being spooled, even if the completely spooled job has a lower priority. This is intended to improve printer efficiency by preventing the printer from sitting idle while waiting for a high-priority job to be completely spooled.

- **Keep Printed Documents**   Configures the spooler to not delete documents after they have been printed. This makes it easy to resubmit a document to the queue. Print documents need to be manually deleted. It is important that the jobs are deleted when no longer needed, because they take up disk space on the hard disk that contains the spool directory.

- **Enable Advanced Printing Features**   Activates EMF spooling and enables printer features such as Page Order, Pages Per Sheet, and other printer-specific features. Advanced printing features are enabled by default and should remain enabled unless you have problems with the printer. EMF spooling can sometimes cause compatibility issues and therefore should be disabled as part of the trouble-shooting process.

- **Printing Defaults**   Configures default document settings for all users of the printer. These settings include such options as orientation (portrait or landscape), page order (front-to-back or back-to-front), number of pages printed per sheet of paper, and paper source.

- **Print Processor**   Configures the print processor and default data type. Recall that the print processor is responsible for processing print documents into a format that is suitable to be sent to the printer, and Windows XP contains only the Winprint processor by default. The default print processor and data types are suitable for the vast majority of printing, and you should not change them unless you have an application that specifies the need for a different print processor or additional data type.

- **Separator Page**   Separates one print job from the next. In some cases, the separator page contains information about the print document and the user who sent it. In other cases, the separator page contains printer commands that can switch a printer between different print modes, such as Postscript and Hewlett Packard's Printer Control Language (PCL).

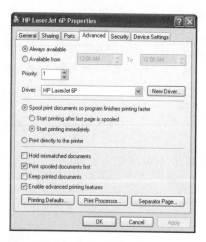

Figure 9-13   Advanced properties vary depending on the type of printer installed.

Configuring Device Settings

The Device Settings tab of a printer's Properties dialog box, shown in Figure 9-14, allows you to configure settings that are specific to the printer. Options available in this tab vary depending on the type of printer that you are using, but you should be aware of one common device setting: the Form To Tray Assignment setting. If the printer has multiple paper trays, you might need to assign different sizes of paper or forms to the different trays. By default, Windows assumes that all paper trays have letter-sized paper. If you need to change this default behavior, you must select the tray and then define the type of paper (such as legal size) that is in it. When users print, they can select the forms they want to use, and the printer knows which forms are in which paper tray.

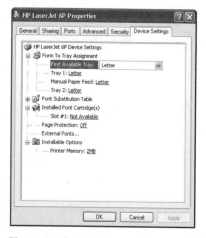

Figure 9-14   Configure printer-specific settings on the Device Settings tab.

Managing Print Jobs

A print job simply refers to a document that is waiting in a printer queue to be printed. You can view the print jobs that are in a queue by double-clicking the printer icon in the Printers And Faxes window. In the queue window, you can manage documents in one of two ways:

- Right-click the document and manage the document by using the commands on the shortcut menu, as illustrated in Figure 9-15.

- Select a document and use the commands on the Document menu.

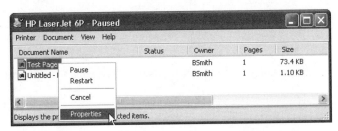

Figure 9-15   Manage print jobs in the printer queue window.

Regardless of which method you use to manage documents, the available commands are as follows:

- **Pause**   Stops printing of the document until you resume or restart the printing

- **Resume**   Causes the document to start printing from the point at which it was paused

- **Restart**   Causes the document to start printing from the beginning

- **Cancel**   Deletes the document from the print queue

- **Properties**   Provides access to the document's Properties dialog box, shown in Figure 9-16. You can use the settings on the General tab to perform the following actions:

  - View basic properties of the print document.

  - Change the user name to be notified when the document prints. By default, this will be the user who printed the document.

  - Reset the document's priority within the queue. This process moves the document up or down the printing order in the queue. The user needs a minimum of Manage Documents permission for this option to be implemented.

  - Change the time that the document is scheduled to print. If the printer itself has time restrictions that are set to limit availability, the documents automatically have the same time restrictions.

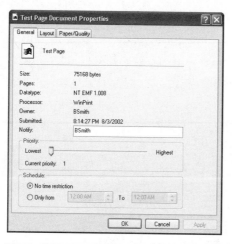

Figure 9-16   Configure settings for a document using the document's Properties dialog box.

Troubleshooting Printers

If a user cannot print, you should first make sure that the print jobs are making it to the print queue. Double-click the printer icon in the Printers And Faxes window to view the list of print jobs waiting to be printed. If the user's jobs are present in the queue, you most likely need to troubleshoot a problem with the print server or printer. If the jobs are not making it to the print queue, troubleshoot the user's printer configuration on the user's local computer.

If you need to troubleshoot the printer, make sure that:

- The printer is plugged in and turned on.
- The cabling connections are secure.
- There is paper in the paper tray or trays that the printer is trying to use.
- The printer does not indicate an error of some sort, such as paper jam or a hardware problem.

If the printer appears to be functioning correctly, turn it off and on. Restarting the printer often resolves many types of problems. If restarting the printer does not work, try restarting the computer to which the printer is connected.

If a user has multiple printers configured, determine which printer is the default printer. If the default printer is configured incorrectly, the user's print jobs might simply be going to the wrong location, and the user is unaware of it.

If a user can print but the output is garbled, most likely an incorrect print driver is the problem. You can view and update the driver that is being used in the Advanced tab of the printer's Properties dialog box. If the appropriate driver is installed, there is a chance that the application that is generating the print job is experiencing a problem. Try printing from other applications. If other applications produce correct print output, you need to troubleshoot the application to correct the problem.

If pages are coming out only partially printed, verify that the printer has sufficient memory to print the document. Also, verify that the page size you are selecting when printing matches the actual size of the paper. Printing an 11" x 17" document to an 8.5" x 11" piece of paper results in an incomplete print job or the job is printed on multiple pages. If text is missing from the pages, verify that the font for the missing text is available to the printer.

EMF format can occasionally cause problems with printing, especially with the printing of graphics. In these situations, consider disabling EMF spooling on the Advanced tab of the printer's Properties dialog box by clearing the Enable Advanced Printing Features check box.

Practice: Configure a Printer

In this practice, you configure settings for a printer on your computer. This practice assumes that you already have a printer installed on your computer. If you do not already have a printer installed, follow the practice at the end of Lesson 1 in Chapter 6, "Installing and Managing Hardware," to install a logical printer in Windows XP, even if you do not have an actual printer to connect.

1. From the Start menu, select Printers And Faxes.

2. In the Printers And Faxes window, right-click the icon for a printer and use the shortcut menu to determine whether the printer is the default printer.

3. On the shortcut menu, select Properties.

4. In the Properties dialog box for the printer, on the General tab, type a location and description for the printer.

5. On the Ports tab, determine whether bidirectional support is already enabled for the printer. If the option is not enabled, enable it now.

6. On the Advanced tab, select the Available From option and configure the printer's availability for normal business hours.

7. Select both the Print Directly To The Printer and Hold Mismatched Documents options, and then click OK.

Lesson Review

The following questions are intended to reinforce key information presented in this lesson. If you are unable to answer a question, review the lesson materials and try the question again. You can find answers to the questions in the "Questions and Answers" section at the end of this chapter.

1. One of your users has a printer with a built-in network adapter. She connected the printer directly to the network, but is unsure what to do next. What should you tell her to do?

   _____

   _____

2. What is the recommended limit to the number of characters used for a printer name?

   _____

3. You have a user with several printers. The user wants to configure those printers to be in a single printer pool. What requirements must the printers meet to establish a printer pool?

   _____

   _____

Lesson Summary

- In Windows XP, the term "printer" refers to the actual hardware device. The term "logical printer" refers to the software interface that Windows creates in the Printers And Faxes window.

- A print server is the computer to which a printer is connected or a computer that controls a printer that is connected to a network.

- Print spooling is the process of saving a print job to the hard disk before sending it to the printer. The process increases user productivity because after the job has been spooled, the application is released, and the user can continue working while the printing process continues in the background.

- Windows automatically detects and installs most Plug and Play–compliant printers. If Windows does not detect a printer automatically, you must install the printer by using the Add Printer Wizard.

- You configure most of the settings for a printer by using the Properties dialog box for the printer, which is available by right-clicking the printer icon in the Printers And Faxes window and choosing Properties.

Lesson 2: Using Print Permissions

As a DST, you must know how to control access to printers by using permissions. Print permissions allow you to control which users can access a printer and which actions the users can perform. Each printer has a discretionary access control list (DACL) associated with it that is similar to the DACL attached to files and folders that you learned about in Chapter 5, "Supporting Windows XP File and Folder Access." A user or group must be listed in the DACL to use the printer.

After this lesson, you will be able to

- Identify basic and advanced print permissions.
- Identify default print permission assignments.
- Calculate effective print permissions.

Estimated lesson time: 15 minutes

Understanding Print Permissions

Although you can assign print permissions to printers in Windows XP Professional, Windows XP Home Edition does not support print permissions. In Windows XP Professional, there is only one set of permissions that applies to printers, and these permissions are in effect when a printer is accessed both locally and remotely. This is unlike file system permissions, where there are potentially two types of permissions at work: share permissions and NTFS permissions.

You can access print permissions on the Security tab of a printer's Properties dialog box, as shown in Figure 9-17.

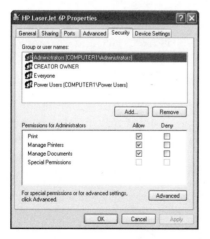

Figure 9-17   Assign print permissions using the Security tab of a printer's Properties dialog box.

Exam Tip   Only Windows XP Professional supports assigning permissions to printers. You cannot assign print permissions in Windows XP Home Edition.

Basic Print Permissions

For each user account or group, you can assign the following three basic print permissions:

- **Print**   Allows users or groups to connect to a printer, print documents, and manage their own documents in the print queue. Managing a document includes the ability to pause, resume, restart, and cancel the document.

- **Manage Documents**   Allows users or groups to connect to the printer, manage all documents in the print queue, and control print settings for all documents. This permission does not include the ability to print documents.

- **Manage Printers**   Allows users or groups to perform all the tasks included in the Print and Manage Documents permissions. In addition, the user can pause and resume the printer, take the printer offline, share the printer, change printer properties, delete a printer, and change print permissions.

You add, edit, and remove print permissions in much the same manner as you would for NTFS permissions on files and folders. To add basic print permission assignments, follow these steps:

1. On the Security tab of a printer's Properties dialog box, click Add.

2.   In the Select Users Or Groups dialog box, enter the user accounts or groups that you want to assign permissions to, and then click OK. Use the Advanced button to search for user accounts and groups if you do not know the exact names.

3. On the Security tab, Windows assigns the Print permission to newly added accounts by default. Modify the permissions as necessary and click Apply.

Advanced Print Permissions

You can provide most printer security requirements by using basic permissions, but sometimes you might need to use advanced permissions. Advanced print permissions include Read Permissions, Change Permissions, and Take Ownership.

To add advanced permission assignments, follow these steps:

1. On the Security tab of the printer's Properties dialog box, click Advanced.

2. In the Advanced Security Settings dialog box shown in Figure 9-18, click Add.

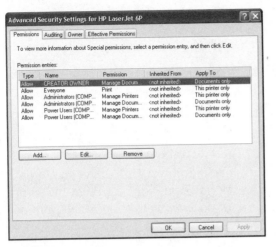

Figure 9-18   Configure advanced printer permissions in the Advanced Security Settings dialog box.

3. In the Select Users Or Groups dialog box, select the user accounts or groups that you want to assign permissions to, and then click OK. Use the Advanced button to search for user accounts and groups if you do not know the exact names.

4. In the Permission Entry dialog box shown in Figure 9-19, modify the permissions as necessary and click OK.

Figure 9-19   Modify the permissions in the Permission Entry dialog box.

5. In the Advanced Security Settings dialog box, click OK to return to the Security tab, and then click OK again.

Default Print Permissions Assignments

After you install a new printer, Windows automatically creates the following default permission assignments:

- The Everyone group has Print permission to the printer.

- The CREATOR OWNER user (which represents the user who installed the printer) has the Manage Documents permission, which permits users to manage their own documents only.

- The local groups' Administrators and Power Users have the Print, Manage Documents, and Manage Printers permissions—giving them full control to use and manage the printer and all print documents that are in the print queue.

If you want to limit access to the printer, you must remove the default permission assignment to the Everyone group and then assign permissions to the appropriate users and groups.

Calculating Effective Print Permissions

You calculate effective print permissions in the same manner as effective NTFS permissions on files and folders. To determine effective print permissions for a user account or group, follow these steps:

1. Combine the Allow permissions from all sources. The user receives the highest possible level of permission from this combination.

2. Apply any Deny permissions. Remember that Deny permissions always override Allow permissions.

Print Permission Inheritance

Inheritance of print permissions controls whether the permissions that you assign to a printer apply to the printer only, to the documents that are printed on the printer, or to both the printer and documents.

You control print permission inheritance by using the Apply Onto drop-down list in the Permission Entry dialog box, as shown in Figure 9-20. You can select from the following settings:

- This Printer Only
- Documents Only
- This Printer And Documents

Figure 9-20   Control print permission inheritance in the Permission Entry dialog box.

Practice: Configure Print Permissions

In this practice, you configure permissions on a printer. This practice assumes that you already have a printer installed on your computer. If you do not already have a printer installed, follow the practice at the end of Lesson 1 in Chapter 6 to install a logical printer in Windows XP, even if you do not have an actual printer to connect. This practice also requires that you use Windows XP Professional because Windows XP Home Edition does not support print permissions.

1. From the Start menu, select Printers And Faxes.

2. In the Printers And Faxes window, right-click the icon for a printer and select Properties.

3. In the Properties dialog box for the printer, on the Security tab, select the Everyone group and click Remove.

4. Click Add, and then, in the Select Users Or Groups dialog box, type **Users** and click OK.

5. On the Security tab, select the Users group and then, in the Permissions For Users section, select the Manage Printers check box in the Allow column.

6. Click OK.

Lesson Review

The following questions are intended to reinforce key information presented in this lesson. If you are unable to answer a question, review the lesson materials and try the question again. You can find answers to the questions in the "Questions and Answers" section at the end of this chapter.

1. List and describe the basic print permissions in Windows XP Professional.

_____

_____

_____

_____

2. What steps must you take to limit access to a printer on a computer running Windows XP Professional?

_____

_____

_____

_____

Lesson Summary

- Windows XP Professional does not distinguish between share and NTFS permissions for printers the way it does for files and folders. There is only one set of permissions for printers. You cannot assign print permissions in Windows XP Home Edition.

- The basic print permissions that are available in Windows XP Professional are Print, Manage Documents, and Manage Printers.

- Windows assigns some user accounts and groups permissions by default. The Everyone group has the Print permission. The CREATOR OWNER user has the Manage Documents permission. Members of the local groups Administrators and Power Users have the Print, Manage Documents, and Manage Printers permissions.

Lesson 3: Sharing a Printer

On a network, many users might need to access a printer. In a business environment, users might require access to a number of different printers that have special features such as color or high-speed capabilities. In a home or small office environment, there might be only a single printer available for all users to share. Most businesses need to control who has access to certain printers, whereas in the home or small office all users normally have unlimited access to the printer. Both Windows XP Professional and Windows XP Home Edition allow you to share a printer. However, as you learned in the previous lesson, you cannot limit access to a shared printer in Windows XP Home Edition.

After this lesson, you will be able to

- Share a printer.
- Install additional printer drivers for a shared printer.
- Connect to a shared printer.

Estimated lesson time: 15 minutes

Sharing a Printer

To make a local printer available to network users, you must share the printer. There are two ways to share a printer:

- During printer installation
- By using the Sharing tab of the printer's Properties dialog box after you have installed the printer

During the installation of a local printer, Windows gives you the option to share the printer on the Printer Sharing page of the Add Printer Wizard, shown in Figure 9-21. To share the printer, select Share Name and then type a share name. You must perform any additional configuration and administration of the shared printer, such as permissions assignments, after the printer is installed. To share a printer during installation, you must be a member of the Administrators or Power Users groups on the Windows XP Professional print server or have a user account of the Computer Administrator type on Windows XP Home Edition.

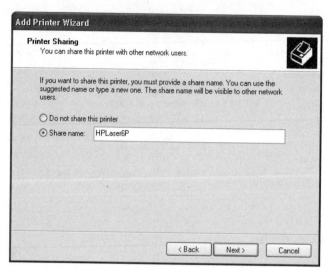

Figure 9-21   Share a printer during installation.

If a printer is already installed, you can share it by using the Sharing tab of the printer's Properties dialog box. To share an existing printer, your user account must have the Manage Printers permission. To share a printer that has already been installed, follow these steps:

1. Open the printer's Properties dialog box.

2. On the Sharing tab, select Share This Printer.

3. Type the share name for the printer, and then click OK.

Installing Additional Print Drivers for Non–Windows XP Operating Systems

Windows XP printer drivers are compatible with Windows 2000, but they are not compatible with previous versions of Windows. If a computer on the network that is running Windows NT, Windows 98, or Windows 95 connects to a shared printer on a computer running Windows XP Professional, the connecting computer cannot use the Windows XP printer drivers. Instead, the computer running the older version of Windows prompts the user to provide drivers.

To avoid forcing users running previous versions of Windows to supply their own drivers, you can supply the drivers for them. Windows XP Professional allows you to install printer drivers for other versions of Windows. When you make drivers for previous versions of Windows available, those drivers are installed automatically when a user of an older version of Windows connects to the printer.

You can install additional drivers by clicking the Additional Drivers button on the Sharing tab of the printer's Properties dialog box. When you select any of the environments that are listed, as shown in Figure 9-22, you are prompted to provide a path to the printer drivers for that operating system. Windows XP then installs the drivers. From that point forward, when users running an operating system for which you have installed drivers connect to the shared printer, they receive the printer drivers automatically.

Figure 9-22   Install non-Windows XP print drivers so other users do not have to.

Connecting to Shared Printers

Windows XP provides many different methods to access shared printers, including the following:

- Using the Add Printer Wizard
- Browsing My Network Places
- Using the Run dialog box
- From within an application

Remember that printer access is controlled through the assignment of permissions. If a user does not have at least the Print permission to a printer, that user cannot establish a connection to the printer.

Connecting by Using the Add Printer Wizard

You can connect to a shared printer by running the Add Printer Wizard. On the Local Or Network Printer page, choose A Network Printer Or A Printer Attached To Another Computer. The Add Printer Wizard asks you to specify the name of the shared printer that you want to connect to. If you do not know the name of the printer, you can use the following search options:

- If the computer is a member of a Windows 2000 Server or Windows Server 2003 domain, you are given the option to Find A Printer In The Directory. This option enables you to search Active Directory directory service for a printer. After you locate the printer that you want to connect to, select it and click OK to continue with the installation.

- Choosing the Connect To This Printer option gives you the opportunity to enter the path of the printer or to click Next to browse My Network Places in search of the printer.

- Choosing the Connect To A Printer On The Internet Or On Your Intranet option allows you to specify the printer's URL.

Connecting by Browsing My Network Places

If you know the name of the computer that shares the printer, you can browse My Network Places to connect to the printer. After you locate the printer, you can right-click the printer and choose Connect, or you can drag and drop the printer to the Printers And Faxes folder on your computer.

Connecting by Using the Run Dialog Box

If you know the location to the printer (or at least the name of the print server that the printer is attached to), you can enter the path in the Run dialog box (available by selecting Run from the Start menu). Entering the full Universal Naming Convention (UNC) path of the printer (for example, \\Computer1\HPLaser6P) automatically connects you to the printer. Entering just the name of the server (for example, \\Computer1) displays all the resources on that computer. You can then right-click the printer and select the Connect option, just as if you had browsed for it in My Network Places.

Connecting from Within Applications

When you are working in an application and it is time to print, you usually have the option to choose any printer that you currently have installed. Some applications also permit you to install a new printer from within the application's Print dialog box.

Figure 9-23 shows the Print dialog box in Notepad. Clicking the Find Printer button opens a dialog box that allows you to locate and install an available printer.

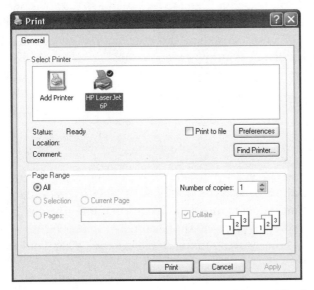

Figure 9-23   Install a printer from within certain applications by using the Find Printer button.

Lesson Review

The following questions are intended to reinforce key information presented in this lesson. If you are unable to answer a question, review the lesson materials and try the question again. You can find answers to the questions in the "Questions and Answers" section at the end of this chapter.

1. List several ways in which a user can connect to a shared printer.

_____

_____

_____

_____

_____

Lesson Summary

- You can share a printer that is connected to a computer running Windows XP by using the Sharing tab on the printer's Properties dialog box.

- Users can connect to a shared printer by using the Add Printer Wizard, by browsing My Network Places, by using the Run dialog box, or from within certain applications.

- To avoid forcing users of previous versions of Windows to supply drivers, Windows XP Professional allows you to install printer drivers for non–Windows XP clients. When those drivers are installed, the installation of the printer on computers with previous versions of Windows is automatic.

Case Scenario Exercises

Scenario 9.1

One of your small-business users has a printer that is connected to his computer running Windows XP Professional. He shares the printer with other users on the network. Often, the other users print large documents that take a long time to print, but sometimes your user and other users have important documents that need to be printed before any long documents that are waiting in the printer queue. What would you suggest to this user?

_____

_____

_____

_____

_____

_____

Scenario 9.2

A user calls to tell you that she just printed a large document to the wrong printer. The printer is a network-attached printer that is used by many people, so the user does not think her document has printed yet. If possible, she wants to stop the document from being printed. What would you suggest to the user?

_____

_____

_____

Troubleshooting Lab

A user cannot print to his regular printer, so he browses the network and locates another printer that is on the same floor as his office. When he connects to the printer, it requests that he select the type of printer so that Windows XP can install a driver for it. He is uncertain about what type of printer it is, so he selects the same printer type as his regular printer. His regular printer is a Postscript printer, and the new printer is an older, non-Postscript HP LaserJet III. When he prints a document to the new printer, each page has one or two characters on it, and the printer does not stop printing. What is the problem, and how do you fix it?

_____

_____

_____

_____

_____

_____

Chapter Summary

- In Windows XP, the term "printer" refers to the actual hardware device. The term "logical printer" refers to the software interface created in the Printers And Faxes window.

- A print server is the computer to which a printer is connected or a computer that controls a printer that is connected to a network.

- Print spooling is the process of saving a print job to the hard disk before sending it to the printer. The process increases user productivity because after the job has been spooled, the application is released, and the user can continue working while the printing process continues in the background.

- Windows automatically detects and installs most Plug and Play–compliant printers. If Windows does not detect a printer automatically, you must install the printer by using the Add Printer Wizard.

- You configure most of the settings for a printer using the Properties dialog box for the printer, which is available by right-clicking the printer icon in the Printers And Faxes window and choosing Properties.

- Windows XP Professional does not distinguish between share and NTFS permissions for printers the way that it does for files and folders. There is only one set of permissions for printers. You cannot assign printer permissions in Windows XP Home Edition.

- The basic printer permissions available in Windows XP Professional are Print, Manage Documents, and Manage Printers.

- Windows assigns some user accounts and groups permissions by default. The Everyone group has the Print permission. The CREATOR OWNER user has the Manage Documents permission. Members of the local groups Administrators and Power Users have the Print, Manage Documents, and Manage Printers permissions.

- You can share a printer that is connected to a computer running Windows XP by using the Sharing tab on the printer's Properties dialog box.

- Users can connect to a shared printer by using the Add Printer Wizard, browsing My Network Places, using the Run dialog box, or by printing from within certain applications.

- To avoid forcing users of previous versions of Windows to supply drivers, Windows XP Professional allows you to install printer drivers for non–Windows XP clients. When those drivers are installed, installation of the printer on computers with previous versions of Windows is automatic.

Exam Highlights

Before taking the exam, review the key topics and terms that are presented in this chapter. You need to know this information.

Key Points

- Users of Windows XP Professional must be members of the Administrators or Power Users groups to install a printer. Users of Windows XP Home Edition must have a user account of the Computer Administrator type to install a printer.

- You can configure multiple logical printers for a single printer to control how the printer is used in different circumstances or by different users. You can also use printer pooling to configure multiple printers for a single logical printer.

- Only Windows XP Professional supports assigning permissions to printers. You cannot assign printer permissions in Windows XP Home Edition.

Key Terms

Add Printer Wizard   A wizard used to install printers.

logical printer   The software configuration that is created in Windows and displayed in Printers And Faxes.

print server   The computer or other remote device that has a network printer physically connected to it.

print spooling   The process of saving a print job to the hard disk before sending it to the printer.

printer   The physical device used for printing. This device is usually a standard printer, but it can also be a fax device, a plotter, or a file. It might also refer to the combination of the physical and logical printer.

printer driver   The software driver containing printer-specific information.

printer permissions   Permissions that enable you to control which users can access a printer and which actions they will be able to perform.

printer pooling   A printing option that permits you to attach two or more printers to a single printer configuration.

Questions and Answers

Lesson 1 Review

Page
9-24

1. One of your users has a printer with a built-in network adapter. She connected the printer directly to the network, but is unsure what to do next. What should you tell her to do?

   The user should start the Add Printer Wizard and begin installing a new local printer. On the Select A Printer Port page of the wizard, the user should create a new Standard TCP/IP Port and then enter the IP address and port name for the network printer. After creating the new port, the user should finish the installation and configure the printer normally.

2. What is the recommended limit to the number of characters used for a printer name?

   You should limit the number of characters used in a printer name to 31 to maintain compatibility with older operating systems or applications.

3. You have a user with several printers. The user wants to configure those printers to be in a single printer pool. What requirements must the printers meet to establish a printer pool?

   Ideally, all the printers should be the same make and model. However, you can create a printer pool if all the printers can use the same printer driver.

Lesson 2 Review

Page
9-30

1. List and describe the basic print permissions in Windows XP Professional.

   The basic print permissions are Print, which allows users to print documents and manage their own documents; Manage Documents, which allows users to manage all documents in the printer queue; and Manage Printers, which provides the combined access of the Print and Manage Documents permissions.

2. What steps must you take to limit access to a printer on a computer running Windows XP Professional?

   First, you must remove the Everyone group from the list of accounts given permission to use the printer. Windows XP gives the Print permission to the Everyone group by default. Next, you must add the user accounts or groups for which you want to configure permissions and then assign the appropriate permissions to those accounts.

Lesson 3 Review

Page
9-35

1. List several ways in which a user can connect to a shared printer.

   Users can connect to a shared printer by using the Add Printer Wizard, browsing My Network Places, using the Run dialog box, or from within certain applications.

Case Scenario Exercises: Scenario 9.1

Page
9-36

One of your small-business users has a printer that is connected to his computer running Windows XP Professional. He shares the printer with other users on the network. Often, the other users print large documents that take a long time to print, but sometimes your user and other users have important documents that need to be printed before any long documents that are waiting in the printer queue. What would you suggest to this user?

> You should suggest that the user configure two logical printers for the printer. He should assign one of the logical printers a higher priority than the other printer. He should also name the logical printers to indicate their use. (For example, he might name the logical printer with the lower priority "Long Document Printer" and the printer with the higher priority "Normal Use Printer.") He should share each of the printers with the network and explain to the other users on the network how the printers are configured. If the long documents that users print are not time-sensitive, you might also suggest to the user that he configure the lower-priority printer to be available only during non-business hours and configure the high-priority printer to be available all the time. That way, users could send long documents to the printer whenever they wanted to, but the documents would not be printed until after the close of business.

Case Scenario Exercises: Scenario 9.2

Page
9-36

A user calls to tell you that she just printed a large document to the wrong printer. The printer is a network-attached printer that is used by many people, so the user does not think her document has printed yet. If possible, she wants to stop the document from being printed. What would you suggest to the user?

> The user should open the print queue for the printer, locate her document, and delete it. Most likely, the user has the Print permission on the printer, which allows her to print to the printer and to manage her own documents in the document queue.

Troubleshooting Lab

Page
9-37

A user cannot print to his regular printer, so he browses the network and locates another printer that is on the same floor as his office. When he connects to the printer, it requests that he select the type of printer so that Windows XP can install a driver for it. He is uncertain about what type of printer it is, so he selects the same printer type as his regular printer. His regular printer is a Postscript printer, and the new printer is an older, non-Postscript HP LaserJet III. When he prints a document to the new printer, each page has one or two characters on it, and the printer does not stop printing. What is the problem and how do you fix it?

> The problem is that the user has installed an incompatible printer driver, and the printer cannot decipher the print job. This incompatibility causes the printer to provide erratic output, potentially a small number of characters per page for a significant number of pages in an attempt to print the job. To fix the problem, start by taking the printer offline and turning it off, which clears the printer's memory and keeps it from accepting any more of the print job. Then, delete the print job from the print queue to prevent it from starting to print again when the printer is powered up. Finally, install the appropriate print driver on the user's computer before he submits any additional print jobs.

10 Supporting Network Connectivity

Exam Objectives in this Chapter:

- Troubleshoot TCP/IP
    - ❑ Answer end-user questions related to configuring TCP/IP settings
    - ❑ Configure and troubleshoot manual TCP/IP configuration
    - ❑ Configure and troubleshoot automated TCP/IP address configuration
    - ❑ Configure and troubleshoot Windows Firewall settings such as enable and disable
- Troubleshoot name-resolution issues
    - ❑ Configure and troubleshoot host name-resolution issues on a client computer
    - ❑ Configure and troubleshoot NetBIOS name-resolution issues on a client computer
- Configure and troubleshoot remote connections
    - ❑ Configure and troubleshoot a remote dial-up connection
    - ❑ Configure and troubleshoot remote connections across the Internet
    - ❑ Configure and troubleshoot end-user systems by using remote connectivity tools
    - ❑ Use Remote Desktop to configure and troubleshoot an end user's desktop
    - ❑ Use Remote Assistance to configure and troubleshoot an end user's desktop

> **Note**   Internet Connection Firewall is the software firewall built into versions of Microsoft Windows XP prior to applying Service Pack 2. After installing Service Pack 2, the firewall is updated to the new (and more robust) Windows Firewall. This chapter focuses on Windows Firewall, and the exam has been updated for Windows Firewall as well. However, the official objectives might still list Internet Connection Firewall.

Why This Chapter Matters

Whether in the home or in a business, you are likely to find networked computers. As a desktop support technician (DST), your responsibilities are to help users connect computers to a network and to troubleshoot network problems when they occur. This chapter provides an overview of Transmission Control Protocol/Internet Protocol (TCP/IP), the networking protocol that is used on the Internet and on most local area networks (LANs). This chapter also teaches you to configure and troubleshoot network connectivity on a computer running Microsoft Windows XP. You will learn how to protect a network computer with Windows Firewall. Finally, this chapter introduces you to using Remote Desktop and Remote Assistance to help troubleshoot computers from a remote location.

Lessons in this Chapter:

Before You Begin

Before you begin this chapter, you should have experience working in a Windows operating system and a working knowledge of the Windows XP interface. You need to be generally familiar with networking technology and should also have a computer running Windows XP on which you can experiment with changing various settings.

Lesson 1: Overview of TCP/IP

As a DST, you must be able to configure and troubleshoot TCP/IP, which is used in the majority of networks and is the preferred network protocol in a Windows XP environment. Many options are associated with this protocol, which the administrator must understand to ensure proper configuration and operation of TCP/IP. Understanding TCP/IP, its configuration issues and options, and how to troubleshoot connectivity problems is necessary to successfully manage a Windows XP network.

After this lesson, you will be able to

- Identify the required and optional parameters that are defined for computers on TCP/IP networks.
- Explain how IP addresses and subnetting work.
- Explain how name resolution works.
- Identify the primary name-resolution mechanisms that are used on Windows networks.

Estimated lesson time: 40 minutes

Understanding TCP/IP

TCP/IP is not a single protocol but rather a group of protocols that work together. A group of protocols working together is called a protocol stack. Transmission Control Protocol (TCP) and Internet Protocol (IP) are two of the most commonly used protocols in the TCP/IP protocol stack.

Windows XP installs TCP/IP automatically when it detects a network adapter. After TCP/IP is installed, you must configure several options for the protocol to function properly. The following are the options that are necessary for a computer to function in a TCP/IP environment:

- IP address (required)
- Subnet mask (required)
- Default gateway (required)
- Domain Name System (DNS) configuration (optional)
- Windows Internet Naming Service (WINS) configuration (optional)

IP addressing and configuration is a comprehensive topic, and there are many texts written strictly on the subject. The following sections provide an overview of TCP/IP information.

IP Addressing

An **IP address** is a number that uniquely identifies a device such as a computer on a TCP/IP network. Devices on IP networks are typically called hosts. An IP address consists of a 32-bit binary number that is logically divided into four groupings of 8 bits each. Each 8-bit grouping is called an octet or a byte.

Binary is a difficult numbering scheme for most people to work with, so IP addresses are normally presented in dotted decimal notation. With **dotted decimal notation**, each octet in an IP address is represented as a decimal number from 0 to 255, and each of these numbers is separated by a period. An example of an IP address is 192.168.0.1, which is represented in binary notation as 11000000 10101000 00000000 00000001.

> **Note**   255 is the largest decimal number that can be represented by an 8-bit binary number (11111111 binary = 255 decimal). You can use the Windows Calculator to translate decimal numbers to binary numbers, and vice versa.

An IP address contains two important pieces of information: the network ID for the network segment to which the computer is connected and the host ID for that computer. The network ID identifies the network on which a host is found. The host ID identifies the host within that network. This addressing scheme is similar to street addresses within a city or town, such as 123 Main Street. The street name is similar to the network ID, and the house number is similar to the host ID.

All devices on the same network subnet must be assigned an IP address that has the same network ID but a unique host ID. This is analogous to the address of each house on a street having the same street name, but a different house number. However, in IP addressing, the network number comes first; in street addresses, the house number is normally first.

The street address analogy can be taken a step further to describe how routers work in a TCP/IP network. The purpose of a router is to move network traffic to the appropriate network in a multiple network environment. When the mail carrier is delivering, the carrier will first ensure that the mail is being taken to the correct street name. After the mail carrier arrives at the appropriate street, she will deliver the mail based on the house number. Routers work in a similar fashion: they first examine the network ID of the IP address and then route the packet to the specified network subnet. After the packet has reached the correct network subnet, the routers forward the packet to the appropriate device based on the device's host ID.

The IP network ID must be unique within a TCP/IP network. If two networks had the same number, the routers would generally attempt to deliver the packet to the network that was the closest to them, which would not necessarily be the correct one. Also, the client's host ID must be unique within the network subnet, so that when a packet reaches the correct IP network, there is no doubt about which device it is destined for.

IP Address Classes   IP addresses are divided into the following classes, with each class having different network ID and host ID properties:

- **Class A addresses**   If the first octet of an IP address is in the range of 1–126, it is a Class A address. By default, the first octet of a Class A address represents the network ID, and the remaining three octets are the unique host ID on that network. An example of a Class A IP address is 10.2.4.78—the network ID is 10, and the host ID is 2.4.78. There are 128 Class A network numbers, each capable of supporting 16,777,214 unique hosts. The first (0.0.0.0) and last (127.0.0.0) network numbers are reserved, leaving 126 potential Class A networks and making the actual range of the first octet 1–126. In a Class A address, the highest order binary bit (the leftmost bit of the 32-bit binary representation) is always *0*.

- **Class B addresses**   If the first octet of an IP address is from 128 to 191, it is a Class B address. By default, the first two octets of a Class B address are the network number, and the remaining two octets are the unique host ID on that network. An example of a Class B address is 172.16.89.203—the network number is 172.16, and the host ID is 89.203. There are 16,384 Class B network numbers, each capable of supporting 65,534 unique hosts. The first (128.0.0.0) and last (191.255.0.0) network numbers are reserved, leaving 16,382 potential Class B networks. The two highest-order binary bits are always *10* in a Class B address.

- **Class C addresses**   If the first octet of an IP address is between 193 and 223, it is a Class C address. By default, the first three octets of a Class C address are the network number, and the remaining octet is the unique host ID on that network. An example of a Class C address is 192.168.0.1—the network number is 192.168.0 and the host ID is 1. There are 2,097,152 Class C network numbers, each capable of supporting 254 unique hosts. The first (192.0.0.0) and last (223.255.255.0) network numbers are reserved, leaving 2,097,150 potential Class A networks. The three highest-order binary bits are always *110* in a Class C address.

- **Class D addresses**   The first octet of a Class D address falls in the range of 224 to 239. Class D addresses are not assigned to individual devices on a TCP/IP network. Instead, they are used for multicasting to a group of IP hosts and also to facilitate the transmission of network control information between certain types of IP devices. The four highest-order binary bits are always *1110* in a Class D address.

- **Class E addresses**   The first octet of a Class E address falls in the range of 240 to 255. Class E addresses cannot be assigned to individual devices on a TCP/IP network. They are reserved for experimental and future use. The four highest-order bits are always *1111* in a Class E address.

- **Loopback addresses**   IP addresses that have 127 in the first octet are called *loopback addresses*. The most commonly used loopback address is 127.0.0.1. Loopback addresses are used for testing TCP/IP configuration and cannot be assigned to individual hosts on a TCP/IP network.

Table 10-1 provides a summary of IP addressing information, using w.x.y.z to generically represent the four octets that are used in dotted decimal notation.

Table 10-1   IP Address Summary

Class	1st Octet Range	Assignable to Hosts?	Network ID	Host ID	Number of Networks	Number of Host IDs per Network
A	1–126	Yes	w	x.y.z	126	16,777,214
B	128–191	Yes	w.x	y.z	16,382	65,534
C	192–223	Yes	w.x.y	z	2,097,150	254
D	224–239	No	N/A	N/A	N/A	N/A
E	240–255	No	N/A	N/A	N/A	N/A
Loopback	127	No	N/A	N/A	N/A	N/A

> **Note**   In dotted decimal notation, IP network IDs are usually presented as an IP address, with the host ID portion configured to all zeros. For example, the Class A network of 10 is referred to as 10.0.0.0, the Class B network of 172.16 is referred to as 172.16.0.0, and the Class C network of 192.168.0 is referred to as 192.168.0.0.

IP Address Validity   You must ensure that the IP addresses that you configure are valid. To make sure that the IP addresses are valid, remember the following rules:

- The first byte of the IP address must fall within the following ranges:
  - ❏ 1–126
  - ❏ 128–191
  - ❏ 193–223
- IP addresses that begin with 0, 127, or 224–255 are invalid.
- The host ID cannot be all binary 0s or 1s. In decimal, it commonly translates to all 0s or all 255s.
- No number in an IP address can be greater than 255.

Table 10-2 displays several invalid IP addresses and gives the reasons why they are invalid.

Table 10-2   Invalid IP Addresses

IP Address	Why IP Address Is Invalid
0.36.78.231	The first octet is 0.
127.54.79.100	The first octet is 127.
126.255.255.255	The host ID is all binary 1s/decimal 255s.
197.34.8.0	The host ID is all 0s.
235.17.234.202	The first octet is between 224–255.
154.12.287.243	The third octet is greater than 255.

In addition, remember that all devices on the same network must be assigned a unique host ID, but the same network ID. For example, if you are using the network ID of 192.168.1.0, all hosts on the network must have 192.168.1 as the first three octets of their IP address.

Choosing an IP Addressing Scheme   The Internet is a huge TCP/IP network, and no two networks or hosts connected to the Internet can have the same full IP address (the combination of network ID and host ID). If your network is directly connected to the Internet, you must follow the specific IP addressing scheme that has been assigned to you by your Internet service provider (ISP) or the Internet Corporation for Assigned Names and Numbers (ICANN). As a DST, it will not be your responsibility to design IP addressing schemes on large networks. However, you should understand the IP addressing scheme that is in place so that you can assist users in troubleshooting network problems.

See Also   For more information about ICANN, see *http://www.icann.org*.

If your network is not directly connected to the Internet, you can theoretically choose any valid IP addressing scheme that you want. However, the governing body of the Internet requests that you choose an addressing scheme that uses one of the private IP address ranges. These ranges are never used on devices that are connected directly to the Internet. Using private IP addresses ensures that data from your network will never accidentally travel across the public Internet. This provides you with privacy and ensures that there will not be any accidental addressing conflicts. The private IP address ranges are as follows:

- 10.0.0.0–10.255.255.255

- 172.16.0.0–172.31.255.255

- 192.168.0.0–192.168.255.255

Although private IP addresses cannot be used directly on the Internet, you will find that many devices with Internet access do use private addressing. When this is the case, a device that translates the private address into a public address is used to facilitate Internet connectivity.

For example, if you use a router at home to connect to your cable or digital subscriber line (DSL) modem, your ISP assigns the IP address that you use for the public network interface on the router (the interface connected to the Internet). The router automatically distributes private IP addresses to the internal devices (devices on your home network) that are connected to the router. Most routers that are sold to the home and small business market use the 192.168.0.0 private range. When an internal device makes a request to communicate with the Internet, the client computer forwards the request to the router, which communicates directly with the Internet resource and then passes information back to the client computer.

Essentially, the router acts as a middleman between the internal client and the Internet resource. The router can perform this function for multiple devices simultaneously. Using a router that functions in this manner reduces the need for multiple unique public IP addresses, and serves to protect internal devices from external threats because the internal devices are never communicating directly on the Internet.

Subnet Masks

The **subnet mask** tells a TCP/IP host how to interpret IP addresses by defining what portion of the IP address is network ID and what portion is host ID. A 255 in the subnet mask indicates that the corresponding octet in an IP address is to be interpreted as part of the network number. A 0 in the subnet mask indicates that the corresponding octet in an IP address is to be interpreted as part of the host ID.

The default subnet masks for Class A, B, and C network numbers are as follows:

- Class A 255.0.0.0
- Class B 255.255.0.0
- Class C 255.255.255.0

If you compare these mask values with the information that was already presented on Class A, B, and C IP addresses, you would notice the correlation between the placement of 255s in the mask and octets that represent the network number. For example, the default Class B subnet mask is 255.255.0.0, indicating that the first two octets are to be interpreted as network number, and the remaining octets are to be interpreted as host ID. In the Class B address of 172.16.89.203, we determined 172.16 to be the network number and 89.203 to be the host ID. The same logic applies to the Class A and Class C IP addresses that we analyzed.

Hosts use the subnet mask to determine their network numbers and also to determine whether a destination host is on the same or a different network. If a destination host is on the same network, the source host will attempt to communicate with the destination directly. If the destination host is on a different network, the source host will use its configured **default gateway** (typically a router) to communicate with the destination host.

The subnet mask can be referenced in either dotted decimal notation or classless interdomain routing (CIDR) notation. Dotted decimal notation is the format used to enter subnet mask values when configuring Windows XP. The subnet mask values of 255.0.0.0, 255.255.0.0, and 255.255.255.0 are in dotted decimal notation.

CIDR notation makes note of the number of binary 1 bits in the subnet mask, and that number of bits is placed at the end of the network ID. For example, the network number 192.168.1.0 with a subnet mask value of 255.255.255.0 is referenced as 192.168.1.0/24 in CIDR notation. The value of 24 represents 24 binary one bits in the subnet mask; each value of 255 represents 8 bits, there are three 255s in the mask, and $3 \times 8 = 24$. Table 10-3 displays several more examples of CIDR notation contrasted with dotted decimal notation.

Table 10-3   Dotted Decimal Versus CIDR Subnet Mask Notation

IP Network Address	Subnet Mask, Dotted Decimal Notation	CIDR Notation
10.0.0.0	255.0.0.0	10.0.0.0/8
172.16.0.0	255.255.0.0	172.16.0.0/16
192.168.0.0	255.255.255.0	192.168.0.0/24

Subnetting an IP Network Number   Subnetting is the process of dividing a single IP network number into multiple IP networks by modifying the subnet mask value. When a subnet mask is modified from the default, it changes how TCP/IP devices interpret the network number and the host ID portion of an IP address.

For example, if a subnet mask of 255.255.255.0 is applied to the Class B IP network address of 172.16.0.0, the first three bytes (172.16.0) are interpreted as network number, and only the last byte is interpreted as host ID. It is still a Class B address, but the third byte of this address can now be used to define several subnetworks, or subnets, that each support fewer host IDs. In this example, up to 254 subnets can be defined, each with up to 254 host IDs.

Table 10-4 outlines the first few ranges of the subnet information for this example. When looking at this table, pay close attention to the third octet because that is where the subnetting occurs.

Table 10-4 Subnet Information for Network 172.16.0.0 with Subnet Mask 255.255.255.0 (172.16.0.0/24)

Subnet Number	Range of Host IDs
172.16.1.0/24	172.16.1.1–172.16.1.254
172.16.2.0/24	172.16.2.1–172.16.2.254
172.16.3.0/24	172.16.3.1–172.16.3.254
172.16.4.0/24	172.16.4.1–172.16.4.254
172.16.5.0/24	172.16.5.1–172.16.5.254

All hosts on the same subnet must have the same subnet mask to communicate correctly with one another. However, the subnet mask can vary from network to network.

Note Do not make the mistake of interpreting a subnet mask to be an IP address. Subnet masks are displayed in dotted decimal notation, but they are not IP addresses.

See Also Further exploration of subnetting is beyond the scope of this discussion. For more information about subnetting, see "Planning Classless IP Addressing" at *http:// www.microsoft.com/technet/prodtechnol/windowsserver2003/library/DepKit/ b5177e77-8fed-453b-9f50-040e279f23b1.mspx.*

Default Gateway

By default, TCP/IP clients can communicate only with other devices on the same network. If you have a multiple network environment or if you are connected to the Internet, you must configure each host with a default gateway address. The **default gateway** is the router to which the TCP/IP client will forward packets that are destined for computers on other networks. The default gateway then examines the destination IP address in the packets and ensures that the packet is routed to the final destination.

Because TCP/IP clients can communicate directly only within their network and they require the default gateway to communicate with other networks, the host's default gateway *must* reside on the same network as the host.

Figure 10-1 depicts a router that connects four networks together, with the IP addresses of each of the router interfaces noted.

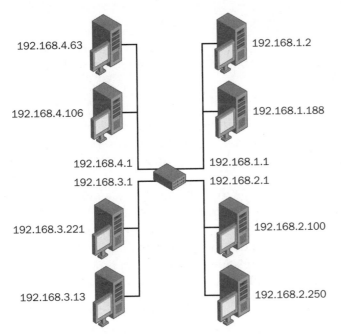

192.168.4.63

192.168.4.106

192.168.4.1
192.168.3.1

192.168.3.221

192.168.3.13

192.168.1.2

192.168.1.188

192.168.1.1
192.168.2.1

192.168.2.100

192.168.2.250

Figure 10-1   A router can connect several IP networks.

The default gateway is a required TCP/IP parameter that is configured only in a multiple network environment. A connection to the Internet is considered a multiple network environment, and a default gateway is required for Internet access. If you neglect to configure the default gateway or if you configure it incorrectly, a TCP/IP client cannot communicate with devices on other networks, including the Internet.

Domain Name System (DNS)

For computers, it is easy to work with numbers such as IP addresses and subnet masks. For people, it is easier to work with names. Host names are standard language names given to TCP/IP devices. Generally, users try to establish connections by using the host name or computer name of the device rather than the IP address. However, for TCP/IP hosts to communicate with one another, they must have the IP address of the device they are connecting to. Therefore, computers must be able to resolve the host names into the IP address of the destination host before the computer can establish a connection. The process of resolving a name into an IP address is called name resolution. **Domain Name System (DNS)** is a network service that is designed to perform name resolution for TCP/IP clients.

Note   In addition to providing name resolution services, DNS also provides service resolution. Clients can query DNS looking for a server that provides a particular service, such as a domain controller or a mail server, and DNS can return the IP address of a device that provides that service.

DNS servers maintain a list of name to IP address mappings called a DNS database. When a client submits a name resolution request to a DNS server, the server searches through the DNS database, locates the host name that was submitted, resolves the IP address, and returns the IP address to the client. In larger private networks and on the Internet, the DNS database is too large to be handled by a single computer. In cases like this, the DNS database is distributed across many DNS servers, and the DNS servers are configured to communicate with one another so that they can resolve a name regardless of where the name to IP address mapping is actually stored. Clients do not need to be aware of the DNS server relationships; they simply submit a request to their DNS server, and the server handles the rest.

DNS is designed to resolve two types of names into IP addresses. A host name is a single-word name, similar to a computer name. Host names can be up to 255 characters long. A fully qualified domain name (FQDN) is a multipart name separated by periods (for example, computer1.contoso.com) that specifies the host name and the host's exact location in the DNS naming hierarchy.

Note   The use of name-resolution methods such as DNS, WINS, hosts files, and Lmhosts files are not necessary in single-network, Microsoft-only environments. Clients automatically perform name resolution by using broadcast packets. This is sufficient in single-network, Microsoft-only environments.

See Also   For more details about DNS structure, see "Understanding DNS" at *http:// www.microsoft.com/windows2000/en/advanced/help/default.asp?url=/windows2000/en/ advanced/help/sag_DNS_und_Topnode.htm.*

TCP/IP Hosts File   In smaller environments, the implementation of a DNS server might not be practical. A standard TCP/IP hosts file can be used to support name resolution if necessary. The hosts file is a simple text file that contains IP addresses followed by the name of the host, as illustrated in Figure 10-2. In Windows XP, the hosts file is stored in SystemRoot\System32\Drivers\etc. There is a default hosts file stored in this path, which contains information about how to create and use the file.

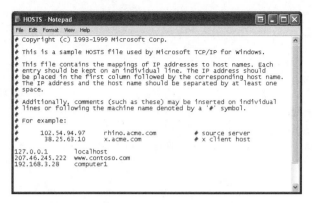

Figure 10-2   A hosts file is a simple text file that stores IP address to host name mappings.

Hosts files are simple to create and use, but they can be difficult to manage. Each computer has an individual hosts file. Whenever a change occurs on the network (such as the addition or deletion of a host, or host name or IP address changes), each individual hosts file must be updated. This can be a time-consuming process, and you must be careful to ensure that all machines receive updates to prevent problems with a client accessing resources.

> **Note**   The hosts file is simply called hosts, and it does not have an extension. If an extension is placed on the file, TCP/IP cannot find it.

WINS

In addition to having host names, computers running Windows also have a **NetBIOS name**. NetBIOS names are based on a protocol called Network Basic Input/Output System (NetBIOS), which assists in the establishment of connections over the network. In a NetBIOS environment, each computer is assigned a NetBIOS name of up to 16 characters in length. The first 15 characters are the actual name of the computer, and the sixteenth character is a reserved character used to represent different resources or services offered by the computer.

In Windows operating systems that are not part of a domain, the Client and Server network services use NetBIOS to establish connections.

Recent versions of Windows, such as Microsoft Windows 2000 and Windows XP, do not require the use of NetBIOS to establish connections, but they support NetBIOS functions to facilitate connections with previous versions of Windows.

In a single-network environment, NetBIOS name resolution is handled by using a broadcast message. The client sends out a packet containing the NetBIOS name of the computer to which the client needs to connect, requesting the computer with that name to send back its IP address. The computer with the requested name sends a packet containing its IP address back to the requesting computer. However, NetBIOS name resolution broadcasts are not forwarded by routers, so the client cannot resolve names that are not on the local network.

In multiple-network environments, a service named **Windows Internet Naming Service (WINS)** can be implemented. The WINS server maintains a database of NetBIOS name to IP address mappings, similar to the way that a DNS server maintains a database of host name to IP address mappings. The WINS server can perform NetBIOS name resolution for clients. If clients are configured with the IP address of the WINS server, the clients send name resolution requests to the WINS server before broadcasting on their local subnet.

The NetBIOS name and the DNS host name are usually the same for a Windows computer. Both name-resolution services might be required in a previous version of Windows because of the different methods that are used to establish connections, not because the names themselves are different.

> ### Real World Dealing with Name Resolution
>
> As a DST, you do not need to get too bogged down in the details of DNS and WINS. On larger networks, one or both of these naming systems may be in place. In a domain running Windows Server 2003, DNS is mandatory. Small business and home networks typically exist on a single network segment and do not require sophisticated name-resolution mechanisms within the network.
>
> However, you do need to understand the service that a DNS server (and to a lesser degree, a WINS server) provide to a network. Any computer that is connected to the Internet has to resolve DNS names in some manner because DNS is used on the Internet. On large networks, you may need to configure a client with the IP address of an appropriate DNS server, but you likely are not expected to do much configuration beyond that. If you discover that a client is not resolving a DNS name on a large network, you can probably just escalate the problem to an administrator. For small network and home users, you might need to determine the correct IP address of the DNS server used by the ISP of the user and configure computers to connect to that server.

Lmhosts File In smaller environments, the implementation of a WINS server might not be practical. Microsoft supports the use of the Lmhosts file to support NetBIOS name resolution, if necessary. The Lmhosts file is a simple text file that contains IP addresses followed by the name of the host, similar to a TCP/IP hosts file. Lmhosts is stored in %SystemRoot%\system32\drivers\etc. There is a sample Lmhosts file called Lmhost.sam stored in this path, which can be used to build a working file. To be recognized by the system, the actual file name has to be Lmhosts without an extension.

Lmhosts files can have support issues similar to those of TCP/IP hosts files. Each computer has an individual copy of the file, and it can be time-consuming to keep all the files updated.

Lesson Review

The following questions are intended to reinforce key information presented in this lesson. If you are unable to answer a question, review the lesson materials and try the question again. You can find answers to the questions in the "Questions and Answers" section at the end of this chapter.

1. List the required and optional parameters that you can assign to a host on a TCP/IP network.

_____

_____

2. List the three primary address classes used for assigning IP addresses to hosts on the Internet and the corresponding range of IP addresses available in each class.

_____

_____

3. Which of the following default subnet masks would be used on a computer connected to the Internet with the IP address 157.54.4.201?

    A. 255.0.0.0

    B. 255.255.0.0

    C. 255.255.255.0

    D. 255.255.255.255

Lesson Summary

- Each host on a TCP/IP network is assigned a unique IP address, typically shown as four decimal numbers ranging from 0 to 255. An IP address is divided into a network ID, which determines the subnet on which a host exists, and a host ID, which uniquely identifies the host on that subnet. The separation of network ID and host ID is determined by a subnet mask.

- A default gateway is the IP address to which a client sends data destined for a host that is not on the same network as a client. The default gateway is typically a router.

- Name resolution is the process of mapping IP addresses to computer or host names. DNS is the primary name-resolution mechanism used on modern Windows networks and on the Internet. WINS is a name resolution mechanism used on older Windows-based networks.

Lesson 2: Troubleshooting Network Connectivity

For a DST, resolving connectivity problems typically involves testing the network cable connections, testing the network adapter in a computer, testing the network configuration on a computer, and verifying that any required servers are online. A user might have several connections configured, including a direct Internet connection through a cable or DSL modem or a network connection to another computer or to a router. You should be able to use the Windows interface to verify connectivity settings and use various tools in Windows XP to isolate different types of network problems.

After this lesson, you will be able to

■ Troubleshoot cable connections.

■ Configure and troubleshoot a network adapter or modem.

■ Identify and use TCP/IP troubleshooting tools.

■ Troubleshoot name-resolution problems

Estimated lesson time: 60 minutes

Troubleshooting Cable Connections

You can resolve a surprising number of network connectivity problems simply by ensuring that the network cable or telephone line is properly connected to the network adapter or modem on a user's computer. This is especially true for an office environment in which the furniture is moved or relocated often, or when a cleaning crew comes in each night and works around users' computers. When a user reports that he or she cannot access the network, always suggest that the user first double-check cable connections.

Besides making sure that the cables are properly connected to a user's computer, you should also verify the following:

■ On large networks, users typically have network jacks on the walls in their offices. Make sure that the network cable is properly connected to the jack.

■ On small networks, computers can be cabled directly to a router instead of to a wall jack. Check the connections at the router to make sure that the cables are securely connected. If other computers are also not connecting to the network properly, check to make sure that the router is turned on and that the cable from the router to the Internet connection device (usually a cable or DSL modem) is secure.

- For users of wireless networks, make sure that the computer is within the acceptable range from the wireless router or access point.

> **Note**   If you notice that a desk, chair, or other piece of furniture is positioned on top of a network cable, or that the cable is crimped, try replacing the cable. The cable could be damaged.

Troubleshooting Networking Hardware

If the cable connections are good, your next step is to check the networking hardware that is installed on the computer so that you can rule out malfunctioning hardware as the cause of the problem. Checking physical hardware connections includes verifying in Device Manager that the connectivity devices are working properly. If they are not, you must troubleshoot those devices. If problems persist, verify that the hardware is installed properly.

Device Manager details the hardware components that are on the computer and denotes any malfunctioning hardware with either a red "X" or a yellow exclamation point. You should use Device Manager if physical connectivity is not the problem and before you attempt other troubleshooting techniques. If you find a problem with a modem or network adapter, you might need to replace the hardware to get the user connected to the network again.

To use Device Manager to locate and troubleshoot hardware devices installed on the computer, follow these steps:

1. From the Start menu, right-click My Computer and select Properties.

2. In the System Properties dialog box, on the Hardware tab, select Device Manager.

3. Check for devices that have red X's or yellow exclamation points overlaid on their icons (see Chapter 6, "Installing and Managing Hardware," for more information about using Device Manager). Figure 10-3 shows Device Manager with the Modems and Network Adapters categories expanded. In this figure, each component is functioning correctly.

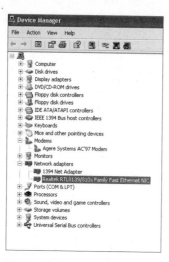

Figure 10-3   Device Manager shows installed hardware, including modems and network adapters.

4. If problems are noted in Device Manager, the component most likely has a device driver issue, is disabled, or has malfunctioned. You should use the troubleshooting techniques detailed in Chapter 6 to troubleshoot the hardware.

> **Tip**   The Help And Support troubleshooting wizards are a great way to troubleshoot hardware because they walk you though current reliable techniques for solving common problems with hardware. In addition, they offer exceptional learning tools for beginning DSTs.

Using the Windows Troubleshooters

The Microsoft Windows Help And Support Center offers a modem troubleshooter that you can use if you believe that a modem is the cause of the connectivity problem. If Device Manager reports that the modem is working properly, you can try using the Modem Troubleshooter to help resolve modem configuration issues.

This troubleshooter guides you through the steps to take if users have problems connecting to the Internet by using the modem, if Windows does not detect the modem, or if the Network Setup Wizard and New Connection Wizard are not working properly. In this case, you would choose to follow the wizard through the options for solving a problem using the modem to connect to the Internet.

To use the Modem Troubleshooter, follow these steps:

1. From the Start menu, select Help And Support.

2. Under Pick A Help Topic, select Fixing A Problem.

3. Under Fixing A Problem, select Networking Problems; from the right pane, select Modem Troubleshooter.

4. On the What Problem Are You Having? page, select I Have Problems Using My Modem To Connect To The Internet. Click Next.

5. Work through the various troubleshooting pages to perform the following:

    a. Verify that the COM port is turned on.

    b. Verify that the modem is functional.

    c. Verify that the physical connection is configured properly.

    d. Verify that the modem is turned on.

    e. Verify that the COM port settings are correct.

    f. Verify that the modem is listed in the Windows Catalog.

    g. Verify that the COM port, modem, or cable is not faulty.

    h. Upgrade the basic input/output system (BIOS) of the internal modem if necessary.

    i. Locate conflicting devices.

    j. Upgrade the modem's .inf file (a file that lists commands the modem supports) or driver.

    k. Verify that the modem is installed correctly.

    l. Re-create dial-up connections.

    m. Visit the Windows Update website or the manufacturer's website.

The Windows Help And Support troubleshooting wizards are quite thorough. If Device Manager reports that a network adapter is working properly, yet you believe the network adapter is causing a network connectivity problem, work through the Help And Support Center's Drives And Network Adapters Troubleshooter. Whenever possible, access these wizards to help you to resolve end-user problems. In your spare time, work through the wizards to learn new techniques for resolving problems.

Configuring Network Connections

Windows XP provides a central location for viewing and configuring Network Connections: the Network Connections window, shown in Figure 10-4. You can open the Network Connections window in several ways, including the following:

- In Control Panel, double-click Network Connections.

- On the Start menu, right-click My Network Places or desktop (if it is displayed) and then select Properties.

- On the Start menu, click Network Connections. (If the Network Connections folder is not displayed on the Start menu, see Chapter 4, "Supporting the Windows Desktop," for more information).

Figure 10-4   The Network Connections window shows local area network and dial-up connections.

The icons that are used for each connection provide visual clues for the type and status of the connection. These visual clues include the following:

- Dial-up connections (such as the Contoso.com connection in Figure 10-4) have a small icon depicting a telephone and modem.

- LAN or high-speed Internet connections (such as the Local Area Connection in Figure 10-4) have a small depiction meant to represent a network cable connection.

- Disabled connections (such as the 1394 Connection in Figure 10-4) are dimmed to show that they are disabled.

- Disconnected connections have a small red "X" on the icon (such as the Contoso.com connection in Figure 10-4).

- Connections that are protected with Windows Firewall have a small picture of a lock (such as the Contoso.com connection in Figure 10-4). You will learn more about Windows Firewall in Lesson 3, "Supporting Windows Firewall."

To view the a connection's properties, open Network Connections, right-click the connection, and then select Properties, as illustrated in Figure 10-5. In addition to the network adapter, the following networking components are installed by default:

- TCP/IP network protocol
- Client for Microsoft Networks
- File And Printer Sharing for Microsoft Networks

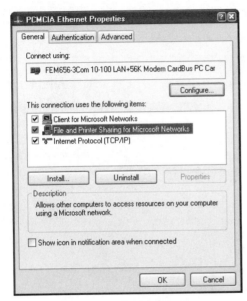

Figure 10-5   Configure a connection by using its Properties dialog box.

Adding, Disabling, and Removing Network Components

You can add and remove network components, such as additional network clients and protocols, by using the Properties dialog box of the network connection. You can have multiple clients, services, and protocols loaded and functioning simultaneously on a single connection.

To add a network component, follow these steps:

1. Open the Properties dialog box for the network connection.
2. Click Install. The Select Network Component Type dialog box appears, as shown in Figure 10-6.

Figure 10-6   Choose network components to install.

3. Select the type of network component that you want to install and then click Add.

4. Select the desired component and click OK, or click Have Disk to install a component that does not appear on the list.

When you add a network component, the component becomes available to all connections automatically. You should disable components that are not used by a particular network connection. This process reduces the amount of network traffic generated on the connection, therefore increasing overall performance. To disable a component without removing it, open the Properties dialog box of the network connection and clear the check box.

When a component is no longer required by any connection, you can remove it. Removing a component removes it from *all* connections.

To remove a network component, follow these steps:

1. Open the Properties dialog box of the network connection.

2. Select the network component that you want to remove.

3. Click Uninstall, and then click Yes to confirm the uninstall operation.

Renaming and Disabling a Local Area Connection

If you have more than one network card installed, Windows names the first connection Local Area Connection, the second connection Local Area Connection 2, and so on. For clarity, consider using a naming scheme that makes it easy to identify what the different connections are for. To rename a connection, right-click the connection in Network Connections and, from the shortcut menu, select the Rename option.

There might be cases in which you will want to temporarily disable a connection without deleting it. To disable a connection, right-click the connection and select Disable.

To enable a connection, perform the same steps and, from the shortcut menu, select Enable.

Configuring TCP/IP for a Network Connection

You configure the TCP/IP settings for a particular connection by first opening the Properties dialog box for the connection. For local area connections, on the General tab of the Properties dialog box, in the This Connection Uses The Following Items section, select Internet Protocol (TCP/IP) and then click Properties. For dial-up connections, you can find Internet Protocol (TCP/IP) on the Networking tab of the dial-up connection's Properties dialog box. For both local area and dial-up connections, the Internet Protocol (TCP/IP) Properties dialog box is the same (see Figure 10-7).

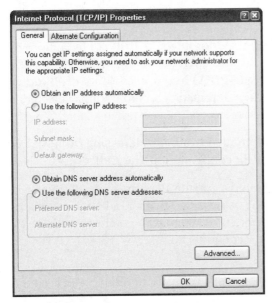

Figure 10-7   Windows XP is configured to obtain TCP/IP information automatically by default.

Obtaining TCP/IP Settings Automatically   By default, TCP/IP is configured to obtain an IP address automatically in Windows XP. When TCP/IP is configured to obtain an IP address automatically, it first attempts to locate a **Dynamic Host Configuration Protocol (DHCP)** server on the network. The DHCP server can be a Windows server or a third-party DHCP service (often built into routers). Administrators configure the DHCP server with a range of IP addresses and other TCP/IP configuration parameters that it will automatically assign to clients. In addition to IP addresses, DHCP servers can assign a subnet mask, default gateway, DNS and WINS configuration, and a variety of other parameters.

DHCP servers lease clients their IP configuration for a period of time specified by the DHCP administrator. (The default lease duration for a Windows-based DHCP server is eight days.) Clients contact the DHCP server to renew their lease every time that the clients are started or when half of the lease time has expired, whichever comes first. Clients lose their TCP/IP configuration if they do not contact the DHCP server before the lease time expires, which can happen if the computer is not started for an extended period of time or if the DHCP server is unavailable due to issues with the server or the network.

DHCP clients communicate with the DHCP server by using broadcast messages. Broadcasts are not forwarded by routers, which means that a client cannot communicate directly with a DHCP server that is not on the local network. Rather than putting a DHCP server on every network in a multiple network environment, administrators can place a service called a DHCP Relay Agent on the local network. DHCP Relay Agents pick up DHCP broadcast messages and forward them to a DHCP server on another network.

If a client that is automatically configured to obtain TCP/IP configuration information cannot locate a DHCP server, there are two alternate configuration methods to choose: **Automatic Private IP Addressing (APIPA)** and a user-defined IP address. These alternate methods are used only when automatic configuration is selected. If manual configuration is being performed, alternate options are not available.

Obtaining TCP/IP Settings from Automatic Private IP Addressing (APIPA)   APIPA is the default method for alternate TCP/IP configuration. The APIPA process is as follows:

1. If the client computer is configured to obtain IP addressing information automatically, but cannot locate a DHCP server, the client randomly assigns itself an IP address from the Class B network 169.254.0.0, with a subnet mask of 255.255.0.0. The range of IP addresses that a computer running Windows XP can assign itself is 169.254.0.1–169.254.255.254.

2. The client sends a broadcast message to verify that no other client on the network has chosen the same address.

3. If the client does not receive any responses to the broadcast (which is likely because there are 65,534 possible addresses in the range), it initializes TCP/IP by using the random IP address and a subnet mask of 255.255.0.0.

If the client receives a response to the broadcast indicating that another client is already using the address, another address is randomly selected and the process begins again. This process continues until the client chooses an address that is not already in use by another computer.

APIPA assigns an IP address and subnet mask only, and configures no additional parameters. This service is very useful in smaller, single-network environments in which there is no need for connectivity to other networks. APIPA provides a very simple way to configure TCP/IP; the network administrator does not need any knowledge of the necessary configuration parameters. However, if connectivity to other networks is required, or if the client requires the name-resolution services of DNS or WINS, APIPA is not sufficient. APIPA does not provide a default gateway, DNS server, or WINS server address to the client.

Exam Tip   If you are troubleshooting a network problem and discover that a client computer has an IP address on the 169.254.0.0 network, the computer has assigned itself that address using APIPA because the computer was unable to locate a DHCP server.

Configuring Alternate TCP/IP Settings   User-configured alternate settings allow you to manually specify the IP address, subnet mask, default gateway, DNS server, and WINS servers to be used when a DHCP server is not available. This is an ideal configuration for portable computers that function with DHCP at one location, but use a static address at another location. If the portable computer is connected to the network that supports DHCP, it automatically obtains an address from the DHCP server. However, if it is connected to a network without DHCP services, it uses the configuration specified here.

Figure 10-8 displays the Alternate Configuration tab of TCP/IP properties, with user-configured settings.

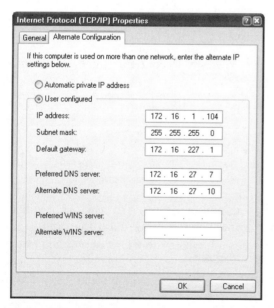

Figure 10-8   Configure an alternate TCP/IP configuration for when a DHCP server is not available.

Manual Configuration of TCP/IP Properties

Automatic configuration of TCP/IP properties is convenient, but there will be times when you want the control that you have in manual configuration. To configure TCP/IP properties manually, on the General tab, select the Use The Following IP Address option, as illustrated in Figure 10-9.

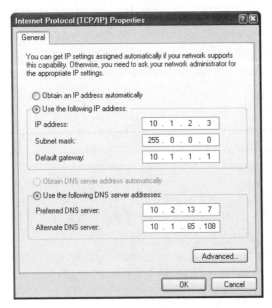

Figure 10-9   Configure TCP/IP information manually.

The General tab of TCP/IP Properties allows you to configure the most commonly used TCP/IP parameters in Windows XP:

- IP address
- Subnet mask
- Default gateway
- DNS servers

You can configure a preferred and an alternative DNS server. The client will attempt to use the preferred DNS server for name-resolution requests. If the preferred server is unavailable or cannot resolve the request, the alternative DNS server will be contacted.

Troubleshooting Modem Connections

Internet connectivity problems that involve modems occur for a variety of reasons. A problem can be caused by something as simple as dialing an incorrect telephone number or having the connection automatically disconnect after a period of time. Or it might be something as complicated as an improperly configured name server address.

Table 10-5 details how to resolve common modem problems using the Properties dialog box for the dial-up connection.

Table 10-5 Resolving Common Internet Connectivity Calls (modems)

Complaint	Possible Solution
My modem does not connect to my ISP.	Call the ISP and verify or obtain a telephone number. On the General tab, retype the telephone number.
When the modem dials, I get an error message that the number is not in service.	Call the ISP and obtain a new telephone number. On the General tab, insert the telephone number.
I cannot hear my modem when it dials.	On the General tab, click Configure. Select the Enable Modem Speaker check box. In Device Manager, double-click the modem; on the Modem tab, configure the speaker volume.
I hear my modem when it dials.	On the General tab, select Configure. Clear the Enable Modem Speaker check box.
I keep getting disconnected from the Internet after 20 minutes of inactivity.	On the Options tab, change the setting for Idle Time Before Hanging Up to Never, 24 Hours, 8 Hours, 4 Hours, or any other setting.
When I get disconnected from the Internet, the connection is not redialed automatically.	On the Options tab, select the Redial If Line Is Dropped check box.
When I disconnect from my ISP at night, the computer redials and connects even if I do not want it to.	On the Options tab, change the value for Redial Attempts to 0. Clear the Redial If Line Is Dropped check box.
I keep getting prompted for my name and password, telephone number, and other information.	On the Options tab, clear the Prompt For Name And Password, Certificate, Etc., Include Windows Logon Domain, and Prompt For Telephone Number check boxes, as applicable to the network.
Sometimes my ISP's telephone number is busy. I have an alternative number. How do I change it?	On the General tab, click Alternates. In the Alternate telephone Numbers dialog box, click Add. Add the new number, and click OK to exit the dialog boxes.

Troubleshooting Cable and DSL Connections

Internet connectivity problems that involve cable and DSL modems also occur for a variety of reasons. A problem can be caused by something as simple as a disconnected cable or something as complicated as troubleshooting a slow connection or identifying the source of DSL interference. Table 10-6 lists common connectivity problems reported with cable and DSL connections.

Table 10-6   Resolving Common Internet Connectivity Calls (cable and DSL)

Complaint	Possible Solution
My Internet connection is unavailable.	Check all physical connections to and from modems, routers, and the computer. Swap out questionable cables for new ones. If problems still exist, right-click the connection in Network Connections, choose Properties, select Internet Protocol (TCP/IP), and then click Properties. Note that if you are using a dial-up connection, the Internet Protocol (TCP/IP) information is on the Networking tab of the network connection's Properties dialog box. Verify with the ISP that the settings are correct. A common setting is Obtain An IP Address Automatically. Click OK to work out of the dialog boxes.
I try to connect, but nothing happens at all.	Verify that all power supplies to modems or routers are plugged in and that all hardware is turned on. Verify that the network adapter and all hardware are functional by using Device Manager, as detailed earlier.
My Internet connection is slow.	Contact the ISP first. The problem could lie in the ISP's capabilities. It is possible that the servers are overloaded. A newer modem might also be available.
I think I am getting interference. Could something be causing that?	Yes. Interference can be caused by lighting dimmer switches, AM radio stations, and other sources.

Using TCP/IP Troubleshooting Tools

Windows XP provides a number of TCP/IP tools for troubleshooting network connectivity problems. As a DST, you should be familiar with the following tools:

- Ping
- Ipconfig
- Net view
- Tracert
- Pathping

Using Ping

When the problem appears to be with TCP/IP (either because you have ruled out problems with cables and network adapters, physical connections, and the other causes detailed in this chapter; or because the Network Troubleshooter pointed out a

TCP/IP address problem), start the troubleshooting process with the Ping command, which allows you to check for connectivity between devices on a network.

When you use the Ping command, you ping from the inside out. You want to find out where the communication and connection fail. For example, you ping the **loopback address** first, then a local computer on the same network, then a DNS or DHCP server on the local subnet if one exists, then the default gateway, then a remote computer on another network, and finally a resource on the Internet. You should be able to find out where the breakdown occurs by compiling the results of these checks.

> **Note**   When using the Ping command, you can use either the computer name or the computer's IP address.

Pinging the Loopback Address   The loopback address (127.0.0.1) is the first detail you should check when a TCP/IP problem appears. If this check fails, the TCP/IP configuration for the local machine is not correct. To ping the loopback address, follow these steps:

1. From the Start menu, point to All Programs, point to Accessories, and select Command Prompt.

2. Type **ping 127.0.0.1**. A successful ping to a loopback address is shown in Figure 10-10.

```
Command Prompt                                               _ □ ×
Microsoft Windows XP [Version 5.1.2600]
(C) Copyright 1985-2001 Microsoft Corp.

C:\Documents and Settings\Walter>ping 127.0.0.1

Pinging 127.0.0.1 with 32 bytes of data:

Reply from 127.0.0.1: bytes=32 time<1ms TTL=128
Reply from 127.0.0.1: bytes=32 time<1ms TTL=128
Reply from 127.0.0.1: bytes=32 time<1ms TTL=128
Reply from 127.0.0.1: bytes=32 time<1ms TTL=128

Ping statistics for 127.0.0.1:
    Packets: Sent = 4, Received = 4, Lost = 0 (0% loss),
Approximate round trip times in milli-seconds:
    Minimum = 0ms, Maximum = 0ms, Average = 0ms

C:\Documents and Settings\Walter>
```

Figure 10-10   Ping the loopback address to verify that TCP/IP is configured correctly.

If pinging the loopback address fails, check the configuration of TCP/IP by following these steps:

1. Open the Network Connections window, right-click the configured connection, and choose Properties.

2. Select Internet Protocol (TCP/IP), and click Properties to view the configuration. If a static address is configured and a DHCP server is available, select Obtain An IP

Address Automatically. If Obtain An IP Address Automatically is selected but a static IP address is necessary, select Use The Following IP Address; then enter the address, subnet mask, and gateway to use. If the configuration is correct, you might have to reset TCP/IP.

3. Click OK in the Properties dialog box and OK in the connection's Properties dialog box. Reboot the computer if prompted.

See Also   If reconfiguring the TCP/IP settings did not help solve the loopback problem, you can try resetting TCP/IP. See Knowledge Base article 299357, "How to Reset Internet Protocol (TCP/IP) in Windows XP," for details.

Pinging Other Resources   To ping any other computer on the network, simply replace the loopback address with the TCP/IP address of the resource on the network. Ping a local computer on the same subnet first, and then ping the gateway address. If you can ping the loopback address (a local computer on the same subnet), but the Ping command to the gateway fails, you probably found the problem. In this case, check the configuration on the local computer for the gateway address and verify that the gateway (or router) is operational.

If the ping to the gateway address is successful, continue to ping outward until you find the problem. For instance, ping a computer on a remote subnet and verify that the DNS server is operational.

Note   For more information about troubleshooting by using Ping and similar commands, read Knowledge Base article 314067, "How to Troubleshoot TCP/IP Connectivity with Windows XP."

Using Ipconfig

You can use the **Ipconfig** command-line utility to view current TCP/IP configuration information for a computer. To use Ipconfig, open the command prompt window and type **Ipconfig** to view basic TCP/IP parameters, **Ipconfig /all** to view the complete TCP/IP configuration (as shown in Figure 10-11), or **Ipconfig /?** to view additional options.

```
Command Prompt                                              _ [] X
C:\>ipconfig /all

Windows IP Configuration

        Host Name . . . . . . . . . . . . : COMPUTER1
        Primary Dns Suffix  . . . . . . . :
        Node Type . . . . . . . . . . . . : Mixed
        IP Routing Enabled. . . . . . . . : No
        WINS Proxy Enabled. . . . . . . . : No

Ethernet adapter Local Area Connection:

        Connection-specific DNS Suffix  . :
        Description . . . . . . . . . . . : Intel(R) PRO/1000 CT Network Connect
ion
        Physical Address. . . . . . . . . : 00-07-E9-45-C4-2D
        Dhcp Enabled. . . . . . . . . . . : No
        IP Address. . . . . . . . . . . . : 192.168.1.2
        Subnet Mask . . . . . . . . . . . : 255.255.255.0
        Default Gateway . . . . . . . . . : 192.168.1.1
        DNS Servers . . . . . . . . . . . : 69.1.30.43
                                            69.1.30.42


C:\>_
```

Figure 10-11   Use the Ipconfig /all command to display a complete TCP/IP configuration.

> **Note**   You must run Ipconfig from a command prompt. If you try to execute it by using the Run command on the Start menu, the command window will close before you have a chance to read the information that is displayed.

Additional Ipconfig options include the following:

■ **/release**   Releases DHCP-supplied configuration information

■ **/renew**   Renews DHCP-supplied configuration information

■ **/flushdns**   Purges the local DNS cache (the area of memory that stores recently resolved names so that the client does not have to contact the DNS server each time the client needs to resolve a name)

■ **/registerdns**   Renews DHCP-supplied configuration information and registers the DNS name to IP address information with DNS

■ **/displaydns**   Displays the contents of the local DNS cache

■ **/setclassid**   Provides for the configuration of DHCP user classes, which can control the way that IP addresses are assigned

Using Net View

The Net View command is another command that you can use to test TCP/IP connections. To use the command, log on with the proper credentials that are required to view shares on a remote or local computer, open a command prompt, and type **net view *ComputerName*** or **net view *IP Address***. The resulting report lists the file and print shares on the computer. If there are no file or print shares on the computer, you see the message There Are No Entries In The List.

If the Net View command fails, check the following:

- The computer name in the System Properties dialog box
- The gateway or router address in the TCP/IP Properties dialog box
- The gateway or router status
- The remote computer is running the File And Printer Sharing for Microsoft Networks Service (this service can be added in the TCP/IP Properties dialog box)

Using Tracert

When a route breaks down on the way from the destination computer to its target computer, communication fails. The **Tracert** command-line utility can help you figure out exactly where along the route the breakdown happened. Sometimes the connection breaks down at the gateway on the local network and sometimes at a router on an external network.

To use Tracert, at the command prompt type **tracert** followed by the IP address of the remote computer. The resulting report shows where the packets were lost. You can use this information to uncover the source of the problem.

Using Pathping

The Ping command is used to test communication between one computer and another; Tracert is used to follow a particular route from one computer to another. The **Pathping** command is a combination of both Ping and Tracert, displaying information about packet loss at every router between the host computer and the remote one. The Pathping command provides information about data loss between the source and the destination, allowing you to determine which particular router or subnet might be having network problems. To use the Pathping command, at the command prompt, type **pathping** followed by the target name or IP address.

> **Note**   The Windows Help And Support Center offers a list of all of the commands that you can perform by using the command line. Search for Command-Line Reference A-Z. Each command reference includes a description of the command and how to use it.

Troubleshooting Name Resolution on a Client Computer

Name resolution is the process that allows network and Internet users to access resources by their names instead of their IP addresses. Names that are used might be (among others) computer names, server names, printer names, or FQDNs. Without name resolution, users would be forced to remember the IP addresses of each resource on the network or on the Internet. Thus, name resolution makes accessing resources much simpler. When problems occur with accessing network resources, often the solution involves troubleshooting these components.

DNS Issues

DNS servers resolve the names of hosts on the network to their respective IP addresses. Administrators install DNS servers and configure the IP addresses of resources on the network. When something is wrong with the DNS configuration on a computer or the DNS server on a network, client computers cannot resolve computer names or FQDNs to their IP addresses, and connectivity to resources fails.

If you believe (because of results of Ping, Ipconfig /all, Tracert, or other command-line tests) that an incorrect DNS configuration is preventing a user or users from resolving names to IP addresses, and you have verified the IP address of the DNS server and that the server is online, you should check the DNS settings on the local computer.

Exam Tip   For the exam, make sure that you understand how to enable automatic configuration of DNS servers and know where to go to specify particular DNS servers.

WINS Issues

In addition to DNS, WINS is sometimes used on a network. WINS servers resolve NetBIOS names to their associated IP addresses. NetBIOS names allow computers running previous versions of Windows (such as Windows NT, Windows Me, and Windows 98) to participate in a network and to access resources.

Note   Not all networks use WINS servers. WINS integration is necessary only if the network includes computers running previous versions of Windows.

If the network includes a WINS server, if you believe that an incorrect WINS configuration is preventing a computer from resolving NetBIOS names to IP addresses, and if you have verified the IP address of the WINS server (and that it is online), you should check the WINS settings on the local computer.

Practice: Resolve Network Connectivity Issues

In this practice, you will create and configure an Internet connection. You will also use the Ipconfig and Ping commands to test network connectivity.

Exercise 1: Configure an Internet Connection

> **Note**   In this exercise, you will configure a nonfunctioning Internet connection by using a modem that does not exist. After you finish this exercise, delete the Internet connection.

1. Log on to Windows XP using an account with administrator privileges.

2. From the Start menu, select My Computer.

3. In the Other Places section in the left-hand pane, select My Network Places.

4. In the My Network Places window, in the Network Tasks section, click View Network Connections.

5. In the Network Connections window, in the Network Tasks section, click Create A New Connection.

6. In the New Connection Wizard, on the Welcome To The New Connection Wizard page, click Next.

7. On the Network Connection Type page, verify that Connect To The Internet is selected, and click Next.

8. On the Getting Ready page, select Set Up My Connection Manually, and click Next.

9. On the Internet Connection page, verify that Connect Using A Dial-Up Modem is selected, and click Next.

10. On the Connection Name page, in the ISP Name text box, type **Contoso**, and then click Next.

11. On the Phone Number To Dial page, in the Phone Number text box, type **1-000-000-0000**. Click Next.

12. On the Connection Availability page, click Next.

13. On the Internet Account Information page, in the User Name text box, type your name. In the Password and Confirm Password text boxes, type **password**. Click Next.

14. On the Completing The New Connection Wizard page, click Finish.

Exercise 2: Use Ipconfig /all

1. From the Start menu, point to All Programs, point to Accessories, and select Command Prompt.

2. At the command prompt, type **ipconfig /all** and press ENTER.

3. For each network connection on your computer, record the following information:

   ❑ Description

   ❑ DHCP Enabled

   ❑ IP Address

   ❑ Subnet Mask

   ❑ Default Gateway

   ❑ DNS Servers

Exercise 3: Use Ping

1. From the Start menu, point to All Programs, point to Accessories, and select Command Prompt.

2. At the command prompt, type **ping 127.0.0.1** and press ENTER. You should see four replies showing response times, followed by statistics for the ping attempts. This response indicates a successful ping of the local computer, meaning that TCP/IP is installed and working correctly.

3. Type **ping www.microsoft.com**. You should see information similar to that in Step 2, but this time showing response times for Microsoft's server.

4. Minimize the command prompt window.

5. From the Start menu, select My Computer.

6. In the My Computer window, in the Other Places section, select My Network Places.

7. In the My Network Places window, in the Network Tasks section, click View Network Connections.

8. In the Network Connections window, under LAN Or High-Speed Internet, right-click Local Area Connection and select Properties.

9. In the Local Area Connection Properties dialog box, on the General Tab, in the This Connection Uses The Following Items section, clear the Internet Protocol (TCP/IP) check box and click OK.

10. In the Network Connections message box, click Yes. This step disables the TCP/IP protocol on the local computer.

11. Minimize the Network Connections window and restore the command prompt window.

12. At the command prompt, type **ping www.microsoft.com** and press ENTER. This time, the Ping command should respond with the text "Destination Host Unreachable," indicating that the ping attempt was unsuccessful (this happens because you disabled the TCP/IP protocol).

13. Minimize the command prompt window and restore the Network Connections window.

14. In the Network Connections window, under LAN Or High-Speed Internet, right-click Local Area Connection and select Properties.

15. In the Local Area Connection Properties dialog box, on the General Tab, in the This Connection Uses The Following Items section, select the Internet Protocol (TCP/IP) check box and click OK.

16. Close the Network Connections window and restore the command prompt window.

17. Type **ping www.microsoft.com** and press ENTER. You should now see the proper ping response again.

18. Close the Command Prompt window.

Lesson Review

The following questions are intended to reinforce key information presented in this lesson. If you are unable to answer a question, review the lesson materials and try the question again. You can find answers to the questions in the "Questions and Answers" section at the end of this chapter.

1. You are troubleshooting a networking problem for a user. Although the user had no problem connecting to the network when she left the office yesterday afternoon, she cannot connect to the network this morning. You know that other users on the network are not having the same problems. What is the first thing you should check?

   _____

   _____

2. A user complains to you that he cannot connect to any network resources after he installed a new network adapter card. You open the Command Prompt window on the user's computer and type **ipconfig /all**. You get the following results:

   ❑ Ethernet adapter Local Area Connection:

   ❑ Connection-specific DNS Suffix

   ❑ Description: Intel(R) PRO/1000 CT

   ❑ Physical Address: 0B-01-C4-32-E1-2C

   ❑ DHCP Enabled: Yes

   ❑ IP Address: 169.254.023.102

   ❑ Subnet Mask: 255.255.0.0

   ❑ Default Gateway:

   ❑ DNS Servers:

What do these results tell you? (Choose all that apply.)

    A. The computer is configured to connect to a DHCP server.

    B. The computer is not configured to connect to a DHCP server.

    C. The computer is successfully connecting to a DHCP server.

    D. The computer is not successfully connecting to a DHCP server.

3. You are troubleshooting a network connectivity problem on a user's computer. At the command prompt, you type the Ipconfig /all command and receive the following results:

    ❑ IP Address......192.168.0.5

    ❑ Subnet Mask.......255.255.255.255

    ❑ Default Gateway......192.168.0.7

Which of these values is most likely configured incorrectly?

_____

_____

Lesson Summary

- To resolve network connectivity problems, you should test network cabling connections, the network adapter in a computer, the network configuration on a computer, and verify that any required servers are online.

- You can configure local area and dial-up network connections using the Network Connections window in Windows XP. Use a particular connection's Properties dialog box to configure the connection settings.

- Windows XP computers can obtain an IP address automatically by searching the network for a DHCP server. If found, the DHCP server provides TCP/IP configuration information to the client. If the computer cannot contact a DHCP server, Windows XP assigns the computer an IP address in the 169.254.0.0 range automatically by using APIPA. You can also configure the TCP/IP information for a computer manually.

- Use the Ping, Tracert, and Pathping commands to test TCP/IP connectivity.

- Use the Ipconfig /all command to show detailed information about the TCP/IP configuration of a computer, including the IP address, subnet mask, default gateway, DNS servers, and DHCP information about every network connection on a system.

Lesson 3: Supporting Windows Firewall

A firewall protects a computer from external network traffic (specifically, the Internet) by blocking all network traffic except that which you specifically configure the firewall to allow through. This section introduces firewalls and looks at the host-based firewall that is included with Windows XP with Service Pack 2: Windows Firewall.

After this lesson, you will be able to

- Explain how firewalls protect computers.
- Enable or disable Windows Firewall for all network connections.
- Enable or disable Windows Firewall for a specific network connection.
- Configure advanced options for Windows Firewall.
- Troubleshoot connectivity problems that are associated with Windows Firewall.

Estimated lesson time: 40 minutes

Introducing Windows Firewall

A firewall acts as a security system that creates a border between the computer or network and the Internet. This border determines what traffic is allowed in the local network or computer. Firewalls help keep hackers, viruses, and other malicious activity from infiltrating the computer and network. A perimeter-based firewall is a device that protects an entire network. A host-based firewall is a program that protects a single computer. Windows XP includes a host-based firewall named Windows Firewall.

Windows Firewall is installed when you install Windows XP Service Pack 2, and is an updated version of the Internet Connection Firewall (ICF) found on versions of Windows XP with Service Pack 1 and previous. Windows Firewall is a stateful, host-based firewall that drops all incoming traffic that does not meet one of the following conditions:

- Solicited traffic (valid traffic that is received in response to a request by the computer) is allowed through the firewall.

- Expected traffic (valid traffic that you have specifically configured the firewall to accept) is allowed through the firewall.

Windows Firewall has the following characteristics:

■ Is enabled by default for all network connections. This differs from Internet Connection Firewall, which was not enabled by default.

■ Limits the network traffic that comes into a computer by blocking transmission over all ports except those specifically configured to allow traffic to reach the computer. When you allow a specific type of traffic into a computer through Windows Firewall, this is called creating an **exception**. You can create exceptions by specifying the file name of an application or by configuring specified ports for which to allow traffic. Windows Firewall lets you create separate exceptions for each network connection. This differs from Internet Connection Firewall, which only allowed you to create global exceptions that affected all connections.

■ Can restrict traffic by IP address (or IP address range), meaning that only traffic from computers with valid IP addresses is allowed through the firewall.

■ Allows you to enable or disable Windows Firewall on each connection configured on a computer running Windows XP, whether that connection is a LAN connection, dial-up connection, or wireless connection. You can also set global configurations that affect all connections. This differs from Internet Connection Firewall, which only allowed you to enable or disable the firewall globally for all connections.

■ Allows you to keep a security log of blocked traffic so that you can view firewall activity.

■ Performs stateful packet filtering during startup, so that the computer can perform basic network tasks (such as contacting DHCP and DNS servers) and still be protected. This differs from Internet Connection Firewall, which did not perform any filtering during startup.

How to Enable or Disable Windows Firewall for All Network Connections

The only users who can make changes to Windows Firewall settings are those who log on to the computer with a user account that is a member of the local Administrators group. To enable or disable Windows Firewall for all network connections, use these steps:

1. Click Start, and then click Control Panel (in Category View).

2. In Control Panel, click Network And Internet Connections.

3. In the Network And Internet Connections window, click Windows Firewall.

4. On the General tab of the Windows Firewall dialog box, shown in Figure 10-12, click On (Recommended) to enable the firewall for all connections. Click Off (Not Recommended) to disable the firewall for all connections.

5. Click OK.

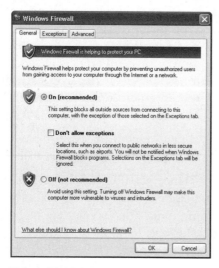

Figure 10-12   Enable or disable Windows Firewall for all network connections.

How to Enable or Disable Windows Firewall for a Specific Network Connection

In addition to being able to enable or disable Windows Firewall for all connections, you can control whether Windows Firewall is enabled on each connection on a computer. To enable or disable Windows Firewall for a specific network connection, use these steps:

1. Click Start, and then click Control Panel (in Category View).

2. In Control Panel, click Network And Internet Connections.

3. In the Network And Internet Connections window, click Windows Firewall.

4. In the Windows Firewall dialog box, click the Advanced tab, shown in Figure 10-13.

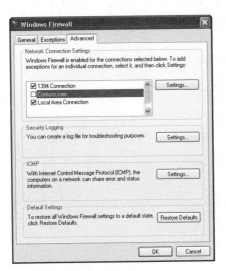

Figure 10-13   Enable or disable Windows Firewall for specific network connections.

5. To enable Windows Firewall for a connection, select the check box for that connection. To disable Windows Firewall for a connection, clear the check box for that connection.

6. Click OK to close the Windows Firewall dialog box.

Windows Firewall Advanced Options

After enabling Windows Firewall, you might need to configure it for a specific situation. You have several options for configuring Windows Firewall options, including the following:

■ Enabling Windows Firewall logging to log network activity

■ Creating an exception for a service or application to allow traffic through the firewall

■ Creating a custom service definition when a built-in exception does not suit your needs

■ Creating an Internet Control Message Protocol (ICMP) exception so that the computer responds to traffic from certain network utilities, such as Ping.exe

How to Enable Windows Firewall Logging

You can configure Windows Firewall to log network activity, including any dropped packets or successful connections to the computer. Security logging is not enabled by default for Windows Firewall. To enable security logging for Windows Firewall, use these steps:

1. Click Start, and then click Control Panel (in Category View).

2. In Control Panel, click Network And Internet Connections.

3. In the Network And Internet Connections window, click Windows Firewall.

4. In the Windows Firewall dialog box, on the Advanced tab, in the Security Logging section, click Settings.

   Windows displays the Log Settings dialog box, shown in Figure 10-14.

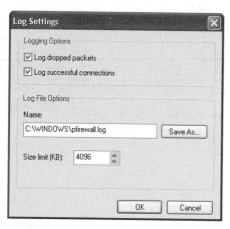

Figure 10-14 Enable security logging for Windows Firewall.

5. In the Logging Options section, select one or both of the following check boxes:

   ❑ Log Dropped Packets. Logs all dropped packets originating from the local network or the Internet.

   ❑ Log Successful Connections. Logs all successful connections originating from the network or the Internet.

6. Note the location of the security log. By default, the log file is named pfirewall.log and is located in the %SystemRoot% folder. Click OK to close the Log Settings dialog box. Click OK again to close the Windows Firewall dialog box.

How to Access the Windows Firewall Log File

After you enable logging, you can access the log file by browsing to its location and opening the file. Log entries provide insight about which packets have been successful in getting into the network and which have been rejected. There are two sections of the log: the header and the body. The header includes information about the version of Windows Firewall, the full name of the Windows Firewall, where the time stamp on the log learned of the time, and the field names used by the body of the log entry to display data. The body details the log data.

There are 16 data entries per logged item, which include information about the date and time the log was written and information about the data that passed. This information tells which types of packets were opened, closed, dropped, and lost; which **protocol** was used in the data transmission; the destination IP address of the data; the port used by the sending computer; the port of the destination computer; and the size of the packet logged.

To locate and open the Windows Firewall log file, use these steps:

1. Click Start, and then click Control Panel (in Category View).

2. In Control Panel, click Network And Internet Connections.

3. In the Network And Internet Connections window, click Windows Firewall.

4. In the Windows Firewall dialog box, on the Advanced tab, in the Security Logging section, click Settings.

5. In the Log Settings dialog box, in the Log File Options section, click Save As.

6. In the Save As dialog box, right-click the pfirewall.txt file, and then click Open.

7. After reviewing the firewall log, close the Notepad window, click OK to exit the Log Settings dialog box, and then click OK again to close the Windows Firewall dialog box.

Exam Tip   You should know where Windows Firewall log files are stored, whether logging is available, and what kind of information you can learn from log files.

▶ **How to Create an Exception for a Service or Application**

By default, Windows Firewall blocks all unsolicited traffic. You can create exceptions so that particular types of unsolicited traffic are allowed through the firewall. For example, if you want to allow sharing of files and printers on a local computer, you must enable the File And Printer Sharing exception in Windows Firewall so that requests for the shared resources are allowed to reach the computer.

Windows Firewall includes a number of common exceptions, such as Remote Assistance, Remote Desktop, File And Printer Sharing, and Windows Messenger. Windows Firewall also automatically extends the exceptions available, according to the programs installed on a computer. You can manually add exceptions to the list by browsing for program files.

To create a global exception that applies to all network connections for which Windows Firewall is enabled, use these steps:

1. Click Start, and then click Control Panel (in Category View).

2. In Control Panel, click Network And Internet Connections.

3. In the Network And Internet Connections window, click Windows Firewall.

4. In the Windows Firewall dialog box, click the Exceptions tab, shown in Figure 10-15.

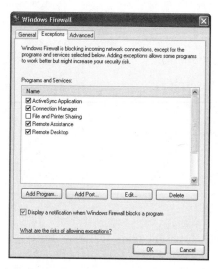

Figure 10-15 Create a global exception for all connections in Windows Firewall.

5. In the Programs And Services list, select the check box for the program or service you want to allow. If you need to add an exception for an installed program that does not appear on the list, click Add Program to locate the executable file for the program, and then enable the exception after the program is added to the list.

6. Click OK to close the Windows Firewall dialog box.

▶ **How to Create an Exception for a Particular Port**

If Windows Firewall does not include an exception for the traffic you need to allow, and adding an executable file to the list does not produce the results you need, you can also create an exception by unblocking traffic for a particular port.

To create a global exception for a port that applies to all network connections for which Windows Firewall is enabled, use these steps.

1. Click Start, and then click Control Panel (in Category View).

2. In Control Panel, click Network And Internet Connections.

3. In the Network And Internet Connections window, click Windows Firewall.

4. In the Windows Firewall dialog box, on the Exceptions tab, click Add Port.

   Windows displays the Add A Port dialog box. To create an exception based on a Transmission Control Protocol (TCP) or User Datagram Protocol (UDP) port number, you must know the proper port number used by an application or service to use this option.

5. Type a name for the exception, type the port number you want to allow access for, and then select whether the port is a TCP or UDP port.

   You can also change the scope to which the exception applies. Your options are to have the exception apply to any computer (including computers on the Internet), the local network only, or a custom list of IP addresses.

6. To change the scope of the exception, click Change Scope to open the Change Scope dialog box, where you can configure the scope options. Click OK to return to the Add A Port dialog box.

7. Click OK again to add the exception and return to the Windows Firewall dialog box.

   After you have added the exception, it appears in the Programs And Services list on the Exceptions tab of the Windows Firewall dialog box.

8. Select the check box for the exception to enable it.

9. Click OK to close the Windows Firewall dialog box.

To create a service exception for a particular network connection for which Windows Firewall is enabled, use these steps.

1. Click Start, and then click Control Panel (in Category View).

2. In the Control Panel window, click Network And Internet Connections.

3. In the Network And Internet Connections window, click Windows Firewall.

4. In the Windows Firewall dialog box, on the Advanced tab, in the Network Connection Settings section, click the connection for which you want to configure an exception, and then click Settings.

   Windows displays the Advanced Settings dialog box, shown in Figure 10-16.

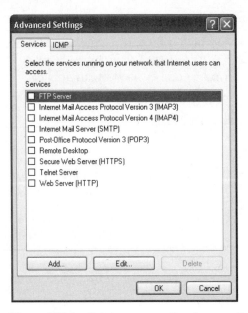

Figure 10-16 Create an exception for a particular network connection in Windows Firewall.

5. On the Services tab, click Add.

   Windows displays the Service Settings dialog box.

6. Type a description of the service.

7. If the computer on which you are configuring Windows Firewall is an Internet Connection Sharing (ICS) host, you can configure Windows Firewall to forward traffic for the port to a particular computer on the network by typing that computer's IP address. If the computer is not an ICS host, you should enter the IP address for the local computer.

> **Tip** Instead of entering the IP address for the local computer, you can also use the loopback address 127.0.0.1, which always refers to the local computer. This is useful should the IP address of the local computer change.

8. Enter the port information for the service.

9. Click OK to close the Service Settings dialog box. Click OK to close the Advanced Settings dialog box. Click OK again to close the Windows Firewall dialog box.

ICMP Exceptions

ICMP allows routers and host computers to swap basic error and configuration information. The information includes whether or not the data sent reaches its final destination, whether it can or cannot be forwarded by a specific router, and what the best route for the data is. ICMP tools such as Pathping, Ping, and Tracert are often used to troubleshoot network connectivity.

ICMP troubleshooting tools and their resulting messages are helpful when used by a network administrator, but harmful when used by an attacker. For instance, a network administrator sends a ping request in the form of an ICMP packet that contains an echo request message to the IP address that is being tested. The reply to that echo request message allows the administrator to verify that the computer is reachable. An attacker, on the other hand, can send a **storm** of specially formed pings that can overload a computer so that it cannot respond to legitimate traffic. Attackers can also use ping commands to determine the IP addresses of computers on a network. By configuring ICMP, you can control how a system responds (or does not respond) to such ping requests. By default, Windows Firewall blocks all ICMP messages.

Table 10-7 provides details about ICMP exceptions you can enable in Windows Firewall.

Table 10-7   ICMP Options

ICMP Option	Description
Allow Incoming Echo Request	Controls whether a remote computer can ask for and receive a response from the computer. Ping is a command that requires you to enable this option. When enabled (as with other options), attackers can see and contact the host computer.
Allow Incoming Timestamp Request	Sends a reply to another computer, stating that an incoming message was received and includes time and date data.
Allow Incoming Mask Request	Provides the sender with the subnet mask for the network of which the computer is a member. The sender already has the IP address; giving the subnet mask is all an administrator (or attacker) needs to obtain the remaining network information about the computer's network.
Allow Incoming Router Request	Provides information about the routes the computer recognizes and passes on information it has about any routers to which it is connected.
Allow Outgoing Destination Unreachable	The computer sends a Destination Unreachable error message to clients that attempt to send packets through the computer to a remote network for which there is no route.
Allow Outgoing Source Quench	Offers information to routers about the rate at which data is received; tells routers to slow down if too much data is being sent and it cannot be received fast enough to keep up.
Allow Outgoing Parameter Problem	The computer sends a Bad Header error message when the computer discards data it has received that has a problematic header. This message allows the sender to understand that the host exists, but that there were unknown problems with the message itself.

Table 10-7 ICMP Options

ICMP Option	Description
Allow Outgoing Time Exceeded	The computer sends the sender a Time Expired message when the computer must discard messages because the messages timed out.
Allow Redirect	Data that is sent from this computer will be rerouted if the path changes.
Allow Outgoing Packet Too Big	When data blocks are too big for the computer to forward, the computer replies to the sender with a Packet Too Big message. Note that this option only applies to networks using the IPv6 protocol.

Security Alert   Generally, you should enable ICMP exceptions only when you need them for troubleshooting and then disable them after you have completed troubleshooting. Make sure that you do not allow or enable these options without a full understanding of them and of the consequences and risks involved.

▶ **How to Enable ICMP Exceptions**

To enable a global ICMP exception for all connections on a computer, use these steps:

1. Click Start, and then click Control Panel (in Category View).

2. In Control Panel, click Network And Internet Connections.

3. In the Network And Internet Connections window, click Windows Firewall.

4. In the Windows Firewall dialog box, click the Advanced tab.

5. In the ICMP section, click Settings.

6. Select the check box for the exception you want to enable.

7. Click OK to close the ICMP Settings dialog box. Click OK again to close the Windows Firewall dialog box.

To enable an ICMP exception for a network connection, use these steps:

1. Click Start, and then click Control Panel (in Category View).

2. In Control Panel, click Network And Internet Connections.

3. In the Network And Internet Connections window, click Windows Firewall.

4. In the Windows Firewall dialog box, click the Advanced tab.

5. In the Network Connection Settings section, click the connection for which you want to configure an exception, and then click Settings.

6. In the Advanced Settings dialog box, click the ICMP tab, shown in Figure 10-17.

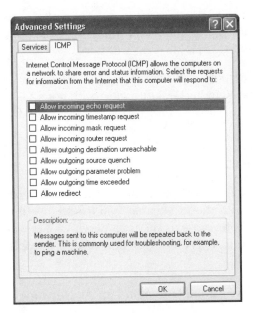

Figure 10-17   Create an ICMP exception for a connection.

7. Select the check box for the exception you want to enable.

8. Click OK to close the Advanced Settings dialog box. Click OK again to close the Windows Firewall dialog box.

Troubleshooting Windows Firewall

There are a few fairly common problems that end users encounter when using Windows Firewall, including the inability to enable or disable Windows Firewall on a connection, problems with file and printer sharing, a network user's inability to access a server on the network (such as a Web server), problems with Remote Assistance, and problems running Internet programs.

When troubleshooting Windows Firewall, make sure that you remember to check the obvious first. The following are some basic rules that you must follow, and any deviation from them can cause many of the common problems that are encountered when using Windows Firewall:

■ Windows Firewall can be enabled or disabled only by administrators. It can be enabled or disabled by a Local Security Policy or Group Policy, as well—sometimes preventing access even by a local administrator.

■ To share printers and files on a local computer that is running Windows Firewall, you must enable the File And Printer Sharing exception.

- If the local computer is running a service, such as a Web server, FTP server, or other service, network users cannot connect to these services unless you create the proper exceptions in Windows Firewall.

- Windows Firewall blocks Remote Assistance and Remote Desktop traffic by default. You must enable the Remote Desktop and/or Remote Assistance exceptions for remote users to be able to connect to a local computer with Remote Desktop or Remote Assistance.

Practice: Configure Windows Firewall

In this practice, you will ensure that Windows Firewall is enabled on all connections on your computer. You will disable and then re-enable Windows Firewall on your LAN connection only. You will then enable an exception in Windows Firewall for all connections. The practices in this exercise require that you have a properly configured LAN connection.

Exercise 1: Ensure That Windows Firewall Is Enabled for All Network Connections

1. Click Start, and then click Control Panel (in Category View).

2. In Control Panel, click Network And Internet Connections.

3. In the Network Connections window, right-click your LAN connection, and then click Properties.

4. In the Local Area Connection Properties dialog box, on the Advanced tab, in the Windows Firewall section, click Settings.

5. In the Windows Firewall dialog box, ensure that On (Recommended) is selected. Also ensure that the Don't Allow Exceptions check box is cleared.

   Leave both the Windows Firewall dialog box and the Local Area Connection Properties dialog box open for the next exercise.

Exercise 2: Disable and Re-enable Windows Firewall on Your Local Area Connection Only

1. In the Windows Firewall dialog box, click the Advanced tab.

2. In the Network Connection Settings section, in the list of connections, clear the check box next to Local Area Connection, and then click OK.

   Windows Firewall is now disabled for the local area connection. A bubble appears in the notification area informing you that your computer is at risk because the firewall is disabled.

3. In the Windows Firewall dialog box, on the Advanced tab, select the check box next to Local Area Connection, and then click OK.

Windows Firewall is now enabled for the local area connection. Leave the Local Area Connection Properties dialog box open for the next exercise.

Exercise 3: Enable an Exception in Windows Firewall for All Connections

1. In the Local Area Connection Properties dialog box, on the Advanced tab, in the Windows Firewall section, click Settings.

2. In the Windows Firewall dialog box, on the Exceptions tab, select the File And Printer Sharing check box.

3. Click OK.

   Windows Firewall is now configured to allow file and printer sharing traffic into your computer.

4. Click OK again to close the Local Area Connection Properties dialog box.

Lesson Review

Use the following questions to help determine whether you have learned enough to move on to the next lesson. If you have difficulty answering these questions, review the material in this lesson before beginning the next lesson. You can find answers to these questions in the "Questions and Answers" section at the end of this chapter.

1. You are troubleshooting a network connection and need to use the Ping command to see if a computer is reachable. Which ICMP exception must you enable on that computer? Choose the correct answer.

   A. Allow Incoming Router Request

   B. Allow Incoming Echo Request

   C. Allow Outgoing Source Quench

   D. Allow Redirect

2. By default, what two types of traffic does Windows Firewall allow into a computer?

   _____

   _____

3. Windows Firewall protects a computer running Windows XP even while the computer is starting up. (True/False)

   _____

   _____

Lesson Summary

- Windows Firewall is a software-based firewall that is included with Windows XP Service Pack 2. Windows Firewall blocks all incoming network traffic except for solicited traffic and excepted traffic.

- You can enable or disable Windows Firewall globally for all network connections on a computer, including LAN, dial-up, and wireless connections.

- You can also enable or disable Windows Firewall selectively for each network connection on a computer.

- Windows Firewall allows you to configure a number of advanced options, including the following:

  ❑ Enabling Windows Firewall logging to log network activity

  ❑ Creating an exception for a service or application to allow traffic through the firewall

  ❑ Creating a custom service definition when a built-in exception does not suit your needs

  ❑ Creating an ICMP exception so that the computer responds to traffic from certain network utilities

- Troubleshooting Windows Firewall typically involves enabling or disabling Windows Firewall and creating exceptions so that specific network traffic is allowed into the computer.

Lesson 4: Using Remote Access Tools

As a DST, you must be able to configure, manage, and troubleshoot Remote Desktop and Remote Assistance. Remote Assistance and Remote Desktop are both Windows XP Professional features that allow remote access to a computer. However, the purpose of each feature, the method of connection establishment, and the tasks that you can perform remotely are different.

After this lesson, you will be able to

- Configure Remote Assistance.
- Configure Remote Desktop.

Estimated lesson time: 25 minutes

Remote Assistance

The **Remote Assistance** feature allows a user to electronically request help from another user. For example, a customer might invite you to provide remote assistance on his computer. Both users must agree to the connection, and after the connection is established, you can take shared control of the user's desktop, chat with the user, and send and receive files. Taking shared control of the desktop requires the user's permission. Remote Assistance can minimize or eliminate the need to physically visit a remote computer to solve a problem.

Establishing a Remote Assistance Session

A Remote Assistance session requires that both the user and the DST actively participate in establishing the connection. The session is established in the following phases:

1. The user that requires support sends a Remote Assistance invitation to the DST.

2. The DST responds to the invitation.

3. The user accepts the DST's assistance.

To send a Remote Assistance invitation, follow these steps:

1. From the Start menu, select Help And Support.

2. In the Help And Support Center, under Ask For Assistance, select Invite A Friend To Connect To Your Computer With Remote Assistance, and then select Invite Someone To Help You.

3. Select the method that you want to use to create the invitation, as shown in Figure 10-18. You can send invitations directly by using Windows Messenger, by using an

e-mail attachment, or by saving an invitation file and transmitting it to the helper user (for example, you could save the file to a shared folder on the network).

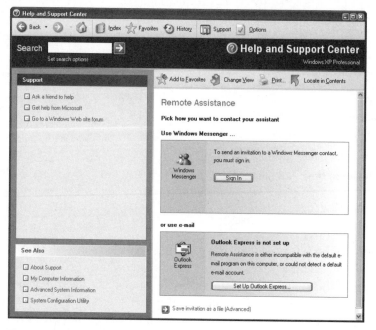

Figure 10-18 Choose the method to create an invitation.

4. When prompted, enter the requested information, including your name, a message, when the invitation should expire, and (optionally) a password to be used to establish the connection.

5. Click Send Invitation.

> **Note** When an invitation is sent through an e-mail attachment or saved as a file, the file has a .MsRcIndicent extension.

When you receive a Remote Assistance invitation, you must respond to continue the process. If the invitation is by using Windows Messenger, you must accept the invitation that is presented in the Messenger pop-up window. If the invitation is sent by e-mail, you must open the attached invitation. If the invitation file is transmitted in some other fashion, you must access and open it. If a password is required, you must enter the password in the Remote Assistance dialog box.

Windows then notifies the user requiring assistance that the request has been accepted. The user must click Yes in the Remote Assistance dialog box as a final indication of acceptance, and Remote Assistance then establishes the connection.

Remote Assistance Console

After the Remote Assistance connection is established, the user requiring assistance sees a User Console and the helper sees a Helper Console.

The User Console is shown in Figure 10-19. You can use the Chat History and Message Entry windows for online chatting. The Connection Status window displays the helper who has connected and the connection's capabilities (Screen View Only or In Control). The functionality of the remaining buttons is as follows:

- **Stop Control (ESC)**   Permits the user to regain control if the helper user has taken control. (This can also be accomplished by pressing ESC.)

- **Send A File**   Sends a file from the user's computer or a network share to the helper's computer.

- **Start Talking**   Enables voice communication on computers with voice capabilities.

- **Settings**   Enables the user to adjust sound quality.

- **Disconnect**   Ends the Remote Assistance connection.

- **Help**   Provides access to Remote Assistance help features.

Figure 10-19   The user requesting assistance sees the Remote Assistance User Console.

Figure 10-20 displays the Helper Console. The Chat History and Message Entry windows are again available for online chatting. The user's desktop is displayed in the

Status window on the right side of the display. The controls for the Helper Console are found across the top of the screen and include the following:

- **Take Control/Release Control**   Sends a request to the user to take shared control of the user's desktop. The user must accept the request and can cancel it at any time by clicking Disconnect on the User Console or by pressing Esc.

- **Send A File**   Sends a file from the helper's computer or a network share to the user's computer.

- **Start Talking**   Enables voice communication on computers with voice capabilities.

- **Settings**   Enables the user to adjust sound quality and console size.

- **Disconnect**   Ends the Remote Assistance connection.

- **Help**   Provides access to Remote Assistance help features.

Figure 10-20   The helper sees the Remote Assistance Helper Console.

Taking Shared Control of the User's Computer

To take shared control, the helper sends a request to the user by clicking Take Control. The user must accept the request and can cancel it at any time by clicking Disconnect on the User Console or by pressing Esc.

When the helper establishes shared control of the user's system, the helper can fully manipulate the computer, including loading and unloading drivers, starting applications, and viewing event logs. However, the helper cannot copy files from the user's hard disk. The only way for the helper to get a file from the user's computer is for the user to send it.

When shared control is established, both users can manipulate the mouse and keyboard simultaneously, so consider using the chat or voice communication functions to coordinate input device usage and minimize overlap. Also, the helper must be careful not to do anything that might affect the network connection, or else the Remote Assistance connection might be disconnected.

Remote Desktop

Remote Desktop is designed to allow users to remotely gain access to their Windows XP Professional desktop, applications, data, and network resources from another computer on the network. Users who have been granted permission can remotely connect. After a connection is established, the local desktop is locked for security reasons, preventing anyone from viewing the tasks that are being performed remotely.

Remote Desktop is designed to allow a user to have full control over his or her Windows XP Professional desktop from another computer on the network. This is useful when a user is working from home, another office, or another site and requires access to information from his or her primary office computer. While a user is remotely accessing his or her computer, local access by another user is not permitted. An exception to this is an administrator. Administrators are permitted to log on locally while another user is connected remotely, but the remote session is then terminated.

Remote Desktop requires the following:

- A remote computer that is running Windows XP Professional and that is connected to a LAN or the Internet. This is the computer to which you want to gain access remotely.

- A client computer with access to the host computer through a LAN, dial-up, or VPN connection that has the Remote Desktop Connection program or the Terminal Services Client installed. A version of the Remote Desktop Connection program is available for most versions of Windows.

- A user account with appropriate permissions. The user must be an administrator or a member of the Remote Users group.

Configuring Remote Desktop

Remote Desktop configuration is a two-part process. First, configure the remote computer to allow Remote Desktop connections. Then, configure the client computer with the Remote Desktop Connection client software.

To configure a computer running Windows XP Professional to allow Remote Desktop connections, follow these steps:

1. From the Start menu (or from the desktop or in Windows Explorer) right-click My Computer and select Properties.

2. On the Remote tab, in the Remote Desktop section, select Allow Users To Connect Remotely To This Computer, as shown in Figure 10-21, and click OK in the Remote Sessions dialog box.

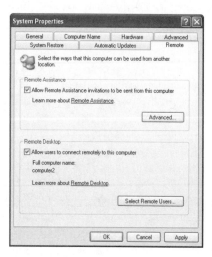

Figure 10-21   Enable Remote Desktop on a computer running Windows XP Professional.

3. If the user account to be used to connect remotely is not a member of the Administrators group, press Select Remote Users, add the appropriate user account, and then click OK.

4. Click OK.

Verify that the user account to be used to connect remotely has a password assigned. User accounts used for remote connections must have passwords.

> **Note**   If you are using Windows Firewall or another personal firewall, you must enable inbound connections on TCP port 3389 to support Remote Desktop connections. You can also change the port on which Remote Desktop accepts connections. More information about changing this port number can be found in the Knowledge Base article, "How to change the listening port for Remote Desktop" (*http://support.microsoft.com/default.aspx/kb/306759*).

After a computer running Windows XP Professional is configured to allow Remote Desktop connections, you can connect to that computer by using the Remote Desktop Connection client software on another computer. From the Start menu, select All Programs, then Accessories, then Communications, and then Remote Desktop Connection. In the Remote Desktop Connection dialog box, click the Options button to display configurable options, as shown in Figure 10-22. The only information that you must enter to establish a connection is the name or IP address of the computer. Other configurable options include the following:

- General options, including the user name, password, and domain name used for authentication and the ability to save connection settings

- Display options, including the configuration of the size of the remote connection display (all the way up to full screen) and color settings

- Local Resources options, including sound and keyboard configuration, and which local devices to connect to when logged on the remote computer

- Programs options, which provide the ability to automatically launch a program when a connection is established

- Experience options, which allow the configuration of the connection speed to optimize performance and provide the ability to control the display of the desktop background, themes, menu and windows animation, and other items that can affect performance

Figure 10-22   Configure options for connecting to a remote computer.

Managing Remote Desktop Sessions

When you establish a Remote Desktop session from a Windows XP Professional computer, use the Remote Desktop Connections client as follows:

1. From the Start menu, select All Programs, then Accessories, then Communications, and then Remote Desktop Connection.

2. In the Remote Desktop Connection dialog box, depicted in Figure 10-23, enter the name or IP address of the remote computer and click Connect.

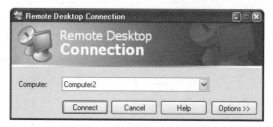

Figure 10-23   Establish a Remote Desktop session.

3. Enter the appropriate user account and password and then click OK.

4. If another user is currently logged on to the remote system, a Logon Message dialog box appears, indicating that in order to continue, that user must be logged off and any unsaved data will be lost. If this occurs, click Yes to continue.

5. The Remote Desktop session is established. Figure 10-24 displays a remote connection window.

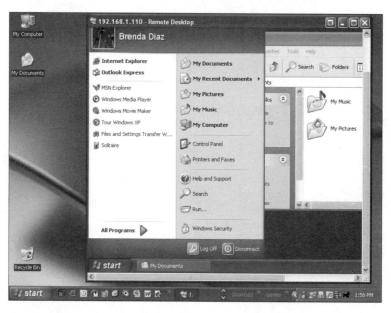

Figure 10-24   After connecting, you have complete control of the remote computer.

After connecting to a remote desktop, you have complete control of the remote computer. When you press the CTRL+ALT+DELETE keys simultaneously during a Remote Desktop session, either Task Manager or the Windows Security dialog box for the local computer appears. To access Task Manager or the Windows Security dialog box on the remote computer, select Windows Security from the Start menu.

There are two ways to end a remote session:

- Log off the remote computer normally, which closes all programs, logs the user off, and then closes the Remote Desktop connection.

- Disconnect by either closing the Remote Desktop dialog box or selecting Disconnect from the Start menu. Disconnecting leaves the user logged on at the remote computer, and all programs continue processing. The user will be reconnected to the same session the next time the user connects.

Lesson Review

The following questions are intended to reinforce key information presented in this lesson. If you are unable to answer a question, review the lesson materials and try the question again. You can find answers to the questions in the "Questions and Answers" section at the end of this chapter.

1. A user calls you to ask for help configuring a hardware driver, but is having trouble following the instructions that you give him over the telephone. You decide that it is easier to show the user how to perform the configuration by taking control of his desktop. What tool is best suited to this task?

   _____

   _____

2. What are the requirements for running Remote Desktop?

   _____

   _____

Lesson Summary

- Remote Assistance enables users to request support from a more advanced user or from computer support personnel. With Remote Assistance, the user providing support can connect to the troubled user's desktop, view what is happening remotely, and take control of the system to resolve a problem if necessary.

- Remote Desktop enables users to remotely access their computers across the network and use the desktop as if they were sitting in front of the computer.

Case Scenario Exercises

Scenario 10.1

A user calls to tell you that he has tried to configure Remote Desktop so that he can use his home computer running Windows Home Edition to connect over the Internet to his office computer running Windows XP Professional. The user enabled Remote Desktop on the office computer, which is one of twelve computers on a small network. He then successfully established a Remote Desktop connection from one of the other computers on the office network. However, when the user tries to connect from his home computer, he receives an error message stating that he cannot connect to the computer, and that the problem is most likely a networking error. What should you suspect?

_____

_____

Scenario 10.2

A user on a small office workgroup has returned from a weeklong vacation. She starts her computer, and everything seems to be functional. As the day progresses, she accesses data from a workgroup file server and prints to a network printer. Later, she tries to access another workgroup resource: a printer that is attached to a user's computer in the office upstairs, but she receives an error saying that the printer cannot be found. She reports that the network cable is connected and that she can access other resources on the network. What is the first thing you should do?

A. Check the status of the network router.

B. Check the status of the computer upstairs.

C. Ping the computer's loopback address.

D. Use the Tracert command at a command prompt to view the route and possible packet losses.

Troubleshooting Lab

You are working as a DST for a technical support company. A user calls to tell you that she cannot access websites from her home computer. While investigating the problem, you determine the following information:

■ The user cannot access any sites on the Internet.

■ The user could access sites previously by using the same computer.

- The user has made no changes recently to Internet Explorer or to any of her network connections.

- The user's computer is connected directly to a cable modem.

Using the information you learned in this chapter, how would you troubleshoot this problem?

_____

_____

Chapter Summary

- Each interface on a TCP/IP network is assigned a unique IP address, which is typically shown as four decimal numbers ranging from 0 to 255. An IP address is divided into a network ID, which determines the subnet on which a host exists, and a host ID, which uniquely identifies the host on that subnet. The separation of network ID and host ID is determined by a subnet mask.

- A default gateway is the IP address to which a client sends data that is destined for a host that is not on the same network as a client. The default gateway is typically a router.

- Name resolution is the process of mapping IP addresses to computer or host names. DNS is the primary name-resolution mechanism used on modern Windows networks and on the Internet. WINS is a name-resolution mechanism used on older Windows-based networks.

- To resolve network-connectivity problems, you should test network cabling connections, the network adapter in a computer, and the network configuration on a computer, and verify that any required servers are online.

- You can configure local area and dial-up network connections by using the Network Connections window in Windows XP. Use a particular connection's Properties dialog box to configure the connection settings.

- Windows XP computers can obtain an IP address automatically by searching the network for a DHCP server. If found, the DHCP server provides TCP/IP configuration information to the client. If the computer cannot contact a DHCP server, Windows XP assigns the computer an IP address in the 169.254.0.0 range automatically by using APIPA. You can also configure the TCP/IP information for a computer manually.

- Use the Ping, Tracert, and Pathping commands to test TCP/IP connectivity.

- Use the Ipconfig /all command to show detailed information about the TCP/IP configuration of a computer—including the IP address, subnet mask, default gateway, DNS servers, and DHCP information about every network connection on a system.

- Windows Firewall is a software-based firewall that is included in Windows XP Service Pack 2. You can enable or disable Windows Firewall for any network connection, and configure what types of traffic it allows to enter or leave the computer.

- Internet Control Message Protocol allows routers and host computers to swap basic control information when data is sent from one computer to another. ICMP tools such as Ping and Tracert are often used to troubleshoot network connectivity.

- Most of the problems you will encounter with Windows Firewall will involve users not being able to enable Windows Firewall for a particular connection, and users having connectivity problems because Windows Firewall is turned on and blocking necessary traffic.

- Remote Assistance enables users to request support from a more advanced user or from computer support personnel. With Remote Assistance, the user providing support can connect to the troubled user's desktop, view what is happening remotely, and take control of the system to resolve a problem if necessary.

- Remote Desktop enables users to remotely access their computers across the network and use the desktop as if they were sitting in front of the computer.

Exam Highlights

Before taking the exam, review the key topics and terms that are presented in this chapter. You need to know this information.

Key Points

- If you are troubleshooting a network problem and discover that a client computer has an IP address on the 169.254.0.0 network, the computer has assigned itself that address using APIPA because the computer was unable to locate a DHCP server.

- For the exam, make sure that you understand how to enable automatic configuration of DNS servers and where you will go to specify particular DNS servers.

- You should know where Windows Firewall log files are stored, whether logging is available, and what kind of information you can learn from log files.

Key Terms

Automatic Private IP Addressing (APIPA)   A method of automatically assigning an IP address to a computer when either no address is assigned or no DHCP server is available.

default gateway   The router to which the TCP/IP client will forward packets destined for computers on other networks.

Domain Name System (DNS)   A network service designed to perform name resolution for TCP/IP clients.

Dynamic Host Configuration Protocol (DHCP)   A service that automatically handles requests for TCP/IP configuration information to client systems.

IP address   A number that uniquely identifies a device on a TCP/IP network.

Ipconfig   A command-line utility that can be used to view TCP/IP configuration information.

loopback address   An address that is used for testing TCP/IP configuration and that cannot be assigned to individual devices on a TCP/IP network. Normally it is 127.0.0.1.

NetBIOS name   A 16-character name assigned to a computer that is used by NetBIOS applications when establishing connections.

Pathping.exe   A command-line utility that is used to trace routes across a series of networks, combining the features of Ping and Tracert.

Ping   A command-line utility for testing basic TCP/IP communications.

Remote Assistance   A service that enables users to request support from a more advanced user or from computer support personnel.

Remote Desktop   A process that enables users to remotely access their computers across the network and use the desktop as if they were sitting in front of the computer.

subnet mask   A method of separating the network portion of an IP address from the host portion of an IP address.

Tracert.exe   A utility used to follow the communication path from router to router between the source and destination hosts.

Windows Internet Naming Service (WINS)   A service that runs on one or more Windows NT, Windows 2000, or .NET servers in the network.

Questions and Answers

Lesson 1 Review

Page
10-15

1. List the required and optional parameters that you can assign to a host on a TCP/IP network.

You must assign each device a unique IP address, a subnet mask, and a default gateway. Optionally, you can also assign hosts the addresses of DNS and WINS servers.

2. List the three primary address classes used for assigning IP addresses to hosts on the Internet and the corresponding range of IP addresses available in each class.

IP addresses are divided into five classes: A, B, C, D, and E. Hosts on the Internet are assigned IP addresses from the first three classes only: A, B, and C. The network IDs for Class A addresses range from 1.0.0.0 to 126.0.0.0. The network IDs for Class B addresses range from 128.0.0.0 to 191.0.0.0. The network IDs for Class C addresses range from 192.0.0.0 to 223.0.0.0.

3. Which of the following default subnet masks would be used on a computer connected to the Internet with the IP address 157.54.4.201?

A. 255.0.0.0

B. 255.255.0.0

C. 255.255.255.0

D. 255.255.255.255

B is the correct answer. The IP address 157.54.4.201 is in the Class B range of addresses. The default subnet mask for Class B addresses is 255.255.0.0. A is not correct because 255.0.0.0 is the default subnet mask for Class A addresses. C is not correct because 255.255.255.0 is the default subnet mask used for Class C addresses. D is not correct because 255.255.255.255 is an invalid subnet mask.

Lesson 2 Review

Page
10-36

1. You are troubleshooting a networking problem for a user. Although the user had no problem connecting to the network when she left the office yesterday afternoon, she cannot connect to the network this morning. You know that other users on the network are not having the same problems. What is the first thing you should check?

You should make sure that the network cable is seated properly in the jack on the back of the user's computer and in the jack on the wall. It is likely that something happened overnight, such as the office being cleaned, that caused the connection to loosen.

2. A user complains to you that he cannot connect to any network resources after he installed a new network adapter card. You open the Command Prompt window on the user's computer and type **ipconfig /all**. You get the following results:

   ❑ Ethernet adapter Local Area Connection:

   ❑ Connection-specific DNS Suffix

   ❑ Description : Intel(R) PRO/1000 CT

   ❑ Physical Address : 0B-01-C4-32-E1-2C

   ❑ DHCP Enabled : Yes

   ❑ IP Address : 169.254.023.102

   ❑ Subnet Mask : 255.255.0.0

   ❑ Default Gateway:

   ❑ DNS Servers:

   What do these results tell you? (Choose all that apply.)

   A. The computer is configured to connect to a DHCP server.

   B. The computer is not configured to connect to a DHCP server.

   C. The computer is successfully connecting to a DHCP server.

   D. The computer is not successfully connecting to a DHCP server.

   A and D are correct. The computer is configured to connect to a DHCP server. However, the computer is not getting an IP address from a DHCP server successfully. You know this because the IP address is in the range assigned by APIPA. B and C are not correct because the computer is configured to connect to a DHCP server, but is not doing so successfully.

3. You are troubleshooting a network connectivity problem on a users computer. At the command prompt, you type the Ipconfig /all command and receive the following results:

   ❑ IP Address......192.168.0.5

   ❑ Subnet Mask.......255.255.255.255

   ❑ Default Gateway......192.168.0.7

   Which of these values is most likely configured incorrectly?

   The subnet mask is configured incorrectly. The IP address displayed is a Class C address (as is the gateway). The default subnet mask for a Class C address should be 255.255.255.0. The subnet mask 255.255.255.255 is an invalid subnet mask.

Lesson 3 Review

Page
10-51

1. You are troubleshooting a network connection and need to use the Ping command to see if a computer is reachable. Which ICMP exception must you enable on that computer? Choose the correct answer.

   A. Allow Incoming Router Request

   B. Allow Incoming Echo Request

   C. Allow Outgoing Source Quench

   D. Allow Redirect

   Answer B is correct. The Allow Incoming Echo Request exception allows a computer to respond to ping requests. Answer A is incorrect because this option provides information about connected routers and the flow of traffic from the computer. Answer C is incorrect because this option allows the computer to send a message to slow the flow of data. Answer D is incorrect because this option allows routers to redirect data to more favorable routes.

2. By default, what two types of traffic does Windows Firewall allow into a computer?

   Solicited traffic, which is received in response to a request by the local computer, and excepted traffic, which is unsolicited traffic that you have specifically configured the firewall to allow.

3. Windows Firewall protects a computer running Windows XP even while the computer is starting up. (True or False?)

   True. Windows Firewall performs stateful packet filtering during startup so that the computer can perform basic network tasks and still be protected.

Lesson 4 Review

Page
10-61

1. A user calls you to ask for help configuring a hardware driver, but is having trouble following the instructions that you give him over the telephone. You decide that it is easier to show the user how to perform the configuration by taking control of his desktop. What tool is best suited to this task?

   Remote Assistance is best, so you should have the user send you a Remote Assistance invitation. When using Remote Assistance, you can take shared control of the desktop, which allows you to perform the configuration while the user watches.

2. What are the requirements for running Remote Desktop?

   The remote computer must be running Windows XP Professional. After enabling Remote Desktop on this computer, you must make sure that the user who will connect remotely is a member of either the Administrators or Remote Users group.

Case Scenario Exercises: Scenario 10.1

Page
10-62A user calls to tell you that he has tried to configure Remote Desktop so that he can use his home computer running Windows Home Edition to connect over the Internet to his office computer running Windows XP Professional. The user enabled Remote Desktop on the office computer, which is one of twelve computers on a small network. He then successfully established a Remote Desktop connection from one of the other computers on the office network. However, when the user tries to connect from his home computer, he receives an error message stating that he cannot connect to the computer, and that the problem is most likely a networking error. What should you suspect?

> Since the user can connect successfully from another computer on the office network, Remote Desktop is enabled and configured correctly. Since the user's office computer is on a small network connected to the Internet, it is likely that a firewall is configured to protect the network from malicious activity from the Internet. If a firewall is in place, it will by default block Remote Desktop traffic. The user needs to open port 3389 on the firewall in order to allow Remote Desktop traffic to pass through to the network.

Case Scenario Exercises: Scenario 10.2

Page
10-62A user on a small office workgroup has returned from a weeklong vacation. She starts her computer, and everything seems to be functional. As the day progresses, she accesses data from a workgroup file server and prints to a network printer. Later, she tries to access another workgroup resource: a printer that is attached to a user's computer in the office upstairs, but she receives an error saying that the printer cannot be found. She reports that the network cable is connected and that she can access other resources on the network. What is the first thing you should do?

A. Check the status of the network router.

B. Check the status of the computer upstairs.

C. Ping the computer's loopback address.

D. Use the Tracert command at a command prompt to view the route and possible packet losses.

> Answer B is correct. Because the user can access other network resources, the problem is probably with the resource itself. The other answers are probably not correct because the user is able to access other network resources.

Troubleshooting Lab

Page
10-62You are working as a DST for a technical support company. A user calls to tell you that she cannot access websites from her home computer. While investigating the problem, you determine the following information:

■ The user cannot access any sites on the Internet.

■ The user could access sites previously by using the same computer.

■ The user has made no changes recently to Internet Explorer or to any of her network connections.

■ The user's computer is connected directly to a cable modem.

Using the information you learned in this chapter, how would you troubleshoot this problem?

> Because this is a home connection on a cable modem, you can be fairly sure that the computer should be configured to obtain an IP address automatically from the ISP. Your first step, therefore, should be to open a command prompt and type **ipconfig /all**. Look for any problems with the IP addressing information. If you see an IP address in the 169.254 range, for example, you know that the computer is configured to obtain an IP address automatically but cannot reach the DHCP server. This probably points to a loose cable or a malfunctioning network adapter or cable modem. If you rule out these problems, there is probably a problem at the ISP.

11 Supporting Internet Explorer in Windows XP

Exam Objectives in this Chapter:

- Configure and troubleshoot Internet Explorer
    - ❏ Configure and troubleshoot Internet Explorer connections properties
    - ❏ Configure and troubleshoot Internet Explorer security properties
    - ❏ Configure and troubleshoot Internet Explorer general properties

Why This Chapter Matters

As a desktop support technician (DST), you will be asked to resolve a wide range of service calls regarding Microsoft Internet Explorer, including configuring Internet Explorer to connect to the Internet, setting security and privacy options, and performing troubleshooting tasks. These calls generally have to do with a user's inability to view Web pages or problems with the speed at which Web pages are loaded, but the requests can also be about performing maintenance tasks such as deleting temporary files or asking for advice on dealing with cookies.

Lessons in this Chapter:

Before You Begin

Before you begin this chapter, you should have a basic familiarity with working with Internet Explorer in Microsoft Windows XP with Service Pack 2. You should also have a computer running Windows XP Professional with Internet Explorer.

Lesson 1: Configuring Internet Explorer

Internet Explorer is the Web browser that is provided with Windows XP. Internet Explorer provides access to local and Internet resources using many protocols, such as Hypertext Transfer Protocol (HTTP) and File Transfer Protocol (FTP). As a DST, you will be called on to help users personalize and maintain Internet Explorer.

After this lesson, you will be able to

- Configure Internet Explorer general settings.
- Configure Internet Explorer security settings.
- Configure Internet Explorer privacy settings.

Estimated lesson time: 60 minutes

Configuring General Settings

You will perform the vast majority of the configuration in Internet Explorer by using the **Internet Options** dialog box. You can access this dialog box in the following ways:

- Right-click the Internet Explorer icon in the Start menu or on the desktop and then select Internet Properties.

- In Internet Explorer, from the Tools menu, select Internet Options.

- In Control Panel, select Network And Internet Connections, and then select Internet Options.

The General tab of the Internet Properties dialog box, shown in Figure 11-1, allows you to configure the following:

- The home page that Internet Explorer opens when you start the program

- How Internet Explorer stores temporary files during browsing sessions

- How long Internet Explorer tracks the history of Web pages you have visited

- The general appearance of Internet Explorer and Web pages

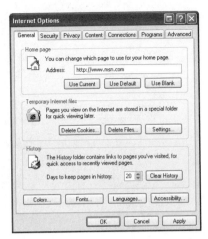

Figure 11-1   Configure basic settings on the General tab of the Internet Options dialog box.

Configuring the Home Page

A **home page** is the website that opens automatically when you start Internet Explorer. You can customize the home page in the following ways:

- **Type an address**   You can type any Uniform Resource Locator (URL) in the Address box to use that URL as the home page.

- **Use Current**   This option sets the home page to the page that Internet Explorer displays. This option is available only if Internet Explorer is open.

- **Use Default**   This option sets the home page to *http://www.msn.com*. Note, however, that on some computers, the computer manufacturer may have changed the default home page to another URL.

- **Use Blank**   This option configures Internet Explorer to not display a home page at all. This is useful if you connect to the Internet with a slow dial-up link and do not want to wait for the home page to download each time you connect.

Managing Temporary Internet Files

Internet Explorer automatically stores (or caches) copies of Web pages that you access to a folder on the local hard disk. These copies are called **temporary Internet files**. The next time you access the same page, Internet Explorer can load the page from the local cache rather than having to connect to the Web server and download it again. This increases performance and decreases Internet traffic.

However, problems occur when the Temporary Internet pages cache is full. Resolving these problems is as simple as deleting the files in the Temporary Internet Files folder. Unfortunately, recognizing problems caused by a full Temporary Internet

Files folder can be difficult. Here are some common warning signs of a full Temporary Internet Files folder:

- An end user reports that he cannot use the Save Picture As command to save a graphics file to his hard disk as a JPEG or GIF, but the file can be saved as a BMP file. The file name might also appear as Untitled.

- An end user reports problems viewing History files by date, or no data appears.

- An end user reports that when he selects Source on the View menu to view the source for a Web page, the source code does not appear as expected.

- An end user reports that when he visits the Windows Update Product Catalog website, he receives the message Cannot Display Page. (This occurs because the user has an earlier version of the site control in his or her browser cache, and the cache is full.)

- An end user reports that he gets unrecoverable errors (faults) when using Internet Explorer.

Although these problems can occur for other reasons, deleting the files in the Temporary Internet Files folder often solves the problem. You can delete temporary Internet files by clicking the Delete Files button on the General tab of the Internet Options dialog box. You can also use the Disk Cleanup utility (discussed in Chapter 8, "Supporting Storage Devices in Windows XP") to delete temporary Internet files.

You can also customize the way that Internet Explorer stores and uses temporary Internet files. On the General tab of the Internet Options dialog box, click the Settings button. This action opens the Settings dialog box shown in Figure 11-2. You have four ways to control when Internet Explorer checks for newer versions of the pages that are stored in its local cache. These four options are as follows:

- **Every Visit To The Page**   This option causes Internet Explorer to connect to the website and check to see whether the page has been updated each time you access the page. If a newer page is available than the one stored in the local cache, Internet Explorer downloads the new page from the website and places it in cache. If the page has not been updated, Internet Explorer loads the page from the local cache instead.

- **Every Time You Start Internet Explorer**   This option causes Internet Explorer to connect to the website and check to see whether the page has been updated only the first time you access the page in any given Internet Explorer session. Subsequent accesses to the page in the same session are always loaded from the cache.

- **Automatically**   This option is similar to the Every Time You Start Internet Explorer option, except that Internet Explorer monitors how often pages change.

If Internet Explorer determines that a page does not change very often, it checks for updates less frequently than once per session.

- **Never** This option causes Internet Explorer to never check for updated versions of the page unless you manually refresh the page.

Figure 11-2 Configure temporary Internet files settings.

The Settings dialog box also allows you to control the amount of disk space that temporary Internet files can consume on a hard disk and the folder that Internet Explorer uses to store the files. You should consider moving the temporary Internet files to another location only if the drive on which they are currently stored runs low on disk space. To view the contents of the folder, click View Files; to view downloaded program files, click View Objects.

Exam Tip Make sure that you understand how to delete temporary Internet files by using Disk Cleanup and from within Internet Explorer. Experiment with the various settings that govern temporary files to make sure that you understand their use.

Managing Internet Explorer History

Internet Explorer automatically stores a list of links to pages that you have recently visited in a folder named History. You can access the recent history by clicking the History button on the Internet Explorer toolbar.

The History section of the General tab of the Internet Options dialog box allows you to manage how long Internet Explorer stores recent links. Use the Days To Keep Pages In History option to specify the number of days the history is maintained. The default value is 20 days. Setting this value to 0 disables the History feature. Use the Clear History button to clear the current History list.

Controlling Internet Explorer's Appearance

The remaining options on the General tab of the Internet Options dialog box allow you to alter the appearance of Internet Explorer and the Web pages it displays. Available options are as follows:

- **Colors** Allows you to manipulate the colors Internet Explorer uses on Web pages for text, background, and hyperlinks.

- **Fonts** Allows you to specify the font Internet Explorer uses to display text on Web pages that do not specify a particular font.

- **Languages** Allows you to control which language is used to display content if a site offers more than one language.

- **Accessibility** Allows you to control additional settings about how Internet Explorer displays colors and fonts. In particular, you can have Internet Explorer ignore settings that are specified by Web pages and use settings you configured. This feature is useful for users who have configured accessibility options.

Configuring Content Settings

The Content tab of the Internet Options dialog box, shown in Figure 11-3, provides controls for managing **Content Advisor**, certificates, and the storage of personal information.

Figure 11-3 Use the Content tab to control Content Advisor, certificates, and personal information.

Using Content Advisor

Content Advisor controls the display of websites based on rating levels defined by the Internet Content Rating Association (ICRA), *http://www.icra.org/*. The most common use for Content Advisor is on a home computer on which parents want to control the websites that their children can view.

> **Note**   The ICRA replaces an older organization named the Recreational Software Advisory Council on the Internet (RSACi). In the Content Advisor dialog boxes in Internet Explorer, you will see references to the RSACi, but the ICRA actually provides the content rating service.

Use Content Advisor to configure the following:

- A supervisor password, which prevents unauthorized users from changing Content Advisor settings.

- Rating levels for language, nudity, sex, and violence. Users must type in the supervisor password to access sites that exceed the configured rating levels.

- Specific sites that Internet Explorer can display regardless of whether the site is rated or not.

- Specific sites that Internet Explorer cannot display, regardless of the rating level, unless the user enters the supervisor password.

Web content providers employ the ICRA and other content rating systems voluntarily. Many sites that contain potentially objectionable content are not rated. Content Advisor provides a method to block all unrated sites, and the approved sites list can then be used to provide access to unrated sites deemed appropriate by the supervisor.

Managing Certificates

The Certificates section of the Content tab provides a method of managing the security certificates that are used to establish secure, encrypted connections using the Secure Sockets Layer (SSL) protocol. Certificates contain the information required to establish a secure connection, such as identification information and encryption keys. Generally, a certificate is required only on the server; however, for some applications, such as secure e-mail, a personal certificate is also required for the client.

Clicking the Certificates button allows you to add and remove personal certificates and to configure what types of server certificates are acceptable. If a server requests a secure connection, but Internet Explorer does not recognize the server's certificate as acceptable, the user receives a warning message and can either allow the connection to continue or terminate the connection before any personal data is transmitted to the server.

When a secure connection is established with a server through Internet Explorer, a lock icon appears in the status bar (lower-right corner of the window) and the protocol in the address bar might be listed as HTTPS (HTTP Secure) instead of HTTP. In some circumstances, a secure connection is established, but the protocol remains HTTP because the secure link is being established through a secondary connection, and the address bar is not updated. However, the lock icon always appears when a secure connection has been established.

Personal Information Management

The Personal Information section of the Content tab allows you to configure the following settings:

- **AutoComplete**   AutoComplete is a feature that helps users work, browse, and purchase items on the Internet faster than normal by automatically listing possible matches for Web addresses, forms, and user names and passwords on forms.

> **Caution**   You should not use AutoComplete when the computer is located in a nonsecure environment, such as a break room, lunchroom, or kiosk; or when two or more people share a computer and computer account.

- **My Profile**   Click My Profile to open Profile Assistant. Profile Assistant stores personal information, which can then be sent automatically to a website when the website requests the information. Profile Assistant saves the information in a secure location on the client's computer and prompts the user to send the information if the website supports this technology. The user can accept or deny this service each time she encounters it. This saves time for the user because she does not have to enter the same information each time she visits a new website, and allows her to determine when and for what sites Profile Assistant is used. As a DST, you might get requests from users who want an easier way to enter personal information than by keying it in manually each time.

Configuring Connection Settings

The Connections tab of the Internet Options dialog box, shown in Figure 11-4, allows you to control how Internet Explorer connects to the Internet. If the computer uses a dial-up or virtual private network (VPN) connection to connect to the Internet, those connections are shown in the Dial-up And Virtual Private Network Settings section. Click Add to start the New Connection Wizard, which you use to configure networking connections (and which you learn more about in Chapter 10, "Supporting Network Connectivity"). When you select one of the displayed connections, you can also configure the following options for that connection:

- **Never Dial A Connection**   Requires that you manually establish a connection before opening Internet Explorer.

- **Dial Whenever A Network Connection Is Not Present**   Causes Internet Explorer to use the current default connection if it detects that there is no existing connection to the Internet.

- **Always Dial My Default Connection**   Causes Internet Explorer to always dial the current default connection.

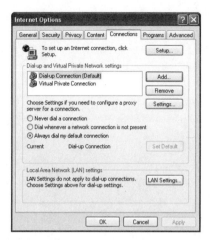

Figure 11-4   Configure the way Internet Explorer connects to the Internet.

To configure the default connection, select a connection from the list and click Set Default.

You can also use the Connections tab to configure proxy server settings. A proxy server is a centralized network device that provides Internet access to the client computers on the network. Proxy servers are used to centralize Internet connection settings, increase security by controlling which resources a client can access, and speed up Internet access by caching Web pages to the server. After you configure Internet Explorer to use a proxy server, Internet Explorer requests Internet content from the proxy server, which in turn connects to the actual Internet resource on the client's behalf, retrieves the information, and forwards it to the client.

To configure Internet Explorer to use a proxy server for dial-up and VPN connections, select the connection and then click Settings. To configure Internet Explorer to use a proxy server for local area network (LAN) connections, click LAN Settings.

Figure 11-5 shows the available proxy server configuration options, which are as follows:

- **Automatically Detect Settings**   Allows the client to automatically receive proxy server configuration from a properly configured Dynamic Host Configuration Protocol (DHCP) or Domain Name System (DNS) server.

- **User Automatic Configuration Script**   Specifies the path to a configuration script containing proxy server information.

- **Use A Proxy Server For This Connection**   Allows you to enter the address of the proxy server and the port that Internet Explorer should use to connect to the proxy server.

■ **Bypass Proxy Server For Local Addresses** Allows the client to connect directly to an address on the local network (such as an internal company Web server) instead of connecting to the proxy server.

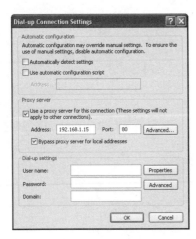

Figure 11-5 Configure proxy server settings.

Configuring Program Settings

The Programs tab of the Internet Options dialog box, shown in Figure 11-6, allows you to configure the programs that are associated with particular services. For example, if a user is browsing a website and selects an e-mail address link, Internet Explorer must launch the appropriate e-mail program. Other configurable services include the HTML editor, the newsgroup client, the program to be used to establish a call across the Internet, and the programs to access the user's calendar and contact list.

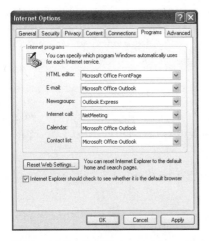

Figure 11-6 Configure programs associated with certain services.

The Programs tab also contains a Manage Add-Ons button. With Windows XP Service Pack 2 installed, Internet Explorer prompts you when add-on software tries to install itself into Internet Explorer. You can view and control the list of add-ons that Internet Explorer can load. Internet Explorer also attempts to detect crashes that are related to add-ons. If an add-on is identified, this information is presented to the user and the user can disable the add-ons to prevent future crashes.

To manage add-ons in Internet Explorer, use these steps:

1. Click Start, and then click Internet Explorer.

2. On the Tools menu, select Manage Add-Ons.

3. In the Manage Add-Ons dialog box (as shown in Figure 11-7), from the Show drop-down list, select one of the following options:

   ❑ **Add-Ons Currently Loaded In Internet Explorer**   This option lists the add-ons that have been loaded into memory within the current Internet Explorer process and those which have been blocked from loading. This includes ActiveX controls that were used by Web pages that were previously viewed within the current process

   ❑ **Add-Ons That Have Been Used By Internet Explorer**   This option lists all add-ons that have been referenced by Internet Explorer and are still installed.

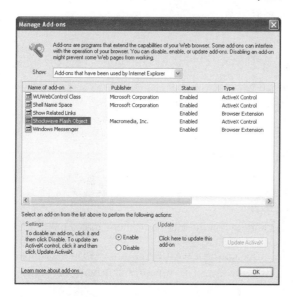

Figure 11-7   Managing add-ons in Internet Explorer

4. Select any add-on from the list by clicking it once, and then perform one of the following actions:

   ❑ Select the Enable option to re-enable a previously disabled add-on. The add-on may have been disabled by the user or by Internet Explorer following a crash.

❑ Select the Disable option to disable an add-on.

❑ Click the Update ActiveX button to update ActiveX controls to their latest version. Windows searches for an update at the location where the original control was found. If a newer version is found at that location, Internet Explorer attempts to install the update.

5. Click OK to close the Manage Add-Ons dialog box.

At the bottom of the Programs tab, you find an option named Internet Explorer Should Check To See Whether It Is The Default Browser. When you enable this option, Internet Explorer checks to see whether it is configured as the default browser each time you open the program.

Configuring Advanced Settings

The Advanced tab of the Internet Options dialog box, shown in Figure 11-8, allows you to configure a variety of Internet Explorer settings. The exact options that are available on this tab vary, depending on whether additional components have been installed. You can right-click any particular setting and select What's This? to see a description of the setting.

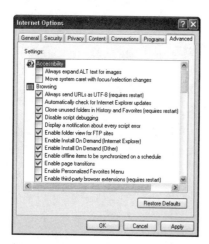

Figure 11-8   Configure advanced settings on the Internet Options dialog box.

Advanced settings are divided into categories such as Accessibility, Browsing, Multimedia, and Security. Following are some of the important advanced settings you should be aware of as a DST:

■ **Browsing: Enable Personalized Favorites Menu**   When enabled, Favorites that you have not recently accessed are hidden from view and are accessible by clicking the down arrow at the bottom of the Favorites menu.

- **Browsing: Enable Third-Party Browser Extensions (requires restart)**   Clearing this option disables non-Microsoft browser extensions, which can be useful when troubleshooting problems with Internet Explorer. Often, browser extensions can cause Internet Explorer to crash or have problems displaying Web pages.

- **Browsing: Enable Visual Styles On Buttons And Controls In Web Pages**   When enabled, button and control styles in Internet Explorer match those set in Display properties.

- **Browsing: Notify When Downloads Complete**   Enabling this option causes Internet Explorer to display a message at the end of a file download, indicating that the download is complete.

- **Browsing: Show Friendly HTTP Error Messages**   Web servers send error messages to browsers when problems occur. When this option is enabled, Internet Explorer will display a detailed message outlining potential solutions for the problem. When this option is disabled, Internet Explorer shows only the error number and name of the error.

- **Browsing: Underline Links**   This option controls the way Internet Explorer displays hyperlinks. Available options are Always (links are always underlined), Hover (links are underlined when the mouse is moved over them), or Never (never underlines links).

- **Browsing: Use Inline Autocomplete**   When this option is enabled, Internet Explorer completes what you are typing in the address bar based on previous entries.

- **Multimedia: Enable Automatic Image Resizing**   When this option is enabled, Internet Explorer automatically resizes large images so that they fit in the browser window.

- **Multimedia: Play Animations In Web Pages**   Enabling this option allows Internet Explorer to display animated pictures. These animations are often slow to load and distracting. Consider clearing this option for smoother access.

- **Multimedia: Show Image Download Placeholders**   When this option is enabled, Internet Explorer draws placeholders for images while they are downloading. This process allows the items on the page to be properly positioned before images are fully downloaded.

- **Multimedia: Show Pictures**   When this option is enabled, Internet Explorer shows pictures normally. For users with slow connections, images can take a long time to download, so you can increase perceived performance by clearing this option.

- **Printing: Print Background Colors And Images** When this option is selected, background colors and images will be printed, which can slow down printing and affect the quality of printing (depending on the printer's capabilities).

- **Security: Empty Temporary Internet Files Folder When Browser Is Closed** Enabling this option causes Internet Explorer to delete temporary Internet files when you close Internet Explorer.

- **Security: Warn If Changing Between Secure And Not Secure Mode** When enabled, Internet Explorer will warn the user when switching from a secure site to a nonsecure site. This warning can prevent the user from accidentally providing personal information across a nonsecure connection.

- **Security: Warn If Form Submittal Is Being Redirected** Enabling this option causes Internet Explorer to warn the user if information entered into a form is being redirected to a website other than the one that is being viewed.

Configuring Security Settings

As a DST, you should be able to help users configure Internet Explorer security settings that control what types of content Internet Explorer can download and use—content such as ActiveX controls, files, and fonts. Internet Explorer contains many settings designed to protect the computer and the user from security hazards when browsing the Internet. Knowing the available configuration options gives you a greater understanding of potential threats and of the methods that you can utilize to help protect users against them.

The Security tab of the Internet Options dialog box, shown in Figure 11-9, provides a method of controlling security based on **security zones**. Security zones contain a list of websites deemed to have similar security settings requirements. You'll be asked to resolve problems that have to do with zone configurations; these problems will mainly be issues regarding the inability to view or access something or to comply with company security directives. To resolve these types of calls, you'll need an understanding of the default settings for each zone.

The four zones provided are as follows:

- **Internet** Contains all websites that you have not placed in other zones.

- **Local Intranet** Contains all websites that are on the local network. By default, this zone includes all sites that bypass the proxy server (if a proxy server is being used) and all local network paths. You can add additional sites to this zone by selecting the zone and clicking Sites.

- **Trusted Sites** Contains websites that are believed to be safe. There are no sites in this zone by default. You can add sites to this zone as you see fit by selecting the zone and clicking Sites.

■ **Restricted Sites**   Contains websites that could potentially be harmful. There are no sites in this zone by default. You can add sites to this zone as you see fit by selecting the zone and clicking Sites.

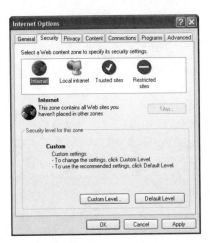

Figure 11-9   Configure security zones in Internet Explorer.

Service calls involving security zones can have to do with an end user's need to have more (or less) access to Web content than she currently has or to place a website in a specific zone and use that zone's default security settings. You might also receive calls to configure users' computers to comply with a company security policy requirement to enable or disable a specific security setting.

Although it is generally a good idea to leave each security zone set to its defaults, you can customize the security level for each site if the default settings are not adequate for a user. For example, some users might enjoy a more secure environment, but would prefer that Internet Explorer give them the option of blocking content rather than blocking the content automatically. Customize the security level of a site by selecting the site and clicking Default Level; then drag the slider that appears to the desired security level.

The security levels that you can configure are as follows:

■ High, which is appropriate for sites that might have harmful content.

❑ Less-secure features are disabled.

❑ The safest way to browse, but functionality is potentially lost.

■ Medium, which is appropriate for most Internet sites.

❑ Prompts before downloading potentially unsafe content.

❑ Unsigned ActiveX controls are not downloaded.

- Medium-Low, which is appropriate for local sites.

  ❑ Most content is run without prompts.

  ❑ Unsigned ActiveX controls are not downloaded.

- Low, which is appropriate for sites that are trusted.

  ❑ Minimal safeguards and warning prompts are provided.

  ❑ Most content is downloaded and runs without prompts.

  ❑ All ActiveX content can run.

Default security levels for each zone are as follows:

- The Internet zone has a Medium security level.

- The Local Intranet zone has a Medium security level.

- The Trusted Sites zone has a Low security level.

- The Restricted Sites zone has a High security level.

Custom Security Levels

You can modify each security level to suit the particular needs of the user or organization by selecting the security level that is closest to what you want to configure and then clicking Custom Level. The Security Settings window is displayed, as shown in Figure 11-10. You can right-click any security setting and select the What's This? command to get information about that setting.

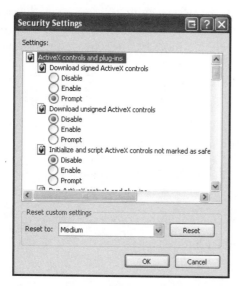

Figure 11-10   Configure a custom security level.

Configuring Privacy Settings

The Privacy tab of the Internet Options dialog box allows you to control how Internet Explorer handles **cookies**, which are small text files stored on your computer by websites. Websites use cookies to store user preferences for personalized sites, and cookies often contain personal information used to identify the user to the website.

Although most cookies are legitimate, some are not. Unsatisfactory cookies are those that are used to provide personally identifiable information for a secondary purpose, such as selling your e-mail address to third-party vendors, or sharing your name and address with other companies. Because there are unsatisfactory cookies, it is important to understand the different types of cookies, how to delete cookies, and how to change privacy settings to prevent different types of cookies from being saved to the computer. Your company might require that changes be made to the default settings for cookies, too, so you need to know how to make changes if asked.

Cookies can be either persistent (they remain after Internet Explorer is closed and can be reused) or temporary (they are deleted when Internet Explorer is closed). Also, there are first-party and third-party cookies. First-party cookies originate from the website that you are currently viewing. Third-party cookies originate from a site different from the one that you are currently viewing but are somehow related to the current website. For example, many sites use advertising from third-party sites, and those sites commonly use cookies to track your website usage for advertising purposes.

Note   Cookies can also store personally identifiable information such as a name, e-mail address, telephone number, or even a person's marital status. However, websites gain this information only by asking for it outright. Make sure that users know that cookies cannot obtain any personally identifiable information from them unless they specifically provide it.

Figure 11-11 shows the Privacy settings for Internet Explorer. You can use the slider to configure the following settings to manage cookies:

- **Block All Cookies**   Blocks new cookies from being created and prevents access to existing cookies. If per-site privacy settings are configured, they do not override this setting.

- **High**   Blocks all cookies that use personal information without the user's explicit consent. If per-site privacy settings are configured, they override this setting.

- **Medium High**   Blocks all third-party cookies that do not have a compact privacy policy or that use personal information without the user's explicit consent, and all first-party cookies that use personal information without implicit consent. If per-site privacy settings are configured, they override this setting.

- **Medium**   Blocks all third-party cookies that do not have a compact privacy policy or that use personal information without the user's explicit consent. First-party cookies that use personal information without implicit consent are allowed, but they are deleted when the browser is closed. Access to first-party cookies is restricted to first-party context if the cookie does not have a compact privacy policy. If per-site privacy settings are configured, they override this setting.

- **Low**   Permits websites to store all cookies on the computer. When the browser is closed, third-party cookies are deleted. Access to first-party cookies is restricted to first-party context if the cookie does not have a compact privacy policy. If per-site privacy settings are configured, they override this setting.

- **Accept All Cookies**   Enables all websites to store and access cookies on the computer. If per-site privacy settings are configured, they do not override this setting.

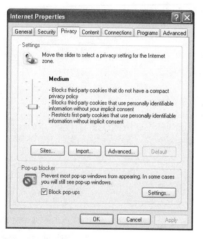

Figure 11-11   Configure privacy settings in Internet Explorer.

Note   If you select a privacy level that does not allow cookies, you might not be able to view certain websites.

You can configure per-site privacy settings by clicking the Sites button. Per-site settings override the way that cookies are handled for specific websites. For example, you can enter the URL for a website and then allow or block cookies for that site, regardless of how Internet Explorer is configured to handle cookies.

Internet Explorer also provides a pop-up blocker for blocking pop-up windows that some sites deploy for advertising purposes. When a site tries to open a pop-up window, Internet Explorer blocks the window from opening and displays a notification in the Information Bar. The Information Bar appears just above the main display of the Web page you are viewing in Internet Explorer. The Information Bar replaces a number of dialog boxes used in previous versions of Internet Explorer. Clicking the Information Bar allows you to show the blocked pop-up, allow all pop-ups on the current site, and configure other settings.

Practice: Configure Internet Explorer

In this practice, you will delete temporary Internet files manually, configure Internet Explorer to delete temporary Internet files automatically, and delete cookies. You will also configure Internet Explorer security zones.

Exercise 1: Delete Temporary Internet Files Manually

1. From the Start menu, select Internet Explorer.

2. In Internet Explorer, on the Tools menu, select Internet Options.

3. In the Internet Options dialog box, on the General tab, in the Temporary Internet Files section, click the Settings button.

4. In the Settings dialog box, click the View Files button.

5. In the Temporary Internet Files folder, on the Edit menu, select Select All. Press DELETE.

6. In the Warning dialog box, click Yes. Close the Temporary Internet Files folder. In the Settings dialog box, click OK.

Exercise 2: Configure Internet Explorer to Delete Temporary Internet Files Automatically on Exit

1. From the Start menu, select Internet Explorer.

2. On the Tools menu, select Internet Options.

3. In the Internet Options dialog box, on the Advanced tab, in the Settings list, in the Security section, select the Empty Temporary Internet Files Folder When Browser Is Closed check box.

Exercise 3: Delete Cookies

1. From the Start menu, select Internet Explorer.

2. On the Tools menu, select Internet Options.

3. In the Internet Options dialog box, on the General tab, in the Temporary Internet Files section, click the Delete Cookies button.

4. In the Delete Cookies message box, click OK.

Exercise 4: Configure Internet Explorer Security Zones

1. From the Start menu, select Internet Explorer.

2. In the Internet Options dialog box, on the Security tab, in the Security Level For This Zone section, click the Default Level button. Note that if settings are already at their default value, the Default Level button may be unavailable.

3. Move the slider to the High position. Click Apply and then click Custom Level.

4. In the Security Settings dialog box, click Cancel.

5. In the Internet Options dialog box, in the Select A Web Content Zone To Specify Its Security Settings section, select Trusted Sites.

6. In the Security Level For This Zone section, click the Default Level button.

7. In the Trusted Sites section, click the Sites button.

8. In the Trusted Sites dialog box, in the Add This Web Site To The Zone: text box, type **https://www.microsoft.com**. Click Add, click OK, and then click OK to close the Internet Options dialog box.

9. In Internet Explorer, in the Address text box, type **http://www.google.com** and press ENTER.

10. On the Google Web page, right-click any hyperlink and select Save Target As. In the Security Alert message box, click OK.

11. In the Address text box, type **https://www.microsoft.com** and press ENTER.

12. On the Microsoft Web page, right-click any hyperlink and select Save Target As. In the Save As dialog box, click Cancel.

Lesson Review

The following questions are intended to reinforce key information presented in this lesson. If you are unable to answer a question, review the lesson materials and try the question again. You can find answers to the questions in the "Questions and Answers" section at the end of this chapter.

1. Match the type of cookie on the left with its description on the right.

1. Persistent	A. These cookies are sent to a computer from the website being viewed. They can be persistent or temporary, and are generally harmless.
2. Temporary	B. These cookies are sent to a computer from a website not currently being viewed. They generally come from advertisers on the website being viewed for the purpose of tracking Web page use for advertising and marketing purposes. They can be persistent or temporary, and most third-party cookies are blocked by default using the Medium privacy setting.

3. First-party   C. These cookies are stored on a computer during only a single browsing session and are deleted when Internet Explorer is closed. They are used by websites to determine which client browser, which language, and which screen resolution is used; and they allow a user to move back and forth among the Web pages at the site without losing previously input information. If these cookies are disabled, a user cannot access a site that requires them.

4. Third-party   D. These cookies remain on a computer even when Internet Explorer is closed, the user has disconnected from the Internet, or the computer has been turned off. These cookies store information such as logon name, password, e-mail address, color schemes, purchasing history, and other preferences. When a site is revisited, this information is available and can be applied.

2. One of your customers enabled Content Advisor on her home computer to protect her child from questionable content on the Internet. However, there are a number of sites with acceptable content that the child cannot access. This is most likely because Content Advisor is not letting Internet Explorer display sites that have not been rated. Your customer wants to let the child view the acceptable sites, yet still maintain control of the sites the child visits. What is the best solution?

   A. Disable Content Advisor and instead set the Privacy setting in Internet Explorer to High.

   B. Configure Content Advisor so that users can see sites that have no rating.

   C. Enter the sites the child needs to access into Content Advisor's list of approved sites.

   D. You cannot configure this using Content Advisor. The customer should purchase a third-party filtering program.

Lesson Summary

- Internet Explorer is the Web browser that is provided with Windows XP. Internet Explorer provides access to local and Internet resources using many protocols, such as Hypertext Transfer Protocol (HTTP) and File Transfer Protocol (FTP).

- Internet Explorer automatically stores (or caches) copies of Web pages that you access to a folder on the local hard disk. The next time you access the same page, Internet Explorer can load the page from the local cache rather than having to connect to the Web server and download it again. You can control how much disk space this feature uses, as well as when Internet Explorer looks for updated pages.

- Content Advisor controls the display of sites based on rating levels defined by the ICRA. The most common use for Content Advisor is on a home computer in which parents want to control which sites their children can view.

- You can use the various tabs in the Internet Options dialog box to control general Internet Explorer settings, security and privacy settings, the way Internet Explorer connects to the Internet, which programs are associated with specific resources, and a number of advanced settings.

Lesson 2: Troubleshooting Internet Explorer Problems

DSTs are often called on to troubleshoot problems with Internet Explorer, and these service calls generally consist of two types. They are user requests to make Internet Explorer work faster and smarter, look better, have more functionality, or resolve simple interface issues; or the calls are user requests to resolve problems that have to do with the inability to view Web pages properly.

After this lesson, you will be able to

- Identify and resolve common user requests involving Internet Explorer.
- Resolve problems viewing Web pages.

Estimated lesson time: 30 minutes

Resolving Common User Requests

End users will have various requests that involve how Internet Explorer looks and performs, and they will ask you to resolve problems with the interface. You can resolve many of these problems by customizing the Standard toolbar, changing what is selected in the View menu, or personalizing the Advanced settings in the Internet Options dialog box.

Note   **Connectivity Issues** This section assumes that Internet Explorer is connected to the Internet properly. Chapter 10 focuses on connectivity problems.

Missing Toolbar, Links Bar, or Status Bar

A common complaint from end users is that an Internet Explorer toolbar is missing, or a toolbar that they used to have is not available anymore. The toolbars that you can configure include the Standard toolbar, the Address bar, and the Links bar. Users might also complain that they cannot see the information at the bottom of the screen that shows which security zone they are in, denoting a missing Status bar. You can add and remove these toolbars by using the View menu, and you can customize the placement of the Standard toolbar, Address bar, and Links bar by dragging and dropping.

To show or hide any of the toolbars, follow these steps:

1. Open Internet Explorer, and from the View menu, point to Toolbars.

2. The Toolbars list contains Standard Buttons, Address Bar, Links, Lock The Toolbars, and Customize selection. Toolbars marked with a check are showing; toolbars without a check do not show. To select or clear a toolbar, select it from the

list. Figure 11-12 shows an example of all three toolbars. In this example, the Links bar is on the same line as the Address bar.

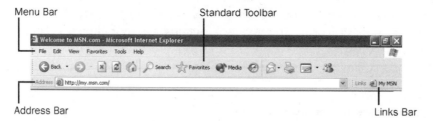

Figure 11-12 You can customize Internet Explorer toolbars to suit any user's needs.

To customize the placement of the Standard toolbar, Address bar, or Links bar, follow these steps:

1. In Internet Explorer, make sure that the toolbars are unlocked by going to the View menu, pointing at Toolbars, and ensuring that the Lock The Toolbars command does not have a check next to it. If it does, choose the command to toggle it off.

2. Position the pointer at the far left of the toolbar you want to move.

3. Click and hold the mouse button; the pointer will change to a four-headed arrow.

4. Drag the toolbar to a new position to combine it with an existing toolbar or to move its position onscreen.

5. Position the pointer on the light dotted lines that separate combined toolbars until the pointer becomes a two-headed arrow. Drag to resize the toolbar.

Note The Standard toolbar, Address bar, and Link bar must remain at the top of the Internet Explorer window. You cannot move them to the left, right, or bottom of the screen (as you can the Windows taskbar).

Locked Toolbar

If a user complains that the toolbar is locked and cannot be moved, click View, point to Toolbars, and clear the Lock The Toolbars command.

Personalizing the Favorites Menu

When users call to report that they cannot access all of their favorites or that they have saved favorites but the favorites are not listed in the Favorites list, it is most likely because the Personalized Favorites menu option is enabled in the Advanced options of

Internet Explorer. Personalized menus keep the Favorites list clean by hiding links that are not used very often. The list shows only the links that are accessed frequently. Tell the users that they can access the less-frequently-accessed links by clicking the down arrow at the end of the Favorites list.

► **Enabling Personalized Favorites Menus**

To disable or enable personalized favorites menus, follow these steps:

1. Open Internet Explorer, and from the Tools menu, select Internet Options.

2. On the Advanced tab, scroll down to the Browsing section, and select or clear the Enable Personalized Favorites Menu check box. Click OK.

> **Note**   Applying the change to personalized favorites might require that you close and restart Internet Explorer.

Importing and Exporting Internet Favorites

If you use Internet Explorer on multiple computers, you can easily share favorite items among computers by exporting them on one computer and then importing them on another. Exporting favorites is also a good way to back them up, share them with a friend, or even create a single Web page with links to all your favorites.

► **Exporting Internet Favorites**

To export Internet Favorites to an .htm file, follow these steps:

1. On the File menu of Internet Explorer, select Import and Export.

2. On the Welcome page of the Import/Export Wizard, click Next.

3. Select the Export Favorites option and click Next.

4. You can specify the primary Favorites folder or any particular subfolder for your export. When you select a folder for export, all subfolders in that folder are also exported. Select the folder you want to export and click Next.

5. Click Browse, select a location and name for the export file, and click Save. Click Next and then click Finish.

6. Internet Explorer informs you that the export is successful. Click OK.

The exported file is saved as a Web page. Double-click it to open it in Internet Explorer, and you can see a list of all your favorites—complete with hyperlinks. You can transfer this file to another computer and import it, back it up to a safe place, or even use it as a Web page.

▶ **Importing Internet Favorites**

To import Internet Favorites from an .htm file, follow these steps:

1. On the File menu of Internet Explorer, select Import and Export.

2. On the Welcome page of the Import/Export Wizard, click Next.

3. Select the Import Favorites option and click Next.

4. Click Browse, locate and select the .htm file you want to import, and then click Save.

5. Click Next and then select a folder in which the imported favorites will be placed. Click Next and then click Finish.

6. Internet Explorer informs you that the import is successful. Click OK.

Using AutoComplete

AutoComplete is a feature that helps end users work, browse, and purchase items on the Internet faster than normal by automatically listing possible matches for Web addresses, forms, and user names and passwords on forms. Although this can be a good feature for a computer administrator who does not share a computer, for the average home user or the owner of a small, home-based business, it is not a good idea under all circumstances.

You should not use AutoComplete when the computer is located in a nonsecure environment, such as a break room, lunchroom, or kiosk; or when two or more people share a computer and computer account. In addition, if a computer is transferred to a new user or sold to another person, the AutoComplete form and password information should be cleared.

▶ **Enabling or Disabling AutoComplete**

As a DST, you will be asked to enable or disable AutoComplete (depending on the circumstance), enable or disable Internet Explorer's capability to save passwords, and clear the AutoComplete history. To do these tasks, follow these steps:

1. Open Internet Explorer, and from the Tools menu, select Internet Options.

2. On the Content tab, and in the Personal Information area, select AutoComplete.

3. To enable or disable AutoComplete, in the AutoComplete Settings dialog box, select or clear the Use AutoComplete for: Web Addresses, Forms, and User Names And Passwords On Forms check boxes.

4. To clear the AutoComplete history for forms, select the Clear Forms button.

5. To clear the AutoComplete history for passwords, select the Clear Passwords button.

6. To remove the capability of Internet Explorer to save any passwords in the future, clear the Prompt Me To Save Passwords check box.

7. Click OK to close the AutoComplete Settings dialog box, and click OK to close the Internet Options dialog box.

Exam Tip   Do not confuse AutoComplete with Inline AutoComplete. Inline AutoComplete completes entries in the Address bar of Internet Explorer as you type (based on entries you used before) and offers a list of choices under the Address bar or other links that start the same way. AutoComplete offers choices under the Address window as well, but does not complete the entry in the Address bar as you type.

Using Inline AutoComplete

Inline AutoComplete completes entries in the Address bar as you type (based on entries you have used before) and offers a list of choices under the Address bar for other links that start the same way.

▶ **Enabling Inline AutoComplete**

You can enable Inline AutoComplete using the Advanced options of Internet Explorer by following these steps:

1. Open Internet Explorer, and from the Tools menu, select Internet Options.

2. From the Advanced tab, scroll down to the end of the Browsing section.

3. Select the Use Inline AutoComplete check box. Click OK.

Using Default Search Actions

Users can perform searches in many ways, including using the Search Explorer bar, using a Web browser or search engine, or typing their requests in the Address bar. If a user's choice is to search for information using the Address bar, there are several ways in which the results for that search can be shown. In addition, searching from the Address bar can be disabled. Following are the advanced choices for searching from the Address bar:

- Display results and go to the most likely site.

- Do not search from the Address bar.

- Just display the results in the main window.

- Just go to the most likely site.

▶   **Changing Default Actions**

The default search action is to go to the most likely site. To change that default, follow these steps:

1. Open Internet Explorer, and from the Tools menu, select Internet Options.

2. Click the Advanced tab and scroll down to Search From The Address Bar.

3. In the When Searching list, select the appropriate choice and then click OK.

Script Errors

Users might report that script error notifications appear on their monitors while surfing websites, and they might also complain that they are continually asked if they want to debug those errors. You might also have users with the opposite problem; a developer or technician might need to see these errors when testing a new website. Whatever the case, script options exist in the Advanced options of Internet Explorer, and they can be easily enabled or disabled.

▶   **Enabling and Disabling Script Debugging**

To enable or disable script debugging, or if a user should be notified of all script errors, follow these steps:

1. Open Internet Explorer, and from the Tools menu, select Internet Options.

2. On the Advanced tab, in the Browsing section, select or clear the following check boxes and then click OK: Disable Script Debugging and Display A Notification About Every Script Error.

3. Click OK to close the Internet Options dialog box.

Download Complete Notification

By default, Internet Explorer notifies users when a download is complete by leaving the download dialog box open and playing a sound. It is possible, however, that a user has turned the notification off (there is a check box on the download dialog box that makes this an easy thing to do), and the user now wants to turn the feature back on.

▶   **Enabling Download Notification**

To enable download complete notification, follow these steps:

1. Open Internet Explorer, and from the Tools menu, select Internet Options.

2. From the Advanced tab, and in the Browsing section, select the Notify When Downloads Complete check box.

3. Click OK to close the Internet Options dialog box.

As you learned in this section, you can resolve many problems by using the View menu or the Internet Options dialog box. The Content tab, Programs tab, and Advanced tab of the Internet Options dialog box allow you to change the program defaults and personalize Internet Explorer. The View menu enables personalization of the toolbars.

Resolving Problems with Viewing Web Pages

There are several reasons why users have trouble viewing Web pages properly, and many times the problem is the result of changes to the defaults that the users have made on their own. Problems can also occur because of default security settings. For example, a site is in the Restricted Sites zone, or the site requires cookies be placed on the computer and cookies are not allowed. Users might report specific errors as well; they get internal page faults; or they cannot hear sounds, see videos, or view pictures. These are common problems, and solutions to them are detailed in this section.

Screen Resolution

If a user reports problems with viewing a single Web page, but other pages look fine, check to see whether there is a note at the bottom of the page that says, "This page is best viewed using 800 x 600 screen resolution" or something similar. If it is a corporate website or one the user relies on heavily, the user might need to reconfigure his or her display settings permanently. Display settings are changed in Control Panel (see Chapter 7, "Supporting Display Devices, I/O Devices, and ACPI," for more).

Cookie Handling

Many websites require that cookies be enabled on a user's computer if the user wants to visit and browse the site. A user cannot view websites that have this requirement if the user's privacy settings are configured to block all cookies, if the privacy settings are set to High, or if the company has a strict cookie policy that blocks first-party cookies or does not allow session cookies. When Internet Explorer blocks content, it notifies the user through the Information Bar.

Allowing a user access to sites requires that the default privacy settings be changed. Changing privacy settings is detailed in Lesson 1, "Configuring Internet Explorer," earlier in this chapter.

The Information Bar

The Internet Explorer Information Bar in Windows XP Service Pack 2 replaces many of the common dialog boxes that prompt users for information and provides a common area for displaying information. Notifications such as blocked ActiveX installs, blocked pop-up windows, and downloads all appear in the Information Bar, which appears below the toolbars and above the main browsing window, as shown in Figure 11-13. Either clicking or right-clicking on the Information Bar brings up a menu that relates to the notification that is presented. A new custom security zone setting allows users to change the settings of the Information Bar for each security zone, including the ability to disable the Information Bar and return to using separate dialog boxes.

Figure 11-13 The Internet Explorer Information Bar provides a common notification area.

Note Microsoft does not use pop-up ads or windows on the Microsoft.com site. The Internet Explorer window in Figure 11-13 was created to show the functionality of the new Information Bar and Pop-Up Blocker features in Windows XP Service Pack 2.

Sounds, Videos, and Pictures

Some of the Advanced options of Internet Explorer restrict what users can and cannot see on a Web page. These settings are often configured to speed up access to a page by not playing videos or showing pictures when the site is loaded, and sound can be disabled as well. If a user reports problems that are associated with sound, video, or pictures, check the advanced options first by following these steps:

1. Open Internet Explorer, and from the Tools menu, select Internet Options.

2. Click the Advanced tab and scroll down to the Multimedia section.

3. Verify that the appropriate items are selected:

   ❑ Play Animations In Web Pages

   ❑ Play Sounds In Web Pages

   ❑ Play Videos In Web Pages

   ❑ Show Pictures

4. On the Advanced tab, verify that the Show Image Download Placeholders check box is cleared. Click OK.

Invalid Page Faults

A page fault is a normal process that occurs when a program requests data that is not currently loaded into the computer's real memory. When this occurs, Windows attempts to retrieve the data from the virtual memory that is stored to hard disk. If the data cannot be mapped to virtual memory, the result is an invalid page fault—and often, a crashed application. Invalid page faults are often difficult to diagnose. Connectivity settings; a full Temporary Internet Files folder; and third-party Internet software including firewalls, file-sharing software, Internet optimizers, and on-screen animation programs can cause page faults. Network protocols, cookies, corrupted Favorites, services, and Internet software installations can also cause invalid page faults.

Invalid page faults can be represented in Internet Explorer by several different types of errors, including the following:

- An actual invalid page fault error

- Iexplore.exe has generated errors and must be shut down

- The page could not be displayed

- Could not open the search page

- An access violation occurred in MSHTML.DLL

If specifics about the error are provided in the error message (as in the last item on the previous list), see the Microsoft Knowledge Base and type in the exact error message as the keywords for a search. Downloading and installing a particular update might solve this particular error. These are the easiest of all page faults for which to find solutions. If no specifics are given, you will have to resolve the errors using trial-and-error troubleshooting techniques.

Note Before you do too much troubleshooting, verify that the user has the most recent version of Internet Explorer and the latest service packs for both the operating system and Internet Explorer. To check the version number and which service packs are installed, open Internet Explorer, and from the Help menu, select About Internet Explorer.

If you are at the user's desk when the error occurs, use the Internet Explorer Reporting tool to report the error, and then view the error details. If the error report gives any indication of the cause of the error, disable the program or service associated with it. If that process does not work, and if the user has the most up-to-date service packs installed, continue troubleshooting in the following order:

1. Verify that the proxy settings for the LAN, if they exist, are correctly configured. You can locate these settings by clicking LAN Settings on the Connections tab of the Internet Options dialog box.

2. Disable third-party browser extensions or other third-party downloaded components. Applications like these can often be disabled from the notification area or from the application itself, and uninstalling the component from Control Panel is the best option if one of these programs caused the page fault.

3. Delete all temporary Internet files. You can do this on the General tab of the Internet Options dialog box.

4. Delete cookies. You can do so on the General tab of the Internet Options dialog box.

5. Troubleshoot the Favorites folder. It is possible that corruption in the Favorites folder or some of the files it holds is to blame. Try moving the contents of the user's Favorites folder to a temporary folder. If that solves the problem, add the shortcuts back to the Favorites folder a few at a time. If the problem recurs, it is usually easy to find the culprit..

6. Verify that the system has enough RAM and that the RAM is performing properly.

Lesson Review

The following questions are intended to reinforce key information presented in this lesson. If you cannot answer a question, review the lesson materials and try the question again. You can find answers to the questions in the "Questions and Answers" section at the end of this chapter.

1. A company has placed a computer in a break room so that users can access the computer during their lunch and coffee breaks. How should the computer be configured? (Choose all that apply.)

   A. Disable AutoComplete.

   B. Clear forms and clear passwords from the AutoComplete Settings dialog box.

    C. Disable Personalized Favorites.

    D. Set Privacy settings to block all cookies.

    E. Configure a custom level for the Internet zone to disable the installation of desktop icons.

2. One of your users has recently upgraded his computer from Windows 98 to Windows XP Professional. The computer is connected to the Internet using a cable modem. The upgrade went fine, but he noticed that the Web pages that he sees in Internet Explorer do not always seem to be up to date. What do you suspect is the problem?

    A. The Temporary Internet Files folder is full.

    B. The Temporary Internet Files settings are not configured to check for newer versions of stored pages.

    C. Internet Explorer is configured to use a dial-up connection instead of a LAN connection.

    D. The network adapter or cable modem is malfunctioning.

Lesson Summary

- Many of the interface requests that you receive can be resolved by customizing the Standard toolbar, changing what is selected in the View menu, or personalizing the Advanced settings in the Internet Options dialog box.

- There are many reasons a user might have difficulty viewing Web pages, including connectivity issues, security zone configuration, privacy settings, Internet Explorer configuration, and even the graphics settings in Windows XP.

Case Scenario Exercises

Scenario 11.1

A customer calls and tells you that she recently got a new broadband DSL connection to the Internet. When the service person came to hook it up, everything was working fine, but whenever the customer opens Internet Explorer, Windows attempts to dial into her old ISP using her standard modem. The customer does not want to disable the standard modem or remove her dial-up network connection because she is not certain how reliable her new DSL connection will be. She does want Internet Explorer to automatically use her new DSL connection when she accesses the Internet. What should you tell this customer to do?

Scenario 11.2

A user reports that each time she accesses a particular website, she is inundated with content she does not want to see. She thinks that this might have to do with ActiveX, Java applets, or scripts running on the site. She reports that the site takes a long time to load, too. She wants to visit this site and only read the data; she has no interest in the other items on the site. You need to make this site available without making any changes to the default settings for the Internet zone. What should you do?

A. Add this site to the Local Intranet zone.

B. Add this site to the Trusted Sites zone.

C. Add this site to the Restricted Sites zone.

Troubleshooting Lab

You are working for a company that provides computer support for several small businesses. You get a call from a user who complains that when she tries to send an e-mail message from within Internet Explorer, it creates a new message using Outlook Express. However, she uses Outlook as her e-mail software. She wants you to configure Internet Explorer so that she can create a message by using Outlook. After talking with her for a few more minutes, you also find that she wants the following programs to be configured to work within Internet Explorer:

- HTML editor: Notepad
- E-mail client: Hotmail
- Newsgroup reader: Outlook Express
- Internet call: NetMeeting
- Calendar: Microsoft Office Outlook
- Contact list: Address Book

How would you configure these programs within Internet Explorer?

_____

_____

Chapter Summary

- Internet Explorer is the Web browser that is provided with Windows XP. Internet Explorer provides access to local and Internet resources using many protocols, such as Hypertext Transfer Protocol (HTTP) and File Transfer Protocol (FTP).

- Internet Explorer automatically stores (or caches) copies of Web pages that you access to a folder on the local hard disk. The next time you access the same page, Internet Explorer can load the page from the local cache rather than having to connect to the Web server and download it again. You can control how much disk space this feature uses, as well as when Internet Explorer looks for updated pages.

- Content Advisor controls the display of sites based on rating levels defined by the Internet Content Rating Association (ICRA). The most common use for Content Advisor is on a home computer in which parents want to control what sites their children can view.

- You can use the various tabs in the Internet Options dialog box to control general Internet Explorer settings, security and privacy settings, the way Internet Explorer connects to the Internet, which programs are associated with specific resources, and a number of advanced settings.

- Many of the interface requests that you receive can be resolved by customizing the Standard toolbar, changing what is selected in the View menu, or personalizing the Advanced settings in the Internet Options dialog box.

- There are many reasons a user might have difficulty viewing Web pages, including connectivity issues, security zone configuration, privacy settings, Internet Explorer configuration, and even the graphics settings in Windows XP.

Exam Highlights

Before taking the exam, review the key topics and terms that are presented in this chapter. You need to know this information.

Key Points

- Do not Confuse AutoComplete with Inline AutoComplete. Inline AutoComplete completes entries in the Address bar of Internet Explorer as you type (based on entries you have used before) and offers a list of choices under the Address bar or other links that start the same way. AutoComplete offers choices under the Address window as well, but does not complete the entry in the Address bar as you type.

■ Make sure that you understand how to delete temporary Internet files by using Disk Cleanup and from within Internet Explorer. Experiment with the various settings that govern temporary files to make sure that you understand their use.

Key Terms

Content Advisor   Controls the display of sites based on rating levels defined by the ICRA.

cookie   A small text file that a website creates and stores on your computer. Cookies detail what users' preferences are, what they purchased, and any personal information offered by the user.

home page   The website that opens automatically when you start Internet Explorer.

Internet Options   The dialog box available in Internet Explorer for configuring program settings.

security zones   Contain a list of websites deemed to have similar security settings requirements. You can configure a different security level for each zone and then place sites into zones according to the sites' levels of trust.

Temporary Internet files   Cached files. Temporary Internet files allow a user to use the Back and Forward buttons, access History, and use offline files and folders. Retrieving information from the Temporary Internet Files folder is much faster than retrieving information from the Internet.

Questions and Answers

Lesson 1 Review

Page
11-20

1. Match the type of cookie on the left with its description on the right.

1. D. 2. C. 3. A. 4. B.

Lesson 2 Review

Page
11-32

1. A company has placed a computer in a break room so that users can access the computer during their lunch and coffee breaks. How should the computer be configured? (Choose all that apply.)

   A. Disable AutoComplete.

   B. Clear forms and clear passwords from the AutoComplete Settings dialog box.

   C. Disable Personalized Favorites.

   D. Set Privacy settings to block all cookies.

   E. Configure a custom level for the Internet zone to disable the installation of desktop icons.

   Answers A, B, and E are correct. Disabling AutoComplete and clearing AutoComplete settings protect users from others obtaining their user names and passwords. Disabling the installation of desktop icons keeps the desktop clean. Answer C is incorrect because the way in which the Favorites list appears is not a security issue. Answer D is incorrect because blocking all cookies will make many websites nonfunctional.

2. One of your users has recently upgraded his computer from Windows 98 to Windows XP Professional. The computer is connected to the Internet using a cable modem. The upgrade went fine, but he noticed that the Web pages that he sees in Internet Explorer do not always seem to be up to date. What do you suspect is the problem?

   A. The Temporary Internet Files folder is full.

   B. The Temporary Internet Files settings are not configured to check for newer versions of stored pages.

   C. Internet Explorer is configured to use a dial-up connection instead of a LAN connection.

   D. The network adapter or cable modem is malfunctioning.

   Answer B is correct. On the General tab of the Internet Options dialog box, click Settings. On the Settings dialog box that opens, configure Internet Explorer to check for newer versions of pages more often. Answer A is not correct because a full Temporary Internet Files folder would not cause this problem. Answer C is not correct because using a dial-up connection would not cause the described problem. Instead, it would prevent Internet Explorer from accessing the Internet at all. Answer D is not correct because a malfunctioning network adapter or cable modem would not cause the described problem. Instead, it would prevent Internet Explorer from accessing the Internet at all.

Case Scenario Exercises: Scenario 11.1

Page 11-33
A customer calls and tells you that she recently got a new broadband DSL connection to the Internet. When the service person came to hook it up, everything was working fine, but whenever the customer opens Internet Explorer, Windows attempts to dial into her old ISP using her standard modem. The customer does not want to disable the standard modem or remove her dial-up network connection because she is not certain how reliable her new DSL connection will be. She does want Internet Explorer to automatically use her new DSL connection when she accesses the Internet. What should you tell this customer to do?

> The customer's best option is to set up Internet Explorer so that it uses the dial-up connection only when the DSL connection is not available, making the dial-up connection an automatic backup connection. On the Connections tab of the Internet Options dialog box, select the modem connection and then select the Dial Whenever a Network Connection Is Not Present option. Tell the customer that when her cable modem connection is not functioning, Internet Explorer will automatically start her modem connection to her old ISP.

Case Scenario Exercises: Scenario 11.2

Page 11-34
A user reports that each time she accesses a particular website, she is inundated with content she does not want to see. She thinks that this might have to do with ActiveX, Java applets, or scripts running on the site. She reports that the site takes a long time to load, too. She wants to visit this site and only read the data; she has no interest in the other items on the site. You need to make this site available without making any changes to the default settings for the Internet zone. What should you do?

A. Add this site to the Local Intranet zone.

B. Add this site to the Trusted Sites zone.

C. Add this site to the Restricted Sites zone.

> Answer C is correct. Adding sites to the Restricted Sites zone disables features such as ActiveX controls and Java. Answers A and B are incorrect because these zones do not restrict websites; they do just the opposite.

Troubleshooting Lab

Page
11-34
You are working for a company that provides computer support for several small businesses. You get a call from a user who complains that when she tries to send an e-mail message from within Internet Explorer, it creates a new message using Outlook Express. However, she uses Outlook as her e-mail software. She wants you to configure Internet Explorer so that she can create a message by using Outlook. After talking with her for a few more minutes, you also find that she wants the following programs to be configured to work within Internet Explorer:

- HTML editor: Notepad

- E-mail client: Hotmail

- Newsgroup reader: Outlook Express

- Internet call: NetMeeting

- Calendar: Microsoft Office Outlook

- Contact list: Address Book

How would you configure these programs within Internet Explorer?

You should configure these programs on the Programs tab of the Internet Options dialog box, shown in Figure 11-14.

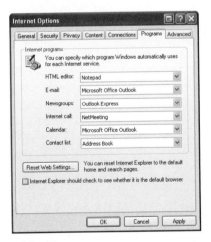

Figure 11-14   Use the Programs tab of the Internet Options dialog box to configure the programs that Internet Explorer uses.

12 Monitoring System Performance in Windows XP

Exam Objectives in this Chapter:

- Monitor and analyze system performance
    - ❑ Answer end-user questions that are related to system performance
    - ❑ Use Help And Support to view and troubleshoot system performance
    - ❑ Use Task Manager to view and troubleshoot system performance
    - ❑ Use the Performance tool to capture system performance information

Why This Chapter Matters

As a desktop support technician (DST), one of your responsibilities is to help users keep their computer running well and to troubleshoot performance problems when they occur. This chapter covers basic measures that you can take to improve operating system performance. It also covers the two major tools that Windows XP provides for monitoring and troubleshooting performance: **Task Manager** and the **Performance tool**.

Lessons in this Chapter:

Before You Begin

Before you begin this chapter, you should have experience working in a Microsoft Windows operating system and a working knowledge of the Microsoft Windows XP interface. You should also have a computer running Windows XP on which you can experiment with changing various settings.

Lesson 1: Configuring Windows XP for Performance

As a DST, you should be able to configure the Windows XP operating system to optimize performance. Windows XP provides a number of methods for increasing actual system performance and the perceived performance to the user.

After this lesson, you will be able to

- Optimize Windows startup.
- Stop unnecessary background applications.
- Optimize hard drive performance.
- Turn off Fast User Switching.
- Disable visual effects to increase performance.
- Configure advanced performance options.

Estimated lesson time: 25 minutes

Optimizing Windows Startup

After you first install Windows XP, the operating system begins to automatically optimize system settings to speed up subsequent startups. Similarly, Windows XP optimizes program files so that applications launch more quickly as you use them. For this reason, you should allow a sufficient number of restarts and launches to let Windows perform these configurations before deciding whether you need to optimize the performance of a computer.

Windows startup is fairly complicated (and you can learn the details about the Windows startup process in Chapter 2, "Installing Windows XP"), but there are many ways that you can optimize the process for a quicker startup time:

- Check the basic input/output system (BIOS) settings for your computer to see if there are unnecessary actions that you can eliminate from the startup process. For example, on many computers, you can skip the memory check that occurs when you turn on your computer—something that can take quite some time when you have a lot of memory.

- If a computer is configured with multiple operating systems, you can reduce the amount of time that Windows displays the menu of operating system choices at startup. Configure this setting by opening Control Panel, selecting the Advanced tab, and then clicking Settings in the Startup And Recovery section.

- Remove any unnecessary applications that start automatically with Windows. Preventing applications from starting with Windows is covered in the section called "Removing Unnecessary Background Applications," later in this lesson.

- When you remove a hardware device from your computer, make sure that you also remove any drivers and software that were installed with the device. You can learn more about working with hardware devices in Chapter 6, "Installing and Managing Hardware."

Removing Unnecessary Background Applications

Many applications install software that runs in the background as you use Windows. Normally, this software is a useful piece of the application, such as the monitor that allows your antivirus software to check files for viruses during download. Often, this software is a program that you could easily live without. When this is the case, it is best to prevent the software from loading with Windows so that the software does not consume system resources.

You can sometimes tell what background programs are running because the programs are represented by icons in the notification area, but this is not always the case. Even if there is an icon present, turning off different programs usually requires different steps, depending on the program.

To prevent unnecessary background applications from running, try the following:

- If there is an icon in the notification area, right-click or click the icon to see if a menu opens. Often, there is a command for setting preferences that you can use to figure out how to prevent the program from loading when Windows starts. You can learn more about the notification area in Chapter 4, "Supporting the Windows Desktop."

- If there is no menu for the icon, check the Startup folder on the Start menu. Often, programs place shortcuts here to load components at Windows startup. You can also try running the program that is associated with the icon to see if there are instructions for preventing the program from loading.

- You should also check the Startup folder for applications that load, but do not place an icon in the notification area.

Windows also includes the System Configuration Utility, which you can use to control Windows startup. Run the program by typing **msconfig** at the Run dialog box or command prompt. The System Configuration Utility, shown in Figure 12-1, contains many tabs that you can use to configure different aspects of the startup process, including the following:

- **General**   Use the General tab to select a type of startup to use the next time that Windows starts. A diagnostic startup is the same thing as starting Windows XP in safe mode. A selective startup allows you to choose which types of components should be loaded (represented by the other tabs on the utility).

- **SYSTEM.INI, WIN.INI, BOOT.INI** These tabs allow you to control the system files that Windows XP uses primarily for compatibility with previous versions of Windows. In earlier versions of Windows, these files were used instead of a centralized system Registry. Turning items on and off by using the tabs is generally safer than editing these files directly.

- **Services** This tab presents a list of services that load with Windows. Although you can use this tab to prevent services from loading, it is much safer (and just as easy) to use the Services node in the Computer Management window.

- **Startup** This is probably the most important tab used for optimizing Windows startup. It presents a list of all program components that load with Windows, whether or not they are represented in the notification area or not. Turn off the programs you do not want to load and restart Windows. You can return and reselect the applications whenever you want.

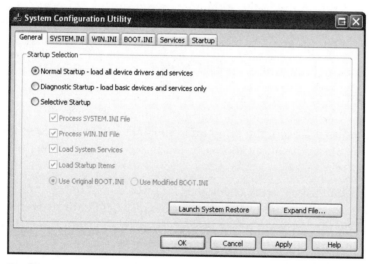

Figure 12-1 Use the System Configuration Utility to control Windows startup.

Optimizing Hard Disk Performance

Many of the functions in Windows XP rely on having enough disk space free to operate, including Windows' virtual memory system and programs that need to create temporary files, to name just two of the most important. In addition, almost every function in Windows relies on quick hard disk access. Windows includes a number of utilities that can help you optimize hard disk performance, including the following:

- **Disk Cleanup Wizard** Scans your hard disk, looking for files that can be safely removed, helping you to free up disk space.

- **Disk Defragmenter**   Rearranges the data on your hard drive so that files are written to disk contiguously. During the defragmentation, it also places more frequently used files toward the front of the disk so that they load faster.

- **Chkdsk**   Scans the files and directory structure of your disk to make sure that they are free of errors.

You can find details on using each of these utilities in Chapter 8, "Supporting Storage Devices in Windows XP."

> **Note**   Disk Defragmenter does not provide a built-in way to schedule the automatic defragmentation of a drive, which is a major selling point of many third-party defragmentation programs. However, with a small Visual Basic script and the Windows Task Scheduler, you can set up an automated defragmentation schedule quickly and easily. The script and instructions for its use are included in the Tools folder on the CD included with this book.

Turning Off Fast User Switching

Fast User Switching in Windows XP allows users to switch between different user accounts without logging off. Each user can even have his own applications running while another user uses the computer. Although this feature presents obvious advantages, it also comes with an equally obvious disadvantage. The more applications that your computer runs at the same time, the slower the computer will perform, regardless of whether those applications are run by one or multiple users. If users frequently have problems with other users leaving applications running, and if this situation tends to slow down the computer, suggest that users turn off the Fast User Switching feature. You can learn more about Fast User Switching in Chapter 3, "Supporting Local Users and Groups."

> **Exam Tip**   When a user who is *not* in a domain environment (especially in a home where multiple home users might use the same computer) complains that a computer performs slowly at some times and performs fine at other times, Fast User Switching is a likely candidate for the problem.

Disabling Visual Effects

Many of the new visual effects that are available in Windows XP can slow the perceived performance of a computer by making dialog boxes, windows, and menus take longer to open and work with. By default, Windows enables visual effects based on the capabilities of a computer, but you can enable or disable specific visual effects to strike your own balance between performance and appearance.

Windows XP provides quick access for enabling and disabling visual effects. From the Start menu, right-click My Computer and then choose Properties. In the System Properties dialog box, on the Advanced tab, click Settings in the Performance section to open the Performance Options dialog box, shown in Figure 12-2.

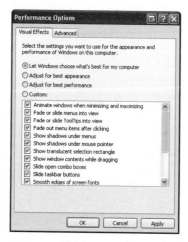

Figure 12-2 Use the Performance Options dialog box to disable unnecessary visual effects.

You can choose from the four options for visual effects:

- Let Windows Choose What's Best For My Computer
- Adjust For Best Appearance, which enables all the effects
- Adjust For Best Performance, which disables all the effects
- Custom, which allows you to enable and disable the effects yourself

Table 12-1 lists the visual effects along with descriptions of those that are not self-explanatory.

Table 12-1 Windows XP Visual Effects

Visual Effect	Description
Animate windows when minimizing and maximizing	Causes a zoom effect when you minimize or maximize a window. Disabling this effect makes windows minimize and maximize faster.
Fade or slide menus into view	Causes menus to fade or slide into view instead of simply appearing. Disabling this effect makes menus appear more quickly.

Table 12-1   Windows XP Visual Effects

Visual Effect	Description
Fade or slide ToolTips into view	Causes ToolTips to fade or slide into view instead of simply appearing. ToolTips are the pop-up descriptions that appear beside certain items when you hold your pointer over them. Disabling this effect makes ToolTips appear more quickly.
Fade out menu items after clicking	Causes menus to fade out after you select a command. Disabling this effect makes menus disappear instantly after selecting a command.
Show shadows under menus	Causes Windows to display a drop shadow behind menus for a three-dimensional effect. Disabling this effect makes menus appear more quickly.
Show shadows under mouse pointer	Causes Windows to display a drop shadow behind the mouse pointer. Disabling this effect can make the mouse more responsive. Also, some older applications do not work well when this feature is enabled.
Show translucent selection rectangle	Draws a filled-in rectangle when selecting multiple items on the desktop instead of just a rectangle outline. Disabling this effect slightly increases the speed with which you can select items.
Show window contents while dragging	Causes Windows to redraw a window while the window is being moved. Disabling this command makes dragging open windows noticeably faster.
Slide open combo boxes	Causes combo boxes to slide open instead of simply appear. A combo box is a drop-down list of items that you open from within a dialog box. Disabling this effect makes combo boxes appear more quickly.
Slide taskbar buttons	Causes taskbar buttons to slide to the left when other programs are closed or to the right when new programs are opened. Disabling this effect makes taskbar buttons appear instantly in the new location instead of sliding. Disabling this effect makes taskbar buttons available more quickly when they change locations.
Smooth edges of screen fonts	Makes screen fonts easier to read, especially at higher resolutions. Disabling this effect increases the speed at which Windows displays windows and dialog boxes.

Table 12-1   Windows XP Visual Effects

Visual Effect	Description
Smooth-scroll list boxes	Causes the contents of a list box to scroll smoothly when you click the scroll bar rather than just jump down a few items in the list. Disabling this effect makes scrolling list boxes faster, but often disorienting.
Use a background image for each folder type	Different types of folders in Windows XP can use different background images. Many of the special Windows folders, such as Control Panel, make use of this effect.
Use common tasks in folders	Causes folders in Windows to display a task pane on the left side of the folder. The task pane lists tasks that are related to the files in the folder.
Use drop shadows for icon labels on the desktop	Creates a transparency effect on text labels for icons, but this transparency really only allows you to see any other icons obscured by an icon on top. The transparency does not allow you to "see through" to the actual desktop background. Disabling this effect causes Windows to display the desktop more quickly.
Use visual styles on windows and buttons	This setting is an important one in that it controls the new look of Windows XP. If you disable it, your desktop will look like previous versions of Windows.

Managing Virtual Memory Paging Files

Like most modern operating systems, Windows XP uses virtual memory, which is created by extending the physical memory assigned to an application to the computer's hard drive. Windows can assign some memory to an application, but not necessarily enough to satisfy all that application's needs. Instead, Windows monitors memory access and continuously reorganizes memory structure to meet applications' needs. By correctly anticipating applications' needs, and by storing pages of memory to hard disk as necessary, Windows uses virtual memory to allow a computer to operate with less physical memory.

When Windows stores memory to hard disk, it uses a special file called a **paging file**. You can configure some aspects that relate to how Windows uses the paging file by using the Virtual Memory dialog box, shown in Figure 12-3. To open the Virtual Memory dialog box, follow these steps:

1. From the Start menu, right-click My Computer and select Properties.

2. In the System Properties dialog box, on the Advanced tab, click the Settings button in the Performance section.

3. In the Performance Options dialog box, on the Advanced tab, click Change.

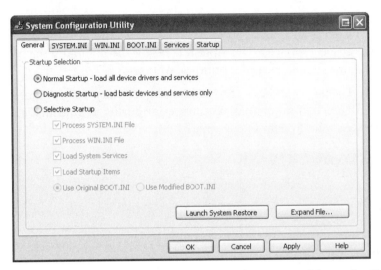

Figure 12-3   Use the Virtual Memory dialog box to control the paging file.

The Virtual Memory dialog box shows the size of the paging file for each disk on a computer and the total paging file size for all the drives combined. The files on all disks are combined and treated as a single area for paging memory to disk. Breaking the paging file up across multiple disks (especially disks on different disk controllers) can decrease the time it takes to write memory information to the paging file. Note, however, that breaking up a file across multiple volumes on the same hard disk can actually decrease the performance of the paging file.

For the most part, Windows does a good job of managing the size of the file itself. Unless you have a good reason for changing the paging file, you should probably just leave it alone. However, if possible, you want to avoid having your paging file on the same disk as your system files.

Exam Tip   You can increase performance by storing the virtual memory paging file on a different physical disk from the Windows system files.

Setting Advanced Performance Options

The Advanced tab of the Performance Options dialog box, shown in Figure 12-4, also contains two other performance options for configuring a computer to run under special circumstances. These options are the following:

■ **Processor Scheduling** By default, Windows optimizes the use of the processor for running programs. You can set this option to optimize the processor for running background services. This option is best if the computer that you are configuring is acting mainly as a file, print, or Web server.

■ **Memory Usage** Windows also optimizes memory for running programs by default. If the computer that you are configuring is running mainly services instead, select the System Cache option.

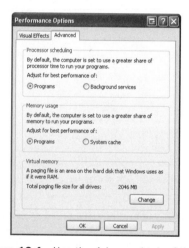

Figure 12-4 Use the Advanced tab of the Performance Options dialog box to adjust processor scheduling and memory usage.

Practice: Configure Visual Effects

In this practice, you configure visual effects on a computer running Windows XP for best appearance and for best performance.

1. From the Start menu, select Control Panel.

2. In Control Panel, select Performance And Maintenance.

3. In the Performance And Maintenance window, select System.

4. In the System Properties dialog box, on the Advanced tab, in the Performance section, click Settings.

5. In the Performance Options dialog box, on the Visual Effects tab, select Adjust For Best Appearance. Click OK.

6. Spend some time opening windows and dialog boxes, starting programs, and configuring options in Windows.

7. Return to the Advanced tab of the System Properties dialog box and, in the Performance section, click Settings.

8. In the Performance Options dialog box, on the Visual Effects tab, select Adjust For Best Performance. Click OK.

9. Perform the same types of actions you performed in Step 6 and see whether you can tell a difference in the perceived performance of your computer.

10. Return to the Advanced tab of the System Properties dialog box and, in the Performance section, click Settings.

11. In the Performance Options dialog box, on the Visual Effects tab, select Custom and then adjust the individual visual effects to best suit your needs. Click OK to return to the System Properties dialog box, and then click OK again.

Lesson Review

The following questions are intended to reinforce key information presented in this lesson. If you are unable to answer a question, review the lesson materials and try the question again. You can find answers to the questions in the "Questions and Answers" section at the end of this chapter.

1. List some common measures that you can take to help improve startup performance.

_____

_____

_____

_____

_____

2. Which of the following tools can you use to control the Windows startup process?

   A. System Information

   B. System Configuration Utility

   C. Chkdsk

   D. Virtual Memory

Lesson Summary

- After you first install Windows XP, the operating system begins to automatically optimize system settings to improve subsequent startup times. After letting Windows start up several times, you can judge and then try to improve the startup performance.

- Many applications install software that runs in the background as you use Windows. You can sometimes tell which background programs are running because they are represented by icons in the notification area, but this is not always the case. Even if there is an icon present, turning the program off usually requires different steps, depending on the program.

- Many of the functions in Windows XP rely on having enough disk space free to operate, including Windows' virtual memory system and programs that need to create temporary files. Make sure to use Disk Cleanup, Disk Defragmenter, and Chkdsk regularly.

- Many of the new visual effects in Windows XP can slow the perceived performance of a computer by making dialog boxes, windows, and menus take longer to open and work with.

Lesson 2: Monitoring Windows XP Performance

In addition to configuring Windows XP for optimal performance, you can also use two tools to monitor performance and troubleshoot performance problems. Task Manager provides a real-time view of certain performance measures, such as the current load on a processor and current memory usage. The Performance tool is a more sophisticated performance-monitoring utility that captures many different types of performance data and allows you to display that data as a graph or save it to a log.

After this lesson, you will be able to

- Use Task Manager to view real-time performance data.
- Use the Performance tool to capture and view performance data.

Estimated lesson time: 30 minutes

Monitoring Performance by Using Task Manager

Task Manager provides information about applications and processes that are currently running on a computer and provides real-time performance information about the processor, memory, and network usage. You can start Task Manager in the following ways:

- Right-click any open area on the Windows taskbar and select Task Manager.
- Press CTRL+ALT+DELETE.
- Press CTRL+SHIFT+ESCAPE.

The two tabs in the Task Manager window that measure performance are the Performance tab and the Networking tab.

Monitoring Processor and Memory Performance

The Performance tab, shown in Figure 12-5, has four gauges that indicate various aspects of system performance:

- **CPU Usage**   Indicates the percentage of processor cycles that are not idle at the moment. If this graph displays a high percentage continuously (and not when there is an obvious reason, such as a big application), your processor may be overloaded. If your computer has two processors, two graphs are shown. If this value runs continuously over 80 percent, you might need to upgrade your processor.

- **PF Usage**   Indicates the percentage of the paging file that is currently being used. If this value runs near 100 percent continuously, you might need to increase the size of the paging file or decide whether you need more memory.

- **CPU Usage History**   Indicates how busy the processor has been recently, although the gauge shows values only after Task Manager was opened. You can use the Update Speed command on the View menu to specify how often the values are refreshed. The High value updates about twice per second; Normal value updates once every two seconds; Low value updates once every four seconds. You can also pause the updates and update the view manually by pressing F5. This is a useful method if you want to monitor some specific activity.

- **Page File Usage History**   Indicates how full the page file has been over time, although it also shows values only after Task Manager was opened. Values that are set using the Update Speed command affect this history as well.

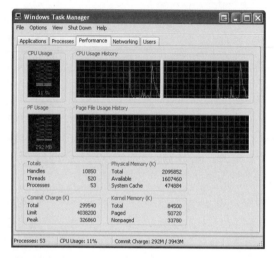

Figure 12-5   The Performance tab of Task Manager shows real-time processor and memory usage.

> **Exam Tip**   If the sustained processor usage exceeds 80 percent, the processor is probably a performance bottleneck on the computer. If the page file usage value runs near 100 percent continuously, you might need to increase the size of the page file or add more memory to the computer.

In addition to displaying these four graphs, the Performance tab also displays the following sections:

- **Totals**   Provides totals for the number of processes, threads, and handles that are currently running. A process is a single executable program. A thread is an object within a process that runs program instructions. A handle represents a specific input/output (I/O) instance. A process may have multiple threads, each of which in turn may have multiple handles.

- **Physical Memory (K)**   Indicates the total and available physical memory, and the amount of memory in the system cache.

- **Commit Charge (K)**   Indicates the memory that is currently committed to running processes.

- **Kernel Memory (K)**   Indicates the memory that is used by the operating system. Paged kernel memory is available only to system processes. Nonpaged kernel memory can be used by applications when necessary.

Monitoring Network Activity

The Networking tab in Task Manager, shown in Figure 12-6, indicates the current network traffic on various network connections on the computer. You can use this information to quickly determine if the network is causing a bottleneck that would result in performance problems for applications that require network connectivity. The detailed information at the bottom of the tab displays current network utilization and link speed for each enabled adapter.

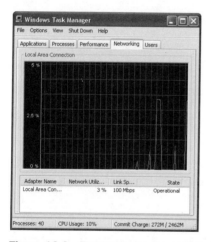

Figure 12-6   The Networking tab of Task Manager shows current network activity.

Monitoring Performance by Using the Performance Tool

When troubleshooting performance issues, you may need more detail than Task Manager provides. If so, you can use the Performance tool to collect vast amounts of performance information. In addition to providing access to more detailed information, the Performance tool allows you to monitor other systems remotely, log information for future analysis, and configure alerts to notify you of potential error conditions.

The Performance tool classifies information in the following areas:

■ **Object**   An object represents a major system component (hardware or software) of the computer or operating system. Examples of objects include physical disks, processor, and memory.

■ **Instance**   Each occurrence of an object is considered an instance. For example, if there are two processors on a computer, there are two processor instances. If there are three hard disks on a computer, each disk is represented by a separate instance.

■ **Counter**   A counter is a particular aspect of an object that the Performance tool can measure. For example, the physical disk object contains the following counters:

   ❏ Percentage Disk Read Time

   ❏ Average Disk Bytes Per Read

   ❏ Disk Reads Per Second

To start the Performance tool, follow these steps:

1. From the Start menu, select Control Panel.

2. In Control Panel, select Performance And Maintenance.

3. In the Performance And Maintenance window, select Administrative Tools.

4. In the Administrative Tools window, select Performance.

When you first start the Performance tool, the graph displays three counters by default (as shown in Figure 12-7):

■ **Pages/sec**   Represents the rate at which pages are read from or written to disk during virtual memory operations. Consistently high values can indicate that not enough memory is present on a system.

■ **Avg. Disk Queue Length**   Represents the average number of read and write requests queued for the selected disk. Consistent values above zero mean that requests are backing up, which may indicate inadequate memory or a slow disk system.

■ **%Processor Time**   Represents the percentage of elapsed time that the processor spends executing nonidle tasks. Consistently high values (over approximately 80 percent) might indicate that your processor is slowing down your system.

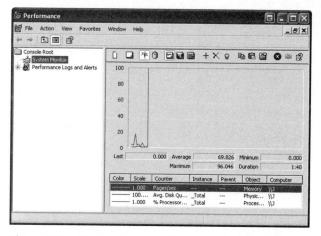

Figure 12-7   The Performance Tool starts working right away.

The three default counters actually do a very good job of representing the basic aspects of a computer's performance. Of course, they are only three of the hundreds of counters that are available in the Performance tool. The counters that you monitor depend on whether you are trying to collect general baseline information, troubleshoot a performance problem, diagnose an issue with an application, and so on. Detailed information on commonly monitored objects and counters is presented later in this section.

To add a counter to the Performance tool, follow these steps:

1. Right-click the graph and select Add Counters.

2. In the Add Counters dialog box, shown in Figure 12-8, select the computer that you want to monitor.

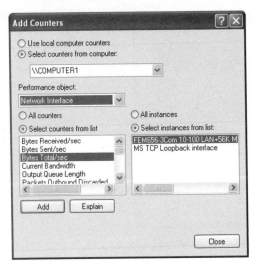

Figure 12-8 Select a counter to add to the Performance tool graph.

3. Select the appropriate Performance Object.

4. Select All Counters or a specific counter from the list. You can use the SHIFT and CTRL keys to select multiple counters. Click Explain for an explanation of any counter.

5. Select All Instances or choose a specific instance of the object.

6. Click Add to add the counter.

7. Repeat Steps 3 through 7 as often as necessary to add all the desired counters.

8. Click Close to return to the Performance window.

In the Performance window, you can view counter data in the following formats:

■ As a graph, similar to the one shown in Figure 12-7.

■ As a histogram, similar to the one shown in Figure 12-9.

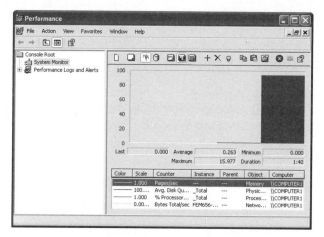

Figure 12-9   A histogram represents values as vertical bars.

■ As a report, such as the one shown in Figure 12-10.

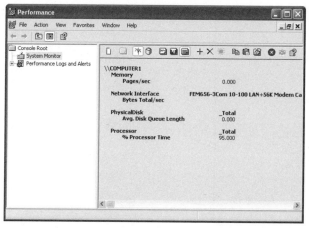

Figure 12-10   A report displays values as simple text.

To change the view, right-click the current view, select Properties, and access the General tab.

Performance Logs and Alerts

The **Performance Logs And Alerts** utility allows you to log counter information to a file and to trigger alerts that are based on configured events. This utility contains three subsections:

- **Counter Logs** Log activity for selected counters at regular intervals

- **Trace Logs** Log activity for selected counters when a particular event occurs

- **Alerts** Log activity and can notify a user when a particular counter exceeds a certain threshold

You can view and analyze performance logs by using the Performance tool or an external data-analysis program such as Microsoft Excel.

To enable performance logging, follow these steps:

1. In the Performance window, expand Performance Logs And Alerts.

2. Right-click Counter Logs and select New Log Settings.

3. In the New Log Settings dialog box, enter the name for the log and click OK.

4. On the General tab, shown in Figure 12-11, add the counters that you want to log. Modify the sampling interval, if necessary.

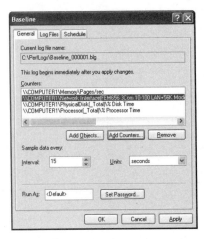

Figure 12-11   Configure general log properties.

5. On the Log Files tab, you can modify the name and location of the log file, as well as the type of file, if desired.

6. On the Schedule tab, shown in Figure 12-12, configure the start and stop times for logging. You can manually stop and start logging or configure logging to start and stop at specified times.

Figure 12-12 Configure log-scheduling properties.

7. Click OK to save the log configuration.

After you create a log, you can load the log into the Performance tool and view it the same way you would view real-time performance data. To view a performance log, follow these steps:

1. In the Performance window, select System Monitor, right-click the data display, and then select Properties.

2. In the System Monitor Properties dialog box, on the Source tab, select Log Files, as shown in Figure 12-13. Click Add and enter the name of the log file that you want to view. Click OK to continue.

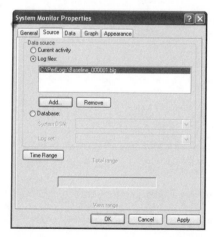

Figure 12-13 Choose the log file to view in System Monitor.

3. Right-click the data display and then select Add Counters.

4. Add the counters that you want to view and then click OK. The available counters are limited to those that are present in the log.

In addition to other monitoring techniques, you can use alerts to notify users or administrators when conditions exceed preset criteria. For example, you can configure an alert to send a message to the administrator when processor utilization exceeds 80 percent.

When an alert is triggered, you can perform the following actions:

- Log an entry in the application event log. This option is enabled by default.
- Send a network message to a particular user.
- Start a performance log that can further monitor the alert condition.
- Run a program that can be used to launch any application program. You can use this option to launch a script that would send e-mail to the administrator.

To configure an alert, follow these steps:

1. In the Performance window, expand Performance Logs And Alerts.

2. Right-click the Alerts folder and select New Alert Settings.

3. Enter a name for the alert and click OK.

4. On the General tab, add the counter(s) and the alert value, as shown in Figure 12-14.

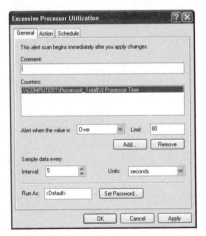

Figure 12-14 Configure an alert to warn you when counters cross performance thresholds.

5. On the Action tab, configure the action(s) to be performed when an alert is triggered.

6. On the Schedule tab, configure the start and stop times for when the alert should be scanned. You can turn scanning on and off manually or configure scanning to occur on a schedule.

7. Click OK to create the alert.

> **Real World   Establishing a Baseline of Performance Data**
>
> It is important to establish a **baseline**, or reference point, of performance data at a time when the computer has adequate resources and is performing well. Having a baseline for comparison is necessary to identify changes in resource usage if computer performance begins to decline.
>
> You establish a baseline by monitoring key counters for an extended period of time—several days to a week is generally adequate. Use the logging feature to gather baseline information. As you analyze your baseline logs, you will notice spikes and dips in the recorded values, but do not focus on them. Instead, look at the averages, identify trends, and define acceptable ranges for each of the counters. When constructing a baseline, use just a few important counters for the disk, memory, and processor objects.

Important Memory Counters

You can detect memory bottlenecks by monitoring and evaluating several important physical memory, paging file, and file system cache counters. Table 12-2 contains a listing of these counters and brief descriptions.

Table 12-2   Important Memory-Related Counters

Object	Counter	Description
Memory	Pages/sec	The number of pages that were either read from disk or written to disk to make room in physical memory for other pages. This counter is the primary indicator of whether the computer has sufficient memory. An average value in excess of 20 can indicate insufficient memory in the computer.
Memory	Available Bytes	Amount of physical memory that is unallocated in the computer. Does not include any memory that is allocated to working sets or file system cache.
Paging File	% Usage	Percentage of the paging file that is currently in use.
Paging File	% Usage Peak (bytes)	Peak percentage of the paging file in use.
Cache	Copy Read Hits %	The percentage of time that information was found in the file system cache and did not have to be read from disk.

Important Processor Counters

Monitoring and evaluating several important counters allow you to detect processor bottlenecks. Table 12-3 contains a listing of these counters and brief descriptions.

Table 12-3 Important Processor-Related Counters

Object	Counter	Description
Processor	% Processor Time	The percent of time that the processor is processing information (processing a nonidle thread). This counter is the primary indicator of processor activity. Sustained values over 80 percent indicate a potential processor bottleneck.
Processor	Interrupts/sec	The average rate per second that the process handles interrupt requests from applications and hardware devices. This counter indicates the activity of the devices in a computer that uses interrupts. When a computer is idle, values average around 100. Averages in excess of 300 indicate a potential problem.
System	Processor Queue Length	Number of threads in the processor queue, waiting to be processed. This counter is a true indicator of processor efficiency. If this counter averages two or more, it indicates that the processor cannot keep up with the number of requests for processing and has become a bottleneck.
System	Context Switches	Rate at which the processor is switched from one thread to another. If this value is high (that is, more than 500), you may have an inefficient application that uses too many threads or a problem with a device driver.
Process	% Processor Time	The percent of processor time used by all the threads of a particular process.

Important Disk Counters

Before you can effectively manage disk concerns in Windows XP, you need to be aware of the following concepts:

- **Physical disk** A physical disk corresponds to a hard disk in the system. If there are two hard disks in a computer, it has two physical disks. Monitoring a physical disk gives an overall indicator of hard disk performance.

- **Logical disk** A logical disk is a volume on a physical disk. A physical disk can have multiple logical disks. Monitoring a logical disk gives an indicator of how often that volume is being accessed by applications or how much disk space is available on that volume.

- **Disk reads** A disk read operation occurs when the operating system requests information from the disk. After information is read from the disk, it can be stored in file system cache. On a system with sufficient memory to support file system caching, the number of disk reads should be relatively low because most read requests are serviced from cache (fast reads).

- **Disk writes** A disk write operation occurs when the operating system receives a request to save data to the hard disk. Windows XP supports write-behind caching, which permits the operating system to gather many disk write requests together and write them to the disk simultaneously, reducing the overall number of disk writes performed.

- **Disk queue** The disk queue is where disk read and write requests are stored while waiting to be processed by the hard disk. The more requests waiting in the queue, the more difficulty the disk has meeting the computer's needs.

You can detect disk bottlenecks by monitoring and evaluating several important physical and logical disk counters. Physical disk counters provide information on the activity of a hard disk as a whole. Logical disk counters report statistics on the volumes (drive letters) that are created on the disks. Table 12-4 lists and briefly describes these counters.

Table 12-4 Important Disk-Related Counters

Object	Counter	Description
Logical Disk	% Free Space	Ratio of free disk space that is available to total usable disk space on a particular logical disk.
Physical Disk	% Disk Time	The percentage of time that the selected physical disk is busy servicing read or write requests. If this value is consistently over 50 percent, the hard disk is having trouble keeping up with the load that is being placed on it.
Logical Disk Physical Disk	Disk Bytes/sec	The rate at which bytes are being transferred. The higher the number, the better the disk is performing.

Table 12-4   Important Disk-Related Counters

Object	Counter	Description
Logical Disk Physical Disk	Avg. Disk Bytes/Transfer	Measures the size of I/O operations. A higher value indicates more efficient disk usage.
Physical Disk	Avg. Disk Queue Length	The average number of both read and write requests that are queued for the selected disk. If this value averages two or more, the disk is a bottleneck.

Lesson Review

The following questions are intended to reinforce key information presented in this lesson. If you are unable to answer a question, review the lesson materials and try the question again. You can find answers to the questions in the "Questions and Answers" section at the end of this chapter.

1. Which of the following pieces of information can you view by using Task Manager?

    A. Current CPU usage

    B. The percentage of time that a physical disk is busy

    C. The amount of available physical memory

    D. The percentage of the paging file currently in use

2. You are using the Performance tool to monitor the performance of a user's computer. You notice that the processor regularly averages over 80 percent utilization when the computer is used normally. You also notice that the Pages/sec counter for the memory object averages around 4. What does this indicate to you?

    A. The processor is a potential bottleneck.

    B. The physical disk is a potential bottleneck.

    C. The memory is a potential bottleneck.

    D. This value is within the acceptable range for normal computer use.

Lesson Summary

- Task Manager provides information about applications and processes currently running on a computer and provides real-time performance information about processor, memory, and network usage.

- You can use the Performance tool to collect more detailed performance information than Task Manager provides. In addition, the Performance tool allows you to monitor other systems remotely, log information for future analysis, and configure alerts to notify you of potential error conditions.

- In the Performance tool, an object represents a major computer component. An instance represents an occurrence of an object. A counter represents a particular aspect of an object that you can measure directly.

Case Scenario Exercises

Scenario 12.1

You receive a call from a user who recently upgraded her computer from Microsoft Windows 98 to Windows XP Professional. After the upgrade, the computer's performance has decreased, and it is functioning at unacceptably slow levels when running resource-intensive applications. The computer is configured as follows:

- Processor: Pentium II/233 MHz

- RAM: 64 MB

- Hard disk: 4 GB EIDE

You start the Performance tool on the computer and configure it to monitor key memory, processor, and physical disk counters. You then launch the applications that are significantly degrading performance. The Performance tool records the following counter values during the test:

- Memory, Pages/sec: 107

- Processor, % Processor Time: 40%

- Physical Disk, % Disk Time: 67%

What is causing the computer performance problem, and how can you resolve it?

_____

_____

_____

_____

_____

_____

_____

Scenario 12.2

You receive a call from a user who reports that his computer seems to run more slowly than it used to. Upon further questioning, you suspect that the problem may not be hardware-based, but that the user probably needs to optimize the performance of his hard disk. What three actions would you suggest to the user for optimizing his hard disk before resorting to using the Performance tool to measure the computer's performance?

_____

_____

_____

_____

Troubleshooting Lab

In this lab, you optimize the performance on your computer by configuring settings in Windows XP. You then use the Performance tool to monitor system performance.

To perform this lab, follow these steps:

1. Check your computer for any unnecessary background applications that may be running, particularly in the notification area. Use the programs' interfaces or the Msconfig command to disable the unnecessary applications. Be careful when using Msconfig that you disable only applications that are truly unnecessary. When in doubt, do not disable an application. Also, you should disable only one application at a time so that you can gauge the effect on your computer.

2. Use Disk Cleanup to free up hard disk space on your computer.

3. Use the Chkdsk command to scan your hard disk for errors.

4. Use Disk Defragmenter to analyze and, if necessary, defragment your disk.

5. Use the Performance Options dialog box to disable any visual effects that you find unnecessary.

6. Start the Performance tool and log your computer's performance for at least four hours under normal usage using the following objects and counters:

   ❑ Memory: Pages/sec

   ❑ Paging File (_Total): % Usage

   ❑ Processor: %Processor Time

   ❑ System: Processor Queue Length

❑   Physical Disk: Disk Reads/sec

❑   Physical Disk: Disk Writes/sec

❑   Physical Disk: Avg. Disk Queue Length

Chapter Summary

■ After you first install Windows XP, the operating system begins to automatically optimize system settings to improve subsequent startup times. After letting Windows start up several times, you can judge and then try to improve the startup performance.

■ Many applications install software that runs in the background as you use Windows. You can sometimes tell what background programs are running because they are represented by icons in the notification area, but this is not always the case. Even if there is an icon present, turning the program off usually requires different steps, depending on the program.

■ Many of the functions in Windows XP rely on having enough disk space free to operate, including Windows' virtual memory system and programs that need to create temporary files. Make sure to use Disk Cleanup, Disk Defragmenter, and Chkdsk regularly.

■ Many of the new visual effects in Windows XP can slow the perceived performance of a computer by making dialog boxes, windows, and menus take longer to open and work with.

■ Task Manager provides information about applications and processes currently running on a computer and provides real-time performance information about processor, memory, and network usage.

■ You can use the Performance tool to collect more detailed performance information than Task Manager provides. In addition, the Performance tool allows you to monitor other computers remotely, log information for future analysis, and configure alerts to notify you of potential error conditions.

■ In the Performance tool, an object represents a major computer component. An instance represents an occurrence of an object. A counter represents a particular aspect of an object that you can measure directly.

Exam Highlights

Before taking the exam, review the key topics and terms that are presented in this chapter. You need to know this information.

Key Points

- When a user complains that a computer performs slowly at some times and performs fine at other times, check to see whether Fast User Switching is enabled. Each running application consumes computer resources, and users often forget to see whether other users have applications running.

- You can increase performance by storing the virtual memory paging file on a different physical disk than the Windows system files.

- If the sustained processor usage exceeds 80 percent, the processor is probably a performance bottleneck on the computer. If the page file usage value runs near 100 percent continuously, you may need to increase the size of the page file or add more memory to the computer.

Key Terms

baseline   A reference point normally associated with computer performance.

paging file (Pagefile.sys)   A section of hard disk space set aside to act as virtual memory; sometimes called a swap file.

Performance tool   A utility that captures performance information for various subsystems on a computer and displays the results graphically or logs the results to a file.

Task Manager   A utility that provides information on currently running applications and processes as well as basic performance and networking information.

Questions and Answers

Lesson 1 Review

Page
12-11

1. List some common measures that you can take to help improve startup performance.

Eliminate unnecessary actions that are performed by the BIOS when the computer starts up (such as memory testing). Reduce the amount of time Windows waits for you to choose an operating system if multiple operating systems are configured on the computer. Remove unnecessary applications that start with Windows. Remove hardware drivers and other associated software whenever you remove a hardware device from a computer.

2. Which of the following tools can you use to control the Windows startup process?

 A. System Information

 B. System Configuration Utility

 C. Chkdsk

 D. Virtual Memory

The correct answer is B. You can use the System Configuration Utility (which you can start by typing **msconfig** in the Run dialog box) to control the startup process. Answer A is not correct because System Information displays configuration information about a computer. Answer C is not correct because Chkdsk scans hard drives for errors. Answer D is not correct because Virtual Memory is not a tool, but a system Windows uses to augment the physical memory on a computer.

Lesson 2 Review

Page
12-26

1. Which of the following pieces of information can you view by using Task Manager?

 A. Current CPU usage

 B. The percentage of time that a physical disk is busy

 C. The amount of available physical memory

 D. The percentage of the paging file currently in use

The correct answers are A and C. Task Manager shows current information on CPU and memory usage. Answers B and D are not correct because you must use the Performance tool to monitor these values.

2. You are using the Performance tool to monitor the performance of a user's computer. You notice that the processor regularly averages over 80 percent utilization when the computer is used normally. You also notice that the Pages/sec counter for the memory object averages around 4. What does this indicate to you?

A. The processor is a potential bottleneck.

B. The physical disk is a potential bottleneck.

C. The memory is a potential bottleneck.

D. This value is within the acceptable range for normal computer use.

The correct answer is A. A sustained processor usage of over 80 percent typically indicates that the processor is a performance bottleneck. Answer B is not correct because this value does not indicate a disk bottleneck. Answer C is not correct because the Pages/sec value indicates that memory is probably not a bottleneck. Answer D is not correct because sustained processor usage values over 80 percent are not in the acceptable range.

Case Scenario Exercises: Scenario 12.1

Page 12-27

What is causing the computer performance problem, and how can you resolve it?

The performance statistics that you obtain by using the Performance tool indicate that the computer is experiencing a shortage of memory. The acceptable level of Pages/sec is under 20. At the current average rate of 107 Pages/sec, the operating system is spending a lot of time moving data in and out of physical memory and the paging file. Also, the % Disk Time statistic indicates a potential hard disk performance issue (67 percent, with an acceptable threshold of 50 percent). The hard disk could be a problem, but it is more likely that the increased paging is causing the hard disk to work much harder than it has to. Increasing the amount of memory in the computer decreases the load on the hard disk, which will most likely cause the % Disk Time counter to drop below the acceptable threshold. It is not surprising that the computer began to have performance problems after the operating system was upgraded. Windows XP requires a higher level of resources than Windows 98. Memory that was previously unused by the Windows 98 operating system and that was available for applications is now being used by Windows XP.

Case Scenario Exercises: Scenario 12.2

Page 12-28

You receive a call from a user who reports that his computer seems to run more slowly than it used to. Upon further questioning, you suspect that the problem may not be hardware-based, but that the user probably needs to optimize the performance of his hard disk. What three actions would you suggest to the user for optimizing his hard disk before resorting to using the Performance tool to measure the computer's performance?

First, the user should use the Chkdsk command to scan the hard disk for errors. Next, the user should use Disk Cleanup to scan the hard disk and locate files that he can safely remove. Finally, the user should run Disk Defragmenter to analyze the level of fragmentation on the hard disk and defragment the disk if necessary.

Part 2
Prepare for the Exam

13 Installing a Windows Desktop Operating System (1.0)

The Installing a Windows Desktop Operating System objective domain focuses on the installation and upgrading of the Microsoft Windows XP operating system. The exam covers three installation types: attended installation, unattended installation, and a Windows operating system upgrade.

As a desktop support technician (DST), you must understand how to install Microsoft Windows XP using the best method for your organization or the method the user requests. You should be comfortable installing the operating system when a user is available to answer setup configuration questions, such as Time Zone and Computer Name. Conversely, by using the unattended installation features available, you should be able to install the operating system when no one is available to answer the setup questions. Lastly, in many situations you will need to upgrade older Microsoft operating system versions to Windows XP Professional. You must be able to troubleshoot those installations that fail by evaluating the boot sequence and reviewing log files.

The Windows XP operating system is a robust and powerful operating system that contains many features. The first step in working with any operating system is being skillful in installing and configuring the system. Troubleshooting an operating system is a lot easier if you are aware of how to install all components.

Tested Skills and Suggested Practices

The skills that you need to successfully master the Installing a Windows Desktop Operating System objective domain on the Supporting Users and Troubleshooting a Microsoft Windows XP Operating System exam include the following:

- Perform and troubleshoot an attended installation of a Windows XP operating system.
    - ❑ Practice 1: Prepare a hard drive for installation using the Fdisk and Format commands, as well as the Windows XP Professional Setup utility. Understand the different file systems that can be configured on a partition or volume, and know when either FAT32 or NTFS should be used.

❑ Practice 2: Copy the Windows XP setup files to a network share. Then, update the setup files by creating an integrated installation with Windows XP Service Pack 2. This process is also known as slipstreaming.

❑ Practice 3: Install Microsoft Windows XP from CD-ROM, and understand the computer hardware requirements. Check for hardware compatibility by using the Microsoft Windows Catalog. Be sure you understand how to start the installation program from MS-DOS if you are installing Windows XP Professional on a computer that does not support a bootable CD-ROM drive. Change the boot order process for a PC using the basic input/output system (BIOS) interface.

❑ Practice 4: After completing the installation in Practice 3, install Windows XP Service Pack 2 on the computer.

❑ Practice 5: Review the steps you should take in troubleshooting a failed installation, and know where to go for assistance. Practice using the Help And Support Center, the Microsoft Knowledge Base, Windows XP newsgroups, and the Microsoft support site.

■ Perform and troubleshoot an unattended installation of a Windows desktop operating system.

❑ Practice 1: Install Windows XP Professional using the **winnt32.exe /unattend** command on a workstation that is running Windows 98. Be sure you understand that all Windows XP Professional configuration settings will be based on your Windows 98 settings, so you will not be prompted as you were when performing an attended installation.

■ Upgrade a previous version of Windows.

❑ Practice 1: Install Windows XP Professional on a computer running Windows 98. During the upgrade, pay close attention to the report that is created indicating possible problems that might occur with your current hardware or software configuration.

❑ Practice 2: Uninstall Windows XP Professional from the workstation you installed in Practice 1 using the Add Or Remove Programs utility in Control Panel. Be sure you understand that this feature is available when an upgrade is made from Windows 98. The uninstall feature returns the computer to its original state if the Windows XP Professional upgrade is unsuccessful.

Further Reading

This section lists supplemental readings by objective. Study these sources thoroughly before taking exam 70-271.

Objective 1.1   "Troubleshoot Windows XP" (available online at *http://www.microsoft.com/windowsxp/pro/using/howto/gettingstarted/guide/troubleshoot.asp*).

"Windows Catalog" (available online at *http://www.microsoft.com/windows/catalog*).

"Microsoft Windows XP Professional Resource Kit Documentation" by Microsoft Corporation (available online at *http://www.microsoft.com/resources/documentation/Windows/XP/all/reskit/en-us/prork_overview.asp*). In particular, look through Part I, "Deployment."

"How to Multiple Boot Windows XP, Windows 2000, Windows NT, Windows 95, Windows 98, Windows Me, and MS-DOS" by Microsoft Corporation (available online at *http://support.microsoft.com/default.aspx?kbid=217210*).

"How to Install or Upgrade to Windows XP" (available online at *http://support.microsoft.com/default.aspx/kb/316941*).

"How to Uninstall Windows XP and Revert to a Previous Operating System" by Microsoft Corporation (available online at *http://support.microsoft.com/default.aspx/kb/303661*).

"Windows XP Service Pack 2 Deployment Information" by Microsoft Corporation (available online at *http://www.microsoft.com/technet/prodtechnol/winxppro/deploy/xpsp2dep.mspx*).

"BDD with Service Pack 2: How Windows XP Service Pack 2 Affects the Solution Accelerator for Business Desktop Deployment Environment" by Jerry Honeycutt and Steve Campbell (available online at *http://www.microsoft.com/technet/itsolutions/cits/dsd/bdd/bddsp2.mspx*). Although you do not need to understand the details of how to create a deployment environment, it is very helpful to understand the deployment options and the overall deployment process.

Objective 1.2   "Microsoft Windows XP Professional Resource Kit Documentation," by Microsoft Corporation (available online at *http://www.microsoft.com/technet/prodtechnol/windowsserver2003/library/ServerHelp/82d599b9-cab8-485a-a914-9e876d6b1246.mspx*). In particular, look through Chapter 2, "Automating and Customizing Installations."

"Microsoft Solution Accelerator for Business Desktop Deployment" by Microsoft Corporation (available online at *http://www.microsoft.com/technet/desktopdeployment/bddoverview.mspx*). In particular, review "Computer Imaging System Feature Team Guide."

"Windows XP Professional Product Documentation" (available online at *http:// www.microsoft.com/resources/documentation/windows/xp/all/proddocs/en-us/ winnt32.mspx*).

Objective 1.3 "Description of Windows XP Upgrade Advisor" (available online at *http://support.microsoft.com/default.aspx/kb/307726*).

"How to Troubleshoot Windows XP Problems During Installation When You Upgrade from Windows 98 or Windows Me" (available online at *http://support.microsoft.com/ default.aspx/kb/310064*).

"How to Prepare to Upgrade Windows 98 or Windows Millennium Edition to Windows XP" (available online at *http://support.microsoft.com/default.aspx/kb/ 316639*).

Perform and Troubleshoot an Attended Installation of a Windows XP Operating System

As a DST, you should be able to install and troubleshoot an attended installation of Windows XP. Before starting the installation, always verify that the computer meets the Windows XP minimum hardware requirements. You should also be able to determine if a computer meets the hardware requirements for installation. It is important that you know how to create a partition and select the appropriate file system.

To answer the questions in this objective, you should know how to install Windows XP Professional from a CD as well as over a network. You should also know how to troubleshoot installation failures using a structured, troubleshooting methodology, as well as using the many available online resources.

After the installation is complete, you need to install software updates to protect the computer from security vulnerabilities. In particular, you should install Windows XP Service Pack 2. Note that many organizations test and approve patches before applying them to client computers. Therefore, you should verify that any patches you installed are appropriate for your environment.

Objective 1.1 Questions

1. You are a DST for a small computer security company. One of your customers has just purchased a custom-made computer from a small business that specializes in building custom computers. There is no operating system on the computer, so she wants you to perform a clean install of Windows XP Professional. The customer informs you that she attempted to load the operating system several times, but the installation failed on all occasions. You suspect that there might be a nonsupported device on the custom-built workstation that is causing the installation errors, but you are not sure which device. The user tells you that they want the installation done. What should you do? (Choose the best answer.)

   A. Remove any nonsupported devices to see if you can get past the installation error.

   B. Inform the user that you must stop the installation and continue when only supported hardware devices are present.

   C. Inform the user that Windows XP Professional cannot be installed on custom computers.

   D. The customer should have installed MS-DOS before installing Windows XP Professional because the new computer did not contain an operating system.

2. Which of the following are valid minimum hardware requirements for installing Windows XP Professional?

   A. 233 megahertz (MHz) processor

   B. 256 megabytes (MB) of RAM

   C. 1 gigabyte (GB) of hard-disk space

   D. Super VGA display (800 × 600 dots-per-inch resolution)

3. You are a DST for a large furniture distributor. On April 15, you installed 12 new computers with Windows XP Professional for the accounting department. The next month you were asked by the branch manager to install a customized accounting software package on all 25 Windows XP Professional workstations, which are located in the accounting department. You receive a telephone call from the branch manager on May 15, who says: "What did you do? Almost half of my staff is not able to start their Windows XP Professional workstations!" You verify that the accountants having the problems were using the workstations you installed in April. What is the most likely cause of this problem?

   A. The accountants who could not start their Windows XP workstations did not have the proper permissions.

B. The workstations that cannot start Windows XP have a boot sector virus.

C. The workstations that cannot start the Windows XP operating system were not activated within the required 30-day period.

D. The workstations that cannot start the Windows XP operating system are not using the NTFS file system.

4.   You are a DST for a help desk. You are installing Windows XP on a client's computer and choose Typical Setting as the installation option. The customer wants to know what the computer's default TCP/IP configuration will be. What will you tell the customer?

A. IP address 192.168.0.100, subnet mask 255.255.255.0.

B. IP address 192.168.0.100, subnet mask 255.255.255.0, default gateway 192.168.0.1.

C. There are no default settings. Windows XP will prompt the user to configure TCP/IP the first time the computer is booted.

D. Windows XP attempts to obtain an IP address automatically.

5.   You are a DST for a small law firm. You installed Windows XP in an office that has 35 computers that are all running Windows XP. After leaving the user's office, you immediately receive a telephone call from her claiming that she cannot connect to the Internet. All the other users are able to connect with no problem. You return to the user's office and type in the ipconfig command at her workstation and see the following IP configuration: IP address 169.254.101.1, subnet mask 255.255.0.0, and no IP address assigned for the default gateway. What could be a possible solution for this problem?

A. You should enter a valid IP address for the default gateway.

B. You should enter the **ipconfig /renew** command at the user's workstation to have TCP/IP configuration information sent to the workstation from the DHCP server.

C. You should configure the IP address for the DNS server.

D. You should contact the Internet service provider (ISP) that the company is using and notify it of the problem.

6.   You are a DST for a help desk. One of your customers has purchased a copy of Windows XP Professional to install on her home computer. You notice that the customer has a copy of Microsoft Flight Simulator on her desk, as well as a joy stick and several other game peripherals. The client tells you that she has several older games on her Windows 98 computer that she wants to continue to use, but that she wants Windows XP Professional to be used for important business applications and tax data because it is more secure. After looking at the configuration of the computer, you note that there are three partitions: C, D, and E. Partition C contains the Windows 98 operating system. Partition D contains games and miscellaneous applications, and partition E is empty. You decide to perform a multiple boot installation and install Windows XP on partition E. What file system should you choose for the user's workstation?

A. You should select FAT32 for all partitions because the user will dual boot between Windows 98 and Windows XP.

B. You should use the NTFS file system on all the partitions because the user is concerned about security.

C. You should run the Fdisk command on the hard drive and create a new partition on C:. You should then run the Format command on the partition and install the NTFS file system on all the partitions.

D. You should install Windows XP Professional on the E: partition and convert the FAT32 file system to NTFS.

7. You are a DST for a small retail company, and one of your customers asks you to install Windows XP Home Edition on his computer, which was previously a Microsoft Windows NT 4.0 Server. He wants you to do a clean install because he does not need any of the files or programs it contains. The computer contains two Pentium III processors, 256 MB RAM, a SVGA display adapter, and three 4 GB disks. He asks if the Windows XP Home Edition operating system will process data more quickly on his computer than his colleague's Pentium III, which has a similar configuration, but only one processor. What should you tell him?

A. You should tell the user that his system would process data twice as fast because there were two processors in his computer.

B. You should tell the user that his computer would process data more quickly if he set the multiprocessor mode to Yes in the Systems Properties dialog box.

C. You should inform the user that he could not install Windows XP Home Edition on his computer because Windows XP Home Edition only supports one processor.

D. You should tell the user that Windows XP Home Edition and Windows XP Professional only support one processor, and that he would need to purchase a copy of either Windows 2000 Server or Windows Server 2003.

8. You are a DST at a local fish distribution company. You are performing an attended installation in a client's office and cannot get the computer to boot from the CD-ROM. The user informs you that the salesperson said the computer had a bootable CD-ROM drive, yet the computer continues to boot from the hard drive. What steps should you take to resolve this problem? (Choose two answers.)

A. You should first confirm that the computer's BIOS supports booting from the CD-ROM, and that the order of boot devices places the CD-ROM before the hard drive.

B. If the computer does not support booting from the CD-ROM, you can create a set of floppy disks that will start the computer and then initiate an installation from the CD-ROM.

C. You should inform the user that he should purchase a new bootable CD-ROM drive before Windows XP can be installed.

D. After confirming that the CD-ROM drive is bootable, you should contact Microsoft and request another installation CD to replace the faulty one.

9. Which two log files can assist you in troubleshooting a failed Windows XP installation? (Choose two.)

   A. System log

   B. Setupact.log

   C. SetupError.log

   D. Setupapi.log

10. You are a DST and you installed Windows XP Professional as a multiple boot so that the user could start her workstation in Windows 98 or Windows XP. After several hours you receive a telephone call from her saying, "I don't know what you did, but I cannot find any of my Microsoft Office applications. I need to create a PowerPoint presentation in two hours!" What is the most likely reason the user cannot find her Microsoft Office applications?

   A. You forgot to create a mapping to the Applications folder.

   B. The user needs to run the Quick Switch utility from the System Properties dialog box.

   C. The user does not have the correct permissions to access the Microsoft Office applications from Windows XP.

   D. You must reinstall the Microsoft Office software, and any other software to which the user needs access, while booted up in the new Windows XP operating system.

11. Which type of installation is done on a computer that has no operating system installed?

   A. An upgrade installation.

   B. A migration upgrade installation.

   C. There must be an operating system present before a new operating system can be installed.

   D. A clean installation is performed on a computer that has no operating system present.

12. You are a DST and are installing Windows XP in the office of a manager who presently does not have Internet connectivity. You have been informed by the network engineers that the wiring of the manager's office will take place in several days. The manager has requested that Windows XP still be installed on her brand new computer so that she can work on a sales presentation. You begin the installation but when you are prompted to activate the program, you remember that you are not connected to the Internet. What should you do to enable the user to run applications as quickly as possible?

    A. Inform the manager that she will have to wait until the engineers connect her computer to the network before you can install Windows XP.

    B. You do not need to activate Windows XP if you enter the 25-digit product ID located at the back of the CD case.

    C. You should continue with the installation and then select the telephone option to activate the product.

    D. You need to activate Windows XP only if you moved it from a different computer than it was originally installed on.

13. You need to deploy Windows XP Professional to ten new computers. All users require Service Pack 2 to minimize the risk of security vulnerabilities. Which is the most efficient way to deploy Windows XP Professional and Service Pack 2 to the new computers?

    A. Install Windows XP Professional from the CD-ROM media. When prompted during setup, choose to download and install Service Pack 2.

    B. Copy the Windows XP Professional installation files to a shared folder. Then, use the **xpsp2.exe /integrate** command, from the service pack installation files, to update the Windows XP Professional files with Service Pack 2. Install Windows XP Professional from the shared folder.

    C. Copy Windows XP Service Pack 2 to a shared folder. Ask a systems administrator to configure an unattended installation of Windows XP Profession, and configure the unattended installation to automatically launch the Windows XP Service Pack 2 setup.

    D. Perform an unattended installation of Windows XP Professional, and then enable Automatic Updates. Wait until Automatic Updates brings the computer up to date.

Objective 1.1 Answers

1. **Correct Answers: A**

   A. **Correct:** Before attempting an installation of Windows XP Professional, you should verify that the hardware and drivers on the computer are listed in the Windows Catalog. If you want to continue an installation that fails, you should try to remove all nonsupported hardware to get past the error, and then reconnect the device after installation.

   B. **Incorrect:** Because the user requested that the installation be done, this is not the best answer. You should first attempt to remove any nonsupported devices to get past the installation error.

   C. **Incorrect:** Windows XP Professional can be installed on any computer as long as the components are listed in the Windows Catalog.

   D. **Incorrect:** Windows XP Professional does not require the presence of an operating system before it can be installed.

2. **Correct Answers: A and D**

   A. **Correct:** A 233 MHz processor is the minimum requirement. However, a Pentium III or better processor is recommended.

   B. **Incorrect:** The minimum required amount of RAM is 64 MB.

   C. **Incorrect:** 1.5 GB of available disk space is required.

   D. **Correct:** Windows XP Professional requires a Super VGA (800 × 600) or higher display.

3. **Correct Answers: C**

   A. **Incorrect:** Not having the correct permissions would not prevent the Windows XP operating system from starting. Also, because the accountants were able to run Windows XP prior to the software program being installed, this is most likely not a permissions problem.

   B. **Incorrect:** It is unlikely that the installation of the software application infected only 12 of the workstations with a virus, and not all the workstations.

   C. **Correct:** Windows XP Professional requires activation within 30 days from the first boot. Because the operating system was installed on April 15 and the manager called the DST on May 15, this is the most likely cause of the problem.

   D. **Incorrect:** Windows XP Professional does not require NTFS as the file system.

4.   Correct Answers: D

A. Incorrect: When you choose Typical Settings as the installation option, TCP/IP is configured to automatically obtain an Internet Protocol (IP) address from a Dynamic Host Configuration Protocol (DHCP) server.

B. Incorrect: When you choose Typical Settings as the installation option, TCP/IP is configured to automatically obtain an IP address from a DHCP server.

C. Incorrect: When you choose Typical Settings as the installation option, TCP/IP is configured to automatically obtain an IP address from a DHCP server.

D. Correct: When you choose Typical Settings as the installation option, TCP/IP is configured to automatically obtain an IP address from a DHCP server. If a DHCP server is not available, a private IP address number is selected from the range 169.254.0.1 to 169.254.255.254. A subnet mask of 255.255.0.0 will also be configured for the workstation, but no default gateway IP address number will be assigned.

5.   Correct Answers: B

A. Incorrect: For a user to connect to the Internet, a valid IP address must be configured for the default gateway. However, the IP address issued to the user in the scenario is a non-routable private IP address generated by the Windows XP operating when a DHCP server is not available.

B. Correct: If the Obtain IP Address Automatically option is selected on a workstation, DHCP will issue the TCP/IP configuration information, such as IP Address, subnet mask, default gateway, DNS, and so on, to the workstation. If a DHCP server is not available, the client's computer will be assigned a private IP in the range of 169.254.0.1 to 169.254.255.254, with a subnet mask of 255.255.0.0.

C. Incorrect: For a client's workstation to be able to use names, instead of IP addresses, to connect to sites on the Internet, a DNS server IP address and a default gateway IP address are required. However, Automatic Internet Protocol Addressing (AIPA) is a private IP address schema that is not routable.

D. Incorrect: Because all the other users can successfully connect to the Internet, you can determine that the problem is isolated to just the user's workstation. You might want to enter the ipconfig command on one of the other workstations that connect to the Internet to determine its configuration.

6.   Correct Answers: D

A. Incorrect: Because the user wants to play games and also have the security features of Windows XP, you can use the FAT32 file system on partitions C: and D:, but use NTFS on the E: partition where Windows XP Professional can be installed. For Windows 98 to boot, it cannot be on an NTFS partition.

B. Incorrect: The NTFS file system is not available for Windows 98. If you installed Windows XP over the Windows 98 operating system, you could use the NTFS file system on all the partitions. However, there is a likely chance that the older game programs and possibly some of the game peripherals will not work properly under the Windows XP operating system.

C. Incorrect: Creating a new partition and formatting the disk will erase the user's programs and data. This was not something that the user requested.

D. Correct: This option will enable the user to boot the workstation in either operating system. If the computer is booted into the Windows 98 operating system, the user would have no access to the NTFS partition because Windows 98 does not recognize the NTFS file system. This option will give the user the security features of NTFS, while allowing her to play the computer games in Windows 98.

7. Correct Answers: C

A. Incorrect: Windows XP Home Edition supports only one processor, so he could not install it on his computer. The user would have to upgrade to Windows XP Professional, which supports two processors.

B. Incorrect: There is no such mode in Windows XP.

C. Correct: Windows XP Home Edition supports only one processor. However, Windows XP Home Edition does support hyper-threading, which makes a single processor appear to be two processors.

D. Incorrect: Windows XP Professional supports two processors. He would not need to purchase server versions of Windows.

8. Correct Answers: A and B

A. Correct: The computer's BIOS must support booting from the CD-ROM, and the BIOS must be configured to boot from the CD-ROM first, followed by the hard drive or floppy drive.

B. Correct: In situations where a computer does not contain a bootable CD-ROM, you can create the floppy diskettes that will start the computer and then initiate an installation from the CD-ROM.

C. Incorrect: Windows XP can be installed by creating the floppy diskettes that will start the computer and then initiate an installation from the CD-ROM drive.

D. Incorrect: After verifying that the BIOS supports booting from the CD-ROM drive, you must confirm that the CD-ROM boots first, followed by the hard drive or floppy drive. If the BIOS is configured to boot from the hard drive first, the computer will never boot from the CD-ROM unless you were performing a clean install in which the hard drive did not contain a bootable partition or operating system.

9.   **Correct Answers: B and D**

   A. **Incorrect:** The System log file will not be available if your installation was unsuccessful. The Setupact.log and Setupapi.log files are created by the Setup utility and help you determine which files or drivers might have caused a problem during installation.

   B. **Correct:** The Setupact.log and Setupapi.log files are created by the Setup utility to help you determine which files or drivers might have caused a problem during installation.

   C. **Incorrect:** There is no such file in Windows XP. The Setupact.log and Setupapi.log files are created by the Setup utility to help you determine which files or drivers might have caused a problem during installation.

   D. **Correct:** The Setupact.log and Setupapi.log files are created by the Setup utility to help you determine which files or drivers might have caused a problem during installation. You can view these text files using Notepad or any other text editor.

10.   **Correct Answers: D**

   A. **Incorrect:** Mappings to folders are done to make them easily accessible to users, not to make programs available in a multiple boot configuration.

   B. **Incorrect:** There is no such utility.

   C. **Incorrect:** Not having the right permissions would not prevent the user from seeing Microsoft Office. In this scenario, the user claims that her Microsoft Office software is missing.

   D. **Correct:** When performing a multiple boot installation, any software that needs to be accessed must be reinstalled into the new operating system. For best results, install Microsoft Office on a different partition from the original installation.

11.   **Correct Answers: D**

   A. **Incorrect:** Upgrade installations are performed on computers that have an operating system present.

   B. **Incorrect:** There is no such installation.

   C. **Incorrect:** An operating system does not need to be present when performing a clean install.

   D. **Correct:** Clean installations can be done on a computer that has no operating system.

12.   Correct Answers: C

A. **Incorrect:** You can choose to activate the product by telephone instead of over the Internet.

B. **Incorrect:** Windows XP must be activated within a 30-day period after installation.

C. **Correct:** Windows XP can be activated at a later time by selecting Start, All Programs, System Tools, and then clicking on the Activate Windows option. You can then select an option to activate using the telephone.

D. **Incorrect:** You must activate Windows XP within 30 days from the first boot up of the operating system.

13.   Correct Answers: B

A. **Incorrect:** Windows XP Setup does not automatically retrieve updates during setup.

B. **Correct:** Integrating service pack files into the operating system installation files, a process known as slipstreaming, is the most efficient way to deliver a new operating system and service pack together. It offers better security, too, because there is less opportunity for an attacker to compromise the computer before known vulnerabilities have been patched.

C. **Incorrect:** While this is a viable option, it is not as efficient as integrating the service pack files into the operating system installation files. Additionally, computers will be more vulnerable to security attacks between the time when the operating system is configured and Service Pack 2 is installed.

D. **Incorrect:** While this is a viable option, it may take several days and multiple reboots for Automatic Updates to retrieve and apply all updates. Therefore, it is not as efficient as creating an integrated installation, and the computers will be more vulnerable to attacks until the latest updates are installed.

Perform and Troubleshoot an Unattended Installation of a Windows Desktop Operating System

As a DST, you might have to assist a user in performing an unattended installation of Windows XP. In an unattended installation, questions that are normally answered during the setup phase are answered through a file or script, appropriately called an *answer file*. The answer file is typically created by an administrator, and not a DST, but you should be prepared to answer questions that a user might ask you in regard to an unattended installation.

In large companies, where hundreds of installations can be conducted in one day, sitting in front of each PC with a CD in hand is not very practical.

To answer the questions in this objective, you should know how Windows XP Professional can be installed using the Remote Installation Services (RIS) server. Be sure you know that a Preboot Execution Environment (PXE)–compliant network interface card (NIC) is needed to connect to a RIS server or that a bootable RIS disk, created by an administrator, can also be used.

Objective 1.2 Questions

1. You are a DST for a help desk. A user calls you and says she is installing Windows XP on five computers in her department. She heard from one of her colleagues that she could create a file that would answer the questions that are normally asked during an attended installation. Another coworker told her that the file is very difficult to create unless one has programming experience. Which utility should you recommend to her that creates a standard answer file as well as a uniqueness database file (UDF)?

    A. You should recommend that she uses the Active Directory Users and Computers Microsoft Management Console (MMC).

    B. You should recommend that she uses the Setup Manager Wizard.

    C. You should recommend that she uses the Setupapi utility.

    D. You should inform her that answer files are created using a text editor, such as Notepad, and that there is no utility available.

2. A RIS client requires which of the following? (Choose one answer.)

    A. A bootable CD-ROM drive

    B. 256 MB RAM

    C. A PXE-compliant NIC or RIS disk

    D. An NTFS formatted partition

3. You are a DST for a large hotel chain and perform a Windows XP Professional unattended installation on 20 workstations in Honolulu, Hawaii. After the installation, you notice that each of the workstations has its time zone set to Tijuana, Mexico. Other than this error, the configurations of the workstations are correct. You will need to install an additional 50 workstations next week and want to correct the time zone error. The manager of the department asks you if it were possible to modify the answer file without having to use Setup Manager. What should you tell him?

    A. You should tell the manager that because the answer file was created using Setup Manager, it will have to be used to modify the file.

    B. You should tell the manager that a new answer file will need to be created to replace the old one because modifications of answer files are not allowed.

    C. You should tell the manager that any text editor could be used to modify the answer file that was created using Setup Manager.

    D. You should tell the manager that editing the answer file should only be done using the regedt32 command and is not recommended or supported by Microsoft.

4.   As the DST for a large textile company, you will assist the network administrator with deploying Windows XP Professional to more than 300 users. She is concerned that an attended installation would not only take an inordinate amount of time, but also would be prone to errors. One of the users is amazed that the computers can be installed without anyone responding to the questions posed during a typical installation. He understands how an answer file responds to common configurations shared by many workstations, such as the time zone and network adapter type, but he doesn't understand how 300 workstations could be configured with the same computer name because you cannot have duplicate computer names on a network. What should you tell him?

   A. You should tell the user that the answer file will name each of the workstations with a default name of computer1, and that these names will have to be changed manually after the installation.

   B. You should tell the user that the answer file contains two sections. One section responds to the common configuration questions, and the other section contains the unique information of each computer.

   C. You should tell the user that a computer programmer will need to create a separate application to handle the duplicate computer names generated by the answer.

   D. You should tell the user that a UDF prevents the computer from identifying multiple workstations with the same computer name, and that the answer file works in conjunction with the UDF.

5.   Which of the following commands would install Windows XP Service Pack 2 without prompting the user?

   A. Xpsp2.exe /O

   B. Xpsp2.exe /Z

   C. Xpsp2.exe /F

   D. Xpsp2.exe /U

6.   You are a DST for a medium-sized business with about 100 desktop and laptop computers running Windows XP Professional. All computers are members of a Windows Server 2003 Active Directory domain, which domain administrators are responsible for managing. You learn that Microsoft has released a new service pack for Windows XP. During lunch, a new systems administrator who has never before deployed a service pack asks you what the most efficient distribution method is. What do you answer?

   A. Group Policy software distribution.

   B. Logon scripts.

   C. E-mail attachments.

   D. Manual installation from a shared folder.

Objective 1.2 Answers

1.   Correct Answers: B

   A. Incorrect: Active Directory Users and Computers MMC is used to create organizational units (OUs), user accounts, groups, and so on. It is not used to create answer files or a UDF.

   B. Correct: Setup Manager Wizard is a program that allows you create an answer file, as well as a UDF. You can specify network settings, computer names, display settings, and so on, through Setup Manager, which creates text files that are later used during the Windows XP setup. This utility is typically used by an administrator, not a DST or a user.

   C. Incorrect: Setupapi.log is a log file used to troubleshoot an installation. It is not a utility used to create an answer file.

   D. Incorrect: Answer files can be created using a text editor, but this method is more complex than using Setup Manager. Many administrators with experience use Setup Manager to create a standard answer file, and then edit the file using a text editor when minor changes are required.

2.   Correct Answers: C

   A. Incorrect: A RIS client connects to a RIS server, which then installs a Windows XP image on the client. A CD-ROM drive is not needed.

   B. Incorrect: The minimum required amount of RAM on a RIS client is the same as that of any workstation that will be installed with Windows XP: 64 MB.

   C. Correct: A PXE-compliant NIC is required for a RIS client to connect to the RIS server, or a bootable RIS disk, which is created by the administrator, if the workstation does not have a PXE-compliant NIC. You should be aware that the RIS disk contains a limited number of NIC drivers.

   D. Incorrect: Because an image of Windows XP will be installed from the RIS server to the RIS client, the RIS client does not need to contain a formatted partition.

3.   Correct Answers: C

   A. Incorrect: Even though the answer file was created using Setup Manager, any text editor, such as Notepad or WordPad, can be used to edit the answer file.

   B. Incorrect: Answer files created with Setup Manager can be modified using the wizard or any text editor.

C. Correct: Even though the answer file was created using Setup Manager, any text editor, such as Notepad or WordPad can be used to edit the answer file.

D. Incorrect: Regedt32 is the utility used to edit and view entries in the Registry, not to edit answer files.

4.   Correct Answers: D

A. Incorrect: Answer files are used to provide common configuration information during setup, but a UDF supplies the unique information for each workstation, such as computer name.

B. Incorrect: Answer files are used to provide common configuration information during setup, but a UDF supplies the unique information for each workstation, such as the computer name.

C. Incorrect: The UDF works in conjunction with the answer file to respond to the setup questions requiring a unique value.

D. Correct: The UDF works in conjunction with the answer file to respond to the setup questions requiring a unique value. As a DST, you will not create an answer file or a UDF, but you should be aware of how and why they are used.

5.   Correct Answers: D

A. Incorrect: The /O parameter overwrites Original Equipment Manufacturer (OEM) files without prompting the user for confirmation. Instead, you must use the /U or /Q parameters to perform an unattended installation of Windows XP Service Pack 2. However, the /O parameter is often used in conjunction with /U or /Q to enable overwriting of OEM files without human intervention.

B. Incorrect: The /Z parameter prevents the computer from rebooting after installation of the service pack is complete. Instead, you must use the /U or /Q parameters to perform an unattended installation of Windows XP Service Pack 2.

C. Incorrect: The /F parameter forces applications to close when the computer needs to reboot after installation of the service pack is complete. Instead, you must use the /U or /Q parameters to perform an unattended installation of Windows XP Service Pack 2. However, the /F parameter is often used in conjunction with /U or /Q to enable the computer to reboot without human intervention.

D. Correct: Use the /U parameter to install Windows XP Service Pack 2 with default options without prompting the user. You can also use the /Q parameter, which functions similarly, but does not display any prompts on the screen to inform the user of the installation progress.

6.   Correct Answers: A

A. Correct: In Active Directory environments, Group Policy software distribution is almost always the most efficient way to distribute a service pack. With just a few clicks, a domain administrator can deploy a service pack, which can automatically install itself on every computer in the organization. Enterprises can also use Microsoft Systems Management Server (SMS) to automate the deployment of a service pack.

B. Incorrect: You can use logon scripts to automatically launch a service pack installation after the user logs on. However, logon scripts are not as efficient as Group Policy software distribution, and some service pack installations might fail if users have restrictive permissions.

C. Incorrect: Service packs are almost always over 100 MB in size, which is too large for e-mail attachments. Additionally, users may ignore the e-mail message, or may not have sufficient permissions to install the service pack.

D. Incorrect: Manual installation enables DSTs to troubleshoot problems as soon as they appear. However, manual installation is extremely time-consuming. In this case, Group Policy software distribution would be much more efficient.

Upgrade from a Previous Version of Windows

As a DST, you will be required to install Windows XP as an upgrade to an older version of Windows, such as Windows 95, Windows 98, or Windows NT. Some older versions of Windows, such as Windows 95, cannot be directly upgraded to Windows XP. Rather, the operating system will first have to be upgraded to Windows 98, and then to Windows XP. You must be able to determine if the computer being upgraded meets the hardware requirements for installation, just as you did for clean installs and unattended installations.

To answer the questions in this objective, you should know how to upgrade previous versions of Windows. You should know that Windows 98, Windows Millennium Edition (Windows Me), Windows NT Workstation 4.0 (Service Pack 5) or Windows 2000 Professional can be directly upgraded to Windows XP. You should also know that Windows XP can recognize both FAT and NTFS partitions, whereas Windows 95, Windows 98, and Windows Me can only recognize FAT partitions.

1. You are a DST and have just completed an upgrade of a Windows 98 workstation to a Windows XP Professional system and notice that several mission-critical software applications do not function under Windows XP. The manager wants to revert back to the original system so that he can produce several reports to give to the CEO tomorrow morning. What should you do?

A. Go to the Control Panel and use the Add Or Remove Programs option to remove Windows XP. This will return the operating system back to Windows 98.

B. You should format the partition Windows XP Professional was installed on and reinstall Windows 98.

C. Install a different computer with Windows 98 and then copy all the manager's data and mission-critical applications from the Windows XP workstation to the new Windows 98 workstation.

D. Use the Microsoft Knowledge Base to search for the appropriate program drivers for the mission-critical applications.

2. Which of the following are actions you should take before performing an upgrade of a Windows operating system to Windows XP? (Choose all that apply.)

A. Verify that any antivirus software is disabled.

B. Verify that the computer being upgraded meets all the hardware requirements.

C. Perform a backup of the current system.

D. Verify that the software on the older system is compatible with the new operating system that you are about to install.

3. You are a DST for a help desk. A user calls your office and says she will be upgrading her computer from Windows NT 4.0 (SP4) to Windows XP Professional. She tells you that she read somewhere that she could generate a system compatibility report before doing the upgrade, but she does not remember the command needed to run the report? What should you tell her? (Choose the best answer.)

A. You should tell her that she will not be able to do a direct upgrade to Windows XP Professional until she first applies Windows NT 4.0 Service Pack 5 or Windows NT 4.0 Service Pack 6a.

B. You should tell her that the command is **winnt32 /upgradecheck**.

C. You should tell her that she could select the Check System Compatibility option on the splash screen that appears after she inserts the installation CD.

D. You should tell her that she should select the Compatibility Report option from the Add Or Remove Programs utility in Control Panel.

4. You are the DST for a small human resources firm that has 30 workstations, each running older Microsoft operating systems. The president of the company has announced that additional monies will be allocated to IT, and that she wants all workstations to be upgraded to Windows XP Professional. Which of the following workstations can be directly upgraded? (Choose all that apply.)

A. Workstations running Windows 98

B. Workstations running Windows NT 3.51

C. Workstations running Windows NT 4.0 (Service Pack 5)

D. Workstations running Windows 95

5. Which tools are available to transfer files and settings to a different computer?

A. Files and Settings Transfer Wizard

B. Migration Wizard

C. File Transfer Utility (FTU)

D. User State Migration Tool (USMT)

6. You are a DST for a small software manufacturing company. Several computer programmers ask you to upgrade their workstations from Windows 98 to Windows XP Professional. After upgrading the workstations, you receive a telephone call from one of the programmers stating that his sound card does not work. You telephone the other two programmers and discover that their sound cards do not work either. What should you do? (Choose the best answer.)

A. Inform the programmers that Windows XP Professional does not support sound cards.

B. Inform the programmers that they should run the Find New Hardware utility from the Systems Properties dialog box.

C. Visit the sound card vendor's website to see if there is a Windows XP Professional driver available.

D. Inform the programmers that they must purchase new sound cards.

7. You are a DST and you installed Windows XP Home Edition on a user's computer in a small downtown law firm that employs 60 attorneys. You receive a call from the network administrator that the user's workstation will need to join the Active Directory domain established by the company so that the attorney can access network resources. You return to the law office to configure the workstation. How should you proceed?

A. Go to the Control Panel, select Systems, and enter the domain name into the drop-down logon dialog box.

B. Upgrade the Windows XP Home Edition to Windows XP Professional.

C. You should right-click the My Network Places icon on the user's desktop and select the Join Domain option.

D. You need to install the Management Console MMC on the attorney's workstation and select the Joining A Domain option.

8. You are a DST and are asked by the network administrator to upgrade a user's Windows 95 workstation to Windows XP Professional. After checking the hardware on the workstation, you determine that the computer's hardware does not meet the minimum compatibility requirements. After informing the administrator of your findings, you are told to install the Windows XP operating system on a new workstation just purchased by the company, and to migrate the user's files from the old computer to the new workstation. You decide to use the Files and Settings Transfer Wizard as a solution to the task. What will you be able to migrate to the new workstation?

A. Only folder and taskbar options

B. Only the My Documents folder

C. Only Internet and mail settings

D. All of the above

9. You are a DST and a user asks you to help her install Windows XP Home Edition on her home computer. She is currently running Windows 98, but does not want to retain any of the programs or data or the operating system. You verify that the workstation meets all the hardware compatibility requirements, but the workstation does not contain a bootable CD-ROM. Because the computer is not on a network, the network installation option is not available. You place the installation diskette into the CD-ROM drive and are able to browse the CD. How could you install Windows XP Home Edition on the user's computer?

A. Copy the i386 folder from the CD-ROM onto the workstation's C:\ drive, and then run the winnt32.ext program by double-clicking it.

B. Copy the i386 folder from the CD-ROM, and then double-click the setup.exe program.

C. Copy the i386 folder from the CD-ROM, and double-click the Install.exe program.

D. Create a RIS boot diskette.

10. You are a DST at an organization with 50 computers. Last week, you completed updating your organization's computers from Windows 98 to Windows XP with very few problems. You used all default settings for the Windows XP upgrade. Last night, a systems administrator deployed Windows XP Service Pack 2 to all the computers by using Group Policy software distribution. This morning, you received several complaints from users that they could not share files directly with other users by using File and Printer Sharing. After discussing the problem with several users, you discover that they could share files yesterday, but haven't been able to since Service Pack 2 was installed. What is the likely cause of the problem?

A. Windows XP by default blocks all inbound traffic, including traffic required to use File and Printer Sharing.

B. Windows Firewall is configured to block file-sharing traffic.

C. A systems administrator chose to disable Windows Firewall.

D. By default, Windows XP disables File and Printer Sharing.

Objective 1.3 Answers

1.   **Correct Answers: A**

    A. Correct: You can uninstall Windows XP after doing an upgrade from Windows 98 by using the Add Or Remove Programs utility in Control Panel. This will return the operating system back Windows 98.

    B. Incorrect: By formatting the partition on which Windows XP Professional was installed, you will lose all the data and mission-critical applications.

    C. Incorrect: Aside from being time-consuming, this solution could also be very costly. A simpler solution is to uninstall Windows XP Professional using the Add Or Remove Programs utility in Control Panel. The system will then revert back to Windows 98.

    D. Incorrect: Drivers are small programs for computer hardware, such as printers, display monitors, and so on, not for application programs. You should uninstall Windows XP Professional using the Add Or Remove Programs utility in Control Panel.

2.   **Correct Answers: A, B, C, and D**

    A. Correct: Antivirus software can cause problems when installing the Windows XP Professional operating system because any attempt of the operating system to write to certain sectors of the hard drive might be misinterpreted by the antivirus software as a boot sector virus.

    B. Correct: Many computers that are running older Windows operating systems do not meet the minimum hardware requirements for an upgrade to Windows XP. Be sure that you have memorized the minimum hardware requirements for memory (64 MB), available disk space (1.5 GB), processor speed (233 MHz), and video display adapter (SVGA-compatible).

    C. Correct: Before conducting an upgrade of an operating system, you should perform a backup of the system in the event there are any problems encountered during the upgrade process.

    D. Correct: Before performing an upgrade installation, verify that the software programs on the system are compatible with Windows XP. The user might have older programs that are critical for the operations of the organization that might cease to function on the new operating system.

3. **Correct Answers: A**

A. Correct: Before upgrading a computer to Windows XP Professional, you can check for possible compatibility issues by typing the command **winnt32 /Check‑upgradeonly** on a command line. However, in this example the user will attempt to upgrade from Windows NT 4.0 with Service Pack 4. You should tell her that she needs to first install Service Pack 5 or later before attempting an upgrade to Windows XP Professional.

B. Incorrect: The correct command is **winnt32 /Checkupgradeonly**, but the user should first be informed that she should apply Windows NT 4.0 Service Pack 5 or later before upgrading to Windows XP.

C. Incorrect: Selecting the Check System Compatibility option is the correct answer for generating a capability report, but this is not the best answer. You should inform her that she needs to apply Windows NT 4.0 Service Pack 5 or later before attempting an upgrade to Windows XP.

D. Incorrect: You can print out a compatibility report by either using the command **winnt32 /Checkupgradeonly** or by selecting the Check System Compatibility option on the splash screen that appears after you insert the installation CD. There is no option in the Add Or Remove Programs utility.

4. **Correct Answers: A and C**

A. Correct: Windows 98, as well as Windows Me, can be directly upgraded to Windows XP Professional.

B. Incorrect: Workstations running Windows NT 3.51 and Windows NT 4.0 with Service Pack 4 and below cannot be directly upgraded to Windows XP Professional. A Windows NT 3.51 workstation will have to first be upgraded to Windows NT 4.0 with Service Pack 5 applied. A Windows NT 4.0 (SP4) workstation will just need to have Service Pack 5 applied before it can be directly upgraded.

C. Correct: Windows NT 4.0 with SP5 can be directly upgraded to Windows XP Professional.

D. Incorrect: Windows 95 cannot be directly upgraded to Windows XP Professional. To upgrade, you must first upgrade the operating system to Windows 98, and then to Windows XP Professional.

5. **Correct Answers: A and D**

A. Correct: This user-friendly utility is mainly for use in small offices or home use.

B. Incorrect: There is no such tool.

C. Incorrect: There is no such tool.

D. Correct: USMT is a utility for larger organizations with many users.

6. Correct Answers: C

A. Incorrect: It is possible that the sound card that was supported in Windows 98 is not supported by Windows XP Professional. You can visit the vendor's website to see if there is a new Windows XP–supported driver available.

B. Incorrect: There is no such utility.

C. Correct: When upgrading a computer from Windows 98 to Windows XP Professional, there is a possibility that some drivers might not be compatible with the new operating system. In this example, you might be able to download a new, supported sound card driver from the vendor's website.

D. Incorrect: This should be the last resort when there is a problem with incompatible hardware. You first attempt should be to contact the vendor to see if newer drivers are available.

7. Correct Answers: B

A. Incorrect: There is no such dialog box in the Systems Properties dialog box. Windows XP Home Edition does not allow users to join a domain.

B. Correct: Windows XP Home Edition does not allow users to join a domain. You will have to upgrade Windows XP Home Edition to Windows XP Professional to meet the requirements.

C. Incorrect: There is no such option. Windows XP Home Edition does not allow users to join a domain.

D. Incorrect: Windows XP Home Edition does not allow users to join a domain. You have to perform an upgrade to Windows XP Professional.

8. Correct Answers: D

A. Incorrect: The Files and Settings Transfer Wizard allows you to migrate folder and task bar options, Internet browser and mail settings, and specific files and folders, such as My Documents and My Pictures.

B. Incorrect: The Files and Settings Transfer Wizard allows you to migrate folder and task bar options, Internet browser and mail settings, and specific files and folders, such as My Documents and My Pictures.

C. Incorrect: The Files and Settings Transfer Wizard allows you to migrate folder and task bar options, Internet browser and mail settings, and specific files and folders, such as My Documents and My Pictures.

D. Correct: The Files and Settings Transfer Wizard allows you to migrate folder and task bar options, Internet browser and mail settings, and specific files and folders, such as My Documents and My Pictures.

9. **Correct Answers: A**

    A. Correct: You can load the Windows XP Home Edition operating system by copying the i386 folder to the hard drive and executing the winnt32.exe setup program.

    B. Incorrect: There is no such program.

    C. Incorrect: There is no such program.

    D. Incorrect: A RIS boot disk is created to connect a workstation to a RIS server if the workstation's NIC is not PXE compliant.

10. **Correct Answers: B**

    A. Incorrect: Windows XP does include a firewall that is capable of blocking traffic (Internet Connection Firewall), however, it is not enabled by default. Therefore, it is not likely to have caused the problem.

    B. Correct: Windows XP Service Pack 2 includes Windows Firewall, which can block all inbound traffic. While the default settings for Service Pack 2 should not prevent file sharing, domain administrators might configure Windows Firewall with overly restrictive settings in the interest of improving security. If you experience such a problem, especially shortly after the installation of Service Pack 2, examine Windows Firewall settings to determine if file-sharing traffic is being blocked.

    C. Incorrect: While it is possible to disable Windows Firewall when installing Service Pack 2, that would not cause file-sharing traffic to be blocked. Instead, disabling Windows Firewall would allow all traffic through. While that would not block user functionality, it can expose the computers to unnecessary security risks.

    D. Incorrect: Windows XP has File and Printer Sharing enabled by default. Additionally, users had shared files successfully earlier. Therefore, the problem is more likely related to the recent installation of Service Pack 2.

14 Managing and Troubleshooting Access to Resources (2.0)

The Managing and Troubleshooting Access to Resources objective domain focuses on the skills that you will need to make network resources, such as folders, files, and printers, available to the users on your network. The exam covers four areas relating to these network resources: file and folder permissions and encryption, shared folder access, printer access, and offline file access.

As a desktop support technician (DST), you must understand how to make resources available to users worldwide. You should also know how to protect these resources from unauthorized access by using file encryption, share permissions, and NTFS permissions. Also, some users will need to access a resource that is located on a network server when they are not connected to the corporate network. You should know how to configure offline folders for such situations and understand how to configure synchronization of the user's files with those files that are stored on the server. You must be able to troubleshoot network access problems that might be caused by incorrectly configured Windows Firewall settings, NTFS permissions, or share permissions and know how to make local and network printers available to your users.

The primary reason why a network exists is to share resources. As a DST, most of your work will be either configuring the network resources so that they are easily accessible to authorized users, or troubleshooting the reasons why a network resource is not available to an authorized user. For you to be successful as a DST, you must be able to do both jobs.

Tested Skills and Suggested Practices

The skills that you need to successfully master the Managing and Troubleshooting Access to Resources objective domain on the Supporting Users and Troubleshooting a Microsoft Windows XP Operating System exam include the following:

- Monitor, manage, and troubleshoot access to files and folders.
    - ❏ Practice 1: Right-click a folder while in Explorer, and select the Sharing and Security option from the drop-down menu. You should know how to change the share name and assign permissions to the folder. You should also be aware that you can assign multiple share names to the same folder and assign the same or different permissions to each share name.

❑ Practice 2: Right-click My Computer, and select Manage from the drop-down menu. From the Computer Management MMC, expand Shared Folders and then select Shares. You should know how to view the folders that are being shared on a workstation or server, and how to access a shared folder using the Universal Naming Convention (UNC) syntax.

■ Manage and troubleshoot access to shared folders.

❑ Practice 1: If you have access to a network workstation, share a folder and try to access it using the Universal Naming Convention syntax: \\server-name\sharename.

❑ Practice 2: You should be able to tell what permissions are assigned to a shared folder by opening the Properties dialog box of the folder and clicking the Permissions button.

❑ Practice 3: In Windows Explorer, map a drive by selecting Tools from the menu bar, and then selecting the Map Network Drive option. Select an available drive letter, and enter the path of the shared folder you created in the previous exercise.

❑ Practice 4: On a computer with Windows XP Service Pack 2 and the default Windows Firewall settings, attempt to share a folder. Do you succeed? Does Windows Firewall block file sharing traffic?

❑ Practice 5: Install Service Pack 2 on a computer, and then manually configure an exception for File and Printer Sharing. From the Control Panel, click Security Center. Then, click Windows Firewall. Click the Exceptions tab and select the File And Printer Sharing check box.

■ Connect to local and network print devices.

❑ Practice 1: Click Start and select Printers and Faxes from the menu. From the Printer Tasks section, select Add A Printer and follow the steps in the Add Printer Wizard. You should practice adding and connecting to a local and network printer using this utility.

■ Manage and troubleshoot access and synchronization to offline folders.

❑ Practice 1: From a workstation running Windows XP Professional, click Start and then click the My Computer icon. On the Tools menu, click the Folders options and then click the Offline files tab. Select the Enable Offline Files check box.

❑ Practice 2: Make a folder you created earlier available offline by right-clicking the folder, and clicking the Make Folder Available Offline option. You should also select the Automatically Synchronize The Offline Files When I Log On And Log Off My Computer option.

Further Reading

This section lists supplemental readings by objective. Study these sources thoroughly before taking exam 70-271.

Objective 2.1   "Best Practices for NTFS Compression in Windows" by Microsoft Corporation (available online at *http://support.microsoft.com/default.aspx/kb/251186*)

"How to Use File Compression in Windows XP" (available online at *http://support.microsoft.com/default.aspx/kb/307987*)

"How to Disable Simplified Sharing and Set Permissions on a Shared Folder in Windows XP" (available online at *http://support.microsoft.com/default.aspx/kb/307874*)

"Encrypt Your Data to Keep It Safe" (available online at *http://www.microsoft.com/windowsxp/pro/using/howto/security/encryptdata.asp*)

Objective 2.2   "How to Convert FAT Disks to NTFS" (available online at *http://www.microsoft.com/windowsxp/pro/using/itpro/managing/convertfat.asp*)

"Use Access Control to Restrict Who Can Use Files" (available online at *http://www.microsoft.com/windowsxp/pro/using/howto/security/accesscontrol.mspx*)

"File and Printer Sharing Does Not Work" (available online at *http://www.microsoft.com/technet/prodtechnol/windowsserver2003/library/Operations/d3cbd31c-6e01-415f-9d7a-d0cbc73baabd.mspx*)

"Troubleshooting Windows Firewall Settings in Windows XP Service Pack 2" (available online at *http://support.microsoft.com/default.aspx/kb/875357*)

Objective 2.3   "Install New or Updated Printer Drivers" (available online at *http://www.microsoft.com/resources/documentation/windows/xp/all/proddocs/en-us/print_drivers_install_updatew.mspx*)

"Security Permissions for Printing" (available online at *http://www.microsoft.com/resources/documentation/windows/xp/all/proddocs/en-us/print_security_permissionsw.mspx*)

"Assigning Printer Permissions" (available online at *http://www.microsoft.com/resources/documentation/windows/xp/all/proddocs/en-us/sag_printconcepts_12.mspx*)

"File and Printer Sharing Does Not Work" (available online at *http://www.microsoft.com/technet/prodtechnol/windowsserver2003/library/Operations/d3cbd31c-6e01-415f-9d7a-d0cbc73baabd.mspx*)

"Troubleshooting Windows Firewall Settings in Windows XP Service Pack 2" (available online at *http://support.microsoft.com/default.aspx?kbid=875357*)

Objective 2.4   "Use Offline Files When You're Off the Network" (available online at *http://www.microsoft.com/windowsxp/pro/using/howto/gomobile/offlinefiles.asp*)

"How to Prepare to Upgrade Windows 98 or Windows Millennium Edition to Windows XP" (available online at *http://support.microsoft.com/default.aspx/kb/316639*)

Monitor, Manage, and Troubleshoot Access to Files and Folders

As a desktop support technician (DST), one of your primary responsibilities will be troubleshooting issues that might arise when users cannot access files or folders stored on their computers. You should understand how NTFS permissions that are incorrectly configured on a Windows XP computer can restrict access to files and folders, and you should know what to do to correct this type of problem. You should also know how to use the Simple File Sharing user interface, and be able to troubleshoot problems a user might encounter when using simple file sharing on a Windows XP Professional or a Windows XP Home Edition computer. Finally, you should be able to troubleshoot problems users might encounter while using the Windows Encrypting File System (EFS).

To answer the questions in this objective, you should know how to troubleshoot NTFS folder and file permissions, manage and troubleshoot simple file sharing issues, and be able to answer end-user questions concerning file encryption.

Objective 2.1 Questions

1. You are a desktop support technician (DST) for a large bank that has several servers running Windows Server 2003 throughout the city. Every day, 30 to 40 tellers must type the path of the servers and share name into the Run command dialog box of their workstations running Windows XP Professional so that they can access the shared folders over the network. This is very time consuming and prone to error because many of the tellers have been typing in the Universal Naming Convention (UNC) addresses incorrectly. The supervisor calls you to ask whether there is an easier way for the tellers to connect to the shared folders without having to memorize the location of the resources. What should you tell her?

    A. Inform the supervisor that mapping available drives to the shared folders would be a quick solution.

    B. Inform the supervisor that DHCP can be implemented on the workstations.

    C. Inform the supervisor that Domain Name System (DNS) must be implemented.

    D. Inform the supervisor that Windows XP Professional does not allow drives to be mapped, only the Windows Server products do.

2. You are a DST for a small law practice and receive a phone call from one of the attorneys, who is running Windows XP Professional on his laptop. He informs you that his hard drive is almost filled to capacity and that he wants to use the compression feature that Windows offers. You walk him through the steps, but when he right-clicks the folder he wants to compress, there is no option on the screen allowing compression. The attorney is logged on to his workstation as local administrator, so you do not think it is a permissions issue. What could be the reason the attorney cannot use the compression feature?

    A. Compression is only available on Microsoft server products.

    B. The attorney's hard disk is too full to do compression.

    C. The attorney's computer is configured with a FAT32 partition.

    D. The attorney's workstation is not assigned to a domain.

3. You are a desktop support technician (DST) for a large auto repair shop franchise and support more than 50 users. The vice president (VP) of the company calls and tells you that he is very concerned that unauthorized personnel are making changes to documents that they should only be allowed to view. The VP wants to restrict access to shared folders that are stored on each of the sales staff's workstations running Windows XP Professional. The share name of the folder is called Status. He wants to allow employees only the Read permission to the shared folder when they connect from home or from anywhere outside the office, and Full Control of the shared folder when they are at work. What should you do to meet the VP's request?

A. Configure the shared folder permission to Read; NTFS permission Full Control.

B. Configure the shared folder permission to Full Control; NTFS permission Read.

C. Configure the shared folder permission to Read; NTFS permission Read.

D. Inform the VP that it is not possible to configure the folder to meet his requirements.

4. You are a desktop support technician for a diagnostic lab. A user calls and asks you why she is not able to encrypt the contents of a folder that contain sensitive archived information. She informs you that she was able to compress the contents of the folder, but she is not able to select the Encryption check box. What should you tell her? (Choose the best answer.)

A. You should tell her that a compressed folder cannot be encrypted.

B. You should tell the user that she is probably not authorized to encrypt the folder.

C. You should tell her that she needs to enable encryption using the EFS wizard.

D. You should tell her that her partition needs to be NTFS.

Objective 2.1 Answers

1.   Correct Answers: A

   A. Correct: Rather than having to retype the UNC path to access a shared resource, it is more efficient to simply map a drive to the resource so that it is always available.

   B. Incorrect: Dynamic Host Configuration Protocol (DHCP) is used on a network to automatically issue IP addresses, subnet masks, default gateway information, and other TCP/IP configuration, to workstations that participate in address selection. DHCP does not map network drives.

   C. Incorrect: DNS is a name resolution solution. When you connect to an Internet address, DNS resolves the host name you enter, such as www.microsoft.com, to an IP address. You can use DNS addresses in UNC paths to map drives; however, it is not as easy for end users as mapping drives to shared folders.

   D. Incorrect: The ability to create a mapped drive is available on Windows 95, Windows 98, Windows Millennium Edition (Windows Me), and other Microsoft operating systems.

2.   Correct Answers: C

   A. Incorrect: Compression is available on client and server Microsoft operating systems that use NTFS file systems.

   B. Incorrect: Compression can be done regardless of the space available.

   C. Correct: The compression feature, as well as disk quotas and NTFS permissions, can only be done on an NTFS-formatted partition.

   D. Incorrect: The workstation does not have to be assigned to a domain.

3.   Correct Answers: A

   A. Correct: When a user connects from outside the organization, the combined shared folder permissions and NTFS permissions will give the remote user Read permission to the folder. Remember that the most restrictive permission is selected. The user will have Full Control permission when accessing the folder from the workstation.

   B. Incorrect: A remote user in this situation would have an effective permission of Read. However, the user would have the same permission when logged on to the local machine.

   C. Incorrect: This would prevent the user from having Full Control access when logged on locally.

   D. Incorrect: Configure the shared folder permission to Read and NTFS permission Full Control to meet the VP's requirements.

4. Correct Answers: A

   A. Correct: Compression and encryption are mutually exclusive.

   B. Incorrect: Because she is able to compress the folder, she has the appropriate permissions to also encrypt it.

   C. Incorrect: There is no such wizard. Encryption is enabled by default.

   D. Incorrect: The fact that she could use compression on the folder indicates that the partition is already formatted as NTFS.

Manage and Troubleshoot Access to Shared Folders

As a desktop support technician (DST), you might have to assist users who call and say they are not able to connect to a network resource, or that they received an Access Deny message. In some cases, the problem might be as simple as a workstation network cable being unplugged from a wall socket. Other times, the problem might be a little more complex. A user might not have the appropriate permissions to access a shared folder, or shared folder permissions combined with NTFS permissions might prevent the user from having the access needed.

As a DST, you typically will not assign NTFS permissions to network resources, but you should have an understanding of how shared permissions can be combined with NTFS permissions to create a more secure environment. You should also know how to create shared folders, and to troubleshoot problems related to Windows Firewall blocking file-sharing traffic.

To answer the questions in this objective, you should know how Windows XP Professional uses both NTFS and shared folder permissions to make network resources available to users.

Objective 2.2 Questions

1. You are a desktop support technician (DST) for a music retail company that has all workstations running Windows XP Professional and one workstation running Windows 98 that is used for timekeeping. A user calls you to ask why he cannot access the SalesRpt folder. He tells you that four of his co-workers cannot access the folder either and that if this isn't fixed, heads are going to roll! What should be the first thing you do? (Choose the best answer.)

A. You should tell the user to reboot his workstation to reestablish any share connections.

B. Determine which workstation is sharing the folder and whether that workstation is accessible over the network.

C. You should determine which workstation is sharing the folder and perform a shutdown.

D. You should determine which workstation is sharing the folder and perform a restart.

2. You are a desktop support technician (DST) for a large bookstore that has only workstations running Windows XP Professional. A Power User wants to share a folder named Inventory, which is located on her FAT32 partition, with four other employees. She wants two of the employees to have Read permission to the contents of the folder because it contains information that the two employees should not be able to modify. She also wants the two other employees to have access to the same Inventory folder, but she wants these two people to have Full Control permission of the folder. She calls you and asks if it is possible for her to accomplish this goal. What should you tell her?

A. You should tell the user that she needs to create a new folder named Inventory2, and that she should copy the contents of the folder Inventory into the new folder. She should then give Read permission to the Inventory folder and Full Control permission to the Inventory2 folder.

B. You should tell the user that she needs to format the hard drive with NTFS to accomplish her goal.

C. You should tell the user that she can accomplish her goal by creating multiple share names for the Inventory folder.

D. You should inform the user that only administrators have the ability to share folders.

3.   You are a desktop support technician (DST) for a small collection agency. A user calls you and says that she is trying to share a folder that she created on her workstation running Windows XP Professional with several other co-workers, but that she doesn't have the option to select individuals or groups to access the shared folder. What could be the reason for this?

    A. Simple file sharing is enabled.

    B. The user does not have permission to share folders.

    C. Windows XP Professional does not allow for the sharing of network resources. Sharing folders can only be done on Windows 2000 Server or Windows 2003 Server.

    D. The user's workstation is not configured with an NTFS partition.

4.   You are a desktop support technician (DST) for an insurance company that has more than 40 workstations running Windows XP Professional. The workstations are configured with two partitions, C and D. The C partition is configured as FAT32, and the D partition is configured as NTFS. A new user calls you and says she is not able to share her status reports folder, which is located on partition C, with any of her peer reviewers. She says that when she right-clicks the folder icon in Windows Explorer, she does not see a Sharing And Security option. What should you do?

    A. Tell the user to copy the folder to the D partition because shared folders are not accessible in FAT32.

    B. Tell the user to disable simple file sharing.

    C. Tell the user to select the Enable Sharing On This Computer option on the General tab of the Systems Properties dialog box.

    D. You should tell the user that she currently does not have permission to create shared folders.

5.   You are a desktop support technician (DST) for a small medical center that has nine workstations running Windows XP Professional. A user calls and says she shared a resource on her computer, but that no one is able to see the share in My Network Places. You go to the user's office to verify the folder is shared, but you are not able to see the shared folder from any other workstations. What could be the possible cause of this problem?

    A. The Server service might be stopped on the user's workstation.

    B. The user does not have the correct permissions to share folders.

    C. High Security is set on the user's workstations, which prevents all shared folders from being visible to network users.

    D. The workstation running Windows XP Professional should be replaced with Windows 2000 Server because workstations cannot share resources.

6. You are a desktop support technician (DST) for a small international bakery. One of the bakers is going to Paris, France, to discuss a secret family recipe for blueberry scones. He will be taking his laptop with him and staying at a world-renowned hotel. What might you want to do to reduce the risk of someone stealing his laptop and copying the secret recipe?

    A. You should consider using an NTFS file system instead of FAT.

    B. You should use EFS on all folders containing sensitive information.

    C. You should select Hibernation mode in Power Options.

    D. You should select Standby mode in Power Options.

7. You are a desktop support technician (DST) for a large real estate company that has 15 workstations running Windows XP Professional. A user calls to ask why she is unable to access a shared folder on her co-worker's workstation. At the co-worker's workstation, you check the shared permissions that are assigned to the folder and verify that the Everyone group has Full Control, yet she is not able to access the resource. You verify that several other employees can access the share with no problems. What could be the reason for this problem?

    A. The user is not a member of the Everyone group.

    B. The user does not have the correct shared permission to access the resource.

    C. You should reboot the workstation sharing the folder to reestablish the share permissions.

    D. The folder might be configured with NTFS permissions that restrict the user's access.

8. Which of the following paths would connect you to a shared folder named EmpShr that is located on partition D: of a workstation named Computer1?

    A. d:\\computer1\ EmpShr

    B. //computer1/empshr

    C. /computer1/empshr

    D. \\computer1\empshr

9.   A user is attempting to look at a folder that is on her Windows XP Professional desktop and gets an Access Denied error. What could be the possible cause of this problem?

    A. The shared permissions on the folder restrict access to the folder.

    B. NTFS permissions are restricting user access.

    C. The user needs to share the file.

    D. The user must have the folder permission of Full Control.

10.   You are a desktop support technician (DST) for a computer training school that has five class rooms. Each of the classrooms contains 12 workstations running Microsoft Windows XP Professional. The Director of the training center wants to share a folder on the training center's Windows Server 2003 server that contains student evaluation forms that can be accessed by students who enroll in a class. She wants the enrolled students to be able to click on an icon on the desktop instead of having them use a network drive to access the shared folder. How can you meet the Director's requirement?

    A. Use Internet Explorer, and create a mapped drive to the shared folder resource.

    B. Use the Systems Properties dialog box, and select to enable shortcut shares.

    C. Create a shortcut on each workstation desktop that has the UNC entered in the Type The Location Of The Item text box.

    D. Create a VBScript that maps each workstation to the training center server.

11.   To which of the following Windows XP Professional local groups must users belong to enable them to share folders? (Choose all that apply.)

    A. Administrators

    B. Print Operators

    C. Power Users

    D. Server Operators

12.   A user with Windows XP Professional and Service Pack 2 needs to share a folder with a colleague on the local network. What is the most efficient way to enable file sharing after Service Pack 2 is installed?

    A. Service Pack 2 permanently disables file sharing. Therefore, the users must copy files to a server to share them between computers.

    B. Use the Netsh command to enable a Windows Firewall exception for File And Printer Sharing. View the properties of the folder the user wants to share. Click the Sharing tab. Enable file sharing. Select the Share This Folder On The Network check box. Click OK.

    C. View the properties of the folder the user wants to share. Click the Sharing tab. Enable file sharing. Select the Share This Folder On The Network check box. Click OK.

    D. From Control Panel, open Windows Firewall. Click the Exceptions tab, and then select the File And Printer Sharing check box. Click OK. View the properties of the folder the user wants to share. Click the Sharing tab. Enable file sharing. Select the Share This Folder On The Network check box. Click OK.

13. A notebook user with Windows XP Professional and Service Pack 2 has configured a Windows Firewall exception to enable them to share files when connected to their company's internal network. They will be traveling soon, and must connect to wireless networks at the airport and at their hotel. They want to minimize the security risks of the file sharing exception and any other exceptions they might have with the least possible effort. How should the user improve the security of their computer while traveling?

    A. From Control Panel, open Windows Firewall. Click the General tab, and then click Off to disable Windows Firewall. Click OK.

    B. From Control Panel, open Windows Firewall. Click the Advanced tab. Click the Restore Defaults button, and then click Yes when prompted. Click OK.

    C. From Control Panel, open Windows Firewall. Click the Exceptions tab. Make note of which check boxes are selected. Then, deselect each exception. Click OK.

    D. From Control Panel, open Windows Firewall. Click the General tab, and then select the Don't Allow Exceptions check box. Click OK.

14. You are a desktop support technician (DST) for a consulting firm that has five employees. Currently, all users have notebook computers running Windows XP Professional and are configured as members of a workgroup. A user recently added a wireless network adapter so that he can connect to networks at airports, coffee shops, and hotels. He would like to use Windows Firewall to prevent unwanted guests from attempting to connect to shared folders across wireless networks. However, he still needs to be able to share files with other users across his wired network adapter when connected to the office network. What do you recommend?

    A. When connecting to wireless networks, the user should select the Don't Allow Exceptions check box on the Windows Firewall properties.

    B. When connecting to wireless networks, disable Windows Firewall.

    C. Configure different exceptions for the wired network adapter and the wireless network adapter.

    D. Configure multiple profiles to create two firewall policies: one for wireless networks and one for the internal network.

Objectives 2.2 Answers

1. **Correct Answers: B**

   A. **Incorrect:** It is unlikely a problem with the user's workstation because four other workstations are unable to connect to the resource.

   B. **Correct:** Because a total of five workstations cannot connect to the resource, it is probable that the network resource is unavailable.

   C. **Incorrect:** Performing a shutdown will prevent any other users from connecting to other resources that might be shared on the workstation. You should first determine if the workstation is connected to the network before shutting it down.

   D. **Incorrect:** Performing a restart will also prevent any other users from connecting to other resources that might be shared on the workstation. You should first determine if the workstation is connected to the network before restarting it.

2. **Correct Answers: C**

   A. **Incorrect:** You do not give share permissions to a folder, but to a shared folder. When you create a shared folder, you must give it a share name. You can create multiple share names for one folder. In this example, the user can give the employees Read permissions to the share name Inventory, and then share the same folder with a different share name and give the other two employees Full Control permission.

   B. **Incorrect:** Formatting a drive with any file system will delete all of its contents. If it were necessary to change a file system from FAT to NTFS, the convert command would be used. In this scenario, NTFS is not needed because folders can be shared on both FAT and NTFS partitions.

   C. **Correct:** You can create multiple share names for a folder and assign different share names to the folder. You could then assign different share permissions to each of the share names.

   D. **Incorrect:** Power Users, Administrators, and members of the Server Operators local group can share folders.

3. **Correct Answers: A**

   A. **Correct:** For a user to be able to assign shared folder permission to specific users or groups, simple file sharing must be disabled. You do this by selecting Appearance And Themes in Control Panel, and then selecting Folder Options. Then click the View tab, and deselect the Use Simple File Sharing (Recommended) option in the Advanced Settings section.

B. Incorrect: If a user does not have the required permissions to share folders, she will not have the Sharing And Security option in the Properties dialog box of the resource. In this scenario, the user said she could not assign permissions to specific users, not that she couldn't share the folder.

C. Incorrect: Windows XP Professional and Windows XP Home Edition allow users to share network resources if they are members of the Administrators (Computer Administrator), Power Users, or Server Operators groups.

D. Incorrect: Even though shared resources should be placed on NTFS partitions for increased security, it is not mandatory.

4.   Correct Answers: D

A. Incorrect: Shared folders can be created on both FAT32 and NTFS partitions.

B. Incorrect: In this scenario, the user does not have the permissions to share folders.

C. Incorrect: There is no such option.

D. Correct: When a user does not have the Sharing And Security option listed in the properties menu of a folder, it indicates that the user is not a member of the Administrators or Power Users groups.

5.   Correct Answers: A

A. Correct: The Server service must be enabled on a workstation so that the workstation can broadcast all the resources it is sharing over the network. You can stop and start this service by using the Services console.

B. Incorrect: In this scenario, the user has shared the folder. The issue here is that no one on the network can see the shared folder, not if the user can share a folder. Even though the share is not visible from My Network Places, users could access it if they knew the network path by either mapping to it or using a UNC.

C. Incorrect: There is no such thing.

D. Incorrect: Users can share resources on workstations running Windows XP Professional if they belong to the Administrators or Power Users local groups.

6.   Correct Answers: A and B

A. Correct: A FAT file system does not provide any security.

B. Correct: Laptops are perfect candidates for using the Encrypting File System.

C. Incorrect: Hibernation mode is not a security feature.

D. Incorrect: Standby mode is not a security feature.

7.   Correct Answers: D

   A. Incorrect: Everyone is a member of the Everyone group—no exceptions.

   B. Incorrect: In this scenario, the user has the Full Control shared permission to the folder.

   C. Incorrect: Other users are connecting to the shared folder, which verifies that the workstation sharing the folder is running.

   D. Correct: Even though a user might have Full Control shared permission, if an NTFS permission is configured to restrict access (Deny Access), the user attempting to connect over the network will not be able to access the folder. When shared permissions are combined with NTFS permissions, the most restrictive permissions are applied.

8.   Correct Answers: D

   A. Incorrect: The correct syntax for an UNC is \\server_name\share_name. In this example, \\computer1\empshr would be the correct syntax.

   B. Incorrect: The correct syntax for an UNC is \\server_name\share_name. In this example, \\computer1\ would be the correct syntax.

   C. Incorrect: The correct syntax for an UNC is \\server_name\share_name. In this example, \\computer1\empshr would be the correct syntax.

   D. Correct: This is the correct syntax for a UNC path: \\server_name\share_name. Users can share resources on workstations running Windows XP Professional if they belong to the Administrators or Power Users local groups.

9.   Correct Answers: B

   A. Incorrect: Shared folder permissions do not apply to someone logged on interactively (locally). Shared permissions only apply to users connecting over a network.

   B. Correct: NTFS permissions can restrict a user from accessing resources on their local workstation.

   C. Incorrect: Files cannot be shared. Only folders are shared.

   D. Incorrect: Because the user is logged on to her workstation and the folder is locally stored, shared folder permissions do not matter.

10.   Correct Answers: C

   A. Incorrect: The director did not want the enrolled student to have to use network drives.

   B. Incorrect: There is no such thing.

    C. Correct: You can use an UNC, such as \\TrainingCenter\Evals, as the value in the Type The Location Of The Item text box.

    D. Incorrect: This does not meet the Director's requirement.

11.   **Correct Answers: A and C**

    A. Correct: A user must be a member of the local Administrators or Power Users group to share folders.

    B. Incorrect: A user must be a member of the local Administrators or Power Users group to share folders.

    C. Correct: A user must be a member of the local Administrators or Power Users group to share folders.

    D. Incorrect: The Server Operators group exists only on Windows Server 2003 computers. On Windows XP computers, a user must be a member of the local Administrators or Power Users group to share folders.

12.   **Correct Answers: C**

    A. Incorrect: Windows Firewall in Service Pack 2 does disable File And Printer Sharing by default. However, Windows XP automatically enables it the first time you share a folder.

    B. Incorrect: While this procedure would work, it is unnecessarily complex. You do not need to manually configure a firewall exception for File And Printer Sharing, because Windows XP automatically enables this exception the first time you share a folder.

    C. Correct: Windows XP automatically enables File And Printer Sharing the first time you share a folder. Therefore, no additional steps are required.

    D. Incorrect: While this procedure would work, it is unnecessarily complex. You do not need to manually configure a firewall exception for File And Printer Sharing, because Windows XP automatically enables this exception the first time you share a folder.

13.   **Correct Answers: D**

    A. Incorrect: Disabling Windows Firewall greatly reduces security, and is the equivalent of configuring exceptions for every application on the computer. Instead, you should temporarily block all traffic by selecting the Don't Allow Exceptions check box on the General tab.

B. Incorrect: This procedure returns Windows Firewall to the default settings, which does disable most exceptions. However, it does not provide a way for the user to easily restore their exceptions the next time they connect to a trusted network. A more efficient technique is to select the Don't Allow Exceptions check box on the General tab.

C. Incorrect: While this procedure would disable all exceptions, it is not very efficient. Additionally, the user has to remember which exceptions were enabled and which were disabled when they want to enable their network applications to run correctly on the trusted network.

D. Correct: Selecting the Don't Allow Exceptions check box quickly disables all exceptions, blocking all unrequested network communications and greatly improving the network security of the computer. Later, when the user reconnects to a trusted network, they can enable their network applications by clearing the Don't Allow Exceptions check box.

14.   Correct Answers: C

A. Incorrect: While this would block all unrequested network communications, it requires the user to manually change a setting each time they connect to a wireless network. The user is likely to forget to change this setting, and therefore may leave themselves vulnerable.

B. Incorrect: Disabling Windows Firewall greatly reduces network security, and would make the user much more vulnerable to network attacks.

C. Correct: Windows Firewall enables you to configure different exceptions for different network adapters. You should use this capability when users connect to internal and external networks by using different network adapters. To configure per-adapter exceptions, open Windows Firewall, click the Advanced tab, click a network adapter, and then click Settings.

D. Incorrect: Windows Firewall does support multiple profiles that enable you to configure different exceptions for different networks. However, the feature is only available in Active Directory domains.

Connect to Local and Network Print Devices

As a desktop support technician (DST), you will be required to support printers that are on a network. Many help calls are made each day when users are not able to print their documents. Companies still rely on hard copy documents to function, and connecting an individual printer to each workstation in an organization is cost prohibitive. To solve this problem, printers are connected to workstations or servers and shared with network users. Permissions may be granted to users that allow them to print, remove print jobs that have been queued, and manage printers that are added or removed from the network.

As a DST, you will typically support users that are experiencing printer problems, but you will not manage printers and the permissions assigned to them. You should still have a basic understanding of the components of printing and the permissions that can be assigned to users so that you can troubleshoot and assist users experiencing printer problems. To support computers that have Windows XP Service Pack 2 installed, you must understand how Windows Firewall can affect the ability to share printers.

To answer the questions in this objective, you should know how local and network printers are installed on a workstation and how permissions can be issued. You should also know the importance of printer drivers and the effect a bad printer driver can have on printing.

Objective 2.3 Questions

1. You are a desktop support technician (DST) for a small community college that has 20 workstations running Windows XP Professional. A professor calls your office and frantically shouts that she cannot print her thesis to the printer connected to her workstation. She tells you that she was able to print yesterday morning without any problem, but that she suspects a colleague who used her computer later that evening might have broken her printer. On the way to her office, a receptionist stops you in the hallway and says she is very upset that her printer is out of paper because a professor printed three copies of a thesis to it. What could be the problem, if any, with the professor's printer?

    A. The professor's print device is configured to print multiple copies.

    B. The professor needs to contact the network administrator because users are not able to select which print device to use.

    C. She needs to have her NTFS permission for the printer changed from Print to Manage Documents.

    D. The professor needs to make her local printer the default printer.

2. You are a desktop support technician (DST) for a small car rental agency and have been asked to install a new printer that will connect to the computer through a USB port. All of the computers are running Windows XP Professional. You were told by one of the employees of the company that Plug and Play is not available for the printer. How would you install a printer that is not Plug and Play compliant?

    A. You should use the Add Printer Wizard.

    B. You should select the Printer Options check box in the Systems Properties dialog box.

    C. You should select Printer Options from the Printer And Other Hardware dialog box.

    D. You should select Add A Printer from the Performance And Themes dialog box.

3. You are a desktop support technician (DST) for a small art supply store, and you receive a telephone call from one of your users saying that the printer is printing pages of unreadable text. He turned off the printer and wants you correct the problem. What should you do? (Choose all that apply.)

    A. Install a new printer driver.

    B. Verify that the computer is connected to the printer.

    C. Remove and reinstall the printer.

    D. From the Systems Properties dialog box, select Clear All.

4.   You are a desktop support technician (DST) for a small retail clothing store that has three workstations running Windows XP Professional, three workstations running Windows XP Home Edition, and two workstations running Windows 98. The owner of the company has purchased a $10,000 color laser printer and has connected it to a workstation running Windows 98. Currently, users that want to print color documents to the printer make copies of the documents from their workstations to a floppy diskette and print the contents at the Windows 98 computer. The owner of the company asks you if there is an easier way to solve her printing problems. What should you tell her?

   A.   You should tell her that if she shared the printer that is connected to the workstation running Windows 98, the other users could access it.

   B.   You should tell the owner that she must connect the printer to one of the workstations running Windows XP Professional for all users to be able to connect to the color printer.

   C.   You should tell the owner that she needs to purchase a print server to solve her goal.

   D.   You should tell the user that she will have to install the LPR Network print driver on the workstation running Windows 98 if multiple users need to connect.

5.   You are a desktop support technician (DST) for small retail music store that has eight workstations running Windows XP Professional. A printer is connected to one of the workstations and permissions have been configured by the network administrator. One of the sales managers starts a print job that is using reams of paper. He is nowhere to be found, and the assistant help desk person's attempts to turn the printer on and off does not stop the print job. The administrator is on leave for two days, but he did inform you before he left that you had the appropriate permissions to remove any print job from the printer queue, but not the permission needed to create or delete printers. Which permission did the administrator give you?

   A.   Print permission

   B.   Manage Printers

   C.   Manage documents

   D.   Admin

6.   What user type must a person be logged on as to install a printer on a workstation running Windows XP Home Edition?

   A.   User

   B.   Administrator

   C.   Computer Administrator

   D.   Admin

7.   You are a desktop support technician (DST) for a company that has 30 workstations running Windows XP Professional. The company has only one printer that is shared on a secretary's computer. The secretary wants to know if there is a way that print jobs submitted by her boss can print before other employees' print jobs. How should you configure the printer?

   A. You could create a logical printer named BOSS, assign the Printer Priority of 1, create a logical printer named EMP, and then assign a Printer Priority of 99. You could then give her boss access to the BOSS printer, and everyone else access to the EMP printer.

   B. You could create a logical printer named BOSS, assign the Printer Priority of 100, create a logical printer named EMP, and then assign a Printer Priority of 1. You could then give her boss access to the BOSS printer, and everyone else access to the EMP printer.

   C. You could create a logical printer named BOSS, assign the Printer Priority of 99, create a logical printer called EMP, and then assign a Printer Priority of 1. You could then give her boss access to the BOSS printer and everyone else access to the EMP printer.

   D. You will have to purchase two different printers.

8.   You are a desktop support technician (DST) for a publishing company that has 200 workstations running Windows XP Professional. The local area network has two subnets, which you refer to as Subnet A and Subnet B. A user on Subnet B has been sharing a color printer with users on both subnets. However, after installing Windows XP Service Pack 2, users in Subnet A can no longer access the printer. Users in Subnet B can successfully print, however. Users in Subnet A can access other network resources in Subnet B. What is the likely cause of the problem?

   A. By default, Windows Firewall in Windows XP Service Pack 2 allows File And Printer Sharing only on the local subnet.

   B. A router is blocking traffic between Subnet A and Subnet B.

   C. Users on Subnet A have Windows Firewall configured to block traffic from Subnet B.

   D. The printer driver does not support Service Pack 2.

Objectives 2.3 Answers

1. **Correct Answers: D**

    A. Incorrect: In this scenario, the professor is attempting to print a document to her local printer, but the document is being sent to a network printer. A quick solution would be to make her local printer the default printer by clicking Start and selecting the Printers And Faxes option from the menu. You can then right-click the local printer you want to print to and choose the Set As Default Printer option from the menu.

    B. Incorrect: In this scenario, the user needs to print to her local printer. Because the document was being sent to the receptionist printer, it is obvious that she has access to multiple printers.

    C. Incorrect: This is not a permissions issue, but an issue of which printer was selected as the default printer. The person that used the professor's computer later in the evening most likely changed the default printer to the network printer located in the receptionist's office and forgot to change it back to the professor's local printer after printing.

    D. Correct: You can make a local printer the default printer by clicking Start and selecting the Printers And Faxes option from the menu. You then right-click the local printer you want to print to and choose the Set As Default Printer option from the menu.

2. **Correct Answers: A**

    A. Correct: For printers that are not Plug and Play compliant, use the Add Printer Wizard.

    B. Incorrect: There is no such option. To add a printer that is not Plug and Play compliant, use the Add Printer Wizard.

    C. Incorrect: For non–Plug and Play compliant printers, you should select the Add A Printer option from the Printer And Other Hardware screen.

    D. Incorrect: For non–Plug and Play compliant printers, you should select the Add A Printer option from the Printer And Other Hardware screen.

3. **Correct Answers: A**

    A. Correct: When a printer prints unreadable or garbled text, it is most likely a printer driver error. To install a new driver, you should click Start, select Printer and Faxes from the menu, and then right-click the printer giving you the problem. From the popup menu, select Properties and choose the Advanced tab. Click New Driver, and install it using the Add Printer Driver Wizard.

B. Incorrect: The fact that text is being printed shows that there is a connection.

C. Incorrect: Garbled text from a printer usually indicates a bad printer driver, not a bad printer.

D. Incorrect: There is no such entry.

4.   **Correct Answers: A**

    A. Correct: The color printer can be shared from the workstation running Windows 98 and accessed by the other workstations.

    B. Incorrect: The printer can be shared from any of the workstations.

    C. Incorrect: Windows 98 can share a printer and folders.

    D. Incorrect: There is no such thing.

5.   **Correct Answers: C**

    A. Incorrect: Print permission would only allow you to remove print jobs that you sent to the printer.

    B. Incorrect: Manage Printers is the highest level permission that allows the user to print, remove all print jobs, and create and delete printers.

    C. Correct: Manage documents permission allows the user to remove his own print jobs from the queue, as well as other users' jobs.

    D. Incorrect: There is no such print permission.

6.   **Correct Answers: C**

    A. Incorrect: To install a printer, your user account must be Computer Administrator for workstations running Windows XP Home Edition.

    B. Incorrect: There is no such account on workstations running Windows XP Home Edition. Your user account must be Computer Administrator.

    C. Correct: The Computer Administrator type account must be used to install a printer.

    D. Incorrect: There is no such account type on workstations running Windows XP Home Edition. To install a printer, your user account must be Computer Administrator.

7.   **Correct Answers: C**

    A. Incorrect: Printer Priority ranges from 1 through 99, with 99 being the highest.

    B. Incorrect: Printer Priority ranges from 1 through 99. You should give the BOSS printer a Printer Priority of 99.

C. **Correct:** The highest priority you can give for Printer Priority is 99.

D. **Incorrect:** You only need one printer, but you could create a logical printer named BOSS, assign the Printer Priority of 99, create another logical printer named EMP, and then assign a Printer Priority of 1. You could then give her boss access to the BOSS printer, and everyone else access to the EMP printer.

8.   Correct Answers: A

A. **Correct:** By default, Windows Firewall blocks File And Printer Sharing connections from remote subnets. To resolve the problem, you will need to adjust the File And Printer Sharing exception in Windows Firewall to enable connections from remote subnets.

B. **Incorrect:** While routers can often cause problems accessing network resources between different subnets, the scenario points out that users on Subnet A can access some resources on Subnet B. Therefore, the network infrastructure is correctly configured.

C. **Incorrect:** The scenario points out that users on Subnet A can access some resources on Subnet B. Therefore, Windows Firewall has not been configured to block traffic from Subnet B. Additionally, Windows Firewall does not typically cause problems when it runs on client computers. Windows Firewall might cause problems when it runs on computers that are sharing resources, however.

D. **Incorrect:** The scenario establishes that users on Subnet B can still access the shared printer. Therefore, the printer driver is functioning correctly, and the source of the problem lies elsewhere.

Objective 2.4

Manage and Troubleshoot Access to and Synchronization of Offline Files

As a desktop support technician (DST), you will be required to support users that want to work with shared folders while they are not connected to the network. In this world of telecommuting, many employees work from home offices and from planes, trains, and automobiles. Making network resources available for these mobile individuals when they are away from the office improves productivity and saves the company money. You should understand how to use the offline files feature and how to troubleshoot potential problems that might arise when it is implemented.

To answer the questions in this objective, you should know how to configure shared folders to be available to users when they are not connected to the Internet. You should understand how these offline files and folders synchronize with one another so changes made in one file will update the other.

Objective 2.4 Questions

1. You are a desktop support technician (DST) for a small hardware store that employs 20 sales representatives. There are only eight workstations running Windows XP Professional in the store, but sales representatives have laptop computers running Windows XP Home Edition to use when they are on the road. The sales manager of the store has heard that it is possible for her sales crew to work on reports that are stored on one of the workstations running Windows XP Professional in the office, even while the sales representatives are on the road. She is very excited and wants you to tell her how to implement the offline files feature. What should you tell her?

   A. You should tell the sales manager that the offline files feature is not available in Windows XP Home Edition.

   B. You should tell her that she could implement the offline files feature using Folder Options in Control Panel.

   C. You should tell her to select Offline Folder from the Systems Properties dialog box.

   D. You should tell the user to modify the Registry to enable the offline files feature.

2. Which of the following would prevent the offline files feature from being implemented on a workstation running Windows XP Professional?

   A. The user is not a member of the Domain Admins group.

   B. Fast User Switching is enabled on the workstation.

   C. The workstation is sharing the My Documents folder.

   D. The workstation is configured with a FAT32 partition.

3. You are a desktop support technician (DST) for a brokerage firm that has 100 sales representatives who work away from the office. Each sales representative has a laptop computer that is running Windows XP Professional. A sales representative calls you and says she is receiving an error message while trying to synchronize her folders with the folders on the server. She tells you that synchronization of her folder with the server's folders usually occurs as soon as she logs off, but this time she gets a message prompting her to either keep the original copy, the offline copy, or both. She doesn't know what to do. What would you tell the user?

A. Inform the user that this is not an error message, but just a warning that someone has changed the contents of the original shared folder.

B. Inform the user that her file has been corrupted and that she should make a backup.

C. Inform the user that she should select to keep the original only.

D. You should tell the user to call the administrator because you are not responsible for offline folder management.

Objectives 2.4 Answers

1. **Correct Answers: A**

    A. Correct: The sales manager wants to implement offline file sharing, which is not available on the Windows XP Home Edition.

    B. Incorrect: The offline files feature is not available in Windows XP Home Edition.

    C. Incorrect: No such option is available.

    D. Incorrect: The offline files feature is not available in Windows XP Home Edition. Her only option would be to upgrade the laptop operating systems to Windows XP Professional.

2. **Correct Answers: B**

    A. Incorrect: A user does not have to be a member of the Domain Admins group to enable the offline files feature.

    B. Correct: For the offline files feature to be implemented on a workstation running Windows XP Professional, Fast User Switching must be disabled.

    C. Incorrect: It does not matter what folders are being shared on a workstation.

    D. Incorrect: The file system that is implemented on the Windows XP Professional workstation does not matter.

3. **Correct Answers: A**

    A. Correct: When changes are made to the contents of a folder that is shared offline, a warning message is displayed. If you do receive this message, you should choose to keep both copies.

    B. Incorrect: If you are prompted with the message shown, you should keep both copies so that you do not overwrite changes that another user has made.

    C. Incorrect: This is not a good recommendation because all changes made to the document will be lost.

    D. Incorrect: Even if offline file management is not your responsibility, the best choice would be to inform the user to save both copies of the file.

15 Configuring and Troubleshooting Hardware Devices and Drivers (3.0)

The Configuring and Troubleshooting Hardware Devices and Drivers objective domain focuses on the skills that you need to be able to troubleshoot and assist users having problems associated with hardware devices and drivers. As management purchases additional peripherals for corporate users, such as display monitors, CD-ROM or DVD-ROM players, memory cards, and so on, you should be able to verify that the proper device drivers are installed and that the new hardware is correctly configured at all workstations.

You should know how to partition and format hard disks and configure various removable storage devices, such as CD-RW and DVD-RW drives. You should also understand how to configure and troubleshoot input/output (I/O) devices, such as modems, mouse devices, universal serial bus (USB)–connected devices, and wireless devices, as well as how to configure printers, keyboards, display monitors, and so on. You should have a good understanding of power options and how to apply them to laptop computers to enhance battery life, using the hibernation or standby features of Microsoft Windows XP Professional. You should also know how to create a hardware profile for company employees who might require one hardware configuration at the office and a different configuration at home.

The exam covers four areas relating to configuring and troubleshooting hardware devices and drivers: storage devices, display devices, power management (ACPI), and I/O devices.

Tested Skills and Suggested Practices

The skills that you need to successfully master the Configuring and Troubleshooting Hardware Devices and Drivers objective domain on the Supporting Users and Troubleshooting a Microsoft Windows XP Operating System exam include the following:

- Configure and troubleshoot storage devices.
    - ❑ Practice 1: Using the Disk Manager utility, create and format a partition on a Windows XP Professional workstation.

❑ Practice 2: Using Disk Manager, right-click the CD-ROM or DVD-ROM icon in the display and select Properties. Be sure you understand the function of each of the tabs, especially the Drivers tab. Select the Drivers tab, and note the Update Driver and Roll Back Driver buttons.

❑ Practice 3: Using the Computer Management console, select Device Manager and look at the entries listed in the details pane. Expand each of the entries, such as keyboard, monitors, network adapters, and so on. Right-click a device and note the Update and Uninstall options on the popup menu. Select the Properties option for the device, and note the options available on the Drivers tab.

■ Configure and troubleshoot display devices.

❑ Practice 1: From Control Panel, double-click Appearance And Themes, and then click the Display icon and select the Settings tab. Change the screen resolution by sliding the bar right or left. Click the down arrow in the Color Quality dialog box, and select and note the available options.

❑ Practice 2: Using Device Manager, expand the Disk Drives icon in the details pane and then right-click one of your available hard disks and select Properties. Note the "This device is working properly" message located in the Device status section of the dialog box.

■ Configure and troubleshoot Advanced Configuration and Power Interface (ACPI).

❑ Practice 1: From the Control Panel, select Performance And Maintenance, and then select Power Options and choose your power scheme using the drop-down dialog in the Power Schemes section of the Power Schemes tab. If you are using a laptop computer, change the default configuration to turn off the monitor after 15 minutes, when running on batteries. If your basic input/output system (BIOS) supports hibernation, configure your laptop or desktop to hibernate after one hour of inactivity.

❑ Practice 2: From the Control Panel, select Performance And Maintenance, select Power Options, and then click the Advanced tab. From the Power buttons section, notice the When I Close The Lid Of My Portable Computer option and choose Standby from the drop-down list. Click the Hibernate tab, and notice the Enable Hibernation check box. Also notice that the Disk Space Required To Hibernate value is equal to the total amount of RAM configured on your workstation because the contents of RAM are copied to your hard disk when Hibernate mode is activated.

- Configure and troubleshoot I/O devices.

  ❏ Practice 1: Using Device Manager, expand Mice And Other Pointing Devices in the detail pane. Select your keyboard from the drop-down list box, right-click it, and select Update Driver from the popup menu. Note that you can insert a CD-ROM or installation diskette at this screen, if you were updating a vendor's driver.

Further Reading

This section lists supplemental readings by objective. Study these sources thoroughly before taking exam 70-271.

Objective 3.1   "How to Troubleshoot Hardware and Software Driver Problems in Windows XP" by Microsoft Corporation (available online at *http://support.microsoft.com/kb/322205/*)

"How to Use Disk Management to Configure Basic Disks in Windows XP" (available online at *http://support.microsoft.com/kb/309000/*)

"How to Partition and Format a Hard Disk in Windows XP" (available online at *http://support.microsoft.com/kb/313348/*)

"Basic Storage Versus Dynamic Storage in Windows XP" (available online at *http://support.microsoft.com/kb/314343/*)

Objective 3.2   "Resources for Troubleshooting Display Problems in Windows XP" (available online at *http://support.microsoft.com/kb/307960/*)

"How to Determine Which Video Driver is Loading in Windows XP" (available online at *http://support.microsoft.com//kb/314854/*)

"How to Troubleshoot the Video Adapter Driver in Safe Mode in Windows XP" (available online at *http://support.microsoft.com/kb/292460/*)

Objective 3.3   "Microsoft Windows XP Professional Resource Kit Documentation, Part II, Desktop Management" (available online at *http://www.microsoft.com/resources/documentation/Windows/xp/all/reskit/en-us*)

"Understanding ACPI BIOS" (available online at *http://www.microsoft.com/windows2000/en/server/help/default.asp?url=/windows2000/en/server/help/understanding_ACPI_BIOS.htm*)

"Use Hibernate and Standby to Conserve Batteries" (available online at *http://www.microsoft.com/windowsxp/pro/using/howto/security/hibernate.asp*)

Objective 3.4 "How to Manage Devices in Windows XP" (available online at *http://support.microsoft.com/kb/283658/*)

"Troubleshooting Device Conflicts with Device Manager" (available online at *http://support.microsoft.com/kb/133240/*)

"How to Set Up Hardware Profiles for Laptop Computers in Windows XP" (available online at *http://support.microsoft.com/kb/308577/*)

"Troubleshooting Device Conflicts with Device Manager" (available online at *http://support.microsoft.com/kb/133240/*)

Objective 3.1

Configure and Troubleshoot Storage Devices

As a desktop support technician (DST), you will need to configure users' hard disks so that data can be stored and retrieved. You should know how to create partitions and format hard disks and have an understanding of the basic and dynamic disk types available in Windows XP Professional. You should also be able configure and trouble-shoot problems that users might encounter with CD-ROM, DVD-ROM, or any removable storage devices that are part of a user's workstation.

To answer the questions in this objective, you should know how to use the Disk Management console to manage your users' hard disks and CD-ROM/DVD-ROM optical drives, and know how to use Device Manager to update hardware devices and drivers.

Objective 3.1 Questions

1. You are a DST for a small automotive shop that has three computers running Windows XP Professional, two computers running Windows 98, and one laptop running Windows XP Home Edition. The manager of the shop has a dual-bootable computer that is running both Windows 98 and Windows XP Professional. The workstation is configured with one hard disk containing two 4-gigabyte (GB) partitions that are both formatted as FAT32. Windows 98 is installed on the C: partition, and Windows XP Professional is installed on the D: partition. While at the Disk Management console, the manager upgrades Disk 0 from a basic disk to a dynamic disk because he heard that it was more efficient. He then types the command **convert d: /fs:ntfs** at the command prompt and reboots the computer. He tries to boot the computer in Windows 98 and receives an error. Why can't the manager start the workstation in the Windows 98 operating system?

    A. The Windows 98 operating system cannot boot on a dynamic disk.

    B. The Convert command formatted both partitions as NTFS, so Windows 98 cannot start.

    C. The manager should have only upgraded the D: partition to dynamic, and not Disk 0.

    D. The manager should have formatted both partition as NTFS, and not just the D: partition.

2. You are the DST for a large recording studio and support 30 users. All the workstations are running Windows XP Professional, except the accountant, who is running Windows XP Home Edition. The accountant's workstation has two basic 8-GB hard disks, with each divided into two 4-megabyte (MB) partitions formatted as FAT32. She decides that she wants to convert the partitions on Disk 0 to NTFS, but leave the partitions on Disk 1 as FAT32. She also wants to upgrade one of the basic disks to a dynamic disk. She calls you and asks if it is possible to upgrade Disk 0 to dynamic and leave Disk 1 as a basic disk. What should you tell her?

    A. You should tell her "Yes," she can upgrade Disk 0 to dynamic and leave Disk 1 as basic.

    B. You should tell her "No" because Windows XP Home Edition does not support dynamic disks, so she cannot upgrade either of the disks.

    C. You should tell her "Yes," but also tell her that she can only upgrade the disk that contained NTFS partitions.

    D. You should tell her "No" because she cannot upgrade a basic disk to a dynamic disk if the disk has partitions formatted in FAT32.

3.   You are a DST for small private investigation firm. The five employees of the company are all running Windows XP Home Edition. One of the users calls you and wants to know how many primary partitions she can create on her 8-GB hard disk. She tells you she currently has one primary partition that is 2 GB and that the rest of the disk has unallocated space. What should you tell her?

    A. Four

    B. Five

    C. Six

    D. Three

4.   How much unallocated disk space must be available on a disk for it to be upgraded from basic to dynamic?

    A. 10 MB

    B. 1 MB

    C. 5 MB

    D. 100 MB

5.   You are a DST for a security firm supporting 50 users. Each user has a workstation that is running dual-boot Windows 98 and Windows XP Professional operating systems. The workstations have two hard disks, both formatted as FAT32. The president of the company calls you into his office and asks you if it is possible to extend his C: partition because it is almost filled to capacity, yet he has almost 2 GB of unallocated disk space on the same disk. What should you tell him?

    A. You should tell him that a partition cannot be extended unless it is formatted as NTFS.

    B. You should tell him the disk needs to be converted into a dynamic disk.

    C. You should tell him that the partition must be part of a volume set.

    D. You should tell him that partitions cannot be extended and that he needs to buy another hard disk.

6.   You are a DST for small brokerage firm and you are supporting 10 users. Each user has a workstation that is running Windows XP Professional. The workstations contain two 4-GB hard disks that are formatted as FAT32. A user calls and says he is concerned about the data that is stored on Disk 0. It contains critical information that is updated every 5 to 10 minutes, and he wants to be sure that in the event of a disk crash, he will be able to recover the information. He asks you if there is a way to mirror the disks so that if one disk crashes, he could still work using the other disk. What should you tell him?

A. You should tell him that the disks can be mirrored, but that he will first have to convert the file type on both disks to NTFS.

B. You should tell him that the disks can be mirrored, but that at least one disk must be converted to NTFS.

C. You should tell him that the disks can be mirrored, but that they will first have to be upgraded to dynamic disks.

D. You should tell him that fault-tolerant volumes are supported only on Microsoft Windows Server products and not on Windows XP Professional or Windows XP Home Edition.

7. Before a basic disk can be upgraded to a dynamic disk, you must:

A. Convert all partitions to NTFS.

B. Confirm that the MBR disk has a minimum of 1 MB of unallocated disk space on it.

C. Confirm that there is a minimum of available hard disk space equivalent to the amount of system memory.

D. Confirm that all files and folders on the disk are moved or copied to a basic disk for access after the upgrade.

8. You are the DST for a help desk, and a user calls saying that her DVD audio is not working on her computer running Windows XP. What are some of the troubleshooting steps you can take?

A. Verify that the sound card is properly configured.

B. Verify that the speakers are plugged in and turned on.

C. Verify that the audio cables connecting the DVD to the sound card are connected.

D. Verify that the Sound Properties Enabled check box is selected in the Power Options dialog box.

Objective 3.1 Answers

1.   **Correct Answers: A**

    A. Correct: Only Windows 2000 products and later can read or boot from a dynamic disk.

    B. Incorrect: Typing the command **convert D: /fs:ntfs** converts the FAT partition of D: into an NTFS formatted partition. Because Windows 98 was installed on partition C:, this will have no effect.

    C. Incorrect: Basic disks can only be upgraded to dynamic disks, not partitions.

    D. Incorrect: Windows 95, Windows 98, and Windows Millennium Edition (Windows Me) cannot read or boot from an NTFS formatted drive.

2.   **Correct Answers: B**

    A. Incorrect: This would be true if she were running Windows XP Professional, but Windows XP Home Edition does not support dynamic disks.

    B. Correct: Windows XP Home Edition does not support dynamic disks.

    C. Incorrect: A disk can be upgraded from basic to dynamic regardless of whether it is formatted as FAT or NTFS, but Windows XP Home Edition does not support dynamic disks.

    D. Incorrect: A disk can be upgraded from basic to dynamic regardless of whether it is formatted as FAT or NTFS, but Windows XP Home Edition does not support dynamic disks.

3.   **Correct Answers: D**

    A. Incorrect: Only a total of four primary partitions can be configured on a basic disk. Because there is already one partition, only three more can be created.

    B. Incorrect: Only a total of four primary partitions can be configured on a basic disk. Because there is already one partition, only three more can be created.

    C. Incorrect: Only a total of four primary partitions can be configured on a basic disk. Because there is already one partition, only three more can be created.

    D. Correct: Because there is already one partition, only three more primary partitions can be created.

4.   **Correct Answers: B**

    A. Incorrect: Only 1 MB of unallocated space must be available for the Master Boot Record (MBR).

B. Correct: Only 1 MB of unallocated space must be available for the MBR.

C. Incorrect: Only 1 MB of unallocated space must be available for the MBR.

D. Incorrect: Only 1 MB of unallocated space must be available for the MBR.

5.   Correct Answers: A

A. Correct: Only NTFS partitions can be extended. To extend the C: volume by 1 GB, you would type the **extend size=1000** command at the DiskPart prompt. The number you type following the size parameter is in MB.

B. Incorrect: To extend a volume or partition, the disk only has to be formatted as NTFS. It does not have to be a dynamic disk.

C. Incorrect: To extend a volume or partition, the disk only has to be formatted as NTFS. It does not have to be a dynamic disk or part of a volume set.

D. Incorrect: He already has unallocated space on his disk, so he does not need an additional hard disk. The partition must first be converted to NTFS and then the C: partition can be extended.

6.   Correct Answers: D

A. Incorrect: Even though NTFS is a better choice of file systems than FAT, it is not required when creating a mirrored drive. What is required is that both disks be dynamic and not basic.

B. Incorrect: Even though NTFS offers such features as file-level security, quota management, encryption, and compression, it is not required when configuring disk mirroring. What is required is that both disks be dynamic and not basic.

C. Incorrect: You cannot create mirrored volumes on computers that are running Windows XP Home, Windows XP Professional, or Windows XP 64-bit Edition.

D. Correct: You cannot create mirrored volumes on computers that are running Windows XP Home, Windows XP Professional, or Windows XP 64-bit Edition.

7.   Correct Answers: B

A. Incorrect: Dynamic disks can contain FAT partitions before and after they are converted.

B. Correct: For an upgrade to take place, there must be 1 MB of unallocated disk space, which will contain database information that is stored on the MBR sector of the disk.

C. Incorrect: For an upgrade to take place, there must be 1 MB of unallocated disk space, which will contain database information that is stored on the MBR sector of the disk.

D. Incorrect: All files and folders will be accessible by the Windows XP Professional operating system after the upgrade. If the workstation is a multiple boot system that also uses Windows 98, any disks that were upgraded to dynamic will be not be accessible while the Windows 98 system is booted. It is not recommended to upgrade basic disks to dynamic disk on multiple boot systems.

8. **Correct Answers: A, B, and C**

   A. Correct: You should verify that the sound card is properly configured and that the audio cable connecting the sound card to the DVD is connected.

   B. Correct: You should also make sure that the Mute All check box is not selected in the Volume Properties dialog box.

   C. Correct: You should also verify that the speakers are plugged in and turned on.

   D. Incorrect: There is no such option. You should verify that the sound card is configured, the audio cables connecting the sound card to the DVD are in place, and that the speakers are plugged in and turned on.

Objective 3.2

Configure and Troubleshoot Display Devices

As a DST, you might have to assist users who call and say they cannot see anything on their display adapters. Users might accidentally install a new display device driver that prevents them from viewing the screen, making it difficult to disable or uninstall drivers. You should be able to view the display device that is installed on a workstation as well as the device drivers that are configured for the computer and know how to start a workstation in safe mode using a generic video driver.

To answer the questions in this objective, you should know how to configure desktop display settings for a user, such as changing the screen resolution, selecting a background and screen saver, and changing the appearance of how text characters or menus are displayed on the screen. You should be able to troubleshoot display device setting errors if an incorrect driver is installed or a driver is overwritten.

Objective 3.2 Questions

1. You are a DST for a large computer retail store and support 20 users who are running Windows XP Professional. A user calls you and says that he upgraded his display video driver but now he cannot see anything on the screen. You visit the office and try to roll back to the previous video driver, but you cannot see anything you type at the keyboard because the video output is not being displayed. What should you do?

   A. Start the computer in safe mode and then disable the video driver.

   B. Change the monitor.

   C. You should download the original driver from the vendor.

   D. You should restore the system from backup tapes.

2. You are a DST for a bicycle repair shop that has three Windows XP Professional workstations. The owner of the shop wants you to change the resolution of the monitor to a higher resolution. He is not happy with the way pictures of bicycles he downloads from the Internet are displayed on his monitor. One of the sites he goes to says that the pictures are best displayed at 1024 × 768. You are seated in front of the owner's workstation. How should you change the resolution of his display?

   A. From Control Panel, select Appearance And Themes, change the desktop background, and then drag the slider to the 1024 × 768 screen resolution.

   B. Depending on the monitor the owner has, screen resolution changes are made from the monitor control buttons, normally located on the front of the monitor.

   C. Tell the user they need to purchase a new monitor.

   D. From Control Panel, select Appearance And Themes, click Display, and then click the Settings tab in the Display Properties dialog box. You can then drag the slider to the 1024 × 768 screen resolution or the one desired.

3. You are a DST for a small cigar manufacturing company that supports 15 users running Windows XP Professional. One of the users mistakenly changed the display resolution to a value that her monitor could not handle. She tried rebooting the workstation, but the monitor did not display the startup or welcome screen. You are sitting in front of her workstation and need to reconfigure the monitor back to its original state. What should you do?

   A. Start the computer in Safe mode and uninstall the display driver.

   B. Start the computer in VGA mode, and select the correct screen resolution.

   C. Use Device Manager to uninstall the monitor.

   D. Use the Add Hardware Wizard to remove the monitor.

Objective 3.2 Answers

1. **Correct Answers: A**

   A. Correct: By starting the computer in Safe mode, you can use a generic video driver and then use Device Manager to disable the device or roll back to the original video driver.

   B. Incorrect: The problem is not with the monitor, but with the video driver. You should start the computer in Safe mode using a generic video driver, and then you can use Device Manager to disable the device or roll back to the original video driver.

   C. Incorrect: You do not need to download the original driver because you can roll back to the driver using Device Manager. The problem is being able to see the output from the display monitor. You must first restart the workstation in safe mode so that you can use a generic video driver that will allow you to view the screen's output. Then you can use Device Manager to roll back to the original display driver.

   D. Incorrect: Restoring the workstation from backup tapes might solve the device driver problem, but it would be difficult to do when you cannot see what you are typing or selecting with your mouse pointer. Also, even if you could perform a restore, it might replace updated information with older information taken when the backup was initiated. Instead, you should restart the workstation in Safe mode so you can use a generic video driver that will allow you to view the screen's output. Then you can use Device Manager to roll back to the original display driver.

2. **Correct Answers: D**

   A. Incorrect: From Control Panel, select Appearance And Themes, click Display, click the Settings tab in the Display Properties dialog box, and then drag the slider to the 1024 × 768 screen resolution.

   B. Incorrect: Screen resolution changes are made by opening Control Panel, selecting Appearance And Themes, clicking Display, and then clicking the Settings tab in the Display Properties dialog box. You can then drag the slider to the 1024 × 768 screen resolution, or the one desired.

   C. Incorrect: Screen resolution changes are made by entering Control Panel, selecting Appearance And Themes, clicking Display, and then clicking the Settings tab in the Display Properties dialog box. You can then drag the slider to the 1024 × 768 screen resolution, or the one desired. You can also view the Display Properties dialog box by right-clicking any blank area on the desktop and selecting Properties from the drop-down menu.

D. Correct: Screen resolution changes are made by entering the Control Panel, selecting Display, clicking the Settings tab in the Display Properties dialog box, and then dragging the slider to the desired screen resolution. You can also view the Display Properties dialog box by right-clicking any clear area on the desktop and selecting Properties from the drop-down menu.

3.   Correct Answers: B

A. Incorrect: There is not a problem with the device driver because the user has not removed or installed a new driver. In this example, the user has incorrectly configured the monitor, so you should restart the computer in VGA mode by pressing the F8 function key before the Windows logo appears, but after startup messages are displayed from BIOS.

B. Correct: In VGA mode, you will be able to make any changes back to the original screen resolution. Restart the computer in VGA mode by pressing the F8 function key before the Windows logo appears, but after startup messages are displayed from BIOS.

C. Incorrect: Because the monitor is not functioning, it would be difficult to do anything before you could view what was displayed after typing commands or moving the mouse. After starting the computer in VGA mode, you could now make changes to correct the errors that were made when changing the screen resolution. There is no need to uninstall the monitor or drivers because the problem is with user configuration errors, not hardware device errors.

D. Incorrect: There is no need to uninstall the monitor or drivers because the problem is with user configuration errors, not hardware device errors. You should start the workstation in VGA mode and then make changes to correct the errors that were made when changing the screen resolution.

Configure and Troubleshoot Advanced Configuration and Power Interface (ACPI)

As a DST, you will be required to support users who need to conserve power on their desktop computers, as well as their laptops that require battery power to function. You should know how to place a workstation in Standby mode as well as Hibernate mode to save battery power, and you should also know how to conserve power by shutting off the monitor and hard disks when there is a certain predetermined time frame of inactivity.

To answer the questions in this objective, you should know how to configure a workstation to Hibernate and Standby modes, and you should be able to troubleshoot issues where Hibernate or Standby modes did not work on a particular workstation. You should be very good in using the Power Options dialog box, and you should know all the options available.

Objective 3.3 Questions

1. You are a DST for a large insurance firm that has more than 200 users running Windows XP Professional workstations. A sales manager calls and says she was working on several important documents and a Microsoft PowerPoint presentation, and that she was interrupted by an important telephone call. During the telephone call, her workstation went into Standby mode, and then she accidentally kicked the power cord from her workstation. She told you that she quickly plugged it back in, but that did not return to the screen where her documents were displayed after logging on, as she usually does. She wants to know why this happened. What should you tell her?

    A. You should tell her that Standby mode only returns you to the state the desktop was in if she selected Enhanced Standby mode.

    B. You should tell her that Standby and Hibernate settings are affected by power outages, and that in either case she will have lost her data.

    C. You should tell her that Standby mode writes the desktop settings to memory and that the power outage erased everything that was stored in memory.

    D. You should tell her that her system BIOS disabled Standby mode when the power was lost on her workstation.

2. You are a DST for a small engineering company that supports ten engineers who travel throughout the United States doing presentations. The engineers are running Windows XP Professional on their laptops and require long battery life due to the air travel time when numerous reports are written. They also attend presentations and conferences where the laptops are sitting on conference room tables for hours on end. The chief engineer is concerned that too many of the engineers are leaving their laptops on when it is not necessary and have asked the engineers to put the workstations in Standby mode when the workstations are inactive. The engineers are complaining that it is too difficult to remember when to do it, and that they do not like it when the workstation automatically goes into Standby mode when they are thinking or analyzing information on the screen and not giving input. What should you suggest to the engineers that would solve this problem? (Choose the best answer.)

    A. You should suggest that the engineers select Hibernate, Standby, or Do Nothing When The Laptop Lid Is Closed.

    B. You can suggest that the engineers configure the laptops to go into Standby mode when 30 minutes of inactivity occur because that would give them more than enough time to think and analyze.

    C. You can suggest that the engineers purchase additional batteries.

    D. You can suggest that the engineers request to plug their laptops into power outlets when in a conference room environment.

3. You are a DST for a small clothing franchise that has seven sales representatives who are running Windows XP Home Edition on laptops. The laptops have been configured with two partitions, C: and D:. The C: partition contains the operating system, and the D: partition contains only reports and presentations to be used by the sales representatives. Each laptop has 512 MB RAM and each partition is 2 GB. The C: partition has 400 MB of available disk space, and the D: partition has 1 GB of available disk space. The sales manager wants to be able to put her laptop into Hibernate mode, due to the problems she is having with her batteries constantly having to be recharged. She calls you and wants to know why she is not able to use Hibernate mode. What should you tell her?

   A. You should tell her that Hibernate mode is not available on Windows XP Home Edition.

   B. You should tell her that she needs more RAM.

   C. You should tell her to copy the hibernate.dll file to the D: partition.

   D. You should tell her that Hibernate mode requires an amount of free disk space on her boot partition (C:) equivalent to the amount of RAM (512 MB) on her workstation.

4. You are a DST for a large grocery store chain that supports more than 400 Windows XP Professional workstations. The owner of the company says that her utility bill has exceeded her budget allocation, and that she has heard that the workstations can be configured to shut off the monitors when there is inactivity for a specified time limit. She does not want the computers to go into Standby or Hibernate mode because she had received too many complaints from users who said it confused them. She wants to know if there is a way that just the monitors could be turned off. What should you tell her?

   A. You should tell the owner that she will have to select Hibernate or Standby mode.

   B. You should tell the owner that she can use the Power Options Properties dialog box to turn off only the monitor after a certain time limit of inactivity.

   C. You should tell the owner that she could use the System Properties hardware option to turn off the monitor.

   D. You should tell the owner that she could use Device Manager to turn off the monitor after a predetermined time of inactivity.

5. You are a DST for a large retail company that supports more than 800 users. To reduce utility costs, a manager asks you if it is possible to control the power consumption behavior of the workstations. What do you tell her?

   A. It is not possible to configure power options on desktop computers.

   B. You can configure both monitors and hard disks to turn off when inactive.

   C. You can select Optimal Power Usage from the Power Options dialog box.

   D. You can select Optimal Power Usage from Power Schemes.

6.   You are a DST for a help desk and have just upgraded the BIOS of a computer running Windows XP to enable Advanced Configuration and Power Interface (ACPI), but are still not able to manage power consumption in Windows XP. What should you do?

   A. Reinstall Windows XP.

   B. Select the Update BIOS option from the Power Options dialog box.

   C. Select the Update BIOS option from the Power Schemes tab.

   D. Select the Upgrade BIOS option from Control Panel.

Objective 3.3 Answers

1. **Correct Answers: C**

    A. Incorrect: There is no such mode. Standby mode did not return her to the original state of her workstation because of the loss of power. Standby mode stores desktop information in memory, not on the hard drive like Hibernate mode does.

    B. Incorrect: Standby mode does not save desktop settings to the disk like Hibernate mode does. When Hibernate is selected, everything that is stored in memory is copied to the hard drive, so data can be saved in the event of a power outage. Because everything in memory is written to hard disk, you must have a minimum of hard disk space equal to the amount of your system memory.

    C. Correct: Standby mode does not save desktop settings to the disk like Hibernate mode does. When Hibernate is selected, everything that is stored in memory is copied to the hard drive, so data can be saved in the event of a power outage. Because everything in memory is written to hard disk, you must have a minimum of hard disk space equal to the amount of your system memory.

    D. Incorrect: Standby mode does not save desktop settings to the disk like Hibernate mode does. When hibernate is selected, everything that is stored in memory is copied to the hard drive, so data can be saved in the event of a power outage. Because everything in memory is written to hard disk, you must have a minimum of hard disk space equal to the amount of your system memory. The system BIOS does not get erased during power losses because it is stored on a ROM (read-only memory) chip that does not rely on power.

2. **Correct Answers: A**

    A. Correct: Using the Power Options Properties Advanced tab, you can select Hibernate, Standby, or Do Nothing When The Laptop Lid Is Closed.

    B. Incorrect: Because the engineers have stated that they did not want the system to automatically go into Standby mode, this is not a good choice. Instead, they can use the Power Options Properties Advanced tab to select Hibernate, Standby, or Do Nothing When The Laptop Lid Is Closed.

    C. Incorrect: Purchasing additional batteries might still not solve the problem because the computers might be left on constantly. A better solution is to use the Power Options Properties Advanced tab to select Hibernate, Standby, or Do Nothing When The Laptop Lid Is Closed.

D. Incorrect: In many instances, availability of power outlets might be limited. Because the chief has requested a way to place the workstations in Standby mode, a better solution is to use the Power Options Properties Advanced tab to select Hibernate, Standby, or Do Nothing When The Laptop Lid Is Closed.

3.   Correct Answers: D

A. Incorrect: Hibernate mode is available in both Windows XP Professional and Windows XP Home Edition, but it requires an amount of free disk space on the boot partition, in this case, C: (where Windows XP Home Edition is installed), equivalent to the amount of RAM on the workstation (512 MB). Because the workstation has 512 MB RAM and the boot partition only has 400 MB of available disk space, Hibernate mode cannot be configured.

B. Incorrect: When Hibernate mode is selected, it copies the desktop settings from RAM to the boot partition, so it requires an amount of free disk space on the boot partition equivalent to the amount of RAM on the workstation.

C. Incorrect: There is no such file. For Hibernate mode to work, it requires an amount of free disk space on the boot partition equivalent to the amount of RAM on the workstation.

D. Correct: When Hibernate mode is selected, it copies the desktop settings from RAM to the boot partition, so it requires an amount of free disk space on the boot partition equivalent to the amount of RAM on the workstation. Because the workstation has 512 MB RAM and the boot partition only has 400 MB of available disk space, Hibernate mode cannot be configured.

4.   Correct Answers: B

A. Incorrect: You can specifically select the Turn Off Monitor option from the Power Options Properties Power Schemes tab dialog box. There, you can choose when the monitor can be turned off based on a value ranging from never to five hours.

B. Correct: You can specifically select the Turn Off Monitor option from the Power Options Properties Power Schemes tab dialog box. There, you can choose when the monitor can be turned off based on a time value ranging from never to five hours.

C. Incorrect: You can specifically select the Turn Off Monitor option from the Power Options Properties Power Schemes tab dialog box. There, you can choose when the monitor can be turned off based on a value ranging from never to five hours.

    D. Incorrect: You can specifically select the Turn Off Monitor option from the Power Options Properties Power Schemes tab. There, you can choose when the monitor can be turned off based on a value ranging from never to five hours. Device Manager can be used to update, roll back, or uninstall the display's drivers.

5.   Correct Answers: B

    A. Incorrect: Power Options can be configured on both desktop computers and portable computers.

    B. Correct: From the Power Schemes tab, you can select the Turn Off Hard Disks and Turn Off Monitor options. There, you can configure when these devices can be turned off, based on a selected time of inactivity.

    C. Incorrect: There is no such option. To turn off hard disks and monitors during inactivity, from the Power Schemes tab, you can select the Turn Off Hard Disks and Turn Off Monitor options. There, you can configure when these devices can be turned off, based on a selected time of inactivity.

    D. Incorrect: There is no such option. To turn off hard disks and monitors during inactivity, from the Power Schemes tab, you can select the Turn Off Hard Disks and Turn Off Monitor options. There, you can configure when these devices can be turned off, based on a selected time of inactivity.

6.   Correct Answers: A

    A. Correct: Because ACPI was not enabled in BIOS when Windows XP was initially installed, you need to reinstall the Windows XP operating system after the BIOS upgrade.

    B. Incorrect: There is no such option. Because ACPI was not enabled in BIOS when Windows XP was initially installed, you need to reinstall the Windows XP operating system after the BIOS upgrade.

    C. Incorrect: There is no such option. Because ACPI was not enabled in BIOS when Windows XP was initially installed, you need to reinstall the Windows XP operating system after the BIOS upgrade.

    D. Incorrect: There is no such option. Because ACPI was not enabled in BIOS when Windows XP was initially installed, you need to reinstall the Windows XP operating system after the BIOS upgrade.

Objective 3.4

Configure and Troubleshoot I/O Devices

As a DST, you will be required to troubleshoot input/output (I/O) devices, such as universal serial bus (USB), mouse devices, modems, and so on. You should be familiar with the wireless technology that is very prevalent in businesses of all sizes and know how to troubleshoot connectivity problems due to I/O device driver errors or configuration errors. You should know how to create and view hardware profiles to allow different hardware configurations to occur on the same workstation, in a situation in which users log on to a docked workstation and an undocked workstation when they work outside of the office.

To answer the questions in this objective, you should know how to configure and troubleshoot I/O device drivers. You should also know how to use Device Manager to view and troubleshoot I/O devices configured on your user's workstation and what to do if a device driver is corrupted or erased from the system.

Objective 3.4 Questions

1.   You are a DST for a large art supply store. There are seven Windows XP Professional workstations running inventory programs, and you recently installed one of the workstations with a new hand-held scanning device to automate data entry. The user of the workstation calls you and says that after the installation, his mouse isn't working. How could you see if there was a conflict between devices?

     A. You should use the Conflict Manager Wizard.

     B. You should use the Advanced tab of System Properties, and select the Performance tab.

     C. Device Manager indicates when there is a conflict between hardware devices.

     D. You should use the Device Troubleshooter Wizard in the General tab of System Properties.

2.   Which tool provides information about the hardware devices that are installed in a workstation and gives the user the ability to update, roll back, or uninstall device drivers?

     A. Device Manager

     B. Disk Management

     C. Disk Defragmenter

     D. Hardware Device Console

3.   You are a DST for a large sporting good store and support 20 users who are all running Windows XP Professional on docking workstations. Because the users are on the road half of the time, they need to have their computers configured differently when they are not at the office in the docking station. The manager calls you late this afternoon and asks if it is possible to have the workstations configured in such a way as to disable certain hardware devices when the computer was in a docking station, but enable those same devices when the computer is not docked. What should you tell the manager?

     A. You should tell the manager that the workstations will have to be configured with two removable hard drives. When the employees are at home, they will need to use the hard drive configured with the enabled devices. They will use the other hard drive when they are at the office and need to disable particular devices.

     B. You should tell the manager that it is possible using hardware profiles.

    C. You should tell the manager that the workstations must be configured in multiple boot mode, and that each operating system can be configured with a different hardware profile.

    D. You should tell the manager that it is possible using Profile Manager Wizard.

4. You are a DST for a large home repair supply store. A user who has Windows XP Professional installed on her workstation calls and says a co-worker installed a new mouse on her computer and that it isn't working. You use Device Manager and notice that there is a yellow question mark next to the mouse, which is listed under the Mice and Other Pointing Devices section. What does the yellow question mark mean?

    A. The yellow question mark means the device is functioning, but the manufacturer is unknown.

    B. Only a yellow exclamation mark is used in Device Manager, not a yellow question mark.

    C. A yellow question mark means the device was not installed, but the driver was installed.

    D. A yellow question mark means the device was installed, but the operating system was unable to find and install a driver.

5. You are a DST for an ISP and support 25 users. One of the employees has installed a new mouse driver for the CEO without checking with the help desk. You get a call from the CEO that his mouse does not work and he wants it fixed immediately. What is the fastest way to fix the problem?

    A. Find the mouse installation software and reinstall the original mouse driver.

    B. You need to reinstall the Windows XP Professional operating system.

    C. You should double-click the mouse driver in the Device Manager utility, click the Drivers tab, and then click the Roll Back Driver button to revert back to the previous mouse driver.

    D. You should use the Delete Hardware Wizard to remove the mouse and then reinstall it.

6. You are a DST for a large book publishing company and support more than 150 Windows XP Professional workstations. Thirty of the users are using docking stations so that they can take their computers out of the office to work remotely. One of the editors had a friend disable the network interface card (NIC) for one of the hardware profiles, but now the user cannot connect to the Internet when he selects either profile. How could you view the hardware profiles configured on the user's workstation?

    A. Select the Add Hardware Wizard from Control Panel, and then select Hardware Profiles.

   B. Select the Hardware tab of the System Properties dialog box, and then click the Hardware Profiles.

   C. Select the Advanced tab of the System Properties dialog box, and click the Settings button.

   D. Select the Hardware Profiles tab on the System Properties dialog box.

7. You are a DST for a large record store. A user says she recently upgraded her Windows 98 computer to Windows XP Home Edition. Now her speakers do not produce any sound when she plays a DVD. What tools can you use to troubleshoot this problem? (Choose two.)

   A. You can use the Add Hardware Wizard, and select the Test Speaker option.

   B. You can use the Add Hardware Wizard, select the hardware device you wish to test, and view the current status of the device.

   C. You can use the Add Or Remove Programs utility and uninstall the device drivers for the speakers.

   D. You can use Device Manager to verify whether the device was working properly.

8. You are a DST for a resort that relies heavily on wireless technology. Several of your users are running Windows XP Professional laptops with IEEE 802.11b NICs, and the rest are running Windows XP Home Edition workstations with IEEE 802.11g NICs. The network administrator has upgraded from an IEEE 802.11b Access Point to an IEEE 802.11g Access Point. The three users with the 802.11b NIC cards are concerned that they will no longer be able to use the wireless network. What will you tell them?

   A. You should tell them that they must upgrade their NICs to 802.11g.

   B. You should tell them that 802.11g is backward compatible with 802.11b.

   C. You should tell them that they need to buy a Wireless Digital Amplifier (WDA).

   D. You should tell them to use a 10/100 megabits per second (Mbps) Ethernet NIC.

9. You are a DST for a nursing home and you support 15 users. The users are all running Windows XP Home Edition. One of the nurses calls you and says that none of his USB-connected devices are working. You suspect that one of the connected devices is drawing too much power and causing the problem. How should you check to see if this is indeed the problem?

   A. You should select Power Options from Control Panel, and click the USB Device tab.

   B. You should use the Power Options utility in Control Panel, select the Advanced tab, and click the USB device button.

C. You should use Device Manager, and select the USB Root Hub from the Universal Serial Bus Controllers node. There, you can select the Power tab and view all attached USB devices.

D. You can use Device Manager and select the Power Management tab of the USB Root Hub Properties dialog box.

10. You are a DST for a private flight school that has four workstations running Windows XP Professional. One of the instructors installed a new USB joystick to his workstation and calls you to say that the joystick is not functioning. He wants to use the original joystick and needs to have it running within an hour. What is the fastest way to resolve this problem?

A. Using Device Manager, uninstall the new device, plug in the original USB joystick and have it automatically install the drivers.

B. Using Device Manager, revert back to the original driver using the Roll Back Driver button.

C. Use the Remove Drivers Wizard to uninstall the new joystick and select the option to install the new one manually.

D. Restart Windows XP Professional, and press the F8 key when prompted to do so.

Objectives 3.4 Answers

1.   **Correct Answers: C**

    A. **Incorrect:** There is no such wizard. Device Manager indicates when there is a conflict between hardware devices.

    B. **Incorrect:** The Performance tab is not used to display device conflicts.

    C. **Correct:** You should use Device Manager.

    D. **Incorrect:** There is no such wizard. Device Manager indicates when there is a conflict between hardware devices.

2.   **Correct Answers: A**

    A. **Correct:** Device Manager is the tool to use when you have problems with a device not functioning, or if you need to update device drivers, uninstall a device, or troubleshoot conflicts that might exist between two devices.

    B. **Incorrect:** Disk Management is used to manage your hard disks and removable storage devices, such as CD-ROM, CD-RW, DVD-ROM, and DVD-R drives. With Disk Management, you can create, remove, and format partitions, change drive letters, convert basic disks to dynamic disks, and check the status or health of each partition or volume.

    C. **Incorrect:** Disk Defragmenter is used to defragment a partition. A fragmented partition is one in which data is not stored in contiguous files. This can slow down disk access speed because data in one file might be spread across multiple areas of the hard disk.

    D. **Incorrect:** There is no such tool. Device Manager is the tool used to troubleshoot problems that you might be experiencing with a hardware device, or if you need to update device drivers, uninstall a device, or troubleshoot conflicts that might exist between two devices.

3.   **Correct Answers: B**

    A. **Incorrect:** You should tell the manager that it is possible using hardware profiles. A hardware profile can be configured on a workstation using the Hardware tab of the System Properties dialog box. There, you can create a different profile name and, through Device Manager, configure which devices you want enabled or disabled if that profile is selected by the user when they are prompted at system startup.

B. **Correct:** A hardware profile can be configured on a workstation using the Hardware tab of the System Properties dialog box. There, you can select the Hardware Profiles button and create a new hardware profile by copying the default profile and editing it. Through Device Manager, you can configure which devices you want enabled or disabled if that profile is selected by the user when prompted at system startup.

C. **Incorrect:** There is no reason to create a dual-bootable operating system because the manager has not indicated one was needed in this scenario. You should tell the manager that it is possible using hardware profiles to have two different hardware configurations. A hardware profile can be configured on a workstation using the Hardware tab of the System Properties dialog box. There, you can select the Hardware Profiles button and create a new hardware profile by copying the default profile and editing it. Through Device Manager, you can configure which devices you want enabled or disabled if that profile is selected by the user when prompted at system startup.

D. **Incorrect:** There is no such wizard. You should tell the manager that it is possible using hardware profiles. A hardware profile can be configured on a workstation using the Hardware tab of the System Properties dialog box. There, you can select the Hardware Profiles button and create a new hardware profile. Through Device Manager, you can configure which devices you want enabled or disabled if that profile is selected by the user when they are prompted at system startup.

4. **Correct Answers: D**

A. **Incorrect:** A yellow question mark means the device was installed but the operating system was unable to find and install a driver.

B. **Incorrect:** A yellow question mark means the device was installed, but the operating system was unable to find and install a driver. A yellow exclamation point means there is a problem with a device.

C. **Incorrect:** A yellow question mark means the device was installed, but the operating system was unable to find and install a driver.

D. **Correct:** A yellow question mark means the device was installed, but the operating system was unable to find and install a driver. A yellow exclamation point means there is a problem with a device, and a red X means the device has been disabled.

5. **Correct Answers: C**

A. **Incorrect:** This will work, but it is faster to double-click the mouse driver in the Device Manager utility, click the Drivers tab, and then click the Roll Back Driver button to revert back to the previous mouse driver.

B. Incorrect: Reinstalling the operating system might or might not correct the mouse driver problem. If a new mouse was installed after the operating system was installed, reinstalling the operating system will not solve the problem. In this scenario, we are only concerned with replacing the mouse driver, not the operating system. Simply double-click the mouse driver in the Device Manager utility, click the Drivers tab, and then click the Roll Back Driver button to revert back to the previous mouse driver.

C. Correct: The Roll Back feature available in Windows XP Professional can save you a lot of time and effort. Double-click the mouse driver in the Device Manager utility, click the Drivers tab, and then click the Roll Back Driver button to revert back to the previous mouse driver.

D. Incorrect: There is no such wizard. To revert back to the original mouse driver, simply double-click the mouse driver in the Device Manager utility, click the Drivers tab, and then click the Roll Back Driver button to revert back to the previous mouse driver.

6. Correct Answers: B

A. Incorrect: Select the Hardware tab in System Properties dialog box, and then click the Hardware Profiles button.

B. Correct: A hardware profile can be configured on a workstation using the Hardware tab of the System Properties dialog box. There, you can select the Hardware Profiles button and create a new hardware profile or see which hardware profiles have been created. Through Device Manager, you can configure which devices you want enabled or disabled if that profile is selected by the user when he is prompted at system startup.

C. Incorrect: The Advanced tab of the System Properties dialog box enables you to configure user profiles, startup and recovery parameters, visual effects, processor scheduling, memory usage, and virtual memory. A hardware profile can be configured on a workstation using the Hardware tab of the System Properties dialog box. There, you can select the Hardware Profiles button and create a new hardware profile. Through Device Manager, you can configure which devices you want enabled or disabled if that profile is selected by the user when he is prompted at system startup.

D. Incorrect: There is no such tab on the System Properties dialog box. To view or create a hardware profile, select the Hardware tab on the System Properties dialog box. There, you can select the Hardware Profiles button and create a new hardware profile.

7.   Correct Answers: B and D

    A. Incorrect: There is no such option. To troubleshoot hardware devices, you should use Device Manager.

    B. Correct: The Add Hardware Wizard can also be used to troubleshoot devices already installed on your computer.

    C. Incorrect: The Add or Remove Programs is used to remove software programs, not hardware devices. Device Manager and Add Hardware Wizard should be used to troubleshoot hardware device problems.

    D. Correct: Device Manager can be used to troubleshoot hardware devices, as well as to update, roll back, and uninstall hardware device drivers.

8.   Correct Answers: B

    A. Incorrect: 802.11g Access Points are backward compatible with 802.11b.

    B. Correct: 802.11g Access Points are backward compatible with 802.11b.

    C. Incorrect: There is no such thing needed. 802.11g Access Points are backward compatible with 802.11b.

    D. Incorrect: A 10/100 Mbps Ethernet NIC will not work on a wireless network. Because 802.11g Access Points are backward compatible with 802.11b, there is no need to do anything.

9.   Correct Answers: C

    A. Incorrect: There is no such tab in Power Options. To troubleshoot USB devices, you should use Device Manager. Expand the Universal Serial Bus controllers' node and then double-click the USB Root Hub. From the USB Root Hub Properties dialog box, click the Power tab and note the attached devices and power-required hardware devices.

    B. Incorrect: The Power Options utility does not contain any references to USB devices. To troubleshoot USB devices, you should use Device Manager. Expand the Universal Serial Bus controllers' node and then double-click the USB Root Hub. From the USB Root Hub Properties dialog box, click the Power tab and note the attached devices and power-required hardware devices.

    C. Correct: To troubleshoot USB devices, you should use Device Manager. Expand the Universal Serial Bus controllers' node and then double-click USB Root Hub. From the USB Root Hub Properties dialog box, click the Power tab and note the attached devices and power-required hardware devices.

D. Incorrect: To troubleshoot USB devices, you should use Device Manager. Expand the Universal Serial Bus controllers' node and then double-click the USB Root Hub. From the USB Root Hub Properties dialog box, click the Power tab and note the attached devices and power-required hardware devices. The Power Management tab displays two options: Allow The Computer To Turn Off This Device To Save Power, and Allow This Device To Bring The Computer Out Of Standby.

10.   Correct Answers: A

A. Correct: USB devices usually take little or no configuration.

B. Incorrect: In this scenario, we want to revert back to the original hardware, not just change the driver.

C. Incorrect: There is no such wizard. You should use Device Manager to uninstall the new device, plug in the original USB joystick, and have it automatically install the drivers.

D. Incorrect: To uninstall the new joystick, you should use the Device Manager to uninstall the new device, plug in the original USB joystick, and have it automatically install the drivers.

16 Configuring and Troubleshooting the Desktop and User Environments (4.0)

The Configuring and Troubleshooting the Desktop and User Environments objective domain focuses on the skills you will need to configure, troubleshoot, and monitor the performance of your users' workstations. The exam covers the following six areas: the user environment, multiple languages and locations, local security policies, local user and group accounts, logon problems, and monitoring system performance.

As a desktop support technician (DST), you must be able to configure the desktop settings of a workstation, which can include toolbar settings, accessibility options, multiple user access configurations, regional settings, and creation of local and group accounts. You must be able to troubleshoot security settings that can prevent a user from logging on to a computer, as well as identify logon problems that might be the result of local or domain policies. You should be able to troubleshoot system startup problems and answer questions that users might have regarding logon issues.

The world has gotten smaller as users conduct business in countries all over the world. As a DST, you must be able to configure workstations to support the use of multiple languages and locations. You should know how to configure a computer to use different currency notations as well as foreign-language representations of time, numbers, and dates.

In many large organizations, groups are configured on networks to facilitate administration. Sometimes users might not have access to a resource because group membership, security settings, or local security policies restrict them. You should be able to troubleshoot these access problems. Finally, the DST must ensure that the user's system is performing at optimum capacity.

Tested Skills and Suggested Practices

The skills that you need to successfully master the Configuring and Troubleshooting the Desktop and User Environments objective domain on the Supporting Users and Troubleshooting a Microsoft Windows XP Operating System exam include the following:

- Configure the user environment
    - ❑ Practice 1: Right-click a blank portion of the taskbar, and select Properties from the menu. Note the options in the Taskbar And Start Menu Properties dialog box. Experiment with checking and clearing the check boxes in the

Taskbar appearance section, and observe the effect of these actions on the taskbar menu. You should practice locking the taskbar, hiding it, keeping it on the top of all windows, and grouping similar taskbar buttons on it.

❑ Practice 2: Click the Start button, and select Control Panel from the menu. From the Pick A Category list, click Accessibility Options. Note the options available on the Accessibility Options screen. Select Accessibility Options, and look at the Accessibility Options dialog box. Practice configuring StickyKeys, Filter-Keys, and ToggleKeys.

❑ Practice 3: From Control Panel, select User Accounts. From the Select Logon And Logoff Options screen, note the options Use The Welcome Screen and Use Fast User Switching.

■ Configure support for multiple languages or multiple locations

❑ Practice 1: From Control Panel, select Date, Time, Language, And Regional Options. Note all of the options listed under the Pick A Task heading. Select Change The Format Of Numbers, Dates and Times, and look at the options available in the Regional And Language Options dialog box. Select French (France) from the drop-down menu, and note the changes made to the date, currency, and other information in the dialog box. Click Cancel to end without applying your changes.

❑ Practice 2: From Control Panel, select Date, Time, Language And Regional Options. From the Pick A Task list, select Add Other Languages. Note the options available in the Regional And Language Options dialog box. Practice adding another language to your computer.

■ Troubleshoot security settings and local security policy

❑ Practice 1: From Control Panel, select Performance And Maintenance. Click Administrative Tools, and then double-click Local Security Policy. Expand the Account Policies and Local Policies nodes. Select an option from the details pane, and double-click it. Select Account Lockout Policy, and change the Account Lockout Threshold from 0 to 3.

❑ Practice 2: Install Service Pack 2 on a computer. Notice any warnings related to virus protection. From Control Panel, click Security Center. Under Virus Protection, click the Recommendations button. On the Recommendation dialog, note that the I Have An Antivirus Program That I'll Monitor Myself check box can be selected to disable the Security Center warnings related to missing antivirus protection.

❑ Practice 3: Install Service Pack 2 on a computer. From Control Panel, click Security Center, and then click Windows Firewall. Browse the different tabs to view the available configuration settings. On the Exceptions tab, experiment by adding different types of firewall exceptions.

- Configure and troubleshoot local user and group accounts

  ❑ Practice 1: From Control Panel, select Performance And Maintenance. Click Administrative Tools, and then double-click Computer Management. Expand the Local Users And Groups node. Right-click the Users folder, and select New User. Practice creating several different local accounts.

  ❑ Practice 2: From Control Panel, select Performance And Maintenance. Click Administrative Tools, and then double-click Computer Management. Expand the Local Users And Groups node. Right-click the Groups folder, and select New Group. Practice creating several different local groups, and add members to the groups.

- Troubleshoot system startup and user logon problems

  ❑ Practice 1: From a Windows XP Professional workstation, log on using an account you created. Enter an incorrect password, and observe the error message you receive after three attempts.

  ❑ Practice 2: Reboot a Windows XP computer, and press F8 before Windows starts. Examine the different options available. Start safe mode, and identify which features are functioning and which have been disabled.

- Monitor and analyze system performance

  ❑ Practice 1: Activate Task Manager by right-clicking a clear area of the taskbar and selecting Task Manager. Click the Performance tab, and observe the CPU and memory usage. Click the Processes tab to see the processes that are running on your system and the resources that they are consuming.

  ❑ Practice 2: Launch the Performance console from Administrative Tools. Click System Monitor, and examine the default counters. Click the Add button on the toolbar, and view the different performance objects and counters available.

Further Reading

This section lists supplemental readings by objective. Study these sources thoroughly before taking exam 70-271.

Objective 4.1   "How to Set Accessibility Features for People Who Are Blind or Who Have Low Vision in Windows XP" by Microsoft Corporation (available online at *http://support.microsoft.com/kb/308978/*)

"How to Configure Desktop Themes in Windows XP" (available online at *http://support.microsoft.com/kb/307855/*)

"How to Change the Behavior of Taskbar Groupings" (available online at *http://support.microsoft.com/kb/281628/*)

Objective 4.2   "How to Change Date, Time, Number, and Currency Value Displays in Windows XP" (available online at *http://support.microsoft.com/kb/307938/*)

Objective 4.3   "How to Audit User Access of Files, Folders, Printers in Windows XP" (available online at *http://support.microsoft.com/kb/310399/*)

"How to Reset Security Settings Back to the Defaults" (available online at *http://support.microsoft.com/kb/313222/*)

"Changes to Functionality in Microsoft Windows XP Service Pack 2, Part 3: Memory Protection Technologies" (available online at *http://www.microsoft.com/technet/prodtechnol/winxppro/maintain/sp2mempr.mspx*)

"Changes to Functionality in Microsoft Windows XP Service Pack 2, Part 6: Computer Maintenance" (available online at *http://www.microsoft.com/technet/prodtechnol/winxppro/maintain/sp2maint.mspx*). Pay particular attention to the content covering problems using Resultant Set of Policy (RSoP).

"Understanding Windows Firewall" (available online at *http://www.microsoft.com/windowsxp/using/security/internet/sp2_wfintro.mspx*)

Objective 4.4   "How to Create and Configure User Accounts in Windows XP" (available online at *http://support.microsoft.com/kb/279783/*)

Objective 4.5   "How to Change a Computer Name or Join a Domain in Windows XP" (available online at *http://support.microsoft.com/kb/295017/*)

"Resources for Troubleshooting Startup Problems in Windows XP" (available online at *http://support.microsoft.com/kb/308041/*)

"How to Troubleshoot by Using the System Configuration Utility in Windows XP" (available online at *http://support.microsoft.com/kb/310560/*)

"Description of Windows XP System Information (Msinfo32.exe) Tool" (available online at *http://support.microsoft.com/kb/308549/*)

Objective 4.6   "Using the Help and Support Center in Windows XP" (available online at *http://www.microsoft.com/technet/prodtechnol/winxppro/support/hsc.mspx*)

"Experience Help and Support" (available online at *http://www.microsoft.com/windowsxp/pro/evaluation/experiences/helpandsupport.mspx*)

"Introduction to Performance" (available online at *http://www.microsoft.com/resources/documentation/windows/xp/all/proddocs/en-us sag_mpmonperf_01.mspx*)

Configure the User Environment

As a DST, you will be asked many questions from users regarding configuration of their desktops because this is where they spend most of their time. The taskbar and the Start menu are the interfaces to the Windows XP operating system. You should know how to customize settings so that your users are comfortable with finding and executing programs. You should also be able to configure settings for users who might have hearing or visual impairments and might require special accommodations to be configured, such as larger fonts, voice-activated menus, and visual warnings. The accessibility options available in Windows XP enable you to do just that.

To answer the questions in this objective, you should also know how to configure a computer to support multiple logon accounts with Fast User Switching so that users can change from one account to another without logging off. You should also know how to configure the taskbar and Start menus, configure and troubleshoot accessibility options, and troubleshoot problems that users might have with a mouse or other pointing device.

Objective 4.1 Questions

1.   You are a DST for a large nonprofit food bank that has more than 30 employees. Two of the employees are hearing impaired and want you to configure their Windows XP Home Edition workstations to generate a visual warning when the system generates a sound. Which three visual warning options are available? (Choose three.)

   A.   Flash the caption bar.

   B.   Flash the Start menu.

   C.   Flash the active window.

   D.   Flash the entire desktop.

2.   How do you display the Quick Launch menu of the taskbar? (Choose all that apply.)

   A.   Right-click a clear area on the taskbar, select Properties, and then select the Show Quick Launch check box in the Taskbar And Start Menu Properties dialog box.

   B.   Right-click a clear area on the taskbar, select Toolbars from the shortcut menu, and then select Quick Launch from the secondary shortcut menu.

   C.   Right-click the Start button, and select Quick Launch from the Programs menu.

   D.   Right-click the desktop, select Properties, and from the Settings tab, select Quick Launch.

3.   You are a DST for a large company that has implemented a Microsoft Windows Server 2003 domain. All of the Windows XP Professional computers have been configured to join a domain. One of the users calls and complains that he can no longer use the Switch User feature when he logs off. What should you tell him?

   A.   You should tell the user that the Fast User Switching was probably removed and that you will add the feature to his workstation.

   B.   You should tell the user that the computer will have to be reconfigured to use Fast User Switching.

   C.   You should tell the user that he will have to be assigned both a local account and a domain account if he wants to use Fast User Switching.

   D.   You should tell the user that Fast User Switching is available only in workgroups, not in a domain environment.

4.   You are a DST for a small garden supply store, and one of your users running Windows XP Professional calls your office. She says that several programs need to be run every morning and that she has difficulty finding the icons on her desktop. Several other employees use her computer, and it is cluttered with shortcuts and programs. She

wants you to add the two programs that she frequently runs to the Quick Launch area of the taskbar. You are now sitting in front of her workstation. What is the quickest way to accomplish this task?

A. Right-click each of the program icons, and select Create Shortcut from the shortcut menu.

B. Right-click and drag the program icon on the desktop to the Quick Launch area of the taskbar, and then select Copy Here from the shortcut menu.

C. Use the Add Or Remove Programs utility, and select Quick Launch as the program destination.

D. Use the Add Or Remove Programs utility, and select Taskbar Properties.

5. In Windows XP Professional, the taskbar is divided into three distinct areas. What are they? (Choose three.)

A. Programs area

B. Taskbar area

C. Quick Launch area

D. Notification area

6. You are the DST for a small nonprofit school for the blind and are supporting more than 30 users. The company has just upgraded all of its Windows 98 computers to Windows XP Professional, and the owner of the school wants you to configure two Windows XP Professional computers that will be used by blind employees. What are some of the features that you might want to configure on the computers? (Choose all that apply.)

A. SoundSentry

B. ShowSounds

C. Narrator

D. ToggleKeys

7. You are the DST for a small movie supply company and support seven users. All the users are using Windows XP Professional computers. One of the users is having difficulty using the mouse and wants to know whether there is a way to control pointer movement by using the keyboard. You tell the user that she can enable MouseKeys by simultaneously pressing which keys?

A. Left CTRL, left ALT, DELETE

B. Right CTRL, left ALT, NUM LOCK

    C. Left CTRL, right ALT, ESC

    D. Left ALT, left SHIFT, NUM LOCK

8. You are a DST for a motorcycle company. One of the mechanical engineers asks you whether it is possible to move the taskbar on her Windows XP Home Edition computer to a different location on her desktop. What should you tell her?

    A. Tell her to right-click a clear area on the taskbar, clear the check mark near the Lock The Taskbar option, and then click and drag the taskbar to the location she chooses.

    B. Tell her to right-click a clear area on the taskbar and select the Move Taskbar menu.

    C. Tell her that Windows XP Home Edition does not support moving the system taskbar.

    D. Tell the user that a Registry modification needs to be made by the administrator.

Objective 4.1 Answers

1.   Correct Answers: A, C, and D

A. Correct: You can flash the caption bar, the active window, or the entire desktop as a visual warning when the system makes a sound.

B. Incorrect: You cannot choose to have the Start menu flash when the system generates a sound. The only options available are to flash the caption bar, the active window, or the entire desktop as a visual warning.

C. Correct: You can flash the caption bar, the active window, or the entire desktop as a visual warning when the system makes a sound.

D. Correct: You can flash the caption bar, the active window, or the entire desktop as a visual warning when the system makes a sound.

2.   Correct Answers: A and B

A. Correct: The Taskbar And Start Menu Properties dialog box enables you to do the following: lock the taskbar, hide the taskbar, keep the taskbar on top of other windows, group similar taskbar options, and show the Quick Launch menu. You can also show the clock and hide inactive icons that are cluttering the taskbar from this dialog box.

B. Correct: By right-clicking the taskbar, you can select Toolbars to activate a second shortcut menu. From here, you can select Quick Launch as one of the menu options.

C. Incorrect: There is no such option. To display the Quick Launch menu, either you can right-click a clear area on the taskbar, select Toolbars from the shortcut menu, and then select Quick Launch from the secondary shortcut menu or you can right-click a clear area on the taskbar, select Properties, and then select the Show Quick Launch check box in the Taskbar And Start Menu Properties dialog box.

D. Incorrect: Right-clicking the desktop, selecting Properties, and selecting the Settings tab enables you to configure screen resolution and the color quality of your display. To display the Quick Launch menu, either you can right-click a clear area on the taskbar, select Toolbars from the shortcut menu, and then select Quick Launch from the secondary shortcut menu or you can right-click a clear area on the taskbar, select Properties, and then select the Show Quick Launch check box in the Taskbar And Start Menu Properties dialog box.

3. **Correct Answers: D**

    A. Incorrect: Fast User Switching allows users to switch from one logon account to another without either user having to log out. It is available only in workgroups, not in a domain environment.

    B. Incorrect: Fast User Switching allows users to change from one logon account to another without either user having to log out. It is available only in workgroups, not in a domain environment.

    C. Incorrect: Fast User Switching is available only in workgroups, not in a domain environment.

    D. Correct: Fast User Switching allows multiple users to log on to a workstation simultaneously and for the users to change back and forth without losing any information or having to log out. This is implemented through the Windows XP Welcome screen, which is not available in a domain environment.

4. **Correct Answers: B**

    A. Incorrect: Creating a shortcut in this case would only create more icons on her already cluttered desktop. You should right-click and drag the program icon to the Quick Launch area of the taskbar, which is located directly to the right of the Start menu, and then select Copy Here from the shortcut menu.

    B. Correct: If the program you want to place on the Quick Launch area is not on the desktop, locate the program using Microsoft Windows Explorer, the Start menu, or the All Programs list, and right-click and drag the icon into the Quick Launch area. You can select Copy Here, Move Here, or Create Shortcut Here from the shortcut menu that is displayed.

    C. Incorrect: There is no such option. Add Or Remove Programs is the utility that you use to install programs on or remove programs from your computer; it is not used to place programs or shortcuts in the Quick Launch area of the taskbar. To copy a program into the Quick Launch area, you should right-click and drag the program icon on the desktop to the Quick Launch area of the taskbar and then select Copy Here from the shortcut menu.

    D. Incorrect: There is no such option. Add Or Remove Programs is the utility you use to install programs or remove programs from your computer; it is not used to place programs or shortcuts on the Quick Launch area of the taskbar. To copy a program into the Quick Launch area, you should right-click and drag the program icon on the desktop to the Quick Launch area of the taskbar and then select Copy Here from the shortcut menu.

5.   **Correct Answers: B, C, and D**

  A. Incorrect: There is no area called the Programs area. The three areas of the task-bar are taskbar, Quick Launch, and notification.

  B. Correct: The taskbar area is where buttons are displayed indicating the applications or documents that can be opened.

  C. Correct: The Quick Launch area is where frequently used programs are listed.

  D. Correct: The notification area is where the clock and icons that represent the status of certain events are located, such as an icon indicating a wireless connection to an access point (AP) or an icon indicating that your desktop firewall software is active or inactive.

6.   **Correct Answers: C and D**

  A. Incorrect: SoundSentry causes Windows to generate a visual warning when the system makes a sound. You would typically configure this feature on a workstation for a hearing-impaired user.

  B. Incorrect: Like SoundSentry, this feature is typically configured on a workstation for a hearing-impaired user because ShowSounds causes Windows to display an icon or a text note to indicate a sound made by the system.

  C. Correct: The Narrator program reads text aloud from the screen and is typically configured on computers for visually impaired users.

  D. Correct: The ToggleKeys feature causes Windows to play a sound when a user presses the CAPS LOCK, NUM LOCK, or SCROLL LOCK key and is typically configured on computers for visually impaired users.

7.   **Correct Answers: D**

  A. Incorrect: Pressing the CTRL, ALT, and DELETE keys simultaneously on a Windows XP Professional computer displays the Windows Task Manager dialog box. To activate MouseKeys, simultaneously press the left ALT, left SHIFT, and NUM LOCK keys.

  B. Incorrect: The keyboard shortcut to activate MouseKeys is left ALT, left SHIFT, NUM LOCK.

  C. Incorrect: The keyboard shortcut to activate MouseKeys is left ALT, left SHIFT, NUM LOCK.

  D. Correct: The keyboard shortcut to activate MouseKeys is left ALT, left SHIFT, NUM LOCK.

8.   Correct Answers: A

A. Correct: By default, the taskbar is locked to prevent users from accidentally moving it. You must first unlock it before you can reposition it in a different location.

B. Incorrect: By default, the taskbar is locked to prevent users from accidentally moving it. You must first unlock it, and then you can click and drag the taskbar to the location you choose.

C. Incorrect: By default, the taskbar is locked to prevent users from accidentally moving it. You must first unlock the taskbar, and then you can click and drag the taskbar to the location you choose.

D. Incorrect: Moving the taskbar is as easy as clicking a mouse button. By default, the taskbar is locked to prevent users from accidentally moving it. You must first unlock the taskbar, and then you can click and drag it to the location that you choose.

Configure Support for Multiple Languages or Multiple Locations

As a DST, you might have to assist users who have multiple languages on their computers. As more and more corporations expand to different areas of the world, computers must be able to format numbers, dates, times, and currencies to reflect these differences. You must be able to configure and troubleshoot regional and language options, as well as answer any questions that users might have about language settings, regional settings, or multiple locations configured on their computers.

As a DST, you should have an understanding of how to troubleshoot and configure the multilingual features of Windows XP. To answer the questions in this objective, you should know how Windows XP implements multilingual support and be familiar with the Regional And Language Options utility available in Control Panel. You should know how to add and remove installed input languages, and you should know how to customize the modifications of numbers, currencies, times, and dates.

Objective 4.2 Questions

1. You are a DST for a small restaurant that has 15 Windows XP Professional worksta-
    tions. The owner of the company is planning on expanding her business to Asia, and
    she wants to know whether she can have her computer display Japanese characters in
    e-mail messages and Microsoft Word documents. How should you configure her com-
    puter to do this?

    A. Select the Install Files For Eastern Asian Languages check box in the Advanced tab
        of the Regional And Language Options dialog box.

    B. Select the Install Files For Eastern Asian Languages check box on the Languages
        tab of the Regional And Language Options dialog box.

    C. Select the Install Files For Eastern Asian Languages check box on the Regional
        Options tab of the Regional And Language Options dialog box.

    D. To configure an Asian language on a Windows XP Professional workstation, you
        must purchase an additional license for that language.

2. You are a DST for an international jewelry company that has offices in the United States
    and France. Several of your sales representatives will be visiting the offices in France
    and want their Windows XP Professional laptops to be configured to display dates and
    currency in the French format. How should you configure the laptops?

    A. You need to purchase two French versions of Windows XP Professional and install
        as a multiboot system.

    B. From Control Panel, you should select Date, Time, Language, And Regional
        Options, click Regional And Language Options, and then select the Regional
        Options tab in the Regional And Language Options dialog box. There you can
        choose a list of options in the Standards And Formats section.

    C. From Control Panel, you should select Date, Time, Language, And Regional
        Options, click Regional And Language Options, and then select the Advanced tab
        in the Regional And Language Options dialog box. There you can choose a list of
        options in the Standards And Formats section.

    D. You need to reinstall the Windows XP Professional operating system and select
        France as the default country.

3. You are a DST for an international grain company and support 25 users. Each user is
    running Windows XP Professional on laptop computers and travels to and from Japan
    on a weekly basis. One of the managers asks whether he can remove Japanese from

his computer because he no longer visits Japan. How should you remove Japanese from his laptop?

A. Use the Add Or Remove Programs option in the Pick A Category section of Control Panel.

B. Reinstall Windows XP Professional.

C. Create a hardware profile, and disable multilanguage support.

D. From the Regional And Language Options dialog box, select the Languages tab, click Details, select Japanese from the Installed Services section of the Text Services And Input Languages dialog box, and click the Remove button.

4. You are a DST for an international language school. You support classrooms that are located in Europe and the United States. The director of the training center has asked you to install Windows XP Professional on his laptop computer. He wants to be able to display dates in both U.S. format (mm/dd/yyyy) and European format (dd/mm/yy). How should you configure the director's workstation?

A. From Control Panel, select Date, Time, Language, And Regional Options, and then select Regional And Language Options. Click the Customize button in the Regional And Language Options dialog box, and change the date format.

B. You need to purchase additional software.

C. You can change the format of dates by using the System Properties dialog box.

D. You can change the format of dates by right-clicking the clock located on the taskbar.

Objective 4.2 Answers

1. **Correct Answers: B**

   A. Incorrect: Most languages are installed by default in Windows XP. To select Asian languages, you must select the Install Files For Eastern Asian Languages check box on the Languages tab of the Regional And Language Options dialog box.

   B. Correct: Most languages are installed by default in Windows XP. To select Asian languages, you must select the Install Files For Eastern Asian Languages check box on the Languages tab of the Regional And Language Options dialog box.

   C. Incorrect: To select Asian languages, you must select the Install Files For Eastern Asian Languages check box on the Languages tab of the Regional And Language Options dialog box.

   D. Incorrect: To install Asian languages on your Windows XP Professional workstation, you must select the Install Files For Eastern Asian Languages check box on the Languages tab of the Regional And Language Options dialog box.

2. **Correct Answers: B**

   A. Incorrect: Windows XP Professional allows for multiple languages to be installed. You should select the appropriate choices from the drop-down list in the Standards And Formats section of the Regional Options tab.

   B. Correct: The Standards And Formats section of the Regional And Language Options dialog box contains a drop-down list of values that you can choose from. If you just want to display the date in a different format, you can click the Customize button and select from four tabs: Numbers, Currency, Time, and Date.

   C. Incorrect: From Control Panel, you should select Date, Time, Language, And Regional Options, click Regional And Language Options, and then select the Regional Options tab in the Regional And Language Options dialog box. There you can choose a list of options in the Standards And Formats section.

   D. Incorrect: From Control Panel, you should select Date, Time, Language, And Regional Options, click Regional And Language Options, and then select the Regional Options tab in the Regional And Language Options dialog box. There you can choose a list of options in the Standards And Formats section. You do not need to reinstall Windows XP Professional.

3.   **Correct Answers: D**

A. Incorrect: To remove a language, select the Languages tab in the Regional And Language Options dialog box, click Details, select the language you want to remove from the Installed Services section of the Text Services And Input Languages dialog box, and click the Remove button.

B. Incorrect: You do not need to reinstall the operating system. To remove the language support, select the Languages tab from the Regional And Language Options dialog box, click Details, select the language you want to remove from the Installed Services section of the Text Services And Input Languages dialog box, and click the Remove button.

C. Incorrect: There is no option to disable multilanguage support.

D. Correct: The Details button also enables you to configure the Language Bar properties and to create shortcut keys, through the Advanced Key Settings dialog box, to toggle between languages configured on your workstation.

4.   **Correct Answers: A**

A. Correct: The Date, Time, Language, and Regional Options dialog box enables you to do just about anything relating to formats and languages.

B. Incorrect: You can change the format of dates by using the Regional And Language Options dialog box.

C. Incorrect: There is no option to change the format of dates in the System Properties dialog box.

D. Incorrect: Right-clicking the clock enables you to adjust the system date and time but not change the date format. To change the format of the date, click Control Panel, select Date, Time, Language, and Regional Options, and then select Regional And Language Options. Click the Customize button in the Regional And Language Options dialog box, and change the date format.

Objective 4.3

Troubleshoot Security Settings and Local Security Policy

As a DST, you will typically not be responsible for configuring security policies, but you will need to troubleshoot issues related to security. Large companies look for ways to centralize administration and simplify the management of hundreds of users by the use of security settings and policies. These security settings make it easier to restrict user access and to control password security as well as logon and audits. A security policy can be configured and applied to a domain or an organizational unit as opposed to individuals. As a DST, you want to be aware of security policies and how they can affect an individual's ability to access a resource or log on to a computer.

To answer the questions in this objective, you should know how local security policies and security settings function and the effect they can have on your users. You should also be aware of several tools that are used in the application of security policies, such as Security Configuration and Analysis and RSoP. Additionally, you must understand the number of changes that Windows XP Service Pack 2 makes to Windows XP security settings and capabilities.

Objective 4.3 Questions

1. You are a DST for a large company that is configured as a Windows 2003 domain. All users are running Windows XP Professional. A user is attempting to execute the Run command at his workstation, but it is unavailable. No local security policies are in effect on his computer. He wants you to tell him what is wrong. What is a possible reason for this problem?

A. There might be a domain policy that is restricting the user from using certain commands.

B. The user might have deleted the Run command from his computer.

C. The Run command has been corrupted.

D. The user needs to run the Security Configuration And Analysis utility.

2. What tool can be used to verify your security settings and make recommendations when problems are detected?

A. Security Policy Wizard

B. Security Configuration And Analysis

C. Local Policy Settings Wizard

D. System Monitor

3. You are a DST for a small art supply store. A user tells you that she is unable to run several computer programs installed on her Windows XP Professional computer. You suspect that multiple policies might be configured for her computer, and you want to see which ones might be preventing her from accessing resources. What command or utility can be used to see which policies are being applied to her computer?

A. Resultant Set of Policy (RSoP) tool

B. Local Policy Wizard

C. Poledit

D. Configpol

4. You are a DST for a home construction business with 50 employees. At your offices, five users have computers running Windows XP Professional with Service Pack 2. One of the users has installed non-Microsoft firewall software and disabled Windows Firewall. However, the user is annoyed by the presence of Security Center warnings informing him that he does not have a firewall installed. How can you eliminate the warnings?

A. Open Control Panel, and then open Windows Firewall directly or from within Security Center. Click the General tab. Select the Do Not Monitor Firewall Presence check box.

B. Open Control Panel, and then open Security Center. In the Firewall area, click the Recommendations button. Select the I Have A Firewall Solution That I'll Monitor Myself check box.

C. When a warning appears, select the Do Not Show This Warning Again check box, and then click OK.

D. Security Center firewall warnings cannot be disabled.

5.   You are a DST for a data-processing services organization with 100 employees. One of the applications you support is a custom data-entry application developed by your internal IT department. Recently, you helped deploy Windows XP Service Pack 2 to all the computers in your organization. Immediately thereafter, users began to complain of error messages that claim the custom data-entry application is causing Data Execution Prevention (DEP) problems. You are not concerned about security risks with the application, so you would like to disable DEP for that application. Which tool should you use?

A. System Properties

B. Security Center

C. Computer Management

D. Windows Firewall

6.   You are a DST for a temporary staffing firm with 40 employees. Earlier in the year, you upgraded all computers to Windows XP with Service Pack 2. Today, a manager asked you to configure everyone's computers so that they could use Windows Messenger to communicate. The users can set up Windows Messenger for themselves, but you need to ensure Windows Firewall will not block instant messages and file transfers. What is the easiest way to configure Windows Firewall to allow instant messages and file transfers while minimizing security vulnerabilities?

A. It cannot be done.

B. Disable Windows Firewall.

C. Manually add an exception for Windows Messenger.

D. Do nothing.

7.   You are a DST for an enterprise with 2,000 desktop and laptop computers running Windows XP Professional. You often use RSoP to troubleshoot problems related to security settings. Recently, domain administrators deployed Service Pack 2 to all computers. Unfortunately, RSoP no longer works. What is the most likely cause of the problem?

    A. Service Pack 2 removes the RSoP tool.

    B. Local security policy disables remote administration.

    C. Windows Firewall blocks RSoP communications.

    D. Domain administrators have reduced your privileges so that you no longer have the rights necessary to run RSoP.

Objective 4.3 Answers

1. **Correct Answers: A**

A. Correct: A domain-level policy would overrule any local policies configured on the local computer.

B. Incorrect: It is unlikely that the user deleted the Run command. Typically, a user will not have access to a resource, rights to perform certain actions, or the ability to run specific applications because of a local, site, domain, or organizational unit policy preventing the user from doing so.

C. Incorrect: In this example, the most likely reason the Run command is not available for the user is because of a security policy.

D. Incorrect: In this example, the most likely reason the Run command is not available for the user is because of a security policy.

2. **Correct Answers: B**

A. Incorrect: There is no such wizard. Security Configuration And Analysis is the tool that can be used to analyze security settings.

B. Correct: Security Configuration And Analysis is the tool used to analyze your system security settings.

C. Incorrect: There is no such wizard. The tool used to analyze security settings is the Security Configuration And Analysis console.

D. Incorrect: System Monitor is the tool used to monitor and collect data about system resources, such as memory, processor, and disk usage. Security Configuration And Analysis is the tool used to analyze your system security settings.

3. **Correct Answers: A**

A. Correct: Resultant Set of Policy (RSoP) can be run to determine which policies are applied to a workstation.

B. Incorrect: There is no such wizard. Resultant Set of Policy (RSoP) is the best choice if you want to determine the policies applied to the user's computer.

C. Incorrect: Resultant Set of Policy (RSoP) is the best choice if you want to determine the policies applied to the user's computer.

D. Incorrect: There is no such utility. Resultant Set of Policy (RSoP) is the best choice if you want to determine the policies applied to the user's computer.

4. Correct Answers: B

   A. Incorrect: You can disable the firewall warnings, but you must do so by clicking the Recommendations button in Security Center and then selecting the I Have A Firewall Solution That I'll Monitor Myself check box.

   B. Correct: You can disable warnings about a firewall not being installed by selecting the I Have A Firewall Solution That I'll Monitor Myself check box.

   C. Incorrect: Security Center warnings do not give you the opportunity to disable warnings directly.

   D. Incorrect: Security Center firewall warnings can be disabled by opening Security Center, clicking the Recommendations button in the Firewall area, and then selecting the I Have A Firewall Solution That I'll Monitor Myself check box.

5. Correct Answers: A

   A. Correct: On the System Properties dialog, click the Advanced tab. Under Performance, click Settings. In the Performance Options dialog, on the Data Execution Prevention tab, click Turn On DEP For All Programs And Services Except Those That I Select. Then, select the data entry application, and click OK.

   B. Incorrect: Security Center does not contain settings for DEP. Instead, you must use the System Properties dialog box.

   C. Incorrect: The Computer Management console does not contain settings for DEP. Instead, you must use the System Properties dialog box.

   D. Incorrect: Windows Firewall settings do not include settings for DEP. Instead, you must use the System Properties dialog box.

6. Correct Answers: D

   A. Incorrect: It can be done by adding an exception for Windows Messenger, which Windows Firewall does automatically.

   B. Incorrect: While this would work, it would expose users to unnecessary security risks. Instead of disabling Windows Firewall, simply allow Windows Firewall to automatically add an exception for Windows Messenger.

   C. Incorrect: While this would work, it is unnecessary. Windows Firewall automatically adds an exception for Windows Messenger and most other applications.

   D. Correct: By default, Windows Firewall automatically adds exceptions for most applications. The first time users connect with Windows Messenger, Windows Firewall will automatically add an exception that will allow users to send and receive instant messages.

7.   Correct Answers: C

A. Incorrect: Service Pack 2 does not directly affect the RSoP tool.

B. Incorrect: Service Pack 2 does not make any changes to local security policy that would disable remote administration.

C. Correct: By default, Windows Firewall blocks RSoP communications. To enable you to run RSoP from a remote computer, domain administrators must enable the Windows Firewall: Allow Remote Administration Exception Group Policy setting. This Group Policy setting is located in Active Directory Group Policy objects in Computer Configuration\Administrative Templates\Network\Network Connections\Windows Firewall\[Domain | Standard] Profile\.

D. Incorrect: While this is a possible answer, the problem is most likely related to the recent deployment of Service Pack 2.

Configure and Troubleshoot Local User and Group Accounts

As a DST, you will be required to create local user accounts and local group accounts on Windows XP computers. These accounts exist in a workgroup environment and are not to be confused with a domain. In a domain, Active Directory is implemented to keep track of all the objects, such as users, groups, and organizational units (OUs). As a DST, you will not be expected to configure and troubleshoot Active Directory, but you should know what components are involved so that you can assist in the trouble-shooting process.

To answer the questions in this objective, you should know how to create local user accounts and local groups, and you should be able to troubleshoot local group accounts. You should also know how to create and add members to a group in Windows XP Professional.

Objective 4.4 Questions

1. You are a DST for a small business that employs 10 sales representatives. A user says that she is not able to log on to her Windows XP Professional computer. From the Computer Management console, you note that there is red circle with a white X in it next to her name. What does this signify?

    A. The account is disabled.

    B. The user account has been deleted.

    C. The user account is locked out.

    D. The account has been suspended.

2. You are a DST for a small real estate company that has 10 computers running Windows XP Professional. One of the Realtors says that he thinks he is a member of a local group called TopSales. Members of the local group have access to a folder on the server called Bonuses. He wants to know whether he is in the group. You are sitting in front of the computer. What should you do to confirm whether he is in the local group?

    A. Click Start, right-click My Computer, and then click Properties. From the shortcut menu, select Users And Groups.

    B. Click Start, Control Panel, and User Accounts. From the Pick A Category list, select Local Groups.

    C. Click Start, right-click My Computer, and then click Manage. In the Computer Management console, expand Local Users And Groups to view the local accounts and local groups on the computer.

    D. Click Start, Control Panel, and User Accounts, and then select Local Accounts And Groups from the Pick A Category list.

3. You are a DST for a small consulting company that has six employees. Five of the employees are running Windows XP Professional and have been configured with local user accounts, giving each user the ability to log on to any computer. One of the users is running Windows XP Home Edition. He calls you and says that he is logged on as Computer Administrator and that he is in the Computer Management console. He wants to create several local user accounts from this screen, but he does not have the Local Users And Groups options displayed. What should you tell him?

    A. Inform the user that he does not have the proper permissions to add local user accounts or groups.

    B. Inform the user that Windows XP Home Edition does not include those options.

   C. Inform the user that he needs to format the partition as NTFS.

   D. You should tell the user to run the Add Or Remove Programs utility.

4. You are a DST for a small law firm supporting 10 attorneys, all running Windows XP Professional. You are asked by the senior partner to create a local group that will contain three attorneys. Members of the local group will have access to financial reports that are located on a computer that is in a locked room. You create the local group on the computer, but only one of the attorneys has a local user account on the computer. How should you add the other attorneys, who have local user accounts on a different computer, to the local group on the computer?

   A. Select the users from the Local Users And Groups tool, and drag them into the local group.

   B. Select the two other attorneys from a drop-down list that appears in the Active Directory Users And Computers console.

   C. Select the two attorneys from a drop-down list that appears in the Computer Management console.

   D. Create local user accounts for the two attorneys on the secured computer. Then place all three attorneys in the local group created on the same computer.

5. You are a DST for a help desk and receive a telephone call from a home user complaining that his computer is very slow. You find out that the customer is running Windows XP Home Edition and that all three family members are using the same computer. The customer tells you that his wife and daughter are usually connected to the Internet when he needs to log on.

After several minutes, you determine that the customer is using Fast User Switching and that this is probably the biggest reason why his system is slow. How should you walk the customer through the process of turning off Fast User Switching?

   A. Tell him to click Start, click Control Panel, select User Accounts, and then click Change The Way Users Log On Or Off. He can then clear the check box for Use Fast User Switching.

   B. Tell him to select No Fast User Switching from the General tab of the System Properties dialog box.

   C. Tell him to select the No Fast User Switching option in the Computer Management console Action menu.

   D. Tell him to select the No Fast User Switching option in the Local Users And Groups tool.

Objective 4.4 Answers

1.   Correct Answers: A

   A. Correct: The account for the user is disabled. You can enable the account by simply double-clicking the user object and clearing the Account Is Disabled check box.

   B. Incorrect: A red circle with a white X in it signifies that the account is disabled.

   C. Incorrect: An account is locked out when an account lockout policy is configured for the workgroup or domain. A lockout policy addresses how many times an incorrect password can be entered before the system locks the user out. You can configure the system not to allow the account to be activated until an administrator releases the lock, or you can set the system to reactivate the account after a designated period of time. To unlock an account, simply double-click the user object and clear the Account Is Locked Out check box.

   D. Incorrect: There is no such designation. A red circle with a white X in it signifies that the account is disabled.

2.   Correct Answers: C

   A. Incorrect: To manage local users and local groups, use the Computer Management console. To run the utility, click Start, right-click My Computer, and then click Manage. In the Computer Management console, expand Local Users And Groups to view the local accounts and local groups on the computer.

   B. Incorrect: To manage local user accounts and local group accounts, use the Computer Management console. To run the utility, click Start, right-click My Computer, and then click Manage. In the Computer Management console, expand Local Users And Groups to view the local accounts and local groups on the computer.

   C. Correct: To verify local user accounts and groups on a workstation, use the Computer Management console.

   D. Incorrect: To verify local user accounts and groups on a computer, use the Computer Management console.

3.   Correct Answers: B

   A. Incorrect: Windows XP Home Edition does not include the Local Users And Groups option.

   B. Correct: The user will have to upgrade to Windows XP Professional if he wants the Local Users And Groups snap-in.

C. Incorrect: It does not matter how the partition is formatted; Windows XP Home Edition does not include the Local Users and Groups option in the Computer Management console.

D. Incorrect: The user needs to upgrade his Windows XP Home Edition to Windows XP Professional if he wants the Local Users And Groups option in Computer Management.

4.   Correct Answers: D

A. Incorrect: A local group can contain only local user accounts from the computer containing the local group. You would have to create local user accounts for the two attorneys on the secured computer and place all three attorneys in the local group.

B. Incorrect: In a workgroup, there is no Active Directory. Local user accounts must be configured on each computer. Local groups configured on a computer can contain only local user accounts configured on the same computer.

C. Incorrect: There is no drop-down list in the Computer Management console.

D. Correct: Remember that local groups can contain only local user accounts, which are on the same physical computer as the local group.

5.   Correct Answers: A

A. Correct: By selecting the Change The Way Users Log On Or Off option, you can also clear the check box for Use The Welcome Screen, for better security.

B. Incorrect: There is no No Fast User Switching option on the General tab. You should tell the customer to click Start, click Control Panel, select User Accounts, and then click Change The Way Users Log On Or Off. He can then clear the check box for Use Fast User Switching.

C. Incorrect: There is no No Fast User Switching option.

D. Incorrect: The Local Users And Groups tool is not available in Windows XP Home Edition; it is available in Windows XP Professional. There is no option in the tool that addresses Fast User Switching.

Objective 4.5

Troubleshoot System Startup and User Logon Problems

As a DST, you will have to troubleshoot local and domain logon issues. When users cannot log on to their computers or log on to their domains, they cannot work. Network resources cannot be accessed until a user is authenticated, either by their local computer or by a domain controller. You should be able to troubleshoot the possible reasons why the logon is not working, and you should also be able to troubleshoot any startup problems that a user might be experiencing.

To answer the questions in this objective, you should know how to reply to questions posed by a user relating to system startup issues. You should also know how to troubleshoot logon issues, both locally and over a domain.

Objective 4.5 Questions

1. You are a DST for a small computer consulting firm that supports 100 users. The company currently has Windows XP Professional computers that have recently joined a domain. Several users have not joined the domain yet, and you are in a user's office sitting in front of one of the computers. How should you configure the workstation to join the domain?

    A. Windows XP Professional workstations cannot join a domain.

    B. Right-click My Computer, and select Properties. From the System Properties dialog box, select the General tab, and then click the Change button.

    C. Right-click My Computer, and select Properties. From the System Properties dialog box, select the Computer Name tab, and then click the Change button.

    D. You can run the Join Domain Wizard from the Windows XP Professional CD-ROM.

2. You are the DST for a company that gives technical support to various businesses. A user calls you and says that she cannot log on. She tells you that she was able to log on yesterday without any problems. The message that she is receiving says that the password or logon is incorrect, but she insists that she is entering the correct information. What is the most likely cause of this problem?

    A. The user is not authorized.

    B. The user needs to reboot.

    C. Caps Lock is on.

    D. The user forgot her password.

3. You are a DST for a small airline that has 30 Windows XP Professional computers and 2 computers that are running Windows XP Home Edition. The administrator recently installed a computer running Windows Server 2003 and created a domain named contoso.msft. One of the users of the Windows XP Home Edition computer calls and says he is not able to join the domain. What should you tell him?

    A. You should tell the user that the administrator needs to add a computer account for his computer.

    B. You should tell the user that his computer needs to be domain enabled, using the Setup Wizard.

    C. You should tell the user that a Windows XP Home Edition computer cannot join a domain.

    D. You should tell the user that he first needs to create a user account on the Windows Server 2003 computer, and then he can join the domain.

Objective 4.5 Answers

1.   Correct Answers: C

A.   Incorrect: Windows XP Professional workstations can join domains. Windows XP Home Edition workstations cannot. To join a domain, click Start, click Control Panel, click Performance And Maintenance, and then click System. From the System Properties dialog box, select the Computer Name tab, and then click the Change button.

B.   Incorrect: You must select the Computer Name tab and then click the Change button to join a domain.

C.   Correct: You can also click Start, click Control Panel, click Performance And Maintenance, and then click System. From the System Properties dialog box, select the Computer Name tab, and then click the Change button.

D.   Incorrect: There is no Join Domain Wizard. To join a domain, click Start, click Control Panel, click Performance And Maintenance, and then click System. From the System Properties dialog box, select the Computer Name tab, and click the Change button.

2.   Correct Answers: C

A.   Incorrect: The error that the user is getting indicates that this is a logon/password issue, not a permissions or rights issue. Access deny errors typically indicate that there is a permissions or rights issue.

B.   Incorrect: Rebooting a computer will not reset passwords.

C.   Correct: Many users leave Caps Lock on when entering a password. This is one of the biggest errors made, so you should always recommend checking Caps Lock.

D.   Incorrect: This is unlikely because the user stated that she logged in yesterday without an error.

3.   Correct Answers: C

A.   Incorrect: Windows XP Home Edition computers cannot join a domain.

B.   Incorrect: There is no such option. Windows XP Home Edition computers cannot join a domain.

C.   Correct: Windows XP Home Edition computers cannot join a domain.

D.   Incorrect: Windows XP Home Edition computers cannot join a domain.

Monitor and Analyze System Performance

Users will turn to you as a DST when they feel that their computers are not performing optimally. Users might complain that their workstations are running slowly or that it takes too long for their computers to start up when they first turn them on. You should understand how certain background programs can slow down a system and what you can do to remedy the problems. You should also know how to use the Help And Support tool to assist in troubleshooting system performance issues.

To answer the questions in this objective, you should know how to optimize Windows XP startup, removing unnecessary background applications or unnecessary applications that start automatically. You should know how to use the System Configuration Utility, Task Manager, the Performance console, Disk Cleanup Wizard, Disk Defragmenter, and Chkdsk. You should also have a good understanding of how important adequate disk space is for both temporary file storage and virtual memory.

Objective 4.6 Questions

1. You are a DST for a small computer consulting company that supports 50 users who have Windows XP Professional computers. One of the users calls and says that the system takes too long to start up when he comes to work in the morning. You want to see which applications or programs are loading at startup that might be slowing down his system. You decide to use the System Configuration Utility. What command do you enter at the Run dialog box?

    A. Ipconfig

    B. Chkdsk

    C. Msconfig

    D. Configms

2. Which of the following utilities scans your hard disks and identifies files that can be safely removed?

    A. Chkdsk

    B. Scandsk

    C. Disk Defragmenter

    D. Disk Cleanup Wizard

3. You are a DST for an enterprise financial services organization. A user, Bob, calls you with a problem:

"I'm running an analysis of a spreadsheet, and it has made my computer unusable. Everything is very slow. I need to continue to use my computer while the analysis happens in the background. How can I stop the analysis from slowing down other applications?"

Bob is using Windows XP Professional with Service Pack 2. What should you tell him?

    A. Press CTRL+ALT+DEL. Click the Applications tab. Right-click the spreadsheet application, and then click Go To Process. Right-click the selected process, and then click End Process.

    B. Press CTRL+ALT+DEL. Click the Applications tab. Right-click the spreadsheet application, and then click Go To Process. Right-click the selected process, click Set Priority, and then click Low.

C. Press CTRL+ALT+DEL. Click the Applications tab. Right-click the spreadsheet application, and then click Go To Process. Right-click the selected process, click Set Priority, and then click Realtime.

D. Press CTRL+ALT+DEL. Click the Applications tab. Right-click the spreadsheet application, and then click Go To Process. Right-click the selected process, and then click End Process Tree.

Objective 4.6 Answers

1.   Correct Answers: C

    A. Incorrect: The Ipconfig command is used to view TCP/IP configuration information. To initiate the System Configuration Utility, enter the Msconfig command.

    B. Incorrect: The Chkdsk command is used to get a status report of a hard disk. To initiate the System Configuration Utility, enter the Msconfig command.

    C. Correct: To launch the System Configuration Utility, enter Msconfig at the Run dialog box.

    D. Incorrect: There is no Configms command. Enter Msconfig at the Run dialog box to initiate the System Configuration Utility.

2.   Correct Answers: D

    A. Incorrect: The command is used to get a status report of a hard disk. To help you free up space on a hard disk, use the Disk Cleanup Wizard.

    B. Incorrect: This is not a Windows XP command. Use the Disk Cleanup Wizard to scan your hard disks to help you free up disk space.

    C. Incorrect: Disk Defragmenter rearranges your files so that they are stored contiguously. The Disk Cleanup Wizard scans your hard disks and identifies files that can be safely removed.

    D. Correct: The Disk Cleanup Wizard scans your hard disks and identifies files that can be safely removed.

3.   Correct Answers: B

    A. Incorrect: Ending the analysis process stops the application from running, which would restore the computer's performance but would not allow the analysis to complete.

    B. Correct: Changing the priority of the process to Low will minimize the process' impact on overall system performance. Performance may still be slightly slower than it would be if the analysis were not running in the background, but performance of other processes will be improved when the priority of the spreadsheet is set to Low.

C. Incorrect: Changing the priority of the process to Realtime would cause Windows XP to give more processor time to the analysis. As a result, other applications would be very slow, and the operating system may even become unresponsive. This is the opposite of what Bob wanted to accomplish.

D. Incorrect: Ending the analysis process stops the application from running, which would restore the computer's performance but would not allow the analysis to complete.

17 Troubleshooting Network Protocols and Services (5.0)

The Troubleshooting Network Protocols and Services objective domain focuses on the skills you will need to troubleshoot and configure Transmission Control Protocol/Internet Protocol (TCP/IP) for your users. As a desktop support technician (DST), you will need to know how to troubleshoot connectivity problems that users might have. If a user cannot connect to a resource on a remote server, you should be adept in using such tools as Address Resolution Protocol (ARP), Ping, Ipconfig, Pathping, Nslookup, and the Repair utility to help you discover the reason why. In some cases, it might be a broken connection. In other cases, a user might be able to connect to a host using an IP address but not a host name. You should be able to troubleshoot name resolution problems involving NetBIOS names or host names for which Domain Name System (DNS) or host files are not configured correctly. As a DST, you will not need to configure these name resolution services, but you should be able to answer end-user questions or troubleshoot problems for which name resolution is an issue.

There is no doubt that network security has become a global concern. It is not unusual to see firewalls, not only in businesses, but in the homes of many nontechnical users. You should be able to support users who have configured Internet Connection Firewall (ICF) or Windows Firewall. You should also know how to troubleshoot remote connections that are made to company servers or workstations and know how to connect to remote users' workstations to offer assistance over the Internet. The use of remote access features can save companies thousands of dollars a year.

Tested Skills and Suggested Practices

The skills that you need to successfully master the Troubleshooting Network Protocols and Services objective domain on the Supporting Users and Troubleshooting a Microsoft Windows XP Operating System exam include the following:

- Troubleshoot TCP/IP. Tools include ARP; the Repair utility; connection properties; and the Ping, Ipconfig, Pathping, and Nslookup commands.
    - Practice 1: From the Run command, practice entering the following commands: ARP –a. Note the IP Address and the MAC (physical/hardware) address displayed. Understand that ARP resolves an IP address to a hardware address. Enter the Ipconfig command, and note the IP address, default gateway, and subnet mask of your workstation. Next, enter the Ipconfig command with the /all switch. Note the additional information displayed when Ipconfig /all is entered.

❑ Practice 2: Right-click My Network Places, and then right-click Local Area Connection and select Properties. From the Local Area Connections Properties dialog box, double-click Internet Protocol (TCP/IP). Note the available parameters that can be configured in the Internet Protocol (TCP/IP) Properties dialog box. Practice entering an IP address, a subnet mask, and a default gateway address. Be sure you understand the valid range of numbers that can be used in each octet of an IP address, that is, 0–255.

■ Troubleshoot name resolution issues.

❑ Practice 1: If your workstation is configured with a static IP address, write down the DNS server address or addresses entered in the Internet Protocol (TCP/IP) Properties dialog box and remove them. Try to connect to a website by using Microsoft Internet Explorer, and observe the error you receive.

❑ Practice 2: If you obtain your TCP/IP configuration automatically, use the Ipconfig /all command to obtain the IP address, subnet mask, default gateway, and DNS server IP address information. Select Use The Following IP Address, and enter the information you wrote down from the Ipconfig /all command. Use Internet Explorer to connect to a website. Next, remove DNS configuration information, and attempt to connect to the same website. Does it work? Try a different website. Understand what happens when name resolution cannot occur.

■ Configure and troubleshoot remote connections.

❑ Practice 1: From a command prompt, try to Ping a remote workstation or website. If your computer is configured with a static IP address, write down the default gateway IP address and then remove it from the properties sheet. Save the new configuration. From a command prompt, attempt to Ping the remote website that you connected to earlier. Note the error message that you receive when a default gateway address is not available and you attempt to connect to a remote host.

■ Configure and troubleshoot Internet Explorer.

❑ Practice 1: Open Control Panel, and then open Internet Options. From the Internet Properties dialog box, observe the options available on the General tab. Change your default Home Page.

❑ Practice 2: From the Internet Options dialog box, select the Security tab. Click on Trusted Sites, and select Sites. Add a site to the list, and then click OK.

❑ Practice 3: Use Internet Explorer to visit a site that uses pop-up windows. When the Information Bar appears, click it, and choose to allow pop-ups temporarily.

❑ Practice 4: Click the Tools menu, and then click Manage Add-ons. Experiment with enabling and disabling add-ons.

- Configure and troubleshoot end-user systems by using remote connectivity tools.

  ❑ Practice 1: From a workstation running Windows XP Professional, right-click My Computer and select Properties. Select the Remote tab, and then select Allow Users To Connect Remotely To This Computer.

  ❑ Practice 2: From a workstation running Windows XP Professional, click Start, and select Help And Support. From the Help And Support Center screen, select Remote Assistance from the Additional Resources heading, and then select Invite Someone To Help You and note the three methods available to send an invitation: Windows Messenger, E-Mail, or Save Invitation As A File (Advanced).

  ❑ Practice 3: Open the Windows Firewall dialog box, and click the Exceptions tab. Note whether Remote Desktop and Remote Assistance exceptions are enabled.

Further Reading

This section lists supplemental readings by objective. Study these sources thoroughly before taking exam 70-271.

Objective 5.1   "How to Troubleshoot TCP/IP Connectivity with Windows XP" (available online at *http://support.microsoft.com/kb/314067/*)

"How to Troubleshoot Home Networking in Windows XP" (available online at *http://support.microsoft.com/kd/308007/*)

"How to Turn On or Turn Off the Firewall in Windows XP" (available online at *http://support.microsoft.com/ kb/283673/*)

"Troubleshooting Windows Firewall in Microsoft Windows XP Service Pack 2" (available online at *http://www.microsoft.com/downloads/details.aspx?FamilyID =a7628646-131d-4617-bf68-f0532d8db131*)

Objective 5.2   "How to Write LMHOSTS File for Domain Validation and Other Name Resolution Issues" (available online at *http://support.microsoft.com/kb/314108/*)

"How to Configure TCP/IP to Use DNS in Windows XP" (available online at *http:// support.microsoft.com/kb/305553/*)

Objective 5.3   "How to Configure and Use Dial-Up Connections in Windows XP" (available online at *http://support.microsoft.com/kb/310410/*)

"Behavior of RAS Connections With the Fast User Switching Feature" (available online at *http://support.microsoft.com/kb/289669/*)

"Dial-Up Connections" (available online at *http://www.microsoft.com/resources/ documentation/windows/xp/all/proddocs/en-us/conn_dialup.mspx*)

Objective 5.4   "How to Uninstall Internet Explorer 6" (available online at *http:// support.microsoft.com/kb/293907/*)

"How to Reinstall or Repair Internet Explorer and Outlook Express in Windows XP" (available online at *http://support.microsoft.com/kb/318378/*)

"Changes to Functionality in Microsoft Windows XP Service Pack 2, Part 5: Enhanced Browsing Security" (available online at *http://www.microsoft.com/ technet/prodtechnol/winxppro/maintain/sp2brows.mspx*)

Objective 5.5   "How to Configure or Disable Solicited Remote Assistance in Windows XP" (available online at *http://support.microsoft.com/kb/306496/*)

"Overview of Remote Assistance in Windows XP" (available online at http:// support.microsoft.com/kb/300546/)

"How to Use Offer Remote Assistance" (available online at *http://support.microsoft.com/ kb/308013/*)

"Get Started Using Remote Desktop" (available online at *http://www.microsoft.com/ windowsxp/pro/using/howto/gomobile/remotedesktop/*)

"How to Turn on Remote Desktop Automatic Logon in Windows XP" (available online at *http://support.microsoft.com/kb/281262/*)

Troubleshoot TCP/IP

As a DST, you should know how to troubleshoot connectivity problems that are the result of a computer on which TCP/IP is incorrectly configured. You should understand the mandatory configuration parameters that must be set when you are doing a manual configuration, namely, IP address and subnet mask. In addition, you should understand that if a workstation needs to communicate outside its local network and deliver packets to a remote network, you must also configure a default gateway address, which is the address of the network router that forwards packets. You should also know how to troubleshoot and configure a computer to obtain its TCP/IP configuration automatically from a Dynamic Host Configuration Protocol (DHCP) server.

To answer the questions in this area, you should be familiar with the available TCP/IP tools, know how to use these tools, and be able to troubleshoot manual and automated TCP/IP address configuration. You should also know how to answer end-user questions pertaining to Windows Internet Connection Firewall (ICF) settings.

Objective 5.1 Questions

1.   You are a DST for a large florist business that supports 25 workstations running Windows XP Professional. The company uses a DHCP server for its TCP/IP configuration. You receive a telephone call from the network administrator asking you to configure a new workstation that has been added. What must you configure on the new workstation running Windows XP Professional?

    A. IP address only.

    B. IP address and subnet mask.

    C. IP address, subnet mask, and default gateway.

    D. Nothing. The DHCP server will assign the necessary parameters.

2.   Which of the following parameters must be manually configured on a workstation running Windows XP Professional if the workstation must be able to connect to the Internet? (Choose all that apply.)

    A. IP address

    B. Subnet mask

    C. Default gateway

    D. DNS address

3.   You are a DST for a large newspaper company that uses DHCP to assign TCP/IP configuration parameters to over 300 workstations running Windows XP Professional. You are troubleshooting a manager's workstation that is unable to connect to any network resources using IP addresses. From her computer, you enter the command Ipconfig and receive the following information: IP Address: 169.254.23.57; Subnet Mask: 255.255.0.0; Default Gateway: <blank>. What is the most likely reason the manager cannot access any resources?

    A. Incorrect subnet mask

    B. No default gateway configured

    C. DHCP server not available

    D. DNS not configured

4.   You are a DST for a marketing consulting firm that supports 20 sales representatives. The sales representatives are using laptop computers running Windows XP Professional. One of the sales representatives wants to know whether it is possible to have her laptop receive its TCP/IP configuration from the DHCP server at the office but use static IP configuration parameters when she is at home. How should she do this?

A. She will need to purchase an additional PC Card network adapter card and configure one with static TCP/IP information and the other as a DHCP client.

B. She can configure a static configuration by using the Alternate Configuration tab of the TCP/IP properties dialog box.

C. She can create a user profile.

D. She can configure multiple protocols on her network adapter.

5. You are a DST for a large publishing company and support 40 workstations running Windows XP Professional. A user is having connectivity problems, and you want to view his current TCP/IP configuration. Which command should you enter at his workstation?

A. Ipconfig /all

B. Ifconfig

C. Msconfig

D. Nslookup

6. Which command is used to update your workstation running Windows XP with new DHCP TCP/IP configuration information?

A. Ipconfig /update

B. Ipconfig /release

C. Config /renew

D. Ipconfig /renew

7. You are a DST for a large IT consulting company that supports more than 300 workstations, all running Windows XP Professional with Service Pack 1. Your company has several firewalls implemented, as well as an intrusion-detection system (IDS). The network administrator has asked you to disable Internet Connection Firewall on a user's workstation. How should you do this?

A. Select Disable ICF from the Security tab of the System Properties dialog box.

B. Deselect Protect My Computer And Network By Limiting Or Preventing Access To This Computer From The Internet on the Advanced tab of the Properties dialog box of Network Connections.

C. ICF can be disabled only through a Registry edit.

D. To disable ICF, you must use the Add Or Remove Programs utility and remove ICF.

8.   You are a DST for a large IT consulting company that supports more than 300 work-stations, all running Windows XP Professional with Service Pack 2. Your company has several firewalls implemented, as well as an intrusion detection system (IDS). The network administrator has asked you to disable Windows Firewall on a user's workstation. How should you do this?

A. From Control Panel, open Windows Firewall. Click the General tab, select Off, and then click OK, to disable Windows Firewall.

B. From Control Panel, open Windows Firewall. Click the Advanced tab. Click Restore Defaults, and then click Yes when prompted. Click OK.

C. From Control Panel, open Windows Firewall. Click the Exceptions tab, and deselect all exceptions. Click OK.

D. From Control Panel, open Windows Firewall. Click the General tab, and then select the Don't Allow Exceptions checkbox. Click OK.

Objective 5.1 Answers

1. **Correct Answers: D**

A. **Incorrect:** Because DHCP is used in the office, you simply need to select the Obtain An IP Address Automatically option in the Internet Protocol (TCP/IP) Properties dialog box (the default option in Windows XP).

B. **Incorrect:** Because DHCP is used in the office, you simply need to select the Obtain An IP Address Automatically option in the Internet Protocol (TCP/IP) Properties dialog box (the default option in Windows XP). IP address and subnet mask are mandatory parameters when manually configuring TCP/IP, but the information will be supplied by the DHCP server when the client workstation starts.

C. **Incorrect:** Because DHCP is used in the office, you simply need to select the Obtain An IP Address Automatically option in the Internet Protocol (TCP/IP) Properties dialog box (the default option in Windows XP). IP address and subnet mask are mandatory parameters when manually configuring TCP/IP, but the information will be supplied by the DHCP server when the client workstation starts. A DHCP server can also assign the default gateway address, DNS server IP address, and Windows Internet Naming Service (WINS) server parameters to a DHCP client workstation.

D. **Correct:** Because DHCP is used in the office, you simply need to select the Obtain An IP Address Automatically option in the Internet Protocol (TCP/IP) Properties dialog box (the default option in Windows XP). IP address and subnet masks are mandatory when manually configuring TCP/IP, but the information will be supplied by the DHCP server when the client workstation starts. A DHCP server can also assign the default gateway address, DNS IP address, and WINS server parameters to a DHCP client workstation.

2. **Correct Answers: A, B, and C**

A. **Correct:** Workstations that have TCP/IP manually configured must have an IP address.

B. **Correct:** Workstations that have TCP/IP manually configured must have an IP address and a subnet mask.

C. **Correct:** Manually configured workstations must have an IP address, a subnet mask, and a default gateway if the workstation will connect to a remote network.

D. Incorrect: Even though DNS should be configured on a workstation connecting to the Internet, it is technically optional. Users can enter the IP addresses of the websites they want to connect to by using Internet Explorer, or a HOSTS file can be populated with the host names and IP addresses of the websites most visited by the user.

3.   Correct Answers: C

A. Incorrect: The address assigned to the manager is an Automatic Private IP Addressing (APIPA) address. This address is assigned when a client workstation is configured to automatically receive TCP/IP configuration from a DHCP server, but a DHCP server is not available. The address 169.254.23.57 is a Class B address. The default subnet mask for a Class B address is 255.255.0.0. Class A addresses have a default subnet mask of 255.0.0.0. Class C addresses have a default mask of 255.255.255.0. There is nothing wrong with the subnet mask in this example.

B. Incorrect: Dynamic Host Configuration Protocol (DHCP) is used on a network to automatically issue IP addresses, subnet masks, default gateway information, and other TCP/IP configuration to workstations that participate in address selection. If a DHCP server is not available, Windows XP will assign an IP address and a subnet mask to the workstation. The IP address will be from the range of private IP addresses: 169.254.0.1 through 169.254.255.254. APIPA does not assign a default gateway address to the workstation because private addresses are not routable.

C. Correct: Dynamic Host Configuration Protocol (DHCP) is used on a network to automatically issue IP addresses, subnet masks, default gateway information, and other TCP/IP configuration to workstations that participate in address selection. If a DHCP server is not available, Windows XP will assign an IP address and a subnet mask to the workstation. The IP address will be from the range of private IP addresses: 169.254.0.1 through 169.254.255.254. APIPA does not assign a default gateway address to the workstation because private addresses are not routable.

D. Incorrect: Domain Name System (DNS) is a name resolution server that resolves host names to IP addresses. In this example, the manager's workstation could not connect to any network resources while using the IP addresses of the resources. Name resolution is not an issue here. If a client workstation is configured to receive its TCP/IP configuration from a DHCP server and a DHCP server is not available, Windows XP will assign an IP address and a subnet mask to the workstation. The IP address will be from the range of private IP addresses: 169.254.0.1 through 169.254.255.254. APIPA does not assign a default gateway address to a workstation, DNS IP addresses, or any other TCP/IP configuration.

4.   Correct Answers: B

A. Incorrect: The Alternate Configuration tab of the TCP/IP properties dialog box allows for a static configuration to be implemented when a DHCP server is not available.

B. Correct: At the Alternate Configuration tab, she can configure the static TCP/IP configuration that will be used when the DHCP server is not available.

C. Incorrect: User profiles are created when a user first logs on to a workstation. User profiles are not used to create alternate TCP/IP configurations but to define a user's desktop settings. The Alternate Configuration tab of the TCP/IP properties dialog box allows you to create an alternate TCP/IP setting for a static configuration that will be used when a DHCP server is not available.

D. Incorrect: This would not solve the manager's problem. If she wants to use DHCP at the office and static IP configuration at home, the best solution would be to configure static IP information on the Alternate Configuration tab of the TCP/IP properties dialog box.

5.   Correct Answers: A

A. Correct: The Ipconfig /all command lists all the TCP/IP configurations for the workstation.

B. Incorrect: This is not the correct command for a Windows XP workstation. The Ipconfig /all command lists all the TCP/IP configurations for a workstation running Windows XP.

C. Incorrect: To display TCP/IP information, use Ipconfig /all. The Msconfig command is used to examine Windows XP system configuration

D. Incorrect: The Nslookup command is the tool that you use for troubleshooting DNS errors. To view TCP/IP configuration information, use the Ipconfig /all command.

6.   Correct Answers: D

A. Incorrect: To renew your DHCP-supplied configuration, use the Ipconfig /renew command.

B. Incorrect: The Ipconfig /release command will remove your current TCP/IP configuration information. You must do a /renew to get new TCP/IP information after executing the /release command.

C. Incorrect: There is no such command as Config /renew. To update your workstation with new TCP/IP configuration information, execute the Ipconfig /renew command from the command prompt.

D. Correct: To update your workstation with new TCP/IP configuration information, execute the Ipconfig /renew command from the command prompt.

7.   Correct Answers: B

A. Incorrect: There is no such option as Disable ICF. To disable ICF, deselect Protect My Computer And Network By Limiting Or Preventing Access To This Computer From The Internet on the Advanced tab of the Properties dialog box of Network Connections.

B. Correct: To disable ICF, deselect Protect My Computer And Network By Limiting Or Preventing Access To This Computer From The Internet on the Advanced tab of the Properties dialog box of Network Connections.

C. Incorrect: To disable ICF, deselect Protect My Computer And Network By Limiting Or Preventing Access To This Computer From The Internet on the Advanced tab of the Properties dialog box of Network Connections.

D. Incorrect: To disable ICF, deselect Protect My Computer And Network By Limiting Or Preventing Access To This Computer From The Internet on the Advanced tab of the Properties dialog box of Network Connections.

8.   Correct Answers: A

A. Correct: This is the proper process for disabling Windows Firewall. Note that disabling Windows Firewall greatly reduces security, and should only be done when alternatively security countermeasures are implemented.

B. Incorrect: This procedure returns Windows Firewall to the default settings, but does not disable Windows Firewall.

C. Incorrect: This procedure disables all Windows Firewall exceptions, but does not disable Windows Firewall.

D. Incorrect: This procedure disables all Windows Firewall exceptions, but does not disable Windows Firewall.

Objective 5.2

Troubleshoot Name Resolution Issues

Because IP addresses can be difficult to remember, services are available to make it easier for us humans. Name resolution services, such as WINS and DNS, enable us to connect to a network resource by using simple names. As a DST, you should be able to recognize whether a connectivity problem is because of an incorrectly configured IP address, subnet mask, or default gateway, or if the problem is a name resolution issue.

To answer the questions in this objective, you should know how to troubleshoot name resolution issues on a client's workstation and understand how DNS and HOSTS files resolve host name resolution. You should also understand how WINS and LMHOSTS files resolve NetBIOS names and how a workstation running Windows XP uses these services and files.

Objective 5.2 Questions

1. You are a DST for a large insurance company that supports more than 100 workstations running Windows XP Professional. On Monday morning, you receive over 30 telephone calls from users saying that they cannot connect to the Internet. From your office, you enter your company's Uniform Resource Locator (URL) from your browser and receive an error. You then enter the IP address of your company in the browser screen and are able to connect without a problem. You attempt to connect to several remote websites by using IP addresses and connect without any errors. What might you try to do next? (Choose the best answer.)

    A. Ping the DHCP server.

    B. Ping 127.0.0.1.

    C. Ping the default gateway.

    D. Manually perform a DNS query with Nslookup.

2. You are a DST for a small dairy farm and support 10 users running Windows XP Professional. One of the users wants to know whether a WINS server or LMHOSTS files are needed on her small nonrouted network. What should you tell her?

    A. Tell her that neither a WINS server nor an LMHOSTS file is necessary.

    B. Tell her that WINS wasn't needed, but that she should create LMHOSTS files on each workstation.

    C. Tell her that WINS should be configured in Single Mode and that LMHOSTS files do not need to be created.

    D. Tell the user that WINS is mandatory for Windows XP networks but that LMHOSTS files are optional.

3. You are a DST for a large furniture outlet and support two workstations running Windows XP Professional. The network administrator informs you that the company will no longer use DHCP for TCP/IP configuration and that all workstations will now use static configuration. You have just configured one of the workstations with an IP address, a subnet mask, and a default gateway. How do you configure the workstation to use the WINS server that is available to the users?

    A. From the General tab, select the Other Parameters button, and use the WINS/DNS wizard.

    B. From the General tab, select the WINS Configuration check box.

    C. Click Advanced on the General tab of the Internet Protocol (TCP/IP) Properties dialog box, and then select the WINS tab.

    D. From the Options dialog box, select WINS under Optional Settings.

4. Which of the following can be used for name resolution? (Choose all that apply.)

    A. WINS

    B. DNS

    C. HOSTS file

    D. LMHOSTS file

5. You are a DST for a large real estate company that has 80 workstations running Windows XP Professional. The company is using DHCP to issue TCP/IP configuration information to all of the users. Today, the administrator moved DNS to a different server, and she added a second router to the network. No one in the company is able to connect to any remote hosts by using the host name, but all of the workstations can connect by using the remote workstation's IP address. What is causing the problem?

    A. The administrator forgot to change the default gateway address after adding a new router.

    B. DNS server IP address is not updated to all DHCP client workstations

    C. The second router should be configured in the Alternate IP Address dialog box.

    D. DNS is configured with no LMHOSTS lookup.

Objective 5.2 Answers

1.   Correct Answers: D

   A.   Incorrect: The fact that your workstation was able to connect to the Web server by using an IP address shows you that your IP configuration was fine. This problem seems more like a name resolution issue. You should try to ping the DNS server to see whether it is available. DNS is used to resolve host names to IP addresses.

   B.   Incorrect: Because you are able to connect to a host by using an IP address, your TCP/IP configuration is fine. You should try to ping the DNS server because the problem seems to be a name resolution one.

   C.   Incorrect: Because you are able to connect to local and remote sites by using IP addresses, the default gateway is correctly configured. You should ping the DNS server because it is responsible for name resolution, and determine whether it is available to the users.

   D.   Correct: Use Nslookup to determine if a DNS server is responding to DNS queries. While you could attempt to ping the DNS server, many servers are configured to not respond to ping requests for security reasons. Therefore, the server may not respond to a ping even if it is functioning properly.

2.   Correct Answers: A

   A.   Correct: There is no reason to configure a WINS server or create LMHOSTS files for each workstation in this scenario because the workstations can discover each other through broadcast traffic. Since there are only 10 workstations on the network segment, there will not be excessive broadcast traffic.

   B.   Incorrect: There is no reason to configure a WINS server or to create LMHOSTS files for each workstation in this scenario because the workstations can discover each other through broadcast traffic.

   C.   Incorrect: There is no such thing as Single Mode with regard to WINS. In a small nonrouted network, there is no need for either WINS or LMHOSTS files.

   D.   Incorrect: Both WINS and LMHOSTS are optional in networks running Windows XP Professional. Because her network contains only 10 workstations and is a nonrouted network, there is no need for either.

3.   Correct Answers: C

A. Incorrect: There are no such options, and there is no such wizard. To configure a workstation's WINS options, click Advanced in the General tab of the Internet Protocol (TCP/IP) Properties dialog box, and then select the WINS tab.

B. Incorrect: There is no such check box. To configure a workstation's WINS options, click Advanced on the General tab of the Internet Protocol (TCP/IP) Properties dialog box, and then select the WINS tab.

C. Correct: The WINS tab allows you to enter WINS addresses in the order you choose and allows you to choose whether to enable LMHOSTS lookup and NetBIOS over TCP/IP.

D. Incorrect: The WINS tab allows you to enter WINS addresses in the order you choose and allows you to choose whether to enable LMHOSTS lookup and NetBIOS over TCP/IP.

4.   Correct Answers: A, B, C, and D

A. Correct: A WINS server is used to resolve NetBIOS names to IP addresses.

B. Correct: Domain Name System (DNS) is used to resolve host names to IP addresses.

C. Correct: A HOSTS file is a text file that is stored on the workstation. It contains host names mapped to IP addresses.

D. Correct: A LMHOSTS file is similar to a HOSTS file. It, too, is a text file, but it contains NetBIOS names mapped to IP addresses.

5.   Correct Answers: B

A. Incorrect: This is not a routing problem because we are able to connect to remote hosts by using IP addresses. It is a name resolution issue. The users are most likely using the IP address for the old DNS server. They should execute the ipconfig /release command, followed by the ipconfig /renew command at their workstations to update their TCP/IP configuration to point to the correct DNS server.

B. Correct: This is a name resolution issue. The users are most likely using the IP address for the old DNS server. They should execute the ipconfig /release command followed by the ipconfig /renew command at their workstations to update their TCP/IP configuration to point to the correct DNS server.

C. **Incorrect:** This is not a routing problem because we are able to connect to remote hosts by using IP addresses. It is a name resolution issue. The users are most likely using the IP address for the old DNS server. They should execute the ipconfig /release command, followed by the ipconfig /renew command at their workstations to update their TCP/IP configuration to point to the correct DNS server.

D. **Incorrect:** LMHOSTS lookup is set in WINS, not DNS. In this scenario, the users are most likely using the IP address for the old DNS server. They should execute the ipconfig /release command followed by the ipconfig /renew command at their workstations to update their TCP/IP configuration to point to the correct DNS server.

Configure and Troubleshoot Remote Connections

As a DST, you will be required to troubleshoot and answer questions that users have regarding their remote connections to the company's network. Because more and more employees are working from home, you should have a good understanding of how to configure workstations to use the dial-up features available in Windows XP. You should also understand how remote connections can be established across the Internet by using DSL or cable modems, and you should be able to answer end-user questions if problems arise.

To answer the questions in this objective, you should know how to troubleshoot modem problems and have an understanding of how users can configure their home or small business networks by using a DSL or cable modem.

Objective 5.3 Questions

1.   You are a DST for a small college that has 20 workstations running Windows XP Professional. One of the evening instructors calls and says he is having problems using his modem to dial into the remote access server located at the university. What should be the first thing you ask the teacher to check?

   A. The Network Properties Configuration dialog box

   B. TCP/IP configuration

   C. Telephone cable connections

   D. The RAS (remote access server) IP address

2.   You are a DST for a small Internet service provider (ISP). A user calls and asks how to connect his home business to the Internet. He has been using a digital subscriber line (DSL) for one of the computers, but he now wants the other two computers to have Internet connectivity. The user said that he made some changes to the router's configuration, and now none of the computers can connect to the Internet. You have the user check the IP addresses on all the interfaces, and he tells you that they are 192.168.0.1, 192.168.0.2, 192.168.0.3 for the three workstation interfaces and that the router's external interface has the IP address 192.168.0.100. What is the problem?

   A. The internal IP addresses are illegal.

   B. The external IP address must be 255.255.255.0.

   C. 192.168.0.1 is reserved for default gateway addresses.

   D. The external interface should be assigned a public IP address.

3.   You are a DST for a small computer security company, and you support 10 investigators who all have laptop computers running Windows XP Professional. One of the investigators wants you to help her configure a new modem that she just purchased to connect to the Internet. The office telephone system requires a caller to dial the number 9 to get an outside line. How should you configure the modem to dial 9 before dialing the telephone number of the workstation that she is connecting to?

   A. Enter the number 9 followed by a semicolon in the Phone Number To Dial of the New Connection Wizard dialog box (for example, 9;555-1212).

   B. Enter the number 9 in the To Access An Outside Line For Local Calls, Dial: section of the General tab of the New Location dialog box.

   C. Enter the number 9 followed by a dash in the Phone Number To Dial of the New Connection Wizard dialog box (for example, 9-555-1212).

   D. The modem will autodetect the number to dial for an outside line.

Objective 5.3 Answers

1.   Correct Answers: C

   A. Incorrect: Remember that the first things you should check when a connection cannot be established are the physical components. Is the telephone cable plugged in to the telephone? Is the phone cable plugged in to the phone jack?

   B. Incorrect: The first things you should check when a connection cannot be made are the physical components. Is the telephone cable plugged in to the telephone? Is the phone cable plugged in to the phone jack?

   C. Correct: The first things you should check when a connection cannot be made are the physical components. Is the telephone cable plugged in to the telephone? Is the phone cable plugged in to the phone jack?

   D. Incorrect: The first things you should check when a connection cannot be made are the physical components. Is the telephone cable plugged in to the telephone? Is the phone cable plugged in to the phone jack?

2.   Correct Answers: D

   A. Incorrect: The internal IP addresses should be private addresses. The IP addresses configured on the internal interfaces are private (192.169.0.1 through 192.169.255.254). The problem here is that the external interface also has a private IP address. It should have a public IP address that is assigned by the ISP.

   B. Incorrect: The external IP address must be a public IP address. 255.255.0.0 is not allowable as a host IP address. It is a subnet mask.

   C. Incorrect: The internal IP addresses are private addresses, and the IP address 192.168.0.1 can be assigned to any host. The problem here is that the external interface also has a private IP address. It should have a public IP address that is assigned by the ISP.

   D. Correct: The problem here is that the external interface also has a private IP address. It should have a public IP address that is assigned by the ISP.

3.   Correct Answers: B

   A. Incorrect: To enter additional numbers for outside local calls and long distance calls, enter the numbers in the Dial Rules section of the General tab of the New Location dialog box.

   B. Correct: To enter additional numbers for outside local calls and long distance calls, enter the numbers in the Dial Rules section of the New Location dialog box.

C. Incorrect: To enter additional numbers for outside local calls and long distance calls, enter the numbers in the Dial Rules section of the General tab of the New Location dialog box.

D. Incorrect: To enter additional numbers for outside local calls and long distance calls, enter the numbers in the Dial Rules section of the General tab of the New Location dialog box.

Configure and Troubleshoot Internet Explorer

As a DST, you will be required to support users that are using Internet Explorer as their Web browser. Because users spend much of their time on the Internet, you should be able to answer any questions that they might have about optimizing Internet Explorer and personalizing it so that it becomes easier for them to use. As more and more users become aware of the misuse of cookies and the dangers of attacks being made over the Internet, you should be able to troubleshoot and assist users with configuring the security properties of Internet Explorer. You should also be able to configure the connection properties and the general properties of Internet Explorer. Many of the questions users will have for you might involve access problems, questions regarding cookies, or general questions regarding why a toolbar or feature is missing from Internet Explorer.

To answer the questions in this objective, you should know how to configure Internet Explorer's general, security, and connection settings. You should also be able to help users personalize their Internet Explorer, making it easier to use. It is also important to understand how Service Pack 2 changes the capabilities and privacy features of Internet Explorer.

Objective 5.4 Questions

1. You are a DST for a small record company and support 20 workstations that are running Windows XP Professional. One of your users comes to your office and asks you whether it is possible to have a different Web page start up when she selects Internet Explorer from her desktop. Currently the company's home page is displayed. How should you modify her current settings?

    A. From the General tab of the Internet Options dialog box, enter the URL of the page that she wants displayed in the Address box.

    B. From the Advanced tab of the Internet Options dialog box, select the Change Home Page option.

    C. From the Security tab of the Internet Options dialog box, enter the new URL in the Address box.

    D. From the Content tab of the Internet Options dialog box, enter the new URL in the Address box.

2. You are the DST for a help desk, and one of your customers calls to ask why he is not able to connect to a website that is using the Secure Sockets Layer (SSL) protocol. He says he is entering http://contoso.msft, but the site cannot be found. What should you tell him?

    A. Tell him to try entering the URL as https://contoso.msft.

    B. Tell him that he might not be authorized to connect to the site.

    C. SSL is not available in Internet Explorer.

    D. Select Allow SSL Traffic from the General tab of the Internet Options dialog box.

3. You are a DST for a brokerage firm that has 100 sales representatives. The network administrator has just installed a local proxy server to enhance security on the network. She has asked you to configure Internet Explorer on each of the workstations running Windows XP Professional to use the new proxy server when connecting to the Internet. How should you configure the workstations?

    A. From the Security tab in the Internet Options dialog box, select Proxy Server, and enter the proxy server's IP address.

    B. Click the Security tab in the Internet Options dialog box, select the LAN Settings button, and then select Use A Proxy Server For Your LAN (These Settings Will Not Apply To Dial-Up Or VPN Connections).

C. To configure Internet Explorer to use a proxy server, click the Connections tab in the Internet Options dialog box, select the LAN Settings button, and then select Use A Proxy Server For Your LAN (These Settings Will Not Apply To Dial-Up Or VPN Connections).

D. To configure Internet Explorer to use a proxy server, click the Advanced tab in the Internet Options dialog box, select the LAN Settings button, and then select Use A Proxy Server For Your LAN (These Settings Will Not Apply To Dial-Up Or VPN Connections).

4. You are a DST for a children's bookstore that has 10 workstations running Windows XP Professional. The network administrator has asked you to configure Internet Explorer to include several websites from other bookstores as trusted sites. How should you configure the workstations?

A. From the Security tab in the Internet Options dialog box, click Trusted Sites, and then click the Sites button. From here, you can enter the URLs for each of the sites that the administrator requested.

B. From the Privacy tab in the Internet Options dialog box, click Trusted Sites, and then click the Sites button.

C. From the Connections tab in the Internet Options dialog box, click Trusted Sites, and then click the Sites button. From here, you can enter the URLs for each of the sites that the administrator requested.

D. From the Content tab in the Internet Options dialog box, click Trusted Sites, and click select the Sites button. From here, you can enter the URLs for each of the sites that the administrator requested.

5. You are a DST for a plumbing company. The company has seven workstations running Windows XP Professional. You are told that the workstations used by the plumbers must be configured not to allow unsigned ActiveX controls to be downloaded. How should you configure this setting on a workstation?

A. From the Security tab in the Internet Options dialog box, click Internet, and then click Custom Level. Under the heading Download Unsigned ActiveX Controls, select Disable.

B. From the General tab in the Internet Options dialog box, click Internet, and then click Custom Level. Under the heading Download Unsigned ActiveX Controls, select Disable.

C. From the Connections tab in the Internet Options dialog box, click Internet, and click select Custom Level. Under the heading Download Unsigned ActiveX Controls, select Disable.

D. From the Content tab in the Internet Options dialog box, click Internet, and then click Custom Level. Under the heading Download Unsigned ActiveX Controls, select Disable.

6. You are a DST for a help desk. A user who is using Internet Explorer on a Windows XP workstation calls and says that she is missing the address area of the Web browser where she enters a URL. What should you ask her to do?

A. Press the F5 key to refresh the Web page.

B. From Internet Explorer, select View, select Toolbars, and then select Address Bar.

C. From Internet Explorer, select Tools, select Toolbars, and then select Address Bar.

D. In Internet Explorer, select Tools, select View, and then select Address Bar.

7. You are a DST responsible for supporting an internal Web application that installs an ActiveX control in users' browsers. All computers are running Windows XP Professional with Service Pack 1. Recently, Purchasing ordered a new computer with Windows XP Professional with Service Pack 2 installed. The user of that computer complains that the internal Web application does not work properly. What should you ask her to do?

A. Log on to the computer as a member of the local Administrators group.

B. Click the Tools menu, and then click Internet Options. Click the Security tab. Adjust the security settings for the Internet zone to Low.

C. Look for the Information Bar. When it appears, click it, and then click Install ActiveX Control.

D. Service Pack 2 disables ActiveX, and it cannot be re-enabled without uninstalling Service Pack 2.

8. You are a DST responsible for supporting 45 users at a health care services firm. All computers have Windows XP Professional with Service Pack 2. Recently, a user installed an Internet Explorer add-on toolbar that she thought would help her perform research more effectively. However, it seems to be slowing her computer. The toolbar does not seem to be listed in Add Or Remove Programs. How should you remove the add-on toolbar?

A. Click the Tools menu, and then click Manage Add-ons. Select the unwanted add-on, click Disable, and then click OK.

B. Click the Tools menu, and then click Internet Options. Click the Security tab, and then click the Add-ons button. Select the unwanted add-on, click Uninstall, and then click OK.

   C. Click the Tools menu, and then click Internet Options. Click the Programs tab, and then click Manage Add-ons. Select the unwanted add-on, click Uninstall, and then click OK.

   D. Uninstall and then reinstall Internet Explorer.

9. You are a DST responsible for supporting users at a managed services enterprise. All computers have Windows XP Professional and have recently been upgraded to Service Pack 2. A user complains that she needs to use a website, but the pop-up window that normally appears does not appear. Which are valid ways to resolve the problem? (Choose all that apply.)

   A. Click the Tools menu, and then click Manage Add-ons. Click the Pop-up Blocker add-on, click Disable, and then click OK.

   B. Click the Information Bar, and then click Always Allow Pop-ups From This Site.

   C. Click the Tools menu, then click Pop-Up Blocker, and then click Pop-Up Blocker Settings. Enter the website's address in the Address Of Web Site To Allow box, and then click Add.

   D. Internet Explorer with Service Pack 2 does not permit pop-ups. Contact the website administrators and have them update their website to not use pop-ups.

Objective 5.4 Answers

1.   Correct Answers: A

A. Correct: The General tab of the Internet Options dialog box enables you to change the home page, delete cookies, delete temporary files, check for newer versions of stored files, allocate the amount of disk space you want temporary Internet files to use, select the number of days you want to store pages in History, and clear History. You can also select the colors, fonts, and languages that your Web browser will use, as well as configure accessibility options from the General tab.

B. Incorrect: From the General tab of the Internet Options dialog box, enter the URL of the page that the user wants displayed in the Address box. The General tab of the Internet Options dialog box also enables you to delete cookies, delete temporary files, check for newer versions of stored files, allocate the amount of disk space you want temporary Internet files to use, select the number of days you want to store pages in History, and clear History. You can also select the colors, fonts, and languages that your Web browser will use, as well as configure accessibility options from the General tab.

C. Incorrect: To change your current home page in Internet Explorer, from the General tab of the Internet Options dialog box, enter the URL of the page that the user wants displayed in the Address box. The General tab of the Internet Options dialog box also enables you to delete cookies, delete temporary files, check for newer versions of stored files, allocate the amount of disk space you want temporary Internet files to use, select the number of days you want to store pages in History, and clear History. You can also select the colors, fonts, and languages that your Web browser will use, as well as configure accessibility options from the General tab.

D. Incorrect: To change your current home page in Internet Explorer, from the General tab of the Internet Options dialog box, enter the URL of the page that the user wants displayed in the Address box. The General tab of the Internet Options dialog box also enables you to delete cookies, delete temporary files, check for newer versions of stored files, allocate the amount of disk space you want temporary Internet files to use, select the number of days you want to store pages in History, and clear History. You can also select the colors, fonts, and languages that your Web browser will use, as well as configure accessibility options from the General tab.

2.   **Correct Answers: A**

> **A.** **Correct:** Because SSL is being used, the site URL might need to be entered by using https instead of http.

> **B.** **Incorrect:** If you are not authorized to connect to a site, you will usually receive an error stating that you are not authorized. In this example, the user is getting a message stating that the site cannot be found.

> **C.** **Incorrect:** When attempting to connect to a site by using SSL, try entering the URL with https instead of http.

> **D.** **Incorrect:** There is no such option as Allow SSL Traffic. Because SSL is being used, the site URL might need to be entered by using https instead of http.

3.   **Correct Answers: C**

> **A.** **Incorrect:** To configure Internet Explorer to use a proxy server, click the Connections tab in the Internet Options dialog box, select the LAN Settings button, and then select Use A Proxy Server For Your LAN (These Settings Will Not Apply To Dial-Up Or VPN Connections).

> **B.** **Incorrect:** To configure Internet Explorer to use a proxy server, click the Connections tab in the Internet Options dialog box, select the LAN Settings button, and then select Use A Proxy Server For Your LAN (These Settings Will Not Apply To Dial-Up Or VPN Connections).

> **C.** **Correct:** The Connections tab is where you configure Internet Explorer to use a local proxy server.

> **D.** **Incorrect:** To configure Internet Explorer to use a proxy server, click the Connections tab in the Internet Options dialog box, select the LAN Settings button, and then select Use A Proxy Server For Your LAN (These Settings Will Not Apply To Dial-Up Or VPN Connections).

4.   **Correct Answers: A**

> **A.** **Correct:** Use the Security tab to add and remove websites to and from the Trusted Sites zone.

> **B.** **Incorrect:** Use the Security tab to add and remove websites to and from the Trusted Sites zone.

> **C.** **Incorrect:** Use the Security tab to add and remove websites to and from the Trusted Sites zone.

> **D.** **Incorrect:** Use the Security tab to add and remove websites to and from the Trusted Sites zone.

5.   Correct Answers: A

   A. Correct: The Custom Level Security Settings dialog box enables you to fine-tune many areas for your Web browser.

   B. Incorrect: From the Security tab in the Internet Options dialog box, click Internet, and then click Custom Level. Under the heading Download Unsigned ActiveX Controls, select Disable.

   C. Incorrect: From the Security tab in the Internet Options dialog box, click Internet, and then click Custom Level. Under the heading Download Unsigned ActiveX Controls, select Disable.

   D. Incorrect: From the Security tab in the Internet Options dialog box, click Internet, and then click Custom Level. Under the heading Download Unsigned ActiveX Controls, select Disable.

6.   Correct Answers: B

   A. Incorrect: You should verify that the user has the address bar selected as a toolbar. In Internet Explorer, she should select View, then Toolbars, and then Address Bar.

   B. Correct: You should verify that the correct toolbars are being selected.

   C. Incorrect: From Internet Explorer, select View, select Toolbars, and then select Address Bar.

   D. Incorrect: From Internet Explorer, select View, select Toolbars, and then select Address Bar.

7.   Correct Answers: C

   A. Incorrect: User permissions do not affect the way Internet Explorer installs ActiveX controls. Instead, the user should click the Information Bar when it appears to install the ActiveX control.

   B. Incorrect: This would reduce the security of the user's computer, and make them vulnerable to potentially malicious websites. Instead, the user should click the Information Bar when it appears to install the ActiveX control.

   C. Correct: After Service Pack 2 is installed, Internet Explorer shows an Information Bar instead of prompting the user to install an ActiveX control. However, the Information Bar is easy for users to overlook, so they may not understand why Web applications do not work correctly.

   D. Incorrect: Service Pack 2 does support ActiveX. However, you must enable it on an object-by-object basis by clicking the Information Bar.

8.   Correct Answers: A

A. Correct: Use the Manage Add-ons tool to enable and disable Internet Explorer add-ons.

B. Incorrect: You cannot use the Security tab of the Internet Options dialog to uninstall add-ons. Instead, you should disable them with the Manage Add-ons tool.

C. Incorrect: You cannot use the Programs tab of the Internet Options dialog to directly uninstall add-ons. However, you can launch the Manage Add-ons tool from this tab. A more direct way is to open the Manage Add-ons tool directly from the Tools menu.

D. Incorrect: Reinstalling Internet Explorer would be overly complex. Instead, you should disable the add-on by using the Manage Add-ons tool.

9.   Correct Answers: B and C

A. Incorrect: The Internet Explorer Pop-Up Blocker is not an add-on, and cannot be configured by using the Manage Add-ons tool.

B. Correct: By default, Service Pack 2 updates Internet Explorer to block all pop-ups. However, you can use the Information Bar to allow pop-ups for a specific site.

C. Correct: By default, Service Pack 2 updates Internet Explorer to block all pop-ups. However, you can use the Pop-Up Blocker Settings dialog to allow pop-ups for specific sites.

D. Incorrect: Internet Explorer with Service Pack 2 can selectively allow pop-ups to support sites that use them.

Configure and Troubleshoot End User Systems by Using Remote Connectivity Tools

As a DST, you might be required to assist users who are not located near your office. In fact, you might have to support a user who is located in a different state or country. Windows XP allows you to use Remote Assistance and Remote Desktop for those cases in which distance might be a factor in how or when support is available for users.

To answer the questions in this objective, you should know how to configure a workstation to send an invitation to an expert and have the expert take control of the user's workstation. You should also know how to use Windows XP Remote Desktop, where control can be taken of a workstation running Windows XP Professional from a client workstation running a version of Remote Desktop Connection software. Remote Desktop allows users to remotely gain access to their own workstations running Windows XP Professional.

Objective 5.5 Questions

1. You are a DST for a large retail store that has offices in five states. An out-of-state user calls you and asks you to help her configure her workstation running Windows XP Professional. You want to administer her workstation by using Remote Assistance. What should you ask the user to do?

    A. Tell the user to right-click My Network Places, select Create A New Connection, and then choose Remote Assistance.

    B. Tell her to click Start, select Help And Support, and then select Remote Assistance from the Additional Resources section.

    C. Tell her to select All Programs and then Remote Assistance from the menu.

    D. Tell the user to select Remote Assistance from Network And Internet Connections of Control Panel.

2. You are a DST for a help desk and receive a call from a user who is attempting to copy a file from another user's hard disk while performing Remote Assistance. The remote helper cannot copy the file and wants to know why he cannot. What should you tell him?

    A. The remote helper (expert) needs permission from the user to copy files from the hard disk.

    B. The user must select Copy Enabled for the helper to be able to copy files from his hard disk.

    C. Remote Assistance does not allow a helper to copy files from a user's hard disk.

    D. The helper must have Full Control Remote Assistance Permissions set.

3. You are a DST for a large retail store and support 100 workstations running Windows XP and Windows 98. One of your Windows XP Professional users calls and says that she wants to establish a Remote Assistance session with a Windows 98 workstation. What do you tell her?

    A. Tell her that she needs to install Remote Assistance client software on the Windows 98 workstations.

    B. Tell her that she needs to run the compatibility utility on the Windows 98 workstation.

    C. Tell her that the Remote Assistance client software can be installed on the Windows 98 workstation from a Windows XP installation CD-ROM.

    D. Tell her that Remote Assistance works only on workstations running Windows XP.

4. You are a DST for a help desk and are using a workstation running Windows XP Professional. You need to connect to your home workstation also running Windows XP Professional to look at some configuration files. Which Windows XP feature can you use to accomplish this?

    A. Remote Assistance

    B. Remote Desktop

    C. Remote Control

    D. Remote Access Service (RAS)

5. How do you configure a workstation running Windows XP Professional to allow Remote Desktop connections?

    A. Right-click My Network Places, select Properties, and on the Remote tab select Allow Users To Connect Remotely To This Computer.

    B. From Help And Support, select Remote Desktop under the Additional Resources heading.

    C. From Help And Support, select Remote Desktop from the Working Remotely dialog box.

    D. Right-click My Computer, select Properties, and on the Remote tab select Allow Users To Connect Remotely To This Computer.

6. You are a DST for a help desk. A user with Windows XP Professional and Service Pack 2 calls you to help troubleshoot a problem. Recently, she edited the Windows Firewall configuration and restored the default settings. Now, she cannot transfer files to others by using Windows Messenger. You attempt to connect to her computer by using Remote Desktop, but you cannot establish a connection. What is the likely cause of the problem?

    A. Resetting Windows Firewall to the default settings removes Remote Desktop permissions from all users.

    B. Resetting Windows Firewall to the default settings removes the Remote Desktop exception, which causes Windows Firewall to block Remote Desktop communications.

    C. Resetting Windows Firewall to the default settings also uninstalls Remote Desktop.

    D. Resetting Windows Firewall to the default settings disables all network communications.

Objective 5.5 Answers

1.   Correct Answers: B and C

   A. Incorrect: To establish a Remote Assistance session, the user can click Start, select Help And Support, and then select Remote Assistance from the Additional Resources section.

   B. Correct: Using Help And Support, the user will be guided through the steps of inviting someone to help her.

   C. Correct: Remote Assistance appears in the All Programs menu of Windows XP.

   D. Incorrect: The Network And Internet Connections screen enables you to configure your Internet connection and home or small office network. It is not where Remote Assistance is established. You can activate Remote Assistance from the All Programs menu and from Help And Support.

2.   Correct Answers: C

   A. Incorrect: Remote Assistance does not allow a helper to copy files from a user's hard disk.

   B. Incorrect: Remote Assistance does not allow a helper to copy files from a user's hard disk.

   C. Correct: If a file must be copied from the user's hard disk to the helper, the user must send it to the helper.

   D. Incorrect: Remote Assistance does not allow a helper to copy files from a user's hard disk.

3.   Correct Answers: D

   A. Incorrect: Remote Assistance works only on workstations running Windows XP.

   B. Incorrect: Remote Assistance works only on workstations running Windows XP.

   C. Incorrect: Remote Assistance works only on workstations running Windows XP.

   D. Correct: Remote Assistance works only on workstations running Windows XP.

4.   Correct Answers: B

   A. Incorrect: Remote Assistance can be established only when both parties participate in the established connection. This would not be possible in the given scenario.

   B. Correct: Remote Desktop allows users to remotely gain access to their own workstations running Windows XP Professional.

C. **Incorrect:** No such feature as Remote Control is available. Remote Desktop allows users to remotely gain access to their own workstations running Windows XP Professional.

D. **Incorrect:** Remote Desktop allows users to remotely gain access to their own workstation running Windows XP Professional.

5.   Correct Answers: D

A. **Incorrect:** Right-click My Computer, select Properties, and on the Remote tab, select Allow Users To Connect Remotely To This Computer.

B. **Incorrect:** Right-click My Computer, select Properties, and on the Remote tab, select Allow Users To Connect Remotely To This Computer.

C. **Incorrect:** Right-click My Computer, select Properties, and on the Remote tab, select Allow Users To Connect Remotely To This Computer.

D. **Correct:** You can get to the System Properties dialog box by selecting Control Panel, selecting Performance And Maintenance, and then clicking System, but the fastest way is to right-click My Computer and select Properties.

6.   Correct Answers: B

A. **Incorrect:** Resetting Windows Firewall to the default settings resets firewall exceptions to their defaults, but does not adjust user permissions.

B. **Correct:** By default, Windows Firewall blocks Remote Desktop communications, which prevents anyone from connecting to a computer with Remote Desktop. Although this reduces security risks, you will need to add the Remote Desktop exception again before you can connect to the user's computer.

C. **Incorrect:** Resetting Windows Firewall to the default settings resets firewall exceptions to their defaults, but does not uninstall Remote Desktop.

D. **Incorrect:** By default, Windows Firewall only blocks unrequested incoming communications. Outgoing communications, as well as incoming Remote Assistance communications, are allowed by default.

Glossary

access control entry (ACE) An entry in the DACL used to determine which security principals have access to a resource.

ACE See access control entry (ACE).

Active Directory A distributed database of user and resource information that describes the makeup of the network. It is also a method of implementing a distributed authentication process. This structure replaced the domain structure used in earlier versions of Windows NT and helps to centralize system and user configurations, as well as data backups on servers in Windows 2000 and Windows 2003 networks.

active partition The disk partition that the system is directed to boot from.

adapter card A printed circuit board that is added to a computer to provide additional capabilities.

Add Printer Wizard A wizard used to install printers.

administrative shares Shares created automatically for administrative access that cannot be unshared through conventional shared folder administration.

Advanced Configuration and Power Interface (ACPI) An open industry specification that defines power management on a wide range of mobile, desktop, and server computers and peripherals. ACPI provides for the OnNow industry initiative that allows system manufacturers to configure a system that will start at the touch of a keyboard. ACPI design is essential to taking full advantage of power management and Plug and Play.

Advanced Options menu The menu displayed during the Windows XP boot-up process. This menu is generated by the Boot.ini file's Boot Loader Menu file. Options in this menu include the variety of operating systems installed on the computer. If no selection is made from this menu after a given time, the default value will be selected.

advanced permissions Permissions that allow the assignment of specific, and potentially unusual, levels of permission.

Advanced Power Management (APM) An advanced Plug and Play that is designed to work with portable computers only, supporting battery status, suspend, resume, and autohibernate functions.

Advanced RISC Computing (ARC) pathname The path found in boot.ini that is used to load Windows XP.

allow permissions Permissions that grant a permission to a resource.

APIPA   See Automatic Private IP Addressing (APIPA).

application events   Events defined by software developers within their applications. Application events can provide information about how an application is functioning, and they vary greatly depending on the application that is generating them.

attended installation   The Windows XP installation process used when a person is actually present and involved in the installation of the operating system.

ATX form factor   The layout and shape of a system board or computer case that meets the ATX standard.

Automatic Private IP Addressing (APIPA)   A method of automatically assigning an IP address to a computer when either no address is assigned or no DHCP server is available.

Automated System Recovery (ASR)   A tool that enables you to back up and restore the system state information and all files stored on the system volume.

baseline   A reference point, normally associated with system performance.

basic disk   A physical disk that can be accessed by MS-DOS and all Windows-based operating systems. Basic disks can contain up to four primary partitions or three primary partitions and an extended partition with multiple logical drives. If you want to create partitions that span multiple disks, you must first convert the basic disk to a dynamic disk using Disk Management or the Diskpart.exe command-line utility.

basic permissions   Permissions that allow users to perform the tasks that are most commonly required.

Bluetooth   A short-range, wireless radio technology designed to coordinate communications between network devices.

boot partition   The disk partition that possesses the system files required to load the operating system into memory.

boot volume   The volume that contains the Windows operating system and supporting files.

Boot.ini   A special hidden boot-loader menu file used by the NTLDR during the boot-up process to generate the Boot Loader menu that is displayed on the screen. If no selection is made from this menu after a given time, the default value is selected.

booting   The process of loading the first set of instructions into a computer.

Bootsect.dos   A Windows XP file used to load operating systems other than Windows NT, Windows 2000, and Windows XP. If an entry from the Boot Loader menu indicates an operating system other than Windows NT is to be loaded, the NTLDR program loads the Bootsect.dos file from the root directory of the system partition and passes control to it. From this point the BOOTSECT file is responsible for loading the desired operating system.

bootstrap loader   Contains code that begins the process of loading the operating system.

cable modem   A type of modem used for broadband Internet connectivity.

CD-ROM   See Compact Disk Read-Only Memory (CD-ROM).

CMOS RAM   A storage area on the system board that is used to determine what types of options were installed in the system. Sometimes referred to as CMOS Setup.

cold boot   The process of starting the computer from an OFF condition.

Compact Disk Read-Only Memory (CD-ROM)   A type of optical disk storage technology. It is used to store approximately 680 MB and comes in various formats. CD-R permits writing to the media, while CD-RW permits rewriting to the media.

Complementary-Symmetry Metal Oxide Semiconductor (CMOS)   A type of semiconductor that requires little power to retain information.

compressed (zipped) folders   Folders that can be created on any FAT, FAT32, or NTFS volume, including floppy disks. Any files copied into them will be compressed.

computer name   The computer name is a unique name given to a computer. It can be up to 63 characters in length. If you are connected to a network, the computer name must be unique.

Content Advisor   Controls the display of sites based on rating levels defined by the Internet Content Rating Association (ICRA).

control set   A section of the Registry that contains Windows configuration information.

cookie   A small text file that a website creates and stores on your computer. Cookies detail what users' preferences are, what they purchased, and any personal information offered by the user.

DACL   See discretionary access control list (DACL).

default gateway   The default gateway is the router to which the TCP/IP client will forward packets destined for computers on other networks.

Device Manager   An administrative tool that you can use to manage the devices on your computer. Using Device Manager, you can view and change device properties, update device drivers, configure device settings, and uninstall devices.

DHCP   See Dynamic Host Configuration Protocol (DHCP).

DHCP Relay Agent   A service that picks up DHCP broadcast messages and forwards them to a DHCP server on another network.

digital video disc (DVD)   A type of optical disc storage technology. A digital video disc (DVD) looks like a CD-ROM disc, but it can store greater amounts of data. DVDs are often used to store full-length movies and other multimedia content that require large amounts of storage space.

discretionary access control list (DACL)   A list containing the users and groups, also known as security principals, that have been assigned permissions to a resource and the permissions that have been granted.

Disk Management   The process of creating, managing, and monitoring disks in Windows XP. Also the name of the Windows XP utility used to perform these functions.

disk partitioning   Disk partitioning is the process of dividing a hard disk into separate sections, with each section functioning as a separate logical storage area.

disk quotas   Quotas that allow you to control the amount of disk space that any individual user can occupy.

Diskpart.exe   A command-line utility used to manage the partitions on your hard disk volumes.

distribution server   A distribution sever is a server that can distribute the installation files to many different computers.

DMA channels   Channels that permit hardware devices to bypass the system processor and access system memory directly.

DNS   See Domain Name System (DNS).

domain   A domain is a logical collection of computers that share a centralized database of user accounts and resources.

domain controller   A domain controller is a server that contains a centralized database of user accounts and resources. There must be at least one domain controller (DC) per domain.

Domain Name System (DNS)   A network service designed to perform name resolution for TCP/IP clients.

dotted decimal notation   A method of presenting binary numbers used in TCP/IP as numbers between 0 and 255, primarily for ease of reading.

Driver.cab   A single cabinet file that contains all the drivers shipped with Windows XP. Having access to these drivers prevents the user from having to access the installation CD whenever a new device is added.

driver rollback A feature in Windows XP that permits you to reinstall (roll back) a previously installed driver. The uninstalled drivers are stored in the system_root\system32\reinstallbackups folder.

driver signing A process in which device drivers that have passed a series of tests by Microsoft are digitally signed, enabling the operating system to determine if the drivers are acceptable for use.

DSL modem A type of broadband modem used on digital subscriber lines.

dual-boot configuration A dual-boot configuration that enables you to have multiple operating systems installed on the same computer.

DualView An extension of multiple monitor support. It enables two devices connected to the same display adapter to display different output at the same time.

DVD See digital video disc (DVD).

dynamic disk A physical disk that can be accessed only by Windows 2000 and Windows XP. Dynamic disks provide features that basic disks do not, such as support for volumes that span multiple disks. Dynamic disks use a hidden database to track information about dynamic volumes on the disk and other dynamic disks in the computer. You convert basic disks to dynamic using the Disk Management snap-in or the DiskPart command-line utility. When you convert a basic disk to a dynamic disk, all existing basic volumes become dynamic volumes.

dynamic disk database A database that tracks the configuration of all dynamic disks in the computer.

Dynamic Host Configuration Protocol (DHCP) A service that automatically handles requests for TCP/IP configuration information to client systems.

effective permissions The permissions level that a user actually has, taking all permission sources into account.

event logs Files that maintain a record of specific events that have taken place on a Windows XP system.

event logs Log files that contain the events recorded by the operating system.

Event Viewer An application used to view the event logs created by the operating system or applications.

extended partition A secondary partition that can be created after the drive's primary partition has been established. It is the only other partition allowed on a disk once the primary partition has been created. However, an extended partition can be subdivided into up to 23 logical drives in a Microsoft operating system.

Extended System Configuration Data (ESCD) A special section of CMOS RAM used to store information about devices found during startup.

File Signature Verification Utility (Sigverif.exe)   A utility that is used to scan a Windows XP system for unsigned files, providing a simple method to identify unsigned drivers.

Files And Settings Transfer (FAST) Wizard   FAST is one of two methods used by administrators to transfer user configuration settings and files from systems running Windows 95 or later to a clean Windows XP installation.

FQDN   See fully qualified domain name (FQDN).

fully qualified domain name (FQDN)   A multiple-part name separated by periods that specifies the host name's exact location in the DNS naming hierarchy.

GPT   See GUID partition table (GPT).

GUID partition table (GPT)   A disk-partitioning scheme that is used in Itanium-based computers. GPT offers more advantages than Master Boot Record (MBR) partitioning because it allows up to 128 partitions per disk, provides support for volumes up to 18 exabytes in size, allows primary and backup partition tables for redundancy, and supports unique disk and partition IDs (GUIDs).

Hardware Compatibility List (HCL)   A listing of devices that have been tested and are supported by Microsoft.

hidden share   A method of preventing users who are browsing the network from viewing the share. If you append the dollar sign ($) to a share name it becomes hidden.

home page   The website that opens automatically when you start Internet Explorer.

host   A device that is functioning in a TCP/IP network.

host name   The name of a device that is functioning in a TCP/IP network.

hosts file   A simple text file that contains IP addresses followed by the name of the host.

i386 folder   The i386 folder contains the installation files for Windows XP.

IEEE 802.11   An IEEE standard defining wireless connectivity. The most common implementations are 802.11a, 802.11b, and 802.11g.

IME   See Input Method Editor (IME).

.inf files   Files that provide the operating system with the information required to install and configure device drivers.

Infrared Data Association (IrDA)   An association that has defined a wireless peripheral connection standard based on infrared light technology.

Infrared Picture Transfer (IrTran-P)   An image transfer protocol used to send images using infrared technology.

Input Method Editor (IME)   A program that enables the thousands of characters in Asian languages to be entered using a standard 101-key keyboard.

Internet Options   The dialog box available in Internet Explorer for configuring program settings.

Internet service provider (ISP)   A business entity that provides Internet connection services for personal and corporate clients.

I/O port   The address that is used to access a device on the system board.

IP address   A number that uniquely identifies a device on a TCP/IP network.

Ipconfig.exe   A command-line utility that can be used to view TCP/IP configuration information.

ISP   See Internet service provider (ISP).

Last Known Good Configuration   The configuration settings that existed the last time the system booted successfully.

Lmhosts file   A simple text file that contains IP addresses followed by the name of the host, similar to a TCP/IP hosts file.

Loadstate.exe   The Loadstate.exe utility is one of two methods used by administrators to transfer user configuration settings and files from systems running Windows 95 or later to a clean Windows XP installation. It is used in conjunction with Scanstate.exe.

local area network (LAN) card   An adapter card that is used to connect the computer to a network.

local print provider   A service that receives print jobs, spools them to the hard disk, and keeps track of job information while the job is in the print queue.

locale   A collection of system settings that reflect regional and cultural conventions.

localized language versions   In Windows XP Professional, the non-English versions of the operating system.

logical drive   A disk storage area that you create within an extended partition on a basic Master Boot Record (MBR) disk. Logical drives are similar to primary partitions, except that you are limited to four primary partitions per disk, whereas you can create an unlimited number of logical drives per disk. A logical drive can be formatted and assigned a drive letter.

logical printer   The software configuration that is created in Windows and displayed in Printers And Faxes.

loopback address   An address used for testing TCP/IP configuration and which cannot be assigned to individual devices on a TCP/IP network. Normally it is 127.0.0.1.

Master Boot Record (MBR)   Also referred to as the Master Partition Boot Sector. A file located at the first sector of the disk that contains a Master Partition Table describing how the hard disk is organized. This table includes information about the disk's size, as well as the number and locations of all partitions on the disk. The MBR also contains the Master Boot Code that loads the operating system from the disk's active partition.

MBR   See Master Boot Record (MBR).

memory leak   A process that occurs when a program requests memory for use but does not relinquish the allocated memory when finished.

Microsoft Magnifier   An accessibility tool used to enhance the readability of the screen.

migration DLLs   Migration DLLs instruct Windows XP Setup on how to handle the Registry and program file differences between the operating systems during the upgrade.

modem   A device used to modulate and demodulate signals between remote systems.

mounted volume   A new volume to be grafted to a folder within an existing volume, rather than assigned a drive letter.

MUI   See Multilingual User Interface (MUI) Pack.

Multilingual User Interface (MUI) Pack   An add-on to the International English version of Windows XP Professional. It supports multiple UI languages.

name resolution   The process of resolving a name into an IP address.

Narrator   A text-to-speech utility for users who are blind or have impaired vision.

NetBIOS   See Network Basic Input/Output System (NetBIOS).

NetBIOS Enhanced User Interface (NetBEUI)   A fast, efficient protocol, suitable for use on small networks.

NetBIOS name   A computer name assigned a 16-character name used by NetBIOS applications when establishing connections.

Network Basic Input/Output System (NetBIOS)   A protocol called to assist in the establishment of connections over the network.

network boot disk   A network boot disk is usually a bootable MS-DOS floppy that contains the DOS-based network client software for the operating system.

Ntbootdd.sys   A copy of the device driver for the SCSI adapter that is required to gain access to the boot partition in the absence of the SCSI BIOS.

Ntbtlog.txt   A log file located in the %system_root% directory containing a listing of all the drivers and services that the system attempts to load during startup.

Ntdetect.com   The Windows NT, Windows 2000, Windows XP hardware detection file, which is responsible for collecting information about the system's installed hardware devices and passing it to the NTLDR program. This information is later used to upgrade the Windows NT Registry files.

NTFS   New Technology File System. This is the native file management system for Windows XP. However, Windows XP is also capable of working with FAT and FAT32 file systems so that it can remain compatible with older Microsoft operating systems.

NTLDR   The Windows NT, Windows 2000, Windows XP bootstrap loader for Intel-based computers running Windows NT, Windows 2000, Windows XP. It is the Windows NT equivalent of the DOS IO.SYS file and is responsible for loading the Windows NT operating system into memory. Afterward, NTLDR passes control of the system over to the Windows NT operating system.

Ntoskrnl.exe   The core part of Windows XP that creates the Registry hardware keys and loads device drivers.

offline files   Files and folders that are available to a user when the user is no longer connected to the network share.

owner   The user who created a file, folder, or printer.

paging file (Pagefile.sys)   A section of hard disk space set aside to act as virtual memory. Sometimes called a swap file.

partition table   The table present at the start of every hard disk that describes the disk's layout, including the number and location of all partitions on the disk.

partitioning   The process of dividing a physical disk into logical sections that function as though they were physically separate disks. After you create a partition, you must format it and assign it a drive letter before you can store data on it.

Pathping.exe   A command-line utility used to trace routes across an internetwork, combining the features of Ping and Tracert.

Performance Logs And Alerts   A utility that enables the user to log counter information to a file and trigger alerts based on configured events.

Performance tool   A utility that captures performance information for various subsystems on a computer and displays the results graphically or logs the results to a file.

Personal Computer Memory Card International Association (PCMCIA)   A standard that defines expansion slots primarily on notebook computers. The card is available in three sizes labeled Type I, Type II, and Type III. Also referred to as PC Card.

Ping   A command-line utility for basic TCP/IP communications testing.

Plug and Play   A technology that enables the system to automatically determine what hardware devices are actually installed in the system and then to allocate system resources to those devices as required to configure and manage them.

power-on self test (POST)   A series of BIOS diagnostic tests performed on the system each time it is turned on or reset to verify that it is operating correctly.

primary partition   A bootable partition created from unallocated disk space. Under Windows 2000, up to four primary partitions can be created on a basic disk. The disk can also contain three primary partitions and an extended partition. The primary partition becomes the system's boot volume by being marked as "Active." The free space in the extended partition can be subdivided into up to 23 logical drives.

print processor   Printing process that makes any necessary modifications to the print job and then calls on the GDI to further render the job if necessary.

print router   A print provider that can service the print job's protocol.

print server   The computer or other remote device that has a network printer physically attached to it.

print spooler   The Windows operating system service that controls the print spooling process.

print spooling   The process of saving a print job to the hard disk before sending it to the printer.

printer   The physical device used for printing. This is usually a standard printer but could also be a fax device, a plotter, or a file. It may also refer to the combination of the physical and logical printer.

printer driver   The software driver containing printer-specific information.

printer permissions   Permissions that enable you to control which users can access a printer and what actions they will be able to perform.

printer pooling   A printing option that permits you to attach two or more printers to a single printer configuration.

process measures   Objects displayed in the Task Manager\Processes tab.

Recovery Console   A command-line interface that gives you access to the hard disks and many command-line utilities when the operating system will not boot. The Recovery Console can access all volumes on the drive, regardless of the file system type. You can use the Recovery Console to perform several operating system (OS) troubleshooting tasks.

Regedit.exe   The editing utility used to directly edit the contents of the Registry (Regedit.exe and Regedit32.exe). This file is located in the \Winnt\System32 folder.

Remote Assistance   A service that enables users to request support from a more advanced user or from computer support personnel.

Remote Desktop   A process that enables users to remotely access their computers across the network and use the desktop as if they were sitting in front of the computer.

Remote Installation Services (RIS)   A service available on Windows 2000 and Windows Server 2003 servers that can be used to automate the deployment of Windows XP Professional.

remote print provider   A service that can forward jobs to remote print servers.

RIPrep images   Images created using the RIPrep Wizard that are similar to the disk images created using third-party disk duplication software.

RIS boot disk   A floppy disk that can be used to boot the computer and that will allow the computer to automatically connect to a RIS server.

RIS Setup Wizard (Risetup.exe)   The utility used to install and configure the RIS software.

router   A network device that moves network traffic to the appropriate network in a multiple network environment.

safe mode   An alternative startup mode that loads a minimal set of device drivers (keyboard, mouse, and standard-mode VGA drivers) that are activated to start the system.

Scanstate.exe   The Scanstate.exe utility is one of two methods used by administrators to transfer user configuration settings and files from systems running Windows 95 or later to a clean Windows XP installation. It is used in conjunction with Loadstate.exe.

security log   An event log in which all the audited events are recorded.

security principal   A term used to describe objects to which you can grant access to resources on a computer. User accounts and groups are major security principals.

security zones   Contain a list of websites deemed to have similar security settings requirements. You can configure a different security level for each zone and then place sites into zones according to the sites' levels of trust.

separator page processor   A printing service that adds separator pages between print jobs as required.

Setup   Windows XP installation utility that guides the operating system installation process. This process exists in two stages: the text mode stage and the GUI mode stage.

Setupcl.exe   A program that is started the first time a computer installed using a disk image is rebooted.

Setup Manager   A utility used to create a standard answer file, which is a batch file for launching an unattended installation.

Shared Documents folder   The folder used in simple file sharing that contains all shared files and folders.

shared folder permissions   Permissions assigned to a shared folder.

shared folders   Folders made accessible to users on the network.

signature syntax   Used in boot.ini when the boot partition is greater than 7.8 GB in size or if the ending cylinder number is greater than 1024 for that partition and the BIOS does not support proper access (extended INT13).

Simple File Sharing   A type of sharing used when a Windows XP computer has not joined a domain or is running Windows XP Home Edition.

simple volume   A dynamic volume made up of disk space from a single dynamic disk. A simple volume can consist of a single region on a disk or multiple regions of the same disk that are linked together.

smart cards   Small, credit card–sized devices that are capable of storing information.

spanned volume   A dynamic volume consisting of disk space on more than one physical disk. You can increase the size of a spanned volume by extending it onto additional dynamic disks.

spool directory   The folder to which print documents are spooled. This is system_root\system32\spool\printers by default.

Stop error   An error that occurs when Windows 2000 detects a condition from which it cannot recover. When a Stop error occurs, the system stops responding and a screen of information with a blue or black background is displayed. Stop errors are also known as blue-screen errors.

striped volume   A type of volume that writes data across 2 to 32 disks in 64-KB chunks.

subnet mask   A method of separating the network portion of an IP address from the host portion of an IP address.

subnetting   The process of dividing a single IP network number into multiple IP networks by modifying the subnet mask value.

Synchronization Manager   The utility used to manage offline files and folders.

Sysprep.inf   An answer file that the Mini Setup Wizard can use to fully automate the installation.

System File Checker (Sfc.exe)   A utility that scans and verifies the versions of all protected system files after you restart your computer.

System Information A utility that allows you to view the status of different components of a Windows XP system, including hardware devices.

system partition Normally the same partition as the boot partition. This partition contains the hardware specific files required to load and start Windows XP.

System Preparation tool (Sysprep.exe) A utility used to prepare master disk images for distribution using a third-party disk duplication utility.

System Restore A process used to roll back a failed Windows XP startup to a previous state.

System_root The System_root is the folder where Windows is installed during Setup.

system state data Data that contains the configuration of the operating system on a Windows 2000 computer. The components that make up the system state data will vary depending on the role of the computer in the network but normally consist of the Registry, the system startup files, the class registration database, the Certificate Services database, Active Directory, and the Sysvol shared folder.

Task Manager A utility that provides information on currently running applications and processes, as well as basic performance and networking information.

TCP/IP See Transmission Control Protocol/Internet Protocol (TCP/IP).

TCP/IP port A mechanism used to manage communication between clients and servers.

temporary Internet files Cached files. Temporary Internet files allow a user to use the Back and Forward buttons, access History, and use offline files and folders. Retrieving information from the temporary Internet Files folder is much faster than retrieving information from the Internet.

Tracert.exe A utility used to follow the communication path from router to router between the source and destination hosts.

Transmission Control Protocol/Internet Protocol (TCP/IP) A routable networking protocol used on the Internet.

universal serial bus (USB) An external serial bus developed to provide a fast, flexible method of attaching up to 127 peripheral devices to a computer.

update packs Update packs (also known as upgrade packs or migration DLLs) are required for Windows 98 applications that implement Windows 98–specific behavior.

User State Migration Tools (USMTs) The User State Migration Tools (USMTs) enable administrators to transfer user configuration settings and files from systems running Windows 95 or later to a clean Windows XP installation.

video display adapter   An adapter card that provides the interface between the system board and the display monitor.

warm boot   The process of restarting the computer from an ON condition.

Windows Internet Naming Service (WINS)   A service that runs on one or more Windows NT, Windows 2000, or .NET servers in the network.

Windows Troubleshooters   A special type of help that is available in Windows XP. This utility allows you to pinpoint problems and identify solutions to those problems.

Winnt.exe   Winnt.exe is the executable used to start a clean installation of Windows XP.

Winnt32.exe   Winnt32.exe is the executable used to upgrade from a 32-bit version of Windows to Windows XP.

WINS   See Windows Internet Naming Service (WINS).

wireless local area network (WLAN)   A network that connects computer nodes using high-frequency radio waves. IEEE 802.11 is an example of WLAN technology.

Wireless Personal Area Network (WPAN)   A wireless network that communicates primarily through the use of infrared devices.

workgroup   A workgroup is a collection of computers that share a common name. Unlike a domain, a workgroup does not have a centralized database of user accounts.

Index

Walter Glenn

Walter Glenn, Microsoft Certified System Engineer (MCSE), Microsoft Certified Desktop Support Technician (MCDST), and Microsoft Certified Trainer (MCT), has been a part of the computer industry for more than 17 years and currently works in Huntsville, Alabama, as a consultant, trainer, and writer. Walter is a regular columnist in Microsoft's TechNet Zone and is the author or coauthor of nearly 20 computer titles, including *Microsoft Exchange Server 2003 Administrator's Companion* (Microsoft Press, 2003), *Mike Meyers' MCSA Managing a Microsoft Windows Server 2003 Network Environment Certification Passport (Exam 70-291)* (Osborne, 2003), and *MCSE Self-Paced Training Kit (Exam 70-297): Designing a Microsoft Windows Server 2003 Active Directory and Network Infrastructure* (Microsoft Press, 2003). He has also written a number of Web-based courses that are geared toward Microsoft certification training.

Tony Northrup

Tony Northrup, CISSP, MCSE, and MVP, is a networking consultant and author living in the Boston, Massachusetts, area. During his seven years as Principal Systems Architect at BBN/Genuity, he was ultimately responsible for the reliability and security of hundreds of Windows servers and dozens of Windows domains—all directly connected to the Internet. Needless to say, Tony learned the hard way how to keep Windows systems safe and reliable in a hostile environment.

As a consultant, Tony has provided networking guidance to a wide variety of organizations, from Fortune 100 enterprises to nonprofit organizations and small businesses. Tony has authored or coauthored a dozen books on Windows and networking. When he is not consulting or writing, Tony enjoys cycling, hiking, and nature photography

Security resources and guidance
—direct from Microsoft

Microsoft® Windows® Security Resource Kit, Second Edition
ISBN: 0-7356-2174-8   Suggested Retail Price: $49.99 U.S., $72.99 Canada

Get the in-depth information and tools you need to help protect your Windows-based clients, servers, networks, and Internet services—with definitive technical guidance from the Microsoft Security team and two industry veterans. You'll learn how to plan and implement a comprehensive security strategy, assess security threats and vulnerabilities, configure system security settings, and more. You'll also find new coverage of service packs, Microsoft Office 2003 Editions, and Internet Information Services (IIS) 6.0. The CD provides must-have tools, scripts, templates, and other key resources.

Assessing Network Security
ISBN: 0-7356-2033-4   Suggested Retail Price: $49.99 U.S., $72.99 Canada

Don't wait for an attacker to find and exploit your security vulnerabilities—take the lead by assessing the state of your network's security. This book delivers advanced network testing strategies, including vulnerability scanning and penetration testing, from members of the Microsoft security teams. You'll find detailed information on how to perform security assessments, uncover security vulnerabilities, and apply appropriate countermeasures. The CD includes time-saving tools and scripts to reveal and help correct security vulnerabilities in your own network, plus a complete eBook.

Microsoft Windows Server™ 2003 PKI and Certificate Security
ISBN: 0-7356-2021-0   Suggested Retail Price: $59.99 U.S., $86.99 Canada

Capitalize on the built-in security services in Windows Server 2003—and deliver your own robust, public key infrastructure (PKI)-based solutions at a fraction of the cost and time. This in-depth reference cuts straight to the details of designing and implementing certificate-based security solutions for PKI-enabled applications. Get the inside information, real-world solutions, and best practices you need to avoid common design and implementation mistakes, help minimize risk, and optimize security administration. You'll find timesaving tools and scripts, plus an eBook, on the CD.

To see more Microsoft Press® products for IT professionals, please visit:

microsoft.com/mspress

Complete planning and migration information
for Microsoft Windows Server 2003

Introducing Microsoft® Windows Server™ 2003
ISBN 0-7356-1570-5

Get a detailed, official first look at the new features and improvements in Windows Server 2003.
Windows Server 2003 provides significant improvements in performance, productivity, and security over previous versions. This official first-look guide shows you exactly what's new and improved in this powerful network operating system—including advanced technologies for XML Web services and components, security, networking, Active Directory® directory service, Microsoft Internet Information Services, support for IPv6, and more. It gives you all the information and tools you need to understand, evaluate, and begin deployment planning for Windows Server 2003, whether you're upgrading from Microsoft Windows NT® Server or Microsoft Windows® 2000 Server.

Migrating from Microsoft Windows NT Server 4.0 to Microsoft Windows Server 2003
ISBN 0-7356-1940-9

Get expert guidance, procedures, and solutions for a successful migration—direct from the Windows Server team. Get real-world guidance for planning and deploying an upgrade from Windows NT 4.0 to Windows Server 2003 for your small or medium-sized business. This book delivers straightforward, step-by-step instructions on how to upgrade to an Active Directory directory service environment; migrate your DHCP, WINS, file, print, remote access, and Web server roles; and implement Group Policy–based administration. Whether you support 10 or 1,000 users, you get the detailed information—plus evaluation software—you need to put Windows Server 2003 to work right away.

To learn more about the full line of Microsoft Press® products for IT professionals, please visit:

microsoft.com/mspress/IT

System Requirements

To follow the practices in this book, it is recommended that you use a computer that is not your primary workstation because you will be called on to make changes to the operating system and application configuration. The computer you use must have the following minimum configuration. All hardware should be listed in the Microsoft Windows Catalog.

- Microsoft Windows XP Professional Edition with Service Pack 2 (an Evaluation Edition is included on the CD-ROM)
- Personal computer with a 233 MHz or higher processor in the Intel Pentium/Celeron family, the AMD K6/Athlon/Duron family, or compatible (300 MHz processor recommended)
- 64 MB of RAM or higher (128 MB or higher recommended)
- 1.8 GB of available hard disk space
- CD-ROM drive or DVD-ROM drive
- Super VGA (800 x 600) or higher resolution monitor
- Keyboard and Microsoft Mouse, Microsoft IntelliMouse, or compatible pointing device

Additionally, several chapters have practices that require you to have an Internet connection.

 Caution   The 120-day evaluation edition of Windows XP Professional SP2 provided with this training kit is not the full retail product and is provided only for the purposes of training and evaluation. Microsoft Technical Support does not support these evaluation editions.

What do you think of this book?
We want to hear from you!

Do you have a few minutes to participate in a brief online survey? Microsoft is interested in hearing your feedback about this publication so that we can continually improve our books and learning resources for you.

To participate in our survey, please visit:

www.microsoft.com/learning/booksurvey

And enter this book's ISBN, 0-7356-2227-2. As a thank-you to survey participants in the United States and Canada, each month we'll randomly select five respondents to win one of five $100 gift certificates from a leading online merchant.* At the conclusion of the survey, you can enter the drawing by providing your e-mail address, which will be used for prize notification *only.*

Thanks in advance for your input. Your opinion counts!

Sincerely,

Microsoft Learning

Learn More. Go Further.

To see special offers on Microsoft Learning products for developers, IT professionals, and home and office users, visit: *www.microsoft.com/learning/booksurvey*

* No purchase necessary. Void where prohibited. Open only to residents of the 50 United States (includes District of Columbia) and Canada (void in Quebec). Sweepstakes ends 6/30/2006. For official rules, see: *www.microsoft.com/learning/booksurvey*

Present this discount voucher to any of 5,000 testing centers worldwide in 130 countries for 15% off your exam fee. Or, use the discount code on the voucher to register online or via phone with the Microsoft Certified Exam Provider of your choice.

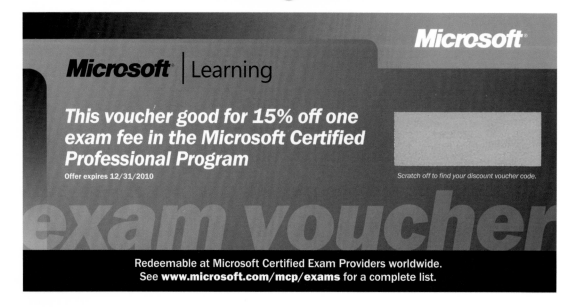

Microsoft

Microsoft | Learning

This voucher good for 15% off one exam fee in the Microsoft Certified Professional Program

Offer expires 12/31/2010

Scratch off to find your discount voucher code.

Redeemable at Microsoft Certified Exam Providers worldwide.
See **www.microsoft.com/mcp/exams** for a complete list.

exam voucher

For more information or the location of a
Microsoft Certified Exam Provider near you, visit:

www.microsoft.com/mcp/exams

Promotion Terms and Conditions:

- Offer good for 15% off one exam fee in the Microsoft Certified Professional Program.
- Voucher can be redeemed online or at Microsoft Certified Exam Providers worldwide.
- Discounted exam must be taken on or before December 31, 2010.
- Promotion is limited to one discounted exam per candidate for each book purchased.
- Inform your Microsoft Certified Exam Provider that you want to use this voucher as payment for your exam at the time you register for the exam.

Voucher Terms and Conditions

- Expired voucher has no value and will not be replaced.
- Voucher code must be used at time of registration.
- This voucher may not be combined with other vouchers or discounts.
- This voucher is nontransferable and is void if altered or revised in any way. It may not be redeemed for cash, credit, or refund, and may not be used for any other exam.
- Any transfer or resale of this voucher is expressly prohibited.

Microsoft

X11-56768